THE TITLES OF JESUS IN CHRISTOLOGY

THE TITLES OF JESUS
IN CHRISTOLOGY

Their History in Early Christianity

by

FERDINAND HAHN

LONDON

LUTTERWORTH PRESS

First published in English 1969

COPYRIGHT © 1963 VANDENHOECK & RUPRECHT, GÖTTINGEN
ENGLISH TRANSLATION COPYRIGHT © 1969 LUTTERWORTH PRESS
LONDON

Lutterworth Press, 4 Bouverie Street, E.C.4.

U.S.A
The World Publishing Company, Cleveland, Ohio.

This book originally appeared as *Christologische Hoheitstitel, Ihre Geschichte im frühen Christentum*, in the series *Forschungen zur Religion und Literatur des Alten und Neuen Testamentes* edited by Ernst Käsemann and Ernst Würthwein.

The English translation is by Harold Knight and George Ogg.

7188 0572 0

*Printed in Great Britain by
The Camelot Press Ltd., London and Southampton*

ABBREVIATIONS

AGSU	Arbeiten zur Geschichte des Spätjudentums und Urchristentums, hrsg. v. Institutum Judaicum Tübingen
ATD	Das Alte Testament Deutsch (Neues Göttinger Bibelwerk)
AThANT	Abhandlungen zur Theologie des Alten und Neuen Testaments
Bauer, Wb	W. Bauer, Griechisch-deutsches Wörterbuch zu den Schriften des Neuen Testaments und der übrigen urchristlichen Literatur
BEvTh	Beiträge zur evangelischen Theologie
BFchrTh	Beiträge zur Förderung christlicher Theologie
BH	Biblia Hebraica, ed. Kittel, Alt u. Eissfeldt
BHTh	Beiträge zur historischen Theologie
Bibl	Biblica. Commentarii editi cura Pontifici Instituti Biblici
BiblStud	Biblische Studien
Bl-Debr	Blass u. Debrunner. Grammatik des neutestamentlichen Griechisch
Bull.J.Ryl.Libr.	Bulletin of the John Rylands Library
BWANT	Beiträge zur Wissenschaft vom Alten und Neuen Testaments
BZ NF	Biblische Zeitschrift Neue Folge
BZNW	Beihefte zur Zeitschrift für die neutestamentliche Wissenschaft und die Kunde der älteren Kirche
CBQ	The Catholic Biblical Quarterly
DtTh	Deutsche Theologie
EvTh	Evangelische Theologie
FRLANT	Forschungen zur Religion und Literatur des Alten und Neuen Testaments
GCS	Die griechischen christlichen Schriftsteller der ersten drei Jahrhunderte
HarvTheolRev	The Harvard Theological Review

Hatch-Redpath	E. Hatch and H. A. Redpath, A Concordance to the Septuagint
JBL	Journal of Biblical Literature
JR	The Journal of Religion
JThSt	The Journal of Theological Studies
Kautzsch	Die Apokryphen und Pseudepigraphen des Alten Testaments hrsg. v. E. Kautzsch
Koehler Wb	L. Koehler u. W. Baumgartner, Lexicon in Veteris Testamenti Libros
LXX	Septuaginta id est Vetus Testamentum Graece iuxta LXX interpretes, ed. A. Rahlfs
Moulton-Geden	W. F. Moulton and A. S. Geden, A Concordance to the Greek Testament
MPTh	Monatsschrift für Pastoraltheologie
NovTest	Novum Testamentum
NtAbh	Neutestamentliche Abhandlungen
NTSt	New Testament Studies
RB	Revue Biblique
RGG	Die Religion in Geschichte und Gegenwart
RHPhR	Revue d'Histoire et de Philosophie Religieuse
RHR	Revue d'Histoire des religions
Riessler	P. Riessler, Altjüdisches Schrifttum ausserhalb der Bibel
RQ	Revue de Qumran
RThPh	Revue de Théologie et de Philosophie
SAB	Sitzungsberichte der Preussischen (Deutschen) Akademie der Wissenschaften zu Berlin
SAH	Sitzungsberichte der Heidelberger Akademie der Wissenschaften
StANT	Studien zum Alten und Neuen Testament
StudBiblTheol	Studies in Biblical Theology
StudTheol	Studia Theologica
ThBibl	Theologische Bibliothek Töpelmann
ThBl	Theologische Blätter
TheolBüch	Theologische Bücherei
ThEx	Theologische Existenz heute
ThLZ	Theologische Literaturzeitung
ThR NF	Theologische Rundschau, Neue Folge
ThRev	Theologische Revue
ThStKr	Theologische Studien und Kritiken
ThSt	Theologische Studien

ThWb	Theologisches Wörterbuch zum Neuen Testament, hrsg. v. G. Kittel bzw. G. Friedrich
ThZ	Theologische Zeitschrift
TU	Texte und Untersuchungen zur Geschichte der altchristlichen Literatur
UNT	Untersuchungen zum Neuen Testament
VetTest	Vetus Testamentum
WMANT	Wissenschaftliche Monographien zum Alten und Neuen Testament
WUNT	Wissenschaftliche Untersuchungen zum Neuen Testament
WZKM	Wiener Zeitschrift für die Kunde des Morgenlandes
ZAW	Zeitschrift für die alttestamentliche Wissenschaft
ZKG	Zeitschrift für Kirchengeschichte
ZNW	Zeitschrift für die neutestamentliche Wissenschaft und die Kunde der älteren Kirche
ZRGG	Zeitschrift für Religions- und Geistesgeschichte
ZThK	Zeitschrift für Theologie und Kirche

On abbreviations for the Qumran Writings see Barthélemy and Milik, *Discoveries in the Judaean Desert I*, pp. 46f.

NOTE

For reasons of space, the original footnotes have been considerably curtailed.

The following are some of the books mentioned in the present Notes which are available in English:

J. M. Allegro, *The Dead Sea Scrolls*, 1956

A. Alt, *Essays on Israelite History and Religion*, 1965

A. Bentzen, *King and Messiah*, 1954

G. Bornkamm, *Jesus of Nazareth*, 1960

G. Bornkamm, G. Barth, H. J. Held, *Tradition and Interpretation in Matthew*, 1963

R. Bultmann, *The History of the Synoptic Tradition*, 1963
—— *Theology of the New Testament*, Vols. I and II, 1952
H. Conzelmann, *The Theology of St. Luke*, 1960
O. Cullmann, *The Christology of the New Testament*, rev. ed. 1963
—— *Baptism in the New Testament*, 1950
—— *Early Christian Worship*, 1953
—— *The State in the New Testament*, 1962
—— *Peter: Disciple, Apostle, Martyr*, 1953
G. Dalman, *Jesus: Jeshua*, 1939
—— *The Words of Jesus*, 1902
W. Eichrodt, *The Theology of the Old Testament*, Vol. I, 1961
J. Héring, *1 Corinthians*, 1962
J. Jeremias, *The Eucharistic Words of Jesus*, 1966[2]
—— *The Parables of Jesus*, rev. ed., 1963
—— *Jesus' Promise to the Nations*, 1958
E. Käsemann, *Essays on New Testament Themes*, 1964
L. Köhler, *Old Testament Theology*, 1956
W. Kramer, *Christ, Lord, Son of God*, 1966
E. Lohmeyer, *The Lord of the Temple*, 1961
M. Noth, *The Laws of the Pentateuch and Other Essays*, 1967
R. Otto, *The Kingdom of God and the Son of Man*, 1938
O. Plozer, *Theocracy and Eschatology*, 1968
J. M. Robinson, *The Problem of History in Mark*, 1957
—— *A New Quest of the Historical Jesus*, 1959
A. Schweitzer, *The Quest of the Historical Jesus*, 1911[2]
E. Schweizer, *Lordship and Discipleship*, 1960
H. E. Tödt, *The Son of Man in the Synoptic Tradition*, 1965
G. von Rad, *Old Testament Theology*, Vol. II, 1965
—— *The Problem of the Hexateuch and Other Essays*, 1966
J. Weiss, *The History of Primitive Christianity*, 1937
Th.Wb. = *A Theological Dictionary of the New Testament*, Vols. I–III, 1965–

CONTENTS

Introduction

9

INTRODUCTION

RESEARCH into the earliest use of Christological titles of
majesty goes back to work that was done preparatory to a
presentation of the theology of the Gospel of Mark. Since in
Mark—the situation is different in Matthew and Luke—there
is no fixed starting-point, and a basis of comparison needed for
a critical examination of this redactional work must first be
determined, two tasks in particular present themselves: on the
one hand, if the determination of the redactional elements is
not to remain more or less arbitrary, clear principles which hold
good in all parts of the Second Gospel have to be obtained,
according to which the redactional framework may be detached;
on the other hand, to grasp the evangelist's thought we have to
enter the field of Christology[1] and, in doing so, to inquire what
were the Christological traditions that have been worked up.

We have here taken in hand the last-named task. It was
obvious that in attempting it we would have to get acquainted
with the Christological titles which occur in the Gospel of
Mark.[2] Assuredly it ought not to be overlooked that other
material of tradition which is not connected with a designation
of majesty can be Christologically significant; but the Christological ideas of the earliest church have nevertheless obtained
far-reaching expression in the strata of tradition which are
stamped with a definite title of majesty. Since a traditio-
historical classification of the material that lay before the
evangelist can be arrived at only if we do not confine ourselves
to the Gospel of Mark—the pieces of evidence for the early
period are as it is scanty enough—the constructive method of
proceeding has led to the problem of the beginnings of the
formation of Christological tradition in general.[3]

The titles of majesty have been dealt with independently of
one another so far as overlappings and contacts have not
emerged in the history of the tradition itself. A convergence of
results has been asked for only in conclusion. It has seemed
advisable to distinguish as carefully as possible from one another
the different Christological conceptions, as also the stages of

tradition within the several views, in order that peculiarities may not be overlooked. In the treatment of the five titles of majesty much could only be sketched, and all the problems could not be taken into account in an equally detailed way. Where a question arises that is essential for a judgment of the whole, an attempt has been made to give a closer argument.

Some definitions are necessary. In the New Testament research of recent decades it has been customary to use the designation "late Judaism" for the Judaism of the period from the Maccabean struggles to the composition of the Mishna. This assumes that the post-exilic period of the Old Testament is characterized as "Judaism", a thing that was generally spread abroad half a century ago in Old Testament research, but today obtains more rarely.[4] Instead of this, in view of the more Talmudic and post-Talmudic stamp of the Judaism of the period from c. 200 B.C. to A.D. 200, the designation "early Judaism" has occasionally been chosen in recent times.[5] It is not to be disputed that this name has various excellent points, nevertheless we have kept to the current term.

For the New Testament age, in place of the old distinction between the Palestinian primitive church and Pauline Christianity, the distinction between the Palestinian primitive church, pre-Pauline Hellenistic Christianity and the Pauline tradition proper has already prevailed for long.[6] Nevertheless the question has to be asked whether this differentiation suffices. Consideration has already been rightly given to the question whether or not a Hellenistic Christianity of a specifically Jewish stamp must be separated from Gentile Christianity.[7] In what follows "Hellenistic Jewish Christianity" is spoken about where the Hellenistic derivation is certainly clearly in evidence, but so firm an adhesion to early Jewish conceptions is still recognizable that this cannot simply be co-ordinated to "Hellenistic Christianity", by which is understood as a rule the early Christianity that was largely severed from Judaism and determined by a Gentile provenance.[8] In more recent times a Christianity in the Palestinian–Syrian outskirts has also been spoken of occasionally.[9] But such localizations of traditions, which are necessary and possible for the student of patristics, prove almost altogether unworkable in the New Testament and rest for the most part on vague conjectures. Consequently it is sounder to do without local fixations, to inquire into the portion of Jewish inheritance and according to that to determine whether the tradition of the Hellenistic church has a Jewish Christian or a Gentile Christian stamp.[10] Hellenistic Jewish Christianity merits careful consideration as an essential link especially in Christology and on some occasions can be dealt with as a quite independent stratum of tradition.[11]

NOTES

1. William Wrede, *Das Messiasgeheimnis in den Evangelien. Zugleich ein Beitrag zum Verständnis des Markusevangeliums*, 1901, has clearly recognized this. In more recent works it has strange to say not been sufficiently observed; that holds good, in spite of many valuable single findings, of James M. Robinson, *Das Geschichtsverständnis des Markusevangeliums* (*AThANT* 30), 1956, and above all of Willi Marxsen, *Der Evangelist Markus, Studien zur Redaktionsgeschichte des Evangeliums* (*FRLANT* NF 49), 1959[2], cf. only p. 66 n. 2: "In our context discussion of the question of Christology can be left out"; in that statement there lies a decisive error.

2. So also Ernst Lohmeyer, *Das Evangelium des Markus* (*Krit.- exeg. Komm. üb. d. NT* 1/2), 1959,[15] pp. 1ff. A presentation of the earliest Christology which starts from the titles of majesty is given by F. J. Foakes Jackson-Kirsopp Lake, *The Beginnings of Christianity* (Part 1), vol. i, 1920, pp. 345ff.; Henry J. Cadbury, *ibid.* vol. v, 1933, pp. 354ff.; Martin Dibelius, *Christologie des Urchristentums*, *RGG*[2] i, 1927, cols. 1592–1607; Vincent Taylor, *The Names of Jesus*, 1953; Reginald H. Fuller, *The Mission and Achievement of Jesus* (*StudBiblTheol* 12), 1954, pp. 79ff.; R. P. Casey, "The Earliest Christologies", *JThSt* NS 9 (1958), pp. 253–277; and above all by Oscar Cullmann, *Die Christologie des Neuen Testaments*, 1957.

3. Cf. now Werner Kramer, *Christos, Kyrios, Gottessohn* (appears in *AThANT* 44), 1963 and the new edition, of Eduard Schweizer's book, *Erniedrigung und Erhöhung bei Jesus und seinen Nachfolgern* (*AThANT* 28), 1962[2].

4. Cf. only *Die Schriften des Alten Testaments in Auswahl neu übersetzt und für die Gegenwart erklärt* II/3: Max Haller, *Das Judentum. Geschichtsschreibung, Prophetie und Gesetzgebung nach dem Exil*, 1925[2].

5. Cf., e.g., Otto Plöger, *Prophetisches Erbe in den Sekten des frühen Judentums*, *ThLZ* 79 (1954), cols. 291–296; Georg Fohrer, *Messiasfrage und Bibelverständnis* (*Samml. gemeinverständl. Vorträge* 213/24), 1957, p. 23.

6. Of fundamental importance is Wilhelm Heitmüller, *Zum Problem Paulus und Jesus*, *ZNW* 13 (1912), pp. 320–337; on the carrying out of

this cf. Wilhelm Bousset, *Kyrios Christos, Geschichte des Christusglaubens von den Anfängen des Christentums bis Irenäus* (FRLANT NF 4), 1921[2], pp. 1ff. 75ff.; Rudolf Bultmann, *Theologie des Neuen Testaments*, 1958[3], pp. 34ff., 66ff.

7. Cf. Rudolf Bultmann, *Die Geschichte der synoptischen Tradition* (*FRLANT* NF 12), 1958[4], pp. 330f.; for a laborious working out of a Hellenistic Jewish Christian tradition see above all Martin Dibelius, *Jungfrauensohn und Krippenkind* (1932), in *Botschaft und Geschichte* (*Ges. Aufsätze*) i, 1953, pp. 1–78. Rather differently Cullmann, *Christologie*, pp. 332f.

8. Cf. further Chapter 5, p. 299.

9. So, e.g., G. D. Kilpatrick, *The Origins of the Gospel according to St. Matthew*, 1946, pp. 124ff. for the community of Matthew.

10. Naturally the question also arises how far Palestinian Judaism threw itself open to the influence of Hellenism. In this regard notice will doubtless be taken of the large collection of material made by E. R. Goodenough, *Jewish Symbols in the Greco-Roman Period* i-viii, 1953–58, above all vols. i and iii; cf. also Jean-Baptiste Frey, *Corpus Inscriptionum Judaicarum* ii, 1952, pp. 113ff., 163ff. Unambiguous literary documents from Palestinian Judaism which reflect syncretism are certainly lacking. Also it may not be overlooked that precisely in New Testament times there were movements which vindicated the exclusiveness of Judaism and very much guarded themselves against all foreign influences. The situation was different in the Judaism of the Diaspora, although there also orthodox circles will not have been lacking; unhappily we cannot make for ourselves any fairly satisfactory picture because only a quite fragmentary tradition remains preserved to us, and this comes largely from the Egyptian-Alexandrian area. For the present nothing more can be secured than a distinction between the Palestinian primitive Christianity, which developed in the area in which Hebrew-Aramaic was spoken, and an early Hellenistic Jewish Christianity to which, with all its adhesion to the tradition it had received, the speech and thought of Hellenism were familiar.

11. The tradition of Hellenistic Jewish Christianity stands out most distinctly in the Kyrios title, in the Son of David tradition and the Son of God conception.

CHAPTER I

SON OF MAN

OF all Christological titles, that of the Son of man has been the most thoroughly investigated.[1] The reason for this is that it has been hoped, by means of this predicate of dignity, to penetrate most deeply to the preaching of Jesus Himself; moreover, the outlook of the early Palestinian community on the person and work of Jesus is discernible in a relatively exclusive context.[2] Hence the consideration of the title of the Son of man is an appropriate starting point for an investigation of the oldest Christological traditions. But of course the history of criticism has shown how many problems are bound up with this stream of tradition, and up to the most recent literature on the subject decisive points are still being debated, so that even here we cannot start from firm conclusions; a short exposition and discussion of the material is necessary.[3]

1. Philological Problems and Problems connected with the History of Religion

The phrase, unusual in the Greek language, ὁ υἱὸς τοῦ ἀνθρώπου, sets the task of philological derivation. Since in the NT we have frequently to reckon with traditions stemming from the sphere of Semitics the explanation does not seem to be difficult. For it is obvious to take into account a collective idea, which by means of the genitival link "son of . . ." is used to denote an individual. This would imply that "Son of man" is nothing other than "man" and represents only a slavish reproduction of the Semitic expression; just like the Hebraic אָדָם the Aramaic אֱנָשׁ would then express the idea of the species, and the form בֶּן אָדָם or בַּר אֱנָשׁ would serve the purpose of distinguishing the individual member of the species.[4]

This point of view has been expressed especially by Wellhausen, who was also of the opinion that in Dan. 7:13 and 2 Esdras 13 the word is used only metaphorically and in the metaphorical speeches of the Ethiopian Enoch only with express

reference to Daniel;[5] hence in the mouth of Jesus, the expression
"Son of man" may have been merely a general expression
denoting an individual man; only the primitive community,
in connection with its expectation of the parousia, stamped it
with titular character.[6]

Lietzmann went a step further, denying altogether a titular
use in the sphere of Aramaic speech, and reckoning with quite
a late emergence of ὁ υἱὸς τοῦ ἀνθρώπου in the sphere of the
Hellenistic community.[7] On the contrary, he regarded בַּר (אֱ)נָשׁ
as a merely pleonastic form side by side with the simple
אֱנָשׁ and rejected any distinction in view of the fact that the
Semitic language is devoid of all conceptual discriminations.[8]

Dalman had, however, maintained the opposing thesis that
the simple אֱנָשׁ was the only currently used word for "man":
"the extraordinary בַּר אֱנָשׁ was not in current use, and was
employed only in imitation of the Hebraic Biblical text, where
בֶּן אָדָם belongs to poetic speech";[9] he considered that the
determinate בַּר (אֱ)נָשָׁא both in Judaic-Galilean and in later
Christian-Aramaic speech was an innovation due to the influence of the Mesopotamian-Aramaic dialect.[10] The consequence of this is that בַּר (אֱ)נָשָׁא cannot simply mean "man",
and in no case is a meaningless mode of speech, but an emphatic
and selected type of expression which may only appropriately
be rendered by such phrases as "son of man" or "child of man".[11]

After these three very different attempts at a solution, the
problem was again taken up by Fiebig, and linguistically
investigated on a broad basis. He showed that a highly varied
use of speech must be assumed for the Aramaic of Jesus' time:
(אֱ)נָשׁ, (אֱ)נָשָׁא), but also בַּר (אֱ)נָשׁ and בַּר (אֱ)נָשָׁא can all be used in
the same sense. The forms with and without בַּר have the same
meaning, hence there is no plain difference between the concept
of the species and that of the individual; but furthermore the
undetermined and the determined forms are not clearly distinguished from each other; they may both convey the idea of
"a" or "the" man.[12] However, where we have an at least
formally precise translation, we must reckon with the fact that
ὁ υἱὸς τοῦ ἀνθρώπου goes back to בַּר (אֱ)נָשָׁא although no special
significance is assigned to the latter expression in Aramaic.[13]
This solution has been widely accepted.[14]

If no specially coined and emphatic mode of expression may be assumed in Aramaic, this by no means precludes the possibility that בַּר (אֱ)נָשָׁא may be linked to a very firmly fixed conception, and in certain contexts even used technically, in some contexts in fact receiving a titular character.[15] Just like the "anthropos" in gnosticism, or the "day" in apocalyptic writings, so also the "man" in apocalyptic contexts implied an unequivocal significance. Dan. 7:13f.; 2 Esdras 13 and the metaphorical speeches of the Ethiopian Enoch furnish proofs of this. The fact that in Dan. 7:13f. and 2 Esdras 13, the "man" is spoken of only in a comparison, hence metaphorically, is no contradiction of this contention.

The only questionable point is whether the כְּבַר אֱנָשׁ of Dan. 7:13 and the *quasi similitudinem hominis* of 2 Esdras 13:3 admits the use of the expression in a titular sense. An unequivocal answer cannot be had from the visionary speeches for the meaning of the demonstrative in "Son of man" is disputed.[16] It can be explained in the sense that the demonstrative serves for the translation of the Greek article since Ethiopic has no special means of determining the article, but this cannot be quite certainly proved.[17] What is undisputed is that in Daniel and 2 Esdras, as in the visionary speeches of the Ethiopian Enoch, what is in question is the stereotyped description of a quite specific heavenly being.

It is not the conception and the technical use that is problematical, only the titular use. The latter is overwhelmingly probable for pre-Christian Judaism; for in favour of the titular use of the word is not only the demonstrative expression in the Ethiopic Enoch, but also the self-explanatory titular use in the whole synoptic tradition. The Aramaic basis בר (א)נשׁא of the Greek expression has indeed no special rank, but perhaps we may say that the individual significance, as also the determination, could most plainly be expressed thus, and this was most clearly to be maintained by the literally faithful translation ὁ υἱὸς τοῦ ἀνθρώπου as distinct from the υἱὸς ἀνθρώπου of the Septuagint (also Dan. 7:13).[18]

Much discussion has taken place in recent times about the so-called corporate interpretation of the figure of the Son of man. It cannot be disputed that in Dan. 7:13f., 27 we have a corporate interpretation, since the Son of man is equated with the "people of the saints of the Most High"; he represents the eternal kingdom of the time of salvation, and by the "saints of the Most High" are probably to be understood the heavenly hosts.[19] But such a corporate idea is not present in 2 Esdras 13 and the visions of the Ethiopic Enoch, and even in regard to Dan. 7 it may be questioned what traditional presuppositions constitute the norm of interpretation. Apart from the later additions in vv. 7, fin. 8, 11a, 20–22, 24f.[20] the real vision vv. 1–7, 9f., 11b–14 must be distinguished from its interpretation in vv. 15–19, 23, 26–28; moreover, in the vision the concept of the four world kingdoms[21] and the view of the divine judgment and the appearance of the Son of man are closely bound together.[22] It must be noted that the corporate understanding results not merely from the interpretation of vv. 15ff. but already from the link between the concept of the Son of man and the vision of the four world kingdoms. But is this true of the concept of the heavenly man in general?

The consideration that behind Dan. 7 and the visions of the Ethiopic Enoch there stands a common individualistic concept of the Son of man, which only in Daniel has received a corporate interpretation, has in any case something to be said for it.[23] However it may be as regards the priority of the collective or individualist interpretation, in the post-Daniel tradition of Judaism there is to be found a clearly individualist conception. In regard to the preaching and person of Jesus the corporate idea in any case raises not inconsiderable difficulties.

T. W. Manson, who above all has urged this interpretation, has to presuppose a direct reference to Dan. 7 and furthermore to assume that Jesus on account of the failure of His disciples at the end of His life Himself vicariously assumed the functions of the corporately understood figure of the Son of man.[24] Hence in the last resort he does not manage without having recourse to a personal exegesis, and notes both a corporate and individualist conception in the gospels. His thesis, which in this form found scant acceptance,[25] was nevertheless at times adopted with certain modifications, for example by Taylor who refers the words about the eschatological coming of the Son of man to "the Elect Community of which He was to be the Head"[26] or by Theo Preiss who ascribes to the figure of the Son of man an inclusive sense as well;[27] similarly, Cullmann speaks of a certain ambiguity in the expression and connects it with the concept of perfected humanity.[28]

However, it should not be overlooked that, quite apart from the definite individualist understanding of the figure of the Son of man in pre-Christian Judaism, the NT words about the Son of man give no indications which demand such an interpretation,[29] that the currency of corporate concepts in Semitic thought[30] together with the one text Dan. 7 is not a sufficient reason and that the primitive Christian statements did not arise with an exclusive reference to Dan. 7[31] but imply a broad stream of tradition which is no longer sufficiently discernible to us.[32]

A further much discussed problem, which has been dealt with especially by Joachim Jeremias and was likewise discussed by T. W. Manson within the framework of his interpretation, is the connection between the concepts of the Son of man and the suffering servant of God,[33] but while the former critic assumes the connection already to exist in late Judaism,[34] the latter sees it effected only with Jesus Himself;[35] R. H. Fuller also makes a similar judgment.[36] Admittedly the influence of the idea of the suffering servant is not to be denied in the Son of man text—Mk. 10:45 and par.,[37] yet this word is quite singular within the corpus of NT Son of man texts; further, Mk. 10:45 can hardly be traced back to Jesus Himself.

In the Son of man idea proper to late Judaism there is lacking, so far as we can see, any clear proof of the assimilation of elements from the suffering servant, for while certain links between Son of man statements and Isa. 42:1ff.; 49:1ff., may be established, this is not so for Isa. 50:4ff., 52:13ff., and in view of the exegesis then prevalent, which did not regard the servant songs as an independent unity, it may not be at once ?? assumed that all the elements of the Deutero-Isaianic conception were taken over. Hiddenness and removal have nothing to do with suffering, and least of all demonstrative is the frequent description of the Son of man as "servant" in 2 Esdras, for neither in the OT nor in Judaism is this name of honour exclusively linked to the servant tradition of Deutero-Isaiah.[38]

A problem which in many respects is still insufficiently clarified is that of the origin of the Son of man concept.[39] The older derivations characteristic of the history of religion school[40] need examination[41] and conclusive recent results have not yet been attained. In any case it is necessary to adhere to the thesis that the Son of man figure in Judaism is not to be explained apart from foreign influences.[42] A certain connection (albeit very broken and modified by some not clearly discernible intermediate stages) with the idea of a primal man cannot be flatly rejected.[43] Yet we must be careful not to accept too quickly a kinship with some developments of the idea of the primal man, e.g. the Adam-Christ typology in Paul.[44] Whatever be the truth about the roots of the concept as far as the history of religion is concerned, in NT times it had for long become a characteristic traditional element in Judaism and also formed a certain point of crystallization for apocalyptic expectations of the end.[45] History of religion problems are therefore of subordinate importance for the NT.

A last question to be touched on here is the relation between the Son of man and the Messiah. In so far as the word Messiah is not loosely used as an inclusive concept for the saviour at the end of time, the supposition of reciprocal dependence involves as a rule certain theses concerning the history of religion and tradition. Thus, in particular, when Riesenfeld or Bentzen propose to trace back not only the Messiah, but also the Son of man conception to ideology centring around the king.[46] Without prejudice to certain points of contact with the concept of the kingly Messiah, that of the Son of man, not only on account of its origin, but still more on account of its independent development and elaboration, must be radically distinguished from true messianism, if we are not to promote confusion about the facts of history and tradition. A derivation from kingly ideology must here quite certainly be excluded. Enquiry must be made into particular cases of mutual influence.[47]

Summary. It must be said that the philological problems may be regarded as clarified: בַּר (אֱ)נָשָׁא is a description of the individual man, but not the only one possible; in any case the phrase has no special significance or emphasis. That does not prevent, however, this general concept from having a clearly defined position as a *terminus technicus* in marked apocalyptic contexts. It is not quite proved, but overwhelmingly probable, that already in pre-Christian Judaism a titular use had established itself which was adopted by Jesus and the primitive community. The collective understanding of the Son of man

which exists in Daniel is lacking in 2 Esdras 13 and the similitudes of the Ethiopic Enoch, and is just as little to be assumed
as far as the NT is concerned. A connection with the idea
of the suffering servant cannot be proved in regard to Judaism;
in the primitive Christian tradition it can be established only in
one single instance. The derivation from the standpoint of the
history of religion has not yet been sufficiently clarified. In
any event, foreign influence will have to be taken into account;
on the other hand, the concept was in a high degree adapted by
Jewish thought, even if it was not widespread. It belongs to its
own characteristic stratum of tradition, and for this reason is to
be fundamentally distinguished from the concept of the
Messiah.

2. *The Son of Man Concept and the Preaching of Jesus*

The Son of man sayings have come down to us almost without
exception as sayings of Jesus Himself. Hence the question
arises in what relation they stand to the preaching of Jesus.
If anywhere in Christological titles, in regard to the "Son of
man", it may be considered that Jesus Himself made use of this
predicate. This does not preclude the fact that a string of
sayings are secondary accretions. But which Son of man sayings may be regarded as the oldest and included in the preaching of Jesus is disputed. It has even been questioned whether
the Son of man concept is to be reckoned at all as part of the
preaching of Jesus. It is always according to how we answer
these questions that the development of tradition must be
estimated. Hence it is advisable to begin with basic considerations rather than detailed discussion of Son of man texts.

There is a certain consensus of critical opinion that the
prophecies of suffering, at least in their present form, arose
only in the community, and as a result the sayings about the
dying and rising again of the Son of man are placed at the
end of the development. It is debated whether the words about
the coming Son of man or those about his earthly work must be regarded as primary and so referred back to Jesus Himself; it is
not very probable that both are equally original.

In regard to the sayings about the earthly deeds of the Son
of man, older criticism frequently asserted their authenticity
on the assumption of an erroneous translation of the Aramaic
phrase. It was thought that from a simple "the man" or "I"

there developed only later a titular of exaltation.[48] But there are difficulties in the acceptance of this view. For, on the one hand, not all these words are intelligible as sayings about man, and often the real point is attained only through the title "Son of man", and, on the other hand, the phrase בַּר (אֱ)נָשָׁא, as a circumlocution for "I", cannot be proved from the Aramaic documents which have come down to us, rather in such cases we have הַהוּא גַבְרָא.[49]

Eduard Schweizer has maintained the thesis that in such sayings "Son of man" is by no means a meaningless circumlocution, but that Jesus deliberately adopted the concept as a means of self-description; such sayings are the most authentic Son of man logia, and are to be regarded as the starting point for a view of the whole development.[50]

Quite apart from the question whether the particular words, from the point of view of content, permit this interpretation, objections may be raised. In the first place the linguistic assumptions compel us to hesitate: בר (א)נשא is regarded as the description of an ordinary man, then, however, it is thought possible that, used instead of an "I", it was "a somewhat unusual circumlocution".[51] Hence the attempt has been made to leave the word with its general meaning, but to derive from its context a certain emphasis.

But in my opinion this cannot be proved in the circumstances; for either the expression was current as a modest self-description, in which case there can be no question of an unusual emphatic circumlocution, or else the expression was not in use as a mode of self-reference, in which case it was to be understood as referring only and plainly to man in general. In any case such a phrase, used to refer to "I", is not provable in Aramaic; moreover, in a string of other Son of man sayings, the "I" of the speaker is very clearly distinguished from the Son of man description.[52]

A further objection to Schweizer's thesis is that, assuming the phrase had become fixed as a title in Judaism, it would be preferable to suppose that the Son of man description was transferred by Jesus to a new context. But Schweizer disputed precisely that a "dogmatically fixed quantity" is here present. He says that Jesus wished to draw attention to the special features of His work and not to give a convenient formula for interpretation. Son of man is "a circumlocution which conceals as much as reveals the secret of His person" and is ambiguous from the start.[53] But how is this ambiguity, which can only be possible under specific firm premisses, to be recognized?[54] Further, it is to be considered that, assuming such a generalized conception, the use of the phrase as a *terminus technicus* always belongs to a quite specific circle of ideas whence it receives its meaning; once it is loosed from this framework, the special meaning is necessarily lost.[55]

If the statements about the coming Son of man stand first in the historical development of the tradition, then an apocalyptic context is presupposed.[56] If, on the other hand, the sayings about the earthly deeds stand first, then such a point of reference and background of understanding is no longer discernible. Schweizer does not of course deny any kind of underlying context. Instead of referring to apocalyptic, he refers to the concept of the suffering and exalted righteous one; in this connection, however, he can only rely on the quotation of the Ethiopic Enoch 70f. and Wisdom 2–5.[57]

He alleges that what is new in Jesus' proclamation is that He applies the title Son of man not only to the exalted righteous one, who will some day confront His enemies before the judgment seat of God, but already to the earthly life of the righteous one.[58] In order to demonstrate this, he must show that it is not the sayings about the parousia, but the sayings about exaltation which belong to the original core of Jesus' Son of man words. His attempt to gain the necessary proofs from Acts 7:56 and the Johannine Son of man words[59] is not, however, convincing; for it can be shown that the sayings about exaltation in the sense of an independent Christological stage of development as contrasted with the parousia sayings are secondary and imply a clear de-eschatologization.[60]

Finally, particular words about the coming Son of man, implying a distinction between Jesus and the Son of man, evince a peculiarity which can only be explained if such logia are placed at the beginning of the development, and if we assess the identification of the Son of man with Jesus as a first step in Christological interpretation. It is precisely in regard to such words that the apocalyptic conception stands most plainly in the background and thus affords an important criterion for the understanding of the Son of man idea.[61]

Hence we must accept the priority of the words about the eschatological working of the Son of man.

But the more ancient character of the words about the coming Son of man does not in itself prove their authenticity. As his chief argument to show that these sayings do not flow from the lips of Jesus Himself, Philipp Vielhauer has attempted to show that they are unconnected with the words about the imminence of the Kingdom of God.[62] But from the point of view of method, caution is here required. It must first be noted that this lack of connection does not apply at any rate to the logia source and the traditional material edited by Mark.[63] This, of course, does not prove their original connection in the words of Jesus Himself, but the fact is that in those sources there are still other elements standing in juxtaposition and without apparent connection.

If, in consequence, Conzelmann for example insists that the eschatological and ethical parts of the teaching of Jesus are intrinsically separate, and that the ethics must not be understood in the light of the eschatology, his view arouses the most serious doubts.[64] But Vielhauer refers not only to the teaching of Jesus, but also to the late Judaic tradition in which the Kingdom of God and the Son of man concepts are consistently unconnected.[65] This is, in fact, of importance but must be interpreted somewhat differently from the way in which he interprets it. The concept of the rule of God belongs by its essential structure to a purely theocratic eschatology, in which the figure of a special Saviour, Messiah or Son of man is missing. If we wish to obtain fairly useful results, three things are to be noted: first, that to confine ourselves to the mere idea of the Kingdom of God is likely to lead us astray, rather our inquiry must be directed to the theocratic idea as a whole;[66] next, that the eschatological rule of God in the sense of a this-worldly expectation must be clearly distinguished from the sense in which it is understood in apocalyptic;[67] finally, that the sayings which appear in late Judaism and especially in Rabbinics about a present Kingdom of God are to be precluded from consideration.[68]

In the preaching of Jesus the reign of God is an eschatological concept—without prejudice to the sayings about its imminent outbreak or its present realization—and it stands within the framework of a transcendental expectation of salvation; in other words, it is moulded by apocalyptic. That the sayings are contained in an exclusively theocratic form is due chiefly to the fact that they stand essentially and by their very nature in a quite specific tradition, in which a connection with the figure of the Son of man (likewise well known in apocalyptic) is not immediately given. But as apocalyptic shows, this does not exclude a certain juxtaposition of elements.

This was already to be expected from the fact that what stood in the foreground in the Son of man development was less the imminent aeon of salvation itself than in the main the end of the world and the final judgment in which all are brought to account. This is especially plain in 2 Esdras 13 where the theme is the judgment executed upon hostile powers and the salvation of the elect, while any statement about the aeon of salvation is missing. In the Ethiopic Enoch also, judgment and salvation are brought to the fore in the Son of man passages[69] and it is interesting to see that all the sayings which are concerned with the handing over of power are directly connected with the function of judge.[70] Admittedly there is then, in view of the aeon of salvation, a reference to an "eating" or "dwelling" with the Son of man,[71] but we must not overlook the modification which is clearly marked in ch. 45: in vv. 1–3 the Son of man acts as judge, in vv. 4–6 God Himself effects the inauguration of the eternal reign of salvation, and it is He who causes the Son of man to dwell among the elect; similarly 62:14: the Lord of spirits dwells enthroned *above* the saved, while the Son of man eats *with them*.[72]

For apocalyptic literature the Son of man is a characteristic but by no means necessary figure. In any case, unlike the Messiah and the concept of a royal era of salvation, he does not stand in a basic tension to a purely theocratic eschatology.[73] Where he does appear, he exercises an independent function only in connection with the Last Day; he is in a certain sense the door-keeper, mediating between the old and the new aeons; in the time of salvation itself, on the contrary, he has a completely subordinate role to play, and God Himself is the ruler.[74]

It must not therefore be asserted without qualification that there is no essential connection between the emergence of the Son of man and the coming of the reign of God, and that there can be no question of the latter where the Son of man plays an active part.[75] Moreover, it must be wide of the mark to say

25

that the idea of עוֹלָם הַבָּא was in late Judaism identified with the Messianic age, but that the idea of the reign of God was "unencumbered by apocalyptic and nationalistic hopes for the future", or that while Jesus "speaks of the reign of God in the *olam* terminology, He replaces the coming *olam* by the concept of the reign of God".[76] The expressions "this aeon" and "the coming aeon" imply a distinction which could be connected equally well with the traditional and with the apocalyptic forms of hope for ultimate salvation.[77]

On the other hand, the idea of the reign of God is by no means a neutral and pure concept; the fact is rather that the ideal of a theocracy could be unfolded both within the framework of the old this-worldly as in that of the transcendental apocalyptic expectation. This implies that the two concepts "the coming aeon" and "the reign of God" were interchangeable—an interchangeability which was not first introduced by the teaching of Jesus. In any event it may be said that the concept of the coming aeon was clearly defined by that of the reign of God. If in the gospels the expression "kingdom of God" is mostly used, while in Jewish literature there appears more frequently that of "the coming aeon" this is primarily a difference of terminology rather than of meaning.

It is not by such considerations that the spuriousness of all the Son of man words can be shown; in apocalyptic the concept of the reign of God is quite compatible with the special function assigned to the judge who appears at the end of the world.[78]

The particular arguments adduced by Vielhauer in connection with the Son of man sayings are to be considered in the following section. As well as referring to the lack of connection between the sayings about the coming Son of man and those about the reign of God, Conzelmann has further pointed out that the idea of the reign of God as formulated by Jesus essentially leaves no scope for an intervening act of judgment and the independent figure of a judge, because no such interval remains.[79]

But it must be carefully considered whether the time scheme of apocalyptic really plays any part in the Son of man sayings of Jesus.[80] For example, in Lk. 12:8. there is not really an allusion to judgment as an independent future event, but, on the contrary, the point is that in an unsurpassable degree men are challenged to make a decision in the face of Jesus Himself. Vögtle very appropriately says: "Jesus explains that the coming of the Son of man in judgment is His own function. He, the present Jesus, is therefore the decisive eschatological mediatorial figure, the final arbiter of weal and woe." For this reason Jesus leaves "the person of the Son of man who executes judgment fully in abeyance".[81]

What Conzelmann says about the indirect continuity of eschatology and ethics, that they confront the hearers directly with God, and that Jesus understands Himself as the instrument of such a confrontation, might thus be more appropriately said in regard to the connection between the proclamation of the Kingdom of God and the coming of the Son of man.[82] For it is just of this that it may truly be said that "the dawn of the kingdom is indicated not by a forensic arrangement", but by "an act of discrimination", in which futurity is not cancelled, but in which it is primarily a question of "so emphasizing the *kairos*, that men think of nothing other than the call to immediate repentance".[83] Just as the announcement of the dawning Kingdom of God contains the promise of coming salvation, so the Son of man words announce the necessity of the eschatological discrimination which is now beginning.

If the words about the coming Son of man can be seen to fit neatly into the preaching of Jesus, if in addition it is clear that no priority can be assigned to the sayings about the earthly deeds of the Son of man, then the work of Tödt, with its analysis of the development of tradition, a work that is independent of the essays of Schweizer, Vielhauer and Conzelmann just discussed, is on the whole confirmed. The great merit of this work is that it demonstrates the essential connection between primitive Christian preaching and the preaching of Jesus Himself. He has shown in detail how in the course of the continued preaching of the message of Jesus and the invocation of His final authority as also in the climate of the early Christian expectation of His second coming there came into being a comprehensive Son of man Christology. The work may be referred to in the following chapters. Our own dissertation which follows is intended to offer a short survey of the development of the tradition; it will renew particular arguments of Schweizer and Vielhauer, and will mark some small deviations.

On the whole, however, it will not be a question of new conclusions.[84]

Summary. It must be established that of the three groups of Son of man words, those about the suffering and rising again of the Son of man can least of all lay claim to authenticity. The words about the earthly deeds may not in general be interpreted, as was customary among older critics, as misunderstood statements about "man", as also the reproduction of "I" by "Son of man" is not provable from contemporary Aramaic. The priority of the sayings about earthly deeds cannot be supported by alleging that the concept of the suffering and exalted righteous one is implied. For it is only within the framework of apocalyptic that unequivocal presuppositions for an understanding of the Son of man idea are to be found, and for this reason the words about the coming Son of man stand necessarily at the beginning of the development. Only after the identification of the future Son of man with Jesus had been made could the Jesus who worked on earth in full power and authority be described likewise as the "Son of man", and this description was finally extended to cover the statements about His suffering and rising again. If the priority of the words about the eschatological working of the Son of man is made clear, then further the origin of some of these words on the lips of Jesus cannot be disputed. Neither the relative lack of connection with sayings about the Kingdom of God nor the peculiar features of the teaching of Jesus furnish essential arguments against authenticity.

3. *Words concerning the future Action of the Son of Man*

The words concerning the coming Son of man stand at the beginning of the evolving tradition. Amongst them two different groups are to be distinguished; for, first, it is a question of the function of the Son of man as judge, secondly, of his appearance at the end of time. In both groups older logia, limited to the indication of the motive, are distinguishable from later ones which have received an apocalyptic recasting.

Among sayings concerned with the motive of judgment, Lk. 12:8f. par. (logia source) and the parallel formula in Mk. 8:38 par. can lay claim to be the oldest. The twofold expression about denial and confession has certainly in Mk. 8:38 received already a recasting which stamps it as secondary.[85] Instead

28

of ἀρνεῖσθαι; we have here the no doubt euphemistic
ἐπαισχύνεσθαι;[86] the being ashamed is also related to the words
of Jesus, and is therefore applied to the post-resurrection
situation of the early church; the expression "this adulterous
and sinful generation" is indeed ancient[87] but none the less
destroys the correlation of the clauses which in Lk. 12:8f.
is emphatically maintained. Finally the parallel statement
about confessing is missing.

Mk. 8:38b also shows in various ways a later expansion for
apocalyptic elements borrowed from Dan. 7:13f. have been
added;[88] there is, moreover, a reference to the "glory of His ✓
Father" which implies a very different Christological outlook.[89]
The more original formulation undoubtedly lies in Lk. 12:8f.
For the parallel passage in Matt. 10:32f. in spite of its closeness
in structure and formulation shows a fundamental transformation, in so far as the "I" has been introduced into the later
clause, hence Jesus has been expressly equated with the future
judge, and the Son of man denomination has been effaced.
For Lk. 12:8f. and even for Mk. 8:38 it is precisely characteristic that Jesus and the Son of man remain clearly distinguished. ✓

This differentiation is such a striking fact, which simply
cannot be explained from the Christology of the primitive ?
community, that we must here reckon with a genuine word of
Jesus. It may not be alleged as an objection that confession
and denial describe a situation which is true only for the
persecuted first church and within the life of Jesus can be true
only at most for Peter at the time of the passion, while for the
disciples as a whole it cannot yet have become acute.[90] It is
on the contrary precisely characteristic and significant that in
connection with the motive of eschatological judgment man's
attitude towards Jesus is spoken of in explicitly forensic terms
and in this way the absolute significance of the judgment here
made is underlined. Furthermore the saying assumes the form
of a principle of sacred law.[91]

In my opinion critics are mistaken when because of the
formal style of the saying they refuse to see it as a word of
Jesus and ascribe it to the prophets of the post-resurrection
community.[92] For while it may well be true that sacred law
played a decisive part in the life and ordering of the primitive
church, this does not by any means imply that Jesus Himself
may not have equally well used this form, as in other respects

also He made use of traditional modes of expression in the formulation of His words. Perhaps the first church was impelled not only by the working of the Spirit but first and foremost by the example of the earthly Jesus to use formulae akin to those of the sacred law in order to make clear to men the absolute character of their decision.

It should not be overlooked that in a saying such as that of Lk. 12:8f. the point at issue is that salvation and undoing are quite directly presented to the hearers and everything is concentrated in a situation of immediate appeal; men are not to wait for judgment in the apocalyptic sense, the Son of man will only later confirm the judgment which is here and now made, and will then make manifest that God's final verdict stands behind the claim and the authority of Jesus. Because in the very preaching of Jesus it is a question of the immediate nearness of God, the eschatological judgment and the Son of man can be alluded to in this way.[93] Tödt has very appropriately spoken of a soteriological relationship.[94] The relation of the person of Jesus to the Son of man remains fully open. As Jesus recedes before the approach of God, so does also the Son of man; the real point of this logion rests on the urgency and the utter seriousness of the judgment which is now beginning.

Hence it is not quite correct of Käsemann to class this word with the conqueror-sayings of the Revelation, with other prophetic law-sayings of the NT or with 1 Cor. 5:3ff.;[95] for in such prophetic law-sayings there is an unmistakable difference; in place of the immediate nearness of God stands the long-expected Lord Jesus.[96] Again, the juxtaposition of the "Son of man" in Lk. 12:8 and the passive denoting the action of God in 12:9 is no reason to doubt the authenticity of the saying.[97] This only serves to make plain how little the action of the Son of man himself occupies the foreground and how little it contradicts theocratic formulae.[98] No really sound reason for denying the authenticity of this logion can be brought forward.

On the other hand, in favour of its genuineness it is sometimes alleged that in this context the Son of man exercises no function as judge but stands as a witness and guarantor of the judgment of God.[99] But this is not certain. Analogies for this are lacking in late Judaic literature,[100] and it is further to be considered whether the statement "him shall the Son of man also confess before the angels of God", and "he shall be denied in the presence of the angels of God" is not simply to be explained from the structure of the sentence which aims to establish a relation of correspondence between the former and the latter clause. If we compare the sayings about the judgment of the Son of man in the Similitudes of the Ethiopic Enoch and in 2 Esdras, there it is always a question of the destruction of the impious and the salvation of the elect. To judge always means the decision about salvation or reprobation. It is just the same that we have in Lk. 12:8: the Son of man makes his final judgment always according to man's attitude to Jesus. Only thus is to be understood the passive referring to God in v. 9, where it is certainly not a question of the function of a witness, but of a decisive judgment. Thus in Lk. 12:8(f.) and Mk. 8:38 the saying refers to the function of the Son of man as judge, in accordance with the apocalyptic tradition from which of course the Son of man figure stems.

A "coming" or an "appearing" of the Son of man is not mentioned in the texts so far discussed. But this motive may also be shown to be part of the preaching of Jesus as is clear from other texts about the Son of man. Only the sayings Lk. 17:24 ‖ Matt. 24:27 and Lk. 17:26f. (28f.) ‖ Matt. 24:37–39 can make a serious claim to authenticity.

In the first mentioned, Lk. 17:24 par., it may well be that the Matthew text has retained the original words in the comparison, the Luke text in the other half of the sentence.[101] The connection with the preceding verse is quite certainly secondary, hence is no argument against genuineness.[102] It is no sound argument to suggest that we may have here a warning stemming from the later church and reflecting the OT idea of the day of the Lord.[103] It is a question of the announcement of a sudden advent of the Son of man, visible to all men, clothed in a tersely figurative formula which is thoroughly typical of Jesus' manner of expressing Himself. In this comparison with the lightning which flashes through the whole firmament it is certain that the coming of the Son of man is thought of in "universal-cosmic" terms, but the saying shows what is observable elsewhere in the teaching of Jesus, namely, a "radical reduction of the tendency to picturesque description which is characteristic of all apocalyptic literature."[104] Again, there is no express identification of Jesus with the Son of man, nor is it originally implied.

31

The case is similar with regard to Lk. 17:26f. par. Apart from the addition 17:28f., found only in Luke, about which there is some uncertainty, there are again no compelling reasons to deny authenticity.[105] Men living carelessly, as in the days of Noah and Lot, will be caught by the utterly un-suspected appearing of the Son of man, which will strike them down to their undoing. It is in the same sense, perhaps, that we should understand the original text of the saying about the sign of Jonah (Lk. 11:30) which is so difficult to interpret.[106]

If we attempt to determine the peculiar features of all these sayings about the appearing of the Son of man, the situation is the same as with those sayings about the function of judgment exercised by the Son of man; in both cases it is a question of a generally well-known motive by the help of which it is intended to express the nearness of eschatological events, and above all to qualify the specific character of the present situation. If in the sayings about the reign of God it is a question of the joyful message that salvation is dawning, if in the words about the judgment exercised by the Son of man the inescapability of the judgment now beginning is emphasized, then what is expressed in the words about the appearing of the Son of man is the unconditional character of Jesus' call to repentance, for the last gracious respite is passing away, and after it final condemnation is no longer to be avoided.

The sayings so far discussed show that Jesus assimilated into His preaching the motives of the sudden all-powerful coming of the Son of man and his exercise of the function of judge. Further sayings about the future action of the Son of man can hardly be shown to be genuine.[107] Nevertheless, from the Son of man texts which stemmed from the primitive church there is one striking indication that they were rooted in the preaching of Jesus; this is that the Son of man sayings are all formulated in the third person singular and placed in the mouth of Jesus Himself. "Son of man" is never found as a mode of address or in any formula of confession.[108]

This severely maintained style of formulation, like the distinction between the person of Jesus and the figure of the coming Son of man, cannot be convincingly explained if we try to find the origin of all the Son of man sayings in the invention of the first church.[109] The tendency which characterizes the post-resurrection period can be observed at work in two ways:

on the one hand the identification between Jesus and the coming Son of man is completed; on the other hand the apocalyptic traits are strengthened, there arises a certain tendency to describe picturesquely the happenings of the end of time, and there is frequent quotation, especially of details of the text, Dan. 7:13f.

This can plainly be recognized in the two secondary Marcan texts which belong here.[110] Mk. 13:26f. shows the "spirit and the literary technique of apocalyptic";[111] but it may not be said that the Son of man, active as judge, is not depicted here, for the sending forth of the angels and the assembling of the elect suggests the judge's act of salvation, corresponding to the judgment of destruction on the world and fallen humanity. The coming on the clouds of heaven is formulated by the use of Dan. 7:13; the phrase "with great power and glory" is probably an allusion to Dan. 7:14, yet here, unlike Daniel, the meaning conveyed is the parousia of the Son of man before the whole world.[112] Mk. 14:62, a text which will have to be discussed in detail in another context,[113] shows what a decisive role the investigation of scripture played, for the answer which Jesus gives to the high priest's question represents a combination of quotations from Dan. 7:13 and Ps. 110:1.[114] The purpose of these apocalyptic elements is to unfold and explain eschatology and Christology.[115]

Summary. The special features of the saying Lk. 12:8f., which refers to the function of the Son of man as judge, show that it may form a point of departure; its genuineness is not to be disputed. Also the sayings Lk. 17:24, 26f. (28f.) and perhaps 11:30 are to be reckoned as belonging to the teaching of Jesus, the former referring to the immediately imminent appearing of the Son of man. In both cases only the motives of the Son of man appearing and judging the world are made use of; there is no attempt at apocalyptic description. Furthermore, it is not primarily a question of prophecy of the future; but rather of qualifying the present, of the judgment about salvation and woe which is now taking place, and of the unconditional character of the call to repentance during the rapidly expiring respite of grace.

Secondly, it must be noted that in none of these texts is there an identification of Jesus with the Son of man, and that in Lk. 12:8f. there is even to be observed a clear differentiation of the two; again, there are sayings of Jesus extant in which the Son of man is spoken of in the third person, a formal characteristic which is retained in all later sayings. The post-resurrection community adhered to this formal style and identified the coming Son of man with the Jesus whose return was expected, so that a special type of self-statement arose.

In the climate of the apocalyptically moulded expectations of an imminent return of Jesus, the church, by means of traditional elements, evolved sayings about the parousia and judgment of the Son of man, placing the emphasis one-sidedly on futurity. In consequence, the action of the Son of man developed into an independent event alongside the breaking in of the Kingdom of God. But it is clear that this is a modification of the original idea.

4. *Words concerning the earthly Deeds of the Son of Man*

The words concerning the earthly deeds of the Son of man cannot be taken as a starting point for a consideration of the whole Son of man concept. As has been shown, such a use of the Son of man title on the lips of Jesus is most unlikely. Where, then, is the place of this group of sayings in the development of the tradition, and what are its characteristic features? We meet with it both in the logia source and in the pre-Marcan collection of disputes, Mk. 2:1–3:6. In both cases it is clear that we are faced by a Christological conception of the early church. The presupposition for this use of the Son of man title was the identification of Jesus with the coming Son of man. Since in Lk. 12:8f., the earthly Jesus in His fullness of power and authority stands over against the coming Son of man who is to judge the world, now on the basis of such an identification the earthly Jesus Himself was described as the Son of man.[116] Tödt has convincingly shown that in this matter we have not, as has in many quarters been asserted, a transference of the idea of the transcendental saviour to the person of the earthly Jesus—Jesus therefore is not to be regarded as a concealed heavenly being clad in human guise—but that rather the claim to full authority made by Jesus Himself, a claim which was to be confirmed by the coming Son of man, is now more particularly defined by the ascription to Him of the Son of man title.[117] The logia source was projected from the polarity between the earthly claim and the return of the Son of man in

34

full power and authority, and in it the Son of man sayings in connection with the growing repercussions of the Jesus tradition have found their most important outcome.[118] The individual logia about the earthly deeds of the Son of man can be summarily treated.[119] Moreover, their secondary character is mostly to be discerned from their intrinsic content.

In Mk. 2:10 the authority of Jesus to forgive sins is underlined by His self-description as "Son of man"; this is only intelligible on the assumption that there was an already firmly established titular use of the expression. Furthermore, the pronouncement occurs in that section of the narrative which plainly stands out as a later addition and must be considered as a product of the community.[120]

In Mk. 2:28 the previous sentence, namely, that the sabbath was made for man and not the reverse (a sentence whose essential meaning was obviously disputed at an early stage, and which Matthew and Luke have even eliminated), has been refashioned in a Christological sense: the Lord of the sabbath is not man, but the "Son of man".[121]

Matt. 12:32||Lk. 12:10, which in its stylized form strikes a soteriological note, discloses itself as an elaboration by the community, whatever be its exact relation to Mk. 3:28.[122] Lk. 6:22 also can make no claim to authenticity, as the comparison with the Matthean form of it suggests;[123] moreover, the whole declaration of blessing in Matt. 5:11f.||Lk. 6:22f. showing a close connection with the situation of persecution most probably first arose in the life of the church.[124] At all events, in the case of Matt. 8:20||Lk. 9:58 and Matt. 11:18f.|| Lk. 7:33f., it may seriously be questioned whether genuine words of the Lord lie at the basis of the text. As regards Matt. 11:18f. par. the mere fact that the Baptist is here neither a witness to Jesus nor His rival can be no convincing ground for authenticity.[125]

What is in question is a comparison of the two figures, which in this form may well have first arisen in the tradition of the community, and above all an attempt is made to characterize summarily the emergence of the two prophets;[126] this does not preclude the fact that in this passage commonly expressed opinions about the Baptist and Jesus have been taken up and used to "characterize this generation and to describe the trivial pretexts by which it seeks to escape the message".[127]

In Matt. 8:20∥Lk. 9:58, it must be considered that the saying, apart from the use of the Son of man title, contains nothing beyond a general maxim.[128] The linking of this simple proverbial statement with the thought of discipleship (Matt. 8:19 par.) might be understood in the sense that the object is to expound the motive of the renunciation of possessions,[129] this finding its sharpest expression in the idea of homelessness. But the pronouncement is here applied to Jesus Himself. Hence at the most it might be a case of disarrangement, as with Mk. 2:27 and 28,[130] but how in that case must the original text have read? In the present form of the passage Matt. 8:19f.∥Lk. 9:57f. it is not merely a question of discipleship entailing loss of home and possessions, but also of involvement in the fate which Jesus Himself bore and which brought Him into an indissoluble tension with the human race and into the position of being outcast and homeless on earth.[131] Such a Christologically heightened expression of the thought of discipleship is only conceivable in the post-resurrection period.

Finally, we have a special case in Mk. 10:45 (par. Matt. 20:28). This applies already to the first half of the text, v. 45a, because here, in contrast with all other sayings about the earthly deeds, deliberate lowliness is stressed.[132] In connection with it, v.45b takes up the motive of the surrender of life as a ransom for many, and the concept of the suffering servant of God is implied.[133]

All the words so far discussed stem, with the exception of redactional elaborations,[134] from the Palestinian tradition. Apart from the logia source and the aforementioned pre-Marcan collection of disputes, there is only one other saying about the earthly deeds of the Son of man, namely Lk. 19:10, a "preacher's maxim" linked to the story of Zacchaeus.[135] This saying to the effect that the Son of man came to seek and save the lost, like the narrative itself, is marked rather by Hellenistic-Judaic Christian features,[136] so that it may be supposed to have sprung up in isolation on Hellenistic ground to be added to the collection of Son of man maxims.[137]

In conclusion, we may point to the relatively ancient date of the sayings concerning the earthly deeds of the Son of man, which explains why the logia source incorporated them. The identification of the coming Son of man with the Jesus whose return was expected must at a very early stage have brought about the identification of the earthly Jesus with the Son of man. This is understandable, since Jesus assumed that His own earthly action and preaching would be confirmed by the coming Son of man. But the sayings about the earthly deeds in their present form and with the use of the Son of man title cannot conceivably be original words of Jesus. They presuppose the firmly fixed Christological use of the Son of man description, and even in detail their origination from the tradition of the primitive church is plainly recognizable.

5. *Words concerning the Passion and Resurrection of the Son of Man*

This last group of Son of man sayings to be discussed stands pre-eminently in the Gospel of Mark, that is, in so far as it is a question of the received tradition and not of redactional elaborations.[138] From the standpoint of the development of the tradition, this very fact suggests that the sayings about suffering are the latest of all the Son of man sayings to have been developed, and therefore failed to find a place in the logia source. It is further to be supposed that the shorter formulae, speaking only of the suffering of the Son of man,[139] which have been absorbed into the later parts of the passion narrative, are the oldest traditional elements in the group.[140] On the other hand, the prophecies of suffering and resurrection in Mk. 8:31, 9:31, 10:33f. represent more recent expansions. The third prophecy will have to be regarded as a sheer redactional development. Finally, in opposition to Tödt who reduces all these prophecies to a single basic structure,[141] two types must be distinguished, according to whether there is a reference to scripture or not.

In a detailed analysis it is best to start from Mk. 10:33f. This prophecy of the suffering and resurrection was invented by the evangelist.[142] We have here an expansion of Mk. 9:31. The ending καὶ ἀποκτενοῦσιν, καὶ μετὰ τρεῖς ἡμέρας ἀναστήσεται, apart from small variants, has been taken over. The παραδίδοται εἰς χεῖρας ἀνθρώπων has been broadly sketched on the basis of the passion narrative; its dependence on Mk. 14f. can be shown even to the wording. It is only the series "mock, spit, scourge" which seems not quite to harmonize; but the evangelist is here concerned to reach his climax in "kill", and it could best be attained in this way.[143] Moreover, the fact that Mk. 10:33f.

begins with the arrest is neither a proof that the prophecy of
suffering must be pre-Marcan, nor, still less, does it show that
the old passion narrative began with the arrest;[144] its explanation is rather that Mk. 10:33f. is concerned with that part of
the passion of Jesus which takes place in public. As in Mk. 9:31
it is a question of the delivering over of the Son of man into the
hands of men, and this is an echo of a characteristic basic element in the older conception of the Son of man.[145]

Mk. 10:33f. belongs to the type of expression concerning the
suffering of the Son of man, in which any allusion to the
necessary fulfilment of scripture is lacking. To the same type
belongs the short form Mk. 14:41b and Mk. 9:31, where it is
connected with a prophecy of the resurrection. The statement
about suffering renewed at the end of the Gethsemane story is
linked with the motive of the hour which gives expression to an
eschatological-soteriological thought alien to the original
tradition of the suffering Son of man.[146] But all the other motives
are characteristic of the Son of man tradition. The παραδίδοται
is already rooted in the old tradition of the passion; there is no
reason to speak of a "proclamatory word" or of a "παρα-
διδόναι-formula", the Biblical expression is primary.[147] It is
just by means of this formula that is most plainly expressed the
contrast, so characteristic of the whole Son of man tradition,
between the exaltation of the Son of man and the hostility of
men—a contrast that Tödt has well brought out.[148]

That the shorter form of the prediction, the mere prophecy
of suffering, must be the older, is shown not only by the fact
that only this one-clause form has found a place in the passion
narrative, but also by the remarkable formulation in Mk. 9:31:
καὶ ἀποκτενοῦσιν αὐτόν, καὶ ἀποκτανθεὶς μετὰ τρεῖς ἡμέρας
ἀναστήσεται. Here the repetitive passive participle is obviously
intended to co-ordinate death and resurrection and marks this
saying as being a more or less independent second member,
distinct from the original expression which ended with the
killing of Jesus.

It is further striking that ἀποκτείνειν and ἀναστῆναι are
distinguished from the terms ἀποθνήσκειν and ἐγερθῆναι which
are the terms currently used in other formulae of the passion.[149]
Here the decisive factor must have been, at least in regard to
ἀποκτείνειν, that it was a fixed technical term like the expression
"to be given up into someone's hand". In the late Judaic

38

tradition of the slaying of the prophets, the term had won a particular emphasis, as is shown in the NT by the quotation in Rom. 11:13, the probably pre-Christian word of Matt. 23:37, and the Pauline expression in 1 Thess. 2:15.[150] Also in regard to ἀναστῆναι the choice of word may well disclose a deliberate attempt at stylization,[151] for its singularity in contrast to other passion formulae is by no means limited to the turn of phrase but contains an essential motive: although Jesus stands in line with the OT messengers of God and their fate, nevertheless as the Son of man He steps through the gate of death; as contrasted with the implication of ἐγερθῆναι here the emphasis lies not on the divine action in the Easter event, but rather on the power of the Son of man to raise himself from the dead.[152] The sovereign action of the one who rises from the dead is set in contrast to his betrayal into the hands of men and his execution.[153] As regards the affirmations of suffering and resurrection, the Son of man conception has found its most strikingly characteristic expression in Mk. 9:31 for the basic conception of this Christology is here most consistently maintained.

The prediction of suffering in Mk. 9:31, together with the short form in Mk. 14:41b, is differentiated from those words about the suffering Son of man which in some way are concerned to allude to scripture and hence belong to the other type. In this type we find elaborations which are markedly mixed in character, for proof from scripture is no specific part of the Son of man conception. But the genesis of these mixed forms can be easily explained. First, the passive παραδίδοται contains a certain allusion to the secret will of God which is fulfilled in the suffering of the Son of man. Further, the formation of this type of saying has been conditioned by the tradition of the passion, and it is just the oldest layer of the passion tradition which was decisively moulded by the motive of the fulfilment of scripture,[154] so that an influence on the sayings about the suffering Son of man was easily exercised.

We find the oldest example of this type in Mk. 14:21, where the formula runs in two parallel statements: ὁ υἱὸς τοῦ ἀνθρώπου παραδίδοται[155] and ὁ υἱὸς τοῦ ἀνθρώπου ὑπάγει καθὼς γέγραπται περὶ αὐτοῦ. In the pronouncement of woe on the betrayer which is coupled with the latter statement there is most abruptly and sharply expressed the contrast between the exaltation of the

Son of man, whose word decides salvation or undoing, and mankind as a whole whose "exponent and representative" "that man" is.[156] In Mk. 8:31 this mixed type is further developed and modified. The second part offers no singularity, but, as in 9:31, completes the prediction of the resurrection. The first part however contains three peculiar features: δεῖ, πολλὰ παθεῖν and ἀποδοκιμασθῆναι ὑπὸ τῶν πρεσβυτέρων κἀὶ τῶν ἀρχιερέων καὶ τῶν γραμματέων. The phrase about being betrayed into the hands of men is here sacrificed in favour of these new elements. The δεῖ undoubtedly echoes the motive of the necessity of scriptural fulfilment[157] and corresponds to the καθὼς γέγραπται of Mk. 14:21. But, unlike that text and many another passage embodying the tradition of the passion, the necessity of scriptural fulfilment is not merely generally presupposed, but elucidated by the ἀποδοκιμασθῆναι κτλ. from Ps. 118:22, the image of the stone rejected by the builders, in which connection it is precisely stated who these builders were.

If the formula is so far clear, the πολλὰ παθεῖν creates some difficulty. It occurs in the NT only in sayings about the suffering Son of man, but merely in texts which are dependent on Mk. 8:31, and which therefore contribute nothing to the understanding of this passage itself.[158] The word πάσχειν in itself is somewhat more frequent and occurs, apart from its use in Lucan elaborations and in the late texts of the Letter to the Hebrews, always in formulae which treat of the sufferings of the Χριστός.[159] The phrase "suffer many things" might well presuppose this use of "suffer" in Christological expressions. Clearly it was introduced into sayings about the suffering Son of man just when the "be betrayed into the hands of men" had been replaced, but the "be rejected of . . ." which was substituted for it could not in the same comprehensive sense embrace the whole passion event—another indication that we have here a mixed type, for precisely in the Χριστός- formulae the thought of the necessity of the fulfilment of scripture is also characteristic and current.[160]

Now the δεῖ must be regarded as a typically Hellenic transcription of γέγραπται; in the Septuagint there is only one comparable text,[161] but in the NT there is more evidence of its use by typically Hellenic authors. Further, πάσχειν is an emphatically Greek word for which in the Semitic languages there is no real equivalent.[162] Thus, as for Lk. 19:10, we have to conclude that the Son of man words assumed a certain expansion and modification on Hellenic ground. Lk. 19:10 and Mk. 8:31 are related inasmuch as in both cases new ideas have been introduced into the Son of man sayings, and further very sharply expressed and meaningful logia have been created.[163] This does not preclude the fact that the Son of man tradition soon lost meaning and declined. Mk. 9:12b cannot be regarded as a further independent Son of man saying. It belongs to the redactional formulation of 9:9b and forms with the latter a self-contained prediction of suffering and resurrection.

In the section Mk. 9:9–13 an Elijah tradition has been used; the γέγραπται of v. 12b corresponds to that of v. 13b. Mk. 9:12b is differentiated from Mk. 8:31 only in that, as in 14:21, γέγραπται is used and instead of ἀποδοκιμασθῆναι (ὑπὸ κτλ.) the synonym ἐξουδενηθῆναι, which was likewise used for the translation of מאס in Ps. 118:22[164] and was here no doubt preferred because it is better fitted to express the use of the word absolutely. This tradition has so little that is characteristic that at best it may have been known to the evangelist as a variant of 8:31.[165]

A mixed formation of quite a different kind is to be seen in Mk. 10:45b, for there the assertion of the voluntary self-humiliation of the Son of man (v. 45a) is interpreted as a vicarious expiation.[166] No other allusion to Isa. 53 is to be found in the texts concerning the suffering Son of man. The euphemistic πολλὰ παθεῖν certainly contains no such allusion. Rather it might be asked whether the absolute ἐξουδενηθῆναι could be a translation of נִבְזֶה in Isa. 53:3;[167] but the fact that if so only a quite subordinate motive from Isa. 53 would have been adopted and that in addition the variant translation of Ps. 118:22 was a more obvious solution,[168] makes this thesis extremely improbable.

Summary. Our starting point is the juxtaposition of shorter and longer forms. In the beginning the sayings were probably concerned only with the suffering of the Son of man, and only later was there included also a statement about his resurrection. For this reason the predictions of the resurrection are fairly unified. On the other hand, in regard to the sayings about suffering, two basic types are to be distinguished. The one closely follows the sayings about the earthly activity of the Son of man, in that here the exaltation of the Son of man and his rejection by men is brought out. To this type belong Mk. 14:41b and 9:31, as well as the redactional imitation in Mk. 10:33f. The other type has been much more strongly influenced by the passion tradition and has taken over from that source the motive of the necessity of scriptural fulfilment, as is especially clear in Mk. 14:21. Both types, as well as the mixed form in Mk. 10:45, can be traced back to the Palestinian community tradition. But in the sphere of Hellenism such sayings have undergone an independent development and expansion, as is clear from the euphemistic formulae of Mk. 8:31 and 9:12b. The whole group of these sayings is undoubtedly the latest. It found no place in the logia source, but on the other hand was incorporated to a relatively large extent in the Marcan traditional material, where only a few words from the other groups have left any trace.

It is easy to discern that the various groups have a common root. In spite of the mixed forms and the somewhat more sharply devious later formations, they show an astonishing unity, a sign of the power exercised by the underlying Christological conception in the primitive church.[169] Their sphere of influence was above all Palestinian Christianity, but also certain circles of the Hellenistic Judaic Christian church lived by their inspiration, and while adopting particular new formations, such circles above all preserved this inheritance to the point of incorporating it into the written gospels, although the Son of man Christology had long been supplanted by other views.

NOTES

1. As regards outlines of the history of the research, reference may be made for the earlier period to Paul Feine, *Theologie des Neuen Testaments*, 1953[9], pp. 52ff., for the more recent research to C. C. McCown, *Jesus Son of Man: a Survey of recent Discussion, JR* 28 (1948), pp. 1–12, and to A. J. B. Higgins, *Son of Man-Forschung since "The Teaching of Jesus"* in *New Testament Essays (Studies in Memory of T. W. Manson)*, 1959, pp. 119–135.

2. It has been uti ized methodically on a broad basis by Wilhelm Bousset, *Kyrios Christos* (1913), 1921[2]; he treats the Son of man title as a characteristic of the Palestinian primitive church in contrast with the

Kyrios title of Hellenistic Christendom which was understood in reference to worship. Cf. Heinz Eduard Tödt, *Der Menschensohn in der synoptischen Überlieferung*, 1959.

3. The presentation that follows is confined to the most important and most discussed literature.

4. In the OT בֶּן אָדָם appears only in the indefinite form. The definite form of the Aramaic אֱנָשׁ בַּר is בַּר אֱנָשָׁא or, with a difference in dialect, בַּר נָשָׁא.

5. There what is said is almost always "this" or "that Son of man".

6. Cf. Julius Wellhausen, *Skizzen und Vorarbeiten* VI, 1899, pp. 187–215, especially pp. 194ff.; *id.*, *Einleitung in die drei ersten Evangelien*, 1911[2], pp. 123–130.

7. Hans Lietzmann, *Der Menschensohn, Ein Beitrag zur neutestamentlichen Theologie*, 1896, pp. 51ff. cf. *id.*, *Geschichte der alten Kirche* i, 1953[3], pp. 46f.

8. Lietzmann, *op. cit.*, pp. 38ff.; sharply attacked by Wellhausen, *Skizzen*, pp. 194ff.

9. Gustaf Dalman, *Die Worte Jesu* I (1898) 1930[2], pp. 191ff.; for the rest cf. also on this Lietzmann, *op. cit.*, p. 31, n. 5.

10. Dalman, *op. cit.*, p. 195; for a critical examination of the Galilean dialect cf. *id.*, *Grammatik des jüdisch-palästinischen Aramäisch*, 1905[2] (reprint 1960), pp. 41f., 43ff.

11. Dalman, *Worte Jesu*, pp. 192, 204f.

12. Paul Fiebig, *Der Menschensohn. Jesu Selbstbezeichnung mit besonderer Berücksichtigung des aramäischen Sprachgebrauchs für "Mensch"*, 1901, especially pp. 53ff., 119f.

13. Fiebig, *op. cit.*, pp. 55f.

14. Cf. Erik Sjöberg, *Der Menschensohn im äthiopischen Henochbuch* (*Acta Reg. Societatis Humaniorum Litterarum Lundensis* XLI), 1946, pp. 40f. Cf. *id.*, בן אדם und בר אנש im Hebräischen und Aramäischen, *Acta Orientalia* 21 (1950/53), pp. 57–65, 91–107.

15. This was admitted by Wellhausen, *Skizzen*, pp. 206ff.; *id.*, *Einl.*, pp. 129f., certainly only for the primitive church.

16. Moreover, here also the metaphorical mode of speech is still preserved in part: "and with Him (*scil.* the One who had a head of days) was another, whose countenance had the appearance of a man" (*Ethiopic Book of Enoch* 46, 1b).

17. Cf. the thorough discussions in Sjöberg, *Menschensohn*, pp. 42ff., especially pp. 56ff.; in a review of this book in *ThLZ* 74 (1949), col. 405 Joachim Jeremias regards the titular use in the Greek text as proved.

18. It remains to consider whether in the Ethiopic translation also with its demonstrative there is not concern to bring out clearly the determinate form of the word.

19. Cf. on this Martin Noth, "*Die Heiligen des Höchsten*", *Gesammelte Studien zum AT* (*Theol. Büch.* 6), 1960[2], pp. 274–290, who has anew advocated this view already earlier championed by Procksch.

20. In the conclusive analysis of Gustav Hölscher, *Die Entstehung*

des Buches Daniel, ThStKr 92 (1919), pp. 113–138, these elements have been eliminated as secondary.

21. The idea of the four empires also underlies the vision of Dan. 2: 31ff. and its interpretation in 2:36ff., confronted there with the "stone", the symbol of the indestructible kingdom, breaking off from the mountain, destroying the empires and filling the earth. Cf. Martin Noth, *Das Geschichtsverständnis der alttestamentlichen Apokalyptik, Ges. Stud.*, pp. 248–276, especially pp. 251ff.

22. As connection there serves on the one hand the contrast of the beasts to the "men", on the other hand the derivation from the sea of chaos and the appearance from heaven.

23. Martin Noth, *Zur Komposition des Buches Daniel, ThStKr* 98/99 (1926), pp. 143–163, especially pp. 144ff., attempted in a literary-critical way to resolve Dan. 7 into two independent sources, one of which (Dan. 7:9, 10, 13) he also regarded as the original of the metaphorical speeches in the *Ethiopic Book of Daniel*.

24. Cf. especially T. W. Manson, *The Teaching of Jesus*, 1935[2], *id.*, "The Son of Man in Daniel, Enoch and the Gospels", in *Studies in the Gospels and Epistles* (ed. M. Black), 1962, pp. 123–145.

25. C. J. Cadoux, *The Historic Mission of Jesus*, 1941, is an exception.

26. Vincent Taylor, *The Gospel according to St. Mark*, 1952 (reprint 1957), p. 384.

27. Théo Preiss, *Le Fils de l'Homme. Fragments d'un cours sur la Christologie du Nouveau Testament*, Montpellier 1951, especially pp. 16ff., 22ff., 69ff.

28. Cullmann, *Christologie*, pp. 157f.

29. For criticism of T. W. Manson's interpretation cf. McCown, *op. cit.*, p. 9; Erik Sjöberg, *Der verborgene Menschensohn in den Evangelien* 1955, pp. 241ff.; Eduard Schweizer, *Erniedrigung und Erhöhung bei Jesus und seinen Nachfolgern* (*AThANT* 28), 1955, pp. 88ff.; cf. in addition the review in Higgins, *op. cit.*, pp. 126f.

30. On the corporate way of looking at things cf. the Excursus in E. Schweizer, *op. cit.*, pp. 153f.

31. R. H. Fuller, *Mission and Achievement of Jesus*, pp. 98ff.

32. Just as little as an exclusive connection with Dan. 7 may a one-sided connection with the Son of man conception be admitted in the metaphorical speeches of the *Ethiopic Book of Enoch*, as in Rudolf Otto, *Reich Gottes und Menschensohn*, (1934) 1954[3], especially pp. 132ff.

33. Cf. Joachim Jeremias, *Erlöser und Erlösung im Spätjudentum und Urchristentum* in *Der Erlösungsgedanke* (*Deutsche Theologie* II), 1929, pp. 106–119; *id.*, article παῖς θεοῦ, *ThWb* V, especially pp. 686f. In addition to the already mentioned investigations of T. W. Manson cf. also his book, *The Servant-Messiah*, 1953, especially pp. 62ff., 73.

34. So also Willi Staerk, *Soter* I, 1933, pp. 72ff., 82ff., Julius Schniewind, *Das Evangelium nach Markus* (*NTD* 1), 1949[5], p. 116; C. H. Dodd, *According to the Scriptures*, 1952, p. 117.

35. Likewise William Manson, *Bist du der da kommen soll?* (≙ *Jesus the Messiah*, 1943), 1952, especially p. 142; Preiss, *op. cit.*, pp. 51ff.,

73f.; Cullmann, *Christologie*, p. 164; also Taylor, *Mk*, pp. 119f. with certain qualifications.

36. Fuller, *op. cit.*, pp. 95ff., 102ff., insists that the ministry of the Son of man is a future one and that Jesus looks out towards his coming.

37. Cf. Excursus I, pp. 56ff.

38. Cf. in particular the detailed criticism of Jeremias' thesis in Sjöberg, *Menschensohn im äth. Henoch*, pp. 116f.; *id.*, *Verborgener Menschensohn*, pp. 70f., 255ff.

39. The attempts that have again been made recently in Anglo-American circles to carry back the New Testament statements about the Son of man to the בן אדם in Ezekiel instead of to apocalyptic, need no serious refutation; cf. on this Higgins, *op. cit.*, pp. 123f.

40. Cf. e.g. Wilhelm Bousset, *Hauptprobleme der Gnosis* (*FRLANT* 10), 1907, pp. 194ff.; Wilhelm Bousset-Hugo Gressmann, *Die Religion des Judentums im späthellenistischen Zeitalter* (*HbNT* 21), 1926[3], pp. 354f., 489f.; C. H. Kraeling, *Anthropos and Son of Man*, 1927.

41. Cf. merely Carsten Colpe, *Die religionsgeschichtliche Schule* (*FRLANT* NT 60), 1961, pp. 16ff., 53ff.

42. A derivation from internal Israelite presuppositions such as W. Küppers, *Das Messiasbild der spätjüdischen Apokalyptik, Internat. Kirchl. Zeitschr.* 23 (1933), pp. 193–256; 24 (1934), pp. 47–72, has attempted is not in any way convincing. External Jewish influences are also rejected by André Feuillet, *Le fils de l'homme de Daniel et la tradition biblique*, *RB* 60 (1953), pp. 170–202, 321–346.

43. Cf. on this especially Walther Baumgartner, *Ein Vierteljahrhundert Danielforschung*, *ThR* NF 11, 1939, pp. 214ff.; Sigmund Mowinckel, *He that Cometh*, 1956, pp. 346ff., especially pp. 420ff., Sjöberg, *Menschensohn im äth. Hen.*, pp. 190ff.; Bentzen, *Dan.*, pp. 62ff.; Gerhard Iber, *Überlieferungsgeschichtliche Untersuchungen zum Begriff des Menschensohns im NT*, Heidelberg Dissertation 1953 (typescript), pp. 6ff., 38ff.; further Higgins, *op. cit.*, pp. 121f. Here there also intrudes the question as to the peculiar tradition of the *Ethiopic Book of Enoch* 71, according to which Enoch is welcomed by God in heaven as Son of man; cf. on this above all Sjöberg, *op. cit.*, pp. 147ff. First of all we are concerned here simply with the idea of withdrawal as in Gen. 5:24; *Jub.* 4:23. But he has been withdrawn who alone was righteous, and for the sake of righteousness all who walk in his ways will live with him in the world to come: *Ethiopic Book of Enoch* 71, 14ff. Enoch, however, is not "identified with the pre-existent Son of man" (p. 186), but as the single righteous man among the first men he is the representative of man created after the image of God and is received by God as "(Son of) man". It looks as if here we had before us a specifically Jewish attempt to explain the primitive man conception which stands in the background by the Biblical doctrine of creation. The *Slavonic Enoch* 22, 1–10; 24, 1ff. and 3 *Enoch* go very much further.

44. Against Cullmann, *Christologie*, pp. 169ff.

45. It is well known that expectation of the Son of man did not acquire significance for apocalyptic simply. There are many apocalyptic writings in which this figure is lacking.

46. Harald Riesenfeld, *Jésus transfiguré* (*Acta Seminarii Neotestament-ici Upsaliensis* XVI), 1947, pp. 63f.

47. On the place of apocalyptic in late Judaism and on the distinction between Son of man and Messiah cf. Chapter 3, pp. 140ff., 147f.

48. Arnold Meyer, *Jesu Muttersprache*, 1896, pp. 91ff.

49. Cf. Dalman, *Worte Jesu*, pp. 204f., 392f.; Sjöberg, *Der verborgene Menschensohn*, p. 239, n. 3. It is altogether unlikely and admits of no proof that Jesus used the demonstrative הֲהוּא בַּר נָשָׁא in distinction from a usual הַהוּא גַּבְרָא, but because of the titular use of ὁ υἱὸς τοῦ ἀνθρώπου the demonstrative became superflous in the Greek; so J. Y. Campbell, "The Origin and Meaning of the Term Son of Man", *JThSt* 48 (1947), pp. 145–155.

50. Eduard Schweizer, *Der Menschensohn*, *ZNW* 50 (1959), pp. 185–209, especially pp. 197ff., 205ff.

51. Schweizer, *op. cit.*, p. 198 with n.46; pp. 201f.

52. Lk. 12:8f.; Mk. 8:38//Lk. 12:26; Mk. 14:62.

53. Schweizer, *op. cit.*, pp. 198, 210f.

54. The assumption of an ambiguous designation or even of a secret name has played a role in more recent research for a long time. Fiebig, *op. cit.*, pp. 66ff., 97ff., e.g. states that "Son of man" is a self-designation of Jesus taken from Dan. 7, but that that passage was merely the starting point and not a barrier to the content of the concept; especially through its transference to Jesus' earthly work and his passion and resurrection it came to have a double meaning, cf. Ernst Percy, *Die Botschaft Jesu. Eine traditionskritische und exegetische Untersuchung* (*Lunds Universitets Årsskrift* N.F. Avd. 1, Bd. 49 no. 5), 1953, pp. 256ff.

55. Cf. on this Sjöberg, *Menschensohn im äth. Hen.*, pp. 58f.

56. Within the developed Son of man Christology of the primitive church then the statements regarding Jesus' work on earth and His passion have their useful place: on the one hand the fixing of titles permits a stable transmission, on the other hand the eschatological reference is maintained, if not in every single saying, yet in the general conception.

57. Since in Wisd. 2–5 the Son of man title is lacking, there are no certain conclusions to be drawn. The otherwise problematical concluding chapters of the metaphorical discourses of the *Ethiopic Book of Enoch* do not bear the burden of proof; moreover there is here an apocalyptic framework.

58. Schweizer, *op. cit.*, pp. 205f. He can reckon even short forms of the predictions of the passion such as Lk. 9:44 to these dominical words.

59. *Op. cit.*, pp. 188ff., 202ff.

60. Cf. on this in detail Excursus II, pp. 129ff. If Schweizer, *op. cit.*, pp. 192ff., points out that Dan. 7:13f. is also to be understood not in the sense of a descent fron heaven but as a heavenly exaltation, it has here to be observed that it is indeed a matter of an enthronement (cf. Bentzen, *Dan.*, p. 64), but that this "exaltation" coincides with the eschatological consummation, whilst the New Testament conception of the exaltation is concerned with a transference of power in heaven before the final consummation. The two need to be carefully distinguished.

Moreover it may not be overlooked that in the New Testament only the phrase "coming on the clouds" has been taken up, doubtless very deliberately, from Dan. 7:13, and so the clouds are understood as a symbol of the epiphany (cf. on this Albrecht Oepke, art. νεφέλη, *ThWb* IV, pp. 904–912); Dan. 7:13 has thus been put at the service of a view of the parousia.

61. It ought not to surprise us that the parousia statements, apart from the words about the Son of man, are poorly attested, a matter to which Schweizer, *op. cit.*, pp. 192ff. refers.

62. Philipp Vielhauer, *Gottesreich und Menschensohn in der Verkündigung Jesu*, in *Festschrift für Günther Dehn*, 1957, pp. 51–79. There follow him Hans Conzelmann, "Gegenwart und Zukunft in der synoptischen Tradition", *ZThK* 54 (1957), pp. 277–296, especially pp. 281ff.; *id.*, "Zur Methode der Leben-Jesu-Forschung", *ZThK* 56 (1959), Beih. I, pp. 9f.; in part also Eduard Schweizer, *op. cit.*, pp. 185ff., 206f.

63. Tödt, *Menschensohn*, pp. 301ff., has rightly emphasized this against Vielhauer.

64. Conzelmann, *ZThK* 56 (1959) Beih. I, pp. 10ff.

65. Vielhauer, *op. cit.*, pp. 71ff.

66 Against Vielhauer, *op. cit.*, p. 76. Cf. Rudolf Schnackenburg, *Gottes Herrschaft und Reich*, 1959, pp. 23ff.

66. Against Vielhauer, *op. cit.*, p. 76.

67. Thus the secular-political foundation of the exclusive dominion of God in Israel (with incorporation of the Gentiles) as perhaps in Deutero-Isaiah; Tobit 14:5ff., *Jubilees* 1:15ff. on the one hand and the apocalyptic expectation of Dan. 2; *Assumption of Moses* 10; *Ethiopic Book of Enoch* 1:3ff. and the like on the other hand.

68. There belongs here the phrase "to take on one's self the yoke of the kingdom of God" as do also reflections on the concealment and shining forth of the kingdom of God, in which an eschatological basic understanding remains the starting point.

69. In addition there is the revelation of secrets in the *Ethiopic Book of Enoch* 46:3; 51:3. But even here it is a matter of the transition from the old to the new aeon and not of the time of salvation itself.

70. Consequently the obscurity also as to whether actually the Son of man is set upon the throne of God, is not accidental; cf. Sjöberg, *Menschensohn im äth. Hen.* pp. 63ff.

71. Cf. *Ethiopic Book of Enoch* 45:4ff.; 62:14; 71:16.

72. The situation is somewhat different in Dan. 7:13f. where the Son of man is enthroned and besides is the representative of everlasting dominion. But precisely in this it appears that the New Testament does not go back primarily to Dan. 7, and indeed the citation of this passage of Scripture also contains a clear modification of the idea; cf. p. 46, n. 60 above.

73. Later rabbinical theology has even provided an adjustment of this; cf. Paul Volz, *Die Eschatologie der jüdischen Gemeinde im neutestamentlichen Zeitalter*. 1934, pp. 71f.; Joseph Klausner, *The Messianic Idea in Israel*, 1956, pp. 408ff.; further Chapter 3, pp. 145ff.

74. Cf. on this Sjöberg, *op. cit.*, pp. 8off.

75. Against Vielhauer, *op. cit.*, pp. 74ff. The situation is somewhat different in the association of the Messiah expectation and an apocalyptic theocratic conception, for then the Messianic time is actually reckoned to this aeon and is marked off even more sharply from the reign of God, as in 2 Esdras 7:28ff.; yet in the sense of a commencing period this belongs to the expected final happenings. Cf. also the *Kaddish* prayer: "May he direct to his royal dominion . . . and bring forth his Messiah". On this Kuhn, *ThWb* I, p. 573; Tödt, *Menschensohn*, pp. 300f.

76. Vielhauer, *op. cit.*, p. 77.

77. Cf. on this Volz, *Eschatologie*, pp. 64ff.

78. There is also a disputing of each and every Son of man statement in F. C. Grant, *The Gospel of the Kingdom*, 1940, and in H. B. Sharman, *Son of Man and Kingdom of God*, 1944.

79. Conzelmann, *ZThK* 54 (1957), pp. 287f.

80. Conzelmann, *op. cit.*, pp. 281f., reckons in my opinion much too much with the particularly apocalyptic conception content.

81. Anton Vögtle, *Grundfragen zweier neuer Jesusbücher*, *ThRev* 54 (1958), col. 103.

82. Cf. Conzelmann, *ThKZ* 56 (1959) *Beih.* 1, pp. 9ff.

83. Conzelmann, *ZThK* 54 (1957), pp. 285, 288.

84. Otherwise Ethelbert Stauffer, *Jesus. Gestalt und Geschichte*, 1957, pp. 122ff., 128ff. on the words about the Son of man. He follows in what is essential the thesis of Rudolf Otto, *Reich Gottes und Menschensohn*, 1954[3], pp. 146f., 171ff., which moreover has also been taken over in Martin Dibelius (-Werner Georg Kümmel), *Jesus*, 1960[3], pp. 78ff., 84f.; against it rightly Sjöberg, *Verborgener Menschensohn*, pp. 122f., 243f.

85. Luke has, in addition to giving this form in 12:8f, reproduced it in 9:26 with a small abridgment; Matt. in 16:27 has decomposed the saying so that it no longer has two members and out of its conclusion has made a promise of the parousia and of the judgment of the Son of man.

86. Cf. Ernst Käsemann, *Sätze heiligen Rechtes im Neuen Testament*, *NTSt* 1 (1954/55), pp. 248–260. their pp. 256f.

87. Cf. concordance.

88. Cf. Tödt, *op. cit.*, pp. 39ff.

89. Cf. Chapter 5, pp. 307ff. This motif has also forced its way into the parallel in Matt. to Lk. 12:8f.

90. Against Vielhauer, *op. cit.*, pp. 69f.

91. Cf. also the recent work of James M. Robinson, *Kerygma und historischer Jesus*, 1960, p. 158(f.) n. 1.

92. So repeatedly Ernst Käsemann, *Die Anfänge christlicher Theologie*, *ZThK* 57 (1960), pp. 162–185.

93. In the two articles that have been mentioned Käsemann does not inquire into the form Lk. 12:8f., but he does not at all regard the Son of man motif as a part of the proclamation of Jesus (*Exeg. Vers.* I, p. 211; *ZThK* 57, 1960, p. 179).

94. Tödt, *op. cit.*, pp. 37ff., 50ff.

95. Käsemann, *NTSt* 1 (1954/55), pp. 257f.

96. That, it is true, does not hold good always, for such a sentence as 1 Cor. 3:17 comes naturally from the primitive church.

97. Cf. also E. Schweizer, *op. cit.*, *ZNW* 50, 1959, p. 188.

98. That in v. 9 it is not simply a judgment executed by God Himself that is spoken of follows from the fact that the phrase "before the angels" (τοῦ θεοῦ is a later addition) must be understood as a circumlocution for "before God"; cf. Dalman, *Worte Jesu*, p. 161.

99. So above all Tödt, *op. cit.*, pp. 40f., 52, 61.

100. With reason Schweizer, *ZNW* 50, 1959, pp. 193f., looks for the roots of this motif. But the allusion to the exalted righteous as witnesses for the prosecution is not valid.

101. παρουσία is a typically Matthean expression within the Synoptic tradition.

102. In Vielhauer, *op. cit.*, pp. 67f., this is the only reason against the genuineness.

103. So E. Schweizer, *ZNW* 50, 1959, p. 190, but with a mark of interrogation which he himself has inserted.

104. Tödt, *op. cit.*, p. 61.

105. In Lk. 17:26ff., there occurs in part a new interpretation conditioned by the context. In the redactional introductory verse 22 the discourse is obviously about Jesus as the Son of man working on earth, thence "the days of the Son of man" (plur.). In v. 24 just as in v. 30 it is a matter of the coming at the end of time (mention is made here of the "day" or "his day" in the sing.), in v. 25 reference is made to the suffering Son of man and in v. 26 to "the days" of the Son of man in the sense of the time immediately preceding the parousia. The evangelist is at pains to assert the different aspects of the Son of man predicate transferred to Jesus and to give the statements severally an exact definition in the history of salvation. When the concept of the parousia is left out of account, Matt. with his exclusive glance at the appearing of the Son of man restores the original intention of the saying.

106. Cf. also Tödt, *op. cit.*, pp. 48ff.; Anton Vögtle, "Der Spruch vom Jonaszeichen" in *Synoptische Studien* (*Festschrift für A. Wikenhauser*), 1953, pp. 230–277.

107. Matt. 10:23; 19:28 are quite certainly creations of the church; cf. Tödt, *Menschensohn*, pp. 56ff. But even the assumption that there is a genuine word of Jesus in Matt. 24:44 par.—so Tödt, p. 50—cannot be upheld, for here relatively to the words of Matt. 24:27, 37, 39 a distinct parenetic conclusion is drawn; the tradition of the parable closely connected with Matt. 24:44 also tells against a great age; cf. E. Schweizer, *ZNW* 50, 1959, pp. 190f.

108. Acts 7:56 represents the only exception; but this text, which has been considerably worked up by Luke, is otherwise a problem in itself and does not cancel what has been said.

109. In favour of a genesis within the church, Vielhauer, *op. cit.*, p. 79, appeals to the eschatological significance of Jesus and for the rest to the conception of exaltation which was preformed by the *Ethiopic Book of Enoch* 71. But the analogy with the disputed chapter of the

metaphorical discourses is highly problematic and the conception of exaltation may not at all be assumed for the period in which the Son of man conception was developed.

110. So also in redactional passages in the Gospel of Matt.; cf. 13:41; 16:27, 28; 19:28 (25:31).

111. Tödt, *op. cit.*, pp. 31f.

112. It is well known that Mk. 13 gives a powerful presentation of the final events, a presentation that has been fed from late Jewish apocalyptic traditions.

113. Cf. Excursus 11, pp. 130f. and Chapter 3, pp. 162ff.

114. Moreover, it is well to recognize here again how largely the motif of the coming of the Son of man on the clouds of heaven was made independent; the Daniel passage was evidently understood only of this motif which had meanwhile been given a new interpretation; cf. p. 46 n. 60 above.

115. The discussion of texts is confined to the early tradition preserved in Q and Mark; Tödt, *Menschensohn*, pp. 62ff., 88ff., is to be compared regarding the redactional developments in Matt. and Luke.

116. Casey, *JThSt* NS 9, 1958, p. 265.

117. Tödt, *op. cit.*, pp. 105ff.

118. A laborious working out of the Christological character of the logia source is one of the most important sections in Tödt, *op. cit.*, pp. 212ff., also pp. 258ff. A systematic building up of it according to subjects and an eschatological adjustment of it had already been well set out by T. W. Manson, *The Sayings of Jesus*, 1949[2].

119. I refer to Tödt, *op. cit.*, pp. 105ff. for all details.

120. Since the analysis by William Wrede, *Zur Heilung des Gelähmten* (*Mk. 2, 1ff.*), *ZNW* 5, 1904, pp. 354–358, vv. 5b–10 has been eliminated by many exegetes. Against that others have supported the view that questions can no longer be carried back behind the present rendering. It cannot actually be disputed that the idea of the story is that of a close connection between the forgiveness of sins and healing; moreover the question as to the relation between sins and sickness was familiar to the Judaism of that period (cf. John 9:2f.). On the other hand, the exceedingly harsh transition from v. 10 to v. 11 is not to be overlooked, also the middle portion has all too clearly the character of a theological reflection. Consequently another demarcation must be made: v. 5b is still a constituent part of the original text and finds in v. 11 (without the introductory σοὶ λέγω) its direct continuation; vv. 6–10 is secondary and has been interpolated. If the forgiveness of sins is regarded as a part of the narrative, it can then be explained more easily how the addition of the middle portion came about. With the justification undertaken by the church of the power of Jesus to forgive sins the Son of man title was also introduced.

121. Cf. also Ernst Käsemann, *Das Problem des historischen Jesus*, *ZThK* 51, 1954, pp. 145f.

122. Tödt, *op. cit.*, pp. 109ff., 282ff. would like to overturn the widely disseminated view that Mk. 3:28 is early as compared with the Q-version; cf. p. 323 n.88 below.

123. Here certainly the Son of man title was not first redactionally added by Luke, on the other hand it has not been cancelled even by Matt. As collectively the Beatitudes show, the Q-tradition reached the evangelists in this passage in two different renderings, in which in Matt. 5:11f./Lk. 6:22f. the agreement is still relatively great.

124. Cf. Bultmann, *Syn. Trad.*, p. 115.

125. Against Schweizer, *ZNW* 50, 1959, pp. 199f.

126. Cf. the twice repeated ἦλθεν; also Bultmann, *op. cit.*, pp. 167f.

127. Tödt, *op. cit.*, p. 106.

128. With Bultmann, *op. cit.*, p. 102, n. 2 (cf. the Supplement, p. 14) against Schweizer, *ZNW* 50, 1959, p. 199; that sentences hold good only for certain situations does not exclude their general validity.

129. Cf. also Herbert Braun *Spätjüdisch-häretischer und frühchristlicher Radikalismus (BHTh* 24) ii, 1957, pp. 73ff.

130. Cf. also Mk. 8:34, the saying about bearing the cross. The understanding that is current among us with reference to the cross of Jesus is to be assumed first for the primitive church. If the saying goes back to Jesus, then he cannot have treated of imitation in this Christological sense. According to Eric Dinkler, *Jesu Wort vom Kreuztragen* in *Neutestamentliche Studien für Rudolf Bultmann*, 1957[2], pp. 110–129, there is doubtless the possibility of understanding the word not of an imitation of the passion but instead in the sense of a mark of ownership; in the case of *taw* (sign of the cross) it is then a matter of an eschatological sign and of belonging to God (following Ezek. 9:4ff.).

131. We cannot on any account make do with the explanations: "Son of man" denotes the "man κατ' ἐξοχήν" or lays emphasis on Jesus' "fellowship with men"; so on the one hand Theodor Zahn, *Das Evangelium des Matthäus (Komm NT* 1), 1922[4], pp. 349ff., 354ff., on the other hand Adolf Schlatter, *Der Evangelist Matthäus. Seine Sprache, sein Ziel, seine Selbständigkeit*, 1929 (1959[5]), pp. 285f.

132. In the original rendering of the saying about serving Lk. 22:27, the Son of man title is wanting.

133. Cf. Excursus I, pp. 56f.

134. Matt. 13:37; 16:13; Lk. 18:8b are to be regarded as redactional logia about the Son of man working on the earth.

135. Cf. on this concept Dibelius, *Formgeschichte*, pp. 60f.

136. Lk. 19:10 takes up the chief catchword of the story, σωτηρία v. 9. In the earliest tradition σῴζειν is used, apart from "deliverance" from sickness, of future salvation, cf., e.g. Matt. 10:22; Mk. 13:13b; in Paul σωτηρία has still to do with the eschatological accomplishment of salvation and σωτήρ is correspondingly used in Phil. 3:20. ἀπώλεια also is understood first of all eschatologically, cf. Phil. 1:28; 3:19; the phrase "the lost sheep of Israel" in Matt. 10:5; 15:24 does not tell against that, it being a matter of a figurative word, and besides it also includes an eschatological component. In Lk. 19:1ff., however, another understanding presents itself. Here σωτηρία is referred to the earthly work of Jesus and as in v. 10 mention is made of a σῶσαι τὸ ἀπολωλός by the Son of man. At the same time we come upon a thought which is dependent on the Old Testament but not specifically Palestinian, for

which reason its derivation from Hellenistic Jewish Christianity is the most likely. In an interesting way there also emerge close connections with the stratum of tradition about Jesus as Son of David; cf. also Chapter 4, pp. 258ff. For the rest the use of $\sigma\omega\zeta\epsilon\iota\nu$, $\sigma\omega\tau\eta\rho\iota\alpha$ and $\sigma\omega\tau\eta\rho$ is in need of a basically new investigation.

137. That on the soil of Gentile Christianity the Son of man designation soon lost its original significance is shown on the one hand by Ign., *Eph.* 20:2: $\dot{\epsilon}\nu\ '\text{I}\eta\sigma\sigma\hat{\upsilon}\ X\rho\iota\sigma\tau\hat{\omega}$, ... $\tau\hat{\omega}\ \upsilon\dot{\iota}\hat{\omega}\ \dot{\alpha}\nu\theta\rho\dot{\omega}\pi\sigma\upsilon\ \kappa\alpha\dot{\iota}\ \upsilon\dot{\iota}\hat{\omega}\ \theta\epsilon\sigma\hat{\upsilon}$, where "Son of man" signifies only the humanity of Jesus (here this understanding appears for the first time), on the other hand by the *Gospel of Thomas* 86: " (The foxes have their holes) and the birds have (their) nests, but the Son of man has no place to lay his head and to rest", where in a close borrowing from the text of Matt. 8:20 par. a generalization to all Christians is assumed and the gnostic motif of "rest" is taken up.

138. Mk. 8:31; 9:9b, 12b, 31; 10:33f.; 14:21, 41b.

139. As against Tödt, *op. cit.*, pp. 134, 137, I am of opinion that both the words about the suffering Son of man in the first part of the passion story (Mk. 14:21, 41b) were not first introduced by Mark.

140. Schweizer, *ZNW* 50, 1959, pp. 196f.

141. Tödt, *op. cit.*, pp. 141f.

142. Otherwise Tödt, *op. cit.*, pp. 186f.

143. Cf. Mark 14:53, 65; then 15:1 (here also "to deliver"); 15:20 (we do not think of v. 31); 15:19 (not to be referred to 14:65); 15:15 (it is of no importance that $\phi\rho\alpha\gamma\epsilon\lambda\lambda\sigma\hat{\upsilon}\nu$ stands here but $\mu\alpha\sigma\tau\iota\gamma\sigma\hat{\upsilon}\nu$ in the prediction of the passion, both denoting the *verberatio* which according to Roman law was associated with the execution). The designation of the Jewish authorities as "the high priests (plur.) and the scribes" is typically redactional, cf. 11:18 (this will be further substantiated in a larger context elsewhere). That the Jewish authorities are named has its prototype in the portion of tradition 8:31, yet the naming there does not show the two representations that are characteristic of Mark.

144. So, e.g. Joachim Jeremias, *Die Abendmahlsworte Jesu*, 1960[3], pp. 88f., a thesis that otherwise is frequently supported.

145. In the whole of the Gospel of Mark a soteriological explication of the death of Jesus is confined to Mk. 10:45 and the Lord's Supper paradosis Mk. 14:22–24.

146. Cf. Karl Hermann Schelkle, *Die Passion Jesu in der Verkündigung des Neuen Testaments*, 1949, pp. 75f., Tödt, *Menschensohn*, pp. 172f.

147. Cf. Excursus I, pp. 59ff.

148. Apparently $\epsilon\dot{\iota}s\ \tau\dot{\alpha}s\ \chi\epsilon\hat{\iota}\rho\alpha s\ \tau\hat{\omega}\nu\ \dot{\alpha}\mu\alpha\rho\tau\omega\lambda\hat{\omega}\nu$ in Mk. 14:41b is already a secondary modification and $\epsilon\dot{\iota}s\ (\tau\dot{\alpha}s)\ \chi\epsilon\hat{\iota}\rho\alpha s\ (\tau\hat{\omega}\nu)\ \dot{\alpha}\nu\theta\rho\dot{\omega}\pi\omega\nu$ as in Mk. 9:31 must be assumed as the most original wording; on this Joachim Jeremias, art. $\pi\alpha\hat{\iota}s\ \theta\epsilon\sigma\hat{\upsilon}$, *ThWb* V, p. 711.

149. Both the last-named concepts are met with frequently in the epistolary literature of the New Testament.

150. On the late Jewish tradition relating to this cf. Hans Joachim Schoeps, *Die jüdischen Prophetenmorde* in *Aus frühchristlicher Zeit*, 1950, pp. 126–143.

151. The "after three days" shows an earlier use which has later been pushed out by the "on the third day".

152. Here Johannine ideas are preformed, perhaps John 10:17f.

153. Cf. Tödt, *op. cit.*, p. 172.

154. Moreover, in the Synoptic tradition Scriptural proof has a secure place only in controversial discourse.

155. Here there is the bare "to be betrayed"; the characteristic addition "into the hands of men (sinners)" is lacking. The reason of this may be in the fact that as regards Judas thought is centred much more concretely on the act of betrayal, whilst the stereotyped phrase is meant to designate the event of the passion generally.

156. Tödt, *op. cit.*, pp. 183f.

157. Tödt, *op. cit.*, pp. 174ff. (cf. also pp. 150ff.), has given further proof that this δεῖ brings to expression the thought of Scriptural necessity and not that of apocalyptic conformity to law.

158. Besides in the Synoptic parallels to Mk. 8:31 it stands in the redactional formations Mk. 9:12b; Lk. 17:25.

159. Cf. Lk. 24:26, 46; Acts 3:18; 17:3; 1 Pet. 3:21 (23); 4:1 (3:18 *v. l*).

160. Cf. only 1 Cor. 15:3b–5; also Chapter 3, pp. 175ff.

161. Dan. 2:28f. and there in place of an original future.

162. Cf. Wilhelm Michaelis, art. πάσχω, *ThWb* V, pp. 906f..

163. Tödt, *op. cit.*, p. 186. also states that in the case of Mk. 8:31 means of testing clearly whether it belongs to the Palestinian tradition can no longer be obtained; it can, however, in my opinion be said that the linguistic evidence points to the Hellenistic sphere.

164. Evidence in Michaelis, *ThWb* V, p. 193, n. 79.

165. That Mark did not regard this tradition as independent also emerges from the fact that side by side with 8:31; 9:31 he has himself in accordance with his plan formulated a third prediction of the passion in 10:33f.

166. Cf. also in detail Excursus I, pp. 56ff.

167. Cf. Jeremias, *ThWb* V. p. 704.

168. Cf. only Acts 4:11.

169. It is beyond question that the two later groups of sayings assume those about the coming Son of man and must be understood from this eschatological point of view, even if there no direct reference is made to the final happenings.

EXCURSUS I

The Idea of the Vicariously Suffering Servant of God in the Earliest Christianity

In connection with statements about Jesus' passion, the question presents itself how far reference is made to the conception of the Servant of God in Isaiah 53.[1] It is well known that clear indications are extremely scanty. In the interest of method it must, moreover, be realized that there is altogether only a single motif on the strength of which an influence of this prophetic statement can be proved with certainty, namely the conception specific for Isa. 53 of vicarious expiatory suffering.[2]

Since in the frequently atomistic exegesis of that time[3] references to items of a text do not in any way involve a taking over of the basic ideas of the section of text concerned, all citations from and allusions to Isa. 53 which do not expressly contain the motif of vicarious atonement must be excluded. That holds good for the bearing of sicknesses Matt. 8:17, for the two allusions to the silence of Isa. 53:7 in Mk. 14:61a and 15:5, and also for the word about being reckoned among the transgressors in Lk. 22:37. Likewise it holds good for the detailed citation in the story of the chamberlain in Acts 8:32f., where mention is made of the slaughter of a lamb and of deliverance from death and yet the idea of vicarious atonement is lacking; also it holds good for the expression ἀρνίον ἐσφαγμένον in Revelation, which, following Isa. 53:7, throws into relief obedience and readiness for death with no words of contradiction.[4] It has rather to be considered whether ὁ ἀμνὸς τοῦ θεοῦ ὁ αἴρων τὴν ἁμαρτίαν τοῦ κόσμου John 1:29(36) is not related to the idea of the expiatory suffering of the Servant of God.[5]

On the other hand, in inquiry regarding the vicariously suffering Servant of God the designation παῖς θεοῦ or ἅγιος παῖς θεοῦ in Acts 3:13, 26; 4:27, 30 must be ruled out, for, in spite of the allusion to the statement of Isa. 52:13 about the glory of the Servant of God (Acts 3:13), the leading thought of Isa. 53 is not decisive here, all reference to the motif of expiation being lacking.[6]

54

Accordingly it remains merely to investigate in the early statements and texts the so-called ὑπέρ-formulae, the word λύτρον in Mk. 10:45b, the eucharistic paradosis, and some phrases connected with παραδιδόναι.

The "ὑπέρ-formulae"[7] give expression to the idea of vicarious atonement and are closely connected with statements about Jesus' death. In primitive Christianity the death of Jesus is understood not always but yet frequently as an expiatory death. The idea does not indeed appear in the earliest stratum of the report of the passion, but it was undoubtedly received in the sphere of the early Palestinian church. In this way the soteriological meaning of the passion could be made intelligible. Its great age is shown not only by the formula of confession 1 Cor. 15:3b–5, which originated among Aramaic speaking Christians—it will be carefully investigated later[8]—but also by the motif of expiation itself.

Some years ago Eduard Lohse pointed out in an impressive way to what an extent the conception of death for one's own sins and as a vicarious atonement was rooted and spread abroad in Palestinian late Judaism.[9] Isa. 53 is indeed the earliest evidence for the idea of a vicarious expiatory death; nevertheless the conception in all its compass cannot be derived from there but boasts a broader stream.[10] Moreover, it needs to be noted that the idea of an atonement "for many (all)"[11] which is characteristic of Isa. 53, does not appear elsewhere in late Judaism. Nothing is said anywhere of an atoning death having universal validity; the expiatory virtue remains throughout restricted to Israel. This means that Isa. 53 has independently carried further what was obviously an older motif.[12] On the other hand, it has to be observed that the whole of late Judaism consistently avoids reference to Isa. 53 in its statements about expiation.[13]

These presuppositions need to be taken into consideration for primitive Christianity; on the one hand, a fairly wide dissemination of the idea of vicarious atonement has to be reckoned with; on the other hand, however, the motif of atonement is by no means necessarily connected with Isa. 53 and consequently does not as a matter of course comprise the idea of a vicarious standing surety "for many (all)".

This means that such formal phrases about the death of Jesus as "for us (you)" and "for our sins" and the like are not

55

derived from Isa. 53, but rather assume the conception of atonement that obtained in late Judaism and was generally spread abroad. Only statements which make mention of a vicarious death "for many" or otherwise comprise a clear reference to the atonement conception of Isa. 53, may be brought into connection with that prophetic chapter.

That it may not be said that in time an original, exact rendering of its statement partially faded to a "for us"[14] follows from this one fact, that 1 Cor. 15:3b is a very early instance, and it, as a firmly fixed and carefully worded confession formula, must at all events contain an exact rendering of what was being thought, especially as in it reference is made expressly to the Scriptures.

The development must have taken place in the opposite direction; the motif of expiation was not taken over by the church of the earliest days from Isa. 53 and at first had nothing to do with Scriptural proof.[15] Only afterwards were atonement statement and Scriptural motif connected with one another. 1 Cor. 15:3b–5 is the earliest indication[16] that Isa. 53 exercised an influence at second hand so that in some passages there came about statements about the death of Jesus in the sense of a vicarious atonement "for many (all)".[17] It needs also to be kept in view that the idea of Isa. 53 cannot have been at all obvious to the particularistic thought of the earliest Jewish Christian church.[18]

As has already been explained, Mk. 10:45 comes from an early saying about service v. 45a, with which the Son of man title was connected and the statement about atonement v. 45b combined.[19] The wording makes it likely that here there is dependence on Isa. 53, yet this has been disputed repeatedly so that an accurate examination is necessary. Büchsel himself, who proceeds from the Old Testament, leaves it open whether what underlies here is a ransom motif or an idea of sacrifice or the conception of the Suffering Servant of God.[20] Even a Pauline influence[21] or an impinging of Hellenistic-Christian redemption doctrine has been reckoned with and altogether an Old Testament Jewish basis has in consequence been disputed.[22]

Recently C. K. Barrett has sought to show that there cannot be an immediate connection with Isa. 53[23]; and his arguments must be gone into somewhat more closely. The fact that Mk. 10:45a has in it no sort of reminiscence of Isa. 53 and its statement about atonement, signifies nothing regarding v. 45b. It is surprising that Barrett has compared δοῦναι τὴν ψυχὴν αὐτοῦ with הֶעֱרָה לַמָּוֶת נַפְשׁוֹ Isa. 53:12, to which it does not naturally correspond, instead of with נַפְשׁוֹ . . . אִם־תָּשִׂים v. 10, especially as here there occurs the concept אָשָׁם. It may not be stated without more ado that λύτρον and אָשָׁם do not answer to one another since LXX evidence for that is lacking. The passages adduced by Barrett in which λύτρον is used in the sense of an equivalent compensation contain either the idea of the giving of a (real) compensation "for" life or they contain the lex talionis motif, according to which the compensation for life can only be life, but nowhere is life given *as* compensation and indeed "for" sins (Isa. 53:11b, 12c).[24] It has then to be maintained that, in spite of a connection in verbal usage which cannot be shown clearly, it is only in respect of content that the thought of Isa. 53:10 can be basic.[25] Likewise the phrase ἀντὶ πολλῶν has no verbal but an essential parallel. The five times repeated רַבִּים in Isa. 52:13–53:12 has also not been overlooked by Barrett. It has already been shown that ἀντὶ (ὑπὲρ) πολλῶν cannot be regarded merely as an expression of the general late Jewish and early Christian conception of atonement,[26] but that precisely because of its inclusive, universal sense it must have a connection with Isa. 53.[27]

In particular, reference can here be made to Jeremias,[28] with whom Eduard Lohse agrees, with undoubtedly sound qualifications, that in Mk. 10:45b we are concerned not with a genuine word of the Lord but with an interpretation by the primitive church.[29] Whether a "ransom in the final judgment" is spoken of[30] is open to question, for the word about the Son of man which occurs here refers to Jesus' earthly work and the salvation already wrought by his death, which is of course preserved for believers at the last judgment. By reference to Isa. 53 the peculiarities of the saying Mk. 10:45 explain themselves, and indeed it needs to be stated that parallels from secular life drop out.[31] It is not said and does not need to be said to whom the λύτρον is offered nor why it has to be offered.

In Old Testament Jewish thought generally and especially in reference to Isa. 53 the אָשָׁם is of course offered to God; on the other hand we are by no means concerned here with something that *must* be done for God, as is asserted in the later satisfaction theory, but simply and solely with the fact that a vicarious atonement is made for many.[32]

The extremely complicated problem of the eucharistic paradosis can be discussed here only in a short section. In particular, the statements about the setting, the invitations to eat and drink, the instruction to repeat the act and the eschatological outlook are left out of account. We are concerned simply with the statements about atonement in the words of institution. These so-called "words of interpretation"[33] are preserved in two essentially different types. On the one hand, there is the rendering in Mark, which is followed in Matthew; on the other hand, the rendering in Paul and in the long text in Luke.

In regard to the word over the bread, the situation is relatively simple; Mk. 14:22 par. has merely "This is my body", whilst 1 Cor. 11:24‖Lk. 22:19 has also a statement about expiation: $\tau\grave{o}$ $\acute{v}\pi\grave{\epsilon}\rho$ $\acute{v}\mu\hat{\omega}\nu$ or $\tau\grave{o}$ $\acute{v}\pi\grave{\epsilon}\rho$ $\acute{v}\mu\hat{\omega}\nu$ $\delta\iota\delta\acute{o}\mu\epsilon\nu o\nu$. This might be a later addition, for, on the one hand, a statement about expiation in this form is impossible in an Aramaic text and, on the other hand, the bringing of a statement about expiation into the word over the bread has its explanation in endeavours to effect a liturgical parallelism between the two words of institution.[34] The $\tau\grave{o}$ $\acute{v}\pi\grave{\epsilon}\rho$ $\acute{v}\mu\hat{\omega}\nu$ ($\delta\iota\delta\acute{o}\mu\epsilon\nu o\nu$) which is added to the word over the bread in the Pauline-Lukan form does not show any dependence on Isa. 53; only the statement about expiation $\acute{v}\pi\grave{\epsilon}\rho$ $\tau\hat{\eta}s$ $\tau o\hat{v}$ $\kappa\acute{o}\sigma\mu o\upsilon$ $\zeta\omega\hat{\eta}s$ which occurs in John 6:51c and is likewise a word over bread, discloses the inclusive character of the thought of Isa. 53.

In the word over the cup, three different elements present themselves in Mark, Matthew and Luke: the blood motif, the covenant idea and the expiation conception; in Paul the expiation motif is wanting in this place. This simpler rendering in 1 Cor. 11:25 results from the expiation motif having been incorporated in the word over the bread. Moreover, the Pauline version of the idea of the "new" covenant is distinguished; at the same time the covenant sacrifice, which finds expression in the $\grave{\epsilon}\nu$ $\tau\hat{\omega}$ $\grave{\epsilon}\mu\hat{\omega}$ $a\H{\iota}\mu\alpha\tau\iota$, plays a part, the reference in the blood being, of course, not to an actual substance but to the death of Christ, the share of which in his work of salvation is assumed.[35] Beyond what there is in Paul, Lk. 22:20b has $\tau\grave{o}$ $\acute{v}\pi\grave{\epsilon}\rho$ $\acute{v}\mu\hat{\omega}\nu$ $\grave{\epsilon}\kappa\chi\upsilon\nu\nu\acute{o}\mu\epsilon\nu o\nu$. This has to be regarded as an assimilation both to the Markan rendering of the word over the cup and to the word over the bread in the Pauline-Lukan rendering. Assimilated to Mark is τό ... ἐκχυννόμενον, assimilated to the word proper over the bread is ὑπὲρ ὑμῶν; on the other hand, the διδόμενον peculiar to the Lukan text in the word over the bread is to be regarded as a redaction that was fashioned to be a parallel to ἐκχυννόμενον.[36]

By this it can be seen that for the Pauline-Lukan rendering as distinct from that in Mark and Matthew the motif of expiation in the sense of an expiation "for you" was constitutive, for which reason Luke did not permit himself to be determined by Mark in this respect. In consequence a connection with Isa. 53 is lacking. On the other hand, a direct allusion to the prophetic text must be assumed for the Markan-Matthaean form of the word over the cup. To that the ὑπὲρ(περὶ) πολλῶν points unambiguously.[37] Further, it has to be observed that the shedding of blood is understood here in the general sense of putting to death,[38] that therefore there is here in reality a parallel to הֶעֱרָה לַמָּוֶת נַפְשׁוֹ Isa. 53:12b, even if no verbal dependence can be proved. The ἐκχυννόμενον may not as a matter of course be regarded as sacrifice terminology; it became that only through its being connected with the covenant idea; here then the death of Jesus is both an expiatory death and a sacrifice that establishes the covenant.[39]

Without being able to follow the traditio-historical problem of the eucharistic words any further, we may hold it fast as a provisional result that two quite different statements were obviously connected with the motif of the shed blood, that namely of the vicarious expiation and that of the sacrifice that establishes the covenant, which were clamped together only at second hand; further, it is to be observed that the expiation motif in the Pauline-Lukan type does not show any dependence on Isa. 53, whilst in the tradition of Mark and Matthew there is a clear allusion to the universal character of the promise of Isa. 53.[40]

The phrases connected with παραδιδόναι have a very varied character and may not be comprised under the arch-concept "παρδιδόναι-formulae".[41] First of all, it has to be observed that the word has its fixed place in legal terminology and is used in this sense as a terminus technicus in the history of Jesus' passion.[42] Hence Judas is described as ὁ παραδιδούς or ὁ παραδούς.[43]

The word first received a "set form" in the Old Testament

Jewish parlance παραδιδόναι (παραδοθῆναι) εἰς χεῖρας τινός, which was incorporated in the words about the suffering Son of man.[44] But παραδιδόναι has also a relatively fixed place in the context of expiation statements. How this came about can perhaps be concluded from 1 Cor. 11:23ff.

In the introduction to the Pauline eucharistic paradosis there stands as a report on the passion narrative ὁ κύριος Ἰησοῦς ἐν τῇ νυκτὶ ᾗ παρεδίδοτο, in which παραδιδόναι may preserve still unaltered the sense of the word in the legal terminology. At the same time, however, it stands in close connection with the words of institution, especially with the expiation statement in the word over the bread, so that from here there can have emerged the formal phrases with the basic structure παραδιδόναι . . . ὑπέρ . . . Moreover, two groups have to be distinguished: in the one it is said that Jesus is "delivered" or that God "delivers" him; in the other that Jesus "delivers himself up".[45] παραδιδόναι thus obtained an essentially different meaning. As there was already contained in the phrase "to be delivered into someone's hands" an allusion to the decree of God and his hidden action in all human doings, so in association with the expiation statements the word came to have a clear reference to salvation history.

Did Isa. 53 exercise an influence here? That in 1 Tim. 2:6, as in Mk. 10:45b, ὁ δοὺς ἑαυτὸν ἀντίλυτρον ὑπὲρ πάντων there is a take-over of the decisive motif of Isa. 53:10, it is not difficult to perceive. The ὑπὲρ ἡμῶν πάντων παρέδωκεν αὐτόν in Rom. 8:32 may also be determined by Isa. 53.[46] On the other hand, however, it cannot be disputed that παραδιδόναι has no actual analogue in the Hebrew text of Isa. 53. It occurs indeed three times in the Septuagint: παρεδόθη εἰς θάνατον ἡ ψυχὴ αὐτοῦ is a very free translation of הֶעֱרָה לַמָּוֶת נַפְשׁוֹ Isa. 53:12b, which certainly does not come into question; κύριος παρέδωκεν αὐτὸν ταῖς ἁμαρτίαις ἡμῶν stands for יהוה הִפְגִּיעַ בּוֹ אֵת עֲוֹן כֻּלָּנוּ Isa. 53:6b and διὰ τὰς ἁμαρτίας αὐτῶν παρεδόθη for וְלַפֹּשְׁעִים יַפְגִּיעַ Isa. 53:12c; it is, however, not to be overlooked that the hiph. of פגע has different meanings in these two places.[47] An influence of the Hebrew text is hardly to be assumed. Still the thought suggests itself that primitive Christian expiation statements which are bound up with παραδίδοται have been influenced by the Greek text of Isaiah.

It cannot be disputed that Rom. 8:32 comes very close to Isa. 53:6b and that Rom. 4:25 with its παρεδόθη διά . . . very much recalls Isa. 53:12c.[48] In the case of 1 Tim. 2:6 the reference is anyhow well known. Whether the idea of self-surrender was also occasioned by Isa. 53 may be questioned in regard to 1 Tim. 2:6. It is true that in Gal. 2:20 this idea is associated merely with a ὑπέρ ἐμοῦ, but there that is necessitated by the context.[49] The association of self-surrender and expiation "for us" with sacrifice motifs in Eph. 5:2 is certainly secondary— παραδιδόναι is thus certainly used in formal connections, but, on the one hand, all passages must be excluded in which the word is used as a term in legal terminology, and, on the other hand, a distinction must be drawn between the various formulae.[50] Only in the association of παραδιδόναι with the idea of expiation have the influences of Isa. 53 come to be at work, at first, however, obviously in the sphere of the Hellenistic church in virtue of the Greek Old Testament.[51]

Detailed investigations have shown that in the earliest tradition reference is made to Isa. 53 only sporadically. For the soteriological statements about Jesus' death are relatively√ seldom combined with the idea of a universal expiation. In more recent times, however, the view has frequently been advocated that in the early primitive Christian tradition this conception had nevertheless a very comprehensive meaning.

Hans Walter Wolff, who opened the recent discussion, advocates energetically the principle that it is necessary to take a general understanding of Isa. 53 into consideration. Jesus had lived intimately with Scripture and especially with Deutero-Isaiah, and since the fate of the prophets stood before his eyes, he cannot have passed by Isa. 53. Consequently Mk. 10:45; 14:24 show to what an extent he had appropriated this Old Testament text; this prophecy was understood by him in a most perfect way and in him it came to be embodied.[52] Moreover, there must have been an instructing of the disciples in regard to Isa. 53, for although the thought became clear to the disciples only with difficulty, it is clear that traits from Isa. 53 unconsciously exercised an influence, above all in the passion narrative. Only gradually then did the Palestinian church appropriate the text of Isa. 53.[53] The hypothetical character of this argument is easily perceived; its conclusions are altogether uncertain.

For this reason Joachim Jeremias has sought to prove the use of the Servant of God conception in the proclamation of Jesus and the earliest church tradition by careful detailed investigation and to make full use of all allusions to or verbal reminiscences of Isa. 53.[54] In his opinion this material leads back consistently to the early Palestinian church, indeed largely to Jesus himself. His conclusion, like that of Wolff, is that Jesus must have wondered about his impending death and, in view of the importance of the theologumenon of the expiatory power of death, must necessarily have come across Isa. 53.[55]

His explanation of the scarcity of reference to Isa. 53 in the Synoptic tradition is that Jesus did not deal with the matter in public preaching but only in esoteric teaching. But weighty objections can be brought against that: in the first place, as Jeremias himself admits, the fact that it is in the earliest Palestinian tradition signifies nothing at all as regards derivation from the mouth of Jesus and additional general considerations likewise cannot provide a proof; in the second place, the Markan prediction of the passion and the eucharistic words in their present form cannot be regarded as authentic, and on the other hand proof of the genuineness of a prediction as e.g. Lk. 13:32f. yields nothing regarding Jesus' occupation with Isa. 53;[56] in the third place, the presence of the conception of expiatory suffering with its diffusion in the Judaism of that time proves nothing regarding a connection with Isa. 53; in the fourth place it must also be asked whether in the actual allusions to Isa. 53 the expiation conception of this chapter has been incorporated; in the fifth place, the Servant of God title and statements about the Servant of God do not require to be associated with Deutero-Isaiah nor in a reference to Isa. 42 or 49 need they imply the expiation motif of Isa. 53.

In spite of all these objections it should not be disputed that Isa. 53, apart from explicit citations, can have exercised an influence on the Gospel tradition, but in the carrying through of the proof regard must be had to unambiguous criteria.[57]

Only brief reference may be made to other recent articles on the problem of the Servant of God conception in the New Testament. In spite of the weak testimony, Oscar Cullmann assumes a close contact of Jesus with Isa. 53: Jesus had to make atonement by living it, not by teaching it.[58] At the time of his baptism he felt conscious that he must assume the role of the Ebed-Jahwe.[59] Erich Fascher's starting point is that Jesus cannot have deceived himself regarding the effect of his deeds and words, consequently he must have recognized his office as the suffering Messiah and have occupied himself with Isa. 53. Because, however, of a want of understanding on the part of the disciples he abstained from speaking before them about the secret of his mission. [60]

But for all these constructions[61] the exegetical basis is extremely small, and by far the main point of the argument is to explain the lack of actually recognizable references to Isa. 53. We observe, however, that the understanding of this chapter in late Judaism was extremely lacking in uniformity and that the expiation statements made there scarcely played any role, a thing that may not be exclusively connected with subsequent anti-Christian endeavours; thus it is easy to understand why Isa. 53 only gradually acquired significance in early Christianity and only at a late date secured its to us self-evident central place in Christology.[62]

NOTES

1. Only a short sketch of the problem can be given here, and only the most important recent works on the subject can be mentioned.

2. Moreover, there must be clearly distinguished one from the other: (1) the very comprehensive "Servant of God" conception in the Old Testament, which could be applied to patriarchs, kings, prophets, etc. (collectively also to Israel), (2) the Servant of God conception in Deutero-Isaiah, which comprises an eschatological task, but is not wholly determined by Isa. 53 (occasionally even different authors have been considered for Isa. 53 and the remaining Servant of God Songs), (3) the conception of the suffering and vicariously atoning Servant of God in Isa. 53, from which alone the statements about the passion could have been borrowed or the statements regarding vicarious atonement for the "many", the subject proper of this section.

3. This is to be assumed not only for late Judaism, but also up to a point for the primitive church.

4. Rev. 5:6, (9), 12; 13:8.

5. The interpretation is much disputed. It may certainly be maintained that what is thought of is not quite generally a sacrificial lamb of the daily tamid; also the goat of the sin offering (Lev. 16) cannot come into question. On the other hand a reference to the passover lamb is

often assumed because a parallel to it presents itself in John 19:33, 36; but the passover lamb has no power to cancel sins, and so for instance Barrett, *John*, p. 147, considers whether by way of a passover interpretation of the Last Supper an association of the conception of the expiatory death and that of Jesus as the passover lamb has here been arrived at. But reference is also frequently made to Isa. 53. Even if the thesis is not accepted that ἀμνός stands for an original טַלְיָא, which means both "lamb" and "servant"—so C. F. Burney, *The Aramaic Origin of the Fourth Gospel*, 1922, pp. 104ff.; Joachim Jeremias, art. ἀμνός, *ThWb* I, pp. 342–344; *id.*," Ἀμνὸς τοῦ θεοῦ—παῖς θεοῦ", *ZNW* 34, 1935, pp. 115–123, and others—it has still to be maintained that both the motif of the (slain) lamb, which originally was doubtless meant metaphorically, and the idea of an achievement of atonement for all men are characteristic of Isa. 53; so recently Hermann Strathmann, *Das Evangelium nach Johannes* (*NTD* 4), 1959[9], p. 48; W. Bauer, *Joh.*, p. 36, also makes the statement: "Recollection of Isa. 53 . . . cannot be banished". Otherwise Bultmann, *Joh.*, pp. 66f.; C. H. Dodd, *Interpretation of the Fourth Gospel*, pp. 230ff.

6. Cf. Appendix pp. 374ff., 379, 381 below.

7. This comprehensive designation in Joachim Jeremias, art., παῖς θεοῦ, *ThWb* V, pp. 704, 707.

8. Cf. Chapter 3, pp. 175ff.

9. Eduard Lohse, *Märtyrer und Gottesknecht. Untersuchungen zur urchristlichen Verkündigung vom Sühntod Jesu Christi* (*FRLANT* NF 46), 1955, pp. 38ff.

10. Lohse, *op. cit.*, pp. 97ff., 104ff.

11. On this inclusive sense of רַבִּים cf. Joachim Jeremias, art., πολλοί, *ThWb* VI. pp. 536–545.

12. Lohse, *op. cit.*, p. 106.

13. Lohse, *op. cit.*, p. 107; Morna Hooker, *Jesus and the Servant*, 1959, pp. 53ff. (cf. the survey of the literature given there pp. 179f., n. 4). On the Targum on Isaiah cf. chapter 3, p. 201, n. 104.

14. So, e.g., Gerhard Kittel, *Jesu Worte über sein Sterben*, *DtTh* 3, 1936, pp. 166–189.

15. Against Jeremias, *ThWb* V, p. 706.

16. Cf. Chapter 3, pp. 177ff.

17. Apart from Mark 10:45b par.; 14:24 par. reference has to be made to 2 Cor. 5:14f.; 1 Tim. 2:6; John 6:51 fin.; furthermore also to 1 Pet. 3:18 (δίκαιος ὑπὲρ ἀδίκων); 1 John 2:2. Paul in Rom. 5:6, 8; 2 Cor. 5:21 (cf. vv. 14f.) shows how the inclusive sense can be taken into consideration even in a ὑπὲρ ἡμῶν.

18. The reference to Isa. 53, that to us is self-evident, was not familiar to the church in the earliest period. This chapter, avoided and given a new interpretation in Judaism, could only be recovered slowly as Scriptural proof. That the conception of the suffering Servant of God was already in pre-Christian times associated with Messianism is still not proved.

19. Cf. Chapter 1, pp. 36 and 41.

20. Friedrich Büchsel, art., λύτρον, *ThWb* IV, pp. 341ff., especially 344.

21. Thus frequently in earlier research. Completely refuted by Martin Werner, *Der Einfluss der paulinischen Theologie auf das Markus-Evangelium* (*BZNW* I), 1923, especially pp. 63ff.

22. So Bultmann, *Syn. Trad.*, p. 154; Klostermann, *Mk.* p. 109; on the history of the exposition cf. Taylor, *Mk.*, pp. 445f.

23. C. K. Barrett, *The Background of Mark* 10:45, in *New Testament Essays* (*Studies in Memory of T. W. Manson*), 1959, pp. 1–18.

24. It is a matter of the following LXX passages: Exod. 21:30; 30:12; also 21:23 and 2 Kings 10:24; further Ps. 48:8 LXX = Ps. 49:8; Isa. 52:3 (*op. cit.*, pp. 6f.).

25. So also R. H. Fuller, *Mission and Achievement*, pp. 57f. which Barrett controverts unfairly.

26. ἀντί exchanges with ὑπέρ, and περί, Aram. חְלַף.

27. Barrett, *op. cit.* pp. 11f., wishes to explain Mk. 10:45 by means of the conception of the suffering and martyr death of the righteous and elect (2 Macc. 7:37f.; 4 Macc. 6:27ff.; 17:22; 18:4).

28. Joachim Jeremias, *Das Lösegeld für Viele* (*Mk.* 10:45), *Judaica* 3, 1947/48, pp. 249–264; *id.*, *ThWb* V, p. 709.

29. Lohse, *op. cit.*, pp. 116ff.

30. So Jeremias, *Lösegeld*, pp. 263f.

31. Adolf Deissmann, *Licht vom Osten*, 1923⁴, pp. 270ff. wishes to explain the passage from the sacral redemption of slaves, Werner Elert, *Redemptio ab hostibus*, *ThLZ* 72, 1947, cols. 265–270, from ancient martial law. Jeremias, *Lösegeld*, p. 250, rightly opposes that.

32. Cf. also Büchsel, *ThWb* IV, pp. 343ff.

33. On this concept and on the matter cf. Günther Bornkamm, *Herrenmahl und Kirche bei Paulus*, in *Studien zu Antike und Urchristentum* (*Ges. Aufs.* II), 1959, pp. 138–176.

34. Jeremias, *Abendmahlsworte*, pp. 160f.

35. Cf. Bornkamm, *op. cit.*, pp. 157f.

36. That also emerges from linguistic observations. The placing of the participle in front corresponds to the word sequence in the Semitic (so Mark); the originally independent τὸ ὑπὲρ ὑμῶν can in this way have arisen only in a Hellenistic speech area (so Paul in the word about the bread) and is now associated in dependence on the Markan word about the cup with a participle that has been placed behind (Luke).

37. Not only εἰς ἄφεσιν ἁμαρτιῶν in Matthew as Hooker, *op. cit.*, pp. 8off. assumes.

38. The idea of the shedding of blood is common in the Old Testament.

39. Jeremias, *Abendmahlsworte*³, pp. 186ff. has recently abandoned the view which earlier he himself supported, that τῆς διαθήκης in Mk. 14:24 must be an addition. Previously he regarded it as decisive that in the Aramaic a noun with a pronominal suffix does not permit a genitive after it (*Abendmahlsworte*², p. 99), whilst now he reckons with another arrangement of the words in the primitive text. But the reasons for a secondary reception of the covenant idea in the word about blood

E

are chiefly of a traditio-historical character; so far then the word sequence, clumsy in the Greek and impossible in an Aramaic text, may nevertheless have its value as indicating a subsequent compilation. We may not reckon in the same matter-of-course way as does Jeremias, *Abendmahlsworte*[3], pp. 213f., with "terms from the language of sacrifice". The idea of sacrifice is indeed firmly combined with the covenant motif, but not with the idea of atonement; cf. also on this Lohse, *op. cit.*, pp. 71f., 124f., 126. In the case of a statement about atonement the concept of atonement-"sacrifice" may not be made use of right away, as it sometimes is; only the association of the statement about atonement and the idea of the covenant sacrifice in the word about the cup in Mk. 14:24 led to the conception of an "atonement sacrifice".

40. For discussion of the traditio-historical problems and of the age of the several motifs cf. the research report of Eduard Schweizer, *Das Herrenmahl im Neuen Testament*, ThLZ 79, 1954, cols. 577–592.

41. Against Jeremias, *ThWb* V, pp. 704f., 708

42. παραδιδόναι τινὰ τινί; so, e.g., Mk 14:10, 11.18; 15:1, 15.

43. Cf. Mk. 14:42, 44; Matt. 10:4 and often.

44. . . . נתן ביד or . . . מסר ביד; cf. Schlatter, *Mt.*, pp. 537f.

45. Cf. on the one hand Rom. 4:25; 8:32; on the other hand Gal. 2:20; Eph. 5:2; 1 Tim. 2:6.

46. Cf. Isa. 53:6b: עָוֹן כֻּלָּנוּ.

47. It is also united with different prepositions: in Isa. 53:6b with acc. and בְּ in the sense "to make something to strike someone"; 53:12c with לְ in the sense "to intercede for".

48. On Rom. 4:25 cf. in detail Otto Kuss, *Der Römerbrief* (1st part, 1957), pp. 193ff.

49. The common atonement statement "for us (you)" and the like intrudes in the later tradition even into contexts determined by Isa. 53, as is shown by the citation from Isa. 53 in 1 Pet. 2:22ff.

50. Accordingly connections between the words about the sufferings of the Son of man and Isa. 53 do not present themselves (apart of course from Mk. 10:45b).

51. Whether this was the LXX is not quite certain.

52. Hans Walter Wolff, *Jesaja 53 im Urchristentum*, 1952[3], pp. 55ff.

53. *Op. cit.*, pp. 75ff.

54. Jeremias, *ThWb* V, pp. 698ff.

55. In particular some predictions of the passion and the eucharistic words are said to prove that; cf. *ThWb* V, pp. 711ff.

56. Cf. also Julius Wellhausen, *Evangelium Lucae*, 1904, pp. 75f., Günther Bornkamm, *Jesus von Nazareth (Urban-Bücher* 19), 1960 [4,5], pp. 141f.

57. The principle defended rightly of course by Wolff, *op. cit.*, pp. 71, 73; Jeremias, *ThWb* V, p. 703, that a limitation to citation is irrelevant, encounters special difficulties precisely in the case of Isa. 53, for the idea that is characteristic of this Old Testament chapter must be clearly pointed out in every instance. Apart, however, from the universal atonement statement there comes into question only the אָשָׁם-

motif and up to a point the association of παραδιδόναι with the idea of atonement. Cf. also the methodical reflections in Hooker, *op. cit.*, pp. 62f.

58. Cullmann, *Christologie*, pp. 59ff., 68f.

59. Cullmann, *Die Tauflehre im Neuen Testament*, 1948, pp. 11ff.

60. Erich Fascher, *Jesaja 53 in christlicher und jüdischer Sicht (Aufsätze und Vorträge zur Theologie und Religionsgeschichte 4)*, 1958, pp. 9ff.

61. There may also be mentioned Christian Maurer, *Knecht Gottes und Sohn Gottes im Passionsbericht des Markusevengeliums, ZThK* 50, 1953, pp. 1–38, who advocates the theory that in the account of the passion "the Servant of God idea already stands right at the beginning of the tradition and already in Mark we have merely a distant but intentional lingering-note" (p. 10); but precisely in Mk. 14f. a very early stage of the passion tradition can still be relatively well recognized, and it presents no allusions to the atonement idea of Isa. 53, not even were we to speak of a "de facto-Scriptural proof" (p. 7); in part Maurer has to fetch his proofs from Hellenistic-Jewish literature (Wisdom of Solomon), from which, in my opinion, nothing at all is obtained for the earliest Palestinian tradition.

62. Morna Hooker also labours to prove that Isa. 53 had no decisive significance either for Jesus himself or for the early church. The collective interpretation of the Isaiah text may be let rest. Much as the authoress is in the right in disputing a recognizable after-effect of Isa. 53 and moreover a Messianic understanding of this passage in late Judaism, she has on the other hand failed to recognize the significance of the atonement motif within the conception of suffering in late Judaism and also in primitive Christianity. The issue is to be sure to the point: "There is . . . very little in the Synoptics to support the traditional view that Jesus identified his mission with that of the Servant of the Songs" (p. 102); but an influence of Isa. 53 on Mk. 10:45b and 14:24 does not by any means permit of its being disputed. The book is very much to be welcomed, for on the basis of careful detailed analysis the limited range of the Servant of God conception in primitive Christianity has been made plain. The clear differentiation of the Son of man and Messiah conceptions (pp. 142ff.) also merits attention.

CHAPTER II

KYRIOS

THE use of κύριος in the NT is many-sided. Apart from the purely profane use of the word,[1] it occurs as denoting God, then as a description of the earthly Jesus, but also as a predicate of the exalted One who is to come again in glory. These various modes of use have in part their own special historical background, yet again they are closely interwoven with each other, and have exerted reciprocal influences. Hence an exact inquiry must be made into the presuppositions and the particular strands of tradition.

This is all the more necessary since as usual the conflicting theses about the origins of the kyrios title have never been finally resolved. If Wilhelm Bousset and Rudolf Bultmann championed exclusively the Hellenistic character of the Kyrios predicate of Jesus,[2] Werner Foerster[3] on the other hand defended the thesis of a Palestinian origin which in its main outlines had been sketched out by Gustaf Dalman[4] and which more recently has again been taken up by Oscar Cullmann[5] and Eduard Schweizer.[6] In fact, it will not be found possible to contest a Palestinian background, but, on the other hand, the considerable change which resulted from the transition to the field of Hellenistic church tradition must not be overlooked.[7]

I. *The Hellenistic and Old Testament Use of the Title of Lord*

In order to be able to determine the special character of the kyrios predicate of Jesus, the conditions in the surrounding world must be briefly elucidated. If we take as our point of departure the use of the word in classical Greek, we notice a fundamental difference from an oriental mode of thought, in so far as κύριος in the sense of possession of power and ownership is primarily defined by the thought of rightfulness, and the contrast to δοῦλος is not really basic.[8] The application of the term to gods is relatively rare, and for the most part has a limited meaning, because the idea implies merely the thought of an authority and responsibility wielded by particular persons or a particular kingdom.[9] The deep and far-reaching changes which were the consequence of the transition from classical Greece to Hellenism are also to be discerned in the use of the kyrios concept.

It now acquires increasing significance in the religious sphere. This results primarily from its use in the Hellenistic mysteries and the cult of the emperor. In the religious mysteries,[10] κύριος, used absolutely, becomes the decisive predicate of divinity. In these cults it is easy to recognize the oriental background: for κύριος implies the god's possession of and sovereign power of disposal over the δοῦλοι who are assembled together and confined in the cultic worship. For Isis and Serapis the use of κυρία or κύριος may be shown to be current already at the beginning of the first century B.C., but for many other cultic deities, even outside Egypt, the title is likewise attested in the first century B.C.[11]

It is, however, to be noted that κύριος is not in general use as the predicate of a cult deity; it does appear in the mysteries of Egyptian and Syrian origin, where it was already acclimatized in the old popular cults, but, for example, it is absent from the Attis mysteries of Asia Minor. It is further to be noted that even where it frequently occurs as in the Isis cult, kyrios is only one title among many.[12] To decide to what extent the kyrios title became the one specific denomination of a mystery god is difficult. In the pre-Christian era this can hardly have been the case; on the other hand, there are examples from the second century A.D., from which it may be inferred that kyrios at least among certain cultic deities had attained the status of the standard predicate for the divine, as the following much quoted instance proves: ἐρωτᾷ σε Χαιρήμων δειπνῆσαι εἰς κλείνην τοῦ κυρίου Σαράπιδος ἐν τῷ Σαραπείῳ.[13] Hence it may be concluded that in the NT epoch the kyrios title was probably still gaining ground rapidly.

Its use in the cult of the emperor leads to similar conclusions.[14] Here again an eastern origin is indisputable. Through Alexander the Great, the Seleucides and the Ptolemies, court ceremonial and the apotheosis of the ruler gradually penetrated to the west. In the first and second centuries B.C. kyrios is found only in the east.[15] But already with Caesar and especially with Augustus, veneration of the ruler gained ground even in the west.[16] No doubt Augustus himself, as Tiberius after him, shunned the ascription to himself of the kyrios title, for the whole oriental conception of the ruler was alien to ancient Roman feeling;[17] in any case, in the eastern part of the empire such veneration of the emperor was suffered.[18] However, from Caligula and with increasing rapidity, from Nero onwards, the kyrios title and the cult of the emperor became prevalent in the west also, and with Domitian, both no doubt became finally established.[19] In Acts 25:26 the procurator unhesitatingly refers to Nero as the kyrios.[20]

Thus here too in the first century A.D. may be observed the strong penetrating influence of the kyrios title. The idea of divinity and of the supreme power of the ruler are in this way conveyed. To consider κύριος as a purely political title and θεός only as a properly religious description in the titles accorded to the emperor would hardly be correct.[21] It is obvious that in Hellenism the kyrios predicate played, if not a singular, yet a most important part in the cultic sphere. And Christianity in the Roman empire, in proclaiming Jesus as the kyrios, must have been coming to terms with this usage.

As regards the OT, our point of departure must be the two basic terms denoting the lord and ruler: בַּעַל describes him who possesses something, while אָדוֹן is the one who disposes of power and authority, especially over men, more seldom over things.[22] In either case it is less the motive of rightfulness than the fact of the exercise of lordship which is predominant; and in both cases total dependence and subordination is basic, on account of which it is precisely the relationship of the master to the slave, absolute bondage, which is characteristic. The concepts may be used both in a profane and a religious sense. בַּעַל in a religious context always denotes the god, to whom man turns as the owner, either of territory or of a city; and the men who inhabit the territory or the city[23] are likewise in his possession. It is otherwise with אָדוֹן which implies the power and the authority of a god, before whom men bow. von Baudissin has made a penetrating study of this concept of lordship from the point of view of the history of religion.[24] However much it may be true that the Baal and the Adon ideas of the OT have their roots and their parallels above all in

Semitic religious forms of thought,[25] it must none the less be
noted that the essential elements of the concept, namely,
absolute power of disposal and complete subordination, are a
standard characteristic throughout the ancient east.

In view of this use of the terms, it is understandable that for
Jahwe only אָדוֹן was in question, בַּעַל could never be used;
precisely at this point there arose even a quite fundamental
debate with the religions of the surrounding Canaanite world.
In the OT אָדוֹן denotes the ruling power of Jahwe. He is the
supreme governor and sole Lord.[26] This is most clearly expressed in the turn of phrase אֲדוֹן כָּל־הָאָרֶץ.[27] But also the special
form אֲדֹנָי expresses this singular claim.[28] The significance which
accrued to this particular expression in the course of time can
be seen in the fact that as the name of Jahwe began to be
avoided, אֲדֹנָי as a *Qerê* took its place. It is, of course, a subject of
contention whether this is not to be regarded rather as a repercussion of the Septuagint translation of the name of Jahwe
by κύριος.[29]

The matter is of some importance because if the replacement
of יהוה by אֲדֹנָי is prior, then we might assume that a genuine
Jewish development lies at the basis of the LXX usage, whereas
if the translation of יהוה by κύριος in the Hellenistic sphere is
original, then we should have to reckon with circumstances
showing a certain Hellenization. It is, however, overwhelmingly
probable that the κύριος of the LXX presupposes that אֲדֹנָי
was already in existence as a term of replacement.[30] For, on
the one hand, κύριος in the Egyptian sphere of origin of the
Septuagint is only attested from the second century B.C.
onwards, and then primarily as a title for the Pharaoh,[31] on the
other hand, it would also in any event have been an obvious
course, as was done at times in regard to the name Baal,
simply to transcribe the name of Jahwe, instead of completely
setting it aside. Yet in this matter it is obvious that other
important developments had already taken place, as also in
other respects the LXX proceeds very consciously and deliberately in the translation of the various denominations of gods
and lords.

Κύριος translates both אָדוֹן and בַּעַל but the latter only when
used in a profane sense: if it denotes a Canaanite god, then

either *Βάαλ* or *αἰσχύνη* or *εἴδωλον* is used. But throughout *κύριος* is used for Jahwe,[32] and has thus become here the specific term for God.[33] Of course the fact that a denomination for God springing directly from Jewish tradition could later be modified in a Hellenistic sense is shown by Philo, who links with the title *κύριος* wide-embracing speculations of a Hellenistic type.[34]

Finally, we must cast a glance at the use of *κύριος* as a title for God in the NT. As far as quotations from the OT are concerned matters are in the main simple: we have simply the adoption of the Septuagint formula. So for example in all the Marcan texts where Kyrios in this sense occurs.[35] In the sole additional text from Lk. 4:18f. (a quotation from Isa. 61:1f.) the OT text has been "freely rendered according to the LXX";[36] so much may be asserted if only for the reason that in the Acts of the Apostles all OT quotations are likewise given in the LXX form.[37] In the older parts of the logia source, Kyrios as a title of God is absent. It occurs only in the later introduction, which in any event raises a number of problems in regard to both tradition and theology; in the story of the temptation (Matt. 4:1–11‖Lk. 4:1–13) it stands in two of the four scriptural quotations; all four quotations literally follow the text of the LXX, Matt. 4:10 (Lk. 4:8) even with a typical LXX deviation from the original text.[38]

The situation is somewhat different in Matthew and Paul, in so far as the Septuagint is not to be presupposed in every case.[39] But the use of Kyrios as a description of God raises no problem, because the term was an obvious translation of the *Qᵉrê* אֲדֹנָי, and furthermore the LXX use had probably already become fully established in Jewish and Christian churches of the Hellenistic sphere; this will no doubt explain the penetration of the LXX formula in those contexts with *κύριος*.[40] Other NT writings show no further special features.[41] Apart from direct quotations, a number of fixed locutions are used following OT Judaic linguistic usage, e.g. *ἄγγελος κυρίου, χεὶρ κυρίου, κύριος ὁ θεὸς ὁ παντοκράτωρ, κύριος τοῦ οὐρανοῦ καὶ τῆς γῆς.*

As well as particular texts where *κύριος* is used as a matter of course as a title for God,[42] there are a number of passages embodying traditional material where the accumulated use of kyrios is striking, especially the introductions of the gospels of Matthew and Luke,[43] and certain sections of the Revelation,[44] which shows not only a preference for Biblical style, but must at least in part reflect a characteristic feature of the traditional material. It is clear that the old denomination of God has a strong repercussion on the NT, and the use of kyrios for Jesus is therefore the more remarkable. But in this matter the various elements of the tradition must first be carefully investigated, in order to see whether and to what extent we have a real transference of the divine predicate.

Summary. In the Hellenistic sphere, the kyrios title, under oriental influence, had attained importance especially in the mystery religions and the cult of the emperor. It denoted the unconditioned power and the divinity of its bearer, and in the NT period was still gaining ground, so that Christianity must have been taking it into account in proclaiming Jesus as the kyrios. The OT also knows the term "lord" in religious contexts. There was no question of using בַּעַל, which denoted the owner, in reference to Jahwe, only the term אָדוֹן which conveyed the idea of authority and sovereign rule was used; as a predicate for God it grew in importance on Palestinian ground, especially in the form אֲדֹנָי by which the name of Jahwe was finally completely replaced. In the sphere of the Diaspora the Septuagint κύριος took the place of the name Jahwe, with the result that eventually it became the standard Biblical name for God. Finally, the repercussion of this is shown in the NT, where κύριος still plays an important part as the title of God.

2. *The Description of Jesus as Lord in the Palestinian Tradition*

In order to begin at the right point a study of the description of Jesus as Lord we must disregard the uses of the term "Lord" as a predicate of deity which have been discussed in the previous section. Nor should we take as our point of departure the linguistic use of the post-resurrection church and its application of the description "my" or "our Lord" to the Jesus whose return was expected. We should rather ask ourselves the question to what extent the term "Lord" was used in address to the earthly Jesus, and in what way this influenced the later development.

In the synoptic tradition there is a surprising parallelism

73

between διδάσκαλε and ὁ διδάσκαλος with κύριε and ὁ κύριος. Hence the use of διδάσκαλε / ὁ διδάσκαλος can be helpful in considering the implication of κύριε / ὁ κύριος The address διδάσκαλε is a translation of the Aramaic רַבִּי which occurs several times in the gospels in a transcribed form.

The fact that ῥαββί in Greek has in part been left untranslated is an indication of the ancient character and currency of this mode of address. ῥαββί and its intensified form ῥαββουνί[45] are to be found in an old stratum of the traditions behind the gospels of Mark and John.[46] There is no evidence of the word in the logia source, but this may be connected with the special character of this strand of tradition.[47] Later it is suppressed. Although Luke does not completely avoid the use of the term "master" in addressing Jesus, he does not incorporate the Aramaic word. Matthew on the other hand has quite deliberately restricted the use of the term; "Rabbi" is the mode of address which is accepted by the scribes, but of which there is no question as far as the disciples of Jesus are concerned; in regard to Jesus it is an address used only by the traitor Judas;[48] in the mouth of the other disciples it is consistently avoided as the comparison with Mark shows.[49]

If we except Matthew, what we have here is a quite unreflective use of the term. In Mark this is suggested by the fact that both a man of the people[50] as well as the disciples, and in similar fashion the traitor use this address. We find a similar state of affairs in John; only in 3:2 as the appended explanation shows, is there a somewhat more emphatic use of the term;[51] perhaps in 1:38 it may be asked in what degree we have the echo of its use as a title of distinction, since in John 1:35ff. the most varied predicates are deliberately ascribed to Jesus and "Rabbi" is included among them; yet in 1:50 this "Rabbi" is surpassed by the "Thou art the Son of God, Thou art the King of Israel",[52] while conversely the address "Rabbi" is quite normally used to the Baptist.

It is certain that in His own lifetime Jesus was addressed as "Rabbi", and in His outward appearance He was not essentially distinguished from the scribes of the day.[53] The address "Rabbi" was in general use at the time, and was especially preferred in respect of the scholars and teachers of the Law, but was not yet limited to the highly accomplished and ordained scholars.[54]

The hypothesis that the later church found the title to convey the special character of the activity and teaching of Jesus as well as of His relationship to the disciples cannot be excluded, but in the traditions which have been preserved for us this is nowhere plainly expressed[55] (apart from John 3:2); even Mk. 10:51f. is brought only secondarily into connection with the idea of discipleship[56]—an indication that the original use of the address is palpably reflected here.[57]

διδάσκαλε is a translation of the Aramaic רַבִּי or רִבּוּנִי, a fact which is expressly mentioned in two passages of John's gospel.[58] It must be borne in mind that the Greek and the Semitic words, in accordance with their semantic development, do not exactly correspond; hence the LXX, despite its use of διδάσκω has almost completely avoided διδάσκαλος.[59] The situation in the NT is very similar to that which we have found in regard to ῥαββί. Again, Matthew at many points has effaced this mode of address and has retained it only in the mouth of the adversaries of Jesus and those who stood aloof.[60] Luke, on the contrary, has adopted διδάσκαλε in many cases,[61] but himself preferred ἐπιστάτα which at times he has editorially inserted.[62] The address διδάσκαλε in any case has no special Christological bearing[63] and in 3:12 it is of course used of the Baptist.

If we compare the oldest examples, ten texts in Mark and four in Luke's special material, then the conclusions reached in respect of "Rabbi" are confirmed: the address διδάσκαλε is found in the mouth of opponents or outsiders,[64] in the petition of one who is seeking help,[65] and equally in address to Jesus by the disciples.[66] Hence there was maintained a widely prevalent, unreflective use, reflecting the fact that Jesus was addressed by the people, the disciples and opponents alike as "Rabbi".[67] The earthly Jesus was recognized as a teacher and master, and even the later church preserved this.

Sometimes ὁ διδάσκαλος is found as a description of Jesus. It is used without special significance by outsiders in their dialogue with the disciples, ὁ διδάσκαλος ὑμῶν.[68] More important is the sententious statement Matt. 10:24f.‖Lk. 6:40. To this may be added the formulation of Matt. 23:8 and the use of the absolute ὁ διδάσκαλος in narrative material.[69]

How has this come about? In Palestinian Judaism רַב was used almost exclusively with the addition of a suffix. Yet we must be cautious about imputing from the start the absolute use of the word to the Greek-speaking community. For we know that in the first century A.D. רַבִּי was used in Palestinian Judaism not only as an address, but also as a title, the suffix having lost in such cases its pronominal meaning.[70] At the start of the development which must here be investigated stands the logion Matt. 10:24f.||Lk. 6:40. If we neglect the addition in Matt. 10:25b, the saying expresses a principle of the Jewish law of the messenger, whereby the latter can fully and completely represent the one whose message he bears;[71] this is clearly formulated in Matt. 10:25a||Lk. 6:40b. It is not surprising that in Matthew disciples and master are related as servants and lord, and there is no need for the supposition that Luke has maintained the original form of the text, which Matthew has modified in view of his Christology.[72] For John 13:16 and 15:20 show that the saying in its formulation as servant and lord was fairly widespread.[73]

What is striking is that ὁ διδάσκαλος, which appears in the first sentence of both the Matthew and Luke texts, has in the second sentence a genitive personal pronoun accompanying it, while in the form employing the terms "servant" "lord" this arrangement is not repeated. However this may be explained linguistically,[74] it is in any case not a question of a properly absolute use for the correlation with "disciples" is essentially decisive. The saying is capable of very varied application.[75]

In Matt. 10:24f. there is given through v. 25b an unmistakable reference to Jesus as the "master" and the "lord"; a singular position is ascribed to him. "Thus Jesus ceases to be a διδάσκαλος in the Jewish sense."[76] And it is hardly a matter of chance that in the saying from the special material of Matthew, (Matt. 23:8) the title "master" is reserved to Jesus alone: ὑμεῖς δὲ μὴ κληθῆτε ῥαββί. εἷς γάρ ἐστιν ὑμῶν ὁ διδάσκαλος, πάντες δὲ ὑμεῖς ἀδελφοί ἐστε.[77] This saying is differentiated from the address ῥαββί/διδάσκαλε as also from the logion of Matt. 10:24, 25a||Lk. 6:40 by the fact that it is no longer in any way explainable from Jewish presuppositions.

Neither the admonition to the disciples not to allow themselves to be called "rabbi", nor the abiding position of Jesus as master, is to be understood in the light of the relation between the Jewish תַּלְמִידִים and their rabbi. What is here at issue is the special character of the discipleship to Jesus, which implies not merely a temporary relation to a master for the purpose of learning the Torah, but rather a total personal surrender. For this reason the connection is valid not merely for earthly fellowship together but extends also beyond the death of Jesus.[78] Hence, in the post-resurrection period μαθητής can be used also as a title of the Christian.[79]

In Matt. 23:8 the term "disciple" does not appear, but the word ἀδελφός likewise conveys indirectly the same idea of subordination and dependence on the one master.[80] There can be no doubt that what is here in question is a problem which only became acute in the post-resurrection period, and which found its answer in the conclusion that the relation to Jesus as the sole authoritative "master" was permanent in character; Matt. 23:8 is thus to be regarded as a formation by the community.[81] Here for the first time is discernible how the term διδάσκαλος became stamped with a specifically Christological content. There is not yet in Matt. 23:8 an absolute use of the word but the presuppositions for this are implied.

A relatively unemphatic use of the absolute ὁ διδάσκαλος is found in Mk. 5:35 par. within the Jairus story; the word refers to the Jesus who is present and thus gains its specific import.[82]

It is different in the story of the preparations for the passover, Mk. 14:14 parr. Jesus sends two of His disciples into the city, foretelling that they will meet a man carrying a jar of water, and ordering them to say: ὁ διδάσκαλος λέγει· ποῦ ἐστιν τὸ κατάλυμά μου κτλ. There can be no question of a prior arrangement.[83] What is expressed here is the singular and characteristic authority of Jesus, who can so advise His disciples and in such a way can make His claim even on a stranger. We have here a markedly Christological use of the title ὁ διδάσκαλος.[84] As with the Jewish רַבִּי but informed by quite a different content there has thus arisen here a titular use, even though this predicate of dignity has not yet by any means attained the same weight of emphasis as the other Christological titles. In any event Matt. 23:8 shows what a decisive affirmation could be bound up with it and Mk. 14:14 illuminates the claim which is rooted in it.

Although in regard to the story of the preparations for the passover it must be assumed that it arose in the sphere of

Hellenism, yet it should not be overlooked that the use of a term stemming from Judaic-Palestinian presuppositions was thus precipitated, for it is certain that the Greek διδάσκαλος-idea was not the standard authoritative one.

The gospel of John is likewise familiar with this tradition, and in view of its independence over against the synoptics this is evidence of the ancient date of the conception. In John, however, it is linked to the Christological idea of the Son of God, as is clear from the explanatory ἀπὸ θεοῦ ἐλήλυθας διδάσκαλος in 3:2 and the juxtaposition of the titles ὁ χριστὸς, ὁ υἱὸς τοῦ θεοῦ and ὁ διδάσκαλος in 11:27, 28.[85] The situation is somewhat different in 13:13f. where ὁ διδάσκαλος is conjoined with ὁ κύριος; to this point we shall have to return.

All in all, the titular use of ὁ διδάσκαλος did not produce any far-reaching effects.[86] Nevertheless, the change from the unreflective use as a mode of address to the term which is used absolutely and filled with a Christological content is still discernible. What is most striking of all is the relatively unconnected juxtaposition of the unemphatic address ῥαββί/ διδάσκαλε and the absolute ὁ διδάσκαλος. But of this there are examples elsewhere.[87] It is precisely Matthew, who consistently removes the term as an address, but on the other hand allows it in Matt. 10:24f., 23:8, 26; 18 (par. Mk. 14:14), who shows that there was no unified usage in this respect. A repercussion of the absolute use of the word on its use as a form of address may only be proved in isolated cases,[88] and in view of the very limited currency of ὁ διδάσκαλος may not be generally assumed.

The term "Lord" underwent a development analogous to that of διδάσκαλε/ὁ διδάσκαλος. To start with, we have its general use as an address and then the absolute use of the word evolved from this.

We must begin with linguistic considerations. In view of the replacement of ῥαββουνί in Mk. 10:51 by κύριε in Lk. 18:41, we might wonder whether κύριε might also be traced back to an original רַבִּי[89] especially as διδάσκαλε was only an inadequate translation of רַבִּי. Yet διδάσκαλε as a rendering of רַבִּי obviously came to prevail and another equivalent of κύριε must be assumed.[90] Behind the use of "Lord" as a form of address there stands the Aramaic מָרֵא whose later form מַר was a word, which like רַב was not used absolutely without a dependent sub-

stantive or suffix.[91] אָדוֹן had gone out of general use and survived only as the specific title for a king, high priest and
so on, but especially as a description of God.

When the rabbis discuss in the second century A.D. the date
at which God was first called אָדוֹן they are intimating what an
exclusive position this description had acquired.[92] On the other
hand, מָרֵא as a description of God played no decisive role in
the NT period. No doubt we find in Dan. 5:23 מָרֵא־שְׁמַיָּא and
in Dan. 2:47 God is described as מָרֵא מַלְכִין, but the form of
address מָרִי or the phrase "thy Lord" (מָרָךְ), etc., is first applied
to God in examples from the Amoraim period.[93] But מַר was
the usual description of the human lord, as was also רַב except
that the latter was very soon confined in application to the
scribes, whereas מַר retained its wider meaning.[94] Hence
מַר is used in the most varied ways. מָרִי like רַבִּי was current as
an address to superiors;[95] but it was also used of equals, so that
it took on the character of an expression of courtesy. In any
case we must reckon with the indiscriminate use of מָרִי and
רַבִּי in the time of Jesus; if רַבִּי was preferred in addressing a
teacher of the law, מָרִי might equally well be used in the same
circumstances.

On the basis of these linguistic considerations we must
suppose that Jesus was addressed not only as רַבִּי but also as
מָרִי. But under no circumstances may we assume that the
address of Jesus as מָרִי/κύριε implied the transference to Him
of a divine title. We have here an originally profane linguistic
use, which only gradually was stamped with a special Christological significance, and which at first was basically distinct
from the application of the term to God. This is confirmed by a
detailed examination of the tradition.

In Mark there is only one example of the address κύριε,
namely in Mk. 7:28. This traditional bit about the Syro-
phoenician woman, in the framework of which the term
κύριε stands, is characterized by the fact that, apart from the
secondary v. 27a, it makes use of no technical terms; the story
is narrated in an emphatically profane way—and this applies
both to the figurative speech and the outline of the story—
not even does the key-word "faith" appear, although an unconditional and unshakeable trust is in fact the issue. Also our

term of address is used in the most general sense, although it expresses real subordination and not only courtesy. ῥαββί/ διδάσκαλε has perhaps been intentionally avoided, for it is here a question of a heathen woman on whose lips the word "Rabbi", emphasizing as it does the special position of a Jewish teacher of the Torah, might have seemed inappropriate to the community which handed on this tradition.

Also, in the one certain example from the logia source, the story of the centurion of Capernaum, Matt. 8:(6), 8||Lk. 7:6, we have this mode of address used by a heathen. Here it is expressly underlined by the motive of the ἐξουσία of a master over his subordinates (Matt. 8:9 par.). But it is clear that the κύριε address cannot have been meant as a predicate of divinity;[96] it expresses rather the thought of authority and dependence, thus implying the true and proper sense of the oriental use of the term. The acceptance of this traditional story into the logia source was probably occasioned by this motive of ἐξουσία.[97] Since the description of Jesus as lord plays otherwise no special part in Q, it may be supposed that here, as in Mk. 7:28, there is evidence of the influence of the ancient form of address which was in fact used to Jesus, and the full meaning of which is here brought out.

It is more difficult to reach a decision with regard to the other examples from the logia source. We may disregard Matt. 7:21||Lk. 6:46 for the original form of the logion must have contained an address to the eschatological judge.[98] As regards Matt. 8:21f.||Lk. 17:4, about reconciliation, the sententious phrasing in Luke, where κύριε is missing, will be the more ancient, while the transformation of it in Matthew serves for the moulding of the passage 18:15–35.

Matters are extremely complicated regarding the discipleship sayings Matt. 8:19–22||Lk. 9:57–62. Here Matthew has two sayings, Luke three, and whereas Matthew has in v. 19 the form διδάσκαλε and in v. 21 the form κύριε, in Luke there is no form of address in the two first sayings. In the third, which has no parallel in Matthew, we find κύριε (9:61). To what extent we must assume in Lk. 9:61f. a traditional nucleus which has been only editorially linked with the Q tradition, may remain an open question.[99] More important is the fact that clearly in such contexts an address of Jesus was implied, so that there is no absolute necessity to allow for editorial additions. In any case it is striking that διδάσκαλε and κύριε are remarkably parallel and hence seem to have been used in the same sense. At the same time it is to be noted that in Matt. v. 19 Jesus is addressed by a γραμματεύς, in v. 21, on the other hand, by a disciple. The result is that v. 19f. expresses the rejection of some one who desires discipleship, while v. 21f. expresses the confirmation of a disciple in the already existing relation of discipleship.[100]

But this arrangement is editorial. The sayings in themselves, as the Lucan version shows, are not concerned with the question whether some one should be accepted as a disciple or not, but only with the unconditional character of the demand involved in discipleship; thus in Luke, the questioners—and this is surely original—are not described in detail. Moreover, the apostrophes in Matt. 8:19, 21 are not absolutely dependent on the specifically Matthean point of view, as Lk. 9:61 shows. Further, Matthew has preserved διδάσκαλε in a number of cases where it occurs in the mouth of opponents and outsiders, but nowhere is to be discerned a tendency for him to insert it editorially.[101] Thus a certain decision cannot be made, but it is at least possible that διδάσκαλε and κύριε in Matt. 8:19, 21 already belonged to the source, and may possibly even reflect an original רַבִּי and מָרִי.[102]

The mode of address κύριε is often to be found in Luke and Matthew, but their gospels give quite a different picture. In a number of places Luke has completed his material by inserting this address, both as regards his Marcan material[103] and his logion source.[104] For this reason it is no longer possible to make any secure judgment about the instances quoted from his own special material.[105] But this point need not be investigated in detail for it is clear that in his own editorial use of it, Luke has maintained the old meaning of this form of address. He does not use it as a divine predicate of exaltation as does Matthew. Of course κύριε is not used as a mere address of courtesy, but implies a genuine subordination and a placing of oneself at the disposal of the person addressed.[106]

In this respect the changes introduced by Luke and Matthew in their use of Mk. 1:40 are very informative. In Mark there is no address, but he speaks of a γονυπετεῖν by the sick man. Luke intensifies this with πεσὼν ἐπὶ πρόσωπον and completes by the addition of κύριε; Matt. 8:2 has likewise inserted κύριε, but in addition has changed γονυπετεῖν to προσκυνεῖν, in order to indicate the divine dignity of the one addressed. At one point Luke too found such a conception in his traditional material, and accepted it, namely in the epiphany story of Lk. 5:1–11, as Peter's words in v. 8b plainly show. But with him this is an exception, and is not really characteristic of his total viewpoint. Rather it is to be concluded from the parallelism with his editorially preferred ἐπιστάτα, which again stands in close connection with διδάσκαλε, that Luke maintained the κύριε mode of address, as suggested by his source, as for instance among other passages in the story of the centurion of Capernaum. But a certain development of the term is observable in him inasmuch as it is placed in emphatic relation to the absolute ὁ κύριος applied to the earthly Jesus,[107] and this point must be examined in more detail.[108]

In Matthew the form of address κύριε has an essentially different meaning.[109] An absolute ὁ κύριος is absent from his gospel apart from 21:3 where he has taken it over from Mk. 11:3.[110] But there is no doubt that the address has now received the "character of a divine name of exaltation".[111] This is shown both by the connection with προσκυνεῖν which has already been illustrated from his use of Mk. 1:40 parr., and which is frequent in other contexts also,[112] and again by the connection with appeals which have the nature of prayer, e.g. σῶσον (με), ἐλέησόν με, βοήθει μοι.[113] For this reason Matthew's use[114] must be excluded from our present investigation, for it presupposes a later stage of development.

The evangelist's understanding of κύριε probably already implies in the background a certain understanding of the "son of David" text, Matt. 22:41–45 (par. Mk. 12:35–37a). Here the κυριότης of Jesus, because of Ps. 110:1, is based on the idea of exaltation, but for Matthew there is no longer any distinction between the earthly kyrios, despite His lowliness, and the heavenly. However, Mk. 12:35–37a presupposes already a later understanding of the kyrios predicate, and may not be traced back to old Palestinian tradition; for the moment therefore we must neglect it.[115]

As in the case of "master", there may be recognized alongside the ancient form of address κύριε a basically corresponding use of ὁ κύριος. Admittedly in this case the transition from the address form to the absolute use is not discernible in detail, but in any event we may refer to Matt. 10:24, 25a where, in the saying about the relationship of master and disciple, we find the parallel statement about lord and servant, even though here an absolute use is missing; however, this dual statement is an indication of the very close connection of the two descriptions. Examples of the absolute ὁ κύριος are to be found in Mark and Luke and also in Paul and John.

The characteristic and, in the gospel of Mark, singular use of ὁ κύριος in the story of the entry into Jerusalem, Mk. 11:3 has always been striking, as also is the parallel with Mk. 14:14. In this case neither may the absolute use of the word be disputed,[116] nor may this ὁ κύριος be referred to the owner of the colt, supposed to be among the disciples of Jesus.[117] We have here a title of dignity in which the authority of Jesus is expressed. It is in virtue of this authority that He can claim the gift of the donkey, and because of it that men in fact obey Him.

This story has many layers in its composition. At the basis of it there probably lies an old story of a more accidental happening on the arrival of Jesus in Jerusalem, in connection with which Ps. 118:25f., recited by pilgrims on the occasion of the passover feast, was applied to Jesus.[118] On the one hand, all this was woven by the later church into the son of David tradition,[119] and on the other was remoulded in the light of Zech. 9:9.[120] This transformation has left its traces especially in the Marcan version in vv. 2–6; here the solemn entry becomes a self-presentation deliberately intended by Jesus and carefully prepared. With marvellous foreknowledge He brings about the event, and the statement in v. 2 that no man had previously used the donkey, points plainly to dependence on the Septuagint, where at the end of the verse Zech. 9:9 we have the phrase πῶλος νέος to which there is nothing corresponding in the Hebrew original.[121]

In the context of these passages there stands the absolute ὁ κύριος. The origin of this in the Hellenistic-Judaic Christian church is indisputable; but an ancient tradition must find its echo here. In any case the kyrios title is not here a transference of a predicate of the exalted Lord to the earthly one, but can only be explained from the ancient address "Lord", in which, as we have shown, it was a question of the special position and authority of the earthly Jesus. It is not fortuitous that the κύριε address received particular weight in a certain strand of the tradition, and expressed the thought of unconditional subordination to the person of Jesus.

It is very suggestive that precisely with Luke, who maintained the old use of the address, as it was contained already in Mark and in the logia source, are to be found a relatively large number of examples of the use of ὁ κύριος as we have just characterized it. Apart from the parallel text to Mk. 11:3, found in Lk. 19:31 and repeated with emphasis in Lk. 19:34,[122] there are fifteen further texts.[123] It is obvious that ὁ κύριος was used by the evangelist in the most varied ways to complete his source; this is shown both by additions to the Marcan material[124] and to the logia source.[125] Added to these eight editorial passages[126] are seven from his own special material.[127] Decision about the originality of particular elements in this special material is always difficult, when there coincides with it a specific tendency peculiar to the evangelist himself; in such a case we often have to remain content with suppositions. But here we are in a favourable position inasmuch as in two texts it can be clearly shown that the title ὁ κύριος was taken over from the traditional material.

In Lk. 16:8 we have the old conclusion of the parable, in which the "Lord", namely Jesus, praises the unrighteous steward;[128] v. 8b is only intelligible if spoken by Jesus. But the praise of such a rascal soon aroused objections, with the result that in vv. 9ff. beginning with a new and emphatic καὶ ἐγὼ ὑμῖν λέγω further comments on the parable follow which sharpen v. 8, and which finally gave rise to the mistaken opinion that the κύριος speaking in v. 8 must be the lord of the steward. It is for us a matter of indifference whether vv. 9–13 were added by Luke himself, or taken over *en bloc*, or whether he expanded an already existing addition. It is plain in any event that v. 8 must belong to the ancient core and cannot be editorial.

A similar assessment is to be made about Lk. 18:6. Here in vv. 6–8a we have an older conclusion of the parable, which has been completed by Luke in v. 8b through a further saying. Since in v. 8b the Son of man title appears, it becomes quite improbable that in v. 6a Luke subsequently inserted ὁ κύριος.[129] In Lk. 7:13 and 13:15 it cannot be excluded that we might have a pre-Lucan tradition, but as in the case of Lk. 10:39,

41, 19:8 we can make no secure decision.[130] That a very old tradition is discernible in Lk. 16:8, 18:6 is in any case indisputable, and it may well be that it goes back to Palestinian sources. Admittedly, the absolute use of מִרָא‎ was not current there, but as in the case of רִבִּי‎ an archaic suffix form may have become established.[131] Even if the absolute use of the term only arose in the Greek speaking communities, there is still a connection with ancient Palestinian tradition.

Where the church in this manner invokes the "Lord", it is concerned to express the word and the authority of the earthly Jesus before whom it bows. Lk. 16:8 and 18:6, as well as Mk. 11:3 may be regarded as conclusive examples of this, and the continuation of this outlook is pre-eminently shown in the editorial idea of Luke. That it was mediated through Hellenistic Judaic Christianity is clear from Mk. 11:3. This is compatible with the fact that here, as will have to be shown, κύριος also attained essential significance as a predicate of the exalted One.

Yet the two types of use are neither to be directly derived from each other, nor without further consideration to be confused, however much they became later on related to each other. In regard to the absolute ὁ κύριος which we have just discussed, the intention was to express the exaltation and the authority of the earthly Jesus, as happened similarly in the conception of the Son of man who was active on earth. But whereas in the latter case the emphasis lay on the position and ἐξουσία conferred by God, which occasions a tension with this generation and finally leads Jesus in the way of suffering, the term ὁ κύριος emphasizes fullness of power which moves human beings to self-surrender and implies the recognition of Jesus. With this view we are led back to the mode of thinking of the first Palestinian church, which thus testifies its abiding loyalty to the work and words of Jesus. From its source in the address מָרִי‎, which brought out in many cases the idea of genuine submission, there followed this meaningful development of the description of Jesus as Lord.

It is not legitimate to assert that Jesus Himself like a wise teacher sketched the picture of service towards a master and slowly instilled it into the souls of His disciples—thus Foerster attempts to define the origin of the kyrios predicate[132]—

85

especially as the title "Lord" was by no means an image for complete dedication derived from everyday life. For the idea that Jesus was not a lord with a number of slaves and that His lordship "in and for itself is simply incomprehensible"[133] rests upon a deep misunderstanding. The idea "Lord" implies not exclusively a determinate sociological relationship, but rather much more generally an authority which claims complete submission.

authority

Lietzmann rightly emphasizes that in the first instance we must think of the pupil or disciple whose relation to his master was understood as one of complete dependence like that of a slave.[134] A "transference" of the concept of the lord was not necessary, and the metaphorical use is only one among others,[135] and by no means a presupposition for the application of the description to Jesus.

It cannot be assumed that Jesus Himself described Himself as "the Lord",[136] and still less is it permissible to draw inferences from the concept of the lord about His own self-consciousness.[137] Doubtless the special characteristics of the emergence and the claim of Jesus were decisive for the formation of the description "Lord". But this was the work of the church, which was faced with the task of defining the reality of the work and person of Jesus.[138]

Examples of the use of ὁ κύριος in this characteristic sense are by no means confined to Mk. 11:3 and Luke. That we must assume the expression to have had a relatively wide circulation is shown especially by the apostle Paul. For apart from the confession of the exalted Lord which is current in his writings and was influenced by Hellenistic ideas, Paul uses the kyrios title in quite other ways which point to an origin in his own stream of tradition.

Paul's use of kyrios:
(1) Hellenistic
(2) Jewish

This is clearest where the apostle refers to words of Jesus; in addition there are passages in which he alludes to the "brothers of the Lord". In this use of ὁ κύριος he has primarily the earthly Jesus in view; it is a question of words which are based on the authority of the earthly Jesus and it is a question of the physical relations of Jesus. It may be assumed that behind ἀδελφοὶ τοῦ κυρίου of 1 Cor. 9:5; Gal. 1:19 there lies a well-known technical expression. The relations of Jesus played a not inconsiderable part in the Palestinian sphere, as is shown by the special position assigned to James in the early period.[139]

If later they were called δεσπόσυνοι[140] this again implies a description of Jesus as Lord, and it is very possible that in both cases it goes back to the same Aramaic root.[141] In any case ὁ κύριος in the expression "brothers of the Lord" signifies the earthly Jesus; such a use of the term "lord" is indeed only understandable if it refers to the earthly Jesus, and is not a title applied to the exalted Lord.

How strongly in the Pauline use of ὁ κύριος the emphasis can lie on the earthly Jesus is shown too in I Cor. 7:10, 9:14. In both cases the apostle alludes to words of Jesus;[142] this is further underlined by the fact that in I Cor. 7:12,25 Paul expressly says that as regards the questions then being debated no words of the Lord have come down to him.[143] This discussion must not be affected by the separate question of the genuineness of the quoted logia. If in I Cor. 7:10 the authenticity of the word about divorce is in fact beyond question, this is not quite certain in I Cor. 9:14 and can hardly be made convincing in I Thess. 4:15ff.[144] But it must be assumed that even as regards I Thess. 4:15 (16f.) the apostle is referring to a traditional apocalyptic saying ascribed to Jesus. Of course, on the other hand, for Paul himself we must bear in mind that the authority of this earthly Jesus is indissolubly bound up with the power and authority of the exalted Lord, and is legitimated by the latter.[145]

It is from this point of view that we should understand the last much debated sentence in the introduction to the paradosis concerning the Lord's Supper, I Cor. 11:23: ἐγὼ γὰρ παρέλαβον ἀπὸ τοῦ κυρίου. There needs no long discussion to show that for Paul the tradition receives its meaning and guarantee not from its earthly bearers, but from the very presence and revelation of Jesus.[146] This does not mean that the content of the tradition must be traced back to the exalted Lord;[147] Conversely, however, the Lord is by no means the first member in a long chain of transmitters of tradition.[148] The point is that the authority of the earthly Lord stands behind these eucharistic words, that nevertheless their perpetuation is effected and legitimated by the exalted Lord.[149] Yet the word ἀπό has its weight,[150] in so far as it suggests primarily the word of the earthly Jesus.

It is very important that the accents should be correctly placed: in this instance it would not be appropriate to say that the exalted Lord is simply the earthly one, it is important to understand the passage from the standpoint of the authority of the earthly Lord, which is but confirmed by the living presence of the exalted Lord. Nor should it be overlooked that in v. 23b with its introductory indication of the time and its reference to the night of the betrayal, we read ὁ κύριος Ἰησοῦς hence the kyrios predicate is used with reference to the earthly Jesus.[151] Thus in Paul we note a consistency of use in all the relevant passages. In this matter Paul was doubtless determined by the tradition already discussed, for with him a very different use of the kyrios title predominates.[152]

It is interesting to note that even in the Letter to the Hebrews this ancient use of the term still finds an echo, when in two places the earthly Jesus is described as κύριος.[153]

Finally, the Gospel of John must be taken into account. For there both the vocative κύριε and the absolute ὁ κύριος have been preserved from an ancient tradition. In detail the question of tradition and editorial redaction will depend on intrinsic factors; to some extent both the vocative form and the title stand out well, because they have not been simply absorbed into the total viewpoint of the evangelist. Yet there is no need to discuss the various texts,[154] since there is one example where the acceptance of a pre-Johannine conception is indisputable, namely John 13:13f., in which we find ὁ διδάσκαλος καὶ ὁ κύριος.[155] That this ὁ κύριος can only be explained from its parallelism with ὁ διδάσκαλος is obvious.[156]

This gives final confirmation to our preceding exposition of the use of ὁ κύριος as referring to the earthly Jesus. For it is clear from this passage that the same development has taken place as that by which ῥαββί/διδάσκαλε developed into the absolute ὁ διδάσκαλος. From the vocative form κύριε there has arisen step by step the title ὁ κύριος applied to the earthly Jesus and it is attested in a clearly recognizable and relatively wide stream of tradition. The parallelism which was already striking in Mk. 11:3 and 14:14, has thus with justification been taken as our point of departure.

Summary. The description of Jesus as Lord in the Palestinian tradition has nothing to do with a predicate of divinity but has grown out of a secular mode of address. The parallel ῥαββί/ διδάσκαλε which was still in the NT period in general currency, even if preferred for a teacher of the law, is shown in the gospels

88

as being in widespread quite spontaneous use. Later this form of address became obsolescent.

With it, surprisingly enough, is contrasted another development according to which on Jesus as "rabbi" a singular position is conferred. In this development the thought of Christian discipleship plays an important part, with the result that the idea of dedication to the one master, lasting even beyond his death, now receives emphasis. Even if the absolute use of the term first became usual in the Hellenistic Judaic Christian tradition, yet an older outlook has here been preserved. The quite titular ὁ διδάσκαλος implies the ascription to Jesus of authority, an authority on which His claim over men is grounded.

In a very similar way the ancient description of Jesus as Lord arose. Here too the use of the term as a mode of address stands first. In the oldest tradition the thought of unlimited power and complete submission is deliberately emphasized. To the address form κύριε there essentially corresponds the absolute ὁ κύριος applied to the earthly Jesus. Peculiar ἐξουσία and the exaltation which has its source in that are implied in this title of dignity; but this has nothing to do with the predicate of the exalted One.

Again it is a question of an ancient Palestinian conception, even if the absolute use of the word only became established later. It is akin to the conception of the Son of man active on earth, although what is implied is less the sense of tension with humanity than the voluntary surrender to the lofty claim of Jesus. ὁ κύριος is still found in this sense in the writings of Paul and John. ὁ διδάσκαλος καὶ ὁ κύριος in John 13:13f. shows for how long a time even the parallelism of the two descriptions found an echo.

3. The "Lord" who is to come again

What distinguishes the use of κύριε and ὁ κύριος from ῥαββί/διδάσκαλε and ὁ διδάσκαλος is the fact that the latter remains confined in its use to the earthly Jesus, whereas the address "Lord" was at a very early stage applied to the Jesus whose return was expected, this in turn leading to an absolute use of the word. On the basis of the texts which have been discussed so far, we have followed only one line of development in the description of Jesus as Lord, and this must now be completed by the study of a second important development. Both types of use were already found side by side and not unconnected in very ancient tradition, nevertheless they were clearly distinguished. The material is not very considerable, but the characteristically eschatological use of מָרִי and מָרַן (מָרְנָא) stands out very plainly.

We shall take as our point of departure a few synoptic texts. The two sayings about those who call Jesus "Lord, Lord", the address "Lord, Lord" in the parable of the ten virgins, and the use of "Lord" as an address in the picture of the last judgment fall to be considered. In the case of three of these four texts, we have a doubling of the title, which is to be regarded as a typically Semitic characteristic,[157] and with regard to the fourth text, that of the last judgment, a very early origin is also certain for intrinsic reasons.

The statement about those who say "Lord, Lord" has been preserved in Matt. 7:21, par. and in Matt. 7:22f. in two distinct versions.[158] It will be best to start from Matt. 7:22f.‖ Lk. 13:(25)26f. If we compare simply the two directly parallel texts, we see that there is no address in Luke. Yet it should be noted that in 13:25 he has a parable-like introduction which includes κύριε which is strongly reminiscent of the parable of the ten virgins and to which there is a corresponding passage in Matt. 25:11f.; here too the address as "Lord" occurs. In Lk. 13:25 what is in question is the eschatological crisis: the doors are shut by the master of the house, the cry κύριε, ἄνοιξον ἡμῖν is rejected with the justification: οὐκ οἶδα ὑμᾶς πόθεν ἐστέ. In Lk. 13:26f. this is followed by the reminder of table fellowship with Jesus and instruction by Him, nevertheless a final rejection ensues.

What we have here is a word of menace, and the situation in which it arose is easily inferred; the intention is to impress clearly upon those who followed Jesus in His lifetime but who after His death do not adhere to the church, the full seriousness of their decision; they will not be able to stand in the hour of final judgment merely by appealing to their attitude towards the earthly Jesus. However much this saying has preserved essentially the original intention, in its form, especially through its connection with the parable-like motive of the closed door, it must be deemed to be secondary.

It is much more likely that it had originally the form of a prophetic word, as is still to be seen in Matt. 7:22f.,[159] where an early Christian prophet speaking in the name of Jesus and therefore in the first person, speaks the menacing word.[160] But on the other hand, in the Matthean version the content has been modified. For here it is a question of a judgment pronounced against false Christian teachers—false prophets and charismatics.[161]

[margin note: false teachers]

In both versions we find ourselves in the sphere of a debate which is taking place on Palestinian ground. This is confirmed by the strongly apocalyptic type of thought. It shows, however, that the address "Lord, Lord" used towards the Jesus who is to return as judge has already at an early date secured a firm foothold.

The situation is somewhat different as regards Matt. 7:21‖ Lk. 6:46. The widespread assumption that the Lucan version here contains the original text is in my opinion mistaken.[162] For, on the one hand, Luke has deprived the saying of its eschatological bearing; on the other, instead of its being a question of doing the will of God, it is a question of carrying out the words of Jesus.[163] Perhaps the saying reached Luke already in this form, though it is also possible that he alone was responsible for casting it in this mould. We must therefore adhere to the Matthean version.

Again the theme is an attitude, a type of conduct which is decisive for eschatological salvation, for the "entering into the kingdom of heaven". We do not propose to dispute that the motive of entering into the kingdom of heaven played a part in the preaching of Jesus Himself;[164] also the close of Matt. 7:21 certainly makes the impression of being ancient.[165] But all the same, the saying in its antithesis of saying "Lord, Lord" and right conduct as the condition for entry into the kingdom of God cannot be accepted without hesitation as possible on the lips of Jesus. No doubt there are here older elements which have been woven into a new saying. The "Lord, Lord" cannot be intended as an address to the earthly Jesus, but as in Matt. 7:22f. we are obviously here faced by a problem which preoccupied the mind of the post-resurrection church.

[margin note: "Lord, Lord" a form of invocatory prayer ✓]

Thus this form of address can only be related to the invocatory prayer of the early Christians;[166] and as is clear from the juxtaposition of Matt. 7:21 and Matt. 7:22f. what is

especially thought of is the eschatological function of Jesus.[167]
We shall have to return to this point later.

With the address to the world judge in Matt. 7:22 the
κύριε κύριε in the parable of the ten virgins Matt. 25:1–12(13)
is closely connected. In the already mentioned parallel text to
v. 11f., namely Lk. 13:25, there is only a single κύριε, but the
double form of the address must be the more original. In Matt.
25:1ff., it may not be considered that we have an authentic
parable of crisis, which was later worked over;[168] the position
is rather that the text as originally drafted, contains already the
problem of the delay in the parousia, and for this reason must
be claimed as a formation by the church.[169]

In the light of this origin are to be explained the clearly
allegorical features, and the repeated emphasis of the meaning
by metaphorical traits. The expected "bridegroom" is of course
the Jesus who is to come again, for whose ὑπάντησις (ἀπάντησις)
His church must be constantly prepared.[170] It is He who as
world judge is appropriately addressed as "Lord, Lord", and
who will pronounce His judgment against the negligent and
dilatory. But conversely it is erroneous to speak simply of a
"late" composition by the church, and for the allegorical
equivalence of bridegroom and Messiah to introduce gnostic
motives.[171]

It will not be possible to deny that this piece of tradition
originated in the first Palestinian church.[172] For in the first
place it cannot be adequately explained without reference to
Palestinian marriage customs; secondly, the figurative word
νυμφίος to which there are no parallels in the OT or in Judaism
discloses a very early allegorical application of the word "Lord"
Mk. 2:(18) 19a, which occurs again similarly in Mk. 2:19b,
20;[173] and finally the Christological eschatological concept
both in Mk. 2:19b, 20 and Matt. 25:1ff. can be explained only
on the presuppositions of the Palestinian first church, which is
not yet familiar with the concept of exaltation.[174]

The delay in the parousia is not surmounted by the church
increasingly assuring itself of the constant presence of its
Lord and living by the faith in His already inaugurated
dominion in heaven; it issues rather in a more yearning expect-
ancy of His return, and the realization that the church is called
to a steadfast vigilance,[175] and readiness to be tested. Salvation
is still for it something to be awaited. Its sole concern is to be

able to share in the marriage feast, its sole anxiety is not to fling away the chance of admission to that ultimate joy. Hence it is precisely He who is to come again who is addressed as "Lord, Lord".

The picture of the great assize in Matt. 25:31–46 which has features suggestive of a parable, is likewise familiar with the address of "Lord". We find the simple κύριε in vv. 37 and 44. Here we have of course only a somewhat weakened repercussion, for the guiding motives are Son of man and royal Messiah. But this text which we shall have to discuss in a later connection belongs equally to the traditional material of the ancient Palestinian church.[176] Here the title Lord as an address to the One who was to come again to judge the world was thus firmly anchored.

We come to the heart of our problem in discussing the use of the formula μαραναθά. In 1 Cor. 16:22 and *Did.* 10:6, it has been preserved in its old Aramaic wording. The thesis, expounded first by Heitmüller and then accepted by Bousset, to the effect that this "Maranatha" stems not from the Palestinian first church but from the bilingual churches of Damascus or Antioch,[177] is untenable and has been repudiated by more recent research. The firmly fixed Aramaic form of the prayer can only be explained if it is here a question of the most ancient primitive church tradition.[178] Also the assertion sometimes made that we have here the formula of an oath, referring to God and used for the purpose of ratification,[179] is to be rejected. The "Our Lord" of the formula is most certainly a reference to Jesus, and on the grounds of the textual material so far discussed this cannot be doubted.

Before essential questions are considered, we shall make brief reference to the linguistic problems involved. For the understanding and translation of it, there are, as Karl Georg Kuhn has penetratingly shown,[180] various possibilities: the first part of the phrase is clear and means "Our Lord", the only point in question is whether we have here the old suffix form מָרַנָא or the more recent popular מָרַן.

The second member of the phrase is more difficult to interpret; for either it is a perfect אֲתָא "he has come", or an imperfect "come", which again might be variously expressed by אֱתָא or תָּא.[181] Thus the most varied combinations result:

93

either the perfect מָרַן אֲתָא. or the imperative מָרַן אֲתָא[182] or מָרָנָא תָא.
A decision about the form and meaning of the phrase is thus
not possible on linguistic grounds. A certain measure of help
is afforded only by the expression ἔρχου κύριε 'Ιησοῦ in Rev.
22:20b which although not quite literally is undoubtedly
derived from μαραναθά. This is contradicted by the fact that the
Coptic translation of the *Didache* renders the μαραναθά of
10:6 by a preterite.[183] But from the point of view of the history
of tradition, Rev. 22:20 is essentially older and merits a certain
preference even if by such considerations alone a final conclusion cannot be reached. More intrinsic reasons must be
sought.

It is important to take into account the context. In 1 Cor.
16:22 and *Did.* 10:6, it is easy to discern that the reference is to
the eucharist. Peterson has especially emphasized the connection of ἀνάθεμα with μαραναθά in 1 Cor. 16:22 and the coupling
of the formula of invitation with the call to repentance and the
following μαραναθὰ ἀμήν in *Did.* 10:6 in order to render probable an apotropaic understanding of the phrase.[184] This can
in fact be proved at a later date from a Christian inscription
found in Salamis and intended for the protection of a grave,[185]
but such a degenerate superstitious use should not be traced
back to the earlier time and inserted into eucharistic traditions.[186]

More important is the investigation of Lietzmann, who
indeed begins with later sources and from thence takes his
inquiry backward, but who himself traces the development
within the liturgy and hence comes to a more useful conclusion.
It is true that in this way he was unable to elucidate the special
meaning of μαραναθά, but he has shown that it has its place in a
bigger liturgical context and is closely connected with the
invitatory formula and the summons to penitence which
preceded the Communion; moreover, he saw that in *Did.* 10:6
we have a *responsorium*, the ἐλθέτω χάρις καὶ παρελθέτω ὁ
κόσμος οὗτος like the εἴ τις ἅγιός ἐστι, ἐρχέσθω· εἴ τις οὐκ
ἔστιν, μετανοείτω· μαραναθά being said by the priest, while the
congregation in the first case answered with ὡσαννὰ τῷ θεῷ
Δαυίδ, in the second with ἀμήν.[187]

Further, Günther Bornkamm by comparison with parallel
texts in the NT and the apostolic fathers has attained addi-

[handwritten margin note: place of maranatha in larger liturgical context]

tional important insights.[188] The elements of the eucharistic
liturgy present in 1 Cor. 16:22 can be shown to be reflected
not only in *Did.* 10:6 but also in Rev. 22:12–20.[189] This means
that the ἔρχου κύριε Ἰησοῦ of Rev. 22:20b just because of its
position in the framework of the Lord's Supper maybe adduced
in elucidation of the "Maranatha". Bornkamm then investigated the firm connection of the "Anathema" with the eucharistic liturgy, and showed that its origin was to be seen in the
conditions of admission to the supper.

For while in the oldest traditional text, *Did.* 10:6, the invitatory formula was adduced to those who were "holy", and the
rest were summoned to repentance and conversion, there soon
developed, as is clear from 1 Cor. 16:22, a formula of rejection,
which as a rule, as in Rev. 22:15, 17 stands parallel with the
invitation. This formula of rejection which belongs to the
sphere of sacred law, and contains no disciplinarian suggestion
of human jurisdiction, was only at a later date replaced by the
rule that only the baptized might be admitted to the Lord's
Supper.[190] To this was added a further development in which
the "Anathema" belonging to the eucharist was applied to
the congregation itself parenetically, whether to warn against
an unworthy use of the Supper as in 1 Cor. 11:27ff., whether to
point out the threatening danger of defection as in Heb. 6:6,
10:29, 13:10, or whether—and in this connection the anathema
retains for long its firm place in the structure of the eucharist—
to contest erroneous doctrines and false prophecies, as is shown
by Rom. 16:17ff. the warning writings dispatched in Revelation, and *Did.* 11–13, etc.[191]

More important for our argument is the question to what
extent "Maranatha" had reverberations beyond 1 Cor. 16:22;
Did. 10:6; and Rev. 22:20b. Very suggestive is the ἄχρι οὗ
ἔλθῃ of 1 Cor. 11:26, indicating the eschatological outlook
which was linked to the words of eucharistic institution; for
this expression, although no longer in the form of an invocatory
prayer, fulfils a similar function to the μαραναθά or ἔρχου
κύριε Ἰησοῦ.[192] Also in the passage Heb. 13:10–16, where by
the use of eucharistic terminology the intention is to illustrate
the status of the Christian which transcends all traditional
cultic rites, in v. 14 there is expressed an expectation, admittedly
not of the Lord who is to come, but none the less of the μέλλουσα
πόλις. In the parenesis 1 *Clem.* 34 which is justifiably quoted in

this connection, and which has strong eucharistic suggestions, there has also been preserved an eschatological note and in v. 3 even an express allusion to the coming Lord.[193] In the despatches of Revelation we twice find a reference, in connection with the polemic against false teachers, to the eschatological feast of the Lord.[194]

From these texts it may be inferred that in fact μαραναθά must be understood as an imperative and emphasizes the eschatological bearing of the eucharistic feast.[195] Although the petition itself ceases to occur, yet only the imperative form of it "Lord, come" suffices to explain the eschatological elements in the texts we have quoted.

Now the conclusion we have reached corresponds to what we know about the oldest eucharistic feast of the primitive Palestinian church. In view of the firm place of the "Maranatha" in the early eucharistic liturgies, we may without hesitation assume that from the beginning it was anchored in the rite. In the first post-resurrection period, a Lord's Supper was celebrated which had a pronounced eschatological character. To the fullest extent, the vision of the worshippers was turned towards that consummation of salvation which was still awaited.

As a result of this insight, difficult problems connected with the evolution of tradition arise. Lietzmann tried to obtain a solution by distinguishing two fundamentally distinct forms of the eucharist, a Jerusalem one and a Pauline one.[196] Lohmeyer too assumed that the eucharist had two distinct roots.[197] But this sharp division into two initially distinct types of the rite has not stood the test and has been given up in recent research.[198] Obviously the various forms of it developed out of each other, and particular elements received varying emphasis, being in part added only in the course of time.[199]

It is especially to be noted that the normal arrangement of the words of institution was attained only gradually, and that, as Paul with his μετὰ τὸ δειπνῆσαι allows us to recognize, the words concerning the bread and wine were originally quite separate from each other.[200] Since the last supper of Jesus can hardly have been a passover meal,[201] it must stand in essential connection with His usual fellowship meals,[202] but on this occasion was especially characterized by the thought of His imminent death,[203] and by an eschatological outlook.[204]

96

In fact the whole weight of emphasis lay at first on the eschatological motive; the Last Supper was an anticipation of the banquet of the Kingdom, and the rite was marked by the note of eschatological joy.[205] Only gradually did the retrospective glance at the death of Jesus and its meaning for salvation receive an independent position, above all through the motive of vicarious atonement which was assimilated still in the Palestinian sphere, and by the thought of the covenant[206] and further, by the motive of memorial.[207]

This sketch may suffice, since we are here only concerned with the primacy of the eschatological element in the earliest eucharistic rite, whence the special meaning of "Maranatha" becomes clear. Cullmann in his essay on the kyrios idea has investigated more deeply this connection.[208] The firm rooting of the formula in the oldest eucharistic rite is for him a plain indication of the fact that already in the first Palestinian church Jesus was an "object of cultic worship", and in this fact he sees the decisive presupposition for, and bridge with Hellenistic Christianity.[209]

But we must guard against including, under one general over-riding conception of the cultic, the use of the description of Jesus as Lord in the Palestinian and Hellenistic spheres, and thus levelling the deep substantial differences between them.[210]

We must especially be clear that a "cultic worship of Jesus", strictly understood, includes two things: first, the motive of exaltation, and secondly the conception of the divine being of Jesus, at least His quasi-divine status.

Cullmann assumes both factors to have been active in the early Palestinian church. Without weakening the intense eschatological expectation, he postulates for the oldest church, on the basis of the resurrection appearances, the consciousness of an already effected transition to the new aeon, and concludes that the "Maranatha" already verges on the "Kyrios Jesus" and must signify as much as "divine ruler".[211]

But in this way the outlook of the Hellenistic church has been woven into the thought of early Palestinian Christianity.[212] Affirmation about the divinity of Jesus were not, however, made in the Palestinian tradition, which was much more concerned with thinking in terms of function. Furthermore, the opinion that the first church already expressed the view that because of the resurrection, Jesus had been installed into a position of

G   97

messianic dignity and authority, can hardly be maintained.[213]

It is perfectly true that for the first church the event of the resurrection was held to be the first meaningful sign of the breaking forth of ultimate happenings. If the immediate nearness of the day of salvation had been proclaimed by Jesus, the message had received its confirmation through the Easter event, the series of salvific events had been set in motion, and the whole expectation of the church was concentrated on the imminent actualization of the Kingdom of God. The church lived not in a time of fulfilment but in a time of expectation and trustful waiting for the future. It realized that it was placed in a peculiar interim condition which it felt to be not a period of time in its own right, but a period of transition. Jesus had been taken away from it and for the moment it must learn to dispense with His earthly presence.[214] Nor do the resurrection appearances suffice to negate this feeling, for, as the tradition consistently shows, they were granted as a respite only, and the story of the ascension, which in its basic structure is very ancient, plainly brings out the orientation of the church towards the parousia.[215]

It was not difficult for the apocalyptic mind of the early church to understand this transitional period in the light of the concept of eschatological travail, as Mk. 13 in particular shows, where according to vv. 9ff. the church has its position in that event, with its miseries and trials, which has still to bring to birth the time of salvation.[216] This church did not yet know a present activity of Jesus rooted in the thought of His exaltation. As a "substitute" the gift of the Holy Spirit had been given it, but this too was a sign and token of the ultimate aeon;[217] only later was the Spirit brought into connection with the heavenly working of Jesus.[218] This gift of the Spirit made the first church certain of its share in the age of salvation and gave it strength to endure the times of woe in this world which was doomed to pass away.[219] For this reason it regarded everything as being decided by attitude towards the Holy Spirit, as the word about blasphemy makes clear, with its affirmation that even the rejection of the earthly Son of man will be forgiven, but not contempt of the Spirit.[220]

Now the Spirit which was primarily understood as an ecstatic phenomenon afforded the possibility of a certain measure of anticipation. In the cultic worship of the church, the end was

98

already experienced in its immediate nearness and reality. For this reason, the future action of Jesus could itself inspire the life of Christians without His earthly presence being really missed. For this reason, the argument that the early church cannot have imagined its Lord as tarrying inactive in heaven is inappropriate in the very terms of its formulation.[221] Since in view of the glowing expectations of the imminent future, time in general played no part, the question of the activity of Jesus during such a period of respite and grace had no actuality.

An independent conception of the present action of Jesus would have tended to push into the background the sense of the pressing nearness of the end. Nor can the present reality of Jesus be inferred from the so-called "eucharistic appearances".[222] Here it was a question of the founding of the church, and the renewal of table fellowship, but this remained something out of the ordinary, something occurring once only which was not thus to be repeated or in any way prolonged; it directed attention rather to the banquet of the kingdom.

Hence the "Maranatha" must in no sense be explained as having the twofold meaning: "Lord, come at last to set up Thy kingdom!" and "Lord, come now, while we are gathered together around Thy table!"[223] And still more is it wrong in this connection to distinguish between lordship over the church and lordship over the world.[224] We must see in the phrase the petition of the church gathered together for worship, imploring the final coming of its Lord and of the Lord of all the world, and realizing itself to be directly confronted with the parousia, while maintaining its eschatological right to celebrate the event in advance.

The conclusion flowing from these considerations is that the linguistically possible understanding of μαραναθά as a historic present: "Our Lord is here, present" is excluded,[225] while also, on the other hand, the understanding of it as an imperative must retain its severely eschatological bearing.[226] The understanding of it a perfect only established itself in early catholicism, and was conditioned by transformations in Christology and in the interpretation of the sacrament.[227] It will, of course, have to be admitted that the enthusiastic anticipation of the final coming prepared the ground for the concept of exaltation, which developed not quite so soon as the delay in the parousia was realized but shortly afterwards.

For the sake of clear differentiation we should not speak of a "cultic worship" of Jesus, when we are alluding to the early Palestinian tradition, despite the fact that the prayer for the eschatological coming of the Lord had its secure position in the cultic framework. The primitive church remained linked to its earthly Lord, and its outlook was orientated to His final appearing. The resurrection was regarded as a pledge of the eschatological reality and office of Jesus, but did not imply any conception of His exaltation and eternal presence, and just as little any idea of His essential divinity.

As a result of these reflections we must demur to the thesis of Eduard Schweizer. He rightly stresses the motive of discipleship for the post-resurrection church, which is clear not only from the ascription of the title "Lord" but equally from that of "Master". But he combines with this, because of the Easter events, the concept of the exaltation of the suffering righteous one, and for him the invocation of Jesus is from the beginning an invocation of the exalted One, of the Lord of the church, of the one who "guides, protects, instructs it, perhaps even causes it to pass through the experience of death, who accompanies it in all distresses and ordeals, until He receives it into the Kingdom as His own bride"; only, he alleges, the divine nature of Jesus plays no part as yet, nor the question of participation in the already completed work of salvation which Jesus has performed.[228] Although he does not go quite so far as Cullmann, yet the characteristic features of the Palestinian tradition are equally concealed.[229]

The continued influence of this Palestinian tradition is shown in many respects. For although the Greek suffixes were willingly shed, as can be seen from the rendering of "Maranatha" in Rev. 22:20b, in many cases "our Lord" was maintained. In the oldest tradition, it was used as an address, now it is used in statements. ὁ κύριος ἡμῶν was no doubt determined primarily by its use in the liturgy. This is to be assumed because it occurs mostly in severely formal expressions,[230] especially in the prescripts, the proems and the postscripts of the NT letters.[231] Just as informative as this use, in which older conceptions are unconsciously to a large extent at work, is the use of the phrase ὁ κύριος ἡμῶν and ὁ κύριος or ὁ κύριος Ἰησοῦς in contexts where the description of Jesus as Lord was already firmly established in the Palestinian tradition. In Paul this is to be seen in statements about the parousia, where the kyrios title appears almost regularly,[232] but also in connection with the invocation of the Lord,[233] and in statements about the eucharist.[234]

Of course with all this usage, later elements have been interwoven, and there are still other modes of use to be found, yet the old structure of the kyrios conception is not simply concealed, but proves to be a persistent and powerful influence. This was the more so, as the Son of man idea was to a large extent not assimilated in Hellenism, the eschatologically understood messianic dignity of Jesus played no longer any decisive part, and statements about the end of the age involved primarily the use of the kyrios title.

An absolute use of ὁ κύριος referring to the ultimate action of Jesus is found in two later parables. The parable of the talents, Matt. 25:14–30, is in Lk. 19:11–27 edited and reshaped by a combination with other motives; Matthew has the relatively more original form, but even with him additions may be discerned. The parable was not originally intended to refer to Jesus: only with vv. 21fin, 23fin, 30 has it received interpretations which make a clear application to Jesus as world-judge.[235] The same applies to the parable of the porter, Mk. 13:33–37 and par., which already in the synoptic tradition was much hacked about, and into a detailed analysis of which it is not necessary here to enter.[236] That in Mk. 13:35 the householder is Jesus is obvious, and in Matt. 24:42 it even says explicitly: ὁ κύριος ὑμῶν.

If we survey the material which has thus been assembled it cannot be doubted that the kyrios predicate of the Hellenistic church not only had a foreshadowing in the Palestinian sphere, but also took over from thence a concept which in some important respects was already moulded with firm features, and which even later was not given up. This does not preclude the fact that the old Palestinian conception was basically distinct from the Hellenistic one, for elements which came to predominate later are completely absent from it.

It is noteworthy that the address of Jesus as Lord and the later titular use of the term were not derived from any specific expectation of a saviour in Judaism, but were rather developed by the church itself on the basis of the earthly activity and the promise made by Jesus. Unlike the concept of the Son of man (and however independently the church proceeded there also) the address of Jesus as Lord has its life-situation less in doctrinal elucidation, than in the cult, where it develops further into acclamation and confession. The early church only gradually assimilated traditional concepts of the saviour, firstly the Son of man concept and then that of the Messiah.[237] The position and dignity of Jesus found its most immediate expression in the invocation of Him as Lord. Here are to be found the roots and the very heart of the most ancient Christology.

The parallel development of the description "master" in view of the earthly activity of Jesus had no such significance, for, so far as we can see, it was not absorbed into eschatological contexts. The reason for this was that the concept of the Jewish teacher and his pupils was too firmly fixed, and despite a widening of the concept to include permanent authority, it was felt to be inappropriate to transfer it to the ultimate activity of Jesus, not least because the eschatological authority concerned not solely the community founded by Jesus but also the whole world.

In the address "my" or "our Lord" both the earthly and the ultimate activity of Jesus were comprised, so that in the description as Lord was included, already on Palestinian ground, a wide-embracing affirmation of the high dignity of Jesus, even if the thought of exaltation was still absent.

Summary. The first church developed the description of Jesus as Lord not only in view of His earthly activity, but above all to express the exalted rank and authority of the One who was to return. The sayings material and the tradition of parables in the early church use the address "Lord" in reference to the judge of the world. Further, He whose return is expected is invoked by the church in its cult as "our Lord", as is shown especially by the prayer "Maranatha" stemming from the most ancient Palestinian tradition. The latter has its secure place in the eucharistic liturgy and at times carries in this context eschatological overtones. "Maranatha" can therefore be understood only as an imperative, the linguistically possible interpretation of it as a perfect or historic present must be excluded. Further, the imperative sense is to be regarded as strictly eschatological and not as a prayer for the presence of Jesus at the eucharist. The most ancient church lived not in a time of fulfilment but in a time of trustful waiting for the final coming of its Lord. No doubt the Spirit had been granted to it as a pledge of the ultimate aeon, and it was able to some extent to anticipate the final consummation, but it was not yet familiar with the concept of the exaltation and the present reality of Jesus. In liturgical usage, "our Lord" was long maintained and even later the description as Lord was preferred in connection with the parousia and the eucharist. With this description the early church forged a Christological conception quite independently of any traditional concept of a saviour, and was able to include in it both the earthly and the ultimate activity of Jesus.

4. The Exalted One as "Kyrios"

From what has so far been discussed it becomes clear that the concept of exaltation cannot stand at the beginning of the development, and expresses rather a basic and far-reaching new Christological interpretation attained by the early church. A critical analysis of those texts which contain the motive of the "sitting at the right hand of God",[238] enables us to appreciate the fact that the concept of messianic enthronement, based upon Ps. 110:1a was secondarily linked with a heavenly office of Jesus conferred upon Him as a result of His resurrection, whereas originally His assumption of messianic dignity and His endowment with royal might belonged to the events of the ultimate aeon. By means of Ps. 110:1b (ἕως ἂν θῶ κτλ.) the eschatological reservation of a divine exaltation and its proleptic character could be given expression. From Ps. 110:1 as a point of departure there arose a combination of the title "Lord" with the motive of exaltation. It must have constituted the point of penetration to those quite new factors which conditioned the transformation of the kyrios title.

The concept of exaltation grew out of the belief in the final messianic work of Jesus, and was conditioned not least by the delay in the parousia. In the Palestinian sphere the title Lord had obviously not yet been combined with the concept of the final messianic work of Jesus, but in Hellenistic Judaic Christianity it was interpreted through Ps. 110:1 and specifically equated with the predicate of Jesus as Messiah.

This conclusion clearly results from a study of the Son of David passage in Mk. 12:35–37a parr. The more original form of the text has certainly been preserved in Mark.[239] Luke has in large measure adopted it without modification; Matthew probably had the feeling that the text in this form was not fully satisfactory and so by changing the introduction gave it the character of a disputation, while adding a new conclusion through the use of Mk. 12:34b. Mark added only διδάσκων ἐν τῷ ἱερῷ[240] but otherwise he was taking up a piece of tradition. The introductory and concluding questions are concerned with the sonship of David, which we shall discuss in detail in a later section.[241]

At the moment we are concerned to explain the meaning of the quotation Ps. 110, 1 and of the kyrios title. Verse 36, as v. 37a shows, is understood as an answer to the opening question of v. 35b, but is then completed by a new question. Verse 37a deduces from v. 36 αὐτὸς Δαυὶδ λέγει αὐτόν— scil. τὸν χριστόν—κύριον. This means that the predicate "son of David" has been disconnected from its traditional equivalence with the title "Messiah" and the latter has instead been made the equivalent of "Kyrios". Messiah and kyrios thus imply the ruler enthroned at the right hand of God, for whom, as is clearly shown from the quotation of v. 1b in Ps. 110, the final subjugation of his enemies is imminent. Hence both predicates are related to the exalted one. A piece of tradition stemming from the Palestinian church cannot possibly be in question here, still less an authentic statement from the mouth of Jesus. Several reasons can be adduced against this. The very fact that Jesus seizes the initiative, and sets a problem concerning the messianic dogma of the Jews, is striking; furthermore, it is to be noted that the question cannot be answered within the framework of Jewish messianic doctrine. The emphatically Christological interest of the passage also tends to disprove its authenticity, as does also in particular the heavy stress which falls on the title of high dignity. Further, the argument proceeds with a markedly sophisticated scriptural erudition which is otherwise alien to the style of Jesus; for no particular reason He here puts a question, gives an answer, and then puts another question, the answer to which must be found.

We see here the precipitate of Christological reflection, which from the apologetic point of view, must be based on scripture, and in this connection the late OT view of the Davidic authorship of Ps. 110 has been made use of. The fact that this piece of tradition cannot have originated in the

Palestinian church may already be inferred from the concept of exaltation. But this is confirmed by the linguistic data.[242]

Mk. 12:36 contains almost word for word the Septuagint version of the text.[243] This might, however, be considered as a secondary assimilation. Yet the stress lies, as is clear from v. 37a, on the title "Lord"; the κύριος takes up the εἶπεν . . . τῷ κυρίῳ μου of the quotation. The basis of this is a Hebraic אֲדֹנִי which in the OT occurs occasionally in an address to the king, but above all in the phrase אֲדֹנִי הַמֶּלֶךְ.[244] In messianic terminology אֲדֹנִי, אָדוֹן plays no part at all. It must further be noted that as regards the citation of the expression נְאֻם יהוה לַאדֹנִי Ps. 110: 1a, in the time of Jesus the name Jahwe was replaced by אֲדֹנִי on which account אָדוֹן was to a large extent avoided in general usage. An emphatic application of just אֲדֹנִי from Ps. 110, 1a to Jesus is therefore hardly conceivable, and the transference of a real divine predicate to Jesus in the Palestinian sphere must be excluded from consideration. But the adoption of אֲדֹנִי is also improbable because in the primitive church מָרִי had so early acquired Christological significance. We should then have to assume with Dalman that in Ps. 110:1 just as יהוה had been replaced by אֲדֹנִי so אֲדֹנִי had been replaced by מָרִי[245] but this is an extremely problematic thesis. This would indeed harmonize with the description of Jesus as Lord elsewhere, but this description, as has been concluded in the previous section, was an independent conception, and showed no influence of messianism. Moreover, it would remain difficult to say how the concluding question about the relationship of the Son of David and מָרִי is to be answered; there would only be the possibility of regarding it as improper, but this again would not be compatible with the fact that precisely in the Palestinian sphere Jesus' sonship of David was an argument brought forward and an attempt was made to prove it by genealogies.[246]

On the other hand, matters are very simple if we begin with the Christological outlook of Hellenistic Judaic Christianity. Here two elements are fused: the ancient description of Jesus as Lord adopted from the Palestinian tradition, and secondly the motive of exaltation developed by the use of Ps. 110:1. Their fusion is grounded, scripturally and theologically, on the

LXX influence
re. Psalm 110

introductory turn of phrase in Ps. 110:1, but it is the Septuagint, rather than the original text which is presupposed. In this way the kyrios title became embedded in the context of the idea of exaltation. Within the framework of the tradition of Hellenistic Judaic Christianity, it is, moreover, reasonable to detach the title "Son of David" from this heavenly messianic dignity of Jesus, for here it was stamped by a quite special use, connoting a present dignity related to the earthly activity of Jesus. On the other hand, the messianic dignity is now, if only for the time being, combined with the heavenly κυριότης of Jesus.[247]

Closely related to Mk. 12:35ff. is Acts 2:34–36, the only other place in the NT where there is a full quotation of Ps. 110:1. Even though we must admit the independence of Luke in the drafting of his speeches, it can hardly be questioned that here he is assimilating a tradition, but we must not at once assume that it is a Palestinian tradition.[248] The meaning of the text Ps. 110:1 is clearly defined by the characteristic expression ὅτι καὶ κύριον αὐτὸν καὶ χριστὸν ἐποίησεν ὁ θεός. Recently Ulrich Wilckens has described the formulation in 2:36 as specifically Lucan.[249]

It is beyond question that the context in v. 36 stems from Luke; the fact that αὐτόν is related to this and that the quoted expression fits in both formally and materially quite smoothly does not preclude the existence of an old and formal expression.[250] It is quite out of the question that Luke has derived from scripture the juxtaposition of "Kyrios" and "Christos" for the only text which might be quoted, Ps. 2:1f. cannot be here adduced for the simple reason that Kyrios is there a description of God. Just as little may it be said, by appealing to Acts 4:27, that the Christ predicate and the title Lord should be understood in the light of baptism, hence in view of the earthly work of Jesus as a whole. Nor is this view supported by the fact that 2:36 is regarded as a summarizing formula concluding the whole speech.[251] For precisely in this specifically Lucan contrast "you have . . . but God has . . ." the statement about the action of God always refers to the sovereign mighty deed after the killing of Jesus.[252] Further, at the end of v. 36 the saying about the crucifixion can hardly be unintentionally related to τοῦτον τὸν Ἰησοῦν. Conversely, in Acts 10:36 κύριος πάντων is certainly an affirmation about the exalted one, and in 2:31 "Christos" is likewise used not of the earthly but of the resurrected Jesus. Hence Wilckens' thesis regarding Acts 2:36 must be rejected, all the more so because the text fits in excellently with that phase in the development of tradition which we have been discussing.

The development of the concept of exaltation and the combination of messianic affirmations with the kyrios title has now been completed in the sphere of Hellenistic Judaic Christianity. Just such an "adoptionist" statement as that in Acts 2:36 is quite characteristic in this connection, for the stress on a sovereignty of Jesus resting on an act of inauguration is genuinely Jewish and such an emphasis would hardly be possible in the sphere of Hellenistic Gentile Christianity.

It must be noted that in both texts Mk. 12:35ff. and Acts 2:34ff. a stage of tradition is discernible in which the kyrios title is not understood as a predicate implying divine dignity. The distinction between the two Kyrios appellations of Ps. 110:1 is still maintained. At the same time, the fact cannot be overlooked that now Jesus, in contradistinction to what characterizes the sphere of the Aramaic speaking church, bears a title primarily applied to God, and this must necessarily lead to assimilations. The mere fact of the translation of מָרַן/מָרִי has thus given rise to a problem which was quite alien to the original description of Jesus as Lord.

However much the early Hellenistic Judaic Christian church may have avoided the interpretation of the person and work of Jesus in a divine sense, a tendency leading in this direction was now present and could not be eliminated. As we have seen earlier, it was just the Hellenistic Judaic Christian community which took over the old Palestinian conception of the earthly activity of Jesus, His authority and fullness of power, as also that of His ultimate office as sovereign Lord, and this conception it carried further. In this connection it developed the marked titular use of "Kyrios" and added to it the further concept of exaltation.

Within this framework which was so firmly fixed that it could for long be maintained, the influence of the Septuagint gradually began to become operative. The divine ascription κύριος is sporadically and later more frequently transferred to Jesus, without this at once leading to a conception of Him as divine.[253] It was only necessary to seize on a few quotations from the Bible illustrating those functions of His which were linked with the description of Him as Lord—and this was an obvious procedure for the Jewish mentality—in order to transfer statements which formerly were applied to God to Jesus as Kyrios.

I confine myself to a few examples. Already in the Palestinian tradition the office of world-judge was linked to the office of Jesus as Lord. Nothing was more obvious than to apply to Him the saying about the ἡμέρα κυρίου, a procedure which would have been unthinkable in the Palestinian sphere, but which in Hellenism suggested itself as something which could be done without scruple.[254] Similarly an OT quotation which included "Kyrios" could be applied to the earthly activity of Jesus. This is true of Isa. 40:3 which in combination with Mal. 3:1 stands at the beginning of a passage about John the Baptist which Mark has adopted *en bloc.*[255] The ἑτοιμάσατε τὴν ὁδὸν κυρίου could simply be transferred as it stands, but in the parallel clause εὐθείας ποιεῖτε τὰς τρίβους τοῦ θεοῦ ἡμῶν had to be changed to τὰς τρίβους αὐτοῦ. The phrase οἱ ἐπικαλούμενοι τὸ ὄνομα τοῦ κυρίου ἡμῶν Ἰησοῦ Χριστοῦ provides a further characteristic instance of this sort of application to Jesus of Septuagint statements with κύριος.[256]

In two places of the NT, Acts 2:21 and Rom. 10:13, there is an express allusion to Joel 3:5, but the calling upon the name of the Lord is an expression such as is found at many other points in the Septuagint, and is throughout referred to God.[257] The Palestinian church was already familiar with the invocation of Jesus and the petition for His coming, but this was clearly separated from prayer to God, whereas now in the Hellenistic sphere the calling upon the Kyrios blurred the boundaries between Jesus and God, and Jesus was increasingly regarded as exalted to the height of divinity.[258] And this certainly took place at a stage of the development where we have not yet to reckon with the influence of Hellenistic cults; rather on the contrary it is to be supposed that an influence exercised by the mystery cults came about in the main because a "cultic worship of Jesus" had already become established or at least the ground for it was fully prepared.

In the Palestinian tradition already the appellation as Lord had its secure place in the cult, and it is not surprising that in the early Hellenistic Judaic Christian church the invocation of the Kyrios played a special part. No doubt as a result of the development and use of Kyrios as a title, and as a result of the concept of exaltation, the point of view became marked with strongly theological-doctrinal features, but this does not supersede its cultic significance. On the contrary it may be said that despite the link with the messianic affirmation of a heavenly enthronement the Kyrios title maintained its independence and realized its most important function in the sphere of worship. Through the concept of exaltation in particular the realization of the eternal living presence of Jesus became a lively conviction.

It is hardly a matter of chance that in Matt. 18:20 a word for which there are many parallels in Judaism, promising the presence of the Shekinah of God, has been transferred to Jesus, so that He promises His presence wherever two or three are gathered together in His name.[259] Equally from now on is current the valid promise that He will be with His disciples always even unto the end of the world, Matt. 28:20b. Hence the acclamation and the confession κύριος 'Ιησοῦς is addressed to this eternally present Lord.[260] According to 1 Cor. 12:3 whoever confesses this is inspired and driven by the Holy Spirit.[261]

But it has to be borne in mind that the oldest church also celebrated its cult under the inspiration of the Spirit and the invocation of the Lord was especially moulded by this conviction, but now the note of eschatological tension recedes. The appellative use of κύριος in connection with the name of Jesus must have emerged at an early stage in the Hellenistic church, for in Rom. 10:9 κύριος 'Ιησοῦς is regarded as the one confession that procures salvation, and in the hymn to Christ of Phil. 2:11 it is presupposed. The conditions for this development were already given in Hellenistic Judaic Christianity. But this acclamation could be filled with varying content, and in itself was not unambiguously fixed.

As far as Hellenistic Judaic Christianity is concerned, it is to be observed that here a primarily functional type of thought was the rule, as is shown especially by the equivalence of Kyrios and Christos in connection with the concept of exaltation. The one enthroned in heaven receives His status and dignity from His office, the question as to His being and divinity was not at first raised. The assimilation of certain sayings from the Septuagint does not alter this fact, although it cannot be disputed that in consequence of it and of the cultic invocation of the ever-present Lord, the way was prepared for a growing understanding of the Kyrios predicate as something implying divinity.

In the sphere of Hellenistic Gentile Christianity there finally developed a conviction of the divine being of the exalted Kyrios. The points of transition were fluid, and the stronger degree of Hellenization on the other hand certainly led to an increased adoption of the divine titles in the Septuagint.[262] It can hardly be doubted that in Gentile Christianity also the Greek OT exercised a very powerful influence.[263]

But only in this sphere did the Kyrios title receive those features which Bousset argued to be characteristic. But this does not imply a completely new departure; it is rather the last stage of a long process of development. The second part of the hymn to Christ in Phil. 2:9–11 seems to belong still to the threshold of Hellenistic Judaic Christianity. For here there is still emphasized the thought of installation in office. The name Kyrios is bestowed on Jesus "by grace" (ἐχαρίσατο) and the sense of ὑπερυψοῦν is precisely that in solemn enthronement God Himself manifests to all the world the position of power conferred on the pre-existent and abased Lord.[264]

On the other hand, an OT passage which originally spoke of the oneness of God as Lord is applied by transference to the exalted Christ.[265] The veneration and universal confession of Lordship which in that passage is seen as befitting God alone is here transferred to Jesus. "Here the προσκύνησις of Jesus is already indicated."[266] In fact it is necessary to speak of a worship of Jesus. To Him as exalted is transferred God's own name, "which is above every other name", and the powers of the world must be subject to Him.[267]

In this connection we have to think of the spiritual powers as rulers over the three kingdoms which constitute all that is.[268] As Κύριος Jesus is the divine Lord of the whole world.[269] But it is not only the Isaianic allusion, and the fact that God Himself has conferred on Jesus His own divine name and dignity[270] that argue for the explicit divinity here ascribed to Jesus, but also the context of the whole hymn, according to which Jesus in His pre-existence was already coequal with God, then emptied Himself, and through God has been made to participate in this ὑπερύψωσις. The origin of the hymn in the sphere of Hellenistic Gentile Christianity, on the grounds of the concepts used and the whole mode of thought, has been demonstrated in detail by Käsemann.[271]

Only against this background can we understand how strongly this passage, with its basic thought of the exaltation of Jesus, implies not only an enthronement, but also already consummated sovereignty,[272] with the result that the eschatological reservation of Ps. 110, 1b has quite receded into the background.

mystery cults

Further developments in the sphere of Gentile Christianity can only be briefly indicated. How far there was an influence exercised by the mystery cults, would have to be investigated above all in individual cases to be found in the Pauline letters. It is not possible roundly to deny any such influence. It is only too plain that the young Christian churches, as the Letters to the Corinthians for example enable us to discern, were drawn from time to time into the maelstrom of Hellenistic conventicle life, and as a result adopted without scruple beliefs typical of the world that surrounded them.

In other respects too, Christology shows so manifold an Hellenistic influence that it is most likely that the Kyrios title was also involved in this play of Hellenistic factors. It is obvious that the invocation of the Kyrios might be understood on the analogy of that of the cult deities. Even a statement like that of Rom. 13:14 about "putting on the Lord Jesus" can only be explained against such a background of religious influences.[273] But however much Gentile Christianity might adopt specific views and undergo specific influences, even reshaping them in appropriate theological terms, the process did not take place without an abrupt differentiation.

From 1 Cor. 8:5f. we may see that at one decisive point in the Christian Kyrios conception, no concession was allowed. Jesus is not one among the many κύριοι but the one κύριος and the Lord of the whole world, which is here even based on the consideration—and the statement goes beyond Phil. 2:9ff. —that He possessed His sovereignty over the cosmos at the moment of creation already.[274] Also in the confessional formula of Eph. 4:5 the εἷς κύριος has its firm place.

Very soon Christianity was then placed in a position of confrontation with the cult of the emperor. The old thesis that the Kyrios predicate of Jesus developed only through the "sense of contrast" to the cult of the emperor, is not tenable.[275]

kyrios Iesous not dev. or contrast ō kyrios Kaisar

"We should not understand the essence of the Christian message, if we proposed to derive it in its origin and basis from this antithesis to the political mythos of the empire and the emperor. It did not receive its main features from this confrontation, however much it proved itself thereby."[276] The terrible ordeal which arose even in the first century through persecution has left its imprint on the Revelation of John.[277] Although in this work "Kyrios" has been widely used as a description of God, in two places of central significance Jesus is spoken of as the κύριος κυρίων καὶ βασιλεὺς βασιλέων.[278] For the church it was a question of cleaving to the confession of the κύριος Ἰησοῦς in contrast to the κύριος Καῖσαρ of the imperial cult, as is impressively shown by the Acts of the Martyrs.[279]

In conclusion, there is one question which must be considered and which we have so far neglected: namely, what are we to think of the use of Kyrios in the resurrection narratives? Might not this be an indication that in the first instance the predicate was assigned to the Risen Christ?[280]

The gospel of John seems to suggest the conclusion most obviously, for whereas the absolute ὁ κύριος occurs very rarely in the first nineteen chapters, in the two chapters 20 and 21 its use is surprisingly frequent.[281] Mark and Matthew make no use of the title in their resurrection stories; only Luke, of the synoptics, has it in two places.[282] Its prevalence in John 20f. by contrast with the synoptics, cannot result exclusively from the intention of the evangelist or the editor, but is rather to be seen as conditioned by the source material, as is also the case in Lk. 24. Nevertheless, there can be no question of an original rooting of the Kyrios title in the traditional reports of the Easter event. But individual instances must be investigated on their merits.

How very little was there any special thought of ascribing exaltation to the Risen Christ is shown first of all in Lk. 24:2 and John 20:2,13, where the women are looking for the dead and buried one. Even in the formulation of Lk. 24:34 ὄντως ἠγέρθη ὁ κύριος the stress lies on the fact of resurrection, so that on the other hand ὁ κύριος must be an appellation of the earthly Jesus. Similarly in the traditional material which we see in John 20:19–23, the writer is referring back to the earthly Jesus, especially as he is emphasizing the point that the Risen

One is identical with the earthly Jesus, ὁ κύριος being used in alternation with ὁ 'Ιησοῦς and indeed at the very moment when it is reported that the disciples recognize Him. In the same sense both John 20:25 and 20:18 are to be understood. Even clearer perhaps is the situation in 21:7 (bis), 12 for by means of ὁ κύριός ἐστιν the moment of recognition is expressly conveyed. In all these cases, the source is traditional material[283] which has been moulded in that stage of the development when the earthly Jesus was spoken of as the Lord.[284]

Yet the evangelist John was not content with this point of view. By the confession of Thomas in 20:28 he imparted to the Kyrios predicate a very different emphasis and an essentially wide range of significance: ὁ κύριός μου καὶ ὁ θεός μου. Here is expressed in its ultimate consequences that note which already sounds in Phil. 2:9ff. in regard to the exalted Lord, and which in the last analysis always lies at the heart of Hellenistic Gentile Christianity; the fact that in the gospel of John it stands in a greater, carefully thought out structure is clearly discernible from the Prologue itself.[285]

In the late conclusion to Mk. 16:19f., we see the reflection of a use of the Kyrios title which is at least similar to that in John 20:28; here the appellation is primarily understood in the light of resurrection and exaltation, but this is a late formulation which must by no means be taken as a point of departure.[286]

In an interesting manner the conception of the divinity of the Kyrios has influenced the description of the earthly activity of Jesus, as was to be seen from the treatment of the Kyrie mode of address in the gospel of Matthew.[287]

Summary. The decisive new interpretation of the Kyrios idea in the Hellenistic area resulted from the thought of exaltation. The concept of the Messiah was applied to denote an independent heavenly office of Jesus and the Kyrios title, on the basis of Ps. 110:1, was linked to this. Against the same background it is also to be explained that in the sphere of Hellenistic Judaic Christianity the κυριότης of the exalted Lord was understood in an emphatically adoptionist and functional sense. At first the title Κύριος did not imply the divinity of Jesus. None the less, Jesus now bore the exalted name of God Himself, and both the influence of the Septuagint and the cultic invocation of the eternally present Christ increasingly prepared the way for this conception. In the sphere of Hellenistic Gentile Christianity the Kyrios title then acquired an impress which was henceforth to prevail, for it came to imply the divine nature and the divine dignity of the exalted Lord. Finally this was developed in such a way as to refer both to the risen and the earthly Jesus. A certain degree of influence exercised by the mystery religions is not to be excluded, but Christianity held fast to the faith that Jesus was not one among many cultic deities, but the one Lord of all the world, a confession of faith which the church was called on to preserve through the ordeal of its opposition to the cult of the Roman emperor.

NOTES

1. Cf. Werner Foerster, art., κύριος, *ThWb* III, p. 1085.
2. Bousset, *Kyrios Christos*, especially pp. 77ff.; Bultmann, *Theol.*, pp. 54f., 123ff.
3. Werner Foerster, *Herr ist Jesus. Herkunft und Bedeutung des urchristlichen Kyriosbekenntnisses* (*Neutest. Forschungen* II/I), 1924.
4. Dalman, *Worte Jesu*, pp. 266ff.
5. Oscar Cullmann, *Urchristentum und Gottesdienst* (*AThANT* 3), 1950², pp. 16f., 19ff.; *id.*, *Christologie*, pp. 200ff.
6. Eduard Schweizer, *Erniedrigung und Erhöhung*, pp. 93ff.; *id.*, "Discipleship and Belief in Jesus as Lord from Jesus to the Hellenistic Church", *NTSt* 2, 1955/56, pp. 87–99.
7. Cf. the short but very carefully weighed considerations in Herbert Braun, *Der Sinn der neutestamentlichen Christologie*, *ZThK* 54, 1957, pp. 341–377, there pp. 351f.
8. Cf. Foerster, *ThWb* III, pp. 1040ff.; also Karl Heinrich Rengstorf, art. δοῦλος, *ThWb* II, pp. 264ff. The proper correlative to δοῦλος is not κύριος but ἐλεύθερος; δοῦλος has no sort of connection with the religious domain in Hellenism.
9. Thus for instance Poseidon is designated lord over the water; only once is Zeus called ὁ πάντων κύριος (Pindar, *Isthm.* 5, 53).
10. On the characteristics of these religious communities cf. Günther Bornkamm, art. μυστήριον, *ThWb* IV, pp. 809ff.; Karl Prümm, *Religionsgeschichtliches Handbuch für den Raum der altchristlichen Umwelt*, 1954², pp. (221ff.) 255ff.
11. Instances in Bousset, *op. cit.*, pp. 95ff.
12. Proofs in Foerster, *Herr ist Jesus*, pp. 79ff.
13. *Pap. Ox.* I, 110; in Bousset, *op. cit.*, p. 96.

14. Cf. especially Prümm, *Handbuch*, pp. 89ff., L. Cerfaux-J. Tondriau, *Le culte des souverains dans la civilisation Gréco-Romaine* (*Bibliothèque de Théologie*, series III, vol. V), 1957, especially pp. 123ff., 269ff.

15. In the second century B.C. in the translation of an old title of Pharaoh: κύριος βασιλειῶν and the like, then in the first century B.C. κύριος βασιλεύς, κύριος θεός.

16. Virgil, *Eclogue* 4 is a clear symptom; cf. also Cerfaux-Tondriau, *op. cit.*, pp. 286ff.; 313ff.

17. Cf. Suetonius, *Caes.* 53; Dio Cassius 57. 8, 2; the citations in Foerster, *ThWb* III, p. 1054.

18. In Egypt in 12 B.C. Augustus was called θεὸς καὶ κύριος Καῖσαρ Αὐτοκράτωρ (*BGU* 1197 i 15); *ThWb* III, p. 1048. In Rome it was not until after his death that Augustus was exalted as *Divus* and a temple erected for his veneration.

19. Nero is called ὁ τοῦ παντὸς κόσμου κύριος, and indeed not in an oriental but a Greek inscription; cf. Adolf Deissmann, *Licht vom Osten*, 1923[4], pp. 301f. Domitian was addressed according to Martial as *Dominus et Deus*; Foerster, *ThWb* III, pp. 1053, 1055.

20. Haenchen, *Apg.*, p. 603, conjectures that here the language of the time of Domitian has been carried back to that of Nero especially in the matter of the absolute use of words.

21. Against Foerster, *Herr ist Jesus*, pp. 103ff.

22. Cf. Gottfried Quell, art., κύριος (*Der at.liche Gottesname*), *ThWb* III, pp. 1056–1080, especially p. 1058.

23. "Baal" can also be god of a spring, of a tree and the like.

24. W. Graf von Baudissin, *Kyrios als Gottesname*, especially vol. III, 1927.

25. In the excavations at Ras Shamra (Ugarit) important new documents bearing on this have come to light.

26. Cf. Ludwig Köhler, *Theologie des Alten Testaments*, 1947[2], pp. 11f.

27. Joshua 3:11, 13; Mic. 4:13; Zech. 4:14; Ps. 97:5.

28. With a long ā at the end.

29. In particular v. Baudissin, *op. cit.*, II, 1926.

30. So Ethelbert Stauffer-Karl Georg Kuhn, art., θεός, *ThWb* III, p. 92, n. 121; pp. 93f.

31. Because of the defectiveness of the early Hellenistic material no quite certain conclusion can be drawn from it.

32. Frequently but not regularly it has not the article.

33. Foerster's assumption in *ThWb* III, pp. 1081f. that the specifically Greek idea of legal provision in the taking over was decisive, can hardly be correct.

34. Cf. Foerster, *Herr ist Jesus*, p. 119.

35. Mk. 11:9 parr. (Entry); 12:10f. parr. (Parable of the Vine-dressers); 12:29 parr. (The Greatest Commandment.)

36. So Erich Klostermann, *Das Lukasevangelium* (*HbNT* 5), 1929[2], p. 63. The Lukan nativity narrative is here left out of account.

37. There are Old Testament citations with Kyrios as the designation of God in Acts 2:20f., 25, 34; 3:22; 13:10; 15:17.

38. προσκυνεῖν instead of φοβεῖσθαι; cf. Deut. 6:13 LXX v. l.

39. For Matthew cf. the work of Krister Stendahl, *The School of St. Matthew and its Use of the Old Testament (Acta Seminarii Neotestamentici Upsaliensis* XX), 1954, for Paul E. Earle Ellis, *Paul's Use of the Old Testament"*, 1957, pp. 11ff.

40. So, e.g., Matt. 27:10: a phrase following Exod. 9:12 LXX at the end of a composition of citations; Rom. 10:16: a citation of Isa. 53:1 after the LXX with an introductory κύριε which is lacking in the Hebrew text.

41. The Old Testament citations which carry κύριος over to Jesus, e.g., Mk. 1:2f., are here left out of account; cf. pp. 107f. above.

42. Reference may be made here to Mk. 5:19, where according to common opinion ὁ κύριος must be referred to God, as follows especially from ὁ Ἰησοῦς in v. 20.

43. Matt. 1:20, 24; 2:13, 19, also 1:22; 2:15. In Luke 1 and 2 the word occurs twenty-six times, twice as a designation of Christ (1:43; 2:11, doubtless redactional), eleven times in stock phrases: 1:6, 9, 11, 66, 67; 2:9 (twice), 22, 23, 24, 39, also in thirteen further passages: Lk. 1:15, 16, 17, 25, 28, 30, 38, 45, 46, 58, 76b; 2:15, 26.

44. Cf. concordance.

45. Cf. Dalman, *Worte Jesu*, pp. 272ff.; *id., Jesus-Jeschua*, 1922, p. 12; Eduard Lohse, art. ῥαββί , *ThWb* VI, pp. 962–966, especially pp. 962f.

46. Mk. 9:5; 11:21; 14:45; also 10:51; John 1:38, 50; 3:2; 4:31; 6:25; 9:2; 11:8; also 20:16; cf. besides John 3:26 (in addressing John the Baptist).

47. Conversations and narratives scarcely occur in Q. The address διδάσκαλε in Matt. 8:19 and 12:38 can possibly go back to Q, but a sure conclusion cannot be drawn here; cf. pp. 80f. above.

48. Matt. 23:7, 8; besides Matt. 26:25, 49.

49. Cf. Günther Bornkamm, "Enderwartung and Kirche im Matthäus-evangelium" in G. Bornkamm-G. Barth-H. J. Held, *Überlieferung und Auslegung im Matthäusevangelium (WMANT* I), 1960, pp. 13–47.

50. Mk. 10:51; the narrative 10:46ff. shows a later revision made from the point of view of the Davidic sonship, cf. Chapter 4, pp. 253ff.

51. In John 3:2, however, this is necessitated chiefly by the noun ὁ διδάσκαλος.

52. The context Mk. 9:5,7 has to be judged in the same way. There an unstressed "Rabbi" stands before the predicate of honour "Son of God".

53. This holds good in spite of a breaking through of customary limits. Thus Jesus gathered disciples about him, availed himself of the teaching and discussion methods of the scribes, and the like; cf. on this G. Bornkamm, *Jesus*, pp. 88f.; Charles Harold Dodd, *Jesus als Lehrer und Prophet* in *Mysterium Christi*, 1931, pp. 67–86.

54. (Hermann L. Strack-) Paul Billerbeck, *Kommentar zum NT aus Talmud und Midrasch* I, 1922, pp. 916f.; *id., ThWb* VI, p. 963.

55. In this regard Lohse, *ThWb* VI, pp. 965f., has already assigned too much importance to the address "Rabbi".

56. Mk. 10:52fin can be shown to be a redactional addition, as

emerges from the language (ἐν τῇ ὁδῷ is typically Markan), and from the close attention paid to the words of dismissal in v. 52a.

57. Both the candid handing down of this address (including διδάσ-καλε) in the mouth of opponents and also the repressing of it, which becomes recognizable later, as an address used by the disciples, show how little any specific Christological statement was associated with this form of address.

58. Cf. John 1:38; 20:16. ;(8:4)

59. Cf. Karl Heinrich Rengstorf, art. διδάσκω, ThWb II, pp. 138–168. especially pp. 138ff., 150ff.

60. Matt. 12:38 (lacking in Lk. 11:29); 19:16 (par. Mk. 10:17); 22:16 (par. Mk. 12:14); 22:24 (parl. Mk. 12:19); 22:36 (par. Lk. 10:25, cf. Mk. 12:32); on διδάσκαλε in Matt. 8:19 cf. under κύριε.

61. Lk. 9:38 (par. Mk. 9:17); 10:25 (par. Matt. 22:36, cf. Mk. 12:32); 18:18 (par. Mk. 10:17); 20:21 (par. Mk. 12:14); 20:28 (par. Mk. 12:19); 20:39 (par. Mk. 12:32); 21:7 (par. Mk. 13:1,4); further from the special material Lk. 7:40; 11:45; 12:13; 19:39. Since Luke has in many cases taken διδάσκαλε over from Mark but has nowhere of himself interpolated it in his tradition material, it may be assumed that the four instances from the special material are also traditional.

62. Lk. 8:24 (instead of διδάσκαλε Mk. 4:38); 8:45 (cf. Mk. 5:31); 9:33 (instead of ῥαββί in Mk. 9:5); 9:45 (in place of διδάσκαλε in Mk. 9:38). Since these passages generally go back to redaction, the two passages in Luke's special material may also be carried back to the evangelist; cf. Lk. 5:5; 17:13.

63. Whether in the taking over of ἐπιστάτης a feeling of a "not complete equivalence" of διδάσκαλος and רַבִּי played a role—so Albrecht Oepke, art., ἐπιστάτης, ThWb II, pp. 619f.—is difficult to decide. It may be rather that this is an attempt to take over an expression familiar to the Hellenistic reader.

64. Mk. 10:17 parr.; 10:20; 12:14 parr.; 12:19 parr.; 12:32 (par. Lk. 20:39, cf. Matt. 22:36//Lk. 10:25); Lk. 7:40; 11:45; 12:13; 19:39.

65. Mk. 9:17 (par. Lk. 9:38).

66. Mark 4:38; 9:38; 10:35; 13:1 (par. Lk. 21:7).

67. Apart altogether from the logically proceeding Matthew, a retrograde tendency hardly appears surprising, for Luke's special material has the address only in the mouth of the risen Jesus and Luke himself has it in the mouth of the disciples certainly not without exception, but yet largely replaced by ἐπιστάτα.

68. Matt. 9:11 (par. Mk. 2:16); 17:24.

69. Mk. 5:35 par.; 14:14 parr.; John 3:2; 11:28; 13:13f.

70. This can be well proved on the strength of sepulchral inscriptions that can be dated; cf. Lohse, ThWb VI, pp. 963f. רַב became later a designation of the Babylonian scribes.

71. Cf. Karl Heinrich Rengstorf, art., ἀπόστολος, ThWb I, especially pp. 414ff.

72. Moreover, with the motif of the altogether perfect or finished being Lk. 6:40b presents a secondary remodelling in the Hellenistic sense.

73. In John 13:16b there is also the very significant parallel statement: ... οὐδὲ ἀπόστολος μείζων τοῦ πέμψαντος αὐτόν.

74. Cf. Dalman, *Jesus-Jeschua*, p. 207; T. W. Manson, *The Teaching of Jesus*, pp. 239f.

75. Julius Schniewind, *Das Evangelium nach Matthäus* (*NTD* 2), 1950[4], p. 132, on the different uses in Matthew, Luke and John.

76. G. Bornkamm, *Enderwartung, op. cit.*, p. 38.

77. In Matt. 23:9 the disciples are forbidden to take the Jewish title of honour אָב.

78. Cf. also above all G. Bornkamm, *Enderwartung, op. cit.*, p. 37.

79. It is beyond question that the majority of the Synoptic passages assume first of all an actual partnership in the life of Jesus with a definite circle of men. That, however, does not exclude the possibility that discipleship was also regarded in the light of the post-Easter existence of the church. The use as a designation of Christians is especially clear in the Acts, cf. concordance; but in Matthew also discipleship in this sense plays a decisive role, as is to be seen not lastly in the μαθητεύσατε of Matt. 28:19.

80. In this Jewish presuppositions are decisive; cf. Hans von Soden, art., ἀδελφός, *ThWb* I, pp. 144–146.

81. Cf. on this especially Ernst Haenchen, *Matthäus* 23, *ZThK* 48, 1951, pp. 38–63, especially pp. 42ff.

82. The Markan text is taken over only by Luke in 8:49. In Matthew, however, there is no cancellation of this expression, but in the considerable abbreviation of the context Mk. 5:35–37 has altogether dropped out.

83. Taylor, *Mk.*, pp. 537f.

84. To speak in this place or in reference to Matt. 23:8 of Jesus as the new Moses, is certainly beside the mark; against Rengstorf, *ThWb* II, p. 159.

85. In John 3:2b reference is also made expressly to the working of miracles; likewise in c. 11 it is a matter of a miracle story.

86. Accordingly Erich Fascher, *Jesus der Lehrer*, *ThLZ* 79, 1954, cols. 325–342.

87. Cf. the Gospel of Mark, where a great significance and fullness of content belong to the concepts διδάσκω and διδαχή, but ὁ διδάσκαλος in redactional formulations is nowhere drawn upon for emphatic Christological statements.

88. So above all John 3:2.

89. So also Matt. 17:4; 20:33, but this stands in Matt. in a special context that has still to be discussed.

90. Cf. Dalman, *Worte Jesu*, p. 269; Foerster, *Herr ist Jesus*, pp. 221f.

91. On this Foerster, *ThWb* III, p. 1084; also Dalman, *Worte Jesu*, p. 268.

92. Forester, *ThWb* III, p. 1083.

93. So Gen. R. 13, 2 or Lev. R. 10, 4; cf. Schlatter, *Mt.*, p. 257.

94. With רַב the form רַבּוֹן was later reserved for God, but this does not yet hold good for the New Testament period, as is shown by the

ῥαββουνί made use of in addressing Jesus, cf. Dalman, *Worte Jesu*, pp. 266f.; also Billerbeck III, pp. 673f.

95. So, e.g. in the New Testament in parables in addressing the father in Matt. 21:30 or an earthly lord in Matt. 25:22ff. Cf. further the address to Pilate in Matt. 27:63.

96. The specifically Matthaean understanding has here to be left out of account; it is a question of the significance of the address "Lord" in the alleged piece of tradition.

97. Cf. Tödt, *Menschensohn*, p. 234.

98. Cf. pp. 91f. above.

99. In my opinion the assumption lying nearest at hand is that Matthew and Luke did not know the logia source in exactly the same form, which also suggests itself in many other passages, cf. Günther Bornkamm. art. *Evangelien synoptische*, *RGG*[3] II, col. 734. Accordingly Lk. 9:61f. possibly also belongs to the Q-rendering that Luke received, whilst this saying was lacking in Matthew's *Vorlage*; it may be then that we should not reckon either with a redactional replacement from special material or with a deletion.

100. Cf. on this Günther Bornkamm, *Die Sturmstillung im Matthäusevangelium* in G. Bornkamm–G. Barth–H. J. Held, pp. 48–53.

101. Even in regard to Matt. 12:38 (–40) this cannot be said, for here it is a question of the reception of a special tradition instead of the Q-rendering of the Jonah sign.

102. With all reservation the thought may be expressed that perhaps occasion was given to the evangelist precisely by the διδάσκαλε to introduce a scribe here and to understand Jesus' answer in the sense of a refusal.

103. "Kyrie" has been added to the Markan material four times at second hand: Lk. 5:12 (an addition to Mk. 1:40); 18:41 (makes good ῥαββουνί in Mk. 10:51); 22:33 (an addition within the denial of Peter Mk. 14:29); 22:49 (an addition in the account of the arrest Mk. 14:46). It is clear that there is Lukan redaction in Lk. 5:12; 18:41; 22:49. In regard to Lk. 22:33 it could be considered whether a special tradition belonging together with 22:31f. does not present itself in vv. 33f.; but Heinz Schürmann, *Jesu Abschiedsrede Lk. 22, 21–38, III Teil einer quellenkritischen Untersuchung des lukanischen Abendmahlsberichtes Lk. 22, 7–38* (*Nt. Abh*, xx/5), 1957, pp. 21ff., especially pp. 27ff., has shown that in vv. 33f. a Lukan revision of the Markan parallel may lie before us.

104. In the context of an introductory or transitional question by a disciple "Kyrie" has been carried redactionally into the tradition material of the logia source in Lk. 12:41: 13:23; 17:37.

105. In the special material the address "Kyrie" occurs in seven places: Lk. 5:8; 9:54; 10:17; 10:40; 11:1; 19:8; 22:38.

106. As a rule it is found in the mouth of the disciples; so Lk. 5:8; 9:54; 10:17; 11:1; 12:41; 13:23; 17:37; 22:33, 38, 49; in the mouth of one seeking help, Lk. 5:12; 7:6; 18:41; further in the saying about treading in the footsteps of Jesus, Luke 9:61, and in the Zacchaeus story, Lk. 19:8.

107. Cf. the juxtaposition of κύριε and ὁ κύριος in Lk. 10:1, 17; 10:39, 40, 41; 12:41, 42; 19:8a, 8b.

108. A somewhat different use of the Kyrie-address presents itself in Lk. 6:46 (par. Matt. 7:21) and 13:25 (par. Matt. 25:11); here it was originally a matter of an address to the Judge of the world, a fact that has certainly been obliterated in Lk. 6:46.

109. The Kyrie-address directed to the Judge in Matt. 7:21, 22; 25:11, 37, 44 has for the present been left out of account.

110. Only for the One who is to come again is ὁ κύριος (ὑμῶν) occasionally used in parables.

111. Cf. G. Bornkamm, *Enderwartung, op. cit.*, pp. 38f.

112. Together with the Kyrie-address it stands in Matt. 8:2 (cf. Mk. 1:40); 14:33 (there a transition from "Kyrie" to "Son of God"; the conclusion of the story as compared with Mk. 6:51 has been much tampered with); 15:25 (cf. Mk. 7:25). Further προσκυνεῖν stands in Matthew in 9:18 (cf. Mk. 5:22); 20:20 (cf. Mk. 10:35); besides in the special material in 2:2, 8, 11. In Mark the word stands only once in association with the title Son of God, namely in 5:6; in this passage, in which homage is paid by demons, Matthew has in an interesting way cut it out. In Matt. 27:30 also the προσκυνεῖν in Mk. 15:19 has been struck out; for Matthew the word is possible only where there is genuine adoration. In Luke the concept is found only in the story of the temptation which has been taken over from the Q-tradition, and there it also appears in Matthew (Matt. 4:9f.//Lk. 4:7f.). If in Matthew the word also occurs in 18:26 in a parable, that is not an indication of a more profane use, but shows how considerably the interpretation of the parable breaks through. In contrast to the bending of the knee and the casting of oneself down before the face of a person, which is the expression of a total subordination to a lord and can be resorted to profanely, προσκυνεῖν exhibits a pronouncedly religious use; cf. Heinrich Schlier, art. γόνυ, *ThWb* I, pp. 738–740; Heinrich Greeven, art. προσκυνέω, *ThWb* VI, pp. 759–767, especially pp. 764ff.

113. So Matt. 8:25 (cf. Mk. 4:38); 15:22, 25 (cf. Mk. 7:24ff., where in v. 28 there stands the simple "Kyrie", which, moreover, Matthew has taken over in v. 27); 17:15 (cf. Mk. 9:17). In Matt. 20:30, 31 the ἐλέησον ἡμᾶς (με) has certainly been taken from the Markan *Vorlage*, yet it is there bound up with the address "Son of David", which Matthew has supplemented with "Kyrie"; cf. chapter 4, pp. 253f.. In the Matthaean special material there occurs in the story of the sinking of Peter 14:28–31, which the evangelist may have taken over from tradition, κύριε σῶσόν με in 14:30, which is such a striking parallel to the phrase in the story of the storm on the sea, Matt. 8:25, that we may certainly assume a redactional addition, which, however, will also hold good for the simple Kyrie-address that precedes in 14:28.

114. In addition to the passages mentioned in the foregoing note and the instances in Matt. 8:8, 21 which have been taken over cf. Matt. 8:6 (//Luke 7:3, where the story has certainly a somewhat different exposition so that possibly not merely Matt. 8:8 but also v. 6 may have been taken over); 9:28; 16:22 (cf. Mk. 8:33); 17:4 (instead of ῥαββί Mk.

9:5); 18:21 (cf. Lk. 17:4); 20:33 (instead of ῥαββουνί Mk. 10:51); 26:22 (cf. Mk. 14:19).

115. Mk. 12:35–37a parr. is discussed in detail on pp. 103ff. above.

116. So Cullmann, *Christologie*, pp. 209f.

117. Still widely-held in English research; e.g. Taylor, *Mk.*, p. 455; C. E. B. Cranfield, *The Gospel according to Saint Mark* (*Cambridge Greek Testament Commentary*), 1959, pp. 349f.

118. Thus already Julius Wellhausen, *Das Evangelium Marci*, 1909², pp. 87f.

119. Cf. on this Chapter 4, pp. 255ff.

120. The tradition in John 12:12ff. still shows a relative want of connection between the early story and the reference to Zech. 9:9.

121. Against Walter Bauer, *The "Colt" of Palm Sunday*, *JBL* 72, 1953, pp. 220–229, who wishes to take πῶλος in Mk. 11:2, 4, 5, 7 according to Greek usage in the sense "horse", the meaning "ass" or "foal of an ass" is to be adhered to for Mk. 11:1ff. Cf. also, Heinz-Wolfgang Kuhn, "Das Reittier Jesu in der Einzugsgeschichte des Markusevangeliums", *ZNW* 50, 1959, pp. 82–91.

122. In opposition to οἱ κύριοι αὐτοῦ (*scil.* τοῦ πώλου) Lk. 19:33.

123. Moreover, the portion of tradition relating to Jesus' Davidic sonship Lk. 20:41–44 (par. Mk. 12:35–37a) is not taken into consideration.

124. Lk. 22:61 (twice) cf. Mk. 14:72 (Peter's denial).

125. It is a matter of 6 passages: Lk. 7:19; 10:1; 11:39; 12:42; 17:5, 6.

126. In regard to Lk. 7:19(ff.) the question has to be asked whether the evangelist took over the narrative in a somewhat different rendering, and also in regard to Lk. 11:37ff. whether the apophthegmatic form came over to him. I do not regard either as likely.

127. Lk. 7:13; 10:39, 41; 13:15; 16:8; 18:6; 19:8.

128. Cf. Joachim Jeremias, *Die Gleichnisse Jesu*, 1958⁵, pp. 34ff.

129. Jeremias, *Gleichnisse*, p. 135, n. 5 reckons v. 8b to the pre-Lukan tradition; otherwise Tödt, *Menschensohn*, pp. 92f.

130. It is beyond question that the whole verse Lk. 19:8 is secondary.

131. Cf. Dalman, *Worte Jesu*, p. 270.

132. Cf. Foerster, *Herr ist Jesus*, pp. 206f., 225f., 227ff.

133. *Op. cit.*, p. 207, n. 1.

134. Lietzmann, *Röm.*, pp. 99f. Cf. Keth. 96a: "All the work which a slave does for his master a pupil should do for his teacher with the exception of the loosing of his shoes," according to Mekh. Ex. 21, 2 the Hebrew slave was not allowed to do this but only the Canaanite slave. Cf. on this Billerbeck I, p. 121.

135. A survey of the different kinds of application (metaphorical, courteous, courtly, sacred, etc.) is given by Ernst von Dobschütz *ΚΥΡΙΟΣ ΙΗΣΟΥΣ*, *ZNW* 30, 1931, pp. 97–123.

136. So, e.g. Foerster, *op. cit.*, pp. 225f.

137. So especially D. A. Frövig, *Der Kyriosglaube des Neuen Testaments und das Messiasbewusstsein Jesu* (*BFchrTh* 31/2), 1928, especially pp. 81ff.

138. Since it is a matter of a closed conception, it is not possible to explain Mk. 11:3 from the king conception; against that there tells the parallelism with 14:14. Against v. Dobschütz, *ZNW* 30 (1931), pp. 111f.

139. Further particulars in Chapter 4, p. 241.

140. Cf. Eusebius, *Hist. Ecc.* I 7, 14.

141. At the same time we must, of course, not proceed from the δεσπότης designation of God in Lk. 2:29; 4:24; these passages go back to the LXX, where for the rest only a guarded use is made of this word. Also the designation of Jesus as δεσπότης in Jude 4 (or designation of God?); 2 Pet. 2:1 has here to be disregarded, it being here a matter of a late reception of this divine predicate.

142. Cf. in substance Mk. 10:11f.

143. In 1 Cor. 7:25 in place of a lacking word that goes back to the authority of the earthly Jesus the authority of the exalted Jesus is claimed indirectly, Paul appealing to the power bestowed upon him by the exalted Jesus.

144. On the delimitation and content cf. Martin Dibelius, *An die Thessalonicher I/II, An die Philipper* (HbNT 11), 1937³, p. 25.

145. This possibly explains the present in 1 Cor. 7:10, although it can also be a matter of the continuing validity of the word of the Lord. I Cor. 9:14 has the aorist.

146. Reference need be made merely to the Pauline use of the traditio-technical terms παραλαμβάνειν and παραδιδόναι.

147. So Hans Lietzmann–Werner Georg Kümmel, *An die Korinther I/II* (HbNT 9), 1949⁴, p. 57.

148. So Jeremias, *Abendmahlsworte*, p. 95; cf. also p. 195.

149. Cf. Günther Bornkamm, *Herrenmahl und Kirche, Studien*, pp. 138–176, especially pp. 146ff.; also Oscar Cullmann, *Die Tradition als exegetisches, historisches und theologisches Problem*, 1954, pp. 8ff.

150. Cf. Lietzmann-Kümmel, *I Kor.*, p. 185; Cullmann, *Tradition*, p. 18; Jeremias, *Abendmahlsworte*, p. 195, for the difference between ἀπό and παρά.

151. The other passages with "Kyrios" which refer to the Lord's Supper have to be judged differently; we shall return to them in the next section.

152. In Paul "Kyrios" is one of the most comprehensive Christological titles. It can designate, although with very different degrees of accentuation, both the earthly and also the exalted Jesus and further-more the Jesus who is to come again.

153. Cf. Heb. 2:3; 7:14.

154. In certain contexts, where the address κύριε occurs frequently, it may have been conditioned by the alleged portions of tradition, so, e.g., in John 4:11, 15, 19; 4:49 (cf. Matt. 8:8 par.); 5:7; 11:1ff., which of course does not exclude redactional use. Likewise we have to regard the ὁ κύριος occurring three times, in 4:1; 6:23; 11:2 (again apart from the occurrence in John 20f.), as a remnant of tradition, hardly as a latter gloss (so Bultmann, *Joh.*, p. 128, n. 4; Taylor, *Names*, p. 43), against which its use in John 13:13f. also tells.

155. An early story lies at the basis of John 13, to which the interpretation of the action in vv. 12–17, 20 also belongs, cf. Bultmann, *Joh.*, pp. 351f.

156. So also Bultmann, *Joh.*, p. 362, n. 2.

157. Cf. Foerster, *ThWb* III, p. 1084.

158. Matt. 7:21//Lk. 6:46 was certainly handed down in Q and has preserved the early setting in association with Matt. 7:15–20, 24–27//Lk. 6:43–45, 47–49.

159. Precisely also the introduction together with κύριε κύριε from Matt. 7:22 will be original; in Luke it has fallen out as after 13:25 it was no longer needed.

160. Cf. on this Ernst Käsemann, *Die Anfänge christlicher Theologie*, *ZThK* 57, 1960, pp. 162–185.

161. So rightly Bultmann, *Syn. Trad.*, p. 123; Klostermann, *Mt.* p. 71.

162. So Bousset, *Kyrios Christos*, p. 51; Bultmann, *op. cit.*, p. 122; Klostermann, *Mt.*, pp. 70f.

163. Cf. the still later apophthegmatic development in *pseudo-Clem.* hom. 8, 4. adduced in Klostermann, *Lk.*, p. 84.

164. Cf. Hans Windisch, *Die Sprüche vom Eingehen in das Reich Gottes*, *ZNW* 27, 1928, pp. 163–192.

165. On the significance of "doing" in the preaching of Jesus cf. Herbert Braun, *Radikalismus* II, pp. 29ff.

166. Werner Georg Kümmel, *Kirchenbegriff und Geschichtsbewusstsein in der Urgemeinde und bei Jesus (Symbolae Biblicae Upsalienses* I), 1943, p. 14, regards Matt. 7:21f. as evidence for the invocation of Jesus in the primitive church. He certainly considers Lk. 6:46 to be earlier and sees in it an indication that the earthly Jesus was addressed by his disciples with "Lord, Lord".

167. That therewith Matthew had thought exclusively of an invocation of Jesus "on that day" as in v. 22, so Klostermann, *Mt.*, p. 71, is in my opinion less likely.

168. So Charles Harold Dodd, *The Parables of the Kingdom*, 1936[2], (reprint 1958), pp. 171ff.; Jeremias, *Gleichnisse*, pp. 43ff., 157ff.

169. On this Günther Bornkamm, *Die Verzögerung der Parusie* in *In Memoriam Ernst Lohmeyer*, 1951, pp. 116–126. Also Erich Grässer, *Das Problem der Parusieverzögerung in den synoptischen Evangelien und in der Apostelgeschichte (BZNW* 22), 1957, pp. 119ff.; Bultmann, *Syn. Trad.*, pp. 190f.; August Strobel, *Zum Verständnis von Mt XXV 1–13*, Nov. Test. 2, 1958, pp. 199–227, and *id.*, *Untersuchungen zum eschatologischen Verzögerungsproblem auf Grund der spätjüdisch-urchristlichen Geschichte von Habakuk 2, 2ff. (Suppl. to Nov. Test. ii)*, 1961, pp. 233ff.

170. Cf. the compilation of the non-explicable traits in Jewish marriage customs in G. Bornkamm, *op. cit.*, pp. 121ff.

171. So Grässer, *op. cit.*, pp. 121f., 126f.

172. Against Strobel, *Verzögerungsproblem*, pp. 235, 250, also pp. 161ff., who regards the parable as a "late creation" and attributes it to the "tradition of a local (Antiochean?) church" in the Hellenistic area.

173. We may not consider that this allegory was taken up for the first time in Paul (2 Cor. 11:2; also Eph. 5:22ff.); against Joachim Jeremias, art. *νυμφίος, ThWb* IV, pp. 1092–1099, especially pp. 1097ff.

174. On this in addition to the following section cf. especially Excursus II, pp. 129ff.; on Mark 2:18–20 cf. p. 133, n. 4.

175. Likewise the use of the parable of the importunate widow (Lk. 18:6-8).

176. Cf. Chapter 3, pp. 166f.

177. Wilhelm Heitmüller, *Zum Problem Paulus und Jesus, ZNW* 13, 1912, pp. 320–337, there pp. 333f.; Bousset, *Kyrios Christos*, p. 84.

178. The same also holds good for *ῥαββί* and *ἀββά*.

179. So Wilhelm Bousset, *Jesus der Herr* (*FRLANT* NF 8), 1916, p. 22. He himself retracts this in *Kyrios Christos*, p. 84, n. 3. Bultmann, *Theol.*, pp. 52f. reckons with a derivation from the Palestinian primitive church, but assumes that originally "Maranatha" was referred to God and was carried over to Jesus only later.

180. Karl Georg Kuhn, art., *μαραναθά, ThWb* IV, pp. 470–475.

181. Other derivations than from the verb אתא are today generally rejected.

182. On -*αθά* as a transcription of the imperative form אֲתָא cf. Kuhn, *ThWb* IV, p. 472, n. 25.

183. Cf. *Die Apostolischen Väter* I, ed. Funk-Bihlmeyer, 1956², pp. XVIIIf.

184. Erik Peterson, *ΕΙΣ ΘΕΟΣ. Epigraphische, formgeschichtliche und religionsgeschichtliche Untersuchungen* (*FRLANT* NF 24), 1926, pp. 130ff. Cf. C. F. D. Moule, "A Reconsideration of the Context of Maranatha", *NTSt* 6, 1959/60, pp. 307–310.

185. *CIG* 9303 (IV/V century).

186. Peterson, *op. cit.*, p. 131.

187. Lietzmann, *Messe und Herrenmahl*, especially pp. 228ff., 230ff.

188. Günther Bornkamm, *Das Anathema in der urchristlichen Abendmahlsliturgie* in *Das Ende des Gesetzes* (*Ges. Aufs.* I), 1958², pp. 123–132.

189. Lohmeyer, *Apk.*, pp. 179ff., especially p. 182.

190. So *Did.* 9, 5; cf. Bornkamm, *op. cit.*, pp. 125f.

191. For all the particulars I refer to Bornkamm, *op. cit.*, pp. 128ff.

192. Cf. Bornkamm, *op. cit.*, p. 129; Neuenzeit, *Herrenmahl*, pp. 120ff., 221ff.

193. Cf. Bornkamm, *op. cit.*, pp. 130f.

194. Rev. 2:7, 17. Cf. also the saying Rev. 3:20f. at the end of the letter.

195. How firmly anathema and maranatha were coupled to one another and how definitely this association maintained its position still later, emerges in Bornkamm, *op. cit.*, p. 127.

196. Lietzmann, *Messe und Herrenmahl*, pp. 249ff.

197. Ernst Lohmeyer, *Vom urchristlichen Abendmahl, ThR* NF 9, 1937, pp. 168–227, 273–312; 10, 1938, pp. 81–99.

198. Cf. Eduard Schweizer, *Herrenmahl im NT, ThLZ* 79, 1954, cols. 577–596.

199. Cf. on this Schweizer, *ThLZ* 79, 1954, cols. 584ff.

200. Cf. G. Bornkamm, *Herrenmahl und Kirche, op. cit.*, pp. 150ff.

201. Otherwise Jeremias, *Abendmahlsworte*, pp. 9ff.

202. That is shown especially by the motif of the "breaking of bread" in the tradition of the Lord's Supper.

203. The words of institution in their original form (without reference to passover, atonement, covenant and sacrifice) are to be understood in this sense.

204. So especially Mk. 14:25 parr.

205. Cf. especially Acts 2:46. On this motif of joy cf. Rudolf Bultmann, art., ἀγαλλιάομαι, *ThWb* I, pp. 18–20.

206. On vicarious atonement and the idea of the covenant in connection with the eucharistic words cf. Excursus I, pp. 58ff.

207. Cf. the detailed material in Jeremias, *Abendmahlsworte*, pp. 229ff.

208. Cullmann, *Urchristentum und Gottesdienst*, pp. 16f., 17ff. *Id., Christologie*, pp. 211ff.

209. Cf. especially Cullmann, *Christologie*, pp. 211f.

210. This danger appears in Adolf Deissmann, *Paulus. Eine kultur- und religionsgeschichtliche Skizze*, 1925², pp. (9off.), 98ff.

211. Cullmann, *Christologie*, pp. 212f., 219; further p. 214.

212. Cullmann reckons to the earliest tradition not only Mk. 12:35ff.; Rom. 1:3f.; Acts 2:36 but also Phil. 2:6ff.

213. Cf. Excursus II, pp. 129ff.

214. Cf. Acts 3:20, 21a; Mk. 2:19f.

215. Acts 1:9ff., especially v. 11.

216. An early Palestinian tradition still relatively intact presents itself in Mk. 13.

217. Cf. Acts 2.1ff., especially also the citation from Joel 3:1ff., which does not fit without strain into the Lukan pentecost discourse; further Acts 5:31; 10:44, 46. The phrase ἀπαρχὴ τοῦ πνεύματος in Rom. 6:23 also belongs here.

218. Cf. above all Acts 2:33.

219. Cf. Mk. 13:11 and the parallel rendering of the logia source in Matt. 10:19f.//Lk. 12:11f.

220. Cf. Mk. 3:28f. as also the corresponding Q-version Matt. 12:31f.//Lk. 12:10.

221. Against E. Schweizer, *Erniedrigung und Erhöhung*, pp. 97f.

222. So Cullmann, *Christologie*, pp. 214f.

223. Cullmann, *op. cit.*, p. 218.

224. *Op. cit.*, pp. 218f.

225. On the possibility of this meaning of the Aramaic wording cf. Kuhn, *ThWb* IV, pp. 472f. We may not in any case with Johannes Weiss, *I Kor.* p. 387, translate מָרַן אֲתָא "our Lord comes" and then adduce ὁ κύριος ἐγγύς Phil. 4:5 as a parallel; there is a similar interpretation in Adolf Schlatter, *Paulus, der Bote Jesu. Eine Deutung seiner Briefe an Korinther*, 1934 (1956²), p. 460. Such a *perfectum propheticum* is not usual in Aramaic; cf. Kuhn, *ThWb* IV, p. 472 with n. 29. On the contrary the question may rather be asked whether

"Maranatha" understood as future does not have an after-effect in Phil. 4:4f.

226. Against Cullmann, *op. cit.*, pp. 218f.

227. The Coptic rendering of "Maranatha" in *Did.* 10:6 is to be judged in this way.

228. Cf. Eduard Schweizer, *EvTh* 17, 1957, especially pp. 1off.

229. Here it still remains an open question how it stands with the application of ὁ κύριος to the risen Jesus.

230. Cf. merely in Paul ὁ κύριος ἡμῶν Ἰησοῦς Rom. 4:24; 1 Cor. 5:4b; 9:1b and often; ὁ κύριος ἡμῶν Χριστός Rom. 16:18; ὁ κύριος ἡμῶν Ἰησοῦς Χριστός Rom. 1:4fin.; 15:6; 1 Cor. 1:9, 10 and often; also the phrase in 1 Cor. 1:2 οἱ ἐπικαλούμενοι τὸ ὄνομα τοῦ κυρίου ἡμῶν Ἰησοῦ Χριστοῦ.

231. Cf. Rom. 15:30; 16:18, 20b; 1 Cor. 1:9 (cf. also 15:57); 2 Cor. 1:3; Gal. 6:18; 1 Thess. 1:3; 5:28 and often.

232. With ὁ κύριος ἡμῶν 1 Thess. 1:3; 2:19; 3:13; 5:23; 1 Cor. 1:7, 8: 2 Cor. 1:14; Phil. 3:20; with ὁ κύριος or ὁ κύριος Ἰησοῦς 1 Thess. 4:15, 16,17; 5:2; 1 Cor 4:4f.; 5:5; 2 Cor. 10:17f.; Phil. 4:5.

233. Besides 1 Cor. 1:2b cf. Rom. 10:12, 13 (OT citation); 2 Cor. 12:8.

234. I Cor. 10:21f.; 11:27, 31f. (16:22); also 11:20: κυριακὸν δεῖπνον. Otherwise where Paul refers to the σῶμα κριστοῦ conception.

235. On this cf. in detail Jeremias, *Gleichnisse*, pp. 5off., 144f.

236. Cf. Jeremias, *Gleichnisse*. pp. 45ff.

237. This acceptance of imprinted ideas was conditioned not least by the missionary preaching. The Son of man conception also afforded a support in the preaching of Jesus.

238. Cf. in detail on this Excursus II, pp. 129ff.

239. I take to be wrong the attempt made by Robert Paul Gagg, *Jesus und die Davidssohnfrage. Zur Exegese von Markus* 12, 35-37, *ThZ*, 1951, pp. 18–30, to regard the Markan version as an abridged text of what was originally a polemical discourse, as also the relevant interpretation which he gives of the pericope.

240. Taken up again word for word in Mk 14:49. "Teaching in the temple" is the redactional leading motif for cc. 11 and 12 together, cf. merely 11:17,27; 12:38a.

241. On this cf. Chapter 4, pp. 251ff.

242. It is surprising how little consideration is given to this problem in commentaries and monographs.

243. Ps. 109:1 LXX, only Mark has ὑποκάτω instead of ὑποπόδιον.

244. So 1 Sam. 26:17; 2 Sam. 3:21; 14:22 and often. The LXX renders this either by κύριε βασιλεῦ or by ὁ κύριός μου ὁ βασιλεύς.

245. Cf. Dalman, *Worte Jesu*, p. 270.

246. Cf. Chapter 4, pp. 20ff.

247. Lucien Cerfaux, *Le titre Kyrios et la dignité royale de Jésus*, *Recueil Lucien Cerfaux* I, 1954, pp. 3–63, especially pp. 35ff., 40ff., wishes to show that in primitive Christianity the designation Lord was associated from the beginning with the idea of royal Messiahship.

248. So in recent times especially Charles Harold Dodd, *The Apostolic Preaching and its Developments*, 1944[2] (reprint 1956), p. 22.

249. Ulrich Wilckens, *Die Missionsreden der Apostelgeschichte* (*WMANT* 5), 1961, pp. 172ff.

250. The αὐτόν may have been inserted by Luke; but both the καί-καί and the use of ποιεῖν, which is not in any way characteristic of Luke, tell in favour of the view that a firmly fixed formulation has been received.

251. When we study the construction of the whole discourse, it emerges that after the broad unfolding of the kerygma the conclusion means to lead back to the situation at the beginning. There it is a matter of the pouring out of the Spirit and this, as could now be shown in vv. 33ff., has its basis in Jesus' exaltation.

252. Cf. Acts 3:13ff.; 4:10; 5:30; 10:40. The action of God is also given precedence in 5:30.

253. The influence of the Septuagint on the New Testament Kyrios title is frequently assumed, but has nowhere been investigated in a comprehensive way.

254. Cf. 1 Cor. 5:5; 1 Thess. 5:2; 2 Thess. 2:2; expressly Christianized in 1 Cor. 1:8; 2 Cor. 1:14.

255. In Mk. 1:2–8 it is not, as is usually assumed, a matter of a redactional composition by Mk. Mal. 3:1 is the early Scriptural evidence for the Baptist; it occurs already in the Q-tradition Matt. 11:10 par. and drew after it the very closely related saying Isa. 40:3, which, however, was possible only on Hellenistic soil.

256. In this form the phrase is found in 1 Cor. 1:2; but quite similarly also in Rom. 10:12f.; Acts 9:14, 21; 22:16; 2 Tim. 2:22.

257. Cf. E. Hatch–H. A. Redpath, *A Concordance to the Septuagint*, 1897 (1954²), I, pp. 521f.

258. What has been said holds good even if it is maintained that in the New Testament period prayer continued to be addressed largely to God.

259. The rabbinical parallels to Matt. 18:20 in Billerbeck I, pp. 794f.

260. No sharp boundary line may be drawn between acclamation and confession in the early period.

261. Cf. Joh. Weiss, *1 Cor.*, pp. 296f. The "anathema of Jesus" will not be inquired into here.

262. On the whole Bousset, *Kyrios Christos*, pp. 101f., would recognize an influence of the LXX on the Kyrios concept only on the strength of an acceptance of the Hellenistic cult concept. But the situation here is very complicated and at all events it must be maintained that for one thing the influence of the LXX preceded that of the mystery cults.

263. The contrary thesis of Walter Bauer, *Der Wortgottesdienst der ältesten Christen* (*Sammlung gemeinverständlicher Vorträge* 148), 1930, pp. 19f., 39ff., is not convincing.

264. Cf. on this Günther Bornkamm, *Zum Verständnis des Christus-Hymnus Phil. 2, 6–11* in *Studien zu Antike und Urchristentum* (*Ges. Aufs.* II), 1959, pp. 177–187.

265. Isa. 45:18–25 represents a unit of tradition.

266. Bousset, *Kyrios Christos*, p. 89, n. 3.

267. Cf. in addition especially Lohmeyer, *Kyrios Jesus*, pp. 56ff.

268. Cf. Dibelius, *Phil.*, p. 79.

269. Ernst Lohmeyer, *Der Brief an die Philipper* (*KrExKommNT* IX/I), 1953[9], pp. 97f.

270. Cf. Bornkamm, *op. cit.*, pp. 183f.

271. Käsemann, *op. cit.*, pp. 65ff.; Bornkamm, *op. cit.*, p. 178, n. 3, follows him.

272. Cf. on this Käsemann, *op. cit.*, pp. 86ff.

273. Cf. *Odes of Solomon* 33.12.

274. Cf. the detailed treatment of this passage in Joh. Weiss, 1 *Kor.*, pp. 219ff.

275. So, e.g., Adolf Deissmann, *Licht vom Osten*, 1923[4], pp. 287ff.

276. Günther Bornkamm, *Christus und die Welt in der urchristlichen Botschaft* in *Das Ende des Gesetzes* (*Ges. Aufs.* I), 1958[2], pp. 157–172 (there p. 165).

277. On this aspect cf. especially Roland Schütz, *Die Offenbarung des Johannes und Kaiser Domitian* (*FRLANT* NF 32), 1933, especially pp. 26ff., 33 ff

278. Rev. 17:14; 19:16. Originally the reference was to a title of the great kings of the Orient. As a divine predicate this designation occurs in 1 Tim. 6:15; cf. on this Martin Dibelius–Hans Conzelmann, *Die Pastoralbriefe* (*HbNT* 13), 1955[3], pp. 68f. Otherwise, apart from ἔργου κύριε Ἰησοῦ Rev. 22:20b and the salutation formula in 22:21, a "Kyrios" referred to Christ but unstressed is used only in 11:8 and 14:13.

279. Cf. only *Mart. Pol.* 8, 2; *Passio Sanctorum Scilitanorum* 5f.

280. So especially Taylor, *Names of Jesus*, pp. 41, 49ff.

281. John 20:2, 13, 18, 20, 25, 28; 21:7 (twice), 12. In John 20:13, 28 there stands ὁ κύριός μου, elsewhere ὁ κύριος. In addition there is the address κύριε in 21:15, 16, 17, 20, 21.

282. Lk. 24:3, 34.

283. For the proof passages in John 20 this is also assumed by Bultmann, *Joh.*, pp. 528ff., 534ff.

284. So also the Kyrie-address in John 21:15ff. is to be understood.

285. Cf. Strathmann, *Joh.*, p. 259; Cullmann, *Christologie*, pp. 239f.,

286. The ἐφανερώθη ἐν ἑτέρᾳ μορφῇ in v. 12 also shows how considerably the whole Markan appendix is stamped with later views about the risen Jesus.

287. The considerable Gentile Christian component in Matthew's Gospel may on no account be overlooked any more than the Jewish Christian tendencies. Kilpatrick, *Origins of the Gospel acc. to St. Matthew*, pp. 101ff., has with good reason spoken of a re-Judaizing.

EXCURSUS II

Psalm 110:1 *and the Idea of the Exaltation of Jesus*

For the most part the exaltation of Jesus has been assumed
entirely as a matter of course for the whole of primitive Christian tradition; modifications conditioned traditio-historically
have hardly been contemplated. But Tödt has now shown
convincingly that an exaltation conception has no place within
the Son of man Christology. Accordingly its use in the earliest
period may not be assumed, at least in all the strata of tradition.[1] On the other hand, Eduard Schweizer has sought to
show from the Jewish conception of the exaltation of the
suffering righteous man that it was used in the primitive
church at an early time.[2]

As to definition, it must be pointed out first of all that "exaltation" does not merely imply the motif of an ascent into
heaven—to the primitive church that was a matter of course
onwards from Easter or the ascension—but denotes principally
the special dignity bestowed by virtue of an act of enthronement and the installation in a position of power. Only if the
concept of exaltation is understood and remains clearly
delimited in this way as a *terminus technicus,* is a serviceable
result to be expected when inquiry is made after the origin and
development of the exaltation conception.[3] For ascent into
heaven by itself could be understood according to the Old
Testament pattern as a withdrawal; and as regards the parousia
expectation this meant that a temporary reception of Jesus in
heaven until he assumed his proper function at the end of time
was thought of.[4]

In the New Testament the exaltation conception is, com-
paratively speaking, easy to follow up because throughout it is
connected with a quite definite Old Testament citation: Ps.
110:1 has become the authoritative statement regarding Jesus'
heavenly dignity and function.[5] As is well known, it is one of
the most used passages of Old Testament Scripture in primitive
Christian tradition.[6] But there are contained in it three different
elements, of which quite diverse applications are seen in the

New Testament. In the leading place there is the motif of sitting at the right hand of God, which in many instances appears without reference being made otherwise to the statements of Ps. 110:1;[7] in addition, there is in the second place the phrase Ps. 110:1b, according to which final subjection of his enemies is promised to him who has been enthroned by God; finally, the introductory formula of Ps. 110:1a, which contains the Kyrios title, is cited only in particular passages. Consequently it must be accurately noted every time which of these three elements from Ps. 110:1 have been taken up and how they have been used.

The sitting of Jesus at the right hand of God already played a role in early Palestinian tradition. In the question of the high priest and Jesus' answer during the examination before the supreme council Mk. 14:61f. there is a peculiar blending of the ideas of the royal Messiah and the Son of man. To the Son of man conception there belongs the coming on the clouds of heaven. The significant elements of Messiahship are the titles ὁ χριστός and ὁ υἱὸς τοῦ εὐλογητοῦ, but there is also the use of ἐκ δεξιῶν καθήμενος τῆς δυνάμεως. The much discussed indistinctness of the statement in 14:62 may be conditioned by this union of Christological motifs of quite different kinds.[8] From a practical point of view it is decisive that in this portion of tradition the sitting on the right hand of God is understood eschatologically. The messianic enthronement, like the coming on the clouds of heaven, is an eschatological event; the handing over of power and the parousia belong together, consequently both take place before the eyes of the world. When Jesus is installed in his messianic office, then the moment has come in which He will appear as the judge of the world.[9]

An eschatological use of the motif of the sitting at the right hand of God such as there is in Mk. 14:61f. is not found elsewhere in the New Testament. We make the interesting discovery that this motif has attained its far-reaching significance on the whole only in connection with the conception of the "exaltation" of Jesus. That the idea of exaltation is completely lacking in the early Palestinian Christology is manifestly no accidental gap in our knowledge of the earliest tradition, a tradition which is preserved only in fragments; rather it is a materially conditioned actuality. It can indeed not be overlooked that the development of the exaltation motif already assumes a radical transformation of the eschatology.[10] As hitherto the resurrection of Jesus had been the anticipation of a final event and the ascension the sign of a merely temporary absence of the risen Jesus until His victorious return, so the ascent into heaven was now connected with the act of enthronement and consequently a new and singular meaning was given to the heavenly stay and work of Jesus.[11] The Old Testament statement about sitting on the right hand of God became the dominating characterization of this heavenly position and dignity that has been made over to Jesus. As the exalted one Jesus has already taken up the place of the Messiah at the right hand of God and now already holds his commanding office in heaven.[12] Here tradition material of the early Hellenistic Jewish Christian church presents itself, a fact that is confirmed by other evidence.

A citation of Ps. 110:1aβ that is quite literal cannot be traced in Mk. 14:62, close as what is said there leans upon that Old Testament word of promise. All the other passages in which the phrase to sit on the right hand of God is taken up in reference to Jesus, show likewise certain deviations from the Old Testament text, and indeed they do so in consequence of the evidently fixed way in which the statement is made, be it in the form of a relative clause, a participial phrase or a preterite formulation.[13] Sometimes the sitting at the right hand of God is also connected expressly with the concept ὑψοῦν.[14] Moreover, in some passages a statement regarding the resurrection is completely replaced by one about Jesus' exaltation.[15] This strange state of affairs has sometimes been taken to indicate that as regards the exaltation we must be concerned with quite an early theologumenon which was ousted at second hand by the idea of the resurrection.[16] But there can be no talk of that. The significance of the resurrection for the earliest tradition is beyond question and cannot be reduced. On the other hand, however, it is quite easy to understand that in the development of the exaltation concept and the consequent repressing of the eschatological expectation the resurrection lost its original datum point[17] and in certain passages may have been absorbed by the idea of exaltation.[18]

A complete de-eschatologizing was not by any means purposed in the exaltation conception and to begin with did not appear. Side by side with the motif of dominion in heaven the expectation of an eschatological fulfilment was by all means adhered to. If not in all the New Testament statements about exaltation, at least in some very significant contexts an "eschatological reservation" is expressed unmistakably, and for that recourse is had surprisingly to the second line of Ps. 110:1: ἕως ἂν θῶ τοὺς ἐχθρούς σου ὑποκάτω τῶν ποδῶν σου. In Heb. 10:12f. (cf. 1:13) this appears in a simple form as far as the outlook there is from the enthronement of Jesus Christ to the final subjection of his adversaries and consequently to the ultimate realization of his dominion. In 1 Cor. 15:25–28 this idea is carried still further; the lordship of Jesus as the exalted and returning one is limited by the eternal lordship of God which begins thereafter; on the other hand, however, just here a βασιλεία of Christ is emphatically spoken of side by side with the βασιλεία of God.[19]

Moreover, the opening phrase of Ps. 110:1aα also came to be accepted. Consequently, the Kyrios title was transferred to Jesus in a new way and connected in especial with the *status exaltationis*.[20] The citation of the whole of Ps. 110:1 thus made possible occurs in Mk. 12:36 parr. and Acts 2:34.

Finally, it must be mentioned that the New Testament lets us see how from the exaltation conception a complete de-eschatologizing can possibly have come about. Ps. 110:1b was no longer connected with the motif of sitting at the right hand of God, which continued to be authoritative, but Ps. 8:7, a statement about the already realized lordship and the actual submission of all creatures.[21] In Eph. 1:20–22a there is a clear instance of this connection of Ps. 110:1aβ with Ps. 8:7 and of the abandonment that went with it of the eschatological reservation that had been associated with the exaltation conception.

The result of our discussion is that the motif of enthronement at the right hand of God was applied at first to Jesus' return and his work as the Consummator, whilst an independent exaltation conception was still completely lacking. To some extent this conception assumes experience of the delay of the parousia, but on the other hand it unfolds the significance of the present ministry of the Jesus who has ascended to heaven. The conception of exaltation which was developed in the early Hellenistic-Jewish church held its ground fairly steadily in the further early Christian tradition, characterized on the one hand by the motif

of sitting at God's right hand and on the other by its outlook
on the parousia. Besides, there came about a connection with
the Kyrios title (by reason of the introductory phrase of Ps.
110:1) and with the concept ὑψοῦν; also there came about a
development of the conception of the βασιλεία Χριστοῦ. A
complete de-eschatologizing and therewith a considerable
transformation of the exaltation motif appear first in the
deutero-Pauline Epistle to the Ephesians.

NOTES

1. Tödt, *Menschensohn*, pp. 258ff.
2. E. Schweizer, *Erniedrigung und Erhöhung*, especially pp. 6off.
3. For this reason the exaltation concept ought to be applied exclusively to the special heavenly status of the risen Jesus; the Messianic
component of this conception must by all means be taken into consideration. As E. Schweizer, *op. cit.*, pp. 38f., shows, the exalting of one who
was abased, therefore the deliverance of a righteous man, represents no
direct parallel, even if occasionally statements about dominion may be
made in regard to the redeemed righteous man. Moreover it needs to be
observed that statements about the exaltation of Jesus do not appear
in the earliest tradition. Cf. for criticism of Schweizer's thesis Tödt, *op.
cit.*, pp. 26of.
4. This can be seen clearly in the passage Acts 3:2of. treated in detail
in Chapter 3, pp. 164ff. But Mk. 2:18-20 is also to be understood in this
sense; for vv. 19b, 20 must certainly be regarded as a subsequent *vati-
cinium ex eventu*. The statement ὅταν ἀπαρθῇ ἀπ' αὐτῶν ὁ νυμφίος in
any case designates, without prejudice to the use of a metaphor, the
time of the withdrawal of Jesus to heaven, so also Acts 3:2of., in a
purely negative sense, with which the custom of fasting when mourn-
ing harmonizes excellently. We may therefore ascribe this portion of
tradition in its present form to a very early Palestinian tradition; that
the original stock of vv. 18, 19a may be carried back to Jesus is beyond
doubt.—Acts 1:9-11 has moreover to be mentioned here; the exaltation
plays no sort of role in this story of the ascension, the outlook is exclusively towards the return of Jesus, and the idea of the Son of man
coming then on the clouds has probably been the pattern here. We cannot
without more ado define this narrative as a Lukan composition as
Haenchen, *Apg.*, pp. 118f. does; that with all its marks of Luke's pen
there is here an early tradition, may not be disputed.
5. Ps. 110 belongs to the so-called Royal Psalms and in consequence
stands essentially in a certain connection with the Messiah conception.

From pre-Israelitish Jerusalm royal tradition an element of the idea of the priest-king remains preserved in v. 4. Regarding its application in late Judaism cf. Billerbeck IV/1, pp. 452ff., an excursus on Ps. 110 in the early rabbinical literature; he reckons with an intentional suppression of this proof passage in anti-Christian polemic. Now it has to be said that the provable non-messianic use of Ps. 110 answers to the former Old Testament meaning of its statements; on the other hand, within the traditional messianism adhered to by the rabbis it would not be surprising if this text also was drawn upon, of course not in the Christian sense of a heavenly enthronement; evidence of that is certainly lacking. Primitive Christianity confined itself to the use of Ps. 110:1, only the Epistle to the Hebrews draws also upon v. 4 in connection with its doctrine of the high priest.

6. Walter Grundmann, art., δεξιός, ThWb II, pp. 37ff., presents merely the material of the passages, but traditio-historically the article is wholly unproductive.

7. It is clear that this motif is nevertheless connected with Ps. 110:1, since for it there is no point of reference of any kind elsewhere.

8. The situation is indeed similar in Acts 7:55f. There comes from Ps. 110:1 only the phrase "on the right hand of God", whilst the much disputed "standing" belongs to the Son of man conception.

9. Grässer, Parusieverzögerung, pp. 172ff. wishes to show that the conception of the exaltation of Jesus already presents itself in Mark 14:61f.; also Olof Linton, "The Trial of Jesus and the Interpretation of Psalm CX". NTSt VII, 1960/61, pp. 258–262, treats the citation from Ps. 110:1 in Mk. 14:62 as an allusion to "the exaltation of Christ to heaven" (p. 260). But this is not to the point as will be shown in detail in the discussion of this text in Chapter 3, pp. 162ff.

10. In Grässer, op. cit., it is not clearly seen that the exaltation conception was reached precisely through conscious remodelling of former parousia statements. He limits himself in a noteworthy way to the treatment of Mark 14:61f. and has not set forth the central significance of Ps. 110:1.

11. It has already been mentioned in Chapter 2, pp. 89ff that the conception of a present ministry of the Jesus who has withdrawn to heaven was not formed in the earliest Palestinian church. It is certainly not to be disputed that the activity of the Spirit, the knowledge of the immediate nearness of the Lord and the call to worship helped to prepare the way for such an idea. Nevertheless, it was the Hellenistic Jewish Christian church that first stated it explicitly.

12. This is presented very effectively in Phil. 2:9–11 without any reference to Ps. 110:1 and associated with the Kyrios title understood in a largely Hellenistic way; cf. Chapter 2, p. 110 above.

13. In place of the imperative in Ps. 110:1aβ there stands ὅς ἐστιν in Rom. 8:34; 1 Pet. 3:22; a participial phrase occurs in Col. 3:1; Eph. 1:20; also in Mk. 14:62; a preterite statement in Mk. 16:19; Hed. 1:3; 8:1; 10:12; 12:2.

14. Acts 2:33; 5:31. Independently of the sitting on the right hand of God "to exalt" occurs especially in Phil. 2:9(ff.) (ὑπερυψοῦν) and in

the Gospel of John, where ὑψωθῆναι and δοξασθῆναι really belong to one another.

15. Unambiguously in Phil. 2:9ff; 1 Tim. 3:16; 1 Pet. 3:18; Heb. 1:4; 2:9f.; 10:12; 12:2 (in Hebrews the resurrection is mentioned only in 13:20); John 3:14; 8:28; 12:32, 34 and often.

16. Thus at first allusively Johannes Weiss, *Urchristentum*, pp. 19f., 56f.; taken up and thoroughly discussed by Georg Bertram, *Die Himmelfahrt Jesu vom Kreuze aus und der Glaube an seine Auferstehung* in *Festgabe für Adolf Deissmann*, 1927, pp. 187–217. The appearances are said to be connected with the exaltation conception; the popular expectation of an immediate reception into heaven after death (Lk. 16:19ff.; 23:43, 46; Phil. 1:23; 2 Cor. 5:1ff.) is the standard background; against it the resurrection and ascension are judged as ideas which on the whole were formed only in the endeavour to ward off docetism. At the same time, however, there is no pertinent treatment of the tradition history of the resurrection statements of the New Testament or of the texts regarding the reception into heaven or regarding the exaltation in the sense of an enthronement, and no correct distinction is made between the conception of an immediate reception of the dead into heaven and the idea of exaltation.

17. After that the connection of the resurrection with eschatology was undone, the resurrection statements were set in another traditio-historical connection and obtained an essentially new meaning beside the death of Jesus within the passion tradition that bore the stamp of the Christos title; cf. on this Chapter 3, pp. 172ff.

18. Following R. H. Lightfoot, Charles Harold Dodd, *Matthew and Paul* in *New Testament Studies*, 1953, pp. 53–66, calls attention to the fact that the Christophany in Matt. 28:16–20 has a character completely different from that of the other resurrection appearances, it being here a matter of "a kind of proleptic παρουσία".

19. Cf. also 2 Tim. 4:1, 18. On that Karl Ludwig Schmidt, art. βασιλεία, *ThWb* I, pp. 581f.; Oscar Cullmann, *Konigsherrschaft Christi und Kirche im Neuen Testament* (*Theol. Studien* 10). 1950[3], especially pp. 5ff., 11ff.

20. The use of the Kyrios title in the framework of the exaltation conception likewise indicates clearly that we are concerned with a tradition of the Hellenistic Jewish Christian church. Cf. Chapter 2, pp. 103ff.

21. This psalm verse 8:7 was originally used in the New Testament only in eschatological connections. Cf. 1 Cor. 15:26f.; Heb. 2:5ff.

CHAPTER III

CHRISTOS

1. The Background in the Old Testament and Late Judaism

THE concept of the Messiah, of all the expectations of a saviour-figure, has the oldest and most meaningful history. It is deeply rooted in the OT and thus far is to be regarded as genuinely Biblical.

The prophetic promises of a Messiah are grounded in the Israelite theory of the kingship. From the beginning, the anointing of the king, probably through Canaanite influences, played a decisive part.[1] The monarchy, which the old Israelite "Amphictyonic Council" for so long resisted, and which it eventually was obliged to adopt,[2] still plainly shows its ancient oriental background, but was none the less transformed to a large extent, and assimilated to the faith in Jahwe.[3]

Whereas the charismatic kingship of the northern kingdom preserved most strongly the traditions of the pre-monarchical period, the kingship of the south also maintained specifically Israelite features, despite the influence of old Jerusalem traditions:[4] the dynasty was based by Nathan on the assent of Jahwe,[5] the old amphictyonic tradition was linked to Zion[6] and even the charismatic element was given scope.[7] The traditional features of the kingship ritual were fitted in to the Jahwistic faith;[8] the king is adopted as a son by Jahwe,[9] entrusted with the lordship of the world created by Jahwe,[10] he receives the promise that he shall overcome all his enemies,[11] and that his kingdom shall stand for ever,[12] and he undertakes the task of maintaining the law.[13]

It was the prophetic task of Nathan—and no doubt later court prophecy understood its mission on similar lines—to affirm the permanence of the monarchical institution and arrangements and of the Davidic dynasty.[14] But from the eighth century onwards the task of the prophets of Jahwe became different: the affirmation of the institution was combined with the threat of judgment; they began to announce that a period of woe would ensue for king and people, only after which the Davidic monarchy and Israel would experience once more the blessings of Jahwe. Hence it is no longer a question of confirming the existing institution, but of proclaiming a new realization of the old promises.

The peculiar characteristic of these prophecies does not depend on whether in individual cases the prophetic theme is about a restitution of the Davidic monarchy within history or at the end of history. What is decisive is that we now have the proclamation of a new saving action of Jahwe which lies in the future. How in the course of this development the structure of promise and fulfilment is changed, how a prophecy about events within history is transformed into a prophecy about the ultimate end of history, is a question to be considered, yet of subordinate importance.[15]

In the OT the concept of the Messiah is nowhere used in prophetic promises about a new recreation of the monarchy. That nevertheless it is legitimate to speak of "messianic" expectation arises from a complex of ideas which is most closely bound up with the concept of kingship.[16]

Messianic promises are first met with in Isaiah and Micah,[17] and in spite of occasional recessions can be traced throughout the whole time before and during the exile. In the post-exilic period they spring for a short time into new life, then rather pale in significance, but are none the less observable up to the period of late OT traditions.[18] Among the Isaianic prophecies, 8:23–9:6 shows most plainly the type of prophetic message of salvation which moves within the horizons of this world and its history.[19] As in 11:1–9(10), what is here proclaimed is a salvation which follows upon judgment and the inauguration of a new Davidic line;[20] for, as is similarly expressed in the message of the prophet Micah, 5:1–3,[21] Jahwe has broken with the old royal dynasty on account of its sin.

In a wonderful holy war, the enemy is to be overcome apart from man's initiative,[22] and a new ruler is to be established over the united people, a ruler whose reign will have permanence.[23] Endowed with the divine spirit, he will procure right for the poor and wretched.[24] In spite of the far-reaching affirmations about the charismatic capabilities of the messianic king, this ruler is no supernatural divine being.[25] He is a creature who at the command of Jahwe has to exercise vicariously the office of rule on the earth and for this purpose the highest gifts are bestowed on him.

In the period shortly before and during the exile, the prophets estimate differently the messianic expectation which is bound up with the prophecy of Nathan and the Davidic dynasty. In the editorial passages of Amos 9:11–15, the writer accepts the idea of a restitution of the Davidic monarchy as a matter of course.[26] But Jeremiah, whatever be our interpretation of the promise 23:5f., expressed in traditional style, proclaimed in his threatening word to the young king Jeconiah, 22:24–30, Jahwe's complete break with the house of David.[27] In other prophets of the exile, the hope of a new king of David's line likewise noticeably recedes, as, for example, is the case in Ezekiel.[28] And in Deutero-Isaiah, it is even completely surrendered; in 45:1 he applies the messianic predicate to the Persian king Cyrus who acts at Jahwe's command,[29] and he no longer has any thought of a kingly bearer of salvation.[30]

In the post-exilic period the messianic hope is fanned into new life.[31] In the disturbed years around 520, and in connection with the building anew of the temple which the prophet Haggai instigated, there arises, after the long period of affliction, a renewed expectation of Jahwe's initiative, and the hope that His power and glory will be manifested.[32] In particular, the prospect of coming salvation connects itself with the Davidic Zerubbabel, who according to the word of Haggai shall assume supreme power on the earth as the signet of Jahwe.[33] Zechariah who develops the prophetic office of Haggai further, goes a step beyond his predecessor, in so far as he assigns, in his promises of coming salvation, a special role at the side of the king to the priesthood, which in the meantime had grown strong and independent: alongside the messianic king Zerubbabel there stands—with differing functions but equal rank—the messianic high priest Joshua.[34]

In spite of the disappointment of these expectations, the messianic hope, in its old and in this specifically post-exilic form, is by no means extinguished, but shows rather in the following period manifold repercussions.[35]

No doubt in official circles of Judaism, as the priestly writings and the work of the Chronicler show, it is in large measure suppressed.[36] But a late OT text such as Zech. 9:9f. shows the reflection of a tradition which is by no means merely conservatory, but still thoroughly alive. Of course it is true that this piece of tradition is formally a compilation of older elements.[37]

But despite such signs that the learning of the scribes was now beginning to operate, it is unmistakable that the picture which is here drawn of the Messiah has its own independent and characteristic features: if the riding upon the ass had previously been the token of the ruler's dignity, it is here the token of humility, which the text expressly states. The collection of predicates in v. 9 (עָנִי, נוֹשָׁע, צַדִּיק) which are affirmed of the Messiah point to a quite specific ideal of piety: the humble and poor, who trusts in Jahwe's help alone, is the righteous one. If previously the Messiah had been the one who espoused the cause of the poor, and secured them justice,[38] he now himself belongs to the circle of these "anawim"; Jahwe shows him to be the "righteous" one and turns on him His wondrous help.[39]

The conception of the poor man as the one about whom God is especially concerned, is ancient, but on the other hand it cannot be overlooked that this motive is brought forward more emphatically precisely in the late Psalms.[40] If we try to date this piece of tradition, we shall probably have to go forward as far as the third century.[41]

The last discussed text is already fairly close to the Maccabean time. Here a very remarkable picture is presented to us.[42] Setting aside the largely secularized priestly caste which was especially liable to Hellenization, we find juxtaposed to each other on the one hand the group of Maccabeans, and on the other the exponents of apocalyptic expectation, without all the forces at work being influenced thereby.

The history and aims of the Maccabean revolt are known especially from the First Book of the Maccabees.[43] In its fundamental attitude it stands in a positive relation to the whole movement occasioned by the Maccabean struggles, and also assents to the later Hasmonaean government. We may therefore expect the book to afford us a relatively reliable account of the basic motives and guiding religious principles involved.[44] Two things are striking: firstly, the principle of zeal for the law and maintenance of the covenant,[45] for the sake of which a holy war was carried on;[46] secondly, the obviously quite uneschatological and so unmessianic attitude.[47] If we wish to explain this we must turn back to the Book of Deuteronomy.

It may be assumed in any case that the governing theological conception of the latter long influenced certain circles, and principally the population which had remained in Palestine.[48] In any event, here too is to be seen a thoroughly uneschatological mode of thought and on the other hand a lively interest in the land appropriated by Israel, in the right worship of God, in strict separation from all Gentiles, as also in the institution of sacred war,[49] all of them motives which characterize the Maccabean revolt. Even the expectation of the prophet sent and legitimated by Jahwe in 1 Macc. 4:46; 9:27; 14:41 may be compared with Deut. 18:15ff., for in both cases what is in question is not the eschatological prophet, but the messenger sent by God from time to time, the type of prophet in fact whose failure to appear the Jews were only too well aware of in the later period.[50]

That the restoration of the monarchy which the Maccabeans lost no time in setting in motion also harmonizes with the Deuteronomic spirit, may be seen from the law concerning the kingship in Deut. 17:14ff. Certain priestly traditions may also have been at work among the Maccabees, but they were certainly not predominant. If we wish to characterize the Maccabean revolt in summary fashion, it would perhaps be best to say that its aim was the restoration of the institution of God's people.

About the same time there appears another quite different basic attitude, that represented by apocalyptic. Whereas among the Maccabees eschatology plays no recognizable part, we have here an eschatological hope carried to an extreme pitch of tension. No doubt it is not legitimate to interpret apocalyptic solely from the point of view of its eschatological aspect, for it is concerned about an understanding of history as a whole, and the realization of salvation for the elect,[51] but it is just the orientation of the outlook towards ultimate salvation which, by contrast with the attitude of the Maccabees, is especially striking.

The apocalyptic outlook did not first arise in the time of the Maccabees, even though it first clearly appears with the Book of Daniel.[52] Its pre-history is complicated and is to be discerned especially in passages such as Isa. 24–27; Zech. 12–14; Joel 3f.[53] It is generally recognized that a not inconsiderable quantity of foreign influences were at work, this being especially reflected in the radical transcendent dualism, and the motive of mystery.[54] There is less unanimity of opinion in regard to assessing the position of apocalyptic in the complex of Israelite traditions.

Recently it has been claimed that the ground from which apocalyptic grew is the wisdom teaching, whereas prophetic influence is admitted merely by way of literary relations.[55] But this one-sided derivation from the wisdom tradition is not truly convincing, however little it is to be denied that a considerable number of points of view typical of the wisdom tradition have been assimilated by apocalyptic.[56] The prophetic inheritance must be more emphatically taken into account, in spite of the considerable modifications which were imposed on it.[57]

It should not be forgotten that already in the pre-Maccabean period the prophetic tradition flowed on in two distinct streams, for alongside the gradually completed transformation of inherited points of view and the adaptation of foreign elements, such as is characteristic of apocalyptic, there is a relatively unchanged continued influence of old prophetic traditions, especially that of eschatology understood from within this world. Hence for the history of the concept of the Messiah, the transition to apocalyptic is not primarily of interest, for in this sphere the expectation of an earthly messianic king was largely given up,[58] what is rather of interest is the continued vitality of old Israelite hopes.[59] This latter is discernible in the Qumran texts, the *Psalms of Solomon* and the rabbinic literature.

The Qumran texts occupy a special position, for here, as little as in the case of apocalyptic, can we speak of a straightforward continuance of prophetic eschatology. In these have been assimilated elements basic to a priestly tradition; further we see an understanding of and an acute exegesis of the Torah, such as may best be compared with the Pharisaic attitude;[60] while again there is a whole group of conceptions which are familiar to us from the apocalyptic tradition,[61] although this does not imply that the Qumran texts either as a *genre* or in their understanding of history and salvation can be characterized as apocalyptic.[62]

The idea of the fellowship conveyed in these writings is to be understood as the remnant community elected by God and destined to salvation, separated from the world which is hostile to God, and about to meet the eschatological struggle against the powers of darkness. However sharply dualistic is the expression of these basic thoughts and however strongly the dualism is emphasized by the awareness of predestination and by eschatological expectation, the outlook never, in fact, led to the apocalyptic antithesis between the earthly and the future heavenly world where salvation is regarded as breaking in only at the end of history, and on the dawning of a completely new aeon.[63] This is shown especially clearly in the teaching on the Messiah, which in its basic structure is thoroughly traditional, and the roots of which are plainly discernible in prophetic eschatology.

The messianism of the Qumran texts is based on the conception of Zechariah, who places by the side of the messianic king a messianic high priest. This teaching of two Messiahs, which had not been forgotten in the intervening period, has received a characteristic expression in the Qumran texts inasmuch as they assign to the high priest a plainly superior position, which was neither intended by Zechariah nor is attested elsewhere in late Judaic literature. However, it fits in excellently with the total picture portrayed of the Qumran community.[64] Also it is not surprising that, at least in those texts so far accessible, the second messianic figure does not bear the appellation king, but alongside (דויד) צמח[65] and שבט[66] the title "prince of the whole community" (נשיא כול העדה).[67] In his position next to the highpriestly Messiah, the משיח אהרן, he is, however, chiefly called משיח ישראל;[68] in one place he also bears the designation משיח הצדק.[69] Really suggestive messianic texts, apart from mere references to the two Messiahs;[70] are CD, VII, 18ff.; XIX, 7ff.; I Q Sa II, 12ff.; I Q Sb V, 20ff. and various fragments from cave 4 of Qumran.[71]

The most characteristic and certainly for the Qumran fellowship the most decisive text is I Q Sa, II, 12–21. Here the eschatological feast of the redeemed Israel is described. Pride of place is given to Aaron, the Messiah; around him the priests are permitted to group themselves; then follows the Messiah of Israel, together with the heads of tribes, the heads of families, and the elders.[72] The representation of the day of salvation under the image of table fellowship is current elsewhere in late Judaism,[73] but what is characteristic here is the analogy the description affords to the fellowship meal of the Essenes,[74] and the so much emphasized superiority of the priestly group, on which account the highpriestly Messiah is allowed to give the blessing and at table to begin the meal.[75] The picture of the Messiah of Israel shows, moreover, extensive traditional features. The OT promises are applied to him;[76] he is regarded as being of the Davidic line,[77] as one whom God has adopted as son,[78] and to whom is entrusted the ultimate lordship,[79] who in the full power of the spirit exercises judgment,[80] and whose throne shall stand for ever and ever.[81] A special part is played by the idea of subjugating the enemy. The war against the "sons of Seth" or the "Kittim" is constantly alluded to, as is also the act of judging the heathen peoples.[82]

Although all this is found in many messianic texts, yet the so-called scroll of the war (1 QM) occupies a special position. With all the caution which is necessary in view of the present stage of research, the following may be said: this manuscript pictures the eschatological triumph over the sons of darkness, combining it with the widely developed tradition of the holy war. It is further presupposed that the people of Israel takes a part and that the services of the temple are properly carried out.[83] Since what is in question is a sacral rite, decisive functions, above all those of sacrifice, prayer and blessing, but also the ordering of the battle array, and the enheartening of the fighters, are assigned to the messianic high priest,[84] with the result that the "prince of the whole community" is noticeably pushed into the background,[85] though as ruler and captain he none the less takes part in the war. Here there is disclosed—setting aside the special position assigned to the high priest—an attitude which strongly reminds us of the Maccabeans and also suggests a certain approximation to the zealots.

We do not intend to discuss in detail the *Testaments of the Twelve Patriarchs*. This strange picture, in which the most diverse streams of influence in late Judaism are absorbed, bears not least the stamp of the theology of the Qumran fellowship.[86] In particular, the messianic ideas show a far-reaching agreement with the messianism of the Dead Sea discoveries.[87] In the *Testaments* also is to be found the juxtaposition of a high-priestly and of a royal Messiah. This is shown especially in the two hymns, *Test. Levi*, 18 and *Test. Jud.* 24; but in many other places too the two messianic figures are mentioned, and once again the messianic high priest occupies the superior position.[88]

143

If the Qumran texts, as a result of their doctrine of the two Messiahs and especially their total theological outlook, occupy a special position, in the *Psalm of Solomon* 17 we have a document of the highest value for the attestation of the almost unmodified continuing influence of the old Israelite messianic expectation.[89]

The psalm begins with an introductory passage praising God as the saviour and deliverer (vv. 1–3). The main part strikes up the theme of the Davidic kingship which it confirms (v. 4); yet God has delivered over the people to the ἁμαρτωλοί, the Hasmonean kings, on account of their disobedience and has destroyed the throne of David (vv. 5f.). He will now raise up against this ruling family a foreigner (ἄνθρωπος ἀλλότριος γένους ἡμῶν), the Roman Pompey, who will carry out a well-deserved punishment and judgment, because children of the covenant have allied themselves with mixed races, and have even persecuted and scattered the pious (vv. 7–10, 15–20).[90]

The second part of the psalm is introduced by the prayer for the coming of the son of David (v. 21), then goes on to speak of the Messiah seizing power, of the destruction of the heathen and sinners (vv. 22–25), of the assembling of the holy people (vv. 26–28) and of their reign over the Gentile world (vv. 29–31). There follows the striking portrait of the 'anointed of the Lord',[91] a through and through human figure,[92] distinguished by righteousness and the fear of God, who places his hope not in earthly power but in God, who is pure from all sin and therefore can maintain authority and effectively rule; who, however, possesses also the gift of the Spirit, so that he is able to preserve and to judge the flocks of the Lord God (vv. 32–43). There then follows in conclusion a blessing pronounced on all those who will have the privilege of living in those days, and the petition that God will soon bring this favour to His people Israel (vv. 44–46). Hence the following basic elements may be noted: the Messiah is the king of Israel, whose emergence and activity begins with the overcoming of his enemies and the establishment of his kingdom; his subjugation of hostile powers and sinners is effected less by warlike action than by his wondrous spiritual power;[93] the Messiah administers his kingly office in the fear of God and in righteousness.[94] The idea of the remnant, the motive of the holy war, and the high-priestly messianic figure are missing here.

Rabbinic literature shows in its oldest Tannaitic stratum a concept of the Messiah which is largely in agreement with *Ps. Sol.* 17.[95] Probably the oldest example is the 14th *berakha* of the 18th petitionary prayer: "Have mercy, O Lord our God, upon us Thy people and upon Jerusalem, Thy city, and upon Zion, the place of Thy glory, and upon Thy temple and Thy dwelling, and upon the kingship of the house of David, Thine anointed." We have here the conclusion of the eschatological prayers.[96] That we are here in the presence of a very ancient liturgical piece of tradition, which in the period after the destruction of the temple only received its final shape, is unquestionable; in date it is very close to the *Psalms of Solomon*.[97] In similar fashion other prayers expressed the messianic expectation.[98] In the Mishnah there are no traditional messianic passages, which, however, does not preclude the fact that the Tannaites concerned themselves with this hope; for in the post-Mishnah tradition the older elements can be relatively clearly distinguished from the specifically Amoraitic views.[99]

To the older conception belong the following features: the setting up of the ultimate kingdom on earth is an event in which God Himself as the גּוֹאֵל inaugurates the days of the Messiah, and brings about the dawning of the new aeon, the consummation of eternal salvation, which will bring to an end all servitude;[100] those peoples who rose in revolt against Jahwe and against His people, will be overcome;[101] Israel securely possesses the whole of the promised land, and the dispersed Jews will be brought back to their home land;[102] under the Messiah who rules over the chosen people and the Gentiles, all will live in peace and the fear of God.[103]

On the whole, this description corresponds to the account of the Messiah, traceable to old prophetic sources, which elsewhere the literature of the time discloses. What is perhaps striking is only the fact that the Messiah himself does not stand much in the foreground, and direct affirmations about his person are made but seldom, that the point of view is rather the messianic era itself which God brings into being.[104] In any event, however, the Messiah is a ruling figure;[105] reflections about a lowly or suffering Messiah are entirely lacking,[106] and only rarely is a priestly messianic figure alluded to.[107]

In addition to the Talmudic literature, we also have the

Targums which, although edited at a late date, preserve nevertheless ancient points of view. Particularly informative for the messianic expectation is the *Targum on the Prophets* of Jonathan ben Uzziel. It approximates quite closely to *Ps. Sol.* 17f. and also to the traditional rabbinic teachings we have just discussed. It shows almost no influence of the apocalyptic mode of thought. "The Messiah awaited by Jonathan is thus wholly included within the national and terrestrial messianic tendency: he is a man, he is a Jew, he is a holy rabbi, he is a mighty king of the time of consolation, he is the son of David promised to the pious Israelites."[108]

Within the same framework is also to be fitted, in spite of all their peculiarities, the attitude of the Zealots. An assessment of this group is certainly difficult because only indirect and not exactly impartial sources are at our disposal. For to a large extent we are forced to rely on Josephus,[109] who in his account of the Zealots is certainly not sufficiently just.[110] In any case the Zealots should not be regarded as mere revolutionaries and nationalist fanatics whose mentality is onesidedly controlled by political interests.[111] Their union under Judas the Galilean on the occasion of the census in the year A.D. 6, chiefly in association with the Pharisees, and their conduct during the decades up to the time of the Jewish war and the revolt under Hadrian,[112] can only be understood in the light of religious motives.[113] As their name indicates, they were concerned to foster a spirit of zeal, a zeal for Jahwe's law and sanctuary,[114] and a zeal for the realization of a certain ideal of what the people of God should be. They doubtless have connecting links with the Maccabean movement.[115] But the human action which is displayed in a holy war[116] remains an important factor along with others, and this differentiates the Zealots from the Maccabees, as far as eschatological expectations are concerned.[117] To what an extent they took into account the ideas of a messianic king and the dawn of the ultimate aeon, is shown equally by the royal entry of Menahem into Jerusalem in the year A.D. 66 and by the significance of the ambiguous oracle about world rule and about patiently waiting in the temple when it should be stormed by enemies.[118] Again this attitude is confirmed by the events of the years 132–135, when Simon ben Cochba[119] was installed and sanctified as the messianic king.[120]

Summary. It may be said that the messianic expectation of the OT prophets was essentially preserved in its main features right into the late Jewish period.[121] There is difference of views only in regard to particular points: first, in the conception of a high-priestly Messiah enthroned alongside the messianic king; then, as regards the way in which the enemies of Israel are to be overcome, which is sometimes seen to be effected by God's own initiative, or by a miraculous intervention of the Messiah, while in other cases it is brought about by the summoning of the pious to fight in a holy war; finally, in the personal attitude of the Messiah, where the type of piety prevailing at a given moment is broadened into an idealistic portrait.

Throughout, however, and this is the constant characteristic feature, the Messiah is a human figure, is a successor of David,[122] takes over a political kingdom and completes his task in the sphere of earthly realities.[123] Wherever the Messiah is spoken of —apart from those plainly indicated contexts where the messianic high priest is meant—it is always a question of this concept, which is unified and self-contained. The suggestion that in the pre-Christian era Messiah had become a generalized title of exaltation to denote the ultimate saviour, is an often repeated but by no means correct assertion.[124] Just as little may it be said that the "earthly-nationalistic" eschatology completely merged with the "apocalyptic-universalist" type[125] so that the title "Messiah" and the title "Son of man" became of equal significance.[126] It is true that within apocalyptic, the expectation of the Son of man occupies the same position as the messianic hope, but it has quite different roots and embraces a quite different complex of ideas. It is therefore necessary clearly to distinguish the two conceptions, and especially to reserve the title "Messiah" for one of them only.

Of course we should not overlook the fact that in individual instances there were connections between the kingly messianism and the apocalyptic eschatology.[127] But such connections must always be precisely determined and limited. Only in the Similitudes of the Ethiopic Enoch was the idea of the Messiah fully merged with that of the Son of man.[128]

But this was not the only and can hardly have been the prevailing conception of apocalyptic literature. 2 Esdras and the Syriac Baruch contain quite a different solution, inasmuch as they assign to the messianic kingdom the character of an interim kingdom between this and the coming aeon, hence attempt to come to terms with traditional eschatology by the conception of a provisional and an ultimate time of salvation.[129]

Thus not even apocalyptic literature offers a unified picture, let alone late Judaic literature as a whole. It is clear that apocalyptic, so far as we can judge, always made certain borrowings from traditional eschatology, but on the other hand it must be noted that the old style messianism long preserved its features uninfluenced by apocalyptic expectations, and for the study of the NT period must certainly be presupposed as existing in its original structure.

2. The Significance of the Messianic Concept in the Life of Jesus

How did it come about that the title and the concept of the kingly Messiah were applied to Jesus? In view of what we have been able to establish as the standard concept of the Messiah prevailing in the first century A.D., it is by no means a matter of course that this description should have been applied to Jesus. The suggestion that it had to be used in order to make at all clear to the Jews the function and the dignity of Jesus as the saviour whom God had sent,[130] is not quite correct, for there was a whole number of other concepts which could have been used, and which in fact were taken advantage of, because they were at least nearer to the work and proclamation of Jesus than was the expectation of the Messiah;[131] and, as a generalized title, "Messiah" was just not in use at that period.

Older scholars took into account the "earthly-nationalistic" concept of the Messiah prevalent in Judaism at that time, and tried to answer the question: In what way did Jesus assimilate and modify this expectation? Various opinions were expressed, as, for example, that Jesus "spiritualized" and "deepened" this hope;[132] or again it was asserted that He Himself combined it with the ideas of the Son of man and the servant of the Lord;[133] sometimes it was also said that messiahship could only be ascribed to Him in a proleptic sense, since the conception was not really applicable to the earthly life of Jesus.[134]

In contrast, today critics are concerned to show that the necessary modifications for the understanding of the NT messianic title belong already to late Jewish tradition, especially the combination with the Son of man idea and the idea of suffering.[135] But again it has rightly been required that NT statements about the Messiah and the Son of man together with their background should be separately investigated.[136]

Wellhausen may well have been right in considering that the combination of the messianic concept with that of the Son of man was a correction of the messianic theory made subsequently by the primitive church, but he also takes into account the possibility that the Jewish messianic concept may have played a certain part in the life of Jesus.[137] Hence the decisive factor is the *interpretatio christiana* of the Judaic messianic idea.[138] It must be borne in mind that we have here to do with a whole complex of ideas,[139] and that therefore the title of Messiah could not be used at will, nor could particular traits of the concept be changed indiscriminately. What modifications the conception of the kingly Messiah gradually underwent, what were the decisive reasons for these changes, and what new elements were merged, are matters which must be investigated and proved. Here there are a number of difficult problems, which so far have hardly been dealt with, or only inadequately so.[140] In what follows, an attempt is made to mark out a few pointers.

To answer the question what significance the concept of the kingly Messiah had in the life of Jesus,[141] we must consider to what extent its characteristic features have left traces in the proclamation and the work of Jesus,[142] secondly, whether the messianic hope was applied to Him and lastly, how the accusation of Jesus on the grounds that He was a pretendant to messiahship must be assessed.

The discussion of the relation of Jesus to traditional Jewish messianic expectations may be reduced in the main to the question of His attitude towards the Zealots. If He had any sympathy with political hopes centred on this world, this would have been clear from His attitude towards that party; further, zealotic features would have been observable in His own work.

The question whether Jesus might have used force for the realization of His aims already played an important part in the research of Reimarus.[143] At the end of the twenties in our own century this opinion was renewed and assumed importance through the works of Robert Eisler and Joseph Klausner.

Eisler tried to prove on the basis of the Slavonic Josephus documents that Jesus Himself had given occasion for a directly zealotic movement: He had indeed at first appeared as the preacher of a better righteousness and of non-resistance, and hoped in a wondrous divine deliverance, but after the sending forth of His disciples He was disappointed with the success of this action, then He decided to embrace homelessness and poverty and to engage in a new exodus, and finally on the occasion of the appeal to the people of Jersualem He became involved in a marked zealotic manner of procedure on the part of His disciples, and on this account He was condemned by the Romans to crucifixion.[144]

Apart from the methodologically wrong structure, it must be observed that even the Slavonic text of Josephus will not bear the burden of proof here assigned to it, and by no means has the value of a historically reliable and original witness.[145]

Klausner gives a different account of zealotic tendencies in the life of Jesus;[146] according to him, Jesus at His baptism attained a consciousness of messiahship; "to be sure, Jesus the Galilean who had grown up in the country of origin of Zealotism, thought at first, like every Jewish Messiah, of this way" (p. 345); but then there penetrates into His mind a more strongly religious ideal of the messiahship, vividly illustrated in the story of the temptations, which, however, "was not merely purely spiritual, but also material and political, hence thoroughly Jewish and messianic" (p. 417); while it is true that open revolt against the Romans was not part of His plan, He decided to cleanse the temple and claimed messianic dignity and functions; He was therefore accused of rebellion, and condemned by Pilate.

Here it is noted that a messianic concept which did not include a this-worldly political aspect was utterly inconceivable; but the attempt to represent in this way the relation of the inner attitude of Jesus and His claim to Zealotism and to indicate on these lines the grounds of His condemnation is, however, not tenable.

And the question becomes all the more pressing: Is the theory of royal messianism at all capable of elucidating the mystery of the person and work of Jesus? Although recently Brandon has assumed as a matter of course that it is, and, even if more cautiously than Eisler, has reckoned with a zealotic element in the procedure of Jesus at Jerusalem, all this is by no means certain.[147] When, on the other hand, Van der Loos, while taking seriously the this-worldly political character of messianism in the Judaism of that time, yet stresses the completely "unpolitical" character of the Kingdom of God which Jesus proclaims and of the claim to messiahship which He raises, regarding in fact the separation of religion and politics as the great original work of Jesus, this again is not quite evident for we have no sort of proof that Jesus transformed stereotyped concepts in this way.[148]

There can be no question that Jesus had in fact to face and deal with the messianic hope of His time. This has been sufficiently emphasized by Cullmann; but again it is doubtful whether Zealotism and the expectation of a kingly Messiah were such a personal temptation for Jesus as he assumes.[149] In order to be in a position to obtain a useful conclusion in the matter, the relevant synoptic texts must be briefly discussed.

The mention of some disciples of Jesus who obviously had formerly been Zealots,[150] does not mean much in the matter under discussion, for there were to be found among the disciples members of the most varied groups and classes, and Jesus accepted both the passionate enemies of the Romans and those, such as the tax-collectors, who were prepared to collaborate with foreign rule.[151] Also the suggestion of a possibly zealotic rising which was suppressed by Pilate (Lk. 13:1-3) is unfruitful.[152]

On the other hand, in Mk. 12:13-17 parr. with the census question a specifically zealotic problem is brought before Jesus. The party of the Zealots had of course been founded in the year 6 A.D. at the time of the assessment and first census levy. The opponents wished to coerce Jesus into adopting a direct political attitude. But He evades the alternative placed before Him. He gives an answer which contains no politico-religious programme, but instead advises man to exercise responsibility and right obedience both towards God and in the transient order of this world.[153] A specifically zealotic attitude can hardly on the basis of this passage be imputed to Jesus.

Did he even radically dissent from Zealotism? Many have understood the obscure saying about violence, Matt. 11:12,[154] in this sense: the phrase ἡ βασιλεία τῶν οὐρανῶν βιάζεται and ἁρπάζουσιν αὐτήν have been understood in the sense of the use of violence in the attempt to bring forcibly to pass the setting up of God's kingdom on earth, and βιασταί has been interpreted as a condemnatory description of the Zealots.[155] But there are difficulties in the way of this interpretation. The linguistic indications would suggest less the thought of a use of violence in order to bring about the kingdom of God than that of a hostile attack on the kingdom of God;[156] if so, then the saying relates to the earthly adversaries of Jesus, [157] perhaps even to demonic opponents.[158]

If the census question and the saying about violence cannot be made to support any thesis on the question, neither do we have in the gospels the reflection of any definite reaction of Jesus to the Zealots, such as we have regarding His relation to the Pharisees. Nevertheless, it remains to be seen whether there are not to be found both in His discourse and His actions certain traces of zealotic conceptions.

Quite recently Otto Betz has proposed, assuming the last-mentioned exegesis of the text, to derive from this saying about violence a quite positive reference of Jesus to the concept of the holy war; he suggests that with the mission and work of Jesus the holy war has begun, and we see the outburst of the attack on the kingdom of God; the βιασταί are said to be both spiritual powers and earthly rulers, and Jesus "with word and deed leads the holy war for the defence and establishment of the kingdom of God".[159] In a similar way he interprets the saying about the attack on the house of the strong man, Matt. 12:25–29, the saying about the bringing of a sword, Matt. 10:34, and even the Matthean version of the saying about the sign of Jonah, Matt. 12:38–40, in which connection he regards Jonah as the champion who overcomes the power of chaos, and correspondingly the Son of man as the one who for three days and nights must go down into the abode of the enemy, in order to seize and judge the latter on his own ground—this being only subsequently brought into relation with the death and resurrection of Jesus.[160]

However, certain objections to this thesis must be made. The texts adduced as proofs from the Qumran writings may indeed help to elucidate some points of detail, but show quite decisive divergences: thus there is not the slightest analogy in the story of Jesus to the preparation of the Qumran community for the holy war by the strictest ritual cleansing.[161] Then the holy war of the sect is no doubt a struggle with earthly and supernatural powers, but is also in every case a concrete summons to arms and an equally concrete military action; the

theory of a holy war conducted by Jesus alone, and supposed
to consist in His preaching, miracles and forgiveness of sins,[162]
has no parallels and can only be regarded as a completely
devious spiritualization of the whole conception. Hence it is
impossible to speak of a holy war in regard to Matt. 11:12,
although it must be agreed that in fact eschatological con-
frontations and struggles are alluded to. Matt. 12:25, 29 (par.
Mk. 3:23–25, 27) is figurative and hence no inferences for the
concept of a holy war as the aim of Jesus can be made.[163]
But in Matt. 10:34 it must be asked whether Jesus may not
have been thinking of a real fight with the sword, especially
as this logion stands in a certain relationship to the word about
the two swords in Lk. 22:36–38.

Although Matt. 10:34 shows a number of specifically Matthean peculiarities, the ending with its βαλεῖν εἰρήνην ἀλλὰ
μάχαιραν is certainly more original here than in the parallel
text (Lk. 12:51).[164] The meaning of βάλλειν may be determined
by a fixed turn of phrase and correspond to the rabbinic
הֵטִיל שָׁלוֹם.[165] With the "casting of the sword" it is, however, not
meant that Jesus puts into the hands of His disciples the
instrument of war; the implication is rather that with the
coming of Jesus the ultimate age of peace has not yet dawned,
but instead the last struggle has broken out.[166] In what way
this struggle is to be carried on is not stated, but the fact that
now more than ever is the time of confrontation, is decisive.
μάχαιρα in its antithesis to εἰρήνη must denote every kind of
dispeace.[167] The disciples are involved in this struggle, but
are not themselves being summoned to a holy war,[168] if indeed
the saying, whose style is moulded by characteristic expressions
and concepts, is to be preserved from excessive reinterpreta-
tion.

Not quite so plain is the passage, Lk. 22:36–38, which contains the mysterious saying about the two swords. For the
point here seems to be that the disciples are invited to carry the
sword, and that in fact weapons are found in their hands, this
being only further emphasized by the conduct of a disciple
at the time of the arrest. That, as far as Luke is concerned,
there is no question of a zealotic motive here can be securely
asserted and proved. It is sufficient to note the following points:
according to Luke's conception, the work of Jesus is a "symbol

of the time of salvation", and is therefore free from every assault of Satan, from struggle and suffering;[169] for this reason, the disciples could be sent forth without any kind of equipment, a point to which 22:35 expressly refers.[170]

Lk. 22:36 indicates that now with the passion of Jesus the time of affliction for the disciples is beginning.[171] For Jesus Himself what scripture says about Him is now to be fulfilled (v. 37), but the threat is directed also to His own, for according to v. 31 Satan intends to sift the followers of Jesus. In v. 36 the allusion to buying a sword can only be meant metaphorically,[172] for the actual use of the weapon at the time of the arrest, v. 49, is rejected by Jesus in v. 51; hence for the evangelist vv. 49–51 are intended to prevent a misunderstanding of the saying about the sword.[173]

It is in the light of all this that v. 38 also must be understood. As in 19:11 a clear misunderstanding on the part of the disciples is to be exposed.[174] ἱκανός ἐστιν, which can be interpreted in three different ways,[175] is therefore neither meant in an ironical sense (satis superque)[176] nor, so to speak, as a pedagogic intimation,[177] but is to be understood only as a formula for the breaking off of the conversation, and thus as a rejection of the answer given by the disciples, for which there are, if not quite exact, yet fairly close parallels.[178]

The idea that Luke is using a special source is as little probable for vv. 35–38 as for vv. 49–51; it must not be forgotten to what a large extent the evangelist has fused these sayings with his own conception. That he is working with transmitted material is, moreover, indisputable:[179] v. 35 uses the saying contained in Lk. 10:4a; in v. 37a Luke may have been seizing on an OT quotation much used in the community tradition of his time, as, in particular, the divergence from the Septuagint suggests, which elsewhere he follows, but the statement which introduces the quotation and v. 37b are certainly redactional;[180] v. 38, on account of its parallelism with 19:11 and its connection with 22:49–51, can only be considered as Lucan.[181]

There remains then v. 36, a saying which may neither be explained as resulting from a "quite special, never recurring situation and mood of Jesus",[182] nor from the outset be described as spurious.[183] It is true that in v. 36a we must admit a Lucan recasting, since this saying corresponds with v. 35; further, v. 36b is not smoothly connected with what precedes, as is clear from the ambiguous reference of ὁ μὴ ἔχων,[184] so that in v. 36a after ἀλλὰ νῦν ὁ ἔχων . . . there probably stood originally something else. We must conclude that this word probably does not belong to the context of the mission sayings and the directives for missionary work. But it is certainly conceived as a disciple-saying, and not only as general instruction for the procedure to be followed in times of apocalyptic woe, as is the case with Mk. 13:16. But what is the meaning of the invitation to buy a sword?

If we recollect that the cloak served several men conjointly as a covering for the night and must on no account be taken from them, as a pawn, for example,[185] the saying must signify that for the disciple of Jesus a situation much more severe than extremest poverty will arise, a situation, namely, in which his life itself is threatened. Hence the disciple is called upon to surrender what is left to the poorest,[186] and to be ready to stake his life. Thus the saying proves itself to be metaphorical, and must on no account be misunderstood in a zealotic sense, or as a straightforward command to the disciples to defend themselves.[187] For as the possession of a cloak merely is the sign of direst poverty, so the sword signifies an extreme threat to life.[188]

If specifically zealotic traits cannot be detected in Jesus, that does not of course in itself mean that the concept of the kingly Messiah can have had no meaning in His life, for already in Jewish tradition the warlike function of the messianic king was by no means an indispensable element.

Jesus may have accepted the image of the peaceful, lowly Messiah, as it is portrayed in Zech. 9:9f. The story of His entry into Jerusalem seems to suggest this. But caution is necessary at this point. It is fitting to take as a point of departure the whole complex Mk. 11:1–33. The story of the cursing of the fig tree and the discourse about the power of faith (vv. 12–14 and 19–25) may be detached with relative ease.[189] But this does not mean that the three other sections form an original unity.[190] Closely bound together are only the cleansing of the temple and the question of authority.[191] The procedure of Jesus in the temple precincts can only be understood as a symbolic action proclaiming judgment and punishment on the Jewish sanctuary if it is connected with the cursing of the fig tree, as it is in the present redactional context.[192]

155

Was it originally really a question of a "cleansing" of the temple? If so, the initiative would have to be understood as an attempt at cultic reform, so that Jesus, in view of the approaching kingdom of God, would have tried to establish a better outward form of the temple services. This interpretation, however, is not very probable in the light of the conduct of Jesus in other matters.

The observation that the action of Jesus took place, not in the sanctuary itself, but in the forecourt of the Gentiles—only there was the sale of sacrificial animals and the exchanging of money allowed—is the most ready indication of Jesus' intention: in this case the temple action would be best understood, as in fact is suggested in v. 17, as a parabolic action referring to the eschatological promise given to the Gentiles.[193]

Is the action messianic? This is often asserted, because both the renewal of the temple cult and the worship of the heathen were expected to characterize the messianic time.[194] But this is not, to say the least, quite clear, since both these features were part of Jewish eschatology, independently of the expectation of a messianic king.[195] A messianic meaning could only be proved in regard to this action of Jesus if a kingly proceeding and appearance were recognizable in other ways also. His action in the temple in itself need be nothing more than a prophetic action.[196] But is not a messianic interpretation commanded by the preceding story of the entry into Jerusalem?

It cannot be doubted that the church strongly reinterpreted this particular occurrence. This is shown firstly by the fact that v. 10 is an emphatically Christian interpretation; further, the story of the finding of the ass, v. 1b–6, was added only in the sphere of the Hellenistic church on the basis of Zech. 9:9 in the LXX.[197] What remains recognizable as the basic constituent is a greeting of Jesus by those keeping the feast, in which connection the εὐλογημένος ὁ ἐρχόμενος ἐν ὀνόματι κυρίου of the pilgrim psalm, 118:25f. was applied to Jesus.

If this is the oldest stratum and the earliest understanding of the event by the church, then the entry cannot have borne any messianic features, and again, it will hardly have caused a sensation, for otherwise the Romans would have taken immediate action and it would be difficult to conceive of Pilate being so hesitant about the arrest of Jesus.[198]

As far as the question of the connection between the

triumphal entry and the temple cleansing, followed by the challenge to Jesus' authority, is concerned, our conclusion must be that neither indications in the text, nor the very different development of the stories in tradition,[199] suggest that there was an original historical and essential link.[200] It would be preferable to ask whether the juxtaposition of the triumphal entry and the restoration of the cult might not have been the motive for the redaction which has combined these texts. But precisely Mark has combined the temple cleansing with the tradition of the accursed fig tree and has marked off these incidents from the triumphal entry; an association of the entry and the temple cleansing—if not original, at any rate pre-Marcan—is not excluded, but there are no plain indications of it.[201]

In any event, the conclusion must stand, that in the story of the entry on the one hand, and in the incidents of the temple cleansing and the challenge to the authority of Jesus, on the other, we have two separate pieces of tradition, neither of which suggest a messianic appearance of Jesus.

Are there any other texts at our disposal which might enable us to make a judgment as to the extent to which the concept of the kingly Messiah played a part in the earthly life of Jesus? Matt. 11:2(ff.) must not be adduced in this connection; the expression $\tau\grave{a}$ $\emph{ἔργα}$ $\tauο\hat{υ}$ $χριστο\hat{υ}$ is a secondary interpretation and presupposes the Christian Messiah concept.[202] In so far as the piece of tradition contained in Mk. 6:14b,15‖8:28 has preserved anything historically reliable, which need not be altogether doubted, it would seem that the people did not unreservedly view Jesus as the fulfiller of messianic expectation.[203]

How did matters stand in the circle of the immediate followers of Jesus? If anywhere at all, we shall find material for a judgment about this in the story of Peter's confession at Caesarea Philippi, Mk. 8:27–33. But here we have a difficult text containing strands. If the analysis made in an excursus is correct,[204] it might be possible to draw some inferences.

So much is plain, that the allusion to the Son of man concept and to suffering must be regarded as an interpretation added by the church, and that the seams of the narrative in vv. 30, 32 have an emphatically Marcan character. If further we may also regard vv. 27b–29 as an independent piece of tradition, then it is not impossible that in vv. 27a . . . 29b, 33 there has been preserved in the form of a biographical apophthegm an incident from the life of Jesus. Jesus repulses any hope of a realization of the messianic, kingdom through Himself as a φρονεῖν τὰ τοῦ ἀνθρώπου, and Peter is even scolded as being Satan because of his use of the title Messiah.

The word of v. 33 rejecting Peter, which would not be transmissible in isolation from the situation, cannot have arisen in the post-resurrection period.[205] Its connection with vv. 27a . . . 29b is therefore most probably to be regarded as original. This is, moreover, confirmed by the fact that even the present Marcan text contains a clear repudiation of Peter's confession, in so far as the title "Messiah" is subjected to the command of silence, and in any case is only accepted under the reservation that it involves suffering.[206] On the other hand, this means that even in this Christianized version the Jewish messianic concept stands in the background.[207]

Hence in this passage the process of Christianization is clearly discernible. The Jewish title of Messiah was as such not tolerable for Jesus and the first church, but in connection with the Son of man concept and the thought of suffering it was assimilated later and correspondingly transformed.

In close relation to the original version of the confession of Peter stands the third temptation of Jesus by Satan, Matt. 4:8–10‖Lk. 4:5–8. It is easy to recognize that the story of the temptations in the logia source is no homogeneous piece of tradition.[208] It is true that all three temptations are built up in the style of a disputation, and the devil is repeatedly repulsed with a word from scripture, but whereas in the first and second case (taking the order given in Matthew) Satan approaches Jesus with a scriptural quotation, and begins his remarks with εἰ υἱὸς εἶ τοῦ θεοῦ, these two features are lacking in the third temptation. Furthermore it is to be observed that the first two temptations presuppose the typically Hellenistic concept of the "Son of God", and are not really intended in a messianic sense,[209] whereas on the contrary in the third temptation the thought of the world rule of the messianic king is the theme.[210]

We may regard this third temptation as a piece of traditional material originating in the early Palestinian church; it is not by chance that we find as in Mk. 8:33 ὕπαγε σατανᾶ appearing.

Here again we see that the church, in this certainly being faithful to the attitude of Jesus Himself, rejected the idea of messianic world rule in the earthly political sense, and indeed regarded it as a possibility plainly contrary to the divine will.

In the Marcan version of Peter's confession, there is sharply outlined the later transformation of the messianic idea effected by the church. How could it undertake such an attempt at all, in view of the fact that Jesus so emphatically declined the title? The suggestion that this title of exaltation, as no other, is rooted in the OT and expresses the fulfilment of OT prophecy,[211] is certainly not false, but does not adequately explain the development. The church had a much more direct reason for assimilating the title of Messiah. For it is indisputable that Jesus was condemned and crucified as a messianic rebel, and that the concept of the kingly Messiah played a decisive role in the trial of Jesus.

On the basis of the conclusions reached so far, it can be said with confidence that the accusation, that Jesus emerged as a messianic pretender, was made quite falsely.[212] So far as we can see, the Jewish authorities took advantage of the popular movement which the appearance of Jesus brought into being, and perhaps also of His conduct in the temple,[213] in order to charge Him before the Romans with being a political insurgent.

The story of the passion handed down to us in Mk. 14f. despite its relatively detailed character is not very informative from a historical and juridical point of view.[214] The supposition that at the basis of this one continuously narrated report there lies a brief historical summary, which was shaped by no kerygmatic interest, but merely proposed to give the sequence of events,[215] is not very probable. No doubt the traditional story of the passion only very slowly grew to its present proportions and consisted to some extent, like most of the materials used by the evangelists, of particular bits of tradition. But already the earliest connected brief account of the passion was moulded by the preaching of the first church, and especially by the proof from prophecy.[216]

The passage, Mk. 14:55-64, so important for the development of the earliest Christology, which narrates the hearing before the high priest, is quite useless from the historical point of view. There is no reason to doubt that Jesus was taken into the high priest's palace and led before the Sanhedrim. But neither could the accusation there made against Him nor the answer which Jesus gave have been ascertained.[217] Further, it is by no means certain that the Jewish authorities pronounced a formal sentence of death of this kind; for it is not improbable that the sitting had a purely informal character, and was only intended to prepare the way for an accusation before the procurator.[218] The much discussed question as to the right of pronouncing a capital sentence in the time of Jesus[219] plays only a subordinate part, because it is possible that the Jews were in any case mainly concerned to bring about a political trial conducted by the Romans, in order to deliver Jesus over to the curse of death by crucifixion.

In essentials we have to rely on the report in Mk. 15:1–27 of the trial before Pilate and the execution.[220] Even though we can accept only relatively few details about the original sequence of events in this trial, nevertheless the decisive motives are clearly recognizable. Jesus was taken by the Jewish authorities before the procurator and accused of political rebellion.[221] Pilate must have been astonished at the prisoner and clearly hesitated to pronounce the sentence demanded. He yielded, however, since the Romans were compelled to proceed with severity against all messianic risings, and might not dispense with the collaboration of the Jewish authorities.[222] Thus in the event he pronounced the verdict customary in such cases. Jesus was condemned to death as a claimant to messiahship and was probably crucified immediately before the passover festival.

According to Roman custom the so-called *titulus* giving the reason for the sentence was drawn up and later nailed to the cross. In the understanding of the heathen, the messianic claim consisted in the attempt to achieve political independence, and kingly rule over the Jewish people. It is characteristic that in this connection the title "Messiah" was avoided, and likewise the fact that the mention was not of the "King of Israel" but of the "King of the Jews"; for ’Ισραήλ was the name by which the Jewish people described themselves, whereas ’Ιουδαῖοι was primarily the name by which the non-Jewish world called them, so that in the latter description there is no religious suggestion whatever.[223] It is very informative that the *titulus* in the mouth of the high priest and the scribes, Mk. 15:32, becomes ὁ χριστὸς ὁ βασιλεὺς ’Ισραήλ.[224]

There is not the slightest reason to doubt the historicity of the inscription on the cross.[225] The whole section, 15:1–20, which in its present form is a broad amplification of the leading thought ὁ βασιλεὺς τῶν Ἰουδαίων, shows how the primitive church accepted and developed this given circumstance.[226] Even the later Christianized messianic concept shows how the first church tried to deal with this very fact of the crucifixion of Jesus as a claimant to messiahship.

Summary. It must be concluded that in the life of Jesus any sort of indication of a zealotic tendency in thought or action is entirely lacking. In other respects too the concept of the kingly messiah had no significance for the work of Jesus; it is extremely probable in fact that Jesus Himself repudiated the messianic title. Moreover, His preaching and activity was little calculated to awaken messianic expectations. But on the other hand Jesus was falsely accused of messianic revolt. However the trial before the Jewish authorities developed, whatever solution must be adopted about the right of capital punishment, it is plain that the decisive sentence was decreed by the Roman procurator, and that Jesus was executed under political suspicion of being the "king of the Jews". The further history of the messianic title in the early church must be understood in the light of this twofold presupposition.

3. *The Messianism of Jesus in the Oldest Tradition*

In the very earliest times the concept and the title of Messiah were not applied to Jesus. This indeed contradicts the widespread opinion that the messianic faith of the early church was centred on the risen Christ and came into use on the basis of the Easter event.[227] For this opinion there can be quoted possibly some texts from the Acts of the Apostles which, however, cannot be accepted without hesitation as testimony to the oldest church tradition;[228] further, Peter's confession and the story of the transfiguration which, however, can hardly be appropriately explained as Easter stories.[229] The whole tradition of the gospels shows rather that in the beginnings of Christianity the concept of the Messiah was not used in reference to Jesus. If the absence of the title from the logia source can, if necessary, be explained on the grounds that there prevails here a one-sided interest in the Son of man Christology, yet the rest of the synoptic traditional material shows that the use of this predicate arose only sporadically and established itself under the influence of the gradually evolving Christology.

"Messiah" as a title of dignity, and equally the messianically understood titles of exaltation such as "Son of David" and "Son of God" can thus not be assumed for the very earliest period. Both the attitude of Jesus Himself as well as the fact of the false accusation will have caused the church to avoid in the first place the messianic conception.

But the question as to how, none the less, it could come about that primitive Christianity did eventually assimilate this conception becomes all the more pressing.[230] The oldest quotations give us a simple answer: the idea of the kingly Messiah was not taken up in its original form, but with a modification flowing from the influence of apocalyptic thought. And, further, the messianic concept was exclusively applied to the ultimate activity of Jesus, to His coming again, and to the hope of salvation connected with this.

The messianic status of Jesus was therefore not at first confessed in view of His resurrection and exaltation, but relatively to His authoritative action at the coming parousia. The statements about a kingly office of ruling were in fact best suited to this purpose, whereas to be made relevant to the exaltation and earthly work of Jesus they still required considerable modification. In this way the messianic predicates came into closest connection with the idea of the coming Son of man, for which apocalyptic literature itself provided a certain foreshadowing.[231]

In the small apocalypse of Mk 13 can still be plainly detected an opposition to every kind of this-worldly messianic hope. Earthly pseudo-Messiahs and pseudo-prophets are placed in contrast to the Son of man who is to come from heaven, Mk. 13:22, 26. At the same time 13:21 suggests that there is no need to give credence to all the rumours about the emergence of a Messiah here or there, because—and it is necessary to complete the sequence of thought in this way—the true Messiah as the heavenly Son of man will appear visibly to all.[232]

The equation of the Messiah with the Son of man is effected *expressis verbis* in the trial of Jesus before the high priest (Mk. 14:61f.) Here, as has been shown, various Christological elements are woven together,[233] which in itself is an indication that the text cannot be traced back directly to Jesus. But as regards the development of tradition, we must not place it too

late, for it represents in any event the oldest form of the
primitive Christian concept of Jesus as the (future) Messiah,
which very soon developed further in a different direction.

That we have here a Christological testimony stemming
from the Palestinian church[234] should be unquestionable.[235]
Details which emerge here are: the question of the high
priest which presupposes the kingly messianism,[236] then the
ἐγώ εἰμι of Jesus, the proclamation of the coming of the Son of
man on the clouds of heaven according to Dan. 7:13 and His
sitting on the right hand of God, from Ps. 110; 1a, both motives
held together by the link ὄψεσθε.[237]

The high priest's question is unambiguous. Jesus' answer
contains many difficulties. First the ἐγώ εἰμι at the beginning
must on no account be diminished in significance because of the
parallel in Matthew; the Marcan text suggests a plain unqualified affirmation, an unequivocal self-confession.[238] On the
other hand this ἐγώ εἰμι must not be detached from the context
of the question, and regarded as an independent formula.[239]
It is not here a question of a formula of introduction as in the
epiphany scene of Mk. 6:50, or as in the warning words of Mk.
13:6, but of a quite straightforward statement of identification,[240] where the predicate noun results from the preceding
question. Further, it is to be noted that the present tense of
εἰμί must on no account be unduly pressed, and placed in
emphatic contrast to the future tense which follows, so as to
suggest that Jesus in His answer means that at present He is the
Messiah, but in future will appear and act as the Son of man.[241]

The first objection to this view is that the text which certainly
goes back to Palestinian tradition can have had no verb at this
point; but a further and a substantial objection is that a quite
essential element of the concept of the messianic king is coupled
precisely with the statement about the coming Son of man,
namely, the "sitting at the right hand of power". The obscurity
of the ὄψεσθε κτλ springs of course from the combination of two
elements which are heterogeneous, but always characteristic
of the concepts of messiah and Son of man.

All this suggests, therefore, that the question about the
messianic character of Jesus put in v. 61 is answered in view of
His future action in such a way as to receive clarification from
the apocalyptic Son of man concept. Not only the coming on the
clouds, but also the ὄψεσθαι is a constitutive element in the

Son of man expectation, so that, as in Mk. 13:21,26, the thought
is that of a return of Jesus from heaven visibly to all the
world.[242]

This, therefore, means that the confession of the messiahship
of Jesus on the part of the primitive church was only possible
and conceivable in so far as it was placed in an apocalyptic
framework and horizon of thought, and made to refer exclusively to the ultimate activity of Jesus at the parousia.[243]
But in this outlook it was not necessary for the kingly office
to be in any way limited and deprived of its "political" features,
for there the thought is of a magisterial function exercised to the
fullest extent. A real transformation of the Jewish messianic
concept has not yet taken place; even the coupling with the Son
of man idea has a certain foreshadowing in Judaism. Thus the
early church could proclaim the messianic status of Jesus even
to the Jews without using from the outset a completely different
and as far as possible spiritualized idea and thus depriving
themselves of any possibility of understanding.[244]

If this application of the messianic idea to the Jesus who is to
return is once appreciated, then it is easier to understand how
there could arise that new understanding of the title "Messiah"
which was soon to prevail, especially its reference to the risen
and exalted Lord.[245]

The messianic title in Acts 3:20, 21a, referring to Jesus'
eschatological work, appears independently of the Son of man
idea but is none the less framed in an apocalyptic context of
thought. It cannot be disputed that we have here a very old
tradition.[246]

The question of its origin has been vigorously dealt with by
Bauernfeind in his analysis of the tradition lying behind it. He
sees in the whole section, Acts 3:19–25, an ancient tradition
concerning Elijah, according to which Elijah is supposed to be
the prophet promised by Moses and to have a messianic status
himself.[247] But this is certainly not quite correct.

Vv. 22ff. at all events go back to Luke, and equally v. 21b
must be ascribed to him; moreover, in v. 19 the first part of the sentence must be Lucan in its phrasing.[248] But not even the section,
vv. (19a) 19b–21a, which the author of the Acts of the Apostles
took over with its characteristic idiom, can be understood
as a completely homogeneous unity. In so far as we come
upon any elements which have their parallels in the Elijah

164

tradition, they are limited to v. 21a; here it is a question of the reception into heaven and of the ἀποκατάστασις πάντων.[249]

As a matter of fact the idea of the eschatological prophet was applied to Jesus, but the expectation of Elijah played no decisive part in this.[250] Even in Acts 3:21a there are merely two individual motives at work. Hence we cannot assume the existence of a stereotyped "Elijah" text, in which it would have only been necessary for an editor to change the name. Moreover, v. 20 has absolutely nothing to do with the expectation of an eschatological prophet.

The "times of refreshing" denote the time of salvation following upon the time of apocalyptic woes.[251] They come "from the presence of the Lord", and are therefore, in accordance with the best apocalyptic thought, a saving good which is held in readiness in heaven.

It is easily discernible that we have here an emphatically Judaic manner of expression; we may even accept that the text has a Semitic source, to which in particular the characteristically broken sentence construction in vv. 20a/20b points.[252] The second half of the sentence in v. 20 treats of the parousia: "He (i.e. the Lord or God) will send the Christ appointed for you." Hence the function of the Jesus who is to come again is that of the messianic king; as such He has been chosen by God beforehand.[253] He too is in heaven, standing in readiness like the saving good of the new aeon, and God will at some time "send" Him.[254] The statements of v. 21a are then linked to this.

The future Messiah chosen by God is the historical Jesus, whom the heavens must now receive until the breaking forth of the eschatological event.[255] The χρόνοι ἀποκαταστάσεως πάντων, which according to Mal. 3:23 must represent an epoch preceding the ultimate aeon, are of course in the context of v. 20 to be referred to the consummation itself,[256] hence are identical with the καιροὶ ἀναψύξεως.[257]

Just as essential as a discussion of the features contained in the text is a consideration of what is missing: Acts 3:20, 21a contains not the slightest allusion to the idea of exaltation. Here we are confronted again by the intermediate character of the post-resurrection status of Christ, to which we have already referred. The being received into heaven of v. 21a is understood on the lines of the translations in the OT, as is especially plain in this passage, hence it is regarded as a temporary and quickly passing condition.[258] Thus far the affirmations of v. 21a can be smoothly integrated with those about eschatological messianism in v. 20.

A further text which brings the messianic status into connection with the eschatological action of Jesus is the description of the world assize in Matt. 25:31-46. It is true that here the title Messiah is not used, but the absolute ὁ βασιλεύς is taken in the same sense. It is clear that this piece of tradition in its present form cannot go back to Jesus Himself, but reveals both characteristic elements of primitive church Christology, and also features of Matthean editorship.[259]

If we attempt to separate traditional from editorial component parts, we must conclude that Matthean characteristics —reserving judgment for the moment about v. 31—are essentially related to phrasing and subordinate motives, that nevertheless the real traditional nucleus must belong to the early Palestinian primitive church; for although this picture of a world judgment in every respect fits excellently into the Christology and eschatology of Matthew's gospel,[260] none the less it contains many ancient elements.

This is shown, on the one hand, by the basic apocalyptic outlook which is suggested especially by the concept of the forensic judgment on all the nations and by the motive of the pre-existence of the βασιλεία (v. 34) promised as an inheritance to the elect; on the other hand, by the Christology itself. It is thus quite impossible to assume as a basis a Judaic text, which, originally referring to God, has secondarily been transferred in reference to Jesus.[261]

No doubt Jewish theology is familiar with the thought that works of love are accounted to the pious as if they had done them to God Himself,[262] but in our text it is precisely not a question of works which man can do for his own justification, and to which he may refer in the presence of God.[263] Also the thought here expressed of a solidarity of Jesus with the poor and suffering is specifically Christian, and no traces of it are to be found either in late Judaism or elsewhere.[264]

Further, the address κύριε which appears in vv. 37, 44 was not usual in reference to God, and is connected with the primitive Christian use of the address "Lord" in reference to Jesus as the One who is to return again as judge.[265] The idea that the absolute "the king" as a title of the Messiah was not customary,[266] is not absolutely certain as far as Jewish tradition is concerned,[267] and is incorrect in regard to later primitive Christian literature.[268]

But also in this early piece of tradition, Matt. 25:31ff., it must be a description of the Messiah, as is clear from the context,[269] and indeed it is applied to the eschatological work of Jesus. There is evident here the same connection of the concept of the Messiah with the apocalyptic tradition, and in particular with the figure of the Son of man, as is found also in Mk. 14:61f. For this reason it is questionable whether the mention of the Son of man in v. 31 is so incongruous as is often supposed, and whether it must necessarily be viewed as a Matthean interpretation.[270] The juxtaposition of the titles of exaltation "Son of man" and "king" (Messiah) is not surprising in this description of the world assize; rather it is well grounded both essentially and as regards the development of tradition.

As a testimony to the early Christian use of the title of Messiah in reference to the parousia of Jesus there must be adduced finally the Revelation of John. In this NT document the title of Messiah occurs four times.[271]

In Rev. 11:15, 12:10 mention is made of the kingdom of God and "His Messiah"; the ultimate victory is celebrated in advance, congruously with the style of the eschatological hymns we have here.[272] Nothing is said about the relation between the rule of God and that of His Messiah; what is clear is simply that the messianic title in these texts denotes the eschatological function of Jesus.

In Rev. 21 the word "Messiah" does not occur. It is also easy to discern that the underlying description of the time of salvation—it is a question of vv. 1–8 and 15–21—sketches a markedly theocratic picture of ultimate blessedness. But in vv. 22–27, there is mentioned along with God the ἀρνίον and in a way which is especially characteristic of this author; similarly in vv. 9–14 are mentioned the "bride" and the "apostles of the Lamb". We cannot speak here of a messianic concept in the traditional sense.

But in the previous chapter, Rev. 20, the idea of the kingly Messiah is taken up in the form of the messianic interim kingdom which is known also in Jewish apocalyptic. As the ultimate Messiah Jesus reigns for a thousand years over those members of His Church who were awakened at the time of the first resurrection

(20:4-6).[273] Then follows the onset of Gog and Magog, the last judgment and the establishment of the final reign of God.

In view of the prior history of messianism in the framework of late Jewish tradition, it is not surprising that such a conception found entrance also into primitive Christianity, once the eschatological messianic character of Jesus had been established. It may be asserted, even though testimonies as a whole are not numerous, that this doctrine of the interim kingdom was not the original and normal conception of Jesus' eschatological messianic work; not even Rev. 11:15, 12:10 reflect this particular idea. The attempt was made to assimilate the original and purely this-worldly form of messianism, though it clearly did not succeed in establishing itself.[274]

Summary. It must be noted that the primitive Palestinian church at first completely avoided the concept of the kingly Messiah, then, however, though within the framework of an apocalyptic outlook, assimilated it and applied it to the ultimate work of Jesus. In this process there took place, in many ways, an absorption with the expectation of the coming Son of man; at least there was a transference of specific characteristic traits of the apocalyptic hope of salvation to Jesus as Messiah. In one special instance the concept of a messianic interim kingdom was adopted. The messianic status of Jesus has at first nothing at all to do with the Easter event.

4. *Jesus as Messiah in the Context of the Concept of Exaltation*

In the texts just discussed the traditional Jewish concept of the messianic king was applied to the eschatological work of Jesus and only to that. For this there are further examples which are to be discussed in the chapters on the "Son of David" and the "Son of God". We are alluding to designations of exaltation which in their origin belong to the complex of ideas concerning the messianic king; accordingly they were adopted by the early church in a messianic sense and at first only related to the coming again of Jesus. The whole hope of salvation in the earliest days of Christianity was focused on the imminent eschatological event; the earthly work and the resurrection of Jesus were conceived only as a prelude to this; His being taken away was a transient state of affairs, which was soon to be ended for the church severely afflicted with the "woes of the latter days".

development

But it was bound to happen that the consciousness of a delay in the parousia and the gradual extinction of hope in a quick return of Jesus should produce an essential transformation in Christology and eschatology. The fact that faith and hope did not collapse as a result of the failure of the parousia to materialize shows, however, to what an extent the Christians were inspired by the salvation already realized through the life and resurrection of Jesus, as also by the experience of His living presence through the Holy Spirit. But they had yet to explain this theologically. A decisive step in this direction was the formation of the concept of exaltation.[275] It must be observed that the oldest tradition of the Palestinian church was unfamiliar with the thought of an enthronement of the Jesus who had ascended to heaven, and of a heavenly reign until the time of the parousia.

It has already been shown that the introductory verse of Ps. 110 became the *leitmotif* of the concept of exaltation; it was also shown that this thought of exaltation was very soon combined in a special way with the Kyrios idea.[276] On the other hand, it is clear that the sitting at the right hand of God was a constituent element in kingly messianology and thus it is easy to see that when the concept of exaltation was developed the idea of the ultimate messianic dignity and function of Jesus was applied to the risen Lord who had been carried away into heaven. Accordingly, it was thought, Jesus did not first enter on His kingly office at the end of the age, after the period of a temporary reception into heaven, but was enthroned before the heavenly powers immediately after His ascension into heaven,[277] and therewith took over His royal functions. He has not yet appeared visibly and powerfully to men, but His church recognizes and knows in Him, now already, the lord and the king of the whole world.

Therefore what we see here is not the detachment and further development of one single motive only in messianology—namely the sitting at the right hand of power—rather the transforming process has embraced the whole concept of the Messiah. But it should be noted that the specifically Jewish basic conception of messianism has been preserved at the one decisive point: a real lordship is bound up with the messianic office; at the same time, of course, the realization of the kingly lordship over the earth is first subordinated to a second period in the royal work of Jesus.[278] One other factor persisted, namely, the idea that the messianic office is undertaken by a human being and by a successor of David.[279] But very new and different elements are combined with the conception of the heavenly lordship. Just as the belief in the messianic function of Jesus at the parousia could be related to the Son of man conception, so the messianic theory, as applied to the exalted Lord, enters into a special combination with the Kyrios title.[280] This is precisely the case in regard to the two texts which use the title "Messiah" in the context of the concept of exaltation, namely Mk. 12:35–37a and Acts 2:36.

But the application of messianic conceptions to the exalted One goes far beyond these two texts and recurs especially where the ancient title "Son of God", still messianically understood, is ascribed to the exalted One.[281] Only through this transformation and the newly developed associations was a real christianization of the kingly messianology effected, for in combination with parousia expectations the Jewish concept, in an apocalyptically modified form, was taken over without essential change.

For the two texts which contain the messianic title as a description of the exalted Lord, the result of our previous inquiry may be recapitulated: in Mk. 12:35–37a, ὁ χριστός must not be understood as a generalized idea; it is a question of the equivalence of this title with the Kyrios predicate. The messianic affirmation of Ps. 110:1 is related to the exalted One.[282] Conversely, "Son of David" is detached from its traditional equation with the title "Messiah" and as a description of the status of the earthly Jesus is differentiated from the appellations of the exalted One.[283] In Acts 2:34–36, in a passage drawing conclusions from the citation of Ps. 110:1, the Kyrios title and the Christos title are clearly applied to the exalted One (v. 36). This cannot be regarded as a characteristic of Lucan theology, since it even contradicts the use of the Christos title elsewhere in Luke.[284]

The ascription to Jesus of messianic dignity through the idea of His heavenly enthronement may not, as has been stressed earlier, be placed at the beginning of the development and associated with the Easter experience. Where is it to be located in the process of developing tradition? On the one hand, it cannot be overlooked that it has markedly Jewish presuppositions; on the other, the combination with the Kyrios concept discloses a plain Hellenistic factor, for the application of Ps. 110:1 to Jesus was only possible on the basis of the LXX text.

Thus we shall at least be able to say that the concept of exaltation became especially effective in the sphere of early Hellenistic Judaic Christianity, and won a home there. Since the sitting at the right hand of God was applied in the oldest Palestinian tradition to the ultimate function of Jesus, it would not be altogether impossible that this development was already completed in the earliest church. The passage Col. 1:12f. might best be chosen as possibly suggesting an old Palestinian affirmation as its basis; but clearly there is here only a consciously archaizing liturgical stylization.[285] In the case of Rom. 1:3f. a primitive Palestinian tradition is not to be thought of on account of the special conception of the Davidic sonship and its combination with the concept of exaltation.[286] The association with the belief in the heavenly lordship of Jesus especially argues against a beginning of the development within Palestinian Christianity.[287]

It must be borne in mind also that the Christology of the earliest church was decisively moulded by the Son of man theory; this was considerably broadened to include the earthly work of Jesus and even His suffering, but failed to absorb the motive of exaltation, which would be difficult to understand if the concept of the exaltation of Jesus had been current on Palestinian soil. So we are led to the conclusion that the application of the messianic idea to the exalted Lord must have been a specific theologumenon of the early Hellenistic Judaic Christian community. Earlier essays in this direction need not be basically disputed, but can only have had the significance of a preparation.[288]

If messianism was first applied to the future work of Jesus and was only secondarily extended to include His present work in heaven, it would not be impossible that, at a still later stage, there was a similar "backdating" of the messianic dignity to the earthly work of Jesus.[289] But the inclusion of the life of Jesus in the confession of His messiahship cannot be sufficiently explained in this way. It is especially difficult if we regard the concept of exaltation as a specific feature of the Hellenistic church; for there the application of the messianic title to the earthly Jesus had played a part very early, especially as a certain time was required for the ossification into a cognomen which was beginning in the pre-Pauline period. The application of the messianic title to the earthly Jesus cannot therefore have taken place by a process of progressive transference to an earlier phase, rather other motives must have been at work. The possibility of a complex use of the messianic concept in the earliest church must be allowed for.

Summary. It must be concluded that the discernible transformation of the messianic idea is connected with the development of the thought of exaltation, while at the same time it is also influenced by the Kyrios title. The use of the messianic title with reference to a heavenly enthronement of Jesus, only after which there will follow at the end of time an establishment of the kingdom on earth, is thus a development which must be imputed to Hellenistic Judaic Christianity.

5. *The Connection of the Passion-Tradition with the Christos Title*

The story of the passion belongs to the oldest part of the gospel tradition. It has come down to us in Mark in a relatively early form and, moreover, the older and later material can in this account be well distinguished from each other. This does not need to be demonstrated in detail here. What characterizes the oldest report of the passion is, as has already been suggested, the consistent use of proof from scripture.[290] The object was to learn to understand the suffering and death of Jesus, which was at first completely incomprehensible to the disciples, in the light of the OT, and on the basis of Biblical testimony to explain it as a divinely willed, necessary happening. The proof from prophecy has been called "the formal principle of the earliest Christian theology",[291] but it must be added that to this formal principle the material principle of scriptural fulfilment indissolubly belongs.

From a Christological point of view none of the Jewish ideas of a bearer of salvation are assimilated in the oldest account of the passion, not even that of the suffering servant.[292] The quotations and the presentation remind us most strongly of the suffering righteous one,[293] but this has to do with an ideal of piety, not with a concept of salvation. This is very significant for the attitude of the early church: the centre of gravity for Christology lay in the expectation of the parousia, even the resurrection of Jesus considered as a foreshadowing of ultimate events belonged less to the story of the passion than to the final eschatological drama; His suffering and death did not stand at the centre of the Christian confession, even though the church had to account for it, and in fact with the help of proof from prophecy overcame its offensiveness.

In this respect it is important to observe, as a matter of form history, that the passion story from the start owes its structure not to missionary preaching, but obviously had its life-situation in the cultic reading of scripture.[294] It is not intended thereby to limit the importance of the passion tradition for the earliest church—its broad development and early cohesion, as well as its far-reaching influence could not otherwise be explained—but in Christology its position is dependent on the primary confession of faith in the eschatological work of Jesus.

It is significant for the oldest stratum of the passion tradition,[295] that a Christological title is completely missing. Only the piece of tradition contained in Mk. 14:55-64, which was added later and was probably originally independent, plainly expressed the eschatological hope in the return of Jesus as Son of man and Messiah, and in the composition of Mk. 14 there were later added two statements about the suffering of the Son of man.[296]

Now the inscription on the cross ὁ βασιλεὺς τῶν 'Ιουδαίων[297] belongs to the basic part of Mk. 15, and it is instructive to see how in Mk. 15:1-20, 32 this has received emphatic amplification. The passage represents a broadening of the still discernible older report contained in vv. 1, 3-5 . . . 15b.[298] The later constituents are thus the confession of Jesus in v. 2, the Barabbas scene in vv. 6-15a, and the mocking of Jesus in vv. 16-20. It is not necessary to discuss here the previous history and the historical value of these sections.[299] The *leitmotif* is the four times repeated "King of the Jews", in vv. 2, 9, 12, 18, foreshadowing the inscription on the cross.

From the formal point of view it could be said that this theme has been elaborated in a number of variations. Denounced by the Sanhedrim, Jesus stands before the procurator as the alleged king of the Jews, then before the criminal Barabbas, next before the people and finally before the Roman soldiery, and constantly the accusation is repeated. In addition, in v. 2 Jesus has Himself admitted this dignity.[300] Hence it is all the plainer that the purpose of the section is to throw into relief,

by means of several "scenes of contrast",[301] the actual kingship of Jesus. Although He is accused of rebellion, equated with
a criminal, rejected by the people and taunted by the soldiers,
yet all must recognize His true dignity, even though they do so
in a state of dazed ignorance. The account is completed by v. 32
where the chief priests and scribes likewise deride the crucified
but replace the profane expression "King of the Jews" by the
terms which convey the Jewish messianic hope: ὁ χριστὸς ὁ
βασιλεὺς Ἰσραήλ.

That this whole section in its present form belongs to a later
stage of tradition, it is easy to discern in view of such an amplification of the motive; this is also confirmed by the fact that in
Mk. 15:1–20 there is no attempt at allusions to the OT. If the
stereotyped report of the passion was concerned, through
its use of proof from scripture, to dissipate the scandal, here
the crucifixion of Jesus as "King of the Jews" has acquired an
eminent theological significance.

In Mk. 15:1–20 we may recognize the turning point in the
interpretation of the messianic character of the earthly Jesus.
If in the earliest church the title Messiah, on account of its
this-worldly political aspect, was strictly avoided in regard
to the earthly life of Jesus, and was assigned to Jesus only in the
apocalyptic context of His office at the parousia, now the fact
that He was crucified as "King of the Jews" begins to have its
effect.[302] Thus is to be explained that, alongside the eschatological use of the title and its transformation by the concept of
exaltation, very soon also the passion tradition and the title
Christos became woven together. In certain cases a clear interpretation is still necessary, as is found even in the late redactional adaptation of Peter's confession, Mk. 8:27–33, where v. 31
expressly refers to the suffering and resurrection of the Son of
man.[303]

The passion tradition in characteristic fashion not only gave
new meaning to the title Messiah, but to a certain extent
influenced equally the Son of man sayings, so that here there
arose as a special group the words about the suffering (and
rising again) of the Son of man.[304] But apart from the use and
wide development of them in the gospel of Mark, these sayings
did not exercise any strong influence, whereas the passion sayings which are bound up with the title Christos have discernible
repercussions throughout almost the whole of the NT.

The nodal point for the combination of the passion tradition with the Christos title is still clearly to be recognized in 1 Cor. 15:3ff.[305] That we have here not only from the standpoint of substance an ancient Christological affirmation, but "an old tradition, moulded as a formula and thus preserved",[306] can be inferred from the introductory expression itself τίνι λόγῳ εὐηγγελισάμην ὑμῖν v. 2,[307] and is generally recognized in modern criticism.[308] What is disputed is the limit of it.

While it is true that Paul has clearly marked the beginning, he has not made clear where the traditional formula ends. In a way highly characteristic for his relation to the common confession of the church and also for his own apostolate, he has carried the statements further and classed himself among the witnesses to the resurrection. It is certain that v. 8 no longer is part of the pre-Pauline tradition. But also v. 6b, the observation that of the 500 brethren many are still alive, must equally be regarded as a Pauline interpretation. Yet the text which remains presents no perfect unity, for the parallel ὅτι-clauses cease in v. 5.[309]

Whatever may be the truth concerning the appearances noted in vv. 6a and 7, whether they belonged to the tradition from the start or were only added later, whether we have here a really chronological series, or whether it is a case of competitive enumerations of the first resurrection witnesses, whether the link with the ancient formula was pre-Pauline or made by him,[310] what is certain is that v. 5 belongs to the old formula of confession.[311] Recently the opinion has at times been expressed that in v. 5 only καὶ ὅτι ὤφθη should be counted as belonging to the formula.[312]

In this way there does indeed arise a formally very regular text,[313] but formal reasons alone cannot and should not here be decisive. ὤφθη as a passive with intransitive meaning[314] always has and must have in the context of NT resurrection assertions a dative to indicate the person concerned, because the resurrection appearances of Jesus are indissolubly coupled with witnesses to the event.[315] Also, if the naming of witnesses were purely secondary, there would subsequently have been given to the formula, whose centre of gravity for Paul rests precisely on vv 5–7(8), a completely new tendency. This hardly seems credible, whereas the addition of further names to an already mentioned group of witnesses is readily explained.

Finally, it must be borne in mind that despite the formal correspondence in vv. 3b and 4a, vv. 4b and 5, the important and primary matter is the correspondence in content. There are four lines of which I and III stand out by the common motive of scriptural fulfilment, but also by their characteristic and parallel interpretations,[316] whereas II and IV occupy a subordinate and consequential position.[317] That Jesus appeared to Cephas and the twelve(v.5) is just as unified a statement as v. 4a, that He was buried. But whereas the terse statement in line II implies that beyond the burial there would seem to lie nothing further, v. 5 with the mention of witnesses points to the new perspective of history disclosed by the miracle of the resurrection. The most probably later continuation in vv. 6a, 7 is essentially made possible by the original conception of the formula. The question of the date of this tradition absorbed by Paul must be regarded as clarified.

The opinion sometimes expressed earlier that it arose in the circle of the first Hellenistic churches of Damascus or Antioch stands on weak ground. For when it is said: "The limitation to the brief scheme of death, burial and resurrection as the main content of the gospel is not understandable for the church to which we owe the sayings source and the basic material of Mark's gospel. It is only intelligible in a circle which was further removed from the riches of the historical reality of the life of Jesus than was the Jerusalem church"[318]—the confessional character of this piece of tradition is disregarded.

Just as little may the Palestinian origin of 1 Cor. 15:3b—5 be disputed on the ground of the implication that Jesus died an expiatory death, because it is plain that the thought of expiatory suffering argues for rather than against ancient Palestinian tradition.[319]

Finally, the objection that the formulation was intended for Greek-speaking missionary churches, and that therefore it would not appear really credible that "such men on such an occasion would have accepted an Aramaic formula in translation",[320] is disposed of both by the traditional way of thinking of the early church[321] and also by the clear indications that there lies behind this passage a basic Semitic text.[322] 1 Cor. 15:11 likewise suggests that the formula must have arisen in the Palestinian church, because Paul here classes himself with the other witnesses to the resurrection and refers to the essential sameness of the proclamation. And, above all, it must be noted that, however the linguistic evidence is assessed, the content itself argues for an early origin in the circle of the first Palestinian church.[323]

The formula 1 Cor. 15:3b–5 is characterized by an abundance of important detailed motives, which must be discussed before their connection with the heading Χριστός can be decided. Each line contains its own verb. The first, ἀπέθανεν, is significant because it avoids speaking of the "way in which the death took place."[324] It was only much later that σταυροῦν became a "gospel word".[325] In the passion story no doubt "crucify" occurs several times, but there it refers quite concretely to the mode of execution. Otherwise it is very rare in the non-Pauline tradition.[326] For Paul, in deliberate contrast to the curse of Deut. 21:23 (Gal. 3:13) and just because of its character as a σκάνδαλον (1 Cor. 1:23), it comprises directly the gospel message. For the oldest church, thinking in terms of such paradoxes is not demonstrable; it may even perhaps, precisely because of the OT assumption, have avoided the word "crucify" in confession and preaching. Conversely the simple ἀποθνῄσκειν is to be found in many Christological statements both more ancient and more recent, both of Pauline and post-Pauline provenance;[327] but as such it is not a "gospel word".[328] The soteriological function of the death of Jesus was explained in various ways.[329] As has elsewhere been suggested,[330] it would not be legitimate to understand ὑπὲρ τῶν ἁμαρτιῶν ἡμῶν in the sense of a reference to Isa.53.[331]

What was important for the oldest passion tradition was only the necessity of the suffering of Jesus, and to convey this conviction it used scriptural proof; also the motive of the persecution and killing of God's messengers by the Jews played initially a certain part,[332] but in both cases the thought of expiation was lacking. It was probably only after the church had learnt to understand the necessity of the death of Jesus, that it took the further step of asking about the meaning of His suffering from the point of view of salvation. It then applied to the death of Jesus the motive of vicarious expiatory suffering which was widespread in late Palestinian Judaism.[333] But scriptural proof and the motive of expiation regarding the death of Jesus must at first have been developed and handed on to some extent independently of each other.

At this early stage Isa. 53 still played no part. A reference to this prophetic chapter of the OT must then have been prepared and eventually made by the fact that gradually the motive of the expiatory death became likewise linked with scriptural proof. Only so can it be explained that already previously particular features of Isa. 53 could have been utilized in the context of scriptural proof for the suffering of Jesus without the theme of expiation in vv. 10f. being fully taken into account.[334]

With the combination of references to expiation and scriptural proof, the door was then opened for the adoption of the motive of the expiatory suffering of the servant of Jahwe, which, so far as we can see, was completely avoided in Judaism, and in no way combined with assertions about vicarious expiation.[335] Naturally it must be asked whether the suggestion that, with the merging of the tradition of expiation and scriptural proof, an influence of Isa. 53 must be allowed for, is not of importance in 1 Cor. 15:3b because the $\kappa\alpha\tau\grave{\alpha}$ $\tau\grave{\alpha}s$ $\gamma\rho\alpha\phi\acute{\alpha}s$ is here expressly added.[336] But this conclusion cannot be drawn, for here we have an older stage of tradition. The plural $\gamma\rho\alpha\phi\alpha\acute{\iota}$ itself would not in this case be justified, and the position of the same phrase in line III also argues against it.[337]

Still more important is an observation relative to the development of the tradition. If we survey the fairly well defined brief formulae whose theme is the death of Jesus, we see an almost regular association with the motive of expiation and in any case a very frequent association with the title Christos; on the other hand, there is missing an express reference to scripture or at any rate the thought of the necessity of Jesus' death.[338] From this it may be inferred that the affirmation of the expiatory death is older, that only later was it combined with the motive of congruence with the scriptures, and thus became so firmly fixed as an independent tradition that in this form it exercised continued influence.

How then did the connection with $\kappa\alpha\tau\grave{\alpha}$ $\tau\grave{\alpha}s$ $\gamma\rho\alpha\phi\acute{\alpha}s$ arise? It is clear at least that this is not primarily an allusion to the scriptural basis for the idea of expiation, and the latter is not intended to be supported in this way. The affirmation of expiation has its own weight and needs no further legitimation. As on the one hand the dying of Jesus was explained by the thought of scriptural necessity, so on the other, was it explained by this soteriological idea. The second prepositional phrase in line I can therefore only refer to the ἀπέθανεν and is to be understood as a further more precise qualification of the death of Jesus.[339] "According to the scriptures" is intended far more basically than would be the case if we had here a reference to Isa. 53. If it is said that the phrase is a mere "postulate", without specific OT texts being already alluded to,[340] this opinion does not quite fit the case. In such traditional confessions, we must think less of an implicit statement than of one which is extremely compressed. But the thought should not be interpreted in such general terms as is implied by the statement that the event "is to be fitted into the divine plan of salvation".[341]

What must be remembered is in what stratum of tradition the motive of scriptural congruity primarily played a part. This was from the outset the passion tradition, and the κατὰ τὰς γραφάς is doubtless to be understood as an allusion to it.[342] Yet in the sense that the basic thought of the ancient passion story is combined with the soteriological statement about Jesus' death: the suffering and death of Jesus happened according to the will and promise of God, the extremest agony and abandonment of Jesus, His shameful death lie in the counsel of God and are therefore to be understood in the light of OT prophetic testimony. Two diverse traditions about the death of Jesus are therefore combined here. How strongly the thought of scriptural fulfilment marks the confession is especially clear from the fact that this point alone occurs twice in a formula which is extremely compressed.

Before the testimony to the resurrection, the fact of the burial of Jesus is placed in line II. Apart from the repeated ὅτι the formula is limited to the passive ἐτάφη. It is probably meant neither by way of contrast to the forbidding of burial to an executed person,[343] nor as an allusion to the pre-eminent rank of the buried man, mentioned by name.[344] In view of the very terse turn of phrase, merely noting facts, and of the subordination of line II to line I, it seems much more sensible to understand the "He was buried" as a confirmation of the death of Jesus; the burial securely affirms "the real death of Jesus, and the *visio* establishes the really ensuing resurrection".[345]

The ἐγήγερται of line III is, unlike the three other verbs, in the perfect tense. This is by no means normal in the references to the resurrection elsewhere, even the resurrection of Jesus is usually spoken of in the aorist,[346] and but seldom in the perfect.[347] It seems questionable whether we should renounce any attempt to discover in this an essential differentiation and regard the two tenses as mere translation variants.[348] At least in the extant Greek text of 1 Cor. 15:3b–5, the perfect has a clear function to perform: in contradistinction to the testimony to the resurrection event alone, there is here also a reference to the repercussions of the Easter miracle, and by this means lines III and IV are most closely bound together.[349] The passive, as is frequent in Jewish tradition, is in this case circumlocutory, drawing a veil over the action of God.

This can be especially well shown in testimonies to the Easter event, because "He was raised up (has been raised up)" alternates fairly regularly with "God raised Him up".[350] Precisely in this respect the use of $\dot{\epsilon}\gamma\epsilon\iota\rho\epsilon\iota\nu$ is distinguished from that of the intransitive $\dot{\alpha}\nu\alpha\sigma\tau\hat{\eta}\nu\alpha\iota$ and perhaps for this reason increasingly prevailed.[351] That the formula, apart from the affirmation of the resurrection in the perfect tense, is concerned to emphasize the once-for-all character of the event, is shown by the addition $\tau\hat{\eta}$ $\dot{\eta}\mu\acute{\epsilon}\rho\alpha$ $\tau\hat{\eta}$ $\tau\rho\acute{\iota}\tau\eta$. As in line I, here too the statement about scriptural congruity must not be specially linked with this qualifying phrase.

Once again the development of tradition shows that the motive of the third day was combined with witness to the resurrection before scriptural proof had been made use of in such a context, a fact which becomes especially clear from the tradition about the suffering and resurrected Son of man.[352] Moreover, it can still be discerned that scriptural proof was originally used only in view of the suffering of Jesus.[353] In consequence there can be no question, from the outset, of deriving the motive of the third day from the use of scriptural proof.[354] Explanations flowing from the primitive Christian calendar of feasts or general reflections having to do with the history of religion are still more inappropriate.[355]

There remains only the one possibility, which in recent times has come to be increasingly accepted, namely, that the mention of the third day rests upon a historical occurrence,[356] and in fact we shall have to refer it to the event of the first resurrection appearance.[357] What function then is fulfilled by the prepositional phrase $\kappa\alpha\tau\grave{\alpha}$ $\tau\grave{\alpha}s$ $\gamma\rho\alpha\phi\acute{\alpha}s$?[358] The miracle of the resurrection of Jesus on the third day is as such an act of God which carries its meaning and salvific power in itself. The testimony to the resurrection was therefore transmitted to a large extent without any kind of reference to the OT. But subsequently here likewise there arose the thought that it was grounded in God's counsel and promise. He who in deepest agony and shame was led into the valley of suffering and death was now seen to have been awakened into new life according to the will and predetermination of God.[359]

Only if we understand the context on these lines, and thus take into account both the parallelism to line I and also the fundamental character of this thought to which we have been alluding, can we escape the inevitable weakening of the confession which is always entailed when κατὰ τὰς γραφάς is referred to the statement about expiation and the third day.

Since in our present argument we may disregard the mention of the witnesses to the resurrection, the only thing that remains is to clarify the ὤφθη. This rare and unusual use of the word in Greek, by contrast with ἐφάνη, has a previous history in the Septuagint and reproduces the Niphal of ראה. In the NT witness to the resurrection, this ὤφθη to a large extent established itself.[360] Is a special meaning involved in its use? Quite certainly wrong is the suggestion that in this way was indicated a purely visionary experience,[361] for precisely in view of the OT the objective reality of what was seen was implied as a matter of course. Neither on the other hand can it be said that ὤφθη denotes the presence of the phenomenon of revelation and the encounter with the self-revealing Lord, without visual perception playing any part in the experience.[362] For the Easter reports are "in agreement in assigning decisive significance to the visual perception of the risen Lord by His friends".[363]

However, the word especially implies a becoming visible in the sense of an unexpected emerging from invisibility, in particular, from the world of God, a becoming visible which does not depend on the one who sees.[364] Despite the occasional occurrence of other words in the description of resurrection appearances, on the basis of the prevailing use of ὤφθη we may argue that it implies the action of the Lord who reveals Himself, a real self-manifestation, but also the creation of the possibility of perception.[365]

That this Christological statement also includes a certain eschatological aspect is fairly obvious in view of the light in which the first church understood the resurrection[366], yet it must be noted that with the concentration of the confession on the death and resurrection of Jesus, the eschatological element somewhat recedes into the background.[367]

The formula I Cor. 15:3b–5 is linked to $X\rho\iota\sigma\tau\acute{o}s$ used without article.[368] At first sight it looks as if this were only possible where the use as a proper name had already become established.[369] Could such a mode of speech, without article and without express identification with Jesus, have been at all possible in the sphere of Palestinian Judaism? The situation, however, is slightly different and more complicated. Two questions are to be distinguished: on the one hand, the equation of the title "Messiah" with Jesus and, on the other, the use of the word, without article, to denote a concept.[370]

As regards the first, it is to be observed that in the Palestinian sphere the equation of the "Son of man" with Jesus prevailed increasingly, and in the two later groups of sayings concerning the earthly work and the suffering and resurrection is as a matter of course presupposed. This identification of the expected bearer of salvation with Jesus does not therefore cancel the titular use of the corresponding name signifying the status of dignity and is accordingly possible in the oldest tradition.

But what is the position as regards the use of $X\rho\iota\sigma\tau\acute{o}s$ without article?[371] Is not this an indication that the titular sense has been lost? Here, however, caution is necessary. For it has been shown that in late Judaic literature משיח without article was likewise in use.[372] It is wrong in such a case to speak of a use as a "proper name".[373] In all circumstances it is a question of the traditional title of exaltation, and it is not by chance that the word is used alternately with and without article often in the same context.[374] This means therefore, that as regards the name $X\rho\iota\sigma\tau\acute{o}s$ without article, both the identification with Jesus and the titular meaning must in certain cases be absolutely presupposed and the word in this use may possibly belong to the Palestinian church tradition, but in the Hellenistic church its use in the same way was maintained. In any event it must not be so quickly assumed, as often happens, that as a matter of course we must take into account the use of $X\rho\iota\sigma\tau\acute{o}s$ as a proper name.

For the precise determination of the function of Χριστός in 1 Cor. 15:3b–5, we must allow for the fact that this formula of confession has a markedly comprehensive character. What is striking is the several times repeated and cumulative ὅτι . . . καὶ ὅτι . . . καὶ ὅτι . . . καὶ ὅτι . . .[375] This introduces a certain prosaic touch into the formula; for this reason, it has often been disputed whether this ὅτι originally belonged to it.[376] But there must certainly be a distinction made between the style of a hymn and that of a credal confession, even if the boundaries between them are fluid.[377] In a hymn such a ὅτι would in any case be disturbing, whereas in a confessional statement it marks the firm, obligatory and common article of faith. Especially in connection with πιστεύομεν, οἴδαμεν, etc., are stereotyped turns of phrase introduced by ὅτι particularly frequent,[378] and the same applies also to the continuity effected by the traditional technical terms παραλαμβάνειν and παραδιδόναι.[379] Thus there is certainly the possibility of regarding ὅτι as suitable in style and of interpreting its regular repetition in the lines of the credal statement as vigorously emphasizing the various points affirmed.

But it must be asked why in such a formula, handed on as a unity, the introduction by a single ὅτι is not sufficient. The only comparable parallel text 1 Thess. 4:14ff. shows[380] that the enumeration there was not a unity originally and was thus co-ordinated by Paul himself. This cannot be said of 1 Cor. 15:3b–5, on account of the very firm technical and formal structure, and the unPauline features. What is to be considered is whether the repeated ὅτι is not an indication that in the pre-Pauline period a number of confessional formulae, originally independent, were fused together.[381] But this contention must be made more precise: only the statements about death and resurrection can have been formal in the strict sense, in view of the independence of their individual components. This is confirmed by the fact that these occur, in the form of short formulae, with relative frequency in the Pauline letters, and are not necessarily joined together.

Among the especially instructive Pauline examples of this,[382] it is clear that the affirmation of Jesus' death and its expiatory effect had its secure place, but that conversely His rising or being raised from the dead is mostly referred to quite simply; that none the less the datum of the three days has its firm place in the tradition, has already been discussed. What is consistently missing is the express mention of congruity with scripture.

Now Χριστός in such brief formulae has a relatively firm, but not an indispensable place.[383] May inferences be drawn from this? With all the caution demanded, when such conclusions *a posteriori* are made, certain points may be noted and their convergence considered.

As has already become clear, the concept of the Messiah in the usual sense was applied to the parousia of Jesus or His exaltation, but not to His earthly life. On the other hand, the connection of the title Christos with His suffering and death is to be explained by the tendency to reinterpret positively the crucifixion of Jesus as a pretendant to the Messiahship; this happened, as has been shown, through attempts within the framework of the ancient tradition of the passion. If now Χριστός occurs in combination with confessional statements about the death and resurrection of Jesus, we shall therefore have to take account of the following component elements.

The starting point is the crucifixion of Jesus as "King of the Jews", which in the meantime, however, led to a clear *interpretatio Christiana* of the messianic title. To this is added the special interpretation of the death of Jesus as a "dying for . . ."; this thought of expiation has its own background in primitive Christian tradition, and did not from the first belong to that stratum of tradition reflected in the ancient version of the passion which has come down to us. Further, within the tradition of confessional statements the affirmation about Jesus' rising from the dead ("on the third day") was associated with the title "Christos", for the one who as "Christos" was led by God into the experience of death was as such called back again to life.[384] Finally, in certain cases the thought of scriptural congruity also occurs, which is to be regarded as an influence of the ancient passion tradition.[385] For although the positive development of the inscription on the cross in Mk. 15:1–20 was not moulded by reference to scripture, yet it was inserted into the old account of the passion which was stamped by the thought of scriptural necessity.

Seen from this point of view, 1 Cor. 15:3b–5 presents a comprehensive formula, which despite its ancient date cannot have stood right at the start of the development. One sign of this is the repeated ὅτι; but a further sign is that the κατὰ τὰς γραφάς has so emphatically been added in two places, and not least significant is the fact that to the confession of the death and resurrection of Jesus have been joined statements about His burial and appearances.

The formula I Cor. 15:3b–5 is a representative formula showing a specific Christological conception. The tradition of the passion story, which in the main sought only to overcome the scandal of Jesus' way of suffering, has here absorbed into itself independent soteriological statements together with the message of the resurrection, and has adopted the Christos title.[386] Thus was formed still on Palestinian ground a further significant tradition in addition to the Son of man idea and the view of Jesus as Lord. Certainly the Son of man Christology played the decisive part in the earliest times, and it may also be asserted that it was probably reproduced in the Hellenistic church, and that echoes of it were still to be heard, but yet it shows no further independent life.

By contrast, the concept of the Kyrios received especially in Hellenistic circles an extremely independent and significant further development, and moreover absorbed into itself some elements of the Son of man theory, especially in connection with the parousia expectation. Provided one does not attempt to understand it in the sense of a hard and fast indissoluble contrast, Bousset's thesis that the Son of man view was characteristic of the Palestinian church and the Kyrios view characterstic of the Hellenistic church, is in a sense quite justified.[387] But what is completely overlooked here is the function which was assigned to the passion tradition in the oldest church already, and the significance which this had acquired in Hellenistic circles. In any case the Christology of Paul and of Peter's First Letter are largely influenced by it.

It should be noted that this Christological conception most of all makes us aware of the continuity between the Palestinian and the Hellenistic church traditions. Perhaps this also explains why the title "Christos" could become the very "point of crystallization for all NT Christological views"—but always the title as linked to the passion tradition and in the meantime Christianized.[388] It must be clearly understood that the Judaic content of the messianic idea is here totally transformed.[389] And in connection with this it must still be shown that in passing into the Hellenistic sphere the Christos title was modified by another factor. But first we must allude to a few important contexts which show the continued influence of the Christos title in its combination with the passion tradition.[390]

Χριστός plays a decisive role in Paul. The usual opinion that in his letters it occurs only as a proper name,[391] is certainly incorrect. Günther Bornkamm has justifiably maintained: "He uses Χριστός—obviously following tradition—almost always in kerygmatic expressions, where it is a question of the death and resurrection of Christ in their saving significance."[392] In detail the problems closely connected with the difficult question of the confluence of the most diverse traditions and their fusion in the Christology of the apostle, have been investigated only in monographs.[393]

What is clear is that Paul, apart from the combinations which were already current in his time, such as Ἰησοῦς Χριστός (Χριστὸς Ἰησοῦς), Ἰησοῦς Χριστὸς ὁ κύριος ἡμῶν, etc., uses above all Χριστός without article while the article is mostly used for purely formal reasons, but also occasionally for the sake of an anaphora.[394] Further, it can be affirmed that Paul's writings already presuppose a thorough *interpretatio Christiana*; the idea derives its content from what Jesus is and effects, for which reason "Christos" is not a title separable from the person and work of Jesus.[395]

Here what must be especially taken into account is that for Paul "Christos" is linked to the passion tradition, which primarily determines his view of the whole earthly work of Jesus.[396] But what is very significant also is that with Paul "Christos" is fused with a whole series of ideas and motives: with ἀπόστολος, with εὐαγγέλιον, with faith, justification and life.[397] Finally, Χριστός has its secure place in the ecclesiological concept of the σῶμα Χριστοῦ and here is essentially determined also by sacramental theories.[398] Thus there is disclosed in Paul a decisive influence and a wide development of this tradition.[399]

The First Letter of Peter, of relatively late date, likewise contains a Christology which is consistently shaped by the passion tradition. This may be seen not only in the clear predominance of Χριστός as opposed to other titles of exaltation, but also in such central affirmations as 1:18–21 or 2:21–25, where *expressis verbis* Isa. 53 is taken up and worked over,[400] and in 3:18–22, where the motive of exaltation as well as the theologumenon of the preaching to the spirits in prison is added.[401] Even in the Letter to the Hebrews, there is to be found a section which, in connection with the theme of the saving significance of the death and resurrection of Jesus, emphatically uses the Christos title (9:11–15, 24–28), hence suggests an influence of this tradition in the midst of a Christology which in other respects is so different in spirit.[402]

Apart from the indirect testimony in Mk. 8:29, 31 parr., examples of this viewpoint in Mark and Matthew are wanting,[403] only Luke has adopted it in his gospel.[404] It will be best to start from observations regarding the Acts of the Apostles.

The four big, similarly constructed missionary speeches to the Jews contain as the constitutive Christological element of their kerygmatic sections affirmations about the death and resurrection.[405] Also the summaries of sermons in Acts 17:3 and 26:22f. refer exclusively to the dying of Jesus and the resurrection event.[406] The title Christos is used only occasionally and takes only a subordinate place in the kerygmatic sections of the missionary speeches,[407] but it controls the formulations in 17:3 and 26:23. Everywhere in these texts is to be found the thought of scriptural congruity.[408] On the other hand, the motive of expiation is completely missing, and elsewhere in the twofold writing of Luke it occurs only in the paradosis of the Last Supper (the long text, Lk. 22:20) and in an expression which occurs in the farewell speech of Paul at Miletus (Acts 20:28).

It must be remembered both that towards the end of the first century the whole concept of expiation is receding into the background,[409] and also that the statements concerning the death and resurrection of Jesus bear strong Lucan features.[410] Nevertheless, it must be asked whether alongside the tradition in which the motive of expiation is adopted, there was not a continuously influential tradition without it. One or two of the short formulae used by Paul might argue in favour of this.[411] But it stands out all the more clearly that in the tradition utilized by Luke there is a combination of the scriptural motive with the Christos title, for the latter is only missing where we have plainly Lucan formulations, not, however, in such formal statements as those of Acts 3:18b, 17:3, 26:23, and equally little in the two important texts of Lk. 24.

Lk. 24:46 fits perfectly into what we have been maintaining: after the assertion of scriptural congruity (οὕτως γέγραπται) prepared in v. 44f. and recurring in v. 46, there follows the expression παθεῖν τὸν χριστόν,[412] then the affirmation of the resurrection from the dead on the third day. πάσχειν[413] in Luke has replaced ἀναθνῄσκειν; it flows from the Hellenistic church tradition, and, as we have already intimated, it has also penetrated into some later forms of the words about the suffering of the Son of man.[414] Lk. 24:46 is especially interesting because here occurs the motive of the third day, which likewise appears in 1 Cor. 15:4 but was nowhere else adopted by Paul. The text Lk. 24:26 has a somewhat different form. Again there is found the thought of scriptural congruity, condensed into the word ἔδει,[415] then the παθεῖν of the Χριστός. But in the second part instead of a mention of the resurrection we find the expression εἰσελθεῖν εἰς τὴν δόξαν αὐτοῦ.

We should not, on account of Luke's strong emphasis on the concept of exaltation, regard this as a Lucan peculiarity, for something similar is in any event found also in 1 Peter; cf. 1 Pet.1:11b: τὰ εἰς Χριστὸν παθήματα καὶ τὰς μετὰ ταῦτα δόξας and 1:18f., 21, where in v. 21a resurrection from the dead and conferment of δόξα are even coupled together. In these texts we see the influence of a Christological pattern of thought, where the earthly saving work of Jesus is set over against His exaltation.[416] Thus Lk. 24:26 indeed belongs integrally to the passion tradition as combined with the title Christos, but it represents a later modified form stemming from Hellenistic circles.[417]

In view of this state of affairs, where we find at a relatively late date the maintenance of the titular significance, and where we can perceive its combination with a quite specific stream of tradition, the generalized use of Χριστός in application to the whole earthly life of Jesus is not readily explained. Hence other factors must have been at work to explain the fact that Χριστός used in a wide comprehensive sense established itself already in the early Hellenistic tradition.

Summary. It is to be noted once more that in the combination of the Christos title with the passion tradition, we see the effect of a completely new initiative. On the basis of the fact that Jesus was crucified as "King of the Jews", there arose a marked Christianized interpretation of the idea of royal messianism. From now onwards the idea that the Messiah must suffer is made part of the conception; the thought of the necessity of this suffering according to the scriptures stands in the background, but in part is directly expressed. In the association of the Christos title with the confessional tradition concerning the suffering and resurrection of Jesus, the thought of expiation was also adopted, a thought which was absent from the old account of the suffering and from one part of the later passion tradition (1 Cor. 15:3b–5). The Palestinian outlook, clearly reflected both in the details and in the whole, shows in regard to Christology a real continuity with the Hellenistic church tradition. The strong influence of the pattern is traceable up to the later NT tradition. Here "Christos" has retained its secure place within this stratum of tradition, nor has its titular meaning been given up. Hence the transition to its use as a proper name is not to be explained from within this historical context.

6. *The Generalization of the Christos Title and its Use as a Proper Name*

It is necessary once more to point out that Jewish messianism furnished no possibility of including the earthly work of Jesus under a title of exaltation. If the theory could be applied at all, it had to be exclusively in regard to the eschatological work of Jesus. The application of it to the dying and rising again of Jesus already presupposed a considerable process of transformation. Even the concept of Jesus as the Son of man was at first developed in a purely eschatological sense, and was only gradually so broadened as to include the authoritative action of the earthly Jesus and His way of suffering. In this process the idea of the earthly work was to a great extent restricted to the special claim of Jesus in His message, to His call to discipleship and His opposition to "this generation", and only exceptionally were the miracles of Jesus also taken into account.[418]

None the less, it is hardly legitimate to say that in the oldest tradition the actions of Jesus played no decisive part, if the quite extensive preservation of narratives about His deeds is to be explained. And in any event it must be expected that the occurrences were not handed on in any sort of way, but rather that they must have been narrated from a Christological standpoint.

Within the theory of the kingly Messiah which grew out of Jewish presuppositions, there was no scope for miraculous deeds; for in Judaism the Messiah was not regarded as a worker of miracles, even if when he came miracles might be expected.[419] The same thing must be assumed as regards the oldest Christian use of the messianic concept. However, it may be shown that the ancient Palestinian church interpreted the earthly work of Jesus obviously in connection with the theory of the eschatological prophet, and that not in the form which reckoned with the return of Elijah, as a preacher of penitence, but in that which expected that at the end of the times a prophet such as Moses would arise who would distinguish himself by miraculous deeds and instruction in the Torah, and who would "redeem" Israel. Demand for a sign, miraculous feeding, the healing miracles of Jesus, but also the oldest forms of the stories of the baptism and transfiguration of Jesus must have belonged to this stream of tradition.[420]

In the transition from the Palestinian to the Hellenistic church all this, however, as an independent tradition was lost so that the constituents of this complex of thought were absorbed and carried on in a different way. Henceforth the Mosaic typology was used in combination with other Christological conceptions.[421] The narrative material primarily became interwoven with the conception of Jesus as the "Son of God". Here Hellenistic and especially Judaic-Hellenistic influences became strongly effective, as will have to be shown.[422] The prevalent association and identification of the titles "Messiah" and "Son of God"—stemming from OT messianism—may have contributed to the fact that the title Christos was likewise used in this context.[423]

The primitive Christian concept of the Messiah underwent a further decisive change through the adoption of important elements characterizing the theory of the eschatological prophet.[424] This afforded the possibility—and it was only this presupposition that did so—of applying the Christos predicate to the earthly work of Jesus as a whole, and, not least, of including under it His deeds and His miracles. Beyond this basic transformation, a highly significant particular motive can be pinpointed which afforded the possibility of contact between the older conception of Jesus as the eschatological prophet and the later (Christianized) view of His earthly messiahship.

If it is agreed that the story of His baptism originally grew out of the theory of the eschatological prophet and the new

Moses,[425] then in the bestowal of the Spirit there is a motive which equally belongs to the concept of the Messiah.[426] Since the use of Isa. 61:1 can most probably be traced back to ancient Palestinian tradition, where the bestowal of the Spirit was connected with the eschatological office of a prophetic figure and was denoted by משח,[427] it is so much the more understandable that such statements about an "anointed" one could be later absorbed into the conception of Jesus as the Christ.[428, 429]

In two synoptic passages the transition from assertions about Jesus as an eschatological prophet to the complex of ideas connected with the Christos title can still be traced. Especially important is Matt. 11:2–6. In Matthew (in contradistinction to the parallel in Luke) v. 2 mentions the ἔργα τοῦ χριστοῦ. That this formulation implies an emphatically Christian standpoint, is unmistakable, for the deeds of Jesus mentioned in v. 5 could not be for Jewish thought any proof of messiahship.[430] So much the more plainly is expressed in Jesus' answer to the Baptist, in this traditional passage, a conception of the work of Jesus according to which He is the miraculous helper of the poor and suffering, and the announcer of glad tidings; in other words, the understanding of His earthly work as that of a new Moses.[431]

If the view is associated with the Christos title, that means, first, that this title can now be extended to cover the whole earthly activity of Jesus,[432] and, secondly, that that ancient interpretation of His action and message has been absorbed into the messianic conception, with the result that the latter has in this way undergone a further deep modification. If we remember that the early Hellenistic church adopted the conception of the eschatological messianic status of Jesus, and elaborated the concept of exaltation, that it developed further the passion tradition interwoven with the title Christos, it is clear to what an extent the Christos title has now become decisive and comprehensive.

This of course does not mean that these various aspects were fused together to form a unified conception; of this there are no signs and such a supposition is contradicted by the relatively independent continued influence of particular points of view. But at a certain stage in the development of the early Hellenistic church, the Christos title must have attained a dominant position so that for this reason believers received the name Χριστιανοί also.[433]

There is a second passage from which it may also be inferred that the view of the earthly Jesus as a second Moses was absorbed into the idea of His messiahship. In the section Mk. 8:27b–29[434] which must be regarded as an independent tradition, the confession of Jesus as the "Christos" is contrasted with all the opinions which admit Him to have held only a prophetic office.[435] In the oldest tradition, such an unqualified application of the messianic idea to the earthly Jesus is utterly inconceivable. But in this text is disclosed the wide use of this predicate in application to Jesus that has now been reached, and that also was precipitated into such confessional formulae as Ἰησοῦς ὁ χριστός or Ἰησοῦς Χριστός. In my opinion, it is out of the question to assign confessional formulae of this type to the beginning of the primitive Christian tradition. The basic confession of the early Hellenistic church must contradict the hypothesis.[436]

On the basis of the general and wide use of the description of Jesus as Messiah there then arose the relatively early establishment of the titular use and of Χριστός as a proper name. It should not be overlooked that on Hellenistic soil, especially after the loosening of contacts with Jewish origins, the tradition of the miraculous earthly work of Jesus which had been absorbed into the Christos title was one-sidedly orientated towards the title of Son of God.[437] No doubt the Christos predicate retains its central position, but it soon fades and becomes rigid; it preserved its true independence only in connection with the passion tradition. The titular sense disappeared last of all in immediate combination with the name Jesus Ἰησοῦς Χριστός, which with time was simply felt as a double name and then frequently combined with other ascriptions of dignity.[438] It is undeniable that the simple Χριστός was likewise used as a proper name. One need only refer to the text Mk. 9:41, where a previous ἐν τῷ ὀνόματί μου has been secondarily changed to ἐν ὀνόματι, ὅτι Χριστοῦ ἐστε.[439] On the other hand, it must be realized that this use at least in the gospels and in the Acts forms an exception, and the titular use of the word is still prevalent there.[440]

Summary. It is clear that this last broadening of the Christianized messianic idea, making possible an application to the work

of Jesus as a whole, first took place in the sphere of the early
Hellenistic church which assimilated to messianism the tradition of the earthly Jesus as the new Moses and the eschatological
prophet. In this way "Christos" could in particular be brought
into connection with the miraculous work of Jesus also. This
led to a use of "Christos" and "Son of God" in a similar sense.
However, the use of the Son of God predicate soon gained the
ascendancy, with the result that "Christos" increasingly faded
and finally was congealed as a proper name.

If in this way the use of the Christos title from the first
beginnings in the earliest church up to the early Hellenistic
church has been traced and if we have given a somewhat rigidly
drawn account of the idea, it must nevertheless be said in
conclusion that this essay has been inspired by the attempt to
disentangle the various strands of tradition and at the same
time to seize upon connections, dependencies and modifications.
We do not wish to deny by any means that many lines of
connection are hidden and that there are many gaps in our
knowledge of the oldest stratum of tradition. But this whole
circle of problems had to be broached and some firm conclusions may have been reached: thus, for example, the absence
of the messianic designation at the first, then the use of the title
only in connection with the eschatological work of Jesus, the
remoulding of it to denote the concept of exaltation, further the
firm connection between the Christos title and the passion
tradition, and finally under the influence of a different standpoint the broadening of the title to include the whole work of
Jesus, which was soon followed by the petrification of "Christos"
and its use as a mere *cognomen*.

NOTES

1. Cf. on the idea and conception Heinrich Weinel, מֹשֶׁה *und seine
Derivate*, *ZAW* 18, 1898, pp. 1–82; further Martin Noth, "Amt und
Berufung im Alten Testament" in *Gesammelte Studien zum AT* (*ThBuch*
6), 1960[2], pp. 309–333, especially pp. 319ff.

2. I refer merely to the fundamental work of Albrecht Alt, *Die
Staatenbildung in Israel* in *Kleine Schriften zur Geschichte Israels* II.
1953, pp. 1–65.

3. Cf. Gerhard von Rad, *Theologie des Alten Testaments* I, 1957, pp. 304ff.
On the thesis advocated in recent English and especially Scandinavian
research that with the acceptance of kingship in Israel there took place a
very considerable influx of oriental sacral conceptions, manifold traces
of which are still recognizable in the Old Testament, cf. Geo Widengren,
Sakrales Königtum im Alten Testament und Judentum, 1955; Ivan
Engnell, *Studies in Divine Kingship in the Ancient Near East*, 1943;
Aubrey R. Johnson, *Sacral Kingship in Ancient Israel*, 1955; *id.*,
"Hebrew Conceptions of Kingship" in *Myth, Ritual and Kingship*,
ed. by S. H. Hooke, 1958, pp. 204–235. For criticism cf. Martin Noth,
*Gott, König, Volk im Alten Testament. Eine methodologische Auseinander-
setzung mit einer gegenwärtigen Forschungsrichtung* (1950), *Ges. Studien*,
pp. 188–229; Karl-Heinz Bernhardt, *Das Problem der altorientalischen
Königsideologie im Alten Testament* (*Supp. to Vet. Test.* vii), 1961,
pp. 51ff., 91ff., 243ff. and in summary pp. 303ff.

4. Cf. Albrecht Alt, *Das Königtum in den Reichen Israel und Juda*
in *Kl. Schriften* II, pp. 116–134.

5. 2 Sam. 7. On this cf. in detail the literary-critical analysis of
Leonhard Rost, *Die Überlieferung von der Thronnachfolge Davids*
(*BWANT* III/6), 1926, pp. 47ff. Considerations against disputing the
unity in Martin Noth, *David und Israel in 2 Samuel 7*, *Ges. Studien*,
1960², pp. 334–345, and Ernst Kutsch, *Die Dynastie von Gottes Gnaden*,
ZThK 58, 1961, pp. 137–153; the latter regards only v. 11b as an older
nucleus and vv. 12b, 13a as a later addition (pp. 144f.).

6. 2 Sam. 6. In addition cf. especially v. Rad, *Theol.* I, pp. 53f.;
Martin Noth, *Jerusalem und die israelitische Tradition*, *Ges. Studien*,
pp. 172–187.

7. The statement about David as a spiritually gifted singer made
(v. 1f.) in the very old portion of tradition of the so-called last words
of David, 2 Sam. 23:1–7, represents a singular tradition. On the one
hand the story in 1 Sam. 16 of the anointing of the young David by
Samuel and his divine designation that thus came about, stands quite
isolated in the account of David's advancement and may be an assimilation to the corresponding story of the anointing of Saul in 1 Sam.
9:1–10:16. The co-operation also of the prophet Nathan in the enthronement of Solomon, 1 Kings 1:34, 45 (otherwise v. 39), a co-operation that is
not accounted for by the coronation ritual, has been supplied at second
hand and has the same purpose.

8. Gerhard von Rad, *Das judäische Königsritual* in *Gesammelte
Studien zum Alten Testament* (*ThBüch* 8), 1958, pp. 205–213.

9. Cf. 2 Sam. 7:13f.; Ps. 2:7; 89:27f.; Isa. 9:5; on this Martin Noth,
Gott, König, Volk in *Ges. Studien*, pp. 188–229, there pp. 211ff., especially
pp. 222f.

10. Ps. 2; 18:44–48; 72:8–11 and often.

11. Here there are statements of different kinds: either victory is
won by the action of the king himself, whose confidence in Jahwe's
help is occasionally emphasized (Ps. 2:8; 18:32–43; 21:9–13), or the
king leaves it to Jahwe to overcome the enemies (Ps. 20:7–9; 110:1;
1 Sam. 2:10). Besides a part is played by traditions of the holy war,

which indeed in later times was understood in the sense of an absolute miracle; cf. Gerhard von Rad, *Der heilige Krieg im alten Israel*, 1952², pp. 43ff., 56ff.

12. Ps. 45:7; 89:5, 30, 37f.

13. In Israel the preservation of law was entrusted to a special institution and was conferred on the king only by degrees; only Jerusalem occupied an exceptional position. There from the outset the members of the David family as the descendants of the city's king had the administration of justice.

14. The history of the succession to the throne of David is told in accordance with this (2 Sam. 9–20; 1 Kings 1f.).

15. Cf. on this especially Gerhard v. Rad, *Theologie des Alten Testaments* II, 1960, pp. 125ff.

16. Hugo Gressmann, *Der Messias* (*FRLANT* NF 26), 1929, p. 1, is of opinion that it is only by chance that the ruler at the end of time is nowhere called "Messiah" in the Old Testament.

17. Gen. 49:8–12 and Num. 24:17–19 may here be left out of account. It is indeed beyond question that these texts also were later understood as messianic, but it is not clear whether from the beginning they were meant in this way. Severally these portions of tradition also present considerable exegetical difficulties.

18. Now and then all messianic prophecies are referred to the post-Exilic epoch. Georg Fohrer, *Die Struktur der alttestamentlichen Eschatologie*, *ThLZ* 85, 1950, cols. 401–420. Mowinckel, *He That Cometh*, pp. 15ff., is somewhat more cautious; he also advocates the thesis of a post-Exilic dating of the messianic hope, but does not dispute the originality of pre-Exilic prophecies, stating merely that "they are not messianic in the strict sense" (p. 17).

19. Cf. for the understanding of this text the fundamental investigation of Albrecht Alt, *Jesaja*, 8:23–9:6. *Befreiungsnacht und Krönungstag* in *Kl. Schriften* II, pp. 206–225.

20. This is unambiguous in Isa. 11:1: from the stock of Jesse a new David will come forth. But even for Isa. 9:5f. it may not be disputed, since after the happenings of Isa. 7:1ff. the reigning king Ahaz assuredly does not come into question as ruler in the time of salvation.

21. There the reference is to Bethlehem instead of to Jesse.

22. Isa. 9:1–4. But also Micah 5:4f., although the connection with vv. 1–3 is not quite smooth and clear.

23. So especially Isa. 9:5f., but also Mic. 5:3. In Isa. 9:5 also the appointment as "Son (of God)" and the bestowal of the royal throne-names.

24. Isa. 11:2–5. In v. 2 in the "resting" of the Spirit a permanent charismatic gift is certainly thought of. The connection with the early Israelitish tradition of the charismatic person is here particularly emphasized.

25. So in a different way Otto Procksch, *Jesaja* 1–39 (*KommAT*), 1930, pp. 124f., 153, who defends the traditional exposition of the Messianic prophecies, and Gressmann, *Messias*, pp. 245f., 247f., as a representative of the religio-historical school.

26. In Amos 9:11–15 there is a series of formally disparate but practically converging sayings.

27. On Jer. 22:24–30 cf. Artur Weiser, *Das Buch des Propheten Jeremia* I (*ATD* 20), 1952, pp. 201f.: "the word says nothing less than that the epoch of the Davidic kingship is at an end". If the promise in 23:5f. of a righteous branch of David comes from Jeremiah, then it must perhaps be put in the time of Jehoiachin, a dating in the period of Zedekiah and of the polemics against him being less likely. Rather it may be considered whether this king, who esteemed the prophet highly, did not, in renaming himself, choose the name that accorded with his plan. Jer. 30:8f., where mention is made not of a branch of David but of the returning David, is to be regarded as a gloss; Jer. 33:14–26 is a post-Exilic supplement composed in Jeremiah's style and language.

28. Cf. v. Rad, *Theol.* II, pp. 247ff., who indeed altogether denies to the prophet the constitution design Ezek. 40–48 (p. 309, n. 23). It may be mentioned that in 21:32 as also in the explanation of the riddle 17:1–10 given in vv. 22–24 Ezekiel avoids one of the usual designations of the Messiah and utters a promise only paraphrastically, while in 34:23f. and 37:15–17, 18–22 (cj. according to the LXX) he speaks not of the king but of a נָשִׂיא.

29. This is already prepared for in Jer. 25:9; 27:6, where it is said: "my servant Nebuchadrezzar".

30. In the centre there stands with him the figure of the servant of God who has to fulfil a prophetic task; cf. on this p. 356 below (Appendix).

31. On the question of the continuity of sovereignty in Israel after the Fall of Jerusalem and following the Exile as also on the problem of legitimation within the Messiah expectation, cf. Klaus Baltzer, *Das Ende des Staates Juda und die Messias-Frage* in *Studien zur Theologie der alttestamentlichen Überlieferungen* (*Festschrift G. v. Rad*), 1961, pp. 33–43, especially pp. 40f.

32. So above all Hag. 1:3ff.

33. Hag. 2:20–23.

34. In Zechariah also the finishing of the temple plays a decisive role, cf. only Zech. 4:7–10; to Zerubbabel there is addressed a demand to abandon all earthly means of power Zech. 4:6, and to him there refers doubtless the original text of Zech. 6:9–14, where in v. 13b reference is made to a priestly figure by his side. On the other hand, in 3:1–7 it devolves upon the high priest Joshua to take a part vicariously in atonement for Israel. The two messianic figures are mentioned in Zech. 4:1–6a, 10b, 11, 13b (so the original text of the section); we are concerned here as it were with a compendium of the statements of this prophet about salvation.

35. Cf. Kurt Schubert, *Der alttestamentliche Hintergrund der Vorstellung von den beiden Messiassen im Schrifttum von Chirbet Qumran, Judaica* 12, 1956, pp. 24–28; Karl Georg Kuhn, *Die beiden Messias Aarons und Israels*, *NTSt* 1, 1954/55, pp. 168–179, especially pp. 174ff.

36. That is well brought out by Otto Plöger, *Theokratie und Eschatologie* (*WMANT* 2), 1959, pp. 41ff.

37. Besides the call to Zion proclaiming God's own royal dominion Zeph. 3:14(f.), there is assumed the messianically understood text Gen. 49:10f. with the motif of the riding on an ass; then in v. 10 the expectation of the destruction of the implements of war plays a role (Isa. 2:4; Micah 4:3; 5:10f.) and in an almost word for word citation from Ps. 72:8 the idea of the world dominion of the Messiah is expressed.

38. Isa. 11:3f.; cf. Ps. 72:2ff., 12ff.

39. There is no occasion of any sort to change נוֹשָׁע on the basis of the LXX into מוֹשִׁיעַ, rather the basic attitude of this text answers precisely to the MT.

40. Cf. on the problem of the *ᵃnāwîm* Johann Jakob Stamm, *Ein Vierteljahrhundert Psalmenforschung, ThR* NF 23, 1955, pp. 1–67, there pp. 55ff.; Kraus, *Psalmen* I, pp. 82f.; Friedrich Hauck-Ernst Bammel, art. πτωχός, *ThWb* VI, pp. 866–915, especially pp. 891ff., 895ff.

41. The difficult text Zech. 12:9–14, which also comes from this period, can here be omitted because it is not even clear whether in fact by "him whom they have pierced" in v. 10 a messianic figure is meant.

42. On the historical events cf. Emil Schürer, *Die Geschichte des jüdischen Volkes im Zeitalter Jesu Christi* I, 1901³,⁴, pp. 179ff.; Noth, *Geschichte Israels*, pp. 322ff., Plöger, *op. cit.*, pp. 9ff.

43. As is generally recognized, 1 Macc. goes back to an original that was written in Hebrew. There is no need here to have recourse to 2 Macc., which, conceived in Greek, is a compendium of the unknown historical work of Jason of Cyrene (cf. 2:20–33) and presents, besides valuable material of tradition, much secondary material.

44. On the characteristics of the history in 1 Macc. cf. Elias Bickermann, *Der Gott der Makkabäer*, 1937, pp. 27ff.; Dietrich Rössler, *Gesetz und Geschichte. Untersuchungen zur Theologie der jüdischen Apokalyptik und der pharisäischen Orthodoxie (WMANT* 3), 1960, pp. 34ff.

45. 1 Macc. 2:27: Πᾶς ὁ ζηλῶν τῷ νόμῳ καὶ ἱστῶν διαθήκην ἐξελθέτω ὀπίσω μου.

46. Cf. only the war speech of Judas in 1 Macc. 3:18–22.

47. The Messianic expectation considered or affirmed for the Maccabees by Volz, *Eschatologie*, p. 183 and Hans Windisch, *Der messianische Krieg und das Urchristentum*, 1909, p. 5, is not confirmed by the texts. When mention is made of σωτηρία attained by the Maccabees (1 Macc. 3:6; 4:25; 5:62), it has to be understood in the sense it has in the Book of Judges, where the word is used likewise in connection with the holy war (cf. Judg. 3:9, 15; 15:18). The fact that according to 1 Macc. 13:41f. a new reckoning of time was begun under Simon, is referred to the independence finally won back and to the deliverance of Jerusalem. The repeatedly mentioned waiting for a prophet who can pronounce final decisions in the name of Jahwe (1 Macc. 4:46; 9:27; 14:41) shows clearly that an eschatological fulfilment was by no means reckoned with.

48. Cf. on this Plöger, *op. cit.*, p. 45.

49. On this v. Rad, *Theol.*, I, pp. 218ff.; *id., Hl. Krieg*, pp. 68ff.

50. On this in detail see Appendix.

51. Cf. Rössler, *op. cit.*, especially pp. 55ff., 100ff. This is an important work for the understanding of the theological conception of apocalyptic.

52. The Book of Daniel in its present form (apart from a few additions) can be dated easily on the basis of 11:40ff. and indeed in the time shortly before 163 B.C.

53. Cf. Plöger, *op. cit.*, pp. 69ff.

54. Cf. only Bousset–Gressmann, pp. 242ff.; Volz, *Eschatologie*, pp. 4ff.

55. v. Rad. *Theol.* II, pp. 319ff.

56. We need, however, merely to compare Ecclesiasticus with the apocalyptic literature to recognize what the specific Wisdom tradition was like in the late Jewish period.

57. So rightly Plöger, *op. cit.*, pp. 56ff.

58. Cf. Chapter 1, p. 20.

59. Plöger has undertaken a noteworthy attempt to bring some light upon these complicated and rarely investigated traditio-historical problems. We can only approve of the contrast he draws between the theocratic attitude of the Jerusalem priestly circle and the unbroken eschatological expectation of other groups (cf. the summary pp. 129ff.). But he equates the bearers of the eschatological hope and at the same time of the developing apocalyptic with the Hasidaeans (חֲסִידִים) mentioned in 1 Macc.; cf. *op. cit.*, pp. 16ff., 66ff. That seems to me open to question. In any case it may not be overlooked that besides the Jerusalem priestly circles and the Maccabees several groups have to be reckoned with at that time. In the first place there were the advocates of a radicalizing exposition of the law with their far-reaching traditional eschatology and messianism, then the circles in which the apocalyptic conception was developed, further there is also to be assumed an independent handing down of the Wisdom material; that there were interactions ought then not to be disputed. The picture of that period is very stratified. In addition there is also the Qumran community in the time of the later Hasmonaean rule.

60. On this in detail Braun, *Radikalismus* I, where side by side he investigates obedience to the law in the Pharisaic *Pirkē Abôth* and in the Qumran texts.

61. Here the problem can only be indicated. Reference may be made to the motif of mystery and to special knowledge, to belief in angels and demons and the part played by Satan, to the significance of belief in election and divine predestination, also to the manner of scriptural exposition. Fragments of apocalyptic writings have been found in the caves of Qumran.

62. It has been emphasized rightly by Rössler, *op. cit.*, pp. 43ff. and often, that an understanding of history and salvation complete in itself belongs to apocalyptic in the proper sense.

63. Cf. the contribution of Karl Georg Kuhn, *Die Sektenschrift und die iranische Religion*, *ZThK* 49, 1952, pp. 296–316.

64. On the functions of the high priestly "Messiah of Aaron" cf.

Gerhard Friedrich, *Beobachtungen zur messianischen Hohepriestererwart-ung in den Synoptikern, Z ThK* 53, 1956, pp. 265–311.

65. So in the Old Testament Jer. 23:5; 33:15; Zech. 3:8; 6:12; cf. 4 Q PatrBless 3f.; 4 Q Flor 2; 4 Q pIs^a fr. D, 1.

66. Following Gen. 49:10; Num. 24:17; cf. CD VII, 20; I Q Sb V, 24, 27; 4 Q PatrBless 1.

67. CD VII, 20; I Q Sb V, 20; I Q M V, I; 4 Q pIs^a fr. A, 2. Here the designation נשׂיא, which occurs for ruler for the first time in the like-wise priestly influenced Ezekiel, is as characteristic as the familiar term עדה of the priesthood.

68. Mentioned together with the high priestly Messiah in CD XII, 23f; XIV, 19; XIX, 10f.; XX, I, separately in 1 Q Sa II, 14, 20 (yet cf. II, 12).

69. 4 Q PatrBless 3.

70. CD VI, 10f.; XII, 23f.; XIV, 19; XX, I; I Q S IX, II; on I Q M see below.

71. Cf. A. S. van der Woude, *Die messianischen Vorstellungen der Gemeinde vom Qumrân (Studia Semitica Neerlandica* 3), 1957, pp. 43ff., 61ff., 96ff., 112ff., 169ff.

72. Cf. on this K. G. Kuhn *NTSt* 1, 1954/55, pp. 168ff.; v. d. Woude, *op. cit.*, pp. 96ff.

73. Cf. Billerbeck IV/2, pp. 1154ff.

74. Cf. 1 Q S VI, 4ff. On this Joachim Gnilka, *Das Gemeinschaftsmahl der Essener, BZ* NF 5, 1961, pp. 39–55.

75. Cf. 1 Q Sa II, 17ff.

76. Expressly cited are Gen. 49:10 in 4 Q PatrBless; Num. 24:17 in CD VII, 19f.; 4 Q Test 9–13; 1 Q M XI, 6f.; Isa. 11:1ff. in 4 Q pIs^a fr. C, 10–13; Amos 9:11 in 4 Flor 12f.; 2 Sam. 7:11b in 4 Q Flor 7; 2 Sam. 7:13f. in 4 Q Flor 10f.; Ps. 2:1f. in 4 Q Flor 18f.

77. Cf. n. 65 above.

78. 4 Q Flor 10f.

79. 1 Q Sb V, 27–29; 4 Q pIs^a fr. D, 1–3; 4 Q PatrBless speaks merely of the covenant of the king's dominion over his people (Israel).

80. 1 Q Sb V, 21–26; 4 Q pIs^a fr. C, 10–13; fr. D, 4–8.

81. 1 Q Sb V, 20f.; 4 Q PatrBless 4; 4 Q Flor 10f.

82. As Biblical evidences there are cited Num. 24:17 (CD VII, 18ff.) and Isa. 10:28ff. (4 Q pIs^a fr. A, I—C, 9). I refer besides to CD XIX, 10ff.; 1 Q Sb V, 24–29; 4 Q Flor 7–9.

83. On the peculiarity of 1 Q M and its difference from the rest of the Qumran writings cf. Leonhard Rost, *Zum "Buch der Kriege der Söhne des Lichts gegen die Söhne der Finsternis*, ThLZ 80, 1955, cols. 205–208; Bardtke, *Handschriftenfunde* II, pp. 121ff.

84. Cf. 1 Q M II, 1–4; XV, 4–8, XVI, 11–14; XVIII, 3–6.

85. 1 Q M V, 1f.; in addition there is the citation of Num. 24:17 in 1 Q M XI, 6f.

86. Moreover, there are in addition the Christian interpolations, for neither with M. de Jonge, *The Testaments of the Twelve Patriarchs*, 1953, can we make the whole work out to be simply a Christian writing nor with M. Philonenko, *Les interpolations chrétiennes des Testaments des Douze Patriarches et les Manuscrits de Qoumrân (Cahiers de la RHPhR*

no. 35), 1960, is it feasible to regard the assumption of Christian additions as altogether unnecessary on the strength of the Qumran finds.

87. Cf. K. G. Kuhn, *NTSt* I, 1954/55, pp. 171ff.; v.d. Woude, *op. cit.*, pp. 190ff.

88. I refer merely to *Test. of Reuben* 6, 7–12; *Test. of Simeon* 7, 2; *Test. of Judah* 21, 2–5; 25, 1f.; *Test. of Issachar* 5, 7; *Test. of Naphtali* 5, 3–5. Kurt Schubert, *Testamentum Juda 24 im Lichte der Texte von Chirbet Qumran, WZKM* 53, 1957, pp. 227–236, presents a comparison of the individual motifs of *Test. of Judah* 24 with the Qumran writings and an attempt to translate it back into their speech.

89. Evidence of this Messiah expectation presents itself also in the *Psalms of Solomon* 18, which, however, is merely a feeble reminiscence of the foregoing song and in grandeur cannot match it. *The Psalms of Solomon* are as a rule regarded as an expression of Pharisaic piety; cf. Herbert Braun, *Vom Erbarmen Gottes über den Gerechten. Zur Theologie der Psalmen Salomos, ZNW* 43, 1950/51, pp. 1–54, now in *Ges. Studien zum NT und seiner Umwelt*, 1962, pp. 8–69. On the question of the employment of the Syriac translation in determining the original form of the text cf. Karl Georg Kuhn, *Die älteste Textgestalt der Psalmen Salomos (BWANT* IV/21), 1937; otherwise Joachim Begrich, *Der Text der Psalmen Salomos, ZNW*38, 1939, pp. 131–164.

90. K. G. Kuhn, *Die älteste Textgestalt der Psalmen Salomos (BWANT* IV/21), 1937, pp. 64f. has shown that vv. 11–14 must be a secondary insertion.

91. The Greek and the Syriac texts have χριστὸς κύριος, but this can be regarded only as an erroneous translation which originated under Christian influence (so also Lam. 4:2 LXX); cf. K. G. Kuhn, *op. cit.*, pp. 73f.

92. Against Willi Staerk, *Soter* I, p. 51, who states that the Messiah gleams here with the splendour of a "superhuman being". The traits taken over from Isa. 11:2ff. may not be understood precisely in that way; cf. Mowinckel, *He That Cometh*, pp. 284ff., 308ff.

93. This holds good at least for vv. 33–36; in vv. 22–25 it is not so unambiguous, for there indeed a destruction ἐν λόγῳ στόματος αὐτοῦ is mentioned, but besides there is also mention of a breaking with iron rods and the like; the reference is to Ps. 2:8f. Here there coincide two traditions which already occur beside one another in the Israelitish royal conception. In the two mentioned passages of *Psalms of Solomon* 17, however, we are chiefly concerned with a dependence on Isa. 11:1ff.

94. H. Braun, *op. cit.*, pp. 7f., 43ff. (pp. 15f., 56ff.), refers to the fact that the Messiah sent by God here stands wholly on the side of the creatures and at the same time reflects in his own person the anthropocentrically orientated piety of the "righteous". That may signify that the (probably "Hasidaeic") line indicated in Zech. 9:9f. has here received its Pharisaic continuation.

95. Cf. on the rabbinical tradition Joseph Klausner, *The Messianic Idea in Israel* 1956, pp. 388–517.

96. Cf. Karl Georg Kuhn, *Achtzehngebet und Vaterunser und der Reim (WUNT* 1), 1950, pp. 10–26.

97. K. G. Kuhn, *op. cit.*, pp. 10f.; also pp. 20f.

98. Habinenu, Kaddisch und Musaph prayers.

99. On this cf. especially Klausner, *op. cit.*, pp. 391ff.

100. That the time of the Messiah is עוֹלָם הַבָּא, answers doubtless to the original idea. As against that the conception that the "days of the Messiah" merely represent a preliminary period of salvation which the future aeon only follows (so R. Akiba and the Amoraim), arose under the influence of apocalyptic.

101. Here both conceptions occur side by side, that the Messiah as the hero in war must himself fight against and defeat the adversaries or that in a wonderful way, in part through God's own intervention, they are overthrown; cf. Billerbeck IV/2, pp. 858ff., 877f. The conception of the Messiah ben David as the hero in war recedes later, this function being ascribed to a Messiah ben Ephraim or ben Joseph who falls in the conflict; this idea can hardly have arisen before the second century A.D. and assumes the experiences of the Bar Cochba war; cf. Billerbeck IV/2, pp. 872ff., also II, pp. 273ff., 292ff.; Klausner, *op. cit.*, pp. 402f., 483ff.

102. Billerbeck IV/2, pp. 881f.

103. In the rabbinical tradition there appears especially the idea of a perfect knowledge of the torah in the time of the Messiah; cf. Billerbeck, IV/2, pp. 882f.

104. Volz, *Eschatologie*, p. 176.

105. Klausner, *op. cit.*, p. 157.

106. The distinction between a coming of the Messiah in splendour and a coming of him in lowliness according as Israel is worthy of his appearance or through sins has polluted itself, belongs to the time of the Amoraim; cf. Billerbeck IV/2, pp. 872ff. To begin with thoughts of suffering are not associated with the Messiah ben David; cf. Klausner, *op. cit.*, p. 405.

107. In the whole of the rabbinical literature the idea derived from Zechariah of the presence side by side of a regal and a high priestly messiah appears only occasionally, so especially the Aboth of Rabbi Nathan 34 (Billerbeck IV/I; p. 457). In later literature the office of the messianic high priest is associated with the figure of the returning Elias; cf. on this Billerbeck IV/2, pp. 789ff.; Klausner, *op. cit.*, pp. 451ff. In line with this Elias and the Messiah ben David occur beside one another in Midr. Ps. 43 § I; Targ. KL 4, 22; Targ. J. I on Deut. 30:4 (Billerbeck I, p. 87; IV/2, pp. 792, 797), in the last named passage as the "two redeemers". In the systematizing statement of bSukka 52b it results that even four anointed persons are placed together: Messiah ben David, Messiah ben Joseph, Elias and כֹּהֵן־צֶדֶק (Billerbeck IV/2, p. 786; similar passages there), so also in PesiqR 8, 1 there is a co-ordination of Messiah ben David and Messiah ben Joseph—following Zech, 4:3 (Billerbeck II, p. 292).

108. Such is the definite result of the investigation of Paul Humbert, *Le Messie dans le Targum des Prophètes*, *RThPh* 43, 1910, pp. 420–447.

109. On the beginnings and aims of the Zealot party cf. Jos., *Bell.*

Jud., I, 204, 304ff.; II, 56, 118; *Ant.* XVIII, 4f, 23–25.; cf. also Hippolyt. *Ref.* IX, 26.

110. The investigation by W. R. Farmer, *Maccabees, Zealotes and Josephus*, 1956, sets out from this fact. He attempts to determine for what reasons Josephus was led to sketch an entirely one-sided picture of the Zealots (pp. 11ff., 126f.).

111. The picture which Bousset-Gressmann, pp. 87f., draw of them is certainly false.

112. On the history cf. Schürer, *op. cit.*, I, pp. 486f., 576, 600ff., 642ff.

113. Cf. Martin Hengel, *Die Zeloten, Untersuchungen zur jüdischen Freiheitsbewegung in der Zeit von Herodes I bis 70 n. Chr. (AGSU* I), 1961, especially pp. 93ff., 151ff., 235ff.

114. Behind there stands the tradition of the fanatic Phineas; cf. Farmer, *op. cit.*, pp. 177ff.; Hengel, *op. cit.*, pp. 154ff.

115. Credit is given to Farmer *op. cit.*, pp. 47ff., 84ff. for having shown this in detail.

116. Many analogies to the Maccabean struggles emerge here: there the motif of "zeal" had also already acquired great significance (1 Macc. 2:24ff., 50ff.; 2 Macc. 4:2).

117. This is the *novum* in comparison with the time of the Maccabees.

118. Cf. Jos., *Bell. Jud.* II, 433; VI, 312; also VI, 286.

119. According to the discoveries in the Wadi Muraba'at the actual name is שמעון בן־כוסבה. In connection with the messianic expectation according to Num. 24:17 this name was altered to בר כוכבא (son of a star), but later to בר־כוזיבא (son of lies), cf. Bousset-Gressmann, p. 224, n.1.

120. R. Akiba participated considerably in this recognition as Messiah; cf. pTa'an 68d (par.) in Billerbeck I, p. 13; in Eusebius *H.E.* IV, 6, 1 Bar-Cochba is dealt with in the same way as the Zealots are in Josephus and so merely as a rebel. On the basis of coins that have been found it is to be concluded that under Bar-Cochba a new reckoning of the years was introduced and indeed under the leading motif of the freedom of Jerusalem; לחרות ירושלם, with which the beginning of the eschatological berachah of the *Shemoneh Esreh* is to be compared: תְּקַע בְּשׁוֹפָר גָּדוֹל לְחֵרוּחֵנוּ (ber. 10 pal.), on this cf. K. G. Kuhn, *Achtzehngebet*, p. 17. Further it may be pointed out that Simon ben Cosba as נָשִׂיא had the high priest Eleazar by his side, as likewise appears from the coins; cf. K. G. Kuhn, *NTSt* I, 1954/55, pp. 174f. Here a two-Messiah-conception has evidently operated; at the same time Bar Cochba has the pre-eminence.

121. This early messianic hope has also left its traces in the writings of Diaspora Judaism, as the LXX, Philo and the *Sib. Or.* show.

122. Bar Cochba represents an exception; in this case history was mightier than dogma.

123. Later there came to be a certain variety in opinion in regard to the question how far the time of the Messiah belongs to the new aeon.

124. So Bousset, *Kyrios Christos*, pp. 3f.

125. It has at last again been emphasized by Rössler, *op. cit.*, p. 64,

n. 6 that the contrast "earthly-national" hope and "apocalyptic-universal" hope is not appropriate. It is indeed a matter of a mundane and a transcendent expectation of salvation; but, without detriment to the fact that it seeks to grasp the whole of world history, apocalyptic is orientated in its hope of salvation to the chosen people in the same way as is prophetic eschatology. Sometimes one is under the impression that there is more room for the coming of the Gentiles in eschatology of the old style than in apocalyptic.

126. So, e.g. Bultmann, *Theol.*, pp. 55f.

127. A useful survey of the various currents that exist side by side in late Jewish eschatology is given by Jean Héring, *Le royaume de Dieu et sa venue* (1937), 1959², pp. 51ff.

128. Cf. Erik Sjöberg, *Menschensohn im äth. Henochbuch*, pp. 140ff., who also shows how apart from the Messiah title (48, 10; 52, 4) some elements of the Messiah expectation have been taken up.

129. Cf. Volz, *Eschatologie*, pp. 71ff. As instances there come into question above all 2 Esdras 7:28ff.; cc. 11f.; also syr. Bar. 29f.; 39:7ff.; cc. 72–74; especially in the *Apo. of Baruch* it is clear how early traditions of the royal messianism were given a new interpretation only at second hand. The destiny of the Messiah is determined in different ways: whilst according to 2 Esdras 7:29 he dies after a rule of 400 years, according to syr. Bar. 30:1 he will return to heaven, yet according to syr. Bar. 74:2 the interval evidently merges immediately into the final time of salvation. Such elements of apocalyptic have also precipitated themselves in the later rabbinical literature, although the royal messianism absolutely predominates.

130. So lastly Cullmann, *Christologie*, p. 113.

131. The Son of man conception and the idea of the eschatological prophet are especially to be mentioned here.

132. In distinct variations in Ferdinand Christian Baur, *Vorlesungen über die neutestamentliche Theologie*, 1864, pp. 93ff.

133. Cf. Heinrich Julius Holtzmann, *Lehrbuch der neutestamentlichen Theologie* I, 1911², pp. 331f.; but also William Manson, *Bist du, der da kommen soll?*, 1952, pp. 136ff., especially p. 142.

134. So Dalman, *Worte Jesu*, p. 259.

135. Principally Joachim Jeremias, art. παῖς θεοῦ, *ThWb* pp. 653–713.

136. Ethelbert Stauffer, *Messias oder Menschensohn?*, *Nov. Test. I*, 1956, pp. 81–102.

137. Julius Wellhausen, *Einleitung in die drei ersten Evangelien*, 1905, pp. 89ff.; 1911², pp. 79ff.

138. Cf. Casey, *Earliest Christologies*, *JThSt* NS 9, 1958, pp. 258ff.

139. This has been emphatically stressed as a principle in method by Ernst Lohmeyer, *Galiläa und Jerusalem* (*FRLANT* NF 34), 1936, p. 93, and has its claims even if Lohmeyer's own prosecution of it cannot be taken as right.

140. The monograph by Philipp Friedrich, *Der Christus-Name im Lichte der alt- und neutestamentlichen Theologie*, 1905, is a stranger to all historico-critical questioning.

141. We can disregard the abortive attempt to derive the conceptions from sacral kingship and corporate personality.

142. We shall not here inquire particularly into Jesus' "understanding of himself". According to what has been said it is at least clear that it need not necessarily have been "messianic" if the title and conception are taken in the strict sense. Moreover, the self-consciousness of Jesus does not permit of its being simply fitted into the case of one of the traditional Jewish conceptions.

143. Cf. Albert Schweitzer, *Geschichte der Leben-Jesu-Forschung*, 1951[6], pp. 16ff.

144. Robert Eisler, *ΙΗΣΟΥΣ ΒΑΣΙΛΕΥΣ ΟΥ ΒΑΣΙΛΕΥΣΑΣ. Die messianische Unabhängigkeitsbewegung vom Auftreten Johannes des Täufers bis zum Untergang Jakobs des Gerechten nach der neuerschlossenen Eroberung von Jerusalem des Flavius Josephus und den christlichen Quellen dargestellt* (Religionswiss. Bibliothek 9) I/II, 1929/30, cf. especially I, pp. 188ff.; II, pp. 687ff.

145. Cf. on this Maurice Goguel, *Das Leben Jesu*, 1934, pp. 27ff. Felix Scheidweiler, *Das Testimonium Flavianum*, ZNW 45, 1954, pp. 230–243, especially pp. 242f.

146. Joseph Klausner, *Jesus von Nazareth*, (1930) 1952[3] with addenda.

147. S. G. F. Brandon, *The Fall of Jerusalem and the Christian Church*, (1951) 1957[2], pp. 101ff.

148. Hendrik van der Loos, *Jezus Messias-Koning. Een speciaal onderzoek naar de vraag of Jezus van Nazaret politieke bedoelingen heeft nagestreefd*, Assen 1942, especially pp. 6off., 254ff.

149. Oscar Cullmann, *Der Staat im Neuen Testament*, 1956, pp. 5ff.

150. The second Simon in the circle of Jesus' disciples was quite certainly a Zealot; the designation ὁ Καναναῖος in Mk. 3:18; Matt. 10:4 is derived from the Aramaic קנאן, and the rendering of it ὁ ζηλωτής in Lk. 6:15 and Acts 1:13 is practically correct. But that (Ἰούδας) Ἰσκαριώθ or ὁ Ἰσκαριώτης formerly belonged to the Zealots is uncertain, for this by-name can just as well indicate derivation as lean upon an Aramaicized σικάριος; cf. Dalman, *Jesus-Jeschua*, p. 26. The interpretation of (Σίμων) Βαριωνά in the sense of "terrorist" advocated by Cullmann, *Staat*, p. 11, is altogether problematic; cf. Hengel, *Zeloten*, pp. 55ff. Βοανηργές, the by-name of the sons of Zebedee, is still unexplained; cf. on this Taylor, *Mk.*, pp. 231f.

151. Cf. G. Bornkamm, *Jesus von Nazareth*, pp. 138f.

152. Cf. Joseph Blinzler, *Die Niedermetzelung von Galiläern durch Pilatus*, Nov. Test. II, 1958, pp. 24–49.

153. The much discussed text does not need to be dealt with here in detail. I refer merely to Martin Dibelius, *Rom und die Christen im ersten Jahrhundert* in *Botschaft und Geschichte* II, 1956, pp. 177ff.; G. Bornkamm, *Jesus von Nazareth*, pp. 110ff.

154. The saying comes from the logia source, but in Lk. 16:16 it is considerably transformed so that the discussion of its original meaning must be confined to the rendering preserved in Matthew. The statement of Matt. 11:12 can be carried back only to Jesus Himself.

155. So Joh. Weiss, *Das Matthäus-Evangelium* in *SNT* I, 1907², p. 317.

156. Cf. Gottlob Schrenk, art. Βιάζομαι, *ThWb* I, pp. 608–613; W. G. Kümmel, *Verh. u. Erf.*, pp. 114f.; just as the meaning "the kingdom of God is striven after with violence" must be excluded, so also must the understanding of it in the middle voice, "the kingdom of God breaks a way for itself with violence".

157. So Schrenk, *ThWb* I, p. 610.

158. So Martin Dibelius, *Die urchristliche Überlieferung von Johannes dem Täufer (FRLANT* 15), 1911, pp. 23ff.

159. Otto Betz, *Jesu heiliger Krieg, Nov. Test.* II, 1958, pp. 116–137, especially pp. 125ff.; parallels from the Qumran texts pp. 116ff.

160. Betz, *op. cit.*, pp. 129ff.; this exposition of the Matthew version of the saying about the sign of Jonah is in my opinion altogether unsuitable. The analysis of Anton Vögtle, "Der Spruch vom Jonaszeichen" in *Synoptische Studien (Festschrift für A. Wikenhauser)*, 1953, pp. 230–277, especially pp. 253ff. is correct. According to it there lies before us an alteration of the original text, an alteration that was taken up by the evangelists, and the three days and nights are conditioned by the prophetic text.

161. Cf. Betz, *op. cit.*, p. 124.

162. Betz, *op. cit.*, pp. 126f.

163. For the rest Betz's whole investigation is altogether happy in hypotheses.

164. Cf. Adolf Harnack, *Sprüche und Reden Jesu (Beiträge zur Einleitung in das NT* II), 1907, p. 62.

165. Cf. Billerbeck I, p. 586; J. Jeremias, *Gleichnisse*, p. 142, n. 2 (on πῦρ βαλεῖν).

166. Cf. the word about the sending of fire, Lk. 12:49f.

167. A life and death struggle is of course also included. But that it is a matter of every kind of discord is made very clear by Matt. 10:35f. par., even if we may not reckon straight away that the two texts belong to one another.

168. Cf. Schlatter, *Mt.*, pp. 349f.; Schniewind, *Mt.*, p. 135.

169. Cf. Hans Conzelmann, *Die Mitte der Zeit. Studien zur Theologie des Lukas*, 1960³, pp. 9, 22, and often, 172ff.—Lk. 4:13 and 22:3 represent the brackets.

170. Cf. Lk. 9:1ff.; 10:1ff. The material is certainly opposed to the Lukan conception, as the idea of the sending of "sheep" among "wolves" 10:3 alone shows.

171. Cf. also Lk. 21:12ff. par. Mk. 13:9ff.

172. So also Conzelmann, *op. cit.*, pp. 74ff.

173. Lk. 22:49,51 go beyond Mark and are to be regarded as Lukan.

174. So rightly Conzelmann, *op. cit.*, p. 75.

175. Cf. Karl Heinrich Rengstorf, art., ἱκανός, *ThWb* III, pp. 296f.

176. So Theodor Zahn, *Das Evangelium des Lukas (KommNT* III) 1920³,⁴, p. 687.

177. So especially Adolf Schlatter, *Die beiden Schwerter. Lk.* 22, 35–38 (*BFchrTh* 20/6), 1916, pp. 71f.

178. In the Old Testament there occurs the phrase לְ רַב and also דִּי likewise mostly with a suffix, but besides רַב עַתָּה (1 Kings 19:4; 1 Chron. 21:15); the simple רַב in the sense "enough" occurs in Gen. 45:28; Exod. 9:28; cf. Brockelmann, *Hebräische Syntax*, 1956, § IIa. In the LXX these passages are as a rule rendered by ἱκανούσθω σοι (ὑμῖν) or νῦν; the simple רַב is in the one place rendered by μέγα μοί ἐστιν and in the other by παυσάσθω. Actually the phrase in Deut. 3:26: ἱκανούσθω σοι, μὴ προσθῇς ἔτι λαλῆσαι τὸν λόγον τοῦτον, comes nearest to Lk. 22:38.

179. Heinz Schürmann, *Jesu Abschiedsrede Lk.* 22, 21–38, pp. 116ff.

180. Cf. in detail Schürmann, *op. cit.*, pp. 124ff.

181. Cf. also the linguistic observations in Schürmann, *op. cit.*, pp. 129ff.

182. Joh. Weiss, *Das Lukas-Evangelium* in *SNT* I, 1907[2], p. 513.

183. Jack Finegan, *Die Überlieferung der Leidens- und Auferstehungsgeschichte Jesu (BZNW* 15), 1934, p. 16: "literary introduction to the sword episode" at the time of the arrest.

184. At a first glance we expect βαλλάντιον καὶ πήραν as object; with μάχαιραν as the object we would rather expect the words to be arranged thus: ὁ μὴ ἔχων μάχαιραν ἀγορασάτω πωλήσας τὸ ἱμάτιον αὐτοῦ; cf. Klostermann, *Lk.*, p. 214.

185. Cf. Billerbeck I, pp. 343f.

186. Schürmann, *op. cit.*, p. 123, regards πωλησάτω τὸ ἱμάτιον αὐτοῦ as "possibly Lukan redaction"; here, however, we may not judge simply from the frequency with which words are used in Luke.

187. By that such an interpretation as is before us in Cullmann, *Staat*, p. 22 is excluded. It is true that the passage is not understood as a confession of Zealotism, yet it asserts that Jesus reckons with occasions "when for the sake of the proclamation of the Gospel it can be necessary for the disciple to carry a sword in self defence".

188. No sort of fundamental significance may be attributed to the fact that according to Mk. 14:47 parr. a disciple had a weapon with him and made use of it to protect Jesus, rather this must be understood from the menacing situation, in which in any case the disciples gave way at every step.

189. Mk. 11; (11) 12, 19 are redactional. An original parable may have lain at the basis of vv. 13f. The transformation of it into a story serves to demonstrate Jesus' power; in the addendum vv. 20–25 it is then interpreted as an instance of the marvellous belief that removes mountains. Mark has undone this connection and related the cursing of the fig tree to the cleansing of the temple.

190. So Jeremias, *Abendmahlsworte*, pp. 84f.

191. The ταῦτα "without connection" in Mk. 11:27 has a character different from that of the ταῦτα in Matt. 11:25, which is often compared with it; for in this second passage an actual definition is indirectly given to it—the divine secret of salvation is hidden and manifest; in Mk. 11:27, on the other hand, the reference is to a concrete occasion. Since moreover the cleansing of the temple and the question about authority

are also associated with one another in John 2:13ff., the two may also have originally belonged together in the Synoptic tradition.

192. Cf. Karl Ludwig Schmidt, *Der Rahmen der Geschichte Jesu*, 1919, p. 300; Lyder Brun, *Segen und Fluch im Urchristentum*, 1932, pp. 75f.; Lohmeyer, *Mk.*, pp. 234f.

193. Cf. the works of Ernst Lohmeyer which appeared after the publication of his Commentary, *Die Reinigung des Tempels*, ThBl 20, 1941, cols. 257–264; *Kultus und Evangelium*, 1942, pp. 44–51; similarly R. H. Lightfoot, *The Gospel Message of St. Mark*, 1950, pp. 6off., who besides the orientation towards the Gentiles especially emphasizes the character of the symbolical action (pp. 68f.); cf. also Joachim Jeremias, *Jesu Verheissung für die Völker*, 1959[2], pp. 55f.

194. I refer merely to Kümmel, *Verheissung und Erfüllung*, p. 111. (further literature there in n. 53).

195. Cecil Roth, *The Cleansing of the Temple and Zechariah XIV. 21*, Nov. Test. 4, 1960, pp. 174–181, understands the text as in fact an explicit rebuff to the endeavours of the Zealots. In Zech. 14:21 mention is made of the expulsion of every כנעני, which was ambiguous and could designate either the "trader, shop-keeper" or the "Canaanite".

196. Rightly emphasized very firmly by Schniewind, *Mk.* pp. 150f., who of late has tended to a messianic interpretation.

197. A detailed discussion of Mk. 11:1–10 follows in Chapter 4, pp. 255ff.; cf. also Chapter 2, pp. 83f.

198. I regard as altogether out of place the popular interpretation that, in view of the hope of a political Messiah entertained by the people and his disciples, Jesus decided upon this entry to demonstrate that his Messiahship accorded with Zech. 9:9 (cf. recently Taylor, *Mk.*, p. 452; similarly Kümmel, *Verh. u. Erf.*, pp. 109f.). For in any case the Messiah expected in Zech 9:9 is an actual ruler at whose coming there commence the conditions of time of the Messiah. It is frequently overlooked that between the Jewish conception of Zech. 9:9 and the later Christian interpretation of it (perhaps in Matt. 21:5) there exists a fundamental difference, in so far as Jesus is not merely a humble and peaceable king, but also a king who renounces all royal dignity and power, who is delivered up even to death and at whose appearing moreover the eschatological consummation did not take place.

199. Rather it is to be conjectured that Mk. 10:46ff.; 11:1ff. were bound together and were obviously connected when taken up by Mark; cf. chapter 4, pp. 253ff.

200. Here the Gospel of John also indicates no sort of association as between the cleansing of the temple and the question of authority.

201. That the story of the entry necessarily ended in the temple— so Jeremias, *Abendmahlsworte*, p. 85—and therefore must have led over directly to the cleansing of the temple, is not convincing. The entry is not primarily orientated to Jerusalem and the temple, but to the Mount of Olives as the place for the coming of the eschatological salvation, cf. Zech. 14:4; on that Klostermann, *Mk.*, p. 113.

202. Cf. pp. 191f. above.

203. Otherwise nevertheless John 6:14f.

204. On Mk. 8:27–33 cf. Excursus III, pp. 223ff.

205. Bultmann, *Syn. Trad.*, p. 277, sees here a polemic from the standpoint of the Hellenistic Christianity of the Pauline sphere against the Jewish Christian view represented by Peter. But this conjecture is not to the point, for the whole narrative, apart from the redactional elements, shows no Hellenistic traits.

206. Mk. 8:32. So far the exegetes who see a rejection of the Messiah title even in the Markan version, are on the right track; cf. Héring, *Royaume de Dieu*, pp. 122ff.; Oscar Cullmann, *Petrus, Jünger-Apostel-Märtyrer*, 1960², pp. 199ff.

207. That, however, no longer holds good for the isolated portion of tradition Mk. 8:27b–29. Accordingly the question suggests itself whether there was a tradition which gave expression to a radical rejection of the Jewish Messiah expectation.

208. Cf. on this Bultmann, *Syn. Trad.*, pp. 271ff.; but Jeremias, *Gleichnisse*, pp. 105f., also reckons with the possibility that the three temptation passages were at first handed down independently. In my opinion the two first temptations belonged together from the beginning.

209. So Bultmann, *op. cit.*; Schlatter, *Mt.*, pp. 95ff.; against Jeremias, *op. cit.*; Schniewind, *Mt.*, pp. 29f.

210. Disputed unfairly by Bultmann, *op. cit.*, pp. 273f.; he wants to see in all three temptations only situations of temptation such as confront every believer. But the pronouncedly Christological orientation of this portion of tradition may not be overlooked.

211. Cf. Cullmann, *Christologie*, p. 127.

212. It is not a matter of the Messiah conception having been "expounded" in the revolutionary, Zealotic sense—so Cullmann, *Staat*, pp. 16ff.—but of Jesus not having made any messianic claim at all in accordance with Jewish messianism, however otherwise his claim to sovereignty may be defined.

213. It can no longer be determined how far Jesus' word about the temple, a word much cited in the New Testament (Mk. 13:2 parr.; 14:58 par.; 15:29 par.; John 2:19f.; Acts 6:14), played a part in this.

214. Even the thorough investigation of Joseph Blinzler, *Der Prozess Jesu*, 1960³, cannot gloss over this. *Id., Das Synhedrium von Jerusalem und die Strafprozessordnung der Mischna"*, *ZNW* 52, 1961, pp. 54–65. But as much as he has thus brought out the historically correct legal state of affairs, as little is the historicity of the account of the proceedings before the supreme council guaranteed in this way. On the problems of the arrest and condemnation of Jesus cf. the recent important work of Paul Winter, *On the Trial of Jesus* (Studia Judaica I), 1961.

215. So Bultmann, *op. cit.*, pp. 301f.

216. Dibelius, *Formgeschichte*, pp. 178ff. has seen this clearly and brought it to prominence. Here indeed the Scripture proof is given not with the help of reflection-citations but by a take-over of the Old Testament wording into the narrative (pp. 187f.).

217. The view sometimes advocated that Mk. 14:60ff. may be a later addition which overlay the earlier account but that at least v. 58 still affords a historical support—cf., e.g., Dibelius, *Formgeschichte*, pp.

182f. or Wellhausen, *Mk.*, pp. 123f., who, it is true, eliminates only vv. 61f. and attaches vv. 63f. to Jesus' silence—is hardly right. As v. 57 and the resumption of v. 56 in v. 59 show, the word about the temple does not belong to the original text; cf. Bultmann, *Syn. Trad.*, pp. 291f. V. 56 must have been followed directly by v. 60, consequently at once by the question that brings into relief the contrast between Judaism and Christianity, so that nothing more is to be ascertained about the actual course of the trial. On Mk. 14:61f. cf. pp. 162ff above.

218. Disputed, it is true, by Blinzler, *Prozess*, pp. 24f.

219. Cf. on this Hans Lietzmann, *Der Prozess Jesu*, now in *Kleine Schriften* II, 1958, pp. 251–276; Blinzler, *op. cit.*, pp. 163ff.; Cullmann, *Staat*, pp. 28ff.; Paul Winter, *op. cit.*, pp. 10ff., 67ff., 75ff., 85ff.

220. Here an early stratum of tradition has been overlaid by a later one; cf. pp. 173ff. above.

221. This is clearly expressed by Lk. in 23:2 in a redactional but altogether pertinent note.

222. According to Winter, *op. cit.*, pp. 36ff., 44ff., 51ff. the initiative in proceeding against Jesus goes back not to the Jews but to Pilate; accordingly the behaviour of the procurator, as it is described in Mk. 15:1ff., may not be historically true, the picture of Pilate having been altogether transformed apologetically in early Christian tradition. I regard as exegetically incorrect this thesis that the Romans carried through the arrest of Jesus and that the Jewish authorities co-operated under pressure, if not unwillingly.

223. Cf. Karl Georg Kuhn—Walter Gutbrod, art., 'Ισραήλ, *ThWb* III, especially pp. 361, 376f.

224. As against that Matt. 27:17,22, where ὁ χριστός occurs in the mouth of Pilate, is secondary.

225. So Bultmann, *op. cit.*, p. 293. But otherwise Martin Dibelius, *Das historische Problem der Leidensgeschichte* in *Botschaft und Geschichte* I, 1953, p. 256 and lastly P. Winter, *op. cit.*, pp. 107ff.

226. Moreover, such a development explains itself most convincingly when the decisive motif has already been given. Besides the profane "King of the Jews" is not to be explained as a late Christological creation.

227. So, e.g. Joh. Weiss, *Urchristentum*, pp. 85f.; Bultmann, *Theol.*, pp. 50f.

228. Cf. especially Haenchen, *Apg.*, pp. 139ff., 163ff. and often; Ulrich Wilckens, *Missionsreden der Apostelgeschichte*, pp. 100ff.

229. Cf. Excursus III and Excursus V.

230. The thesis advocated by Lohmeyer, *Galiläa und Jerusalem*, especially pp. 92ff., of the existence side by side of two primitive churches, which are to be distinguished by different kinds of Christologies, must be regarded as having failed as a whole, but also largely in its treatment of individual texts.

231. Corresponding to the different kinds of connection in apocalyptic parallel uses permit of their being traced in early Christianity, as is shown for instance by Mk. 14:61f. and Rev. 20:4-6.

232. How far in Mk. 13:21ff., 24ff. elements of Jewish apocalyptic

are used, is of subordinate significance because in any case the identification of Jesus with the coming Son of man must be assumed as obvious.

233. Cf. Excursus II, and on the analysis of the text see note 217 above.

234. Apart from the content of this portion of tradition the twice repeated paraphrase of God's name in v. 61 and v. 62 goes to prove its great age.

235. This relates only to the early portion of tradition Mk. 14:55f, 60–64.

236. "Son of the Blessed" is also to be understood as messianic.

237. The "seeing" at the parousia here supposed may not be given a new interpretation or be qualified, as it is in Taylor, *Mk.*, p. 568.

238. But even the σὺ εἶπας of the Matt. text (26:64) must be understood in this sense; against Cullmann, *Christologie*, pp. 118ff., who, following Adalbert Merx, interprets this as an evasive answer.

239. Against Stauffer, *Nov. Test.* I, 1956, p. 88, In his opinion Jesus here completely ignores the Messiah question and answers with the Old Testament theophany formula ANI HU and a word about the Son of man.

240. Cf. on these definitions Bultmann, *Joh.*, p. 167, n. 2.

241. Otherwise Matt. 26:63f.

242. H. K. McArthur, *Mark xiv. 62*, NTSt 4, 1957/58, pp. 156–158, joins issue with Glasson and others in defence of the eschatological understanding of the phrase about the coming on the clouds of heaven, and in this he is doubtless in the right. Cf. T. F. Glasson *The Reply to Caiaphas (Mark XIV: 62)*, NTSt 7, 1960–61, pp. 88–93.

243. Consequently we are concerned with a "proleptic" statement about the Messiah—cf. on this Dalman, *Worte Jesu*, p. 259—but in a sense other than may have been assumed for it in the original version of the Caesarea Philippi story, where the concern is that Jesus should take in hand an actual mundane-messianic task in his lifetime.

244. It is difficult to say how far precisely the Jewish mission resulted in the originally avoided Messiah conception becoming popular.

245. J. Héring, *Royaume de Dieu*, pp. 128ff., quite rightly rejects all use of it in a positive sense within the life of Jesus. On the other hand, however, he reckons with an immediate "spiritualized" use of it in reference to the exalted Jesus by the primitive church. The difficulties which result from that are clear.

246. Against Haenchen, *Apg.*, pp. 170f.; with Wilckens, *Missionsreden der Apostelgeschichte*, pp. 152ff.

247. Otto Bauernfeind, *Die Apostelgeschichte* (ThHdKomm V), 1939, pp. 65ff.; Wilckens, *op. cit.*, who agrees in the main, but with a restriction to Acts 3:20f. Cf. also E. Schweizer, *Ern. u. Erh.*[2] p. 94, n. 330.

248. The composition of the mission discourses in Acts is to a large extent Lukan; cf. Martin Dibelius, *Anfsätze zur Apostelgeschichte* (FRLANT NF 42), 1951, p. 142; Wilckens, *op. cit.*, pp. 32ff., 72ff. The section commencing at v. 22, which contains the Scripture proof, shows this in detail very clearly, even if there the idea of Jesus as the new Moses has been taken over. In the section "Exhortation to Repentance" vv. 17–21, which belongs to the scheme of this discourse, Luke takes up

an eschatological kerygma besides the phrase in v. 18b drawn from the tradition of the passion. V. 17 is specifically Lukan (motif of the ἄγνοια of the Jews); in v. 19a the association of μετανοεῖν and ἐπιστρέφειν, which occurs again only in Acts 26:20, is characteristic of the author (doubtless as a hendiadys; somewhat differently Haenchen, *Apg.*, p. 168). The exhortation to repentance itself, especially v. 19b, is pre-Lukan, so also its connection with the eschatological proclamation, as the pre-Pauline phrase in 1 Thess. 1:9f. makes it possible for us to recognize. In v. 21b Luke takes up the thought that salvation had been proclaimed in advance by the prophets and with that he forms a transition to vv. 22ff.

249. The motif of the eschatological mission, which also has its place in the Elias tradition, is here connected closely with the appearance of the χριστός.

250. Only single features of the Elias expectation could be applied to Jesus. Otherwise it was above all the idea of the eschatological prophet as the new Moses that was applied to him (so indeed in Acts 3:22–26).

251. To that there corresponds the motif of v. 19, which has as its basis the Jewish idea that repentance is a condition of the coming of the time of salvation and can even hasten it; cf. Volz, *Eschatologie*, pp. 103f.; Billerbeck I, pp. 165ff., 599f. On καιροὶ ἀναψύξεως Hans Hinrich Wendt, *Die Apostelgeschicht e(KrExKommNT* III), 1913⁹, p. 106, rightly refers to 2 Thess. 1:7; Heb. 4:3–11; against Bauernfeind, *Apg.*, p. 68, who wants to see a breathing-space indicated in the necessity of the messianic throes. Even if the latter may perhaps have been the original implication of the concept, yet it does not come into question in the present connection.

252. This passage does not permit of its being understood as a simple Septuagintismus, so frequently does Luke make use of it elsewhere in Acts; against Haenchen, *Apg.*, p. 168, n. 4.

253. The concept προχειρίζεσθαι, especially in the emphatically temporal sense, is possibly Lukan.

254. This motif, which is associated in later Christology with the earthly appearance of the Son of God, still stands here in an eschatological connection. On the "sending" of the Son of God cf. Chapter 5, pp. 304ff.

255. The δεῖ shows that there has been some touching up in the Hellenistic style, but does not by any means do away with the thoroughly ancient character of this portion of tradition, for the word often plays a role precisely in apocalyptic connections as the translation of Dan. 2:28 in the LXX shows, also Mk. 13:7, 10, 14; Rev. 1:1 and often.

256. That possibly speaks even against an Elias conception proper, although on the other hand Elias is also occasionally expected at the beginning of the time of salvation (*Apo. of Elias* 42f. or when he is put on an equality with the messianic high priest), and that can have led to the taking over of the concept of "restoration". In the Old Testament the idea of removal to heaven is not associated exclusively with Elias.

257. With Heinrich Julius Holtzmann, *Die Apostelgeschichte (Hd*

CommNTI/2), 1901³, pp. 42f.; Wendt, *Apg.*, pp. 106f.; Bauernfeind, *Apg.*, p. 69; against Erwin Preuschen, *Die Apostelgeschichte* (*HbNT* IV/I), 1912, p. 21, who has taken over the exposition given by Overbeck, according to which it is a matter of the date of the conversion of the Jews.

258. Here Haenchen, *Apg.*, p. 168, enters unfairly into controversy with Preuschen, *Apg.*, p. 21.

259. I refer merely to Bultmann, *Syn. Trad.*, pp. 130f.; Klostermann, *Mt.*, pp. 204ff.; Jeremias, *Gleichnisse Jesu*, pp. 172ff.

260. Cf. G. Bornkamm, *Enderwartung* in Bornkamm–Barth–Held, pp. 21, 34f., 36f.; Tödt, *Menschensohn*, pp. 68ff.

261. So Bultmann, *op. cit.*; Vielhauer in *Festschrift für G. Dehn*, pp. 57f.

262. Even remote Egyptian parallels from the Books of the Dead can be pointed out as Bultmann, *op. cit.*, shows.

263. Cf. on this G. Bornkamm, *Jesus*, pp. 101f.

264. This has been set out above all by H. Braun, *Radikalismus II*, p. 94, n. 2.

265. Cf. Chapter 2, pp. 89ff above.

266. So Vielhauer, *op. cit.*, p. 58, n. 2.

267. Cf. only the מַלְכֵּךְ in Zech. 9:9 on the one hand and the relatively frequent מלכא משיחא in the rabbinical writings on the other hand.

268. Cf. Lk. 19:38; John 6:15; 18:37 (19:12, 15); further ὁ βασιλεύς σου following Zech. 9:9 in Matt. 21:5; John 12:15, also βασιλεῦσαι in Lk. 1:33; 19:14, 27.

269. This has been correctly seen by Sherman E. Johnson, *King Parables in the Synoptic Gospels*, *JBL* 74, 1955, pp. 37–39: Matt. 25:31ff. "is originally a parable of King Messiah"; he regards Son of man in v. 31 as secondary.

270. So Jeremias, *Gleichnisse*, p. 172; Tödt, *Menschensohn*, pp. 71f.

271. Rev. 11:15; 12:10; 20:4, 6. The use of Ἰησοῦς Χριστός in Rev. 1:1, 2, 5, can here be left out of consideration.

272. Cf. Bousset, *Apk.*, p. 331; there is here a "complete prolepsis". This has to be distinguished clearly from an exaltation conception which reckons with two different periods.

273. Cf. in detail Bousset, *Apk.*, pp. 437f.; Lohmeyer, *Apk.*, pp. 161f.; Hadorn, *Apk.*, pp. 195ff.

274. On Rev. 20 cf. Cullmann, *Christologie*, pp. 136f.

275. Grässer, *Parusieverzögerung*, pp. 76ff. has pointed out how the fact of the delayed parousia has precipitated itself in many individual features of the tradition of the early primitive church; but he has not seen clearly that, apart from the thought of a purely temporary postponement, already before "Luke's special outline" a theologically singular conception had been secured in the idea of exaltation, which attempted to cope with the delay of the parousia; cf. *op. cit.*, pp. 172ff.

276. Cf. Excursus II, pp. 129ff. and Chapter 2, pp. 103ff.

277. Cf. only the second portion of the hymn Phil. 2:9–11, which is oriented towards the Kyrios title.

278. This modification was relatively easy to carry out in virtue of

the apocalyptic background of the statements about messiahship associated with Jesus' parousia.

279. Cf. Mk. 12:35–37a and above all Rom. 1:3f. On this especially Chapter 4, pp. 246ff. below.

280. At the same time the Kyrios title minted afresh by the LXX naturally has an effect.

281. So in Rom. 1:4; Acts 13:33; 1 Cor. 15:25; Col. 1:13; Heb. 1:5; 5:5; cf. on this Chapter 5, pp. 286ff.

282. Cf. Chapter 2, pp. 103ff.

283. The Davidic sonship of Jesus certainly plays a certain part in connection with the parousia expectation, but not within the exaltation conception, rather by that precisely it is limited consistently to the earthly work of Jesus; cf. Chapter 4, pp. 246ff.

284. Cf. Chapter 2, pp. 106ff.

285. Cf. Martin Dibelius—Heinrich Greeven, *An die Kolosser, Epheser, an Philemon* (*HbNT* 12), 1953³, p. 9; Ernst Käsemann, *Eine urchristliche Taufliturgie* in *Exegetische Versuche und Besinnungen* I, 1960, pp. 43f.

286. Against Michel, *Röm.*, pp. 30f.; on this text and its classification cf. also Chapter 4, pp. 246ff.

287. Mk. 12:35–37a and Acts 2:36 must quite certainly be adjudged to the tradition of the early Hellenistic church.

288. Here one has to think above all of the experience of the present ministry of Jesus, which has precipitated itself progressively especially in the Kyrios title, perhaps also of the motif of the predestination of Jesus to the office of the eschatological Messiah as it presents itself in Acts 3:20 (there, however, indisputably without the idea of exaltation).

289. Thus earlier it was sometimes assumed that the Messiah conception, which was associated originally only with Easter, was connected step by step with the revelation given in advance in the transfiguration, then with the earthly work of Jesus onwards from his baptism and finally with the whole of Jesus' earthly life onwards from his birth; cf. Bousset, *Kyrios Christos*, p. 268, n. 2; Bultmann, *Syn. Trad.*, p. 279.

290. Cf. p. 159 above.

291. Friedrich Karl Feigel, *Der Einfluss des Weissagungsbeweises und anderer Motive auf die Leidensgeschichte*, 1910, p. 121, cf. pp. 116ff.

292. So especially Leonhard Goppelt, *Typos. Die typologische Deutung des Alten Testaments im Neuen* (*BFchrTh* II/43), 1939, pp. 120ff.; Christian Maurer, *Knecht Gottes und Sohn Gottes im Passionsbericht des Markusevangeliums*, *ZThK* 50, 1953, pp. 1–53.

293. Cf. E. Schweizer, *Erniedrigung und Erhöhung*, pp. 47ff., also pp. 81ff.

294. Cf. Dibelius, *Formgeschichte*, pp. 25,102.

295. To it there may perhaps be reckoned Mk. 14:1f., 10f., 18 . . . 26f., 43–52, 65; 15:1, 3–5 . . . 15b, 20b–24, 26f., 29a, 32b, 34 (35f.) 37.

296. Mk. 14:21,41.

297. Cf. on this pp. 160f. above.

298. That Mk. 14:55–64 competes with 15:1 and Mk. 15:2 with 15:3–5, has been rightly established by Bultmann, *Syn. Trad.*, pp. 290, 293.

299. I refer to Bultmann, *op. cit.*, pp. 293f.; P. Winter, *On the Trial*, pp. 91ff., 100ff.

300. A false interpretation may not be put on this passage so that σὺ λέγεις is interpreted in the sense of an evasive answer.

301. Cf. Bertram, *op. cit.*, p. 67.

302. There runs parallel to that a tendency in this underlining of the Messiahship of Jesus to emphasize nevertheless his political innocence and to claim Pilate as a witness for Jesus; so especially Matthew and Luke. Cf. on this Ellis E. Jensen, "The First Century Controversy over Jesus as a Revolutionary Figure", *JBL* 60, 1941, pp. 261–272; also P. Winter, *op. cit.*, pp. 51ff.

303. Similarly indeed in Mk. 14:61f. the Messiah title is interpreted by the Son of man conception.

304. Cf. Chapter 1, pp. 37ff.

305. This text must be discussed somewhat more in detail because of its importance in a material and traditio-historical respect.

306. Hans Frhr. von Campenhausen, *Der Ablauf der Osterereignisse und das leere Grab, SAH (phil.-hist. Kl.)*, 1958², p. 9.

307. τίνι λόγῳ does not mean "for which reason"—so Joh. Weiss, *I Kor.* p. 346; Lietzmann, *I Kor.*, p. 76 —but refers to the wording and therefore indicates the formal character of the tradition that follows; cf. Dibelius, *Formgeschichte*, p. 17; Lietzmann-Kümmel, *I Kor.*, p. 191.

308. The first thorough investigation of the passage as a fixed pre-Pauline tradition is in Alfred Seeberg, *Der Katechismus der Urchristenheit*, 1903, pp. 45ff.

309. Eduard Norden, *Agnostos Theos*, 1913 (1956⁴), p. 270, n. 1, has already attached great importance to this.

310. Some important treatises on 1 Cor. 15:3ff. busy themselves for the most part with these questions, above all Karl Holl, *Der Kirchenbegriff des Paulus in seinem Verhältnis zu dem der Urgemeinde* in *Ges. Aufsätze zur Kirchengeschichte* II, 1928, pp. 44–67; C. H. Dodd, "The Appearances of the Risen Christ" in *Studies in the Gospels (in Memory of R. H. Lightfoot)* ed. D. E. Nineham, 1955, pp. 9–36, especially pp. 27ff.; v. Campenhausen, *op. cit.*, pp. 13ff.; Hans Grass, *Ostergeschehen und Osterberichte*, 1956, pp. 94ff.; E. L. Allen, "The Lost Kerygma", *NTSt* 3, 1956/57, pp. 349–353; Paul Winter, "I Corinthians XV, 3b–7", *Nov. Test.* 2, 1958, pp. 142–150.

311. Jean Héring, *La première épitre de Saint Paul aux Corinthiens (Commentaire du Nouv. Test.* VII), 1949, p. 134, wishes to regard only vv. 3b, 4 as the sure stock of tradition.

312. So Michaelis, *op. cit.*, p. 12 and above all Ernst Bammel, *Herkunft und Funktion der Traditionselemente in I Kor.* 15, 1–11, *ThZ* II, 1955, pp. 401–419, especially pp. 402f.

313. Bammel, *op. cit.*, p. 402, mentions analogues "in equal number of words, homoioteleuton, and a *parallelismus membrorum* that is at the same time synthetic and antithetic".

314. Cf. Blass-Debrunner § 313 and § 191, I; otherwise Karl Heinrich Rengstorf, *Die Auferstehung Jesu*, 1960⁴, p. 57.

315. Against the ending of the formula at ὤφθη already v. Harnack,

op. cit., p. 64, n. 4; also v. Campenhausen, *op. cit.*, p. 9, n. 4; Grass, *op. cit.*, p. 94, n. 2—It may not be disputed that ὤφθη may also be used occasionally without the dative in the context of descriptions of visions, thus in Lk. 9:31 (cf. v. 30); Rev. 11:19; 12:1, 3; but this use is lacking not accidentally in the accounts of the resurrection.

316. In which case ὑπὲρ τῶν ἁμαρτιῶν ἡμῶν and τῇ ἡμέρᾳ τῇ τρίτῃ are completely analogous neither essentially (we are concerned with a statement regarding soteriology and one regarding salvation history) nor syntactically (in spite of the accidentally equal number of words).

317. Thorough reflections on the structure of the formula in Ernst Lichtenstein, *Die älteste christliche Glaubensformel*, ZKG 63, 1950/51, pp. 1–74, especially pp. 3ff.

318. So Wilhelm Heitmüller, *Zum Problem Paulus und Jesus*, ZNW 13, 1912, p. 331.

319. Bousset, *Kyrios Christos*, p. 73, has already admitted this, although he maintains (p. 76) that in 1 Cor. 15:3b–5 we must be concerned with a Gentile Christian tradition.

320. So Dibelius, *Formgeschichte*, p. 18.

321. Cf. on this Cullmann, *Die Tradition*, pp. 12ff.

322. Cf. in detail Jeremias, *Abendmahlsworte*, pp. 95ff.

323. Besides Jeremias there reckon expressly with an Aramaic *Vorlage* Lietzmann-Kümmel, *I Kor.*, p. 191; Rengstorf, *op. cit.*, pp. 47f; Lucien Cerfaux, *Le Christ dans la théologie de St. Paul*, 1954², pp. 24f.; Bammel, *op. cit.*, p. 418; Grass, *op. cit.*, p. 95; v. Campenhausen, *op. cit.*, pp. 9f. ("probably"); P. Winter in *Nov. Test.* 2, 1958, p. 143.

324. Schlatter, *I Kor.*, p. 394.

325. Cf. on this Schelkle, *Passion Jesu*, pp. 240ff.

326. The question of a full literal sense arises only in Mk. 16:6 parr., possibly also in Rev. 11:8.

327. Cf. the concordance. Besides a "putting of Jesus to death" is frequently mentioned.

328. The simple ἀπέθανεν can possibly have been once used in connection with the resurrection of Jesus; so I Thess. 4:14; similarly Rom. 14:9.

329. Cf. Bultmann, *Theol.*, pp. 47ff.

330. Cf. Excursus I.

331. So as the likely solution Joh. Weiss, *I Kor.*, p. 348; Lietzmann, *I Kor.*, p. 77; with emphasis especially Jeremias *Abendmahlsworte*, p. 97; *id.*, *ThWb* V, pp. 704f., 707.

332. Cf. Chapter 1, p. 39.

333. It is difficult to say how far the picture of the suffering righteous man has given occasion to that. Vicarious atonement was adjudged to the righteous man in late Judaism. Cf. Lohse, *Märtyrer und Gottesknecht*, pp. 78ff.

334. So Mk. 14:61a; 15:5; but also Lk. 22:37; Acts 8:32–35, further Matt. 8:17. In the atomistic exegesis of that time this is not at all surprising.

335. This point of view also merits consideration. Cf. on the avoidance of the statements about expiation in Isa. 53 Lohse, *op. cit.*, pp. 108ff.

336. For this reason Lohse himself, *op. cit.*, pp. 113ff., has brought the statement about expiation in 1 Cor. 15:3b into association with Isa. 53.

337. Cf. pp.180f. above.

338. Cf. Rom. 5:6, 7; 14:15b (15:3, 7b); 1 Cor. 8:11b; 2 Cor. 5:14b, 15a, 15b (21); Gal. 1:4a; Eph. 5:2, 25b; 1 Thess. 5:10a; 1 Tim. 2:6; Tit. 2:14a; 1 Pet. 2:21a; 3:18a and often. In association with "Son of God", e.g. Rom. 8:32; Gal. 2:20b.

339. This also suggests itself on grounds of style, for it would be surprising if one prepositional phrase was elucidated by a second.

340. So, e.g., J. Héring, *I Kor.*, pp. 134f., who, moreover, pertinently disputes the reference to Isa. 53.

341. So Rengstorf, *op. cit.*, p. 50.

342. Naturally a reference to written presentations of the history of the passion does not come into question; γραφαί doubtless denotes the Old Testament.

343. So Schlatter, *I Kor.*, pp. 395f.

344. So Rengstorf, *op. cit.*, pp. 51f.

345. Cf. v. Harnack, *op. cit.*, p. 64.

346. Cf. Mk. 16:6 parr.; Lk. 24:34; John 2:22; 21:14; Acts 3:15; 4:10; 5:30; 10:40; 13:30, 37; Rom. 4:24, 25; 6:4, 9; 7:4; 8:11 (twice), 34; 10:9; 1 Cor. 6:14; 15:15 (twice); 2 Cor. 4:14; 5:15; Gal. 1:1; Eph. 1:20; Col. 2: 12; 1 Thess. 1:10; 1 Pet. 1:21.

347. 1 Cor. 15:4, 12, 13, 14, 16, 17, 20; 2 Tim. 2:8; in 1 Cor. 15 there is the influence of the traditional formula, and in 2 Tim. 2:8 there may likewise be a stereotyped phrase.

348. So Rengstorf, *op. cit.*, pp. 54f.

349. Quite similarly in the secondary Markan conclusion 16:14: οἱ θεασάμενοι αὐτὸν ἐγηγερμένον.

350. ὁ θεὸς αὐτὸν ἤγειρεν and the like is read in all the instances from Acts in the passages named in n. 346 above, also in Rom. 4:24; 8:11 (twice); 10:9 (described as a confession formula); 1 Cor. 6:14; 2 Cor. 4:14; Gal. 1:1; Eph. 1:20; Col. 2:12; 1 Thess. 1:10; 1 Pet. 1:21. The transitive use referred to God of ἀνιστάναι in Acts 2:24, 32; 13:33f.; 17:31 may be a Lukan speech peculiarity.

351. That ἀναστῆναι was also used in very early tradition is obvious and is seen especially in words about the suffering and rising Son of man.

352. The early version of the words about the suffering and rising Son of man in Mk. 9:31 (Mk. 10:33f. is worded according to this) is independent of the Scripture proof, but it contains the μετὰ τρεῖς ἡμέρας. For the present there is no need to prove that there is no difference between this and τῇ τρίτῃ ἡμέρᾳ. The latter together with ἐγείρειν asserted itself more and more as the Matthaean and Lukan versions of the predictions of the passion show. The motif of the 3rd day also occurs in Mk. 16:1f. parr.; John 20:1; Matt. 12:40; 27:63(f.); Lk. 24:7,46; Acts 10:40.

353. This is shown by the early passion tradition in contrast to the Easter tradition; cf. Mk. 16:1ff. parr. Further it is shown by the short formulae about the suffering Son of man Mk. 14:21, 41; in Mk. 8:31

the ἀναστῆναι is certainly dependent on the superposed δεῖ, but actually it is only loosely connected with it. 1 Cor. 15:4 first repeats the idea of conformity to Scripture in its statement of the resurrection.

354. Against Grass, *op. cit.*, pp. 134ff., who recently has again vigorously advocated this interpretation.

355. Cf. on this Grass, *op. cit.*, pp. 127ff.

356. So lastly in particular v. Campenhausen, *op. cit.*, pp. 11f.; Héring, *I Kor.*, p. 135.

357. Cf. Joh. Weiss, *I Kor.*, pp. 348f.; v. Campenhausen would like to connect it with the discovery of the empty grave, but this is open to question; for 1 Cor. 15:4f. the close connection between the resurrection and the appearance is at any rate indisputable.

358. That this must be connected with ἐγήγερται and does not have the 3rd day in view, has already been stressed emphatically by Joh. Weiss, *I Kor.*, p. 348.

359. In this texts such as Hos. 6:2 or Jonah 2:1 have not played a special part, but statements such as Ps. 16:10; 49:16; 73:24, passages therefore which already in the original text promise most clearly life after death.

360. Here, however, otherwise than in the case of ἐγήγερται, we are by no means concerned with a passive as a "veiling statement about God", for occasionally the Appearing One (even Jahwe) is named as the subject; against Rengstorf, *op. cit.*, p. 57.

361. So v. Harnack, *op. cit.*, p. 70.

362. So Wilhelm Michaelis, *Erscheinungen*, pp. 103ff.

363. Rengstorf, *op. cit.*, p. 117; instances from the LXX and rabbinical texts on pp. 119ff.

364. Rengstorf, *op. cit.*, pp. 56f.; also reference to a possibly clear difference between ראה and מצא in the Old Testament and Judaism on p. 122.

365. On the strength of the not quite uniform terminology Grass, *op. cit.*, pp. 186ff., has concluded too quickly that nothing at all is to be gathered from the ὤφθη regarding the nature of the appearances.

366. Lichtenstein, *op. cit.*, p. 52.

367. There lies here, otherwise than in the case of the exaltation conception, no deliberate de-eschatologizing; the statements about salvation, however, are now no longer connected exclusively with the future, but are independently developed in reference to Jesus' death and resurrection.

368. The texts discussed thus far in Chapter 3 have all ὁ χριστός; even Acts 2:36 is no exception, κύριος and χριστός being there predicate nouns.

369. It is therefore widely assumed that the subject of this formula is actually a mere proper name. For that reason the exegetes frequently do not make any inquiry into this Χριστός in discussing this formula. The use as a proper name seems to suggest itself because occasionally even the simple name Ἰησοῦς can stand in brief formulae; so in Rom. 8:11a; 1 Thess. 4:14; but as will be shown, these circumstances have to be explained otherwise.

217

370. Cf. the very useful grouping of the different kinds of application of the Christos title in the New Testament in Ernest de Witt Burton, *The Epistle to the Galatians (ICC)*, 1921, Appendix III. 3: *ΧΡΙΣΤΟΣ*, pp. 395ff.

371. It is very rare in the Synoptic Gospels: Mk. 9:41; Lk. 2:11, also the vocative Χριστέ Matt. 26:28; in addition there is Ἰησοῦς Χριστός in Mk. 1:1, Matt. 1:1, 18; 16:21, as well as Ἰησοῦς ὁ λεγόμενος Χριστός in Matt. 1:16; 27:17, 22.

372. Rengstorf, *op. cit.*, 1960[4], pp. 129ff.

373. So Dalman, *op. cit.*, pp. 239f.; but also Rengstorf, *op. cit.*, 1960[4], pp. 129f.

374. Cf. Charles C. Torrey, Χριστός in *Quantulacumque (Studies presented to Kirsopp Lake)*, 1937, pp. 317–324, an article which is concerned almost exclusively with philological questions. "In the native Semitic speech of the Bible times 'Messiah' was not used by the Jews as a proper name"; also proof that precisely in the Babylonian Talmud forms with and without the article appear in the same connections (p. 319). But besides in passages of the Babylonian Talmud משיח without the article can be pointed out in Palestinian writings and indeed in Midrash literature, now and then already in the Tannaite period; cf. instances in Billerbeck I, p. 6. Torrey, *op. cit.*, pp. 320ff. would like on the strength especially of the New Testament passages to prove an early use in the Palestinian sphere. Even if we cannot reckon to the same extent as he does with written Aramaic *Vorlagen* of the Gospels and Acts, we must nevertheless take seriously into consideration the possibility that a משיח without the article can have been applied to Jesus already in the Palestinian church. Instructive in this regard are John 1:41: εὑρήκαμεν τὸν Μεσσίαν ὅ ἐστιν μεθερμηνευόμενον Χριστός and John 4:5: οἶδα ὅτι Μεσσίας ἔρχεται ὁ λεγόμενος Χριστός, where Μεσσίας is used once with and once without the article.

375. There is no occasion to understand the ὅτι at the beginning of line III as adversative; against Jeremias, *Abendmahlsworte*, p. 97.

376. Cf. A. Seeberg, *op. cit.*, p. 57.

377. Cf. on this E. Schweizer, *Erniedrigung und Erhöhung*, p. 52, n. 221.

378. Cf. only Rom. 6:9; 10:9; 1 Thess. 4:14; also Jas. 2:19; 1 John 5:1, 5; further Rom. 6:3 (ἢ ἀγνοεῖτε ὅτι); Phil. 2:11 (ἐξομολογεῖσθαι ὅτι).

379. Cf. I Cor. 11:23. With regard then to I Cor. 15:3b–5 we do not need to say that the ὅτι-clauses depend "ideally" on ἐπιστεύσατε, as does Norden, *op. cit.*, p. 271.

380. Norden appeals to this passage; there it is said: πιστεύομεν ὅτι ... λέγομεν ... ὅτι ... ὅτι ... καὶ ... ἔπειτα ...

381. So lastly Wilckens, *Missionsreden der Apg.*, pp. 73ff.

382. I refer on the one hand to Rom. 5:6, 8; 8:32; 14:15; I Cor. 8:11; 2 Cor. 5:14, 15a, 21; Gal. 1:4a; 2:20b; I Thess. 5:10a; on the other hand to Rom. 6:4, 9; 7:4; 8:11 (twice); 10:9; I Cor. 15:12(ff.), 20; 2 Cor. 4:14; Gal. 1:1; I Thess. 1:10a.

383. Thus Ἰησοῦς stands in Rom. 8:11a; I Thess. 1:10; 4:14; "Son of God" in Rom. 8:32; Gal. 2:20; κύριος in I Cor. 6:14; κύριος Ἰησοῦς

($Χριστός$) in 2 Cor. 4:14; Gal. 1:4; 1 Thess. 5:9 in the already mentioned brief formulae.

384. The independence of the early passion tradition and the Easter accounts must here be assumed.

385. Besides 1 Cor. 15:3b–5 cf. above all the Lukan texts.

386. That is the more significant because first of all, as the passion predictions show, a certain connection had begun with the Son of man title.

387. Cf. especially Bousset, *Kyrios Christos*, pp. 75ff.

388. The citation from Cullmann, *Christologie*, p. 111; he has failed to see the transformation of the title.

389. Nils Alstrup Dahl, *Der gekreuzigte Messias* in *Der historische Jesus und der kerygmatische Christus*, 1960, pp. 149–169.

390. Here we must dispense with detailed discussions as occasionally independent further developments and complicated connections with other views present themselves.

391. Characteristic of this older view is, e.g., the treatment of the Christos title in the excursus *Paulinische Formeln für Gott und Christus* in v. Dobschütz, *Thess.*, p. 61.

392. Günther Bornkamm, *Taufe und neues Leben* in *Das Ende des Gesetzes (Ges. Aufs.* I), 1958[2], p. 40.

393. As yet there lies before us only Nils Alstrup Dahl, *Die Messianität Jesu bei Paulus* in *Studia Paulina (in honorem Johannis de Zwaan)*, 1953, pp. 83–95; Cerfaux, *Le Christ*, pp. 361ff.

394. Cf. on this Dahl, *op. cit.*, p. 85.

395. Cf. Dahl, *op. cit.*, pp. 86f., 89.

396. The connection of "Christos" with this definite stratum of tradition has not been clearly seen by Dahl in the two works that have been mentioned.

397. This is emphasized especially by Cerfaux, *op. cit.*, pp. 361ff.

398. Cf. 1 Cor. 10:16ff.

399. Also the prepositional phrases particularly frequent in Paul $ἐν$ $Χριστῷ$, $σὺν$ $Χριστῷ$ and $διὰ$ $Χριστοῦ$ need a fresh classification and clarification in the light of these connections.

400. Without the inclusive "for many (all)", which is here so characteristic of the atonement statements from Isa. 53, coming to expression; it is a matter of deliverance and atonement for those who have returned to the shepherd and bishop of their souls (v. 25).

401. That in 1 Peter we have to reckon with firmly fixed tradition has been shown by Rudolf Bultmann, *Bekenntnis- und Liedfragmente im ersten Petrusbrief* in *Coniectanea Neotestamentica* XI (*Festschrift Anton Fridrichsen*), 1947, pp. 1–14.

402. It should then not be disputed that typical traits of the Christology of Hebrews are found in the section named, nevertheless there is a distinct precipitate of the earlier underlying conception. This needs further investigation since in Heb. 9:14 as in 1 Pet. 1:19 it is associated with the motif of the "blood of Christ".

403. Apart of course from Mk. 15:1ff. parr.

404. It has certainly to be observed that all formulations of this

stratum of tradition have chiefly the character of confession statements and therefore were hardly suitable for incorporation in the Synoptic tradition, quite in contrast to the Son of man logia, which are worded throughout as self-assertions. Luke has fitted the only two Christos words into the chapter on the resurrection and put the phrases in the mouth of Jesus Himself with the instruction of the disciples in view.

405. Cf. Acts 2:22–24; 3:13–15; 10:37–42; 13:27–31.

406. On the striking formulation in Acts 26:23 cf. Haenchen, *Apg.*, p. 613.

407. In Acts 2:31 ἀνάστασις τοῦ χριστοῦ; in 3:18, in connection with the statement of the prophecy that had been fulfilled, παθεῖν τὸν χριστὸν αὐτοῦ (*scil.* τοῦ θεοῦ).

408. In the great mission discourse before the Jews there is included a full Scriptural proof proper to each point (only 10:43a has an exceptional position); in 3:18 and 26:22 reference is made directly to the prophetic prediction, in 17:3 this motif comes to expression in ἔδει.

409. So Lohse, *Märtyrer und Gottesknecht*, pp. 187ff.

410. This holds good above all for the "him have ye slain" (in confronting the Jews), which is not traceable in the rest of the New Testament and is characteristic of the Lukan conception; but the phrase "God has raised him from the dead" with the active ἀνέστησεν has also to be mentioned here.

411. Cf. the passages Rom. 14:9; 1 Thess. 4:14.

412. Here not the ὁ χριστὸς τοῦ θεοῦ sometimes preferred by Luke and typical of him.

413. Besides Lk. 24:26, 46; Acts 3:18; 17:3; 26:23 (παθητός) also in 1 Pet. 2:21 (23); 3:18 (v. l); 4:1 in passion formulae, therefore no Lukanismus; cf. also Acts 1:3; Heb. 2:18; 5:8; 9:26; 13:12.

414. Cf. Chapter 1, pp. 39ff.; there also the argument that πάσχειν, for which there is no actual Semitic equivalent, must be regarded as a term of the Hellenistic church.

415. Cf. besides vv. 25b, 27.

416. It is a matter of a schema such as we are acquainted with in Phil. 2:6–11; 1 Tim. 3:16, even if there in the first part the idea of the incarnation occasionally stands in the foreground; in Phil 2:8 Jesus' death is certainly also mentioned, yet in association with a way-motif which is of another nature.

417. For that reason Luke 24:26 should not be cited, as it sometimes is, as an example of the passion tradition.

418. In Mark 2:1–12 it is primarily a matter not of the working of miracles, but of the forgiveness of sins; thus there actually remains only Matt. 8:5–13//Lk. 7:1–10.

419. Cf. on this Klausner, *Messianic Idea*, pp. 502ff.

420. A detailed discussion of this view and of its application to Jesus follows in the Appendix, pp. 372ff.

421. The most important testimonies are the Gospel of Matthew and the discourse Acts 3:12–26 composed by Luke, also the discourse of Stephen in Acts 7.

422. Cf. Chapter 5, pp. 288ff.

423. On the equating of "Christos" with "Son of God" cf. Matt. 16:16; Lk. 4:41; Acts 9:20, 22; John 11:27; 20:31.

424. Otherwise than in the case of the oldest form of the exaltation motif and in that of the Son of David or Son of God conception, there are as regards the generalized use of "Christos" no criteria for a co-ordination with the Hellenistic Jewish Christian or the Gentile Christian Church.

425. Cf. Excursus V.

426 The bestowal of the Spirit is found already in Isa. 11:2ff. and then in late Judaism fairly regularly in messianism.

427. Cf. on this Appendix, pp. 381f.

428. The story of the baptism itself contains "Son of God" used in the same sense.

429. W. C. van Unnik, *Jesus the Christ, NTSt* 8, 1961/62, pp. 101–116, proceeds on the assumption that "Messiah" was a firmly established title in Judaism and cannot have been carried over to Jesus at will.

430. Cf. Klostermann, *Mt.*, p. 94.

431. That this was not the only statement about Jesus does not need to be emphasized, for the expectation of his return determined the life and thought of the earliest church in a decisive way. But the primitive church also sought to comprehend Jesus' earthly work with the help of certain categories of interpretation. In summary it can be said that it understood the Jesus expected at the end of time as Son of man, Lord and Messiah, at the same time as the prophet who immediately precedes the end of time.

432. The titular character is clearly given prominence in Matt. 11:2 through the use of the article, and that may not be effaced by writing χριστός with a capital letter.

433. Cf. Acts 11:26 (also Tacitus, *Ann.* XV, 44). According to the more probable interpretation it is to be assumed that this designation was coined by non-Christians and not that the name was claimed by the church itself, even if χρηματίζω can have been used, in the sense "to bear a name".

434. Cf. pp. 157f. above and Excursus III.

435. This takes place in the form of a pronouncedly teaching conversation. The dependent relationship of Mk. 6:14–16 and 8:27b–29 is mutual. For 6:14a and 16 is certainly a redactional Markan formation which follows on 6:6–13 (in virtue of the sending out of the disciples Jesus' "name" is known everywhere) and leads over to the story of the death of the Baptist vv. 17–29. Mark has drawn the motif of this popular opinion about Jesus from the stereotyped portion of tradition Mk. 8:27b–29; on the other hand he assumes in 8:28a, in the assertion that Jesus is John the Baptist, the closer elucidation of 6:14b. It is not altogether excluded that the conclusion of 6:14b regarding the miraculous powers may be a redactional addition, but the reference to the Baptist (risen again) was taken over so that Mark found occasion to make full use of the tradition in the context of c. 6. The equations with the prophetic figures, apart from the return of Elijah, are difficult to explain in detail.

436. There also the detachment from the firmly fixed secular-political

royal messianism of the Palestinian tradition explains itself in the best way by far.

437. Nevertheless it must be observed that a considerable inheritance of Hellenistic Jewish Christianity has been preserved in the Son of God concept; also the close linkage of "Christos" and "Son of God" in statements about the earthly Jesus may have been domiciled there first of all.

438. Above all with ὁ κύριος ἡμῶν, but also with other designations of majesty.

439. That is suggested by a comparison with v. 39 and to a certain extent also by the *varia lectio.*

440. The Jewish Christian Matthew, who assuredly came from the Diaspora, has quite emphatically retained the titular usage in his Gospel; cf. Matt. 1:17; 2:4; 11:2; 16:16, 20; (22:42) 23:10; 24:5 (23); 26:63. Luke, who works up all sorts of tradition material from Hellenistic Jewish Christianity, assumes it; in the Gospel he largely follows Mark; he underscores the titular character in that in Lk. 3:15; 23:2; Acts 17:7 he emphasizes the contrast with the Jewish Messiah concept; moreover, in tension with Lk 2:11, 26, he connects the Christos dignity with the baptism, as Lk. 4:14, 18; Acts 4:26f.; 10:38 show, perhaps also the phrase ὁ χριστὸς τοῦ θεοῦ Lk. 9:20; 23:35, which is characteristic of him, is associated with this emphasized functional understanding; cf. Acts 9:(20)22; 17:3fin.; 18:5, 28. Reference may also be made to the usage in the Johannine writings. In John 1:35–51 "Messiah" (v. 41) is one of the many usual titles of majesty which are all carried over to Jesus. The Christian title is defended against the Jewish Messiah dogmatics, cf. John 7:27, 31, 41f.; 12:34. Moreover the union of "Christos" and "Son of God" is clear, as John 11:27; 20:31, also 1:49 expressly, and yet other text connections indirectly, make it possible for us to recognize. The Christos title undergoes a very interesting sharpening in John 20:31; 1 John 2:22; 5:1, whilst it crops up regularly in statements of a confessional kind, and indeed over against a docetic Gnosis, the danger of which had to be averted (cf. 1 and 2 John). Among the heretics the man Jesus was distinguished from the Spirit-Christus—for that the use as a proper name perhaps provided some support. To the author of the Johannine writings it is thus of great importance to prove their identity, whereby the titular meaning of "Christos". is again expressed realistically. That Jesus is "the Christ" is identified with the statement, "Jesus Christ has come in the flesh" (1 John 4:2; 2 John 7; apart from 1 John 2:22; 5:1, 1 and 2 John have elsewhere only Ἰησοῦς Χριστός).

EXCURSUS III

Analysis of Mark 8:27–33

THE narrative of Peter's confession outside Caesarea Philippi has a complicated structure and is by no means easily analysed traditio-historically.

Today, certainly, it should no longer be disputed that the Markan text is original as compared with that of Matt. and cannot on any account be conceived as an abridgement.[1] Indeed on making a comparison with Matthew we recognize that the text Mk. 8:27–33, being full to the utmost and not patient of any further development, breaks asunder; for in Matthew a new paragraph begins with 16:21 (par. Mk. 8:31), whilst in Mark the really characteristic feature is that Peter's confession and the prediction of the passion belong to one another.[2]

On the other hand, it is beyond question that Mk. 8:27–33 in its present form represents a composition and that in it several portions of tradition have been put together. This indeed is frequently acknowledged on principle, yet an analysis which inquires into the past history of the individual components is generally not carried out. In the case of this section of text such a dispensing with this cannot in my opinion be justified. Even if no absolutely certain results are obtained, yet it may perhaps be possible to realize more keenly how distinctive the text is.

First of all, the prediction of the passion in v. 31 proves form-critically to be a portion of tradition of a peculiar character.[3] The parallels in Mk. 9:31; 10:33f. show that here we are concerned with quite independent traditions.[4] 8:32a is closely connected with the prediction of the passion; together with the instruction to keep silence v.30 and the transition v.32b it is first of all to be set aside. The text vv. 27–29, 33 that remains after the elimination of vv. 30–32 does not represent a unity and cannot possibly be regarded as an independent portion of tradition.[5] V. 33 clearly contains a reference back to something and cannot simply be detached; on the other hand, however, vv. 27–29

223

do not absolutely require a continuation. In the contrast between what men say and the answer which the disciples give, the confession "Thou art the Christ" has its place as the climax and conclusion. By means of a question which to a certain extent is Socratic Jesus desires to lead the disciples to the correct answer.

What presents itself here is, judged form-critically, a teaching conversation. The fact that Jesus takes the initiative gives rise to the conjecture that we are concerned with a later formation,[6] and this is confirmed by the pronouncedly Christological content of the section. The parallel passage in 6:14–16 (14b, 15) shows that we are concerned with a portion of tradition that was formerly independent.[7] Observing that there is a double introduction in v. 27, we may see the proper beginning of the teaching conversation in v. 27b, in which doubtless the ἐν τῇ ὁδῷ, which occurs several times in the further course of Mk. 8–10, must be viewed as a redactional addition.[8]

If we eliminate vv. 30, 31, 32a, b as also vv. 27b–29, the question naturally arises whether completely disconnected fragments do not remain. Actually it is only hypothetically that we may venture a judgment regarding the rest of the text. A possibility nevertheless very much suggests itself and should be considered. V. 33 certainly belongs to an earlier portion of tradition and was not first drafted subsequently for the context that lies before us.[9] The point rests upon v. 33b, but even v. 33a does not give the impression of a secondary formation; at the same time v. 33b is hardly conceivable as an isolated logion. What can have preceded it?

As has already been mentioned, v. 27 contains a double introduction. V. 27b belongs to vv. 28f. V. 27a cannot possibly be referred to the foregoing narrative;[10] it can therefore be the old beginning of a portion of tradition which had its climax and conclusion in v. 33. A gap must then be assumed between them. If we wish to find out something about this, help is perhaps given by a consideration which precisely the interpolation of vv. 27b–29 makes possible.[11]

It seems to be not out of the question that in some way the discourse may have been about the hope of an earthly fulfilment by Jesus of Messianic expectations and therefore that a statement in the form of v. 29b can very well have had its original place here. The blunt rebuff in v. 33 then pillories all secular-political messianism as human striving.[12] Form-critically a biographical apophthegma would then present itself in vv. 27a . . . 29b, 33.[13]

However it may stand as regards the historicity—v. 33b does not give the impression of a subsequent formation—a portion of tradition of that kind could explain excellently how it is that in the very earliest period the Christos title plays to our surprise no role at all.

Moreover, from the apophthegma Mk. 8:27a . . . 29b, 33 that has been disclosed the formation of the present version of Mk. 8:27–33 can be well understood. If originally the Messiah title as such was rejected, it was adopted little by little and was reshaped by the church in such a manner that it could also be applied to the earthly Jesus. This had found its expression among other things in the teaching conversation vv. 27b–29. Nevertheless there was still reserve and the necessity of an exact definition of the Messiah title was obvious.

Thus, a positive judgment on the Christos title as compared with all the other designations named in v. 28 could be taken over, but at the same time through the prediction of the passion in v. 31 a practical "interpretation" of the Messiah confession was interpolated.[14] The rebuff of Peter was now referred only to the ignorance which he showed when confronted with the necessity of the passion, not to his confession itself.

If we consider the clamps which hold the text together in its final redaction, we must then ascribe the fusion to the evangelist. For v. 30 contains one of the instructions to silence which are typical of Mark:[15] the Messiah title is not rejected, but a demand is made that it be concealed. Also the introduction to the prediction of the passion in v. 31 can be shown to be redactional, both by the use of $\check{\eta}\rho\xi\alpha\tau o$ with the infinitive and by the catchword $\delta\iota\delta\acute{\alpha}\sigma\kappa\epsilon\iota\nu$.[16] V. 32a stands in connection with the Markan conception that everything befalls the people in parables, but the disciples receive an $\epsilon\pi\acute{\iota}\lambda\upsilon\sigma\iota s$ through esoteric instruction.[17] Finally, in v. 32b Mark has fashioned a transition which, connected again with $\check{\eta}\rho\xi\alpha\tau o$, takes up the $\epsilon\pi\iota\tau\iota\mu\hat{\alpha}\nu$ which has already been used in v. 30 and then follows again in v. 33a, whereby a fine word response is attained.[18]

A classification according to genre of this story composed of so many strata and so ingeniously, is not possible. Mark has

225

here created out of very different building-stones a scene which he was able to place in the centre of his Gospel as an important Christological statement.[19]

NOTES

1. With an abridgement by Mark there reckon not merely exegetes who assume the priority of Matthew, but also Bultmann, *Syn. Trad.*, p. 277; other supporters of the view are mentioned in the Suppl. Vol., p. 36. In favour of the greater age of the text of Mark there have rightly appeared recently: Oscar Cullmann, *Petrus*, pp. 196ff.; *id.*, *Christologie*, pp. 122ff; *id.*, art., Πέτρος, *ThWb* VI, pp. 104f.; *id. L'apôtre Pierre instrument du diable et instrument de Dieu: la place de Matt. 16:16–19 dans la tradition primitive* in *New Testament Essays (Studies in Memory of T. W. Manson)*, 1959, pp. 94–105; Anton Vögtle *Messiasbekenntnis und Petrusverheissung. Zur Komposition von Mt 16, 13–23 par.*, *BZ* NF I, 1957, pp. 252–272; II, 1958, pp. 85–103.

2. Cf. the ἀπὸ τότε Matt. 16:21. The Markan text may not on any account be torn asunder into vv. 27–30 and vv. 31–33, as it is in K. L. Schmidt, *Rahmen*, pp. 215ff; Lohmeyer, *Mk.*, pp. 161ff.

3. So also Dibelius, *Formgeschichte*, pp. 41, 112, who foregoes a determination of the genre of Mark 8:27–33 because of its compositional character, but on the other hand omits an analysis of this section of text.

4. On the predictions of the passion cf. Chapter 1, pp. 37ff.

5. This view was frequently defended in earlier times; so Arnold Meyer, *Die Entstehung des Markusevangeliums* in *Festgabe für Adolf Jülicher*, 1927, p. 44; Sundwall, *Zusammensetzung des Mk.*, pp. 54f.

6. Cf. also Bultmann, *Syn. Trad.*, pp. 69f. This may not in any case be understood as a *petitio principii*, but in a noteworthy way almost all portions of tradition in which Jesus takes the initiative show pronouncedly secondary features.

7. Mk. 6:14a. 16 is redactional. Cf. p. 221, n. 435.

8. Cf. Mk. 9:33, 34; 10:32, 52fin.

9. Against Bultmann, *op. cit.*, pp. 276f.

10. Against Bultmann, *op. cit.*, pp. 275f. K. L. Schmidt, *Rahmen*, p. 216, himself reckons with a new beginning, although elsewhere he frequently toys with so-called "diversions". Even the statement of place must be regarded as original here since no tradition-tendency can have been decisive for the naming of so definite a place.

11. In form-historical work more attention should be given to this formulating of the question.

12. Only for the underlying portion of tradition may it be said that v. (32)33 is the actual point of the story, but not for the present version as is done in Cullmann, *Petrus*, pp. 200f.

13. In an interesting way this disclosure of an early apophthegm is to a certain extent confirmed by the version of Peter's confession handed down in John 6:66–71. Certainly there is there a radical remodelling and a connecting with specifically Johannine traits, but the basic structure of the story shows surprising parallels to Mk. 8:27a . . . 29b, 33. In the beginning, John 6:66, it is said that the disciples "went back and walked no more with Jesus", and in Mk. 8:33 that is assumed; the middle portion vv. 67–69 contains the actual confession of Peter, where the original σὺ εἶ ὁ χριστός in pre-Johannine tradition has certainly been replaced by σὺ εἶ ὁ ἅγιος τοῦ θεοῦ in order to make the disciple's assertion acceptable; as in Mark Peter is finally snapped at as "Satan", so here the one who is to become the traitor is spoken of as "diabolos". The Johannine version clearly assumes the biographical apophthegm that is basic in Mark. On the other hand, similarly as in the teaching conversation Mk. 8:27b–29 a positive remodelling of the confession is given, except that John 6:66–70 belongs to an earlier stage. Here the Messiah title, which first of all was not transferable to Jesus' earthly work, is replaced by the designation ὁ ἅγιος τοῦ θεοῦ which was used of the eschatological prophet; on this cf. pp. 231ff., 380. According to what is stated in Chapter 3, pp. 189ff. precisely this early conception of Jesus as the eschatological prophet made possible at second hand the new version of the Christos title and its application to the earthly Jesus, therefore finally the confession of Jesus as the Christos with the rejection of all merely prophetic predicates Mk. 8:27b . . . 29. Consequently we have before us in John 6:66–70 the link between Mark 8:27a . . . 29b, 33 and Mark 8:27b–29. Mark has connected the earliest version of the story and this school conversation and besides has incorporated the passion tradition.—A form-historically interesting further moulding of Mark 8:27b–29 is found in the *Gospel of Thomas* logion 13, where the setting over against one another of the opinion of men and the confession of the disciples (or their representatives) is replaced by the setting over against one another of the views of different disciples (Peter and Matthew) and that of the true recipient of revelation (Thomas), who certainly formulates no confession but emphasizes the unspeakableness of the secret of Jesus. The *Gospel of Thomas* 13 is of course not directly dependent on the early portion of tradition taken up in Mark, but, as the continuation shows, on Matt. 16:13–20 (cf. p. 223 above); in place of the promise to Peter there appears a likewise inexpressible revelation of Jesus ("three words") to Thomas.

14. At the same time the passion tradition, which in any case had connected itself progressively with the Christos title, had an effect.

15. Wrede, *Messiasgeheimnis*, pp. 33ff.

16. On ἤρξατο c. inf. cf. Taylor, *Mk.*, p. 48; on διδάσκειν cf. Mk. 1:21, 22b; 2:13; 4:1f.; 6:2, 6b, 30, 34; 9:31; 10:1; 11:17; 12:35; 14:49.

17. Cf. Mk. 4:10ff., 33f., 7:17ff.

18. A sign that word responses are not at all significant merely as a symptom of portions of tradition that have been fashioned orally and been already transmitted to the evangelist, as is asserted (*passim*) in the already mentioned work of Sundwall. A clearly redactional oral

response occurs, e.g. in Mk. 1:45; 2:1f. There exists also a certain response between οἱ ἄνθρωποι 8:27b and τὰ τῶν ἀνθρώπων 8:33.

19. From this analysis it appears extremely improbable that the reference can be to an original resurrection story; so especially Bultmann, *Syn. Trad.*, pp. 277f. Just as little of course do we get along by going back for the whole Markan text to a "recollection of Peter" as Taylor, *Mk.*, pp. 374f. has recently done.

EXCURSUS IV

*The Conception of the High Priestly Messiah and the
Primitive Christian Tradition*

After having inquired into the royal messianism, its application to Jesus and its Christian remodelling, we must briefly investigate whether the idea of a messianic high priest has not left traces in early primitive Christian tradition.

It has been shown that in the post-exilic period the figure of a high priestly Messiah first appears in Zechariah and played a not unauthoritative role in the Judaism of the time of Jesus. The documents found in the Qumran caves show, as do the *Damascus Writing* and the *Testaments of the Twelve Patriarchs*, a setting of the high priestly Messiah over the royal. This, however, is to be regarded as a peculiarity of the Messiah expectation of the Qumran community, wherein it clearly differs from the doctrine of two Messiahs which occasionally crops up even in rabbinical literature.[1]

Within the New Testament a high priestly office of Jesus is spoken of explicitly only in Hebrews; in addition there are some fixed phrases in the First Epistle of Clement.[2] It has repeatedly been asserted that in both cases early traditions have been taken up.[3] Accordingly it has been asked whether elements of this view have not precipitated themselves elsewhere in early Christian tradition.[4]

On account of the significance of the Qumran discoveries for the illumination of thought in the Palestinian sphere, Gerhard Friedrich in especial has looked into the influence of high priestly messianism on the earliest tradition about Jesus as it remains preserved in the Synoptic Gospels.[5]

It is advisable not to detach the investigation of the Synoptics from the high priestly statements about Jesus which occur elsewhere in the New Testament, for there the derivation is not by any means clear and is certainly not settled by reference to the Qumran texts. This emerges from a closer consideration of Hebrews.

In all the strata of Palestinian late Judaism, and especially in the Qumran texts, the messianic high priest is a figure who appears only along with the messianic king.[6] If we assume their influence upon the Christology of Hebrews, that forces us to an assumption that is indeed not impossible and yet is not obvious without more ado, the assumption that the different "messianic aspects of the Messiah doctrine of the Qumran people" have been carried over to a single person.[7] Beyond that, however, it has to be considered that Hebrews is not acquainted with the derivation, essential for the Qumran texts, of the messianic high priest from Aaron, therefore from the family of Levi;[8] that assuredly is connected not alone with the fact that Jesus did not belong to the family of Levi;[9] rather the priestly office after the order of Melchizedek assumed for him stood as a matter of course in antithesis to the Aaronic priesthood.[10]

The whole conception of the high priestly office after the order of Melchizedek may have had roots very different from those of the two-Messiah doctrine of Palestinian late Judaism. For of vital importance in this is the contrast between what is heavenly and what is earthly, which led on the one hand to the spiritualizing of the cult conceptions[11] and on the other hand to opposition to the earthly priesthood. A clear indication of this is the fact that the high priest of the Melchizedek tradition has pronouncedly superhuman features and is almost a heavenly figure.[12] If we search after the previous history of this view, we shall turn to Hellenistic Judaism, a relationship with certain traditions worked up by Philo being also unmistakable.[13]

From Hebrews it is to be gathered that the idea of Jesus' high priestly office represents a development of the exaltation conception. Jesus' atoning passion and His ascent into heaven are certainly included in His high priesthood, but there emerge several tensions and defects in balance[14] so that it may be assumed that the author of Hebrews has himself built the statements about the passion into the high priestly doctrine;[15] in doing so he has doubtless allowed himself to be led, not by the co-existence of the death and resurrection of Jesus, but by the co-existence of His death and exaltation determined by a way-schema.[16] Doubtless, however, the emphasis is on Jesus' priestly office in heaven, in especial on His appearance before God for His own (7:25; 9:24).[17]

For this, but only for this, there are some pieces of evidence outside Hebrews. The ἐντυγχάνειν ὑπὲρ ἡμῶν Rom. 8:34 is related to Heb. 7:25 down to its wording. The motif of the heavenly intercession likewise occurs in 1 John 2:1.[18] Also the three passages in 1 Clement respectively refer to the function of the heavenly mediator and helper.[19] In Rom. 8:34 the ἐντυγχάνειν is expressly connected with the exaltation statement of Ps. 110:1 ὅς ἐστιν ἐν δεξιᾷ τοῦ θεοῦ. It can no longer be said with certainty how this connection was arrived at;[20] it is at least quite explicable how the later tradition was able to incorporate the Melchizedek conception once priestly functions had been carried over to the exalted Jesus. Evidently, however, it was only with the help of this Melchizedek tradition that the idea of Jesus' high priestly office was independently developed, whilst previously it was only a matter of the use of a single motif.

A dependence on the Qumran texts and their high priestly messianism cannot be shown to be likely either for Hebrews or for the motif of the heavenly intercessor. Moreover, we must understand that the transference of a cult trait to Jesus' work of salvation would not necessarily have resulted in Jesus being also regarded as a high priest.[21]

The feature repeatedly mentioned in the New Testament that by his death Jesus has obtained the προσαγωγὴ πρὸς τὸν θεόν[22] is sometimes understood in line with a high priestly function.[23] This would mean that already before the composition of Hebrews not only the work of the exalted Jesus but also Jesus' death was regarded as high priestly action. This phrase has, however, no exclusively cultic significance, but has likewise its place in legal terminology and in court ceremonial.[24]

It is a disputed question how far priestly traits are incorporated in the Christology of the Gospel of John. At least it must be seen that they have been considerably reminted and built into the author's total conception;[25] in my opinion it is little likely that an independent pre-Johannine conception of Jesus as high priest has been incorporated.[26]

Turning to the Synoptic Gospels, we must take one passage into serious consideration and investigate it accurately, the salutation of Jesus with ὁ ἅγιος τοῦ θεοῦ in Mk. 1:24, in the story of the casting out of a demon. The single parallel to this in the New Testament occurs in the Johannine version of Peter's confession, John 6:69, where in the Synoptics the Christos title is used.[27]

It is beyond question that John uses a portion of tradition;[28] on the other hand it is not difficult to recognize that this confession statement has been built into the theological context of the Gospel and must now be understood from there: "the Holy One of God" is equated with "Son of God" (10:36), he is sanctified by the Father and sent into the world (10:36) and has himself the function to sanctify others (17:19b).[29] But ὁ ἅγιος τοῦ θεοῦ is doubtless an earlier predication, for the origin and meaning of which we must make careful inquiry; for in Mk. 1:24 the phrase is already assumed in a fixed sense. An understanding of it as active[30] is not to be assumed here, the reference can only be to the One who has been sanctified by God.

That the designation must be a "Messiah predicate" because the magical aim requires a salutation that is as relevant as possible,[31] may hold good for the present context; but it says nothing regarding the idea that underlies the phrase; the same holds good for the interpretation that Jesus here encounters the unclean spirits as the bearer of the Holy Spirit and therefore stands over against them as a "pneumatic being" whose "divinity" they must recognize.[32] In this a Hellenistic understanding is taken as standard, it being decisive for the evangelist, but it cannot answer either to the early Palestinian tradition of this exorcism story[33] or to the original meaning of the predication "the Holy One of God".

Friedrich states emphatically that on the one hand the notion of holiness refers to the cultic sphere and in particular has a parallel in the designation of Aaron; that on the other hand the vanquishing of demons is regarded in the *Testaments of the Twelve Patriarchs* as the task of the messianic high priest.

So far as the destruction of the demons is concerned, the instances adduced from the *Test. of Levi* 18, 12 and the *Test. of Dan* 5, 10f. are not convincing and do not represent actual parallels. For there quite a different understanding of the evil spirits presents itself: in the stories of exorcisms in the Gospels the πονηρὰ πνεύματα are the authors of sickness (possession), but in the *Testaments* they are the followers of Beliar who must be vanquished by the messianic high priest in a holy war (*Test. of Dan* 5, 10); consequently the special dualistic conception of the Qumran texts is behind these statements,[34] whilst in the exorcism narratives we are concerned with the general belief in demons of late Judaism.[35] Accordingly these connections drop out.

How stands it then with the designation ὁ ἅγιος τοῦ θεοῦ? In Old Testament Jewish tradition "holy" is particularly a cultic concept, yet it may not be confined to that. Generally the reference is to what is separated from the world and belongs to God.[36] Thus Jeremiah can be "sanctified" a prophet (Jer. 1:5).

First of all, then, it is clear that we are concerned with a designation which points to a definite separation to a special task in God's name. Since the concept of holiness already occurs in late Judaism more frequently in eschatological statements,[37] we may in the case of "the Holy One of God" think specially of a function at the end of time.

But is it actually a matter of a priestly characteristic? It can be pointed out that in Ecclus. 45:6 Aaron is called ἅγιος and in Ps. 105:16 LXX even ὁ ἅγιος κυρίου, which brings us very near to Mk. 1:24. On the other hand, however, it must be observed that in 2 Kings 4:9 (LXX) it is said of Elisha: ἄνθρωπος τοῦ θεοῦ ἅγιος οὗτος; further in Wisd. 11:1 Moses is spoken of as προφήτης ἅγιος;[38] and in addition there is above all the statement of Samson according to Judg. 16:17 B: ἅγιος θεοῦ ἐγώ εἰμι ἀπὸ κοιλίας μητρός.

It thus appears that mention could be made of holy persons in connection not merely with the priesthood but also with the prophetic office[39] and that the titular ὁ ἅγιος τοῦ θεοῦ has a very close parallel in Judges 16:17 B.[40] If we add to this that the τί ἡμῖν καὶ σοί in Mk. 1:24 likewise has a connection with the tradition of Old Testament charismatic persons and men of God[41] and that precisely the narratives of the wonderful deeds of Jesus now and then bear traces which recall these figures, then ὁ ἅγιος τοῦ θεοῦ may be regarded very much rather as the equivalent of the designation of a charismatic person than as a parallel to the designations of Aaron that have been mentioned. It also tells in favour of that that the conception of the eschatological prophet was evidently carried over to Jesus at an early time,[42] and precisely from this a taking-over of elements of the charismatic tradition suggests itself.[43]

A connecting of Mk. 1:24 with the idea of the messianic high priest may be justified only if the influence of the high priestly messianism permits of its being identified elsewhere in the earliest tradition.

Friedrich has referred, apart from Mk. 1:24, to fifteen other Synoptic passages.[44] The address to Jesus "Son of God" in the exorcisms may certainly be assigned just as little as "the Holy One of God" to the context of the high priest conception.[45] That the baptism of Jesus was an act of priestly consecration is established neither by the parallel in the *Test. of Levi* 18[46] nor by Heb. 5:5–7, for this last-named text shows in its use of Ps. 2:7 that high priestly doctrine was later superimposed on the idea of exaltation.[47] A connection of the temptation story in Mk. 1:12f. with the *Test. of Levi* 18, 10 is altogether improbable.

As regards Jesus' inaugural preaching in Nazareth, Lk. 4:16ff., Friedrich himself allows that in Isa. 61:1 it is strictly speaking the prophets who are thought of. The discourse about the Son of David is said to prevent popular expectation of the messianic king and to point instead to the messianic high priest, but that can be made clear only by bringing in v. 4 of Ps. 110 which is not cited. "Here is more than the temple", Matt. 12:6, can hardly have the doctrine of the high priest in view.

In connection with the examination before the supreme council, the word about the Son of man is regarded as secondary because only the conception of the high priestly Messiah fits into the context with its word about the temple, Mk. 14:58, and the question v. 61,[48] but this analysis is not tenable.[49] Also the mockery of Jesus, Matt. 26:28, cannot be regarded as a typical mockery of a high priest.[50] In Mk. 15:35, Elias must be thought of, not as the high priest at the end of time, but as an helper in need at the present time.

It is not at all to the point to say that in Mk. 2:5ff. "Son of man" has again been brought in at second hand since the forgiveness of sins is a high priestly task.[51] The same holds good of the reflection regarding the connection of the high priest, temple and church in Matt. 16:18ff. That Mk. 1:40ff. must be understood as the activity of the eschatological high priest whom the earthly priests do not recognize, does not carry conviction. The blessing of the children in Mk. 10:13ff. likewise cannot be regarded as a specifically high priestly doing. Finally, the appearance of Jesus in the temple is certainly not represented as an act of the messianic high priest,[52] as also the temptation in Matt. 4:5–7 par. Lk. 4:9–12 cannot be explained from such a connection.[53]

Consequently, not one of the passages to which Friedrich has recourse is conclusive.[54] More than ever the simple ὁ χριστός signifies nothing regarding the messianic high priest.[55] The assumption that the idea of Jesus as the high priestly Messiah has been absorbed and covered over by the Son of man conception,[56] cannot be substantiated, for the Son of man conception is undoubtedly one of the earliest fixed Christological traditions and is largely self-dependent; priestly elements are altogether lacking.[57]

Moreover, that the early church face to face with Jews avoided speaking of Jesus, who did not stem from Levi, as the messianic high priest and that in consequence only a few pieces of evidence have been preserved, is an argument that carries little conviction.

When the New Testament material is surveyed, it has to be stated that apart from the high priest doctrine in the Epistle to the Hebrews, which stems from other roots, there are at hand no indications of an interpretation of the work of Jesus in accordance with high priestly messianism.[58] Only the function of the exalted Jesus, His interceding for the church before God, has probably been understood as priestly service, but, like the conception of exaltation itself, this may have ensued first on Hellenistic soil and stands in no recognizable connection with the idea that obtained in Palestinian Judaism. The earthly work of Jesus and His death have just as little been interpreted from that.[59]

It is not surprising that Jesus' work on earth has not been expounded with the help of this conception. For, on the one hand, what has to be said in regard to royal messianism holds good, namely that the appearance of the messianic high priest assumes the final dawning of the time of salvation. On the other hand, in His entire demeanour Jesus was altogether different from a priestly figure, so that a high priestly messianism did not in any way suggest itself.

An influence of the conception of the messianic high priest such as confronts us in the Qumran texts, cannot be shown to be likely in the New Testament.

1. On the idea of the messianic high priest cf. especially Karl Georg Kuhn, *Die beiden Messias Aarons und Israels*, *NTSt* I, 1954/55, pp. 168–179; Gerhard Friedrich, *Beobachtungen zur messianischen Hohepriester-erwartung in den Synoptikern*, *ZThK* 53, 1956, pp. 265–311; Kurt Schubert, *Die Messiaslehre in den Texten von Chirbet Qumran*, *BZ* NF I, 1957, pp. 177–197, especially pp. 181ff., 188ff.; A. S. van der Woude, *Die Mess. Vorstellungen* s.a.; Cullmann, *Christologie*, pp. 82ff.; Burrows, *Mehr Klarheit*, pp. 257ff.; Joachim Gnilka, *Die Erwartung des messianischen Hohenpriesters in den Schriften von Qumran and im Neuen Testament*, *RQ* 2, 1960, pp. 395–426, especially pp. 396ff., 405ff. Cf. also Chapter 3, pp. 141ff. and p. 201, n. 107.

2. Cf. Heb. 2:17; 4:14f.; 5:5–10; 6:19f. cc. 7–10; 1 Clem. 36:1; 61:1; 64:1.

3. Cf. Alfred Seeberg, *Der Brief an die Hebräer*, 1912, pp. 28, 156; Rudolf Knopf, *Die zwei Clemensbriefe* (*HbNT* Erg.-Bd. I), 1920, 106; Ernst Käsemann, *Das wandernde Gottesvolk* (FRLANT NF 37), 1957[2], pp. 107f., 124ff.; A. J. B. Higgins, "Priest and Messiah", *Vet. Test.* 3, 1953, pp. 321–336; Gottfried Schille, *Erwägungen zur Hohepriesterlehre des Hebräerbriefs*, *ZNW* 46, 1955, pp. 81–109.

4. So especially Olaf Moe, *Das Priestertum Christi im NT ausserhalb des Hebräerbriefs*, *ThLZ* 72, 1947, cols. 335–338; C. Spicq, *L'origine johannique de la conception du Christ-Prêtre dans l'Épître aux Hébreux* in *Aux sources de la tradition chrétienne* (*Mélanges M. Goguel*) 1950, pp. 258–269.

5. Friedrich, *op. cit.*, pp. 275ff.

6. Certainly the royal Messiah appears alone, but the high priestly Messiah nowhere does so; cf. Billerbeck IV/2, p. 789, which still holds good after the discovery of the Qumran writings.

7. So, e.g. Kurt Schubert, *Die Gemeinde vom Toten Meer. Ihre Entstehung und ihre Lehren*, 1958, pp. 136f. (following Y. Yadin); Hebrews may have been addressed to Jewish Christians "who came from the circle of the Qumran Essenes or from a circle of Jews whose Messiah doctrine resembled that of the Qumran Essenes".

8. Even for the Elias expected as the high priestly Messiah a derivation from Levi was postulated by the rabbis; cf. Billerbeck IV/2, pp. 789ff.

9. Heb. 7:13f.

10. This does not permit of its being explained by saying that the New Testament linkage of the idea of the high priest with the conception of the suffering Servant of God, who was in truth able to redeem men by the sacrifice of himself, a thing that the priestly service of the Aaronites was unable to do, had given occasion to such an antithesis; against Gnilka, *op. cit.*, pp. 420f.

11. This is also to be recognized everywhere in Hebrews.

12. Cf. only Heb. 7:1ff., where borrowing from tradition that had been

transmitted is very clear. The messianic high priest of the Qumran texts is, without detriment to his eschatological function, a human figure.

13. Cf. on this especially Hans Windisch *Der Hebräerbrief* (*HbNT* 14), 1931[2], pp. 61f.; Käsemann, *op. cit.*, pp. 125ff.

14. Cf. the celebrated dispute whether only the exalted Jesus or already the earthly Jesus is to be regarded as high priest; on this Käsemann, *op. cit.*, pp. 140ff.

15. Cf. Chapter 3, p. 187.

16. Cf. Phil. 2:6–11, also 1 Tim. 3:16.

17. Friedrich Büchsel *Die Christologie des Hebräerbriefs* (*BFchrTh* 27/2), 1922, p. 66, has rightly stated with emphasis that "the decisive thing in the priestly doings of Jesus is that he appears in the presence of God".

18. Connected there with the designation of Jesus as παράκλητος but this word is not used in the specifically Johannine sense.

19. Here ἀρχιερεύς is everywhere placed together with προστάτης. In spite of the dependence of 1 Clem. on Hebrews (especially clear in 36:2ff.) these phrases must be ascribed to the fixed language of liturgy.

20. It can be questioned whether the Old Testament motif of the free request of the king has here had an effect. In Ps. 110:4ff. there is no mention of priestly intercession, for which reason we cannot simply derive the idea from Ps. 110.

21. That holds good, e.g. for Rom. 3:25.

22. Cf. Rom. 5:2; Eph. 2:18; 1 Pet. 3:18.

23. Moe, *op. cit.*, cols. 337f.; Friedrich, *op. cit.*, pp. 267f.

24. Karl Ludwig Schmidt, art., προσάγω, *ThWb* I, pp. 131–134.

25. For a discussion of the above mentioned work of Spicq cf. Joachim Gnilka, *Die Erwartung des messianischen Hohenpriesters in den Schriften von Qumran und im Neuen Testament*, *RQ* 2, 1960, pp. 421ff.

26. The high priest title is lacking in John 1:35–51, where the different predicates of majesty are carried over to Jesus. The two most important passages which are adduced in favour of an acceptance of the high priest idea by John are 17:19 and 19:23.

27. Otherwise we have only to compare: ὁ ἅγιος in 1 John 2:20; Rev. 3:7; ὁ ἅγιος παῖς Acts (3:14) 4:27, 30; besides τὸ γεννώμενον ἅγιον in Lk. 1:35.

28. It has been mentioned in Excursus III that there are instructive connections between the Synoptic and Johannine renderings of Peter's confession.

29. Behind that, there stands the thought of the oneness with God made possible by the revelation.

30. Therefore in the sense of ὁ ἁγιάζων Heb. 2:11, as also is assumed in John 17:19a.

31. So Otto Bauernfeind, *Die Worte der Dämonen im Markusevangelium* (*BWANT* III/8), 1927, pp. 16f.

32. So Otto Procksch, art., ἅγιος, *ThWb* I, 102f.; he is followed by Gnilka, *op. cit.*, p. 410. Similarly Taylor, *Mk.*, p. 174; Barrett, *Joh.*, p. 253.

33. This is to be understood from Lk. 11:20 par., therefore in a functional sense, without reflection on essence. Cf. chapter 5, pp, 292ff.

34. Cf. on this Karl Georg Kuhn, *Die Sektenschrift und die iranische Religion*, *ZThK* 49, 1952, pp. 296–316, especially p. 301(f.), n. 4.

35. Cf. Bousset-Gressmann, pp. 339f.; Billerbeck IV/I, pp. 501–535, especially pp. 521ff.

36. In the Greek the word ἅγιος, which in any case is rare, is never applied to men; cf. Procksch, *ThWb* I, p. 88.

37. Cf. Bultmann, *Joh*, p. 344(f.), n. 6, also n. 5.

38. Here we should read ἐν χειρὶ προφήτου ἁγίου in the singular with the Vaticanus against the Alexandrinus, as it alone answers to the context.

39. We may also recall the "holy anointed" = prophets of CD II, 12; VI, 1f.

40. Eduard Schweizer, *"Er wird Nazoräer heissen"* (*zu Mc* 1, 24; *Mt* 2, 23) in *Judentum-Urchristentum-Kirche* (*Festschrift für Joachim Jeremias, BZNW* 26) 1960, pp. 90–93, has referred to Judges 16:17 B and for Mk. 1:24 has likewise pointed out an association with the expectation of the eschatological prophet.

41. It comes from the Elias story, cf. 1 Kings 17:18 (LXX): τὶ ἐμοὶ καὶ σοί, ἄνθρωπε τοῦ θεοῦ.

42. cf. Appendix, pp. 372ff. It may not then be said that "the Holy One of God" has no connection at all with the common Messiah, Saviour and Redeemer titles of the Jewish and Hellenistic tradition; so Bultmann, *Joh.*, p. 344.

43. If elsewhere exorcisms do not belong to the picture of the eschatological bringer of salvation, cf. Friedrich, *op. cit.*, p. 278, it has to be observed to what an extent they are characteristic of Jesus' earthly work, as Lk. 11:20 par. alone shows. They certainly fit nicely into the picture of the eschatological prophet and are mentioned in such a traditio-historical connection in Acts 10:38. On the other hand, many of the distinctive features of Jesus' demeanour may also have recalled those Biblical charismatic persons.

44. Friedrich, *op. cit.*, pp. 279ff.

45. Cf. on the derivation and character of the Son of God designation of Jesus in the miracle stories Chapter 5, pp. 288ff.

46. Cf. Excursus V., p. 346, n. 49.

47. Friedrich, *op. cit.*, pp. 283f.

48. Friedrich, *op. cit.*, pp. 289ff.

49. The word about the temple fits very loosely into the structure of this story; cf. Chapter 3, p. 208, n. 217.

50. Friedrich, *op. cit.*, p. 291.

51. It is a matter here of a prerogative of God on which Jesus encroaches.

52. Then Jesus had himself to enter into the sanctuary, cf. on this text Chapter 3, pp. 155ff.

53. Cf. Chapter 5, p. 295.

54. Gnilka, *op. cit.*, pp. 409ff., also comes by the same result, although he sometimes judges the texts differently.

55. Against Friedrich, *op. cit.*, pp. 302f.

56. Friedrich, *op. cit.*, 305ff.

57. As regards the words about the Son of man, elements of the passion tradition have been included only in the later groups of sayings, sporadically in Mk. 10:45b the idea of the vicarious suffering Servant and in Lk. 19:10 the conception of Jesus as σωτήρ.

58. Moreover, considerable doubts arise against the consideration that Jesus had applied to himself the idea of an ideal priesthood after the order of Melchizedek; so Cullmann, *Christologie*, pp. 87ff.

59. We must, moreover, realize that the idea of the self-sacrifice of the high priest is unusual and may be an extension of a view already accepted in virtue of Jesus' history.

CHAPTER IV

SON OF DAVID

THERE is no comprehensive recent study of the "Son of David" tradition.[1] In order to be in a position to understand the significance of this title of dignity and of the Christological statements connected with it, we must make a short survey of its total, but not very frequent use in primitive Christianity.

1. *Jesus as Son of David in the Oldest Tradition*

Assertions of the status of Jesus as Son of David go back to the early Palestinian church, where an important part must have been played by genealogical trees and the attempt to demonstrate the descent of Jesus from the house of David. Family registers are "in substance and form a native element in the Jewish inheritance".[2] The genealogies preserved in Matthew and Luke have of course been several times worked over, and cannot be simply regarded in their present form as documents emanating from the Palestinian, Jewish-Christian church. Nevertheless, in spite of their complex development, their original intention stands out so plainly that an analysis can be undertaken.

In Matthew the genealogy (1:1–17) has in v. 16 been pierced at the decisive point by the acceptance of the theologumenon of the virgin birth;[3] further, the thesis of sonship of David has been relativized by the continuance of the line of the fathers up to Abraham, as a result of which the thought of divine election has been brought into prominence;[4] finally, the whole has been set in an apocalyptic framework.[5] The basic constituent must have been a family tree from David through Joseph to Jesus.[6]

Also in Luke (3:23–38) an originally shorter genealogy is to be presupposed, reaching back probably only to the Davidic Zerubbabel.[7] Here the tracing of the descent backwards went through David as far back as Adam, by which means a typological parallelism of Adam and Christ was meant to be attained;[8] further, here again a hebdomadal system has been imposed;[9] 3:23 in its present form is Lucan, and in v. 38 the evangelist has added τοῦ θεοῦ in order to obtain an indirect testimony to the status of Jesus as Son of God, and so a link to the story of the baptism. For our present purpose all these modifications are to be disregarded.[10]

In their original form both genealogies presuppose the fatherhood of Joseph; only so are they at all meaningful, and thus the direct natural connection of Jesus with the house of David. It is true that we cannot assume that we have here in every detail genuine family traditions, for the difference between the two genealogies contradicts the idea.[11] But it may be inferred that the family of Jesus was conscious that it belonged to the lineage of David and that Jesus in fact sprang from David's line.[12]

It is indisputable that in the time of Jesus the question of family descent still played a part even among the people,[13] and for the family of Jesus this is confirmed by the information of Hegesippus concerning the relations of Jesus who were introduced to the emperor Domitian.[14] This, however, does not explain the significance attributed to this fact in the early Palestinian church and which gave the impulse to the development of continuous genealogies carried back as far as David or Zerubbabel. This phenomenon is only understandable if the descent from David was brought into connection with the view that Jesus had the dignity and office of a royal Messiah.

It has already been seen that the ancient messianic expectation which was thoroughly this-worldly in its roots, was able to be linked to the eschatological work of Jesus. It is true that this did not happen in the very first stages of the formation of Christological tradition, yet it took place relatively early and in any case on Palestinian soil. As our study of the title "Messiah" suggested, the declarations were as a rule placed in an apocalyptic setting, and in part also connected with the Son of man concept.[15] In view of the substantial involvement of the messianic hope with the promises which were specially given to the posterity of David and which concerned the restoration of the Davidic kingship, it is not surprising if such elements found application to Jesus. That the descent of the Messiah from the house of David played a decisive part in OT and late Jewish times and belonged to the really permanent elements in royal messianism was likewise noted.[16]

It must not, of course, be forgotten that the description "Son of David" is markedly infrequent and in a clearly pre-Christian context occurs only in *Psalms of Solomon* 17:21; only in post-Christian times does it become more frequent in Jewish traditions.[17] Even the primitive Christian tradition does not offer a thoroughgoing use of the title υἱὸς Δαυίδ[18] but makes use of all sorts of variants.[19] Nevertheless, it need not be assumed that "Son of David" first struck root in the soil of earliest Christianity;[20] it was certainly adopted but obviously goes back to a not very ancient linguistic use.

Again, it must be borne in mind that apart from Davidic descent as a messianic qualification, the promise of the restitution of David's rule over Israel shows plain this-worldly political features. If such assertions were not altogether avoided by the early church, it is manifest that a very concrete ultimate transformation of things was looked for. Of course, only the connection with the thought of the return of Jesus offered a specifically apocalyptic background, and brought such expectations under a definite sign, but in the awaited cosmic revolution the old messianic promises were not cancelled but rather fulfilled. Thus what were clearly this-worldly elements in the messianic expectation could be absorbed into the pattern of the basic apocalyptic thesis, and in fact there was precedent for this in Judaism.

If, moreover, the Davidic descent of Jesus had to be taken into the account, then it is quite understandable why the early church, despite its original repudiation of the messianic idea, despite the prevalence of the Son of man conception, found itself compelled to absorb royal messianism into its eschatological expectations, and why it seized upon the old Jewish promise of a new Davidic kingdom.

One of the most suggestive pieces of material for the Son of David tradition is to be found in the introduction to the Gospel of St. Luke. In the form in which it has come down to us, it stems, apart from some editorial elements, from the early Hellenistic Jewish-Christian church, but it contains older material which deserves close attention.

The first part of the Benedictus, Lk. 1:68–75, is an eschatological hymn, as Gunkel has recognized and has proved in detail.[21] Hope is directed to a successor of David as the promised bearer of salvation. In accordance with ancient Israelite tradition, there lies at the heart of this a markedly this-worldly conception of salvation, such as is precisely characteristic of royal messianism. God wills to visit His people, and to procure for them redemption, He will set up a "horn of salvation" in the "house of David, His servant", He will send an earthly ruler, whose mission it will be to free the people from their enemies and from all adversaries,[22] and He will restore the holy covenant so that a worship of God in holiness and righteousness may take place.[23]

It is quite possible and even probable, that this text is pre-Christian.[24] The earliest church could none the less appropriate this hymn, and doubtless referred it to the eschatological office of Jesus.

The fact that the Benedictus is no solitary exception is shown by the existence of an ancient bit of tradition which later became embedded in the annunciation of the birth of Jesus, namely, Lk. 1:32f. Here again the thought is that of an earthly kingly rule over Israel, which will last for ever; the ultimate king will accede to the "throne of his father David", he will be "great"[25] and will be called "the Son of the Most High".[26]

This last predicate is especially informative, because it expresses a typical element in the messianic concept; for of course the idea is that of adoption to sonship of God in the sense of Ps. 2:7, and in connection with the process of enthronement.[27] In contrast with the preterite mode of expression found in Lk. 1:68–75, which is adapted to the style of the eschatological hymn[28] we find here direct future tenses.

In regard to this passage too there can be no doubt that the promise, because of the careful, formal structure and the lofty style in which it is expressed, must be regarded as a stereotyped traditional piece which perhaps was likewise derived from Jewish tradition. In any case it was not first conceived for its present context, as may be seen from the unmistakable difficulties which have been experienced in adjusting it to the latter.[29]

That this tradition, which in the later version of the Lucan introduction, was referred to the earthly mission of Jesus, belonged in fact originally to the context of the eschatological creed of the first church, may be supposed not only from the corresponding use of Christos and Son of God but also is to be inferred from the fact that in the Revelation of John the

Son of David concept is in three places expressly referred to the eschatological work of Jesus.[30]

In Rev. 5:5 the expression ὁ λέων ὁ ἐκ τῆς φυλῆς Ἰούδα, ἡ ῥίζα Δαυίδ is used. This is the predicate of the Lamb, standing before the throne of God, that was found worthy to open the seven seals. One cannot fail to recognize that we have here a characterization of the dignity and the authority of the Messiah. The first phrase has been coined by adaptation of the messianically understood text Gen. 49:9(f.) The origin of the second description ἡ ῥίζα Δαυίδ is more difficult to determine. What is certain is that here ῥίζα, corresponding to the Hebrew equivalent, denotes not the root itself, but the young shoot or sprout of the root; David is the origin from which the scion springs. Whence arises this motive? There are no unequivocal linguistic examples of an original צֶמַח דָּוִד[31]. In the LXX ῥίζα is found as a translation of שֹׁרֶשׁ.[32] So we might think of Isa. 11: (1a)1b, 10, though we should have to note that instead of the shoot from the stump of Jesse we have here a shoot springing from David himself, a substitution which will probably not have taken place wholly without the influence of צֶמַח דָּוִד.[33]

The context introduces thoughts which are characteristic of the Revelation; the motive of the Lamb, the idea of the sealing and the opening of the book. If we set aside the connection with the death of Jesus which is suggested by ἀρνίον ἐσφαγμένον and the *terminus technicus* νικᾶν,[34] then the ascriptions refer to the eschatological work committed to the lamb seen in vision. The same situation is found in Rev. 22:16b: ἐγώ εἰμι ἡ ῥίζα καὶ τὸ γένος Δαυίδ, ὁ ἀστὴρ ὁ λαμπρὸς ὁ πρωϊνός. The predicate ἡ ῥίζα (Δαυίδ) has been completed by the qualification τὸ γένος Δαυίδ which must not be weakened to "from the house of David",[35] but has been rightly understood by Büchsel as being a parallel to υἱὸς Δαυίδ;[36] thus perhaps it could still more directly be traced back to צֶמַח דָּוִד. As in Rev. 5:5 further motives of royal messianism are adopted. The expression ὁ ἀστὴρ ὁ λαμπρὸς ὁ πρωϊνός is in fact based on the oracle of Balaam in Num. 24:17, even though in its formulation we may detect an influence of Isa. 14:12. The whole authorizing statement of Rev. 22:16, together with the response in v. 17, shows plainly that the ascription to Jesus in v. 16b is again an allusion to His eschatological office.

The text Rev. 3:7 is a further illustration of the point. The very fact that in the visions of the Revelation, and also in chapters 1–3 Jesus appears always as the future One confirms that in 3:7 the words ὁ ἔχων τὴν κλεῖν Δαυίδ, ὁ ἀνοίγων καὶ οὐδεὶς κλείσει, καὶ κλείων καὶ οὐδεὶς ἀνοίγει are an allusion to an eschatological function. The "key of David" is to be distinguished from the "keys of death and Hades", mentioned in 1:18, and of course still more from the "key of the bottomless pit" of 9:1 and 20:1.[37] Just as the underworld and the kingdom of the dead were thought of as being locked by keys, so in a similar fashion was the world of the future.[38] What in Matt. 16:19 is described as the "keys of the kingdom of heaven", is here called with a clearly messianic emphasis "the key of David", on which account Isa. 22:22 is here quoted also. It is therefore hardly probable that it is a question of the "key to the ultimate abode of God";[39] one might rather say that it must be the key to the city of David, the new Jerusalem;[40] the most obvious thing is to speak in quite general terms of the key to the still future and therefore locked kingdom of the Messiah.[41] Hence it is here too a question of the future office of Jesus, even though it is possible to speak already of the open door of the church (3:8).

Summary. It is to be concluded that the Davidic descent of Jesus cannot be disputed, and that, just like the title Christos and other features of the royal messianic expectation, so also the promise of the restoration of the Davidic rule was applied to the eschatological work of Jesus.

The fact of the descent of Jesus from David's line could thus be understood in the sense of a legitimate presupposition, for the one chosen by God had to be of the house of David; but the descent of Jesus will have acquired quite simply the value of a legitimation, and not least will have contributed to the fact that the specifically this-worldly elements of the Davidic promise and the royal messianism in general were in spite of everything accepted and absorbed after some hesitation. Jesus, sprung of the house of David, is therefore not only the expected Son of man and Kyrios, but also the king promised in the OT, and on Him ultimate power is conferred. In this process, features of the messianic concept which expressed a purely this-worldly realization of salvation were accepted as well; in most cases, however, the latter were fitted into an apocalyptic framework, as is plainly to be seen from the Revelation of John.

From the juxtaposition of Jesus' earthly descent from the line of David, and the eschatological realization of the Davidic reign which it was hoped He would bring about, there arose from the first what was clearly a tension; the characterization "Son of David" could already be applied to the earthly Jesus on the ground of His descent, but the fulfilment of the promises granted to the shoot of David, on the other hand, was expected only in the future. This tension characterizes the whole primitive Christian tradition of Jesus as Son of David and will also explain in an essential degree the further development of the tradition.

2. *Jesus as the Son of David in Hellenistic Jewish Christianity*

The view of Jesus as the Son of David received its most characteristic expression in the sphere of Hellenistic Judaic Christianity.[42] It shows throughout a close dependence on the Jewish background, especially the OT promise, but none the less reveals some essential deviations from the oldest Palestinian tradition. In the first place, the status of the earthly Jesus as Son of David acquires an independent objective importance; secondly, the expectation of ultimate enthronement is stimulated by the motive of exaltation connected with the resurrection. This latter has already shown itself in another connection to be a pointer to acclimatization in the early Hellenistic church.[43]

Rom. 1:3f. occupies a key position in the thesis of Jesus as Son of David. If the characteristic significance of this Christological formula can be elucidated, then the other Son of David affirmations can be interpreted accordingly. The traditional passage taken over by Paul has in recent times been treated in different ways.[44] In studying it we shall start with some general considerations. The structure of this confessional formula has been appropriately described as showing a "Christology built up in two stages".[45] Paul has somewhat obscured this by his introductory expression περὶ τοῦ υἱοῦ αὐτοῦ which has to be understood in the sense of a superior title of dignity; hence this must be disregarded. Further, the concluding predicates Ἰησοῦς Χριστὸς ὁ κύριος ἡμῶν which are frequently to be found in Pauline proems,[46] must be separated off. Both these points have been widely conceded.

But the question, whether within the piece of tradition there are still further secondary elements, has been variously answered. Eduard Schweizer[47] has convincingly shown that κατὰ σάρκα and κατὰ πνεῦμα ἁγιωσύνης may not be regarded as Pauline additions.[48] But he regards ἐν δυνάμει as a subsequent interpolation, because by this means the concept of a sonship of superior degree arises, and the formula is thus brought into appropriate relation with the main Son of God idea.[49] However, this is hardly conceivable within the pattern of Pauline Christology. Hence we shall have to regard ἐν δυνάμει also as a constituent part of the original formula, and consequently shall not need to take interpolations into account at all.

The first line presents in detail no special problems. γίνεσθαι ἐκ is current in genealogical statements,[50] and occurs also in Christological contexts,[51] where the participial formulation is in characteristic style.[52] σπέρμα to denote posterity is frequent both in Jewish OT and Greek linguistic usage; the singular is understood collectively. ἐκ σπέρματος Δαυίδ occurs further in the NT at John 7:42; 2 Tim. 2:5 and, somewhat differently phrased, in Acts 13:23. So far the formula contains no peculiarities and follows the ancient traditional pattern recognizable as basic in genealogies.

It is only the κατὰ σάρκα which gives the phrasing of the first member a new accent, since the genealogical expression is here marked by a very essential, more precise qualification. σάρξ and πνεῦμα are used in this formula to denote the earthly and heavenly spheres.[53] This has its analogy in 1 Tim. 3:16 and 1 Pet. 3:18b,[54] though it must be noted that here the distinction between the fleshly and spiritual kingdoms is linked to quite other Christological ideas.[55]

In Rom. 1:3 the prepositional phrase declares that the descent from the line of David qualifies precisely the time of the earthly life of Jesus. But this is not understood only in the sense that physical descent from David is the presupposition and legitimation of the future messianic function.[56] The fact that there are assigned to the status as Son of David and to that as Son of God two different spheres of operation, and that these are juxtaposed in such a way as to suggest a "first"—"then", has the consequence that the idea of a Davidic reign as the true description of the messianic office of Jesus disappears, while the predicate "Son of David" on the other hand is used especially to denote His earthly mission. It is thus not strange that the title "Son of David" straightaway denotes "the Messiah in the condition of His humanity and lowliness",[57] and thus a specifically Christian sense is imposed on the Jewish predicate of dignity.

The second line, Rom. 1:4, offers manifold difficulties. The ὁρισθῆναι at the beginning is of course clear; it means "to be appointed, designated",[58] and is substantially parallel to the κληθῆναι of Lk. 1:32. υἱὸς θεοῦ must accordingly be understood in the sense of the conferring of a dignity and office; again we have here a clearly OT Jewish mode of thought. In any case the conception of a sonship of God must not be taken in the physical sense. The kingly predication of Ps. 2:7 has here been assimilated. The decisive break with the old Palestinian view which was explained at the beginning, lies, as has already been intimated, in the transference of the predicate which was at first referred to the eschatological work of Jesus to His present reality, or to be more precise, to His exaltation. There is no reason to dispute the presence of an adoptionist idea, if it is borne in mind, firstly, that this term must be understood in the light of OT Jewish thought, and not in the light of later Christological controversies, and, secondly, that this adoption as Son of God is preceded by a special emphasis on the status of Son of David, hence by a preparatory Christological stage.[59]

The way is now paved for an explanation of the other ideas in v. 4. From a purely formal point of view ἐν δυνάμει can be referred either to the verb or to the title "Son of God". No decision can be made on grammatical lines, hence we must investigate the content for criteria. Our starting point is the observation that ἐν δυνάμει occurs in the logion about the coming of the kingdom of God in Mk. 9:1;[60] the phrasing is quite similar, with trifling variants, in the prediction of Mk. 13:26, where it is said that the Son of man will come μετὰ δυνάμεως πολλῆς καὶ δόξης.[61] Thus in these cases the expression denotes the ultimate event by which the work of salvation will reach its final consummation.

Also in 1 Cor. 6:14 we read of the divine δύναμις in regard to the future general resurrection of the dead, but in the same passage and in 2 Cor. 13:4 the expression refers also to the resurrection of Christ. These Pauline texts throw light on our present context in so far as eschatological statements are here used proleptically in the framework of Christology, which in the case of the resurrection of Jesus, regarded as an anticipation of the general resurrection, was an obvious course.

In Rom. 1:4, however it is a question not of resurrection, but of exaltation, of the conferring of a messianic dignity which has already taken place, and this again can be regarded only as a first step in de-eschatologization. For not only the predicate "Son of God" but also the eschatological description of the authoritative appearing and effectual reality are applied to the risen Lord raised to heaven. Hence there certainly exists the possibility of connecting the ἐν δυνάμει with the title "Son of God", not in the sense that to the status "Son of God in power" there must correspond a present, hidden status as Son of God, but in the sense that the exalted Lord even now takes over His messianic function in its fullest range.[62]

"Designated Son of God in power" means therefore that in any event the adoption and the enthronement for the assumption of messianic power coincide. There is thus no essential difference if ἐν δυνάμει is linked to τοῦ ὁρισθέντος υἱοῦ θεοῦ as a whole, and thus understood adverbially, which perhaps is the interpretation to be preferred.[63] On the grounds of parallelism to v. 3 κατὰ πνεῦμα ἁγιωσύνης ἐξ ἀναστάσεως νεκρῶν must be regarded as a unified expression. As far as πνεῦμα is concerned, what is necessary has already been said in connection with the σάρξ idea. The Semitic turn of phrase πνεῦμα ἁγιωσύνης replaces (τὸ) πνεῦμα (τὸ) ἅγιον[64] which is usual elsewhere in the NT and already in the Septuagint, as correspondingly the shortened formula ἐξ ἀναστάσεως νεκρῶν instead of ἐκ (τῆς) ἀναστάσεως αὐτοῦ (τῆς) ἐκ νεκρῶν is used.[65] In view of the parallel to κατὰ σάρκα in v. 3, it needs no further proof to show that πνεῦμα should not be understood individually, nor κατὰ instrumentally. If σάρξ and πνεῦμα are descriptions of the human and the divine kingdoms, hence also descriptions of the earthly and the heavenly worlds, then κατὰ πνεῦμα ἁγιωσύνης must be regarded as a description of the heavenly mode of existence.

We must at once make it clear, however, that this statement should not be interpreted in the sense of a heavenly divine "nature", for such a conception is foreign to the formula and to the Jewish mode of thought which lies at its basis. Nor should we bring into it the antithesis of corporeality and non-corporeality; it is solely a question of the contrast between the sphere of weakness, transience, sinfulness, and the sphere of divine power, life and salvation.[66] Hence κατὰ πνεῦμα ἁγιωσύνης implies that the authoritative designation as Son of God has taken place, not under earthly conditions, but under the exclusive operation and within the unlimited rule of the spirit of divine holiness. In His heavenly mode of existence the One born of the seed of David and risen from the dead has taken over the authoritative function of the Son of God and has assumed the office of Messiah.

In regard to the concluding shortened expression ἐξ ἀναστά-σεως νεκρῶν, it is an old debate whether the ἐκ should be understood temporally or causally;[67] at times a middle way has been sought, namely, a combination of temporal and causal meaning.[68] Now, of course, it must not be said that the resurrection cannot be "the ground of the exaltation, but only its first manifestation",[69] for the event of the resurrection is the presupposition for the exaltation in its true sense, that is, enthronement at the right hand of God. But neither may we speak of an exaltation "in virtue of" the resurrection, as if the resurrection were not only a presupposition but a real *causa efficiens*, for the older tradition shows that just such a mutual coinherence of resurrection and messianic function is by no means a matter of course.[70] We should then have to assume a very faint causal meaning in the sense of priority and co-ordination, and should come very near to the above mentioned middle solution. But this is not convincing, and the temporal understanding of ἐκ can be supported by exegetical considerations.

First, we must again be reminded that the affirmation of the resurrection cannot imply the thought of exaltation but rather the converse is true;[71] there would therefore be no necessity to mention the resurrection here for substantial reasons. Secondly, the structure of this two-line statement shows that as regards the two Christological stages, a characteristic event for each is named, in v. 3 the birth of Jesus and in v. 4 His heavenly enthronement. If in the first line the prepositional qualification κατὰ σάρκα was sufficient, then in the second line there was needed alongside the κατὰ πνεῦμα ἁγιωσύνης an unequivocal temporal qualification, if the designation as Son of God were to be unmistakably understood in the sense of exaltation and not in the sense of the parousia, even though this has already been intimated by the use of the aorist participle.

Hence it is here a question of the current "initiatory acts" of this two-stage Christology, of the birth as the beginning of the earthly reality as Son of David, of the exaltation as the beginning of the mode of existence κατὰ πνεῦμα ἁγιωσύνης as Son of God and messianic king, and in this process the resurrection marks the temporal turning-point between the lowliness and the exaltation of Jesus.[72]

The peculiarity of the piece of tradition contained in Rom. 1:3f. is twofold: firstly, the adoption of the thought of exaltation, and of the de-eschatologization of the messianic office of Jesus that is bound up with this and, secondly, the independent development of a Christological stage preceding that of exaltation, in connection with which the status as Son of David is regarded as the decisive characteristic.[73] In this way both "Son of David" and "Son of God" are in a high degree Christianized, and no longer to be understood directly in the light of Jewish tradition.[74] Traces of a similar two-stage Christology are also to be recognized in 2 Tim. 2:8,[75] but here there is no firmly stereotyped unified piece of tradition, but we have two particular modes of expression[76] and, moreover, the resurrection is mentioned before the descent from David's line.

While the statement about Davidic origin is in line with the tradition contained in Rom. 1:3f., the resurrection motive, which here admits no thought of exaltation as well, stems from quite a different tradition to which already the precedent (Ἰησοῦς) Χριστός points. Old traditional material has here been seized upon and exploited, but the various Christological conceptions from which these formulations has grown, have lost their compulsive force. The current expressions which however have become mere formulae are combined at will.[77]

Following the results attained from our investigation of Rom. 1:3f., the texts of the synoptic tradition, excluding the birth stories which represent a group on their own, must now be studied and considered from the point of view of the history of tradition.

Mk. 12:35–37a has already been discussed in connection with the Kyrios title, and was briefly touched on in our consideration of the Christos title.[78] We must now go into a detailed examination of the meaning implied in the sonship of David in this passage. It is precisely this which is the aim of the whole section, with its introductory and concluding questions, and this must not be overlooked, however central and emphatic may be the affirmation of the Lordship of Jesus. It has for long been disputed in what sense the title "Son of David" is included here alongside the other titles of exaltation. The thesis, that in this argument the title "Son of David" is altogether rejected, was especially expounded by Wrede. He invokes a series of later witnesses, the most important of which he regards as Barnabas 12:10f.[79] In fact here the "Son of David" title is repudiated as unsuitable, and Ps. 110:1, as a prophecy of David, who himself fears the error of sinners, is cited in opposition.

But there is no plain indication that this kind of debate goes back to the earliest Christian times, for in the gospel of Mark and also in Matthew and Luke, in connection with the son of David question, affirmations of Jesus' being Son of David are calmly and unhesitatingly accepted, and this fact cannot be argued away by simply referring to the very varied origins of the traditional material;[80] further, the point of view of the Letter of Barnabas is better explained against the background of the situation in the second century.[81] However, it is equally unacceptable to see in Mk. 12:35-37a a rejection, not indeed of the title, but of the politico-nationalistic ideas bound up with it, as has recently been contended by Cullmann,[82] for it must be presupposed that the title "Son of David" like the titles Kyrios and Christos are taken in a specifically Christian sense.[83]

If we are not willing to accept a "paradoxical unity" between the Son of David and the transcendent Kyrios (which is an improbable hypothesis to postulate for the thinking of that time),[84] then it must be considered whether the text cannot be explained in the sense of the two-stage Christology.[85] It has already been seen that the quotation from Ps. 110:1 in v. 36, and consequently the Kyrios title, is meant to be referred to the exalted Lord. The two questions in v. 35b and v. 37aβ especially the interrogative particles πῶς and πόθεν must be carefully differentiated.[86]

πῶς is certainly to be understood in a very general sense. This means: the starting point for the passage is the traditional thesis, that the Messiah must stem from the house of David: "How can the scribes say that the Christ is the son of David?" The answer is given in connection with the OT quotation in v. 37aα: "David himself calls him Lord (i.e. Christ)." From this is to be inferred the already discussed equivalence of Christos and Kyrios; both titles are used in connection with the messianic enthronement in heaven, hence with the act of exaltation.

But to this is added now a special question: πόθεν αὐτοῦ (scil. Δαυίδ) ἐστιν υἱός; πόθεν, "whence", will be best translated here as "in what sense, from what point of view". The concluding question then means: in what sense can Jesus be spoken of as the "Son of David", in view of this statement of David which describes Jesus as his Lord, as the Christ? To this no answer was given.

It is just this silence which gave rise to the supposition that the sonship of David was in general to be repudiated. But since elsewhere in the primitive Christian tradition there is no question of this and since we have Rom. 1:3f. as an outstanding parallel, we shall have to understand the answer implied in v. 37aβ as something on the lines of our two-stage Christology.[87]

Messianic dignity and Lordship are assigned to the Risen and Exalted One; but this lofty dignity and function of rule over all mankind and the whole world does not exclude that Jesus in His lifetime was Son of David and that as such He occupied a quite special position of dignity. Consequently the sonship of David is a characteristic of the earthly reality of Jesus, and has the value of a prior stage of exaltation existing alongside the confession of the messianic power of the exalted One.

We have no description of the earthly office of Jesus implied in the "Son of David" dignity. But we do possess two other pieces of traditional material which unfold and qualify the earthly activity of Jesus in His capacity as Son of David, namely, Mk. 10:46–52 and 11:1–10. The Bartimaeus story, as is easy to recognize, is not homogeneous in its present form and reveals a later redaction; but it is precisely these secondary portions which are important and which show that this story was subsequently drawn into the Son of David tradition.[88] What is significant is the combination of the address υἱὲ Δαυίδ ('Ιησοῦ) with ἐλέησόν με. It is the cry of the sick and suffering who expect, and in fact receive, help from Jesus.

When the title "Son of David" is combined with this almost formal expression, then it becomes clear that the earthly work of Jesus is interpreted in the light of His compassion with men and the outreach of His loving assistance. To what extent a specifically Christian interpretation is here imposed on the "Son of

David" theory, is seen when it is realized that the messianic king of Judaism was not expected to be a doer of miraculous deeds.[89] But the Christian community attempted to explain the idea of the Son of David by applying it to the earthly life of Jesus and to pour into it the rich content of Jesus' special earthly activity. It is not only the humanity of Jesus and the physical relationship with the great king of the past which the predicate is meant to express, but the peculiar features of His marvellous appearance on earth. The tradition which combines the truly messianic function of Jesus with His exaltation is far removed from simply transferring to the earthly Jesus the predicates of exaltation proper to the kingly Messiah. And yet it is concerned to speak of the earthly Jesus in such a way as to suggest that already the splendour of the imminent messianic glory falls upon Him and that the latter is adumbrated symbolically.[90]

How has this come about? Quite certainly it is not yet the case that, as could be observed in regard to the messianic title, by appeal to the wonderful work of Jesus as an eschatological prophet and a new Moses the messianic concept has been transferred to the earthly Jesus.[91] On the other hand, it will have to be appreciated that an incipient influence and independent elaboration of that tradition is beginning. In view of the formation of the concept of exaltation, it was no longer possible to speak as unhesitatingly as in the oldest tradition about the restoration of the Davidic kingdom; rather, the fact of messianism, especially in connection with Ps. 110, 1, was clearly interpreted in the sense of heavenly dignity and power. The fact that the substance of the Davidic promise was now linked to the earthly activity of Jesus is probably mainly to be explained by His descent from David's line.

However, the church stemming from Judaism did not at first undertake to apply to the earthly Jesus truly messianic traits. Instead it combined the picture of His work as a performer of miracles, which had already been developed in the Palestinian tradition, with the motive of His sonship of David. And just as in the oldest tradition, the earthly work of Jesus was brought into relation with His future messianic office, so now here the Davidic sonship was linked with the heavenly enthronement of Jesus after His resurrection. That we are here in the presence of a relatively independent conception is shown not least in the relevant miracle stories by the already firmly fixed exclamatory cry: υἱὲ Δαυίδ ἐλέησόν με which in the primitive Christian tradition has only here found a fairly secure place.[92]

The petitionary cry ἐλέησόν με which frequently occurs in the Psalter,[93] should not be understood in such a way as to suggest that divine dignity is thus conferred on Jesus.[94] It occurs also in Lk. 16:24 in address to "Father Abraham", and in any case can be shown to have existed in the linguistic usage of the time as a formula of request to earthly lords.[95] No doubt the cry acquired the meaning of a prayer,[96] but that must not be presupposed for the beginnings of this tradition.

The fact that in Mk. 10:47f. we have no isolated formula but that we have to allow for the wider prevalence of this conception, may be inferred from the relatively independent parallels in Matt. 9:27(f)., 15:22 (17, 15). Since the evangelist himself likes to use for such petitionary cries the κύριε mode of address,[97] we must assume as regards the address to the Son of David that we have the influence of a specific tradition.[98]

Further, the story of the triumphal entry into Jerusalem, Mk. 11:1–10, of which only vv. 9f. are to be investigated in detail, belongs to our present connection. The understanding of the acclamation of the people depends essentially on the expression: "Blessed be the kingdom of our father David that is coming!" The interpretations which have been given of this formula are for the most part very tentative and unsatisfactory.

So much is clear, that a statement of this kind is markedly unJewish.[99] This is especially true of the description of David as a father;[100] but also to speak of the "coming" Davidic kingdom was an unusual mode of expression.[101] The latter could of course be an analogy to the idea of the coming kingdom of God,[102] but it is much more likely that in this expression of v. 10a we have a parallel to ἐρχόμενος ἐν ὀνόματι κυρίου (Ps. 118:26) of v. 9b, as of course the words ἐρχόμενος/ἐρχομένη in the two lines correspond with each other. ἡ βασιλεία τοῦ πατρὸς ἡμῶν Δαυίδ presupposes without any doubt a quite specific Christological conception. For obviously "father" David is spoken of only because of the current description of Jesus as David's Son. The hoped-for bringer of salvation comes of David's line and in accordance with the promise made to David.

Hence the patriarchs as a whole are not, as in Judaism, the decisive figures in the divine plan, but David is the one father to whom Christianity appeals.[103] The connection with the old covenant remains intact, but is understood in a special way from that vantage point where a bridge is built towards fulfilment in Christ. But what does this acclamation imply? The parallelism with v. 9b must be noted. It is a matter of indifference whether in contemporary Judaism Ps. 118:26 was already understood messianically[104] or not; in this text the surrender of the originally collective meaning in favour of the relation to Jesus is unequivocal. Verse 10a can only be understood as the appropriate interpretation—in other words, the affirmation of the coming Davidic reign is likewise referred to Jesus.[105] There is here, therefore, an indirect allusion to His Davidic sonship, and this dignity and office is at the same time more precisely indicated.

The result of our study so far can be resumed thus: Son of David has become especially a designation of the earthly Jesus; the intention is to make thus a clear differentiation from the messianic office, yet this title, although in a different way, is intended likewise to be a title of exaltation.

This is shown far more clearly in the story of the triumphal entry than in any other of the passages discussed. Here indeed the sonship of David seems to be plainly identified with an earthly kingly dignity. It may therefore be asked whether this still fits into the pattern of the two-stage Christology, whether here the combination of a prior dignity in lowliness and the messianic function assumed only in heaven is not surrendered and with the result that the text is already a witness to the unlimited transference of the messianic dignity to the earthly Jesus.[106] The situation, however, in this passage is somewhat different and a connection with the two-stage Christology can still be detected.

We must refer back to our earlier observation that the description of the eschatological messianic office of Jesus as a Davidic kingship tended to be pushed into the background as a result of the concept of exaltation. Since the messianic dignity of Jesus was of a purely heavenly kind, since on the other hand Jesus was the promised Son of David, descended in fact from the royal house, His earthly function, in which the future exaltation is already foreshadowed, could be described plainly as a Davidic "kingship". Doubtless deep far-reaching changes in the ancient Jewish conception are present. It is easy to see from the story that Zech. 9:9, although not expressly cited by Mark, stands in the background. In the LXX version, the motive of the "helper, rescuer" (σώζων) plays a part, and this is reflected in that understanding of Jesus' mercy and miraculous healings which we have been speaking of. The presupposition of an actual political kingship which is still a matter of course for the promise of Zech. 9:9 is here given up.[107]

If Jesus is the representative of the promised Davidic kingdom, His earthly kingly dignity receives its legitimation solely from the heavenly power and authority towards which He is only as yet approaching.[108] It is not by chance therefore that the statement in Mk. 11:9f. is formulated in such a notably indirect way.[109] The earthly kingly dignity was not meant to take the place of the heavenly one, but a prior, provisional office was to precede the ultimate messianic lordship.[110]

It must be specifically emphasized once more that this view of the earthly kingship of Jesus has absolutely nothing to do with the thought of hiddenness and secrecy;[111] on the contrary it is a question of a kingship which is enthusiastically celebrated, and in Mk. 11:9f. it is hardly by chance that the acclamation is placed on the lips of the people.[112] This tradition was concerned not with the hiddenness but precisely with the openness of the function of Jesus.[113] What is at issue is not a secret kingship, but a provisional one,[114] in which the future sovereignty is nevertheless visible and clearly mirrored.[115]

Summary. We must once more refer to the tension (mentioned in the first section) between the descent of Jesus from David's house and His eschatological messianic dignity, for this has received its theological formulation in the two-stage Christology of Hellenistic Judaic Christianity. The two-stage Christology acquired its characteristic form firstly by the fact that the eschatological messianic office of Jesus was replaced by the idea of exaltation and, secondly, by the fact that the Davidic sonship of Jesus was elaborated into a special preliminary stage of exaltation.

The basic structure of this Christological standpoint is seen in Rom. 1:3f. and in the Son of David question of Mk. 12:35–37a. The idea of exaltation is in both cases plainly expressed whether by the combination of the messianic enthronement with the crucial event of the resurrection, or by the quotation of Ps. 110:1.

The special elaboration of the motive of the Davidic sonship is seen principally in stories which present Jesus as the helper of the sick and suffering and contain the fixed characteristic cry: "Son of David, have mercy on me".

Then comes the story of the triumphal entry, where the earthly dignity of Jesus is plainly described as a preliminary Davidic kingship, which precedes the heavenly kingly office; doubtless at this point, where the splendour of the heavenly messianic office already irradiates the earthly work of Jesus the pattern of the two-stage Christology is stretched to the limit,[116] and it could not fail to happen that soon, even within the Son of David tradition, the messianic dignity would be assigned without qualification to the earthly Jesus, as likewise happened in connection with the titles Christos and Son of God.

The texts we have discussed show as a whole to what an extent the concept has been Christianized, so that on the basis of Jewish presuppositions alone a true explanation is no longer possible; but they also show how strongly a predicate which previously belonged to a similar idea of the kingly Messiah has in the sphere of the primitive Christian tradition received an independent elaboration.

3. The Davidic Sonship of Jesus in the Nativity Narratives of the Gospels of Matthew and Luke

Within the nativity narratives of the Gospels of Matthew and Luke there is a series of pieces of tradition which contain the motif of the Davidic sonship of Jesus. Besides the genealogies there come into question the birth story, Lk. 2:1–20, the two announcements of the birth of Jesus in Matt. 1:18–25 and Lk. 1:26–38, further, the story of the magi, Matt. 2:1–12. The traditio-historical evolution can still be recognized relatively well. The motif of the Davidic sonship of Jesus unites with Jesus' birth in the city of Bethlehem, and thereby for the time being the early structure of the conception as we have recognized it in the story of the healing in Mk. 10:46–52 is preserved. But then there comes about a union with the idea of the virginity of Mary, and that leads to essential alterations.

Jesus' birth in Bethlehem is spoken about explicitly only in the two stories, Lk. 2:1–20 and Matt. 2:1–12.[117] Since in Matt. 2:1ff. this motif is associated with various later elements, we must confine ourselves to an investigation of the original form of this idea in Lk. 2:1–20. There is no explicit citation of Old Testament prophecy, but a reference to Scripture is unmistakable both in the Bethlehem motif and in the shepherd motif.[118] The virgin birth is not assumed in this story; accordingly there is no connection with Lk. 1:26ff.[119] Joseph moves with his wife to Bethlehem for the ἀπογραφή. There the birth of Jesus takes place and it is marked by a heavenly message to shepherds.

The analysis of the text is not easy; there are various secondary linings and trimmings, and the original story can no longer be reconstructed in all its parts.[120] Vv. 1–5 is much superimposed by the redactional work of Luke; the old beginning of the story has been broken off. The comprehensive, cosmohistorical horizon of the present introduction is pronouncedly Lukan; there exists, however, no reason to dispute the census as the occasion of the journey in the early story.[121] The brief report of the birth of Jesus vv. 6f. is wholly designed for the shepherd scene that follows and in its present form is certainly original. Vv. 8–14 brings with the heavenly message the actual culmination of the story, which again is closely bound up with the conclusion vv. 15–20, where the confirmation of the sign of recognition, the spreading abroad of the message and the giving of praise to God are reported. In this concluding part, v. 19 is certainly redactional, as 2:51b shows; otherwise the section, which is set out plainly, proves itself to be original.

The situation in the middle portion is more difficult. Vv. 8f. gives no trouble. Also there are no objections to v. 10, for εὐαγγελίζεσθαι is frequent in the Septuagint and need not have its later technical missionary sense.[122] As its clear reference to v. 7 and vv. 16f.—the child wrapped in swaddling clothes and the manger—shows, v. 12 belongs to the old stock. The same holds good of the praise of the heavenly hosts in vv. 13f., where in v. 14 a clearly Semitic piece of tradition has been used.[123]

The essentially problematic passage is v. 11. In the time of Paul σωτήρ was used only of the coming finisher of salvation and was carried over to the earthly Jesus only in the post-Pauline period under the influence of Hellenistic epiphany conceptions.[124] The Christmas story cannot on any account be classified as so late. The question has therefore to be asked whether as it occurs here σωτήρ is not used in a very different way and, in accordance with its Old Testament meaning, designates the helper and supporter who is sent by God.[125] This would connect excellently with the observations made in regard to Mk. 10:46ff. (11:9f.); further the basic form of the story of Zacchaeus, Lk. 19:1–7, 9, also presents a parallel to this motif of "help" and "today".[126] In σωτήρ in Lk. 2:11 then there may be no specifically Christological title of dignity. But how does the designation of the new-born child as "helper" stand in relation to the predicates "Christos" and "Kyrios"?[127] It has frequently been considered that in accordance with Lk. 2:26 χριστὸς κύριος might be taken as χριστὸς κυρίου.[128] But the text gives no support to a transference of the Messiah title to the new born child;[129] that gained ground only with the help of the idea of the virgin birth, which has no effect here.[130] Elsewhere in the story κύριος is a designation of God; in the rest of the Lukan nativity narrative also this use of κύριος holds its ground.[131] The only exception in Lk. 1:43 within the story of the meeting of Mary with Elisabeth proves to be Lukan.[132] Accordingly it is very likely that the relative clause ὅς ἐστιν χριστὸς κύριος in Lk. 2:11 is textually not corrupt in its present form, but it is to be regarded as redactional.[133] The evangelist quite clearly felt that the original statement of the Christmas story had no Christological fullness of meaning; for that reason he added two important titles for its interpretation and in doing so made the best, as he has done in Lk. 1:39ff., of the tension with the κύριος designation of God.[134]

With such an analysis it is possible to regard the narrative as a relatively early portion of tradition, and that is suggested by its content, its style of narration,[135] and also its relation to the Davidic sonship tradition as examined thus far. In favour of a Palestinian origin there can be claimed only the short hymn Lk. 2:14, otherwise the story shows no sort of Semitic reminiscences in its language.[136] Lk. 2:1–20 is part and parcel of the Son of David tradition of the early Hellenistic Jewish Christian church which has precipitated itself in the texts that have already been dealt with. The story provides on the one hand for the development of the Bethlehem motif, on the other hand for the portrayal of the birth of the σωτήρ sent by God and proved by a message from heaven and special signs of identification.

As in Rom. 1:3 the birth of Jesus stands here for all his earthly work, and as in Mk. 11:9f. it is "all the people" who as the "men of the (divine) good-will" are to receive joy and salvation. In the story there is all the tension of the two-stage Christology, the co-existence of heavenly brightness and angelic praise being in striking contrast with Jesus' inconspicuous birth and earthly lowliness.

With the taking up of the motif of the birth at Bethlehem the conception of Jesus' Davidic sonship underwent a homogeneous development. It was otherwise with the incorporation of the theologumenon of the virgin birth.[137] The earliest evidences certainly show a union which still preserves the assumption of the two-stage Christology. The natural descent of Jesus from David's family no doubt breaks up the virginity of Mary, but the more emphatically is the lawfulness of the betrothal or marriage of Joseph, a descendant of David, with Mary now set forth.

The genealogy, Matt. 1:1–16, brings this very well to expression in that, apart from the apocalyptic schema which has in view the thought of the history that fulfils itself in Christ, it exhibits two groundlines which alike are marked at the beginning by the mention of the David sonship and the Abraham sonship: the one is the special election of God that has become an actuality in Abraham, the different women of the old covenant, and the mother of Jesus; the other is the connection through Joseph with the family of David.[138] The New Testament is not acquainted with the idea of a derivation of Mary from the stem of David which is again and again seized upon in later ecclesiastical tradition.[139] Rather it is there a matter, in a sound Jewish sense, of the lawful, therefore now decisive membership of Jesus in the tribe of David.

For this reason, emphasis is laid in Matt. 1:18–25 both on the fact of the betrothal, which according to Jewish law had binding power and counted as the beginning of marriage,[140] and on the call upon Joseph to take to himself the expectant Mary and assume the paternity of her child. Now this portion of tradition shows in a certain regard a later coinage as compared with Lk. 1:26ff. inasmuch as the virgin birth is here assumed whilst there it is reported and explained;[141] in Matt. 1:18ff. one almost gets the impression that the intention is to defend it apologetically.[142] But it is precisely the presumed apologetic traits which especially set forth a connection willed by God of the child conceived by the Holy Spirit with the family of David. The accent lies less upon the motif of the virgin birth than upon a Davidic sonship that nevertheless exists.[143] The pregnancy of the virgin is represented as a solid reality, the Davidic sonship on the other hand is regarded as effected through the command of the angel and the obedience of Joseph.

In the present text of Matthew, Mary's virginity is certainly underlined by the thought of the fulfilment of the prophecy in Isa. 7:14, but this reflection-citation interrupts the continuity of the narration and proves to be redactional.[144] It can nevertheless be said that the Old Testament text is included here with good reason, for doubtless it stands, precisely in the Septuagint form,[145] behind the theologumenon of the virgin birth received by the Hellenistic Jewish Christian church. Also the καὶ καλέσουσιν τὸ ὄνομα αὐτοῦ ᾽Εμμανουήλ, ὅ ἐστιν μεθερμηνευόμενον μεθ᾽ ἡμῶν ὁ θεός takes up appropriately and with no shifting of the emphasis the instruction regarding the giving of the name and the interpretation given in v. 21 of the name Jesus. The chief stress in the original story falls, that is to say, precisely on this giving of the name side by side with the motif of the Davidic sonship. We are not concerned here, as in Lk. 1:31, solely with the fact that the name Jesus was determined in advance by the angel, but with the fact that this name has a quite definite content of meaning.

Moreover, in an interesting way there again appears, if also indirectly, the σωτήρ predicate; mention is made anew of the λαός,[146] and in this case deliverance from sin is named as the result of salvation. As regards this last idea we may not think of the expiatory suffering of Jesus. Rather we must go back to the story of Zacchaeus, Lk. 19:1ff., which has been adduced once already. There σωτηρία is understood in the sense of the pardon of the sinner, and this Jesus grants by receiving the repudiated person into his fellowship.[147]

Thus, without prejudice to the acceptance of the idea of the virgin birth of Jesus, we still move wholly within the framework of the Son of David tradition so far discussed.[148] Membership in David's family is emphatically adhered to, and ascription to the earthly Jesus of a messianic predicate of dignity is avoided. The statements which are made regarding Jesus' earthly activity are obtained from an explication of the name Jesus, but essentially they fall in with the other statements in this stratum of tradition.

Nevertheless, very different tendencies were comprised in the motif of the virgin birth, and these immediately broke through. This can be recognized in Lk. 1:26ff. and Matt. 2:1ff. Apart from the clamping with the story of the Baptist in vv. 36f., the account of the annunciation of the birth of Jesus to Mary, Lk. 1:26–38, can be regarded as homogeneous. In this portion of tradition what is emphasized is that the special character of the conception at the same time establishes the divine sonship of the child. The result is that the originally eschatologically intended messianic statements in vv. 32f. are now carried over to the earthly Jesus;[149] therefore the tension adhered to in the portions of tradition so far discussed between the Davidic sonship and the divine sonship or Messiahship of Jesus is here given up. It is indeed not yet a question of a divine sonship in the physical sense,[150] but the κληθήσεται υἱὸς θεοῦ as also the promise of installation on the throne of David is already meant for the child brought by Mary into the world.[151]

How stands it now with the Davidic sonship of Jesus? In v. 27 it is expressly said of the virgin Mary that she was betrothed to a man named Joseph of the house of David. But it is disputed whether this phrase belongs to the early story: the mention of the name of Mary seems very much to have been brought in later so that it is not known exactly whether Davidic derivation is accredited to Joseph or to Mary; further, Joseph is not mentioned elsewhere in the story; finally, the question in v. 34 is said to be conceivable only if Mary knew nothing at all of a man.[152]

Nevertheless these arguments are not convincing: the naming of Mary at the end of the exposition answers to the style of the narrative;[153] the reference of ἐξ οἴκου Δαυίδ to Joseph, and indeed to him alone, is quite unambiguous; in view of the sexual sense of γινώσκειν and the fact of the mere betrothal the question of Mary, πῶς ἔσται τοῦτο, ἐπεὶ ἄνδρα οὐ γινώσκω, is certainly sensible.[154]

There remains then only the question whether the mention of Joseph, who is named nowhere else in the story, is well founded or proves to be a redactional clamp. Here, however, Joseph must be considered because of the Davidic sonship. Only because the lawful betrothal to Joseph, a descendant of David, stands in the background can a promise be given that the throne of David will be handed over to this child. As on the one hand the virgin conception, so on the other hand membership in the house of David substantiates the messianic office of Jesus. The Davidic sonship as such is not ousted by the conception of the virgin birth, only the idea of a preliminary stage in the majesty of the earthly Jesus, to whom the full messianic dignity does not yet fall, is undone.[155]

Matt. 2:1–12 already assumes the transference of the messianic dignity to Jesus. Very various elements are woven together in this narrative: in addition to the story of the magi and their star, there is the opposition between king Herod and the new-born "king of the Jews"; further, the motif of the birth in Bethlehem and the virginity of Mary are included. It is quite likely that at the basis of the whole there lies an afore-time independent magi story,[156] for after all a twofold direction is given as to the place of Jesus' birth, one given by Herod and one given by the star.[157] The motif of the birth in Bethlehem is linked directly with the story of Herod, which is indeed to be regarded not as an afore-time independent tradition but as an expansion of the story of the magi.[158]

The question, $\pi o \hat{v} \ \dot{o} \ \chi \rho \iota \sigma \tau \dot{o} s \ \gamma \epsilon \nu \nu \hat{a} \tau a \iota$, put apparently in full accordance with Jewish Messiah dogmatics, is answered by the scribes with the citation of Mic. 5:1, 3.[159] Yet as the wording $\dot{o} \ \tau \epsilon \chi \theta \epsilon \grave{\iota} s \ \beta a \sigma \iota \lambda \epsilon \grave{v} s \ \tau \hat{\omega} \nu \ '\mathit{Iov}\delta a \dot{\iota} \omega \nu$ shows, the messianic predicates are applied to the child that has just been born,[160] as cannot possibly have been done either in the Jewish or in the earliest Christian tradition. The process of transformation which there has clearly been in Lk. 1:26ff. is here in essentials concluded, so that the Messiah designations of Jesus can be put quite openly in the mouth even of the magi and of Herod. The virgin birth is not mentioned explicitly, but is yet indicated by the phrase $\tau \dot{o} \ \pi a \iota \delta \dot{\iota} o \nu \ \mu \epsilon \tau \grave{a} \ \tau \hat{\eta} s \ \mu \eta \tau \rho \dot{o} s \ a \dot{v} \tau o \hat{v}$. Throughout the story Joseph is not mentioned at all; the motif of the Davidic sonship has indeed wholly passed over to that of the birth in Bethlehem.[161] The contours of the several elements of tradition are even already quite blurred.

Finally, it has to be added that the *proskynesis* (adoration), which belongs to the story of the magi, appears in association with the messianic predicates of the child; consequently a divinity of Jesus in the Hellenistic sense is possibly already thought of. Nothing can any longer be recognized here of the independently fashioned conception of the earthly work of Jesus as the Son of David.[162]

Summary. We have again to call attention to the significance for the Palestinian primitive church of the actual derivation of Jesus from David's family and the eschatological expectation connected with it. It has been shown that the decisive step to an independent development of the Son of David idea was taken in the sphere of the Hellenistic Jewish Christian church by way of the so-called two-stage Christology. Even where a co-ordination of the earthly Davidic sonship and the heavenly Messiah-ship of Jesus is not explicitly brought to expression, the Davidic sonship is regarded for the most part as a temporary stage of dignity wherewith Jesus' earthly office must be described. At the same time a special role is played by the motif of the God-sent "deliverer" ($\sigma\omega\tau\acute{\eta}\rho$), who is sent to the people Israel as once were the judges and the charismatic persons of the old covenant. He brings help in sickness and want, to the sinner also he brings companionship and enables him to experience the divine grace.

The Son of David stories in the nativity narratives are determined by two further motifs, the birth of Jesus in Bethlehem and the virginity of Mary. The birth in Bethlehem underlines Jesus' status as Son of David and the divine prophecy which is being fulfilled. The theologumenon of the virgin birth is also determined by the idea of the fulfilment of Scripture. It was first of all balanced with the Davidic sonship of Jesus so that the legal paternity of Joseph was emphasized. But the idea of the virgin birth of Jesus soon outweighed that. If the Davidic sonship of Jesus was not simply abandoned, yet on the ground of the special character of Mary's conception divine sonship and Messiahship were adjudged to the new-born child and so to the earthly Jesus. The independent concept of the Davidic sonship of Jesus in the sense of a temporary stage of dignity was thus undone.

NOTES

1. Even the essay of Wilhelm Michaelis, *Die Davidssohnschaft Jesu als historisches und kerygmatisches Problem* in *Der historische Jesus*

und der kerygmatische Christus, 1960, pp. 317–330, does not cancel this statement. William Wrede, *Jesus als Davidssohn* in *Vorträge und Studien*, 1907, pp. 147–177, is still fundamental. Beside it there are to be mentioned Ernst Lohmeyer, *Gottesknecht und Davidssohn* (*FRLANT* NF 43), 1953², especially pp. 64ff.; Taylor, *Names of Jesus*, p. 24; Cullmann, *Christologie*, pp. 128–144; by way of addition I refer to Evald Lövestam, *Son and Saviour* (*Coniect. Neotest.* XVIII, 1961.

2. Schlatter, *Mt.*, p. 2.

3. The idea of the virgin birth cannot be reckoned with certainty to the tradition of the early Palestinian church. Alike the traditio-historical consideration of the portions of text that come into question and also the fact that the later Jewish Christianity strictly rejected this theologumenon, clearly go to prove that.

4. The idea of election also underlies the mention of the four women in Matt. 1:3, 5a, 5b, 6. That the naming of them corresponds to the mention of Mary in v. 16 is obvious. In the case of these women it was of course their extraordinary call that was decisive and not their sinfulness, especially as the latter would by no means have been applicable to Mary.

5. This schema expressly emphasized in Matt. 1:17 of 3 periods each of 2 times 7 members, has led, as is well known,'to the omission of several generations as compared with the Old Testament accounts and genealogies.

6. In any early text of the Gospel of Matthew we may of course not expect the natural fatherhood of Joseph to be asserted in 1:16. That holds good also in regard to the much discussed text of the Sinaitic Syriac, in which the intention is to emphasize the genealogical connection simply in accordance with legal fatherhood.

7. So with good reasons Gottfried Kuhn, *Die Geschlechtsregister Jesu bei Lucas and Matthäus, nach ihrer Herkunft untersucht*, *ZNW* 22, 1923, pp. 206–228, especially pp. 208f.

8. Cf. Joachim Jeremias, art., Ἀδάμ, *ThWb* i, p. 141.

9. Cf. Rengstorf, *Lk.*, p. 61: the 77 members from Adam to Christ can hardly be accidental; moreover in 2 Esdras 14:11f. the Messiah is expected at the end of 11 world-weeks.

10. An apologetic justification of the historicity of the two genealogies in their present state, such as is attempted by Karl Bornhäuser, *Die Geburts- und Kindheitsgeschichte Jesu*, 1930, pp. 6ff., 22ff., is untenable.

11. It is a vain undertaking to attempt to work out the basic stock of each of the two genealogies and then to ascribe them in accordance with early ecclesiastical tradition to the families of Joseph and Mary.

12. To show this is the main concern of Michaelis, *op. cit.*

13. Cf. the texts—they are instructive in this respect—regarding the supplies of wood for the temple arranged according to family units in Wrede, *Vorträge*, pp. 149ff.

14. This notice preserved in Eusebius, *H.E.* III, 19f. may be dealt with quite positively; cf. Cullmann, *Christologie*, pp. 130f.

15. Cf. Chapter 3, pp. 161ff.

16. Cf. Chapter 3, p. 147.

17. On this especially Dalman, *Worte Jesu*, pp. 26off.; Billerbeck I, p. (12f.) 525.

18. So Mk. 10:47f. (par. Matt. 20:30f.; Lk. 18:38f.); Mk. 12:35 (par. Lk. 20:41 cf. Matt. 22:42); Matt. 1:1 (1:20); 9:27; 12:23; 15:22; 21:9, 15; *Barn.* 12, 10.

19. ἐκ (τοῦ) σπέρματος Δαυίδ John 7:41; Rom. 1:3; 2 Tim. 2:8; Ign. *Eph.* 18, 2; Ign. *Rom.* 7, 3; ἐκ γένους Δαυίδ Ign. *Eph.* 20, 2; Ign. *Trall.* 9, 1; Ign. *Smyrn.* 1, 1; τὸ γένος Δαυίδ Rev. 22:16; ἡ ῥίζα Δαυίδ Rev. 5:5; 22:16.

20. υἱὸς Δαυίδ in *Ps. of Sol.* 17, 21 must then be regarded in the same way as χριστὸς κύριος in v. 32 as a later correction of a Christian copyist and perhaps an original צמח דויד (so the Qumran texts, cf. p. 199, n. 55 above) or the like is to be assumed. But the later rabbinical application has hardly been borrowed from Christianity.

21. Hermann Gunkel, *Die Lieder in der Kindheitsgeschichte Jesu bei Lukas* in *Festgabe für Harnack*, 1921, pp. 43–60, especially pp. 53ff.

22. The connection of v. 71 is not quite smooth; cf. Klostermann, *Lk.*, p. 27. Provided that v. 70 is taken as a parenthesis, v. 71 belongs as apposition to κέρας σωτηρίας; but then it is not clear whether to deliver from enemies is the task of the Messiah or the work of God himself. In view of the almost verbal parallels to v. 70 in Acts 3:21 with their specifically Lukan intention, Lk. 1:70 may be regarded as a redactional addition; cf. Joachim Gnilka, *Der Hymnus des Zacharias*, *BZ* NF 6, 1962, pp. 215–238, there pp. 220f.

23. Cf. on Lk. 1:68–75 Schlatter, *Lk.*, pp. 173ff.

24. Gunkel, *op. cit.*, p. 57.

25. On μέγας cf. Martin Dibelius, *Jungfrauensohn und Krippenkind* in *Botschaft und Geschichte* (*Ges. Aufs.*) I, 1953, pp. 4f., 15f.

26. ὕψιστος is already a designation of God in the Old Testament and can be shown to have been so also in late Judaism (עֶלְיוֹן); cf. Billerbeck II, pp. 99f.

27. Cf. on this Chapter 5, pp. 284ff.

28. On this Gunkel, *op. cit.*, pp. 53ff.

29. Thus the divine sonship is understood in Lk. 1:32f. as adoptionist; on the other hand in v. 35 it is established by the miraculous procreation. Moreover the κληθήσεται in vv. 32f. refers to the eschatological enthronement, but in v. 35 to the birth.

30. As is well known, early Palestinian church tradition is preserved more than once in Revelation.

31. In the LXX צמח (דוד) is usually rendered by ἀνατολή. cf. Heinrich Schlier, art., ἀνατολή, *ThWb* I, 354f. In other connections ἄνθος, ἰσχύς and the like appear for צמח, but never ῥίζα.

32. Cf. Hatch-Redpath, *LXX-Konkordanz* II, pp. 1251f.

33. In Isa. 11:1 in a synonymous *parallelismus membrorum* mention is made of a shoot from the root-stock of Jesse (v. 1a גֶּזַע, v. 1b שֹׁרֶשׁ both rendered by ῥίζα in the LXX). Then in 11:10 in the secondary שֹׁרֶשׁ יִשַׁי reference is made to a branch from the root of Jesse. By that the promised Messiah is meant. Certainly in late Jewish times he

obtains more and more the designation צֶמַח דָּוִד; cf. Billerbeck II, p. 113; now also established in three passages in the Qumran texts (4 Q PatrBless 3f.; 4 Q Flor II; 4 Q pIsᵃ fr. D, I). This has found its most beautiful expression in the additional (15th) berachah in the Babylonian recension of the Shemoneh Esreh: אֶת־צֶמַח דָּוִד [עַבְדְּךָ] מְהֵרָה תַצְמִיחַ; cf. Willi Staerk, Altjüdische liturgische Gebete (Kl. Texte 58), 1930², p. 18. —Since in Rev. 5:5 no dependence on the LXX is to be assumed, ῥίζα Δαυίδ will be connected at least indirectly with צֶמַח דָּוִד. On the other hand ῥίζα τοῦ Ἰεσσαί in Rom. 15:12 stands within an unambiguous LXX citation.

34. In my opinion Bousset, Apk., p. 256, is incorrect in relating ἐνίκησεν to the death and resurrection of Jesus. For, just as in the case of the sayings about the conquerors, νικᾶν is referred only to the trial in death, which there likewise implies an eschatological promise; cf. Rev. 2:7, 11, 17, 26; 3:5, 12, 21; 21:7. Where the death of Jesus and his eschatological work are spoken of side by side, the resurrection can possibly be passed over since then it plays a role only as an anticipated final happening. The position of the resurrection in the earliest tradition certainly needs to be thoroughly investigated.

35. Rightly emphasized by Lohmeyer, Apk., p. 181; but his interpretation of Christus as the representative of the whole family of David is not convincing.

36. Friedrich Büchsel, art., "γίνομαι etc.", ThWb I, p. 684.

37. Cf. Lohmeyer, Apk., p. 35; Joachim Jeremias, art. κλείς, ThWb III. pp. 743–753.

38. Jeremias, op. cit., pp. 745, 747f.; in Revelation, Jesus is distinguished as the possessor of the keys of both realms.

39. So Jeremias, ThWb III, p. 748. For the rest he points out that Isa. 22:22 does not find any sort of messianic application in late Jewish texts, as has repeatedly been maintained.

40. So Lohmeyer, Apk., p. 35. But the conception of the new Jerusalem in Rev. 21 is considered pronouncedly non-messianic.

41. It has here to be taken into consideration that, as elsewhere in Revelation in the case of messianic statements, it is a matter of elements which have been taken over but have not been worked into the author's conception; apart from 20:1–6, on which see pp. 167f. above.

42. Within Hellenistic Gentile Christianity only isolated aftereffects permit of their being recognized (2 Tim. 2:8; Ignatius).

43. Cf. Excursus II, pp. 129ff. as well as Chapter 3, pp. 168ff.

44. There is a first allusion to its pre-Pauline character in Joh. Weiss, Urchristentum, p. 89 (he had expressly called for an extraction of the material of tradition from the epistles of Paul, cf. id., Die Aufgaben der neutestamentlichen Wissenschaft in der Gegenwart, 1908, p. 29); Norden, Agnostos Theos, p. 385; Hans Windisch, Zur Christologie der Pastoralbriefe, ZNW 34, 1935, pp. 213–238, there pp. 214ff.; Dodd, Apostolic Preaching, p. 14; Rudolf Bultmann, ThR NF 8, 1936, p. 11; id., Theol., p. 52; Günther Bornkamm, Das Bekenntnis im Hebräerbrief, ThBl 21, 1941, now in Studien zu Antike und Urchristentum (Ges. Aufs

II), 1959, p. 199. n. 25; Werner Georg Kümmel, *Kirchenbegriff und Geschichtsbewusstein in der Urgemeinde und bei Jesus (Symbolae Biblicae Upsalienses* I), 1943, p. 48, n. 38; Nils Alstrup Dahl, *Die Messianität Jesu bei Paulus* in *Studia Paulina (in honorem Johannis de Zwaan),* 1953, p. 90; M.-E. Boismard, *Constitué Fils de Dieu (Rom. 1:4), RB* 60, 1953, pp. 1–17; Michel, *Röm.,* pp. 30ff.; Eduard Schweizer, *Erniedrigung und Erhöhung,* pp. 55f., 62f., 86f., 101, 131f., 137f.; *id., Röm. 1:3f, und der Gegensatz von Fleisch und Geist vor und bei Paulus, EvTh* 15, 1955, pp. 563–571; *id.,* art. πνεῦμα, *ThWb* VI, p. 415; *id.,* art. σάρξ, *ThWb* VII, pp. 125f.; Cullmann, *Christologie,* pp. 243f., 299; Franz-J. Leenhardt, *L'Épitre de Saint Paul aux Romains (Commentaire du Nouveau Testament* VI), 1957, pp. 22f.; Kuss, *Röm.,* pp. 4ff.; James M. Robinson, *Kerygma und historischer Jesus,* 1960, pp. 68f., 139, 175, 177.

45. So Eduard Schweizer, *Der Glaube an Jesus den „Herrn" in seiner Entwicklung von den ersten Nachfolgern bis zur hellenistischen Gemeinde, EvTh* 17, 1957, pp. 7—21, there p. 11.

46. 1 Cor. 1:9; 2 Cor. 1:3; 1 Thess. 1:3.

47. E. Schweizer, *EvTh* 15, 1955, pp. 563ff.

48. This opinion is supported by Bultmann, *Theol.,* p. 50; Dahl, *op. cit.,* p. 90; Michel, *Röm.,* pp. 30f.

49. *Op. cit.,* pp. 563f. Also Cullmann, *Christologie,* pp. 242f., 299.

50. Cf. Bauer, *Wb. s.v.* γίνομαι I, I.

51. Cf. especially Gal. 4:4; Phil. 2:7.

52. By hard work Eduard Norden, *Agnostos Theos,* pp. 166ff., 201ff., 380ff. has obtained what is important regarding that. He has indeed cited Rom. 1:3f. merely as an instance and has not discussed it closely.

53. I refer above all to E. Schweizer, *op. cit. EvTh* 15, 1955, pp. 564, 568ff.

54. Cf. on this Dibelius-Conzelmann, *Past.,* p. 50 ("it is a matter of the sphere of being"); Rudolf Bultmann, *Bekenntnis- und Liedfragmente im ersten Petrusbrief* in *Coniectanea Neotestamentica* XI *(In honorem A. Fridrichsen),* 1947, p. 4.

55. In 1 Tim. 3:16 it is a matter of an epiphany conception, in 1 Pet. 3:18b of the passion tradition (the presence side by side of death and resurrection).

56. So Dodd, *op. cit.,* p. 14 on Rom. 1:3.

57. G. Bornkamm, *Jesus von Nazareth,* p. 206.

58. Cf. on this usage Acts 10:42; 17:31.

59. With E. Schweizer, *ThWb* VII, p. 126, n. 225 we can speak of a "preliminary stage of dignity".

60. Michel. *Röm.,* p. 32.

61. Cf. also 2 Thess. 1:7.

62. Similarly as in Phil. 2:9–11 it is the condition of being subject to the powers that is thought of.

63. The apprehension that in this way "such a thing as a devious adoptionism" could "emerge"—so Karl Ludwig Schmidt, art., ὁρίζειν *ThWb* V, p. 454, n. 7—need not alarm us.

64. πνεῦμα ἁγιωσύνης occurs in the *Test. of Levi* 18, ii and answers to the Hebrew רוּחַ הַקֹּדֶשׁ (Isa. 63:1of.; Ps. 51:13; but in both places the LXX has τὸ πνεῦμα τὸ ἅγιον), without a real difference as compared with πνεῦμα ἅγιον being assumed.

65. Lietzmann, *Röm.*, p. 25.

66. E. Schweizer, *EvTh* 15, 1955, p. 568, points out that only under Hellenistic influence does the conception of corporality and incorporality connect itself with the Biblical concepts of "flesh" and "spirit". But the few pieces of evidence adduced by him for late Judaism are in my opinion by no means conclusive. How under Jewish presuppositions conceptions of the kind were warded off is shown for instance in 1 Cor. 15. But this question which became acute in connection with the resurrection does not count at all for Rom. 1:3f. A glance at the material in Billerbeck III, pp. 48of. shows how little the motif was received in the sphere of Judaism. I Thess. 4:16f. knows only a bodily resurrection, a removal to heaven and a being for ever with the Lord; in Rom. 1:4 also the resurrection of Jesus may be spoken about in the same way. But even if a transformation is thought of, non-fleshliness may not on any account be equated to non-corporality in any of these passages.

67. The former is advocated above all by Lietzmann, *Röm.*, p. 25, the latter firmly by E. Schweizer, *Erniedrigung und Erhöhung*, p. 62.

68. So M.-J. Lagrange: "Less than causality and more than mere succession"; according to Kuss, *Röm.*, p. 6, who considers this interpretation, but inclines more to the purely temporal one.

69. So Lietzmann, *Röm.*, p. 25.

70. It could possibly be said that resurrection and removal to heaven belong together. But at the same time a break is soon marked with the help of the conception of ascension.

71. Cf. Excursus II, p. 131.

72. The temporal succession is plainly constitutive for this Christological statement and may not be understood as "dialectic contrast" as it is by Robinson, *op. cit.*, pp. 175, 177.

73. Besides interpretations in accordance with the doctrine of the two natures and a distinction between Son of God of the seed of David and Son of God with power, there naturally also drops out the exposition which would understand the text from Phil. 2:6ff.—so Lietzmann, *Röm.*, p. 26—for if the motif of eminence presents itself in both texts, yet the motif of pre-existence and resignation of rights and further the schema of descent and ascent are altogether foreign to the text of Rom. 1:3f.

74. Reference may be made to the investigation of the Catholic, M.-E. Boismard, who expressly refuses to utilize improperly the presence side by side of "Son of God", in v. 3, and "Son of God with power"; *Constitué Fils de Dieu* (*Rom.* 1:4).

75. Cf. on this Windisch, *ZNW* 34, 1935, pp. 214ff. Dibelius-Conzelmann, *Past.*, p. 81; E. Schweizer, *Erniedrigung und Erhöhung*, p. 104.

76. ἐκ σπέρματος Δαυίδ is here so formal that not even a verb stands with it.

77. Reference may be made to the after-history of the motif in Ignatius of Antioch. The phrase ἐκ σπέρματος or ἐκ γένους Δαυίδ occurs frequently: Ign., *Eph.*, 18, 2; *Trall.* 9; 1; *Rom.* 7, 3; even united with κατὰ σάρκα in *Eph.* 20, 3; *Smyrn.* 1, 1b. The last named passage Ign., *Smyrn.* 1, 1b in particular clearly recalls the Pauline portion of tradition Rom. 1:3f., because there beside ἀληθῶς ὄντα ἐκ γένους Δαυίδ κατὰ σάρκα there also appears the phrase υἱὸν θεοῦ κατὰ θέλημα καὶ δύναμιν θεοῦ. But a two-stage Christology no longer presents itself, for precisely this double statement is referred to the earthly Jesus and the text proceeds: γεγεννημένον ἀληθῶς ἐκ παρθένου, βεβαπτισμένον ὑπὸ Ἰωάννου κτλ. Likewise in Ign., *Eph.* 20, 2 the ἐν Χριστῷ Ἰησοῦ τῷ κατὰ σάρκα ἐκ γένους Δαυίδ is interpreted by τῷ υἱῷ ἀνθρώπου καὶ υἱῷ θεοῦ. In Ign., *Eph.* 18, 2: Ἰησοῦς ὁ χριστὸς ἐκυοφορήθη ὑπὸ Μαρίας . . . ἐκ σπέρματος μὲν Δαυίδ, πνεύματος δὲ ἁγίου the expression about the Holy Spirit has nothing at all to do any longer with the tradition of Rom. 1:3f., rather we have to think here of the story of the birth Lk. 1:26ff., especially v. 35.

78. Cf. Chapter 2, pp. 103ff. and Chapter 3, p. 170.

79. W. Wrede, *Vorträge*, pp. 166ff.

80. Wrede, *Vorträge*, p. 176.

81. Already in the Hellenistic church of the first century divine sonship (in the physical sense) was predicated of the earthly Jesus. Ignatius speaks of the Davidic sonship almost regularly only in such a way that he unites the motif of divine sonship with it. Soon, however, the divine sonship was one-sidedly moved into the foreground. The ἐν Χριστῷ Ἰησοῦ τῷ κατὰ σάρκα ἐκ γένους Δαυίδ, τῷ υἱῷ ἀνθρώπου καὶ υἱῷ θεοῦ in Ign., *Eph.* 20, 2 becomes Ἰησοῦς, οὐχὶ υἱὸς ἀνθρώπου, ἀλλὰ υἱὸς τοῦ θεοῦ in *Barn*, 12, 10a (it is clear that in both places the early Son of man title no longer presents itself, but a statement regarding the humanity of Jesus formulated in dependence on that).

82. Cullmann, *Christologie*, pp. 132ff.

83. The view advocated by Robert Paul Gagg, *Jesus und die Davidssohnfrage. Zur Exegese von Markus* 12, 35-37, *ThZ* 7, 1951, pp. 18–30, that Son of David and Kyrios are not theologically crowded concepts, that on the contrary "Have you already heard that the Father calls the Son Lord?" was asked "simply by way of disconcerting the hearers" and said on the strength of every-day wont, and that this was then interpreted Christologically only at second hand by the church, is untenable.

84. So Lohmeyer, *Gottesknecht und Davidssohn*, pp. 74f.

85. We must disregard all interpretations which connect the Davidic sonship in any way with the conception of the Son of God or of the Son of man or even of the messianic high priest, since no clues to that are to be found in the text.

86. Against Gagg, *op. cit.*, pp. 19f.

87. Cf. G. Bornkamm, *Jesus*, p. 206; *id.*, "Enderwartung" in Bornkamm-Barth-Held, p. 30. Similarly also Joachim Jeremias, *Jesu Verheissung für die Völker*, 1959[2], p. 45, who speaks here of a haggada question in which a contradiction between Scriptural statements is

cleared up by the claim of each being emphasized but reference being made to their different kinds of connection; cf. on this David Daube; *The New Testament and Rabbinic Judaism*, 1956, pp. 158ff.

88. Mk. 10:46–52 shows earlier and later elements side by side, but the original rendering of the story no longer permits of its being reconstructed because the revision conceals it. Vv. 51, 52a makes an impression of age; the address "Rabbuni" stands in distinct tension with the address "Son of David". Formerly the point of the middle portion may have lain less in the word of petition than in the persistence of the cry. Also the exposition v. 46 is overloaded in its present form, which, however, is in part to be ascribed to the redaction.

89. Cf. on this Chapter 3, pp. 189f. Albert Descamps, *Le messianisme royal dans le Nouveau Testament* in *L'attente du Messie* (*Recherches Bibliques*), 1954, pp. 57–84, especially pp. 58ff., wishes to find the popular Messiah expectation bound up with the conception, traceable in antiquity and the Middle Ages, of a king who performs miracles.

90. One may therefore not have recourse without more ado to texts which belong to the two-stage Christology as evidence for the idea of a life of Jesus understood "non-Messianically", as do Wrede, *Messiasgeheimnis*, pp. 214ff.; Bultmann, *Theol.*, pp. 28f. For although no transference of the conception of the royal Messiah to the earthly life of Jesus takes place here, it is yet a matter, as the stratum of tradition on the whole shows, of a distinct first step to his messianic splendour.

91. Cf. Chapter 3, pp. 189ff.

92. So Mk. 10:47, 48//Matt. 20:30f.//Lk. 18:38f., as well as Matt. 9:27; 15:22. Otherwise only in Lk. 17:13 united to the ἐπιστάτα which is typical of Luke and in Matt. 17:15 in association with κύριε which Matthew prefers (in this place also the "have pity" is redactional, as Mk. 9:17 shows).

93. Cf. the LXX concordance.

94. Against Lohmeyer, *Gottesknecht und Davidssohn*, p. 69.

95. As a parallel Jos. *Ant.* ix, 64 is especially important.

96. Cf. on this Peterson, *ΕΙΣ ΘΕΟΣ*, pp. 164ff.

97. Cf. G. Bornkamm, *Enderwartung* in Bornkamm-Barth-Held, pp. 38f.

98. Lohmeyer is the only one who inquires somewhat accurately into this "Son of David, have mercy on me"; cf. *Gottesknecht und Davidssohn* pp. 69ff., 75ff.

99. Lohmeyer, *Mk.*, p. 231, gives a fruitful analysis of this acclamation.

100. Cf. Billerbeck II, p. 26.

101. According to Lohmeyer, *Mk.*, p. 231, the kingdom of David "comes" at most "again" or, as it is usually worded, it is "again set up".

102. An application of the expression "coming" to an eschatological entity, and the new kingdom of David is that according to Jewish understanding, is not completely excluded.

103. In the New Testament in Acts 4:25 according to the Hesychian text.

104. So Billerbeck I, p. 850.

105. For the understanding nothing is to be obtained from ὡσαννά or ὡσαννὰ ἐν τοῖς ὑψίστοις because here only formally used phrases present themselves.

106. The birth narratives, which have still to be discussed, show that this also happened in connection with the Son of David tradition.

107. On the original sense of Zech. 9:9(f.) cf. Chapter 3, pp. 138f. That Mark 11:1–10 assumes the LXX text is seen especially in v. 2b, where it is said that till then no man had sat on the beast, which answers to the πῶλος of νέος the LXX (without equivalent in the MT); moreover σῴζων brings a new emphasis into the context.

108. Obviously the ἐρχομένη does not have a future sense; that emerges from the parallel wording in v. 9b.

109. This is abandoned in Matthew and Luke. Matthew cites Zech. 9:9 explicitly in 21:5 and connects the title "Son of David" with it in vv. 9,15. Luke has included the designation βασιλεύς in 19:38 and consequently has abandoned the connection with the Son of David tradition.

110. At least the narrative of the Entry is connected with Jesus' work in Jerusalem, and perhaps the same is true of other stories belonging to the Son of David tradition (Mk. 10:46ff. is indeed already included with 11:1ff. in pre-Markan tradition); cf. on this Lohmeyer, *Gottesknecht und Davidssohn*, pp. 82f.

111. So in a different way especially Schniewind, *Mk.*, pp. 149f.; Lohmeyer, *Mk.*, pp. 232f.

112. In the miracle stories also "Son of David" is used by common people.

113. Wrede, *Messiasgeheimnis*, p. 237, sets that out clearly for the story of the Entry.

114. Here also the temporal components may not be set aside. Indeed it may be said that for the church the recognition of the kingship of Jesus on the earth corresponds to his position of dominion in heaven and the latter finds its echo in earthly praise. But as from the earthly Davidic kingship Jesus has passed through to the heavenly and the former was only the first step to the final position of majesty, so is also the earthly recognition of Jesus only the first step to final entrance into his messianic kingdom on the other side. In this time structure genuine Jewish thought is seen, even if it is connected in places with thought that is characteristic of Hellenism.

115. There is also to be noted the interesting coincidence of the Kyrios designation for the earthly Jesus and the Son of David motif in Mk. 11:3, 9f. It was of consequence to both traditions to incorporate the earthly life of Jesus also in their Christological statements.

116. It must be observed that it is an entirely different matter whether statements of dignity which hold good for the returning or exalted Jesus are carried over to his earthly life, or whether regarding the dignity of the earthly Jesus a statement is made which stands to the former in a relation of correspondence and is meant to be understood in the sense of a preliminary stage of dignity.

117. Besides in Matt. 2:1, 5, 6, 8, 16 and Lk. 2:4, 15 Bethlehem is

S

mentioned only in John 7:42, there in accordance with Jewish Messiah dogmatics.

118. That the shepherd motif has no Hellenistic presuppositions has been shown conclusively by Martin Dibelius, *Jungfrauensohn* in *Botschaft und Geschichte* I, especially pp. 64ff.; we have to think rather of an allusion to David, who watched his flock on the fields of Bethlehem and there was called by Jahwe.

119. Reference is nowhere made to the singularity of the pregnancy. Joseph and Mary appear in v. 4 as married people travelling together.

120. Besides to the already mentioned work of Dibelius and the critical commentaries reference should be made to Dibelius, *Formgeschichte*, pp. 119ff.; Bultmann, *Syn. Trad.*, pp. 316ff. (suppl. vol., pp. 44ff.); Gottfried Erdmann, *Die Vorgeschichten des Lukas- und Mattäus-Evangeliums und Vergils vierte Ekloge* (*FRLANT* NF 30), 1932, for the analysis of the nativity narratives.

121. Against Dibelius, *Jungfrauensohn*, pp. 55ff. The census was needed for exposition, to provide a special direction to Bethlehem; in view of the style of the narrative a resumption of it is not at all to be expected.

122. Cf. only Lk. 1:19. On that Gerhard Friedrich, art. εὐαγγελίζεσθαι, *ThWb* II, pp. 710f.

123. So already earlier Billerbeck II, p. 118; Joachim Jeremias, *Ἄνθρωποι εὐδοκίας* (*Lc. 2, 14*), *ZNW* 28, 1929, pp. 13–20. For this there are now interesting parallels in the Qumran texts, cf. Claus-Hunno Hunzinger, *Neues Licht auf Lc 2:14 ἄνθρωποι εὐδοκίας*, *ZNW* 44, 1952/53, pp. 85–90; id., *Ein weiterer Beleg zu Lc 2:14 ἄνθρωποι εὐδοκίας* *ZNW* 49, 1958, pp. 129f.; Reinhard Deichgräber, *Ἄνθρωποι εὐδοκίας*, *ZNW* 51, 1960, p. 132. The reference is of course to the men in whom God is well pleased.

124. Cf. Phil. 3:20 or 2 Tim. 1:10; Tit. 3:6. In all these places σωτήρ means the bringer of final redemption. In Paul the outlook in σωτήρ as in σωτηρία is toward the consummation of salvation.

125. In the Old Testament judges, for example, have this designation; cf. especially Judges 3:9, 15; 12:3.

126. That Lk. 19:10 is a relatively independent saying which at any rate later became overgrown, is easily recognized; the narrative had its essential point originally in v. 9. There are doubts even about v. 8: for one thing besides ὁ Ἰησοῦς which occurs three times, in vv. 3, 5, 9, the absolute ὁ κύριος is used here in a striking way (the address κύριε is less objectionable), for another thing v. 9 does not follow smoothly upon the foregoing word of Zacchaeus, but fits in excellently as an answer to the objection in v. 7, in which we need merely to assume a former πρὸς αὐτούς in place of the present πρὸς αὐτόν.

127. The large investigation of René Laurentin, *Structure et Théologie de Luc* I–II (*Études Bibliques*), 1957, proceeds in its detailed interpretation from the present text and consequently handles the Christological statements of v. 11 as expressing the Messiahship and divinity of Jesus (pp. 120ff.).

128. So Joh. Weiss, *Lk* in *SNT²* I, p. 426; Bousset, *Kyrios*

Christos, p. 79; Vielhauer, *ZThK* 49, 1952, p. 266 ("possibly").

129. Here I do not inquire into the very different problems of the section of text Lk. 2:25ff.

130. Here it may not be argued that the birth in Bethlehem already necessarily implies the statement about the full Messiahship of the child.

131. In Lk. 2:9, 15 κύριος is a designation of God. It occurs twenty-four times in this sense in the whole of the Lukan nativity narrative.

132. Lk. 1:39–45 (and the independent Magnificat vv. 46ff.) serves to connect the narrative about the Baptist and the one about Jesus. In my opinion the scene certainly does not go back as a whole to Luke; against Dibelius, *Jungfrauensohn*, pp. 13f., who nevertheless indicates clearly that in detail secondary redactional work presents itself; but the possibility granted in principle of an early *Vorlage* is not actually taken seriously by him. Bultmann, *Syn. Trad.*, p. 322, regards Lk. 1: 39ff. as pre-Lukan, but again does not reckon with redactional interferences. In any case this narrative shows that the two childhood stories were already connected before Luke. Luke's share must, however, be clearly demarcated. First of all v. 41c καὶ ἐπλήσθη πνεύματος ἁγίου ἡ ᾿Ελισάβετ is redactional, for through it there results a noticeable doubling of the introduction to the discourse in v. 42a καὶ ἀνεφώνησεν κραυγῇ μεγάλῃ; and moreover there is a genuinely Lukan motif in v. 41c, cf. Heinrich von Baer, *Der Heilige Geist in den Lukasschriften* (*BWANT* III/3), 1926, p. 54. The second interpolation occurs in v. 43 καὶ πόθεν μοι τοῦτο ἵνα ἔλθῃ ἡ μήτηρ τοῦ κυρίου μου πρὸς ἐμέ, through which it is brought to expression unambiguously, and indeed in accordance with later Christology, that the place of Jesus is above that of the Baptist. This almost prophetic utterance of Elisabeth necessitated the first interpolation in v. 41c. The remaining text yields a seamless connection; vv. 41 and 44 refer to Gen. 25:22 LXX (the leaping of the child in the mother's womb); v. 42b (blessing of the mother) has many parallels in Judaism, cf. on this Bultmann, *Syn. Trad.*, pp. 29f.; v. 45 reverts to the Mary scene so that the "Kyrios" referred to God is altogether significant (1:38), but the more abruptly does the "Kyrios" referred to Jesus fall out.

133. Dibelius, *Jungfrauensohn*, pp. 62f., also regards the ὅς ἐστιν χριστὸς κύριος as a Lukan addition. On purely formal grounds, however, no one can disapprove of the phrase.

134. It is certainly not altogether out of the question that the two predicates were already added in pre-Lukan tradition, but the presence of very similar redactional elements in 1:39ff. goes rather to prove that the addition was made by Luke himself.

135. Above all the Old Testament stories about the happenings prior to the births of Samson and Samuel will have been a pattern.

136. Dibelius, *Jungfrauensohn*, p. 73. The question as to the original language of the *Vorlage* of Lk. 1 and 2 has been dealt with frequently in recent times and cannot be discussed here in detail. In several investigations Paul Winter especially has advocated a Hebrew original text, cf. in particular: "Some Observations on the Language in the

Birth and Infancy Stories of the Third Gospel", *NTSt* 1, 1954/55, pp. 111–121; "The Proto-Source of Luke 1", *Nov. Test.* 1, 1956, pp. 184–199; "On Luke and Lukan Sources", *ZNW* 47, 1956, pp. 217–242; R. Laurentin, *op. cit.*, pp. 12f., 19f., also reckons with ultimately Hebrew beginnings, although he undertakes no detailed philological investigations. Otherwise, e.g. Nigel Turner, "The Relation of Luke I and II to Hebrew Sources and to the Rest of Luke-Acts", *NTSt* 2, 1955/56, pp. 100–109, who wants to show that in style the language of the Lukan nativity narrative is Greek. But the question cannot be decided for Lk. 1 and 2 as a whole. R. McL. Wilson, "Some Recent Studies in the Lucan Infancy Narratives" in *Studia Evangelica* (*TU* 73 = V/18), pp. 235–253, has rightly made out that the story about the Baptist and the lyric portions most easily permit us to conclude that they had Semitic originals (pp. 252f.).

137. Cf. the work of Hans Frhr. von Campenhausen, *Die Jungfrauengeburt in der Theologie der alten Kirche* (*SAH phil.-hist. Kl.* 1962/3), 1962, especially pp. 7ff., 19ff.

138. In the genealogy Lk. 3:23ff. the motifs are not so clearly recognizable, although there also the Davidic sonship and the virgin birth stand side by side, but are considerably covered over by the Adam-Christ typology or the continuing backwards of the genealogy to God.

139. Cf. the principle of the Mishna adduced by Billerbeck I, p. 35, that on the declaration of a man a child counts as his child (*Baba B.* 8, 6). Moreover, it may be pointed out that in the levirate marriage it is not natural extraction but legal membership that is decisive for the child.

140. Cf. Billerbeck II, pp. 393ff., also I, pp. 45f. Besides Matt. 1:18 note also vv. 20b, 24.

141. In Lk. 1:26ff. the angel appears directly before Mary; on the other hand the appearance in Matt. 1:18ff. takes place in a dream, which also points to a somewhat late and very reflective stratum of tradition. Appearances in dreams are characteristic of the whole of Matthew's nativity narrative, cf. Matt. 1:20; 2:13; 19:22.

142. This has been emphasized above all by Dibelius, *Jungfrauensohn*, pp. 23f., who even considers whether the evangelist is not responsible for the whole of this apologetic representation. That, however, may not be said, for the character of an independent narrative is very well preserved even if the virgin birth is assumed as well known.

143. This holds good although Jesus is not directly characterized as Son of David; but it is hardly by chance that in Matt. 1:20 the pious Joseph receives the honorific "son of David".

144. From here there emerged in the early church the dispute as to whether vv. 22f belongs or not to the angel's discourse. Since Matt. 21:4f. also contains such a citation-interpolation (cf. Mk. 11:1ff.), 1:22f. is likewise to be regarded as redactional.

145. παρθένος takes the place of עַלְמָה.

146. As αὐτοῦ shows, it is Israel the people of God who are thought of; again a sign of an early Jewish-Christian tradition. Cf. also Matt.

15:22b, 24. Later the church referred ὁ λαὸς αὐτοῦ to itself; so the evangelist Matthew also understands it.

147. Cf. especially Lk. 19:6f., 9, but also the σῶσαι τὸ ἀπολωλός in the explanatory statement given in v. 10.

148. The Davidic sonship and the σωτήρ-motif occur side by side only in Lk. 2:1ff. and Matt. 1:18ff.; generally each of the two motifs can represent the other.

149. On Lk. 1:32f. cf. p. 243.

150. Cf. on this in detail Chapter 5, pp. 295ff.

151. Here then the line from Mk. 11:1-10 is carried further. Only now, together with the Davidic kingship, Jesus receives the messianic dignity at the same time and in all its fullness. The futures of the promise made in Lk. 1:32f. refer, as v. 35 shows, to the birth of Jesus and hold good for the whole of his earthly life.

152. So Dibelius, *Jungfrauensohn*, pp. 11f.

153. Thus a report is given in the first place of the sending of Gabriel, then of the city of Galilee named Nazareth, then of a virgin betrothed to Joseph, a descendant of David, and only at last is the name of this virgin given; thereupon v. 28 follows directly.

154. The ἰδού in v. 31 is also to be noted here, for it indicates that the announcement refers not to something of uncertain date but to something that is now becoming operative. On v. 34 cf. the important article by Josef Gewiess, *Die Marienfrage Lk. 1:34*, BZ NF 5, 1961, pp. 221-254. Reference may also be made to the essay, instructive in family history, of Jean-Paul Audet, *L'annonce à Marie*, RB 63, 1956, pp. 346-374, who compares the parallels in the Old Testament, especially the annunciation of the birth of Gideon.

155. On Lk. 1:26ff. cf. further Chapter 5, pp. 296ff.

156. Above all there can be claimed for this Matt. 2:9b-11 together with the exposition in vv. 1b, 2b, the limits of which can no longer be determined quite clearly; cf. for the analysis Dibelius, *Formgeschichte*, pp. 125f.

157. V. 8 and v. 9b; it can be said for the present narrative that it is a matter first of the place and then of the house; but in view of the leading of the star the magi had no need of information from Herod.

158. To this there belong especially vv. 1a, 2a, 3-9a, 12.

159. Here it must also be asked if vv. 5b, 6 is not a secondary citation due to reflection.

160. See v. 1a.

161. In the present Matthean context the Davidic sonship is of course assumed on account of the legal position of Joseph. But 1:18ff.; 2:1ff. and the section 2:13-23, which assumes the Moses typology, represent no original unity. 2:1ff is quite certainly thought of as an independent narrative. As regards 2:13ff. we may prefer to wonder whether it is material that has been added.

162. Finally it may be pointed out that, except in the passages that have been discussed, the Davidic sonship of Jesus appears only in the discourses of Acts. Acts 13:22f. is concerned with the prophecy made to David which has been fulfilled in the sending of the σωτήρ

'Ιησοῦς. In two passages, Acts 2:25–31 and 13:32–36, in connection with the exaltation conception the words οὐδὲ δώσεις τὸν ὅσιόν σου ἰδεῖν διαφθοράν (Ps. 16:10) spoken prophetically by David are taken up by Luke as a prophecy of the resurrection of Jesus. Further, within the discourse of James to the Apostolic Council, Acts 15:14–18, the words of Amos 9:11f. regarding the re-erection of the tabernacle of David are quoted to establish the statement ὁ θεὸς ἐπεσκέψατο λαβεῖν ἐξ ἐθνῶν λαὸν τῷ ὀνόματι αὐτοῦ. No instances of the two last named kinds of application can be produced from elsewhere in the New Testament, and probably they go back to Luke himself. On the other hand, the first mentioned passage, Acts 13:22f., fits excellently into the picture obtained above of Jesus' earthly work as Son of David and σωτήρ. On this cf. especially Lövestam. op. cit.

CHAPTER V

SON OF GOD

THE designation of Jesus as Son of God presents a problem which has long been discussed in historico-critical research. Already there has been much debate as to whether this title ought to be regarded as having a Palestinian or a Hellenistic origin.[1] It may certainly not be doubted that it had a previous history on Palestinian soil, but it is indisputable that on Hellenistic soil "Son of God", in the same way as "Kyrios", received a meaning that was essentially different.[2] While in the Hellenistic church Son of God was aligned first and foremost with the unique being of Jesus, it may not be assumed that the Palestinian church viewed it in this way.

Opinions with regard to the earliest use of the title now differ widely: is "Son of God" derived from royal messianism,[3] or from the expectation of a messianic high priest,[4] or from the Son of man conception?[5] Does there stand behind "Son of God" an original "servant of God",[6] or are we concerned here with a designation of dignity which grew out of Jesus' singular belief in the Father?[7] A convincing account of the further evolution of this title of majesty within the Hellenistic church can only be given when its use at the commencement of the early Christian tradition has been clearly determined.

1. *The Presuppositions of the early Christian Title Son of God*

In our discussion a fundamental distinction has to be drawn between the title "Son of God" and the absolute title "the Son". Both designations have, as will yet appear, different roots and do not permit of their being identified without more ado. Only with "the Son" is the designation of God as "Father" found as correlative in the New Testament; here then it is in order to ask what significance the conception of the fatherhood of God has in the proclamation of Jesus and of the early church. There is, however, no clear reference to the designation of God as Father in any place where the title "Son of God" is used.[8] However it may be as regards the relation of "the Son" to "Son of God" in the later history of the tradition, they certainly do not permit of their being derived from one another.[9] The title of dignity "Son of God", which is to be dealt with first, has presuppositions different from those of the designation "the Son" and has to be tested for its own roots.

The servant of God conception, which may in fact have played a part in the original form of the narratives of the baptism and transfiguration, does not suffice to explain the earliest history of the primitive Christian title, Son of God. The baptism and the transfiguration cannot be taken as the starting point, for in their present form these narratives represent a later phase of the tradition, and in their earlier form they are not so clear a proof that the ideas, Son of God and servant of God, belong to one another as in recent times has occasionally been asserted.[10]

The question has been considered whether the conception of the Son of God may not fit into the compass of the late Jewish conception of the Son of man and then from its origin have to be understood in the sense of a metaphysical sonship existing from eternity. In orthodox Judaism at any rate the motif of divine sonship, although an early element in the conception of the king is involved here, had been given a wide berth as being a denial of the much emphasized antithesis of God and man; and indeed even the Messiah also was regarded unreservedly as a man.[11] The idea of the Son of God must instead have been at home in less orthodox, possibly even semi-Gentile, circles and have belonged there to the conception of the heavenly primitive man. Nevertheless, against this thesis it has to be said that there is no really clear evidence for it;[12] this derivation also has then to be abandoned.

The idea of the messianic high priest is likewise out of the question as a starting point. The designation "son" applied to the priest occurs by the side of "servant" in Mal. 1:6, but there in figurative speech.[13] Its occurrence side by side with servant and minister in the *Testament of Levi* 4:2: ". . . that thou shouldest become to him (the Lord) a son and a servant and a minister of his presence",[14] shows already that here there can be no thought of a special dignity of the son or even of a status and function as in Ps. 2:7.[15] In the *Midr. Ps.* 2 §3

(13a) it is merely a matter of an application of Ps. 2:2 (משיח יהוה))
to the high priest, and here, in view of the exegesis of that time,
Ps. 2:7 may not be tacitly included. Finally it may not be
denied that the "Father's voice" of the *Testament of Levi*
18:6f., in spite of the striking parallels in these verses to
the story of the baptism, does not without more ado
declare anything regarding the divine sonship of the high
priest, the designation of God as Father being much too
widely disseminated for that in Old Testament Jewish
tradition.[16]

The statement that Ps. 2:7 has to be brought in here because
the high priest has also "traits that are quite royal",[17] is
inapposite. For on the one hand, the dignity of the Son referred
to in Ps. 2:7 includes, as vv. 8ff. show, the motif of dominion,
and it is precisely in this connection that it has found its
proper expression in royal messianism, for which reason it is
hardly by chance that evidence for the carrying over of Ps. 2:7
to the messianic high priest is lacking. On the other hand, the
carrying over of isolated motifs of royal messianism to the
high priestly Messiah ought not to deceive us into regarding such
elements as characteristic; rather it was only general messianic
traits that were taken over, and this certainly took place for the
reason that the high priest could be clearly distinguished as an
eschatological and messianic figure[18] and not with a view to
adjudicate royal functions to him himself.[19] But, however it
may stand as regards the dependence of the conception of the
messianic high priest on royal messianism, already in a different connection it has emerged that a carrying over of the idea
of the messianic high priest into New Testament Christology
cannot be demonstrated with certainty in any single passage,[20]
and the evidence discussed here cannot invalidate this judgment, for Mal. 1:6, the *Testament of Levi* 18,6f. and the *Midr.
Ps.* 2 §3 drop out completely, and the *Testament of Levi*
4,2 can on no account bear the burden of proof.

If the divine sonship does not sufficiently permit of its being
derived from any of the associations which have been indicated
thus far, there remains only royal messianism,[21] and in fact
it is from this that the use of the title Son of God in the primitive
Christian tradition has to be explained. Before the New Testament texts are dealt with, an answer must certainly be found
to the question whether the designation Son of God for the

royal Messiah was at all current in late Judaism, for this has been contested with weighty reasons.[22]

It has indeed to be granted that the evidence from the *Ethiopic Book of Enoch* 105,2 and II Esdras 7:28; 13:32, 37, 52; 14:9, which earlier was frequently drawn upon, drops out, for the Enoch passage is lacking in the fragment of the Greek translation which doubtless goes back directly to the Semitic original, and the various passages from II Esdras which have *filius meus* as designation of the Messiah have, as the other early versions of this writing show, to be carried back to an original עבדי[23] But after all there is now some evidence of the use in rabbinical literature of the form of address in Ps. 2:7, and it is not allowable to characterize this as late.[24] A *baraita* from *bSukkah* 52a has been preserved which may reach back at least to the second century after Christ;[25] there Ps. 2:7 is expressly referred to Messiah ben David. Above all, however, the anti-Christian polemic shows that, alongside radical discussion of the question of divine sonship in the physical sense, the reference of Ps. 2:7 to the Messiah must have been rooted fairly securely; it may even be that this emphatically adoptionist statement alone was adhered to precisely for polemical reasons, in order to avoid all reference to the later Christian Son of God conception.[26]

There is now a piece of clear evidence that we must reckon with an application to the royal Messiah, already in pre-Christian times,[27] of passages from the Old Testament which contain the title Son of God. It is the florilegium from the Qumran Cave 4. There the promise to David in 2 Sam. 7:11f., 14a is quoted and applied to the coming of the צמח דויד, who is to appear with the "investigator of the Torah";[28] finally the promise in Amos 9:11 of the re-erection of the tabernacle of David is also included in this place.[29] This important piece of evidence from the Qumran texts is moreover a sign that in the idea of the appointment of the royal Messiah as Son of God the use of Ps. 2:7 can never be reckoned on exclusively as is suggested in the rabbinical writings; on the other hand, however, it may be concluded that in virtue of the *indicia* that have been discussed the use of Ps. 2:7 in pre-Christian times may be assumed, 2 Sam. 7:14a having also been used. To our regret the exposition of Ps. 2 in 4 QFlor, which begins at the end of column 1, has not been preserved. Only this much is clear,

that this psalm, in the same way as 2 Sam 7:11–14, was understood eschatologically.

Yet another text from the Qumran writings may suggest to
us the use of the motif of divine sonship. It is 1 Q Sa II, 11:
"This is the seating arrangement of the men named, of those
called to the assembly, for the community council when is
born[...] the Messiah..."; it is true that יוליד is not undisputed,
but it is nevertheless extremely probable that in this passage,
similarly as in Isa. 9:5, the thought of the adoption of the
messianic king lies before us, and therefore that the conception
of the divine sonship stands in the background.[30] Thereby it is
certainly not yet proved that "Son of God" was also used as an
independent title, for not only 2 Sam. 7:14a but also Ps. 2:7
contain the motif of divine sonship in the compass of a statement of adoption.

Nevertheless the earliest New Testament pieces of evidence
do not give us the impression that only the thought of the
divine sonship of the Messiah was taken over from Judaism,
and that on the other hand the titular use of "Son of God"
came first into use in the primitive church. Moreover two late
rabbinical passages are preserved in which the Son of God
designation occurs in independence of Ps. 2:7. The one is in
Mekh Ex 15,9 (48b)—repeated somewhat more in detail in the
mediaeval compilation *Yalqut Shim'oni* Ps. 2:2 (2 § 620)—
where the "son of the king" is spoken about allegorically;[31]
the other occurs in *TargPs* 80:16, where וְעַל בֵּן is interpreted by
מַלְכָּא מְשִׁיחָא.[32] Here at least there lie before us indications that
even a use of the Son of God designation for the royal Messiah
that is independent of Ps. 2:7 (2 Sam. 7:14a) is not to be completely ruled out for New Testament times. The possibility that
we are concerned here with early tradition is not to be challenged on principle although there is no absolutely positive
evidence. An evolution similar to the one that took place in the
case of the Davidic sonship may be assumed in the case of the
messianic king.

The motif that the promised Messiah is a son of David
took shape above all in the perfectly formal "offspring of
David"; yet there came about in pre-Christian times, as the
Psalms of Solomon 17,21 shows, a use of "son of David" in the
titular sense. In the case of the divine sonship the statement of

adoption did on the whole clearly play a part within the compass of royal messianism. But here also the titular use can in the end have gained a certain acceptance. It is true that to a certain extent there stood against that the custom, which was pretty thoroughly naturalized, of avoiding the name of God,[33] yet this could be got round by a circumlocution such as we meet with, for instance, in Mk. 14:61.[34]

Summary. It emerges that the motif of the divine sonship in its distinctive form, therefore in the sense of appointment to office and assignment of dominion, practically belongs to royal messianism within the sphere of Palestinian late Judaism. It is extremely probable that there also the titular use of "Son of the Blessed" and the like had come to be common already in pre-Christian tradition.

2. *Son of God as Designation of the Jesus who is to come again and of the Exalted One*

Observations made in earlier connections may be resumed on the basis of these reflections regarding the late Jewish use of the Son of God conception. In the Palestinian primitive church the idea of the royal Messiah was related most of all to the future work of Jesus. This has emerged in the investigation both of the Messiah title and of the Son of David title. Moreover it is supported by its association with the statement about the coming Son of man; in this connection there crops up above all the citation of Ps. 110:1 referred to the one who is to come again.[35] Since the Son of man and Kyrios conceptions also have an intent that is primarily eschatological, this consequence is not at all surprising.

The designation "Son of God" was also originally applied to Jesus' eschatological function. Indeed, strictly speaking, the divine sonship was not an independent idea, but one of the constituent parts of royal messianism and therefore was applied in the same way in the primitive church. So far as I can see, this conclusion has until now not hit the mark anywhere; rather it has as a rule been considered that from the beginning the appointment to divine sonship was bound up with the Easter event.[36] Those New Testament passages which treat of the eschatological work of the Son of God certainly do not permit of their being satisfactorily explained in this way; often they are not even so much as noticed.[37] No further research on

284

messianism is needed. The New Testament portions of tradition which contain "Son of God" in the eschatological-messianic sense have, however, to be assembled.

The earliest text, which still preserves the peculiarities of Jewish thought in all their strength, is the little messianic hymn, Lk. 1:32f., which may even go back to Jewish tradition. The mention of the "throne of his father David" and of his endless reign over the house of Jacob shows how clearly royal messianism has here been realized, particularly in its early secular-political structure. The nomination as "Son of the Highest" of the king appointed to the dominion, shows in its formulation and matter dependence on the Old Testament Jewish way of thinking.[38]

The second passage, Jesus' confession before the supreme council, Mk. 14:61f., shows that instructive blending of the Messiah and Son of man conceptions which results not only from the relation of v. 61 and v. 62, but above all from the association of Ps. 110:1 and Dan. 7:13 in v. 62 itself.[39] There is no doubt that the question of the high priest σὺ εἶ ὁ χριστὸς ὁ υἱὸς τοῦ εὐλογητοῦ is to be understood in the sense of a hendiadys.[40] At the same time, however, the Christos title is not explained, as it is perhaps in Matt. 16:16, by the later Son of God title of Hellenistic Christianity, but the titles Son of God and Christos are here assumed in their original messianic sense. It is not difficult to recognize that the periphrastic phrase "Son of the Blessed" also points directly to the early Palestinian tradition.[41] In v. 62 the Messiah title is accepted by the person questioned.

But the answer cannot be otherwise understood than as an "interpretation" of the Messiah question in terms of the eschatological expectation of the Son of man, consequently as an acceptance, in reference exclusively to the eschatological work of Jesus, of the dignity of the Messiah, the terrestrial setting being thereby replaced by the transcendent conception of apocalyptic. Jesus thus professes messiahship and divine sonship in that he speaks of his eschatological office and of his appointment to the dignity and power of the one who, appearing in splendour, brings salvation.[42]

The early messianic tradition which is evident in Lk. 1:32f. and Mk. 14:61f. did not wholly die out even in the early tradition of the Hellenistic church. That emerges from a text which as a rule has not been sufficiently valued in respect of its significance in this regard, namely I Thess. 1:9f. It is indeed recognized that here we are concerned with a portion of primitive Christian missionary preaching that is not strictly speaking characteristic of Paul himself;[43] nevertheless, strange to say, it is always utilized only with a view to the penitential homily and eschatological proclamation, but not for Christology. The resurrection of Jesus and eschatological judicial activity being near to one another, reference is made to the parallel in Acts 17:31, but not to the previous history of this motif in the primitive Palestinian church.

Yet we are concerned here with one of the few texts in which the correlation of the resurrection of Jesus and eschatological happenings comes unambiguously to expression. Furthermore, here as in Mark 14:62, the eschatological function of Jesus, envisaged according to an apocalyptic mode of thinking, is explicitly connected with the messianic Son of God title.

Reference is not made to the earthly work of Jesus and his death, and the resurrection is not understood, as is the case in Acts 17:31, as proof offered to all men of the election of Jesus,[44] but in this exclusively eschatologically orientated statement of I Thess. 1:10 as an anticipated final happening which all the more certainly refers us to the beginning of the eschatological events. The coming "from heaven" indicates fusion with the Son of man tradition, as does also the function of Jesus as "Redeemer" ($\dot{\rho}\nu\acute{o}\mu\epsilon\nu o s$) from "the wrath to come", which has to be understood here in the sense of the apocalyptic judicature of the world.[45] But the Son of God title remains decisive; in this we can see how the Messiah conception, far from being a general designation, was used especially to describe the eschatological office of Jesus.

From I Thess. 1:9f. it emerges that a use, eschatologically orientated, of the Son of God title continued to be made in the missionary preaching of the Hellenistic church. Nevertheless it may not be overlooked that there the already discussed process of fusion set in relatively early, and the expectation of the parousia receded in favour of the idea of the exaltation of Jesus.[46] At the same time the statements originating in royal messianism were detached from the eschatological work of Jesus and transferred to his present dignity and function in heaven.

286

With that, however, elements that hitherto had been connected separated from one another: the Son of man conception does not incorporate the motif of exaltation[47] and is confined to statements about the parousia and the earthly works or the passion of Jesus; the Son of David title, which was originally linked up with phrases about the future messianic kingdom, is applied, within the compass of the two-stage Christology, to the earthly life of Jesus in especial. On the other hand, Ps. 110:1 and the strictly messianic statements of sovereignty and dominion are transferred to the exalted Jesus; henceforth Ps. 110:1 remains firmly united to the theologumenon of the exaltation of Jesus.

The titles of dignity "Christos" and "Son of God" are now likewise applied to the exalted Jesus, but they soon undergo a further transformation so that it is not surprising if they occur relatively seldom as titles of the exalted Jesus. There are instances of "Christos" in Mk. 12:35ff. and Acts 2:36.[48] For "Son of God" there comes into question most of all the important passage Rom. 1:3f., which has already been dealt with in detail;[49] there is also the application of Ps. 2:7 to the risen Jesus in Acts 13:33 (cf. vv. 32–37) in the speech of Paul at Pisidian Antioch, a speech which was certainly formulated by Luke, but in which nevertheless older material is worked up.[50]

There is also an echo of such an application of the Son of God title in the Epistle to the Hebrews, especially in 1:5 and 5:5, where Ps. 2:7 (also 2 Sam. 7:14) is quoted with regard to the heavenly position of Jesus, although the author himself adjudicates the sonship to the pre-existent and also to the earthly Jesus.[51] Finally, there have to be adduced from Col. 1:13 the words: to be translated εἰς τὴν βασιλείαν τοῦ υἱοῦ τῆς ἀγάπης αὐτοῦ. There the time between the resurrection of Jesus and the parousia is thought of, and, similarly as in 1 Cor. 15:25–28, a dominion of Christ as king is mentioned.[52] In 1 Cor. 15:28 the designation Son also appears and, although there it is a question of an eschatological act, the return of the dominion to God, it clearly refers back to the βασιλεύειν of vv. 25ff. Through the explicit citation of Ps. 110:1 the original association of this designation of dignity with the conception of exaltation is here again clearly in evidence.[53]

That exhausts the New Testament texts which declare the

divine sonship particularly of the exalted Jesus, for if elsewhere in Pauline contexts a work of the heavenly Christ is spoken about in association with the title "Son of God", it is not the *status exaltationis* exclusively that is thought of, rather "Son of God" is understood as a comprehensive title of honour, one to be associated with all the work of Christ.

Summary. Hitherto it has not been observed that the use of the title "Son of God" in primitive Christianity was connected initially with the eschatological conception of the Messiah and was made first of all only with an eye on the eschatological work of Jesus. This use of it was continued in the missionary preaching of Hellenistic Jewish Christianity (1 Thess. 1:9f.). But the process of transformation which we have had to recognize in the case of the Messiah concept also wrought here, with the result that "Son of God" became a characteristic title of the exalted Jesus who has been adopted by God and installed in his heavenly office. This has played a large part within the compass of the two-stage Christology (Rom. 1:3f.), though otherwise also it has had a considerable after-effect.

3. *The Son of God Conception in Hellenistic Jewish Christianity*

The development of the theologumenon of the exaltation of Jesus came about within the sphere of the early Hellenistic church. In the long run it could not but come about that there influences should assert themselves which were conditioned by the attempt to come to grips with the realm of ideas that was characteristic of paganism. To speak religio-phenomenologically, we are concerned here with the taking over of elements of the θεῖος ἀνήρ-conception into the traditional Son of God concept. The extent to which the idea of the divine man was alive in Greek antiquity and also in Hellenistic syncretism has been graphically described by Windisch and Bieler.[54]

That this conception had long since been associated with the motif of divine sonship, is not astonishing.[55] From this there resulted considerable impingements upon the early Christian proclamation of Jesus as the Son of God.[56] If indeed we mean to sketch a history of the Son of God conception in Hellenistic Christianity, it is inadmissible to refer at once to the pronouncedly pagan cast of the θεῖος ἀνήρ-idea.[57] Hellenistic Judaism represents a not unessential intervening link in so far as in it Hellenistic ideas of various sorts were already accepted

288

and transformed in order to render feasible an association of them with the Biblical tradition.

Since the "Son of God" title of primitive Christendom was applied on Hellenistic soil to the earthly Jesus, the question has to be asked in what way this was prepared for and made possible by the Judaism of the Diaspora.

In Hellenistic Judaism the Old Testament "men of God" were very soon put on a par with the θεῖοι ἄνθρωποι. Windisch has devoted a special section of his investigation to these men of God and the understanding of them that obtained in Hellenistic Jewish circles.[58] At the same time he has certainly made a mistake in treating the "men of God" according to the Old Testament representation as θεῖοι ἄνθρωποι in the literal sense.[59] There tell against that two characteristics which distinguish the old Israelitish nebiism fundamentally from all Graeco-Hellenistic thought about phenomena of a similar kind: on the one hand, there is here no sort of participating by man in what is divine, but only complete subordination to God; on the other hand, the special abilities of the "men of God" are carried back to the action of the divine Spirit;[60] accordingly these abilities are understood not as signs of an ἐνθουσιασμός but as χαρίσματα.[61] Quite definitely the constitutive element of the θεῖος ἀνήρ-conception, the divinity of man or the possibility of his participating in what is divine, indeed of his deification, is unthinkable in the Old Testament, and for that reason this concept is not at all suited to describe the Old Testament circumstances.[62]

It is, however, instructive to compare with the Old Testament the interpretation which the Israelitish men of God met with in Hellenistic Judaism. It is available only in cuttings, but these are sufficiently instructive.[63] In the *Epistle of Aristeas* 140 it is stated by Egyptian priests that only the Israelites as worshippers of the true God have a right to the designation ἄνθρωποι θεοῦ; there precedes a polemic against polytheism, idols, and probably also against the deification of man.[64] The wider context indicates in its moralizing tendency as also in its use of that title of honour a disintegration of the idea of the divine man. Nevertheless the restriction to the Israelites is itself very significant. Here there is reflected the conflict against the pagan views of gods and godliness. The testimony of Josephus is discordant; on the one hand, he says emphatically:

κοινωνία θείῳ πρὸς θνητὸν ἀπρεπής ἐστιν,[65] on the other hand,
however, he uses θεῖος as an attribute of Moses and the
prophets.[66]

Whilst here then the Jewish structure of thought is retained
in principle, special phenomena of the religious life of Israel are
nevertheless described in the terms of Hellenistic abstract
thinking; actually then a far-reaching Hellenization has set in.[67]
In Philo this is carried out quite consciously. Abraham and
Moses and also the prophets are no longer mere men of this
earth. On the other hand, he seems to avoid the concept
θεῖος ἀνήρ consciously[68] and speaks instead of the θεσπέσιος
ἀνήρ. This may not indicate any fundamental difference, but
after all it may rather permit thoughts of a divine infusion and
inspiration.[69] In a way Philo also wishes to take into account the
divine leading in the life of the man of God, in the conversion of
Abraham, the ascent of Moses on Sinai and the like; but here he
again makes use of a Hellenistic idea, being able, when dealing
with such passages, to speak in accordance with what was said
about the initiation ceremonies of the mystery religions,
accordingly to speak of a deification, a transformation of the
human nature into the divine. As regards this intervention of
God and the equipment of the man of God that is effected
thereby there is, however, no thought in any case of a divinity
that is a natural endowment of these specially elected men.
Philo has doubtless gone very far in the matter of Hellenizing
and may not be immediately authoritative for our context. It
is significant that in all the instances that have been dealt with
there has been a more or less considerable attempt to come to
terms with the Hellenistic spirit, and Philo certainly stands not
at the beginning but at the end of this process of assimilation.

A first acceptance in Christology of traits of the θεῖος ἀνήρ-
conception came about in Hellenistic Jewish Christianity. At
the same time Old Testament Jewish ways of thinking were
adhered to quite consistently, and accordingly miraculous deeds
and authoritative teaching were legitimate only in virtue of the
electing and inspiring Holy Spirit and in the name of the one
God. The inheritance of Diaspora Judaism, which had already
taken the specifically pagan edge off the θεῖος ἀνήρ-conception,
could be accepted as well.[70]

On the other hand, its adoption was prepared for in that the
early Palestinian church had already developed side by side

with the Son of man Christology of the logia source, which restricted itself in the main to what Jesus proclaimed, a Christological conception in which the working of miracles stood in the foreground; Jesus was regarded as the new Moses and was characterized in detail according to the conception of the charismatic men of God of the old covenant.[71]

This understanding remains preserved most clearly in the story of the casting out of a demon in Mk. 1:23ff.[72] There the word of the demon in v. 24, both by the τί ἡμῖν καὶ σοί and by the address ὁ ἅγιος τοῦ θεοῦ, permits lines of connection with these Old Testament figures to be clearly recognized.[73] What would have been absolutely impossible in early Palestinian Christianity is the coupling of such a view with the title Son of God. On the other hand, it has to be borne in mind that in the sphere of the Diaspora the Old Testament men of God had taken over very fully the attributes of the θεῖοι ἄνθρωποι. In addition to this Jesus was already regarded there as the exalted One and the heavenly Son of God. Above all, the presentation of his miracles as the activity of a specially gifted charismatic person pressed increasingly in this direction.

The story of the exorcism in Mk. 5:1ff. shows by its reception of the title Son of God in the word of the demons that this step was taken immediately. In respect of its local colour as of the judgment passed on the swine this story of the legion of demons doubtless arose out of the presuppositions of Palestinian Judaism. Certainly it is also related very closely to Mk. 1:23ff. and again shows Jesus as the spiritually mighty vanquisher of demons.[74] The address in 5:7 contains the same basic elements as 1:24, which certainly goes back to a common tradition. But in place of the address ὁ ἅγιος τοῦ θεοῦ there appears Ἰησοῦ, υἱὲ τοῦ θεοῦ τοῦ ὑψίστου. This formulation is extraordinarily instructive for the history of the tradition. For the divine predicate ὕψιστος is indeed already known in the Old Testament, but in the Judaism of the Diaspora it gains a special significance and is frequently a sign of Jewish influence.[75] In our passage it signifies that we are in the sphere of early Hellenistic Jewish Christianity, in which the idea of Jesus as a man of God and the "Holy One of God" has now been exchanged for the conception of him as "Son of God".[76] The reserve maintained in Mk. 1:23ff. in the Christological interpretation of an exorcism is here abandoned. Nevertheless we come here upon a stage of the tradition at which the Jewish presuppositions are still very considerably in evidence and the Hellenistic elements are incorporated in an extremely wilful manner.[77] For now as ever the thought of the equipment with the Spirit bestowed by God, wherewith Jesus has obtained power over the "unclean spirits", is of vital importance.[78]

In this place some reflections are needed in regard to the earliest understanding of the exorcisms of demons. That Jesus actually wrought as an exorcist cannot be called in question.[79] Apart from the stories of exorcism, this can be verified by the portion of tradition Mk. 3:22–30, which in Matthew and Luke is associated with a parallel tradition from the logia source, in which there is also the early saying Lk. 11:(19)20 par.[80]

The most original version of this discussion about the exorcising of demons is to be found in the Q-tradition best preserved in Luke; Mark already presents a very different and certainly a later understanding of it. In spite of the variations in formulation the figurative expressions are common to all; they are intended to show the impossibility of the reproaches that have been directed against Jesus.[81] The accusation runs: $\dot{\epsilon}\nu$ $B\epsilon\epsilon\zeta\epsilon\beta o\dot{\nu}\lambda$ $\tau\hat{\omega}$ $\ddot{a}\rho\chi o\nu\tau\iota$ $\tau\hat{\omega}\nu$ $\delta a\iota\mu o\nu\acute{\iota}\omega\nu$ $\dot{\epsilon}\kappa\beta\acute{a}\lambda\lambda\epsilon\iota$ $\tau\grave{a}$ $\delta a\iota\mu\acute{o}\nu\iota a$ Lk. 11:15 par.[82] In the logion Lk. 11:20, which, while it is authentic, hardly arises out of a situation marked by controversy, it is a matter of the casting out of demons "by the finger of God" as a sign of the opening up of the kingdom of God.[83] Both in the formulation of the charge and in this $\dot{\epsilon}\nu$ $\delta a\kappa\tau\acute{\nu}\lambda\omega$ $\theta\epsilon o\hat{\nu}$ $\dot{\epsilon}\gamma\grave{\omega}$ $\dot{\epsilon}\kappa\beta\acute{a}\lambda\lambda\omega$ $\tau\grave{a}$ $\delta a\iota\mu\acute{o}\nu\iota a$ the same basic idea comes to expression: the $\dot{\epsilon}\nu$ answers to a Hebrew בְּ and designates the agent who grants power for such an act and makes men to be his own instruments.[84] God and Satan are in opposition. That is shown by the interpretation of the name $B\epsilon\epsilon\zeta\epsilon\beta o\dot{\nu}\lambda$ as also by the typically Semitic parlance $\delta\acute{a}\kappa\tau\nu\lambda os$ $\theta\epsilon o\hat{\nu}$, by which God's own action is paraphrased.[85]

In this place Matthew or his tradition already presents a certain dislocation, for instead of this in Matt. 12:28 the divine power of the $\pi\nu\epsilon\hat{\nu}\mu a$ is spoken of, and so it is explained more closely how Jesus has been made fit for his doings.[86] The functional idea is doubtless still preserved, the Spirit of God is the power that falls suddenly on men and works through them and the $\dot{\epsilon}\nu$ signifies the agent—the statement can, it is

292

true, also be understood in an instrumental sense, and then what comes to expression is that Jesus vanquishes the demons by virtue of the Spirit of God which is available to him.

That this modification actually asserted itself is shown by Mk. 3:22–30. There at the beginning the accusation preserved in Lk. 11:15 par. in a more original wording is transformed into a parallel formulation; in v. 22fin the early formulation is received in ἐν τῷ ἄρχοντι τῶν δαιμονίων ἐκβάλλει τὰ δαιμόνια, but now the phrase Βεεζεβοὺλ ἔχει is set in front of that.[87] To that there also corresponds the wider context in Mark, one that goes beyond Q; the concluding v. 30 once again expressly receives this statement in πνεῦμα ἀκάθαρτον ἔχει; above all the once independent saying about the blaspheming of the Holy Spirit in vv. 28f., whatever its earliest form and its original meaning,[88] has also to be understood now on these presuppositions: it is a matter of the Spirit of God whom Jesus "has" and through whom he effects his exorcisms, wherefore every one who blasphemes against this power of God is lost for ever.[89] Here what is thought of is no longer just a passing seizure but a permanent possession by the Spirit.[90]

The view last stated of a permanent possession by the Spirit does not necessarily point to Hellenistic tradition,[91] but is still possible on the presuppositions of Old Testament thought.[92] But from this understanding there comes about the decisive next step in the Hellenistic Jewish Christian tradition: Jesus, who is not only inspired as the "Holy One of God" to do unusual doings but as the bearer of the Spirit has power over the demons, is called "Son of God". What comes to expression in Mk. 5:7 within the compass of a single happening is stated in the narrative of the baptism as fundamental for the earthly life of Jesus. Mk. 1:9–11 did not originate first on Hellenistic soil, but has a long and complicated previous history.[93] There, however, the text obtained its final form and meaning on the presuppositions just mentioned.

The descent of the Spirit and the content of the voice from heaven have a decisive importance. The Spirit of God descends in person through the opened firmament in the form of a dove[94] and unites with the human person of Jesus.[95] Through this permanent endowment Jesus is appointed to his eschatological office. On the basis of such an indwelling and singular equipment he obtains the messianic dignity of the Son of God. God has pleasure in him and has therefore in this way conveyed to him the status and function of the Son mighty in the Spirit. It is very significant that on the one hand the divine sonship is determined by the conception of a quite special supernatural power and ability, a power which henceforth remains united inextricably with the person of Jesus, and that on the other hand it rests upon an act of appointment.

Here lines of different kinds converge: first of all the early conception of Jesus' work as that of a charismatic person laid hold upon by God, further the Hellenistic-Jewish interpretation of the men of God mighty in the Spirit in the sense of θεῖοι ἄνθρωποι, in which, however, subordination to God is preserved and all thought of deification remains averted, finally the conception of the Messiah as the Son of God, as is shown by reminiscence of Ps. 2:7 as well as of Isa. 42:1.[96]

But this very passage shows how considerably the messianic conception of the Old Testament tradition, which has to do with a royal dominion in the time of salvation, has now been transformed. There remains preserved only the adoption as Son of God understood in the sense of an appointment to office and the bestowal of the Spirit.[97] Yet this also stands under other stars, for everything is switched over to the bestowal of the Spirit; on this the divine sonship rests and by this the divine sonship gives proof of itself. Thus early and late elements interpenetrate in quite a remarkable way.

A noteworthy parallel to the association of an official appointment with a pronouncedly Hellenistic-Jewish Christian understanding of the pneumatic person, occurs in the use of ἄνθρωπος θεοῦ in the Pastoral Epistles (1 Tim. 6:11; 2 Tim. 3:17). The designation doubtless also stands in relation to the θεῖος ἀνήρ-conception, but again the reference is to the act of appointment, the ordination of Timothy.[98] Käsemann rightly states that "man of God" is a variant for πνευματικός, but that may not in any case be understood from the rebirth mysteries and so in a purely Hellenistic sense, but is to be interpreted on the already mentioned presuppositions of Diaspora Judaism: the "man of God" is the holder of the office not in consequence of a process of transformation but rather because he has been equipped with the Spirit of God, who works through him and whose bearer he is in a special measure.[99] As in particular the titles of God in vv. 15f. show, the Hellenistic-Jewish background of the portion of tradition I Tim. 6:11–16 is quite unmistakable.

The assertions about the divine sonship of Jesus did not spring from Gentile Hellenism and were to remain protected against it. The warding-off of a falsely understood Son of God concept can be recognized especially in the first two temptations of Jesus in Matt. 4:1–7 par.[100]

They are conceived uniformly and, in the formal way in which in them Satan is warded off by a word of Scripture, they have taken the earlier third temptation as pattern; it is something new that now there arises nothing less than a dispute regarding passages from Scripture and their correct understanding and that the title Son of God is included in Satan's address to Jesus. It is not altogether certain whether the mention at the beginning of the bestowal of the Spirit belongs to the Q-tradition, there being in Matthew and Luke overlappings with Mark's version of the story of the temptation; but it is extremely likely that it does so.[101]

But even without this motif a connection with the Son of God conception last dealt with is clear. For it is a matter of a commitment to God which cannot be broken. The Son of God may not misuse his power either in helping himself or in working a spectacular miracle, but must use it only in what he is commissioned to do. Thus divine sonship in the context of equipment with the wonderful power of the Spirit is stamped with the thought of obedience.[102]

Certainly these temptations, in which again early Jewish thought and Hellenistic thought strangely interpenetrate, are actually significant only in view of discussion regarding the θεῖος ἀνήρ-conception, discussion which set the commission and the work of Jesus in a clear light and saved them from all foreign influence.[103]

Nowhere in the passages that have been dealt with is any mention made of a divine sonship in the physical sense. Here, however, a logically imposed limit has to be stated, one that was conditioned by the traditional Jewish assumptions. In the sphere of Gentile Christianity such a conception immediately intruded and more and more asserted itself, as will be shown in the concluding section.

A not unimportant first step towards that was doubtless facilitated by Hellenistic Jewish Christianity with its theologumenon

of the virgin birth.[104] It has, however, to be put on record
that what lies before us is not a mythological understanding
such as we are acquainted with in Hellenistic syncretism,[105]
and therefore it is not an intrinsic divine sonship constituted
by the union of the Spirit with the virgin that has to be thought
of.[106] That we proceed to show in detail from the important
text Lk. 1:26ff.

The basic motif of the whole of this portion of tradition is the
virginity of Mary.[107] This is mentioned expressly at the beginning
in vv. 26f., in v. 31 it is underlined through the reference to
Isa. 7:14, and in v. 35 it is defined more closely in the answer
given by the angel. The annunciation of the birth of a son
links up with the instruction about the name-giving in v. 31b
and with the promise in vv. 32f., which is once again resumed in
v. 35 fin. Mary's submissive word in v. 38 in reference to what is
said in v. 35 completes the narrative.[108]

Dibelius has shown convincingly that precisely in v. 35, which
is decisive for the understanding of the whole, the terms and
motifs appropriate ideas from the Septuagint. That holds
good both for the $\dot{\epsilon}\pi\dot{\epsilon}\rho\chi\epsilon\sigma\theta\alpha\iota$ and for the $\dot{\epsilon}\pi\iota\sigma\kappa\iota\dot{\alpha}\zeta\epsilon\iota\nu$ of the
$\pi\nu\epsilon\hat{\upsilon}\mu\alpha\ \ddot{\alpha}\gamma\iota\sigma\nu$ or the $\delta\dot{\upsilon}\nu\alpha\mu\iota\varsigma\ \dot{\upsilon}\psi\dot{\iota}\sigma\tau\sigma\upsilon$, neither of which denotes
sexual connection, but in both of which the aim is to give
expression to approach or epiphany.[109] "The fact of the divine
begetting stands in the foreground; the fulfilment itself remains
a mystery and is to remain a mystery"; everything is described
merely "in a paraphrastic and allusive manner".[110]

The divine Spirit indeed steps in directly and a conception is
effected without a man being involved. It is, however, not as if
the pagan conception of a $\iota\epsilon\rho\dot{\sigma}\varsigma\ \gamma\dot{\alpha}\mu\sigma\varsigma$ were entertained and
supernatural seed took the place of the natural, but through the
creative power of God a begetting without natural seed is made
possible.[111] Here mention is made of the start of a pregnancy
similar to what was predicated in Hellenist Judaism of the
remarkable motherhood of certain women of the Old Testament, in which cases the complete humanity of the children
begotten in this extraordinary way was not in the least called in
question.[112] Here the Holy Spirit is understood not as inspirat-
ory power but as "creative vital energy".[113]

On the basis of this begetting by the Spirit divine sonship
is now predicated of Jesus. Here then, otherwise than in the
story of the baptism, the divine sonship is not established by the

indwelling Spirit, by virtue of whom Jesus is installed in his earthly messianic office, but by a special act which precedes the whole of his work on earth.

Dibelius maintains that nevertheless no really new concept of divine sonship presents itself here. That may actually prove to be right. Nevertheless, doubts arise as regards his argument; he wishes to understand the miraculous begetting merely as a sign whereby Mary will recognize that her child is a child of God: "as security for the one miracle that can be recognized only later, the Messiahship", there is "mentioned a special, early ascertainable miracle, the begetting of the Spirit".[114]

Here, however, it is a matter not of a "sign", but of the act that establishes the divine sonship. Does the relation between the begetting and the divine sonship not permit of its being defined in a better way? In any case it has to be observed that what is spoken of is divine sonship in a pronouncedly adoptionist formulation: $\kappa\lambda\eta\theta\acute{\eta}\sigma\epsilon\tau\alpha\iota$ $\upsilon\acute{\iota}\grave{o}s$ $\theta\epsilon o\hat{\upsilon}$. That can certainly be regarded as a purely formal borrowing from v. 32, but it may nevertheless have a deeper matter-of-fact meaning.

The future $\kappa\lambda\eta\theta\acute{\eta}\sigma\epsilon\tau\alpha\iota$ certainly does not refer directly to an appointment to office, but gives expression to the fact of Jesus' divine sonship onwards from the day of his birth. But even this status and dignity rests nevertheless on a special creative act of election and separation which has already taken place in the mother's womb. The use of the phrase $\tau\grave{o}$ $\gamma\epsilon\nu\nu\acute{\omega}\mu\epsilon\nu o\nu$ $\mathring{\alpha}\gamma\iota o\nu$ may not be accidental, for the motif of holiness always comes into an action that selects and claims for the service of God,[115] and the idea of election in the mother's womb is genuinely Jewish.[116] Thus, as in Mk. 1:11, the divine sonship is founded on an act of appointment and is therefore understood as thoroughly messianic.[117] In accordance with Jewish thought the question as to the "nature" of the child who has been miraculously begotten is not put at all.[118]

But how then is the relation of v. 35 to vv. 32f. to be determined? As is shown in another place, we are concerned with an early messianic prophecy, which was understood originally in an eschatological sense and may even come from Jewish tradition.[119] At the same time it was a matter of eschatological enthronement and ruling activity; Jesus' descent from David's family was simply a pledge of this eschatological messianic dignity. Later the Davidic sonship was regarded as a status obtaining in particular for the earthly life of Jesus, in which his forthcoming exaltation and royal dignity in heaven was adumbrated.

Now, however, with the Son of God title full messianic dignity is transferred to the earthly Jesus.[120] As in Rom. 1:3 his earthly ministry is considered inclusively from his birth. Naturally vv. 32f. cannot at the same time retain its original meaning unaltered any longer. Already in Mk. 11:1–10 it was recognizable that the promise of the earthly Davidic dominion has been referred to Jesus' work on earth, but manifestly on the assumption of the two-stage Christology.[121] Here the full messianic predicates of Lk. 1:32f. are now applied to the earthly Jesus, and that has spiritualization as its sequel. This new spiritualizing interpretation of traditional Jewish motifs again points to the sphere of Hellenistic Jewish Christianity.[122]

But above all there emerges thence the esential unity of this narrative, which on the assumption of motifs of the Septuagint and ideas of Hellenistic-Jewish midrash has unfolded the idea of the virgin birth without giving way to a pronouncedly Hellenistic manner of thinking.

Summary. The transference to the earthly Jesus of the conception of the divine sonship took place first within the sphere of Hellenistic Jewish Christianity. In the Judaism of the Diaspora the θεῖος ἀνήρ-conception was already adopted and had undergone a very significant reminting in being applied to the Old Testament "men of God", their distinction and mighty works being considered as wrought only by the Spirit granted by God. Since in the primitive Christianity of Palestine Jesus' working of miracles was already understood according to the idea that was entertained of the Old Testament charismatic person, a connection easily emerged. Consequently acceptance of the Son of God title comes clearly to light in the portions of tradition which treat of the exorcisms of demons. As these were first of all understood as divinely wrought miraculous doings and were then attributed to the permanent possession of Jesus by the Spirit, so predication of divine sonship was now associated with them.

The narrative of the baptism is representative of this stratum of tradition, for there an appointment to office and an adoption as Son of God are associated with the bestowal of the Spirit, and that permits of the Jewish background and the connection with the early messianic conception being still clearly recognized.

The divine sonship was provided with another basis in the theologumenon of the virgin birth in the narrative of the annunciation to Mary. There it is a matter of the life-giving power of the Spirit, who effects the conception without the participation of any man. The divine sonship rests upon the creative act of election and separation in the mother's womb. Here also the messianic basic understanding is preserved to a certain extent, although the statements of dignity are incorporated only in a largely figurative sense. A divine sonship in the physical sense certainly does not yet present itself.

4. *Jesus as Son of God in Hellenistic Gentile Christianity*

Transitions are as a rule fluid. That certainly applies in this passage in which the ideas regarding Jesus' divine sonship that were formed in Hellenistic Jewish Christianity and those developed in Gentile Christianity are to be distinguished from one another. It may of course not be denied that, as Philo shows, considerable Hellenizations were possible in the sphere of Judaism itself or that, as can be seen from the Epistles to the Galatians and the Colossians, the danger of syncretistic foreign influence in Jewish Christian churches was by no means small. Also it cannot be called in question that in the early period of Hellenistic Christianity the proportion of church members who had been won from the Jewish Diaspora was certainly extraordinarily great in most churches.

But in the distinction that we have taken in hand it is a matter of something else: it has to be asked where, on the one hand, the Jewish inheritance is still so considerable that Hellenization is kept within definite limits, and where, on the other hand, the Jewish presuppositions step into the background and a typically Hellenistic mode of thought asserts itself among Christians, which soon moves into the foreground in a dominating manner and is pondered over dogmatically on a broad basis in the early church. In connection with the Son of God concept the Hellenization has to be recognized especially in a twofold way: first the divine sonship established through the bestowal of the Spirit is understood in the sense of a pervasion in being, and this then leads on to the idea of an original giftedness in nature.

The transition to a typical Hellenistically understood divine sonship took place first of all, without the influence of the motif of the virgin birth, in pursuance of a Christology which adhered to the story of the baptism and the conception of a bestowal of the gift of the Spirit. But the apprehension by the Spirit was no longer understood in the sense of equipment and endowment but—expressed Hellenistically—as an apotheosis.[123] One was not satisfied with the idea of a permanent indwelling of the Spirit, rather one understood the bestowal of the Spirit in the sense of a pervasion in being.[124] It can be said positively that this way once entered upon, here received its logical continuation, for Jesus had, by the Spirit that was given to Him and qualified Him for His office, to be honoured by God in a manner that was unique and comprehended His whole person.[125] Thereupon the step was taken from a concept of the divine sonship that was messianically and therefore functionally determined to one that was understood in reference to being, even if to begin with an act of appointment was still adhered to.

The earliest testimony to a concept of the divine sonship understood in reference to being is presented in the version preserved in Mk. 9:2–8 of the story of the transfiguration. Analysis of this narrative shows that an early stratum of tradition was associated with such ideas only at second hand.[126] In the present version of the narrative, apart from the redactional additions κατ' ἰδίαν μόνους in v. 2 and the whole of v. 6, two motifs stand in the foreground: the statement about transformation in v. 2fin and the predication of divine sonship in v. 7b. As it were a presentation, with οὗτός ἐστιν the transfigured Jesus is identified as the Son of God by the voice from heaven. As in the voice that proceeds from heaven at the time of the baptism of Jesus, there is an original reference to Isa. 42:1, which is still to be recognized in ὁ ἀγαπητός; in place of the statement about divine approval there is the ἀκούετε αὐτοῦ from Deut. 18:15. But hardly any special importance is attached to these two elements. For principally it is a matter of the Son of God title, which here comes probably only indirectly from Ps. 2:7 and has been taken over from the later version of the story of the baptism. What this Son of God is in truth comes to expression in the transformation motif. The μεταμορφοῦσθαι is doubtless used as a *terminus technicus*.[127]

Since it occurs in this way only in pronouncedly Hellenistic connections, the motif of metamorphosis, as we know it from the mystery cults and the incantation texts, must also stand in the background in Mk. 9:2fin.[128] Now a certain idea of transformation no doubt already lies at the basis of the portion of early tradition in v. 3, but for v. 2fin we do not manage with a reference to Old Testament-Jewish, particularly apocalyptic tradition. Above all the idea of a simple shining in which heavenly splendour is adumbrated but which again disappears[129] must here be kept out. Rather the conception of an eschatological transformation is involved here, but at the same time it also has to be distinguished carefully: for, as the ideas of the resurrection of the dead show, it is primarily a revivification that is thought of in Judaism, even if the old body is to be honoured with perfection, heavenly splendour and the conditions of new existence.[130] In contrast with that the idea of a literal transformation such that the man raised from the dead comes to have a new body enabling him to have a part in the heavenly world, rests on other presuppositions.[131]

An argument and development such as lies before us in 1 Cor. 15:(35ff.), 44ff. is intelligible only on Hellenistic presuppositions, for there also in the terms εἰκών and σῶμα ψυχικόν or πνευματικόν statements about being are certainly implied.[132] Accordingly mention is made in Rom. 8:29 and Phil. 3:21 of a transformation of being at the eschatological consummation (cf. also 1 John 3:2f.). Yet a further step and one that can by no means be altogether explained merely on the basis of Hellenistic modes of thought, is taken by Paul in the places where he speaks, as he does in 2 Cor. 3:18 and Rom. 12:2, of a transformation of being that begins or completes itself in the time of the believer's earthly existence.[133]

We shall not examine these passages in detail; they indicate, however, very accurately the religio-historical circle whence the μεταμορφοῦσθαι of Mk. 9:2fin is also to be understood.[134] That here it is a matter not merely of a change in appearance, as in the Greek mythology of the classical period, but rather of a transformation in reference to being, cannot be called in question. In view, however, of the context an exact definition is required: Mk. 9:2fin is doubtless not to be understood in analogy with an act of consecration whereby divine being is obtained,[135] but Jesus already possesses this and allows it to be visible only to his intimate disciples. As by such a metamorphosis he unveils what his true being is, it becomes manifest that the epiphany of divine being takes place on this earth in the human person of Jesus, that here the beloved Son of God has appeared in whom alone salvation can be obtained. Thus far the Hellenistic motif has undergone a very significant variation and been made subservient to a Christology that is orientated toward the question as to the being of the Son of God.[136]

That in this way pronouncedly Hellenistic conceptions intruded into the primitive Christian tradition, is shown by such a narrative as Mk. 5:25–34. It is true that here there is no title of majesty and no theological reflection, and here only a traditio-historical incorporation in the early Christology is possible.

In the story of the woman with an issue of blood, Jesus appears pervaded to such an extent with divine being that a mere touching of his garments suffices for participation in his supernatural power and for recovery. All ancient and early oriental thought was well aware of the transference of power through touching, wherein especially the laying on of hands, also the taking by the hand and certain manipulations in healings have their origin, and for Palestinian tradition also this cannot be bluntly gainsaid.[137] But once more Mk. 5:25ff. stands on another level; for here a gift is not bestowed and a power is not transferred intentionally, rather the divine δύναμις is amassed to such a degree and is itself so mighty that it appears almost independent of its bearer and can flow out rapidly at any time. The person is a chosen vessel; the dynamic substance fills it completely and consequently determines its being.

It has been pointed out that above all early Egyptian motifs of a divine fluid which accumulated almost materially in its bearers, have exercised an influence.[138] Ideas of the kind had combined in Hellenistic times with the θεῖος ἀνήρ-conception, and thereby these persons were distinguished from ordinary men. In the New Testament one needs merely to recall Mk. 6:56 par.; Acts 5:15; 19:12 to indicate what an influence was secured even in early Christianity by such popular views as later lingered on in the cult of martyrs and relics.[139] It cannot escape notice that in any case an extremely massive conception was received here, which could give only very imperfect utterance to the Christological assertion.

The fact that it was nevertheless taken over into the Gospel tradition in addition to the more sublime and directly Christological conception of the story of the transfiguration, shows how very much statements regarding divine being mattered to the Christendom of that time, however insufficient they might severally be.[140]

The same presuppositions permit of their being recognized in the epiphany narratives. It is beyond question that in the Old Testament-Jewish sphere there was a conception of divine epiphany; but when it was carried over to Jesus, the idea of His divinity was assumed, and that was first possible on Hellenistic soil. A nature miracle such as the stilling of the storm in Mk. 4:35–41 may certainly have been thoroughly domiciled in early Palestinian tradition, in which case an act of conjuration, therefore a charismatic action, has to be thought of.[141] But when, as in the story of the walking on the sea in Mk. 6:47–52, perhaps a later reproduction of that narrative, the fundamental superiority of Jesus over earthly conditions is exhibited and the absolute ἐγώ εἰμι combines therewith, then the characteristic features of a real epiphany narrative are clear.[142] For that reason Matthew has added quite consistently in 14:33 both the worship of the disciples and their recognition of Jesus as the Son of God.[143]

The texts last treated of assume an intrinsic divine sonship without substantiating it in further detail. On the basis of the story of the transfiguration it may however be accepted that they stand in a real connection with the narrative of the baptism, that therefore a pervasion in being is understood of the bestowal of the divine Spirit. But in course of time Hellenistic Christendom became no longer satisfied with this answer. It interpreted the divine sonship in the sense of a giftedness in nature, and to that two approaches were open: the one proceeded from the event of a virgin begetting, the other from the idea of pre-existence; and in this connection it is to be observed that the two were unconnected at the beginning and were developed independently side by side.

Regarding the virgin birth, very cautious statements were made at least in one definite stratum of Hellenistic Jewish Christianity, as we were able to show in dealing with Lk. 1:26ff.[144] The narrative Matt. 1:18–25, which represents an early stage of tradition with regard to the Davidic sonship of Jesus,[145] has formulated the motif of the virgin birth very much more carelessly and spoken of an ἐν γαστρὶ ἔχειν ἐκ πνεύματος ἁγίου or of a γεννηθῆναι ἐκ πνεύματος ἁγίου (vv. 18,20). It was easy indeed in a usage of that kind to understand the statement as the expression of a procreation act in which a supernatural seed unites in substance with the virgin.[146] It is then not surprising if Ignatius in *Eph.* 18, 2: ἐκυοφορήθη ὑπὸ Μαρίας . . . ἐκ σπέρματος μὲν Δαυίδ, πνεύματος δὲ ἁγίου, or 7, 2: σαρκικός τε καὶ πνευματικός . . . ἐκ Μαρίας καὶ ἐκ θεοῦ, puts ἐκ and ἐκ in emphatic parallel,[147] and if in the *Symbolum Romanum* Jesus is described as γεννηθεὶς ἐκ πνεύματος ἁγίου καὶ Μαρίας τῆς παρθένου, a description which was first given exact definition in the context of the later Christological controversies.[148]

More important for the Hellenistic church was the view that the divine sonship has its basis in *pre-existence*. With this a decisively new stage is reached which involves many problems and needs to be unfolded at length, but in this place is to be touched upon only briefly. With the conception of pre-existence Christology obtained the contours which henceforward were decisive for theological explication and in the compass of which urther evolution took place. That this conception sprang out of the soil of the Hellenistic church cannot be gainsaid.[149] In an interesting manner it can still be perceived in what way this conception was arrived at, for the transition is marked by the motif of the "sending" of the Son of God. Alfred Seeberg has already seen that both the emphatic statements in Paul, that God sent His own Son (Gal. 4:4; Rom. 8:3), must represent a firmly stereotyped phrase.[150]

Now the concept of sending as such contains first of all merely the idea of commissioning, and in this sense Jesus' earthly work could be spoken of as a "sending", without the idea of a pre-existence in heaven playing any part in it.[151] So for example in Mk. 12:1–9 it is said that God sent His servants to the wicked vine-dressers and then sent His own Son. Close borrowing from the baptism and transfiguration stories is unmistakable, and the Son of God concept is accordingly to be understood as it is in them.[152]

But the motif of the sending of the Son of God receives an entirely new accent the moment it is associated with the idea of the incarnation, for thereby it is related to the conception of pre-existence. What is put allusively in Gal. 4:4 in the juxtaposition of ἐξαπέστειλεν ὁ θεὸς τὸν υἱὸν αὐτοῦ and γενόμενος ἐκ γυναικός is made plain in Rom. 8:3: ὁ θεὸς τὸν ἑαυτοῦ υἱὸν πέμψας ἐν ὁμοιώματι σαρκός, in such a way that the divine and the human natures are set in an appropriate relation to one another. In a considerable development of the statements about divine being and pre-existence, Phil. 2:6ff. has given expression to the full humanity of Jesus onwards from the incarnation.[153]

Finally, John 1:14 gives complete expression to the idea of incarnation,[154] as also in the Gospel of John there is a manifold pursuit of the motif of the "sending" of the Son of God, which in a characteristic way is equated with a καταβαίνειν ἐκ τοῦ οὐρανοῦ.[155] Here we see most clearly how the early motif of sending has united with the idea of a descent of the Redeemer from heaven and his appearance on earth, and how in primitive Christian tradition the pre-existence and revelation conception is now consistently orientated to the idea of incarnation in opposition to all the docetic thought of Hellenism. With all its borrowing from the thought forms of the world of the time Christendom gave to its proclamation and theology a form that was all its own in what was crucial, and in this way sought in the Hellenistic sphere also to do justice to the actuality of the revelation of God in Jesus Christ.[156]

A glance has still to be taken at the interpretations of the individual Gospels, in which the divine sonship of Jesus has altogether a leading role.[157]

Mark represents the earliest view. He presents the baptism in the sense of an appointment to office and a bestowal of the Spirit at the beginning of Jesus' ministry. At the same time, however, the evangelist is aware of the conception of a pervasion in being by the Spirit of God, as can be seen in particular from the miracle narrative Mk. 5:25ff. and the transfiguration story.

Luke has a very peculiar conception, the distinctiveness of which has frequently not been seen clearly enough. On the one hand, he accepts the early history and does not shrink from applying messianic predicates to the child Jesus; but obviously he means this proleptically, as indeed he also adheres to the early meaning of Lk. 1:26ff., according to which Jesus is the Son of God in virtue of the vital power of the Spirit that effects the conception, and does not think of divine sonship in the physical sense.[158] On the other hand, he emphatically accepts the conception of appointment to office at the baptism and of a special equipment by the Spirit,[159] being concerned to define in a special way the public work of Jesus that begins therewith. The κληθήσεται υἱὸς θεοῦ in 1:35 thus receives a very exact sense in the total setting, since it refers to the baptism happening. Above all, Luke of set purpose carries further the idea of special equipment by the Spirit:[160] Jesus is led into the wilderness "full of the Holy Spirit" and tempted of the devil (4:1), Jesus returns to Galilee "in the power of the Holy Spirit" (4:14), and in his preaching at Nazareth Isa. 61:1 is quoted: "The Spirit of the Lord rests upon me, because he has anointed me" (4:18).[161]

Matthew has abandoned the early view and understands the divine sonship of the virgin begetting. That is shown by the baptism narrative 3:16f., which he has converted into a public proclamation made by the Spirit and the voice from heaven. For him, then, the virgin birth has a very considerable importance and directly establishes the divine sonship. On that account the messianic title and the designation Son of God are used of the child even quite openly in the nativity narrative.[162]

It needs merely to be mentioned once again that John has accepted the idea of the sending of the Son of God and of the incarnation. In him the Christology of pre-existence is outlined and resurrection and exaltation understood as return to the heavenly world.

Summary. Directly the Jewish presuppositions stepped into the background a strong Hellenistic mode of thought asserted itself. That is seen first of all in the fact that the bestowal of the Spirit was understood in the sense not just of an equipment but of a pervasion of being. Therewith the step was taken from a divine sonship that was thought of as primarily functional to one that was in being, even although at first an act of appointment was still adhered to. In the transfiguration Jesus let His divine being be visible to His disciples in a secret revelation, and in a whole series of miracle narratives He appears in His divine power and majesty. The later tradition goes still further, carrying back a physical divine sonship to a special manner of conception or understanding it from the idea of pre-existence and incarnation. All four Gospels are acquainted with the conception of a divine sonship that has reference to being, but whilst for Mark and Luke the appointment and equipment at the time of the baptism are decisive, Matthew and John see the divine sonship grounded in birth or pre-existence.

5. *Jesus as "the Son"*

The absolute ὁ υἱός has to be examined separately. It is found in the Synoptic Gospels only three times, in Paul only in one place, in the Epistle to the Hebrews it occurs five times; on the other hand it appears frequently in the Gospel of John and the Epistles of John.[163] The Synoptic passages and the majority of the Johannine ones show a close relationship in that a correlation of Father and Son at times presents itself.

In detailed investigation we must proceed from the designation of God as Father. In the New Testament this is relatively frequent, and all the ways in which it is used do not need to be discussed.[164] We shall now adduce only the Aramaic אַבָּא and then "our Father", "your (thy) Father" and "my Father".

The Aramaic form of address ἀββά can be regarded with certainty as a mark of Jesus' manner of speech, for this diminutive form which arises from the speech of children is absolutely unthinkable in the prayer language of contemporary Judaism.[165] It is therefore not accidental that this Aramaic word maintained itself in the speech of the Christian church; further it was used in the Hellenistic churches in the sphere of the Pauline mission (Rom. 8:15; Gal. 4:6). That it was translated into Greek doubtless even at an early time, is shown particularly by the Lord's Prayer.

The simple πάτερ of Luke's version goes back to an original אַבָּא, whilst πάτερ ἡμῶν with the addition ὁ ἐν τοῖς οὐρανοῖς represents a recasting that is secondary and follows the liturgical tradition of Judaism.[166] Otherwise an "our Father" is lacking in the whole of the early tradition. Even in Matt. 6:9 it represents the common address of the band of disciples, and it cannot at all be shown that Jesus joined with His disciples in saying, "Our Father".[167] This might be a clear indication that the early parlance, which goes back to Jesus Himself, "your Father" (or "thy Father")[168] was adhered to intentionally and without alteration. Here that does not need to be further investigated.

Of great importance in the present connection is the expression "my Father", which likewise occurs frequently. Can it also be carried back to Jesus Himself? The fact that אַבָּא could represent the form of address "my Father" does not mean much, for here we are concerned with the language of prayer and such a "my Father" would be parallel to the "our Father" of the disciples; moreover, in the only passage which comes into question for that, Mk. 14:36, there stands ἀββὰ ὁ πατήρ, which Matthew has altered at second hand into a πάτερ μου, whilst Luke gives the simple πάτερ, as in the Lord's Prayer. But "my Father" occurs repeatedly, as does also "your (thy) Father", in texts in which Jesus is not addressing God but making statements about God.

If a comparison of the Synoptics is made, then of 19 passages only there are 10 in the text of Matthew in which "my Father" has been inserted subsequently, as the parallel passages in Mark and Luke show.[169] As instance from the logia source we have at our disposal only Matt. 11:27//Lk. 10:22; in Luke alone "my Father" occurs twice in material of tradition that is clearly secondary and in a further passage in the statement of a redactor.[170] The four passages show that in Luke there is no intentional avoidance of this phrase, and from that the conclusion may be drawn that in fact "my Father" scarcely occurred in the logia source, but was only subsequently brought into its material by Matthew. The same holds good of the five passages in Matthew's special material, for no one of which can it be claimed that in the form in which it has been preserved to us it goes back to Jesus.[171] The last passage Mk. 8:38 parr. has still to be considered. There the coming of the Son of man in the glory of "his Father" is spoken of; the parallel passage Lk. 12:8f., which is preserved in the logia source, shows clearly that we are concerned here with a secondary addition, and the transference to the third person and the association with a quite different Christological tradition go to prove that.[172]

On the question of the authenticity of "my Father" we are thus directed to Matt. 11:27//Lk. 10:22. In this very much disputed portion of tradition there also occurs at the same time the absolute use of "the Father" and "the Son". The question of the composition of the section Matt. 11:25–30 par., which was brought into the foreground by Norden's investigation,[173] may here be dealt with briefly.[174]

In Matthew's version we are concerned with a tripartite

section of text, which begins with an ἐξομολόγησις in which God is addressed as "Father" (πάτερ in v. 25 or ὁ πατήρ in v. 26);[175] upon that there follows in v. 27, in the manner of a word of the Lord, a statement about the full power bestowed by the Father, which debouches into a more instructively worded explication regarding knowledge and revelation.[176]

The whole is concluded with an address to the hearer, the Saviour's Invitation as it is called (vv. 28–30). This conclusion is wanting in Luke and was doubtless associated only subsequently with the two other logia, which are closely held together by the motif of revelation.

That certainly does not exclude the possibility that these first two sections also represent traditions that were originally separate. The question of origin can be answered most easily in the case of Matt. 11:28–30, for there, as clear parallels show, a portion of tradition from late Jewish philosophy has been received and carried over to Jesus.[177] On the other hand, vv. 25f. and v. 27 can be understood only from Christian tradition.

Certainly in the motif of concealment and revelation in vv. 25f. dependence on an apocalyptic view is very considerable; also the setting of the "wise and understanding" over against the "babes" who become sharers of the revelation has its prototype, as especially parallels from the Qumran texts show, in late Jewish tradition.[178] We shall have to adjudge this aphorism to the Palestinian primitive church and to reckon with an originally Aramaic rendering.[179]

The question of derivation in the case of v. 27 is disputed: here not only is the authenticity defended,[180] but an origin in the sphere of the Palestinian primitive church is also given consideration,[181] and frequently also a derivation from Hellenistic Christendom is asserted.[182] Into v. 27 there crowds an abundance of substantial and difficult concepts.

The early history of the text already shows that this logion was felt to be remarkably overloaded; accordingly variants to ease it gained ground.[183] In more recent times also text alterations of many kinds have been proposed.[184] But we must desist from all violent interference. We must keep to the renderings preserved in Matthew and Luke, which are to a large extent in agreement.[185]

Matt. 11:27a has a certain exceptional position as compared with v. 27b and v. 27c. That is seen on the one hand in the fact that there an actual statement regarding self presents itself, whilst the attendant statements are made in the third person; on the other hand, there then results from that the juxtaposition of "my Father" in v. 27a, whilst in vv. 27b, c, there stands twice the absolute "the Father" and thrice the absolute "the Son".[186] The παραδοθῆναι in v. 27a certainly cannot be understood in the sense of a "delivery" of doctrines or even of any secrets that are to be revealed.[187] The very word πάντα is an objection to that.

As in the text Matt. 28:18(f.), which is in fact quite intimately connected with the present one and in which the absolutes "the Father" and "the Son" likewise occur, πᾶσα ἐξουσία is given to Jesus.[188] Authority and power are spoken about here. The ἐξουσία is not simply claimed, as usually from the tradition about Jesus we know it to be,[189] it is affirmed by Jesus *expressis verbis* and named as the prerequisite to His doings. This itself is an objection to the authenticity of the statement, so that therewith the last piece of evidence for "my Father" must also be regarded as not authentic. This will obtain its confirmation from v. 27b, c as the meaning and origin of "my Father" are determined more closely.

In Matt. 11:27b and 27c the motifs are curiously intertwined. Before the predicates "the Father" and "the Son" are discussed, the conceptions of knowledge and revelation have to be explained. The concept of knowledge as such is, of course, not strange to Old Testament Jewish tradition.[190] From that we see that it is not necessary to infer a Hellenistic origin of the logion. But now in the text that is under discussion it is a matter of mutual knowledge.

To that there are many analogies in the Hellenistic sphere, and in Paul there are similar statements, which are frequently explained on Hellenistic presuppositions.[191] On the other hand, it has been stated rightly that the idea of such mutual knowledge is not impossible even in Judaism, although there are no verbal pieces of evidence.[192]

For a practical judgment it must above all be observed how in our passage this is associated with the idea of revelation. The motif of the mutual knowledge of the Father and the Son stands indeed on the whole only in the background; it is also understood, not in the sense of a participation in revelation, but of full powers for revelation and so once again takes up the thought of v. 27a. And the actual intention tends to this, that the knowledge of God is bound to the Son's purpose to reveal and therefore can be communicated exclusively by the Son.

All this can be intelligible only when the specifically Hellenistic concept of knowledge is disregarded. For in Matt. 11:27 it is not a matter of illumination and vision. The "knowing" of the Son by the Father can only mean that God has chosen and legitimated Him, and on the other hand the "knowing" of the Father by the Son signifies that the Son alone really acknowledges the Father and has life from fellowship with the Father.

Here then we must proceed from the meaning of the Old Testament ידע in order to reach an appropriate interpretation.[193] Only then do the concluding words "he to whomsoever the Son willeth to reveal him" also become clear. The revelation depends on the unique legitimation of the Son, wherefore "knowledge" of God can be given to men only through revelation by the Son.

The idea of revelation must also be explained on Old Testament Jewish or specifically Christian presuppositions: in the Son God turns to men, enters His claim and grants to them forgiveness and salvation.[194] When one proceeds from such premises, v. 27b, that no one knows the Son save the Father, is unmistakable; here it is a matter of a choice and authorization which is and remains absolutely independent of men, as also according to v. 27c the revelation work of the Son remains related simply and solely to God and communicates the "knowing" of the Father, the experience of his work of salvation and the recognition of his glory. If instead of this we take the Greek concept of knowledge, then in v. 27b, provided we do not at all cross out or alter this part of the sentence, we come to extremely problematic considerations regarding the secrecy of the revealer.[195] But we are concerned with the idea of a unity of purpose in the Father and the Son which is characterized by a complete subordination of the Son to the Father,[196] who yet in His authority altogether represents the Father.[197] Vv. 27b, c may then explicate and define the basic idea of v. 27a.[198]

The idea of subordination to the Father is also found in Mk. 13:32, the second passage in the Synoptics which contains the absolute "the Father" and "the Son".[199] Here the subordination is so emphatically brought out that the statement is almost in a certain contradiction to the πάντα μοι παρεδόθη ὑπὸ τοῦ πατρός μου of Matt. 11:27a, but the Christological basic conception is nevertheless the same. Mk. 13:32 expresses the dependence of the Son on the Father by a massive restriction of the authority of Jesus; on the other hand Matt. 11:27 attempts to say that the unrestricted authority and total dependence are in one another. We shall regard the very much differentiated text of the logia source as traditio-historically the later, all the more so since the saying of Matt. 28:18, which certainly originated only somewhat later and to which we have yet to come back, contains the idea of unlimited authority and to that extent it and Matt. 11:27 belong to one another.

From these exegetical considerations the designations "the Father", "the Son" and "my Father" can now find their explanation. As Matt. 11:27 shows, the phrase "my Father" stands in a very close association with the absolutes "the Father" and "the Son". To a certain extent it expresses the relation which is indicated by the juxtaposition of "the Father" and "the Son" and quite certainly assumes this absolute use of the words. As the texts show, "the Father" and "the Son" are as a rule employed near to one another. The Son is spoken of where the Fatherhood of God is also mentioned expressly. It is a matter of the relationship to one another of Father and Son. "The Son" is Jesus from the Father, and "the Father" is God by reason of and through the Son. More precise definitions can be given: the Sonship of Jesus is to be understood of His unique status and the authority granted to Him. Since He is united wholly to God and at the same time "all is given over" to Him, He alone can reveal God and communicate "knowledge" of the Father.

It cannot be overlooked that this stands in a certain opposition to Jesus' unaffected conversation about "your (thy) Father".[200] Here indeed a Christological narrowing has obviously taken place. Originally every one could say "Father", now access to the Father is tied to Jesus.

On the other hand, however, it has also to be said that the church wished to guard the message of Jesus from the misunderstanding of a general Fatherhood of God and a natural filiation of men from God. The Fatherhood of God, His love, His forgiveness and turning towards men, as it encircles them from their first beginnings, manifests itself just in the authority of the Son. For that reason the "knowledge" of the Father is inseparably united to the Son's work of revelation.

The question as to the origin of this conception is very difficult to answer. To begin with, the fact may be instructive that the two decisive pieces of evidence in the Synoptic tradition Matt. 11:27 par. and Mk. 13:32 are in contexts which have preserved the heritage of the early Palestinian church, namely in the logia source and the so-called Synoptic Apocalypse. It is hardly accidental that the standard motif of the authority of Jesus fits especially into the Son of man Christology which is dominant in the logia source.[201] The conception of the Son of man also dominates in Mk. 13, and, as has already been shown,[202] a peculiar association of a Son of man saying with the statement about the glory of "his Father" presents itself in Mk. 8:38.

Is then the conception to be derived from the idea of the Son of man? The suggestion has been made repeatedly in recent times.[203] But it cannot be overlooked that the motif of the Fatherhood of God has absolutely no roots there.

No doubt then it permits of its being explained very much rather from messianism. The "my Son" of the baptism and transfiguration stories implies the idea of fatherhood and besides the Father-Son-relation can also be pointed out in the messianic tradition of the Old Testament;[204] also the idea of authority perhaps permits of its being explained from there.[205]

Yet on the other hand it must be observed that in all the tradition about Jesus as the "Son of God" the fatherhood of God and his union with the Father do not play any recognizable role; a distinction has therefore to be drawn between "Son of God" and "Son—Father".[206] Also the motif of authority is very differently understood in Matt. 11:27 par. and Mk. 13:32 and is coupled with the idea of revelation, which is not domiciled in the messianic tradition. Consequently the conclusion must be drawn that the designation "the Son" has been obtained chiefly from the אַבָּא that was characteristic of Jesus.[207]

Thus an altogether singular conception of the early church may here present itself, one that has its nearest parallels in ὁ διδάσκαλος and ὁ κύριος, of which likewise no previous forms are met with. Whether the absolute verbal use of "the Father" and "the Son" arose on Palestinian soil, I do not venture to decide; the presuppositions of the early Palestinian church tradition will need, however, to be taken fully into account.

The frequently emphasized "Johannine" character of the saying in Matt. 11:27 par. ceases to be any longer surprising when it is observed that this conception of Jesus as the Son and of His union with the Father, which is recognizable only sporadically in the Synoptic tradition, is accepted in the Johannine writings. This may be illustrated shortly in some instances.

First of all, here also co-ordination to "the Father" is characteristic of almost all texts in which the absolute "the Son" occurs.[208] In the 1st and 2nd Epistles of John the confession or the denial that Jesus is the Christ can be equated with the confession or the denial of the Father and the Son; he who confesses in the right way "has" the Father and the Son.[209] A formal usage of the kind is lacking in the Gospel of John, but the tradition itself is extensively developed: the Father loves the Son, He has committed to Him judgment and quickening power, indeed the Son has life in Himself, even if He can do nothing but what God Himself does.[210] Wherefore the Son is to be feared, all must believe on Him, for the Father has honoured the Son as on the other hand the Son also honours the Father.[211] The statements doubtless go a step beyond Matt. 11:27 par. This holds good first of all of the status which the Son occupies for believers beside the Father, without detriment to the complete unity of the two; indeed even the motif of knowledge has hereby been given a somewhat different orientation. John 10:15a also assumes, as does Matt. 11:27, the mutual knowledge of the Father and the Son, and again the communication of the knowledge of God is associated exclusively with the Son. But, otherwise than in that text from the logia source, a "knowing" of the Son by believers is now spoken of, although this knowledge of Jesus also includes directly the knowledge of God.[212] The Johannine conception differs most clearly in having this line of tradition fused with the idea of Jesus as "Son of God".[213] Consequently motifs so significant as mission or self-sacrifice are now carried over to the "Son".[214]

To the same stratum of tradition there also belong of course those passages in the Gospel of John in which mention is made not expressly of the "Son" but of the "Father", particularly when Jesus speaks of Himself in the first person; the phrase "my Father" also occurs very frequently.[215] In this respect the Gospel of John is an interesting instance of the lingering on of traditions which are available to us in the Synoptics at an earlier stage.

The after-effects of the tradition of Jesus' sonship can also be recognized in other parts of the New Testament. In the Epistle to the Hebrews its singularity is still preserved particularly in the linguistic usage, the relation to the Father remains preserved only in a single passage and that within an Old Testament citation.[216] Otherwise there is always an equating of "Son" with "Son of God", as is shown by the change in the terminology as also by the application of the messianic citations to the "Son".[217] In addition to this equating there is also a fusion with the doctrine of the high priest.[218]

Reference may also be made to the theme: the Son and the sons, which has undergone an extensive development.[219] In regard to the sonship of Jesus it is especially important that here, on the one hand, the heavenly enthronement and the motif of eminence play a part, but that, on the other hand, Jesus' earthly life, not last His passion, is under the idea of sonship.[220] In Matt. 11:27 par. and Mk. 13:32 an authority and sonship are indeed also thought of which have reference to the activity of the earthly Jesus, although certainly not restricted one-sidedly to that.

A further dislocation presents itself where the sonship is associated with the heavenly reign of Christ, as it is in 1 Cor. 15:23–28 and Matt. 28:18–20. In 1 Cor. 15:28 the dominion of the exalted Jesus is definitely thought of.[221] The correlation with "the Father" is indeed still preserved in v. 24, but it no longer stands in the foreground; at all events ὁ θεός stands in immediate connection with the predicate ὁ υἱός. The individual motifs are taken from the Messiah conception, so that fusion with "Son of God" is again to be recognized.

The traditio-historically latest passage is Matt. 28:18–20. However it may stand with the early history and the different elements of this complex,[222] this much is clear, that in v. 18 the idea of ἐξουσία again presents itself and in v. 19 the Father-Son-relation is still recognizable. But the ἐξουσία-idea is understood, as in the passage from Paul, in the sense of the power of the exalted Jesus, wherefore ἐν οὐρανῷ καὶ ἐπὶ τῆς γῆς has been added.[223] Above all v. 19 presents in place of the juxtaposition

of the Father and the Son the triadic formula: "in the name of
the Father and of the Son and of the Holy Spirit".[224] In the
form first associated with the baptism liturgy the statement
regarding Jesus as "the Son" received a traditio-historically
quite new place and then in this context gained a decisive
significance in the doctrine of the Trinity of the early church.[225]

Summary. It has emerged that the designation "the Son"
belongs to a relatively independent stratum of tradition and
was associated only secondarily with the conception of the Son
of God. The independence shows itself in a series of characteristic interfused motifs: above all in the juxtaposition of "the
Father" and "the Son", then in the concepts of authority,
knowledge and revelation.

The authority, knowledge and revelation ideas are to be
understood from the Old Testament Jewish tradition, and it is
hardly accidental that the earliest instances occur in the logia
source and in the Synoptic Apocalypse. But the same idea has
also precipitated itself in the Johannine writings. It is a matter
of the union of the Son with the Father and at the same time of
the unique authority which the Father has granted to the Son.
The Son has his legitimation from the Father, and the fatherhood of God depends on the revelation that comes about
through the Son. As regards the derivation of the conception
neither the Son of man conception nor messianism comes
directly into question.

Similarly as in the case of "the Master" and "the Lord" it
may be a matter of a far-reaching independent tradition of the
primitive church, in which the especial emphasis on the fatherhood of God and the address "Abba" used by Jesus played a
part. Certainly there came about at the same time a Christological narrowing, as also the thoroughly secondary mode of expression "my Father" shows.

The early view with its different motifs, and certainly fused
with the conception of Jesus as the "Son of God", is still clearly
preserved in the Gospel of John. The after-effect also shows itself
here and there elsewhere in the New Testament and finally
flows into the triadic formula of Matt. 28:18f., where the idea of
the sonship of Jesus is set in an entirely new context.—Looking
back once again over this whole section regarding the Son of
God predicate, we see how different sorts of elements have here
met together and how very stratified the material is. A

316

levelling is here more disastrous than in the case of the other titles of dignity. The individual elements need to be accurately investigated and discriminated. Only so can the traditio-historical place of the respective texts be rightly determined.

NOTES

1. The use of the Son of God title in the Palestinian church is entirely disputed, e.g., by Gillis P. Wetter, *Der Sohn Gottes. Eine Untersuchung über den Charakter und die Tendenz des Johannesevangeliums (FRLANT NF 9)*, 1916, pp. 138f.; cf. also Bousset, *Kyrios Christos*, pp. 54f.

2. Cf. on this especially Bultmann, *Theol.* pp. 130ff.; Herbert Braun, *Sinn der neutestamentlichen Christologie, ZThK* 54, 1957, especially pp. 353ff. or *Studien*, pp. 255ff.

3. So Joh. Weiss, *Urchristentum*, pp. 85f.; Staerk, *Soter* I, pp. 47, 89f.; Feine, *Theologie*, pp. 45ff.; Ethelbert Stauffer, *Die Theologie des Neuen Testaments*, 1948⁴, pp. 93f.; Bultmann, *Theol.*, pp. 52f.; Werner Georg Kümmel, *Das Gleichnis von den bösen Weingärtnern (Mark 12, 1–9)* in *Aux sources de la tradition chrétienne (Mélanges M. Goguel)*, 1959, pp. 120–131, especially p. 131.

4. Friedrich, *Beob. z. mess. Hohepriestererwartung, ZThK* 53, 1956, pp. 279ff.; Walter Grundmann, *Sohn Gottes. Ein Diskussionsbeitrag, ZNW* 47, 1956, pp. 113–133.

5. So Mowinckel, *He That Cometh*, pp. 293f., 366ff.

6. Considered especially in connection with the baptism and trans-figuration stories; cf. Dalman, *Worte Jesu*, pp. 226ff.; Bousset, *Kyrios Christos*, pp. 56f. (especially p. 57, n. 2); Cullmann, *Tauflehre*, pp. 11ff.; id., *Christologie*, p. 65; Jeremias, *ThWb* V, p. 699.

7. Büchsel, *Theologie*, pp. 51ff.; William Manson, *Bist du, der da kommen soll?* pp. 125ff.; Joachim Bieneck, *Sohn Gottes als Christus-bezeichnung der Synoptiker (AThANT 21)*, 1951, especially pp. 42ff., 72ff.; also Cullmann, *Christologie*, pp. 288ff. Manson, Bieneck and Cullmann reckon with a connection of Jesus' belief in the Father with the consciousness that he must assume the office of the suffering Servant of God. Otherwise E. Schweizer, *Erniedrigung und Erhöhung*, pp. 87f., who assumes "that this title was fashioned quite early on the one hand by Jesus' special relation to the Father and on the other hand by Ps. 2:7". Similarly B. M. F. van Iersel, *Der Sohn' in den synoptis-chen Jesusworten. Christusbezeichnung der Gemeinde oder Selbstbezeich-nung Jesu?* (Suppl. to *Nov. Test.* III), 1961; according to him the authentic "Son" is the root of the "Son of God" title, which arose through reflection on the Old Testament.

8. To "Son of God" there are also to be reckoned the passages in which "my Son" occurs (Mk. 1:11; 9:7; 12:6b); in addition the υἱὸς ἀγαπητός in Mk. 12:6a assimilated to the baptism and transfiguration

narratives. Naturally these belong also the predicates in which God's name is paraphrased, as in Mk. 14:61; Lk. 1:32. The lack of the Father designation is the more surprising as the correlation of Father and Son seems to be suggested by the Old Testament (Ps. 2:7; 2 Sam. 7:14).

9. In this respect Bieneck and Grundmann are quite careless. For the latter the Son consciousness of Jesus is also an element of his esoteric teaching and possibly even the substance of what Judas betrayed; cf. *ZNW* 47, 1956, p. 128.

10. So especially W. Manson, *op. cit.*, pp. 133f.; Cullmann, *Christologie*, pp. 282f., 290.

11. In the framework of royal messianism, according to Mowinckel, *op. cit.*, pp. 293f., only isolated traces of the motif of the divine sonship can have maintained themselves and moreover be emphasized expressly in accordance with a special election and adoption.

12. As texts Mowinckel, *op. cit.*, pp. 368ff., has recourse to Mk. 5:7 and 14:61ff. As regards the address by the demons "Son of the most high God", it can be clearly recognized that the idea of the "most high God", in spite of its use in the Old Testament, has deep roots in Canaanite soil—accordingly the location in the semi-heathen region of the Gergesenes has much in its favour—but must belong there together with a natural divine sonship and so far with the Son of man conception. Likewise the trial before the supreme council is said to indicate that "(Messiah) the Son of the Blessed" is meant in the Son of man sense, because only so, and not in the event of a claim to be the Messiah in the traditional Jewish sense, would the condemnation for blasphemy explain itself.

13. Cf. Elliger, *Kl. Propheten* II, pp. 182, 184.

14. τοῦ . . γενέσθαι αὐτῷ υἱὸν καὶ θεράποντα καὶ λειτουργὸν τοῦ προσώπου αὐτοῦ. Moreover, υἱός is not even altogether certain textually; it is lacking in the first recension of the Armenian text, cf. Charles, *Testaments*, p. 36.

15. Against Friedrich, *ZThK* 53, 1956, p. 280.

16. The fatherhood of God is as a rule referred to Israel, but can also be asserted in reference to the royal Messiah. Surprisingly, however, the father motif no longer plays any part in the later messianism.

17. Friedrich, *op. cit.*, p. 282.

18. The motif of the opening of the heavens and of the bestowal of the Spirit is found in the *Test. of Judah* 24, 2 in the same way as in the *Test. of Levi* 18, 6f., therefore in reference to the royal Messiah; but apparently neither was firmly combined with any of the messianic conceptions.

19. The conception of an eschatological priest-king is foreign to Judaism. *Jub.* 31:14ff. cannot be drawn upon in support of it, for in vv. 18ff. there follows the parallel word of promise regarding Judah; and the purely priestly function is quite clear in *Jub.* 30:18. In the *Test. of Levi* 18, 3 mention is made of a king only in a simile; in the *Test. of Reuben* 6, 7a the statement regarding the dominion of Levi is certainly defined more closely in view of the eschatological "anointed high priest" v. 8, the problematic v. 7b being left out of account: the

mention made in the *Test. of Simeon* 5, 5 of the function of Levi in the wars of Jahweh has its parallel in 1 Q M. Against Friedrich, *op. cit.*, p. 283.

20. Cf. Excursus IV, pp. 229ff.

21. The Son of God conception in the Old Testament is an element of the Jerusalem royal tradition of the house of David and goes back in its history beyond the usage of the Canaanite court to early oriental, to a considerable extent mythologically stamped, royal ideology. We must certainly beware of assuming a uniform "ritual pattern" such as is assumed in particular in recent Swedish research; cf., e.g. Geo Widengren, *Sakrales Königtum im Alten Testament und im Judentum*, 1955; for criticism Noth, *Ges. Studien*, pp. 188ff. Already in the early Orient the Son of God concept was expressed in very different ways. Only in Egypt was an immediate physical sonship thought of, whilst in the Mesopotamian area it was a matter of the divine glory and the legitimacy of the king; cf. Henry Frankfort, *Kingship and the Gods*, 1948.

22. Cf. especially Kümmel, *op. cit.*, pp. 129ff. (with information about literature); doubts were raised even earlier, thus Dalman, *Worte Jesu*, pp. 219, 223; Bousset, *Kyrios Christos*, pp. 53f.; cf. van Iersel, *Der Sohn*, pp. 4f., n. 7.

23. Cf. Bruno Violet, *Die Apokalypsen des Esra und Baruch in deutscher Gestalt (GCS* 32), 1924, pp. 74ff.; Jeremias, *ThWb* V, p. 680, n. 196. It has certainly to be noticed that this "my servant" in II Esdras has nothing to do with Deut.-Isa., but as in Ezek. 34:23f.; 37:24f. (צבדי דוד); Zech. 3:8 (עבדי צמח) must be regarded as a designation of the royal Messiah; so far also the translation *"filius meus"* is not altogether unsuitable.

24. Against Kümmel, *op. cit.*, p. 130.

25. Cf. the passage in Billerbeck III, p. 19.

26. On the anti-Christian polemic cf. Billerbeck III, pp. 20ff.

27. Cf. Erminie Huntress, *"Son of God" in Jewish Writings prior to the Christian Era, JBL* 54, 1935, pp. 117–123.

28. "Investigator of the Torah" is here a designation of the high priestly Messiah.

29. 4 Q Flor 10–14; whence vv. 11, 12a: אני [אחיה] לוא לאב
[. . .] בציון והוא יהיה לי לבן הואה צמח דויד העומד עם דורש התורה אשר
באחרית הימים "I [will] be a father to him and he will be a son to me. This is the shoot of David who will appear with the teacher of the law, who [. . .] in Zion in the end of the days" (as written, Amos 9:11 follows).

30. Cf. Maier, *Texte* II, pp. 158f.

31. Cf. Billerbeck III, pp. 676f., 19.

32. Cf. Billerbeck III, p. 19(f.).

33. Cf. on this Karl Georg Kuhn, art., θεός, *ThWb* III, pp. 93ff.

34. Besides Mk. 14:61 cf. also Lk. 1:32.

35. Cf. in addition Chapter 3, pp. 163ff. and Excursus II, pp. 129ff.

36. So Joh. Weiss, *Urchristentum*, pp. 85f.; Bultmann, *Theol.*, pp. 52f.

37. An attempt to do justice to the various applications of the Son of God concept in Paul, therefore to its relation to the earthly, the exalted and the returning Jesus, is made by Cerfaux, *Le Christ*, pp. 329ff.

But a uniform picture is attained only by assuming the conception of the supernatural nature of the Son of God wholly as a matter of course and by taking no sort of traditio-historical considerations into account.

38. In detail cf. Chapter 4, p. 243.

39. This tells against Mowinckel's derivation of the Son of God predicate from the Son of man conception, *op. cit.*, pp. 369f., for in Mark 14:61f. the motif of the sitting at the right hand of God, therefore precisely the adoptionist element in royal messianism is incorporated.

40. Rightly emphasized by Friedrich Hauck, *Das Evangelium des Markus* (*ThHdKomm* II), 1931, p. 178.

41. The same holds good for the (ἐκ δεξιῶν . . .) τῆς δυνάμεως in v. 62.

42. The alterations made in Matthew and Luke are very instructive. Matthew wishes of course to have the dignity both as Christos and as Son of God carried over to the earthly Jesus in the same way as in 16:16; accordingly in 26:64 he splits the answer of Jesus into an affirmative answer to the question and a promise of the parousia, the πλὴν λέγω ὑμῖν indicating a distinct caesura. Luke goes still further in that he splits the question into one as to the Messiahship and one as to the divine sonship so that the former is answered with a reference to the exaltation, whilst the latter is directly answered in the affirmative, and consequently divine sonship holds good of the earthly Jesus.

43. Cf. Alfred Seeberg, *Katechismus der Urchristenheit*, pp. 82f.; v. Dobschütz, *Thess.*, pp. 76ff., 81f., Albrecht Oepke, *Die Missionspredigt des Apostels Paulus*, 1920, pp. 64, 158, 210; Dibelius, *Thess.*, pp. 6f.; Bultmann, *Theol.*, pp. 77, 81; Béda Rigaux, *Les Épîtres aux Thessaloniciens* (*Études Bibliques*), 1959, pp. 392ff.; also with reservations Charles Masson, *Les deux Épîtres de Saint Paul aux Thessaloniciens* (*Commentaire du Nouveau Testament* XIa), 1957, pp. 23f.; Wilckens, *Missionsreden*, pp. 80ff.

44. Cf. Haenchen, *Apg.*, pp. 463f.

45. Moreover, precisely 1 Thess. 1:9f. shows how little the conception of the messianic high priest can be assumed in the Son of God predicate.

46. Cf. especially Chapter 2, pp. 103ff.; Excursus II, pp. 129ff.

47. Apart from some Lukanisms; cf. Lk. 22:69; Acts 7:56.

48. Cf. Chapter 3, pp. 168ff.

49. Cf. Chapter 4, pp. 246ff.

50. Cf. pp. 277f., n. 162.

51. Cf. especially Heb. 1:2f.; 5:8.

52. Cf. Dibelius-Greeven, *Kol.*, p. 9. That a certain eschatological aspect remains preserved is shown by Col. 3:4.

53. It is true that the Son of God title does not stand in 1 Cor. 15: 28, but ὁ υἱός; both the lack of a corresponding ὁ πατήρ (there may certainly be an after-effect of v. 24) and the material connection with Ps. 110:1 and exaltation show, however, that in this place the independent tradition of the absolute ὁ υἱός may not be assumed.

54. Hans Windisch, *Paulus und Christus. Ein biblisch-religionsgeschichtlicher Vergleich* (*Unters. z. NT* 24), 1934, pp. 24–89; Ludwig Bieler. ΘΕΙΟΣ ΑΝΗΡ. *Das Bild des „göttlichen Menschen" in Spätantike und Frühchristentum* I, 1935; II, 1936.

55. Cf. on this especially Bieler, *op. cit.*, I, pp. 134ff.

56. The problem of the Hellenizing of the Son of God concept does not permit of its being settled in the way in which, e.g., Stephan Lösch, *Deitas Jesu und Antike Apotheose*, 1933, attempts to settle it. He asserts that from the beginning the early Christian church opposed all apotheosis.

57. So especially G. P. Wetter, *Sohn Gottes*, especially pp. 137ff.; H. Braun, *ZThK* 54, 1957, pp. 353ff. (*Studien*, pp. 255ff.).

58. Windsch, *op. cit.*, pp. 89–114.

59. Ecstasy, prophecy and the working of miracles are indeed in either case characteristic forms of expression. Cf. in the Old Testament especially the figures of Elias and Elisha; but Moses also and at a later time David were accounted men of God.

60. Cf. the parallel אִישׁ הָרוּחַ Hos. 9:7 (LXX ἄνθρωπος ὁ πνευματο-φόρος).

61. I refer only to Walther Eichrodt, *Theologie des Alten Testamentes* I, 1957[5], pp. 204ff.

62. Even Bieler, *op. cit.*, II, pp. 3ff., has not carried through a quite clear distinction between the Old Testament and the Hellenistic-Jewish tradition.

63. I use the material collected by Windisch and Bieler. For the rest cf. the references in Joachim Jeremias, art., ἄνθρωπος, *ThWb* I, pp. 365f.

64. The text *Epist. of Aristeas* 136 that comes into question for this last idea is unfortunately corrupt, cf. *Epistula Aristeae*, ed. Paul Wendland, 1900, *in loc.*

65. Jos., *Bell. Jud.* VII, 344.

66. So Saul is once called ἔνθεος (Jos., *Ant.* VI, 76) or the θεία διάνοια of Solomon is spoken of (*Ant.* VIII, 34).

67. Bieler, *op. cit.*, II, pp. 25ff., shows how in the *Antiquities* additional haggadic material is used, whilst there is a twisting into new forms in accordance with the Hellenistic θεῖος ἀνήρ-conception.

68. The simple θεῖος is used by Philo, but does not occur in all the connections where from the matter in hand it is expected; following Exod. 7:1 Philo uses even the θεός-predicate for Moses; cf. in detail Windisch, *op. cit.*, pp. 103f., 108f.

69. Cf. also Windisch, *op. cit.*, p. 110.

70. Cf. on this Bultmann, *Theol.*, p. 133. So far as literary documents are preserved to us, in Hellenistic Judaism the Son of God predication is lacking in such a connection, but there were the relevant assumptions.

71. To that reference has already been made in the concluding section of Chapter 3 and in the Appendix it will be investigated thoroughly; cf. pp. 189ff., 372ff.

72. We may with certainty regard Mk. 1:23–26 as traditional. There, apart from εὐθύς at the beginning, there are no additions of any kind. On the other hand the introduction vv. 21f. is to be ascribed to the evangelist, likewise the concluding v. 28. A decision is more difficult in the case of v. 27: at least διδαχὴ καινὴ κτλ must be redactional, but apparently also the ὥστε clause.

73. Especially worthy of note is 1 Kings 17:18 in the LXX: *Ti*

ἐμοὶ καὶ σοί, ἄνθρωπε τοῦ θεοῦ, only ἄνθρωπος τοῦ θεοῦ has already been replaced by ἅγιος τοῦ θεοῦ, which falls into the context of the Nazaraean conception.

74. Mk. 5:1ff. shows clamps in vv. 1a, 2a, 18, which go back either to the Markan redaction or to a pre-Markan association of the miracle stories 4:35–5:43.

75. It is certainly wrong to regard "Son of the most high God" as a syncretistic predicate, as does Mowinckel, *op. cit.*, pp. 368f.

76. The προσκυνεῖν in Mk. 5:6 may also be connected with that; otherwise the narrative has fully preserved its early character.

77. The investigation of Otto Bauernfeind, *Die Worte der Dämonen im Markusevangelium* (*BWANT* III/8), 1927, proceeds in its judgment of the defensive sayings, as also of the names of dignity, much too largely from the analogy of the Hellenistic incantation texts and emphasizes one-sidedly the magical character of this motif.

78. πνεῦμα ἀκάθαρτον is a decisive catchword in Mk. 1:23, 26; 5:2, 8, 13; other designations are lacking in these stories. In the two other accounts of exorcisms, Mk. 7:24ff.; 9:14ff., on the other hand, the designations of the demons vary. In redactional passages Mark uses δαιμόνιον; cf. 1:34; 3:15; 6:13. The narratives Mk. 7:24ff.; 9:14ff. contain no words spoken by the demons and consequently no Christological statements of dignity; the address by the demons in Mk. 3:11 is redactional.

79. Cf. G. Bornkamm, *Jesus*, p. 120.

80. The literary-critical and traditio-historical relations in Mark 3:22–30 and the parallel passages Matt. 12:22–32//Lk. 11:14–23 (12:10) associated with the Q-tradition, are somewhat indistinct and may therefore be presented in a brief review. Mk. 3:22–30 has the form of a controversial conversation. This, however, is not carried through in a rigorous manner, and after the reproach of the opponents, for which no concrete occasion is reported (otherwise in Matt. 12:22 par.), there follows a series of metaphors and aphorisms. Vv. 22a, 23a have been worked over redactionally, otherwise the text connection may be pre-Markan. To the reproach v. 22b Jesus answers with the two-fold metaphor vv. 24f., on which in vv. 23b, 26 interpretations have already grown; a further metaphor follows in v. 27, then the saying about blaspheming the Holy Spirit in vv. 28f. and the concluding formulation in v. 30. The parallel tradition of the logia source is very close to the Markan tradition (Matt. 12:23 and Lk. 11:16, 18 fin, which have no direct equivalent words, may here be left out of account). It is distinguished by an introduction of its own Matt. 12:22 par., a transition of another kind Matt. 12:25a par., the somewhat divergent form of the metaphor Matt. 12:25b par. and the independent sayings Matt. 12:27f. par. and 12:30 par.; on the other hand Matt. 12:26 par. has been interpolated doubtless on the strength of Mk. 3:26 (23b), likewise Matt. 12:29 on the strength of Mk. 3:27; the relatively independent parallel saying Lk. 11:21f. may on the other hand rest on special tradition (Q?). Finally in 12:31f., in analogy with Mk. 3:28f., Matthew has appended the Q-version of the saying about blasphemy, while Luke has preserved in this place the original connection of the logia source and adduces in

11:24–26 the saying about relapse. From the presence side by side of Markan and Q tradition it is clear that the metaphors Mk. 3:24f. (Matt. 12:25 par.) with their introduction Mk. 3:22b (Matt. 12:22, 24 par.), the metaphor Mk. 3:27 par. (Lk. 11:21f.) as also the saying Matt. 12:(27) 28 par. and the word Mk. 3:28f. (Matt. 12:31f.//Lk. 12:10) were originally independent. For an analysis cf. Bultmann, *Syn. Trad.*, pp. 10ff., on the matter R. H. Fuller, *Mission and Achievement*, pp. 37ff.

81. The characterizing of the opponents as Pharisees (Matt. 12:24) or as scribes who had come down from Jerusalem (Mk. 4:22a) is secondary; originally a closer designation was lacking as is the case in Lk. 11:15a.

82. It is not out of the question that τῷ ἄρχοντι τῶν δαιμονίων is an explanatory addition; cf. Lk. 11:19 par. (also v. 18fin).

83. On the difficult problems connected with the exposition of Lk. 11:20b cf. W. G. Kümmel, *Verheissung und Erfüllung*, pp. 98ff.; Fuller, *op. cit.*, pp. 25ff.

84. The conception of the accomplishment of miracles "in the name of . . ." is again somewhat different and should not be brought in here, against Bultmann, *Syn. Trad.*, p. 11.

85. Cf. on this Heinrich Schlier, art., δάκτυλος, *ThWb* II, p. 21.

86. That Lk. 11:20 is original emerges from the concept of the kingdom of God; as in v. 20b so also in 20a we are concerned with God's own action.

87. Similarly also in the case of the demoniacs, on the one hand ἄνθρωποι ἐν πνεύματι ἀκαθάρτῳ are spoken of (Mk. 1:23; 5:2), whilst on the other hand it can be said that a man "has" a demon (e.g. Mk. 9:17). The logical subject is in the first case the demon, in the other case the man.

88. The saying Mk. 3:28f. with its introductory ἀμήν indicates a very ancient motif, cf. Joachim Jeremias, *Kennzeichen der ipsissima vox Jesu in Synoptische Studien (Festschrift für A. Wikenhauser)*, 1953, pp. 86–93; even if the logia source may actually have had a tendency to do away with the phrase, yet on the other hand it cannot be disputed that this form of composition was also taken over by the church, and the genuineness of a word is not certain as a matter of course in view of an introductory ἀμήν. The relation of Mk. 3:28f. to the version of the logia source Matt. 12:31f.//Lk. 12:10 is disputed. Now the question is not decided with a simple either-or. It is indisputable that linguistically Mk. 3:28f. exhibits later features (cf. Tödt, pp. 285ff.), on the other hand an ἀφεθήσεται τοῖς υἱοῖς τῶν ἀνθρώπων (Mk. 3:28) cannot have arisen subsequently out of an ἀφεθήσεται τοῖς ἀνθρώποις (Matt. 12:31), at the same time that phrase must stand in some connection with the Son of man title in Matt. 12:32 par. Practically we must likewise adjudge a relative priority to the Markan text, for the dividing into periods of the salvation history in Matt. 12:32 par. is to be explained as a recasting of a statement such as Mk. 3:28f. very much rather than by assuming that Mark has "blurred" the original understanding of the saying (so Tödt, p. 111). Matt. 12:31 is evidently dependent on Mk. 3:28f., but on the other hand Mk. 3:28a (without καὶ αἱ βλασφημίαι κτλ) is a first step to Matt. 12:32a//Lk. 12:10a, whilst in Matt. 12:32b

the earlier version of the concluding sentence as compared with Mk. 3:29 is preserved; Lk. 12:10b unites elements from Matt. 12:31b (Q) and Mk. 3:29. Now Mk. 3:29 will have been applied only at second hand to the earthly work of Jesus (in this Tödt is right even if this understanding may hardly be ascribed first to the evangelist), whilst originally as in Matt. 12:32b par. it was possibly referred to the post-Easter situation and probably domiciled as an article of sacred law in church prophecy; on the significance of church prophecy and sacred law in the earliest primitive Christian tradition cf. the investigations already mentioned of E. Käsemann, *NTSt* 1, 1954/55, pp. 248ff.; *ZThK* 57, 1960, pp. 162ff. —Reference may be made to the remodelling of the saying in the *Gospel of Thomas* 44: "He who blasphemes the Father will be forgiven; and he who blasphemes the Son will be forgiven. But he who blasphemes the Holy Spirit will not be forgiven either on earth or in heaven." Apart from the influence of trinitarian thought there is to be observed a giving of precedence to the Holy Spirit such as is conceivable only among gnostics.

89. Matthew, who adds this saying in a double rendering in 12:31f., has not brought about any actual organic unity, for the statement about the Spirit refers in v. 28 to the earthly work of Jesus, but in v. 32 to the post-Easter period.

90. This understanding has perhaps already precipitated itself in the stories of the exorcisms, where, it is true, mention is made not of Jesus' possession of the Spirit but emphatically of his power over the "unclean spirits". Even the motif that the demons scent in Jesus the divine Spirit that is superior to them, may point in this direction; spirit stands against spirit and the spirit understands the spirit, as Wrede, *Messiasgeheimnis*, p. 24, has correctly interpreted it, only this does not hold good for Mark alone but is already traditional.

91. Bultmann, *Syn. Trad.*, p. 11, has also alluded to the variety of ways in which in Mk. 3:22 the accusation is formulated, but for Βεεζεβοὺλ ἔχει he refers one-sidedly to the Hellenistic magician conception.

92. For the conception of a continuing possession of the Spirit reference can be made both to Isa. 11:2ff. and to Isa. 42:1; 61:1; in the one case it is a matter of the Messiah as the bearer of the Spirit, in the other of the prophetic Servant of God.

93. In an analysis in Excursus V, pp. 337ff. an attempt is undertaken to determine the elements of the narrative in detail traditio-historically.

94. With σωματικῷ εἴδει Luke has rightly interpreted this intention of the Markan text.

95. The εἰς αὐτόν has to be understood quite concretely and may not be weakened as it has already been in Matthew and Luke (in dependence on Isa. 42:1 LXX ?).

96. In Lk. 3:22 D this element has been strengthened at second hand; it is not just an effort to secure exactness in the agreement of the Old Testament citation with the text of the *Vorlage* that is decisive here.

97. Besides Ps. 2:7, Isa. 11:2ff. especially plays a role, also the *Psalms of Solomon* 17:37 and the like.

98. Naturally the appointment to office is understood otherwise in the institutional thought presupposed in the Pastorals. Nevertheless, to a surprising extent the basic structure remains a common possession.

99. Ernst Käsemann, *Das Formular einer neutestamentlichen Ordinationsparänese* in *Exegetische Versuche und Besinnungen* I, 1960, pp. 101–108, especially pp. 107f.; consequently the evidences drawn upon from the *Corp. Herm.* and also from Philo, which have likewise been adduced by Dibelius-Conzelmann, *Past.*, pp. 66f., do not come into question.

100. For the analysis cf. Chapter 3, pp. 158ff.

101. Lk. 4:1a in redactional, vv. 1b,2 lean on Mark. Matthew also shows an influence of Mk. 1:13.

102. The motif of obedience is rightly emphasized by Bieneck, *Sohn Gottes*, p. 63, but traditio-historically the text is judged quite wrongly.

103. It has already for long been seen that the story of the temptation Matt. 4:1ff.//Lk. 4:1ff. occupies a special place within the logia source; cf. Harnack, *Sprüche und Reden Jesu*, pp. 169f.

104. See Chapter 4, pp. 261ff. The motif of the virgin birth stood first of all in connection with Jesus' Davidic sonship, but broke up this independent preliminary stage of majesty. For originally the Davidic sonship stood in correlation with the divine sonship of the exalted Jesus, but then in virtue of the virgin birth divine sonship was conferred upon the earthly Jesus.

105. The religio-historical material is assembled especially in Eduard Norden, *Die Geburt des Kindes*, 1924 (= 1958³); we cannot agree with his evaluation of it.

106. To have pointed this out is above all the merit of Dibelius, *Jungfrauensohn* in *Botschaft und Geschichte* I, pp. 1–78; consequently with convincing reasons he refers the narrative to Hellenistic Jewish Christianity. Peculiarities of the idea of the virgin birth in Lk. 1:26ff. as compared with Gentile mythology are also pointed out by von Baer, *Heilige Geist in den Lukasschriften*, pp. 124; John Martin Creed, *The Gospel according to St. Luke*, 1930 (reprint 1953), pp. 19f.; Gerhard Delling, art. παρθένος, *ThWb* V, 833f.

107. That the theologumenon of the virgin birth does not belong to the early Palestinian tradition, can be stated with certainty, for in the first place this motif stands in close connection with Isa. 7:14, but exclusively with the LXX version, which renders עַלְמָה by παρθένος; in the second place the conception of a procreation with the exclusion of a man was completely foreign to the Palestinian-Jewish mode of thought, but is traceable in Hellenistic Judaism (cf. Dibelius, *op. cit.*, pp. 25ff.); to that it answers in the third place that late Jewish Christianity passionately rejected and fought against the idea of the virgin birth of Jesus (cf. Chapter 4, p. 266, n. 3). Cf. von Campenhausen, *Jungfrauengeburt*, pp. 7ff.; whether John 1:13 may be made use of as evidence against this theologumenon, I am not so certain.

108. It has already been shown that vv. 36f. is to be regarded as an addition.

109. Dibelius, *Jungfrauensohn*, pp. 18ff.

110. *Op. cit.*, pp. 20, 39f.

111. Emma Brunner-Traut, *Die Geburtsgeschichte der Evangelien im Lichte ägyptologischer Forschungen*, *ZRGG* 12, 1960, pp. 97–111, alludes to the basic structure of all mythic modes of statement in which the "biological" conception may neither be isolated nor excluded, but rather stands in the framework of a comprehensive mode of thought, which holds good also for the conception of a pneumatic procreation and virgin conception (pp. 107f.). If in this way, certainly not in the content of their statement but in its form, we equate Egyptian texts and Lk. 1:26ff., then in doing so we misunderstand the extent to which in this early Christian portion of tradition the mythic structure has been shattered by theological reflection.

112. With this there are to be compared in detail the ample investigations of Dibelius, *Jungfrauensohn*, pp. 25ff. The co-ordinating of this conception with Hellenistic Judaism has recently been disputed by Otto Michel-Otto Betz, *Von Gott gezeugt* in *Judentum-Urchristentum-Kirche* (*Festschrift für J. Jeremias*, *BZNW* 26), 1960, pp. 3–23, especially pp. 11ff., 15ff.; the Qumran community was also acquainted with the begetting of the Messiah as "a wonderful, supernatural happening", and, as David Daube, *Evangelisten und Rabbinen*, *ZNW* 48, 1957, pp. 119f. has shown, ἐπισκιάζειν is to be understood in accordance with the spreading out of the cloak in the story of Ruth. It is true that in 1 Q Sa II, 11 there occurs the statement that God "will beget" the Messiah "among them (*scil.* the Qumran community)", but here יוליד has to be understood not otherwise than in the adoptionist statement of Ps. 2:7. Michel and Betz themselves state that as in the case of the spiritual adoption of believers we must reckon with a juxtaposition of spiritual and natural begetting (pp. 12ff., 20); and in my opinion the arguments in favour of a wonderful supernatural begetting of the Messiah (p. 16) are not telling. But above all it has to be noted that all the parallels to Lk. 1:35 do not remove the fact that according to vv. 27, 31 and especially v. 34 the reference is to a virgin birth, therefore that Isa. 7:14 LXX and the ideas pointed out by Dibelius of an exclusion of the man in the conception stand in the background, and that points clearly to the sphere of Hellenistic Judaism or Jewish Christianity.

113. Dibelius, *Jungfrauensohn*, p. 30.

114. Dibelius, *Jungfrauensohn*, pp. 16f.

115. τὸ γεννώμενον ἅγιον is of course the subject and ἅγιον may not be connected with "Son of God"; cf; Dibelius, *op. cit.*, p. 16.

116. Cf. Judges 13:5; Isa. 49:1b; Jer. 1:5; Gal. 1:15.

117. It may be pointed out that endowment with the Spirit in the mother's womb is not spoken of here as in Lk. 1:15 in the case of John the Baptist. The story of the virgin birth is so far no rectilineal extension of the statements about Jesus as the bearer of the Spirit. Rather the Spirit is understood here not as a gift but as the creative power, and otherwise than in the story about the Baptist it is just in this that the divine Sonship of Jesus rests. It is of interest that in the narrative

of the birth of Jesus in Lk. 1 and 2 statements about His possession of the Spirit are avoided.

118. H. Braun, *ZThK* 54, 1957, p. 354, n. 3 (*Studien*, p. 256, n. 42) advocates the view that Dibelius has not established a Jewish-Hellenistic origin because in Hellenism also, side by side with grossly sensual conceptions of a begetting by God, there are very many sublime views (in Plutarch, Jamblichus and others). But the Jewish-Hellenistic character does not depend on this single motif, but emerges from the total character of the story. Cf. for the rest Dibelius. *Jungfrauensohn*, pp. 33ff.

119. Cf. Chapter 4, pp. 243f.

120. It was shown in Chapter 4, pp. 263f. that, in spite of the abandonment of the preliminary stage of honour, the motif of the Davidic sonship continued to be adhered to.

121. Cf. Chapter 4, pp. 255ff.

122. Hans Wenschkewitz, *Die Spiritualisierung der Kultusbegriffe Tempel, Priester und Opfer im Neuen Testament* (Angelos-Beiheft 4), 1932, shows that spiritualizing made its way especially on Hellenistic soil in Judaism and Christianity.

123. Allusion has been made on p. 290 above to parallels in Philo. The pronouncedly Hellenistic comparison material in Richard Reitzenstein, *Die hellenistischen Mysterienreligionen*, 1927[3] (reprint 1956), pp. 38ff.; 220ff.; 262ff. and often.

124. The difficult questions as to the relation to the human person of Jesus do not present themselves at this stage.

125. A simple indwelling could also be asserted of the unclean spirits in possessed persons.

126. For an analysis and all the questions of detailed exegesis cf. Excursus V.

127. On this cf. Ernst Lohmeyer, *Die Verklärung Jesu nach dem Markus-Evangelium*, *ZNW* 21, 1922, pp. 185–215.

128. What is said here holds good for v. 2fin, not for v. 3, for there earlier motifs manifestly present themselves.

129. So Exod. 34:29; on this finally Noth, *Exodus*, p. 220. Cf. also 2 Cor. 3:7ff.

130. There belongs here the "transformation" of Mk. 9:3, where Jesus appears attired in heavenly garments, but a statement about a transformation of the countenance and the body is lacking; cf. on this Excursus V.

131. Cf. on this Bousset-Gressmann, pp. 274ff.

132. Cf. Friedrich-Wilhelm Eltester, *Eikon im Neuen Testament* (*BZNW* 23), 1958.

133. Cf. on this Martin Dibelius, *Paulus und die Mystik* in *Botschaft und Geschichte* II, 1956, pp. 134–159, especially pp. 140ff., 156.

134. Religio-historical comparison material in Behm, *ThWb* IV, pp. 764f.; Reitzenstein, *Mysterienreligionen*, pp. 357ff. Yet it is worthy of note that the conceptualism of these New Testament passages with μεταμορφ-, μετασχημ-, συμμορφ-, συσχημ-is lacking in the LXX apart from a single passage; the exception is, again significantly, IV Macc. 9:22 (μετασχηματιζόμενοι εἰς ἀφθαρσίαν).

135. Cf. on this Windisch, *op. cit.*, pp. 57f., 104ff.; Martin Dibelius, *Die Isisweihe bei Apuleius und verwandte Initiationsriten* in *Botschaft und Geschichte* II, pp. 30–79, especially pp. 52ff.; Lohmeyer, *ZNW* 21, 1922, pp. 203ff.

136. We could think of the pseudo-Homeric *Hymn to Demeter* 275ff. or of Euripides, *Bacchae* 1329, where gods staying on the earth disclose their identity. But we may not overlook the radical difference, for here the human figure is an outer veil chosen by chance, whereas in the other case we are concerned with a complete permeation of the human being by the divine essence, the humanity being constitutive. In later Christology on the other hand it is thought that the divine essence enters wholly into the humanity, and that the idea of incarnation especially brings to expression.

137. We cf. merely the stories about the miracles of Elias and Elisha. Cf. also for religio-historical material Bultmann, *Syn. Trad.*, pp. 237f.

138. Friedrich Preisigke, *Die Gotteskraft in frühchristlicher Zeit* (*Papyrusinstitut Heidelberg Schrift* 6), 1922.

139. Cf. Preisigke, *Gotteskraft*, pp. 12ff.

140. Walter Grundmann, *Der Begriff der Kraft in der neutestamentlichen Gedankenwelt* (*BWANT* IV/8), 1932, pp. 26ff., 61ff., 65ff., advocates the thesis that the non-personal manistic understanding has been overcome by the personal; cf. *id.*, art. δύναμις, *ThWb* II, pp. 301ff. But this cannot be asserted so generally for the New Testament; even if the principle be preserved in many passages, for Mk. 5:25ff. and similar texts it may not be advocated without more ado.

141. There are parallels to the Stilling of the Storm in rabbinical tradition, cf. Bultmann, *Syn. Trad.*, pp. 249f.; there instances of the power of prayer are dealt with.

142. Cf. Dibelius, *Formgeschichte*, pp. 91f; Lohmeyer, *Mk.*, pp. 133f.

143. On the characteristic features of the story in Matthew, where also the motif of the sinking Peter is interpolated, cf. Heinz-Joachim Held, "Matthäus als Interpret der Wundergeschichten" in G. Bornkamm-G. Barth-H. J. Held, pp. 193ff.

144. Cf. Chapter 4, pp. 263f. and especially Chapter 5, pp. 295ff.

145. Cf. Chapter 4, pp. 261f.

146. Cf. Bauer, *Wb. s.v.* ἐκ 3a, according to which with ἐκ in such phrases there is brought in the man's part in bringing about the procreation. It could of course also be understood as in Lk. 1:26ff. as the bringing about of a virgin conception without the participation of a man; but undoubtedly the formulations were unprotected and in the Hellenistic sphere must have met with misunderstanding as signifying a literal procreation function of the Spirit; cf. Norden, *Gebsrt*, pp. 76ff.

147. As for Ignatius the divinity and the humanity of Jesus are indeed obvious assumptions of his Christology, in which the divine essence clearly stands in the fore-ground; ἐν σαρκὶ γενόμενος θεός, (*Eph.* 7, 2); θεός ἀνθρωπίνως φανερούμενος (*Eph.* 19, 3); ὁμολογῶν αὐτὸν σαρκοφόρον (*Smyrn.* 5, 3; similarly also Clement of Alexandria.

148. In an interesting way Justin resists with all firmness the idea of a conception by God or the divine Spirit: τὸ πνεῦμα ... ἐλθὸν ἐπὶ τὴν

παρθένον καὶ ἐπισκιάσαν οὐ διὰ συνουσίας ἀλλὰ διὰ δυνάμεως ἐγκύμονα κατέστησε *Apol.* I 33, 6b (cf. v 3.f.: εἰ γὰρ ἐσυνουσιάσθη ὑπὸ ὁτουοῦν, οὐκ ἔτι ἦν παρθένος); on the other hand, however, in defence against an adoptionist Christology it was important for him to state that already from His birth Jesus possessed His special power of the Spirit, so especially *Dial.* 87f.

149. That does not exclude the possibility that at the same time Jewish traditions, especially from the Hellenistic-Jewish speculation about wisdom, were taken up; cf. only Eduard Schweizer, *Zur Herkunft der Präexistenzvorstellung bei Paulus*, *EvTh* 19, 1959, pp. 65–70.

150. Alfred Seeberg, *Katechismus der Urchristenheit*, pp. 59ff.

151. Cf. Karl Heinrich Rengstorf, art., ἀποστέλλω (πέμπω), *ThWb* I, pp. 397ff.

152. That there is in Mk. 12:1–9 no genuine parable, but an allegory formed by the church, has once again been thoroughly demonstrated by Kümmel, *Gleichnis von den bösen Weingärtnern*, *op. cit.*, pp. 120–131, against Dodd, *Parables of the Kingdom*, pp. 124ff.; Jeremias, *Gleichnisse*, pp. 59ff.

153. Even if the Son of God title is lacking in Phil. 2:6ff., the passage may be included here, for as in the case of the Son of God concept what is at issue is the question as to the divine essence and its relation to Jesus' humanity.

154. That here a genuine Christian idea presents itself, with which no comparable statements are found in heathen mythology, is by no means to be disputed; I refer to Ernst Käsemann, *Aufbau und Anliegen des Johanneischen Prologs* in *Libertas Christiana* (*Festschrift für Friedrich Delekat*, *BEvTh* 26), 1957, pp. 75–99.

155. Religio-historical material in Wetter, *op. cit.*, pp. 82ff. Cf. also Bultmann, *Theol.*, pp. 385ff.

156. To the methodical procedure of Bieneck, *Sohn Gottes als Christusbezeichnung der Synoptiker*, objection must be made on principle. Apart from the fact that no distinction is drawn between the title "Son of God" and "the Son" used absolutely, all religio-historical dependence is flatly disputed and a traditio-historical judgment has not been carried through even in its initial stages.

157. If the question is asked as to the age of the actual confession of Jesus as the "Son of God", it has to be stated that in Paul, whom the conception itself influenced considerably, it is lacking. It is connected with the confession-tradition of Hellenistic Jewish Christianity where "Christos" and "Son of God" are used beside one another, in which case, however, the Son of God predicate interprets the Christos title and not the other way round; cf. Chapter 3, pp. 189f. In Mk. 15:39 it shows a clearly Hellenistic background as far as the death of a godlike, specially distinguished man is thought of (cf. the analogies in Bieler, *op. cit.*, I, pp. 44ff.; it may not be said that it must be a confession that is figurative and answers to the understanding of the heathen centurion, so Hauck, *Mk.*, pp. 188, 190). Certainly onwards from the second half of the first century the confession of the Son of God steps clearly into the foreground and has its fixed place in the baptism liturgy, as is

shown above all by the Western tradition of Acts 8:37 and Hebrews (Heb. 1:2ff.; 4:14; 6:6; 10:29); on this Günther Bornkamm, *Das Bekenntnis im Hebräerbrief* in *Studien zu Antike und Urchristentum*, 1959, pp. 188–203. In 1 John 4:15; 5;5; also 1:3b; 3:23 this confession plays a role in anti-heretical conflict.

158. Cf. the brief observation in Conzelmann, *Mitte der Zeit*, p. 160.

159. Thus far the Western tradition of Lk. 3:22 is thoroughly significant; even if it is a secondary remodelling, it has retained the original intention.

160. On the other hand it can hardly be by chance that in his nativity narrative Luke has avoided statements regarding Jesus' possession of the Spirit—very much in contrast with the tradition about the Baptist which was appropriated unaltered; cf. Lk. 1:15, 80 with Lk. 2:40, 52. Moreover it is to be observed that the passages Lk. 4:1a, 14 subsequently cited are clearly redactional as is also the arrangement of the special tradition in 4:16ff.

161. Cf. Lk. 4:36; 5:17; 10.21.

162. Cf. Matt. 2:15, also 1:1, 16, 18; 2:2, 4.

163. Matt. 11:27//Lk. 10:22; Mk. 13:32//Matt. 24:36; Matt. 28:19; 1 Cor. 15:28; Heb. 1:2, 8; 3:6; 5:8; 7:28 (partially without the article); the Johannine passages cf. p. 332 below.

164. Cf. Gottfried Quell-Gottlob Schrenk, art., πατήρ, *ThWb* V, pp. 946–1024, especially pp. 983ff.; van Iersel, *Der Sohn*, pp. 93ff.

165. Joachim Jeremias, *Abba*, *ThLZ* 79, 1954, cols. 213f.: not merely Abba but the address "my Father" in prayer is altogether foreign to Judaism down to the Middle Ages.

166. Cf. Karl Georg Kuhn, *Achtzehngebet und Vaterunser*, pp. 32, 34f.

167. Cf. on this G. Bornkamm, *Jesus*, pp. 114ff., especially p. 118.

168. Cf. concordance and Schrenk, *ThWb* V, pp. 987f. The rooting in a quite old stratum of tradition that goes back to Jesus himself, is not to be disputed.

169. Matt. 12:50; 15:13; 20:23; 26:29, 39, 42, 53; with Matt. 7:21 cf. Lk. 6:46 and Mk. 3:35; Matt. 10:32f. is a secondary remodelling of the saying about the Son of man in Mk. 8:38 par. or Lk. 12:8f.

170. Lk. 2:49; 22:29 in the special material; redactional in Lk. 24:49. The passages with the address πάτερ have to be judged somewhat differently.

171. Matt. 16:17; 18:10, 19,35; 25:34. A relatively great age can be maintained most easily for Matt. 16:17; but the most recent investigation of the promise to Peter has shown that this does not hold good for v. 17 in the same way as for vv. 18f.; cf. Anton Vögtle, *Messiasbekenntnis und Petrusverheissung*, BZ NF I, 1957, pp. 252–272; II, 1958, pp. 85–103, especially pp. 90ff.

172. Cf. on this Tödt, *Menschensohn*, p. 39. Likewise also Matt. 12:32f.

173. Norden. *Agnostos Theos*, pp. 277ff.

174. Against Norden's thesis of an original unity Bousset, *Kyrios Christos*, pp. 44f.

175. In the Synoptics this address is found in the introduction

to the Lord's Prayer Lk. 11:2, in the prayer in Gethsemane Mk. 14:36 par., and in the words from the cross Lk. 23:34, 46.

176. On this transition to the didactic style cf. especially Joh. Weiss-W. Bousset, *Das Matthäus-Evangelium* in *SNT*³ I, p. 310.

177. Cf. on this Bultmann, *Syn. Trad.*, pp. 171f.

178. Cf. especially Sjöberg, *Der verborgene Menschensohn*, pp. 185ff.

179. So also Bultmann, *Syn. Trad.* p. 172. That this stems from a Jewish writing, which can be said with some justification of vv. 28–30, is very unlikely. Even the ταῦτα does not authorize this conclusion, for from the context it must refer to the revelation secret.

180. So Zahn, *Mt.*, pp. 441f.; Schlatter, *Mt.*, pp. 383ff.; Schniewind, *Mt.*, pp. 151ff.; Bieneck, *op. cit.*, pp. 75ff.; Percy, *Botschaft Jesu*, pp. 259ff.; Cullmann, *Christologie*, pp. 292ff.

181. Sjöberg, *op. cit.*, pp. 187ff., 230ff.

182. Norden, *op. cit.*, pp. 290ff.; Bousset, *Kyrios Christos*, pp. 45ff.

183. Cf. on this Harnack, *Sprüche und Reden Jesu*, pp. 189ff.; Klostermann, *Mt.*, p. 103; Paul Winter, "Matthew xi. 27 and Luke x. 22 from the First to the Fifth Century. Reflections on the Development of the Text", *Nov. Test.* I, 1956, pp. 112–148.

184. So Julius Wellhausen, *Das Evangelium Matthaei*, 1914², pp. 57f; Joh. Weiss, *Mt* in *SNT*² I, pp. 321ff. (cancelled by Bousset in *SNT*³ I, pp. 309ff.); Harnack, *op. cit.*; Bultmann, *Syn. Trad.*, p. 171.

185. Luke has γινώσκειν, but the ἐπιγινώσκειν in Matthew has also to be understood in the sense of the simple verb, as is frequent in the Koine. The τίς ἐστιν in Luke is significant; we shall come back to this.

186. The pronoun μου after ὑπὸ τοῦ πατρός in Matt. 11:27a‖Lk. 10:22a is textually not quite certain; cf. Winter, *Nov. Test.* I, 1956, p. 128.

187. So Wellhausen, *Mt.*, p. 57; Joh. Weiss, *Mt* in *SNT*² I, p. 321.

188. Bousset, *Kyrios*, p. 47, n. 2; Schniewind, *Mt.*, p.151; Percy, *op. cit.*, pp. 263f. also understand the passage in accordance with Matt. 28:18.

189. G. Bornkamm, *Jesus*, pp. 52ff. and often.

190. Cf. Julius Schniewind, *Zur Synoptikerexegese*, *ThR* NF II, 1930, pp. 169f.; *id.*, *Mt.*, pp. 152f.; also Rudolf Bultmann, art. γινώσκω, *ThWb* I, pp. 688–715, especially pp. 696ff.

191. Gal. 4:8; 1 Cor. 8:3; 13: 12.

192. Dalman, *Worte Jesu*, pp. 232f.; Schniewind, *Mt.*, p. 152.

193. It is certainly insufficient to appeal to the Old Testament ידע and speak onesidedly only of an "ultimate inner connection between Jesus and God"; so Bieneck. *op. cit.*, p. 84. Cf. on the other hand the interpretation of the cognition concept in R. H. Fuller, *Mission and Achievement of Jesus*, pp. 92f.

194. The idea of revelation is foreign to Greek religion and gained a certain significance only in Hellenistic times under oriental and not lastly Jewish influence; cf. Albrecht Oepke, art. ἀποκαλύπτω, *ThWb* III, pp. 571ff.

195. This is found already in Joh. Weiss, *op. cit.*, pp. 322f., but also in Schlatter, *Mt.*, pp. 382f.; Schniewind, *Mt.*, 151. But in all these cases the component of understanding and knowledge in the concept of

cognition is taken more or less largely as starting point. Hannelis Schulte, *Der Begriff der Offenbarung im Neuen Testament (BEvTh* 13), 1949, pp. 15ff., in spite of her assumption of Hellenistic influences, attempts at the earliest to throw off these presuppositions and to proceed from cognition in the Old Testament sense, which depends on the conquest of sins and being under forgiveness; it is true that in this place she also brings in the motif of the messianic secret.

196. The motif of subordination is completely misunderstood in Herman Mertens, *L'Hymne de Jubilation chez les Synoptiques*, Gembloux 1957, pp. 58ff.

197. From this a solution must be found of the textual problem of the variants (ἐπι-)γινώσκει and ἔγνω.

198. It cannot be overlooked that Lk. 10:22 with its γινώσκειν τίς ἐστιν ὁ υἱός or ὁ πατήρ already imparts to the logion an accent that is foreign to it and starts from the Greek cognition concept.

199. That, as Kümmel, *Verheissung und Erfüllung*, pp. 35f., asserts, there is here a statement which is not intact in its wording but which in content is characteristic of Jesus' own view, is not convincing.

200. The reverse development, that "your (thy) Father" was put in the mouth of Jesus only at second hand, is absolutely impossible.

201. Cf. Tödt, *Menschensohn*, p. 236.

202. Cf. p. 308 above.

203. So Percy, *Botschaft Jesu*, pp. 270f.; Sjöberg, *Verborgener Menschensohn*, pp. 187f.

204. Reference may be made merely to 2 Sam. 7:14.

205. Reference to the royal messianism is made above all by Schniewind, *Mt.*, pp. 151ff.

206. The derivation of the Son of God title from the designation "the Son", as it has been advocated by B. M. F. van Iersel, is to be disputed on principle. He is completely astray in his antithesis, either "the Son" must be derived from "Son of God" or "Son of God" from "the Son" (cf., e.g., "*Der Sohn" in den synoptischen Jesusworten. Christusbezeichnung der Gemeinde oder Selbstbezeichnung Jesu?* (Suppl. to *Nov. Test.* III), 1961, pp. 18off.). We have to do here with two strata of tradition which developed side by side and only later came into contact with one another.

207. There lies here the relative justice of the statement of Bieneck, *Sohn Gottes*, especially pp. 52ff., 58ff., and of Cullmann, *Christologie*, pp. 281ff.

208. Cf. John 3:35; 5:19–23 (7 times), 26; 6:40; 14:13; 17:1; also 1:18 (according to the variant that is to be preferred). "The Son" stands alone only in 8:35f., beside "God" in 3:16f.; 3:36.

209. Cf. 1 John 2:22–24; 5:12; 2 John 9.

210. Cf. John 5:35; (5:20) 5:21, 22; 5:26; 5:19.

211. Cf. John 5:23; 3:36 and 6:40; 14:13 and 17:1.

212. It ought, however, not to be overlooked that the cognition concept still retains here its early Semitic structure as also that γινώσκειν τινά is used otherwise than in Luke. Moreover it needs to be observed that the change-over from γινώσκειν to ὁρᾶν and πιστεύειν

(14:9; 17:8) serves to check the Hellenizing of the cognition concept, for this ὁρᾶν is very different from the one in Hellenistic Mysticism and Gnosis and πιστεύειν defines recognition in its specifically Biblical sense, as on the other hand the πίστις-concept is interpreted by γινώσκειν and guarded from misunderstanding.

213. "Son of God" occurs in John 1:34, 49; 3:18; 5:25; 10:36; 11:4, 27; 19:7; 20:31.

214. That is seen twice in the formulation in John 3:16–18 (also in 1 John 4:14), but it also holds good for the Johannine understanding as a whole.

215. Cf. Schmoller, *Handkonkordanz*, p. 392 or p. 391.

216. Cf. Heb. 1:2, 8; 3:6; 5:8; 7:28 and the citation from 2 Sam. 7:14 in Heb. 1:5b.

217. Cf. Heb. 4:14; 6:6; 10:29; the O.T. citations in 1:5a, b; 5:5.

218. Cf. especially Heb. 4:14; 7:3, 28.

219. I refer to Ernst Käsemann, *Das wandernde Gottesvolk. Eine Untersuchung zum Hebräerbrief* (*FRLANT* NF 37), 1957². pp. 58ff.; Günther Bornkamm, *Sohnschaft und Leiden* in *Judentum-Urchristentum-Kirche* (*Festschrift für J. Jeremias, BZNW* 26), 1960, pp. 188–198.

220. Cf. Heb. 3:(1ff.)6, above all 5:7f.

221. Cf. Excursus II, p. 132.

222. Besides the commentaries cf. Otto Michel, *Der Abschluss des Matthäusevangeliums, EvTh* 10, 1950/51), pp. 16–26.

223. It could of course be discussed whether the reference to the exalted Jesus was not there at the beginning and was carried over to the earthly Jesus only subsequently. But then, in view of the firm connection of the exaltation conception with royal messianism, it would be possible only with difficulty to explain the independence of the idea, especially since there, the fatherhood of God plays no sort of recognizable part. Accordingly we must regard this connection with Jesus' exaltation as a secondary assimilation to the conception of the "Son of God" enthroned in the heavens, the motif of exousia having presented a bridge. Moreover, a greater age is to be assumed for Mk. 13:32 and Matt. 11:27 par.

224. As is well known, it is disputed whether the trinitarian formula represents the original text of Matthew. But the variant found in Eusebius and containing a purely Christological abbreviation is all too weakly attested; for another thing 2 Cor. 13:13 presents an analogy and shows that statements of the kind had already got under way in the middle of the first century.

225. The designation of Jesus as "the Son" is as a rule not investigated specially. Either it is incorporated in the Son of God conception or the whole Son of God conception is interpreted by a "Son-consciousness" of Jesus.

EXCURSUS V

Analysis of the Transfiguration and Baptism Narratives

(*a*) Mk. 9:2–8. Precisely as is to be expected in a text that is Christologically very significant, we have here a narrative that is very compressed in motif and statement. It may not be doubted that while its basic stock is early, there have been various transformations of it; since, moreover, the transfiguration story in Mark has so central a place near Peter's confession, redactional embellishments must also be reckoned with.

It is, however, by no means a simple matter to distinguish in detail earlier and later parts, earlier and later meanings of the statements. It is not accidental that the proposals of a traditio-historical analysis deviate widely from one another and are occasionally withdrawn by their authors. While Lohmeyer eliminated vv. 2fin, 3 and 6,[1] Bultmann has detached vv. 5f.,[2] and recently v. 6 and v. 7b have been separated by Baltensweiler,[3] to mention only the most important theses.[4] Now v. 6, regarding which there is a certain agreement in opinion, cannot be taken as the starting point of an investigation and for the present is to be set altogether aside. The remaining elements of the narrative are closely united to one another and may not be simply torn asunder.[5] On the other hand, there are unevennesses which call for explanation.

It is advisable to start from a general appreciation of the story as it now lies before us in Mark. The mountain is the place of revelation, and the choice of its top suggests the extraordinary event that is imminent. The statement of time marks an unmistakable relation to Peter's confession, even if originally this mention of the six days had another meaning.[6] Jesus takes with him only the three intimate disciples, it being a matter of a pronouncedly esoteric revelation. The decisive happening is the transformation; the white garments are the sign of that. In addition there is the appearance of Elias and Moses. As the representative of the disciples Peter merely stammers nonsensical words, being unable to understand the miracle. Finally, the clouded appearance designates the transformed

Jesus as Son of God, an explicit, divine confirmation of this Christophany; as supplement there follows the instruction, "Hear him". A brief concluding observation indicates the end of this revelation occurrence. The whole weight falls upon the transformation and the divine proclamation; the conception of the divine sonship is a Hellenistic one, for Jesus is here Son of God in His being and is manifest as such before His disciples.[7]

It must be observed that in this version of the story some existing motifs have moved completely into the background. Especially is that true of v. 5, which is almost cancelled by v. 6. Also the appearance of Elias and Moses becomes by the side of the transformation a secondary element.[8] The question must therefore be asked whether formerly very much more weight did not lie on vv. 4f. and whether perhaps an even earlier understanding of the story can be recovered from there.

Moreover, it has at all times been evident that in v. 3, which follows the brief mention of a metamorphosis in v. 2fin, only the glistening white garments are mentioned, but nothing is said of a shining of the face.[9] If v. 2fin is dropped, then vv. 3 and 4 unite very much more closely: Jesus is dressed in heavenly[10] garments and with Him are Elias and Moses, whose bodily removal to heaven must here be assumed.[11] As Jesus is favoured with a white robe, He is ranked with these two Old Testament men of God; expression is also given to that by the fact that Elias and Moses talk with Jesus; we are concerned here with a sign of fellowship and equality.[12] There is no thought at all of a transformation, none at all of reflection regarding the heavenly and the earthly natures.[13] Decisive for the understanding of the whole of this happening is the eschatological task assigned to Elias and Moses.

Now the juxtaposition of these two Old Testament men of God in late Jewish texts is indeed not altogether easily verified, but it can nevertheless be inferred.[14] In the context of a primitive Christian portion of tradition the appearance of Moses and Elias can only mean that by this Jesus' eschatological function is to be indicated. Peter's word in v. 5 follows directly, this disciple having understood that it was a matter of an eschatological happening. His suggestion that tabernacles be erected for the consummation[15] is answered and corrected by the voice in the cloud: it still counts "to hear" Him who has here been revealed. It is true that Jesus' earthly work already

335

bears eschatological traits, but as yet it directly precedes the dawning of the time of salvation. Elias and Moses legitimate Him as the eschatological prophet.[16]

In the background there may probably stand the further thought, suggested by the heavenly garments, that like these two Old Testament figures Jesus belongs to those who are carried away to heaven and then appear again when a new aeon begins.[17] But the chief stress rests doubtless on the definition of the earthly mission of Jesus, and this is associated by the voice in the cloud with Deut. 18:15.

At the same time a predicate of honour is addressed to Jesus, which originally can hardly have been "Son of God", for applied to the earthly activity of Jesus this would be inconceivable in early tradition that had developed from a Palestinian-Jewish mode of thought.[18] Here ὁ υἱός μου may go back to a former עַבְדִּי, which is quite possible in translation, but is also suggested by the first part of the statement of the voice from heaven, which leans quite heavily on Isa. 42:1 MT.[19] In this place then there may be no allusion to Ps. 2:7, but a combined citation of Isa. 42:1 and Deut. 18:15. This would have considerable consequences for the understanding, for in His earthly activity, consequently in analogy with Elias and Moses, Jesus would be understood as an eschatological prophet.[20]

Whilst the original form of this section of text certainly goes back to Palestinian tradition, the version in Mark derives from the Hellenistic church, assumes the Son of God concept, and indeed, as the motif of metamorphosis shows, assumes it in the sense of divine being.[21] On this ground it may be concluded that v. 2fin is a secondary addition.[22] From this the Son of God title[23] now included in v. 7 received its unambiguous interpretation.

With that there came about a considerable displacement of the accent; the eschatological character of the narrative was weakened and certain motifs stepped completely into the background. Elias and Moses are merely witnesses of the fulfilment which with the bodily manifestation of the Son of God has already taken place; in their appearance reference is no longer made to the speedy beginning of the time of salvation, which Jesus' earthly work immediately precedes.[24] Accordingly in the redactional framework this revelation is correlated not with eschatology but with the resurrection of Jesus (Mk. 9:9).[25]

According to this determination of earlier and later elements[26] it is easy to recognize the redactional additions within the narrative. Since v. 6 not only gives a new interpretation of the preceding word of Peter but is also in the service of the Markan motif of the misunderstanding of the disciples which continues up to the time of the resurrection, an embellishment by the evangelist certainly presents itself here.[27] In v. 2 the underlining and very dragging κατ' ἰδίαν μόνους goes back decidedly to Mark. It is again a matter of one of his typical motifs, which crops up even in a tolerably fixed formulation.[28] Whether the introduction of the three intimate disciples is also to be carried back to Mark, is not quite certain. It is true that in some texts he has certainly introduced these intimate disciples subsequently, but their introduction may already have been handed down in certain contexts, and in the case of the story of the transfiguration that is not out of the question.

If we disregard v. 6 and the mention of the isolation in v. 2, we have a piece of tradition that is complete in itself, in which, it is true, an early stratum and a late interpretation can be recognized, but which otherwise shows no longer any seams or cracks. As genre for the transfiguration story the legend comes into question. It is a narrative in which, as Lohmeyer has excellently put it, "the inner significance of the figure of Jesus for believers is 'to be read' ".[29]

(b) Mk. 1:9–11. The narrative of the baptism of Jesus has in its main part vv. 10f. been taken over unaltered by the evangelist; the εὐθύς, which is frequent in Mark, could possibly have been inserted, but it often crops up in the popular style of narration and therefore may not on principle be regarded as redactional.[30] It is difficult to decide how far additions present themselves in the exposition v. 9, but that does not need to be investigated here; v. 9fin, the concise description of the baptism of Jesus by John in the Jordan, belongs assuredly to the stock that was handed down, it being the actual presupposition of vv. 10f. To the coming up out of the water there are joined three closely related events, which determine the character of the narrative, the opening of the heavens, the descent of the Spirit in the form of a dove and the sounding of a voice from heaven, which designates Jesus as the beloved Son of God on whom the divine pleasure rests. Here also it has to be asked how far in its present form the text represents the understanding of the later

Hellenistic church, to which the application of the Son of God title to the earthly Jesus no longer presented any difficulty; but behind that another meaning of the motif could possibly conceal itself.

The elements of the narrative permit of their being explained in quite different ways according as we reckon with the early Palestinian mode of thought or set out from the ideas of the Hellenistic church. It is easy, as in Mk. 9:2–8, to carry back the wording of the voice from heaven only to Isa. 42:1, accordingly to assume again a former "my servant" and then to disregard Ps. 2:7. According to late Jewish apocalyptic understanding the opening of the heavens, the appearing of the Spirit and the issuing of a voice directly from heaven all stand in relation to the end of time, and originally it is a matter of a threefold paraphrase of the one wonderful event that is being realized in this person who is baptized. The motif of the opening of the heavens that had been current since Isa. 63:19b[31], is united directly with the sounding of a voice from heaven, for example in Rev. 4:1.[32] And of course the voice from heaven in the narrative of the baptism[33] is not to be explained as a *Bath qol*, which was merely a substitute for the speech of God which no longer issues directly; rather, as follows clearly from what is said, it is to be explained as God's own speaking which begins again at the commencement of the end of time.[34] To that there belongs likewise the idea of the Spirit, for according to a widespread view the Spirit had been extinct since the last prophets of the Old Testament and was not to step into world affairs again until the end of the times.[35] Thus this threefold-one description permits it to be recognized that the time of the salvation of God is dawning and that the person here baptized by John enters as the "servant of God" upon His eschatological office. He is laid hold of by the Spirit[36] and can accomplish his word and work with real authority.[37]

It is not to be overlooked that the motivation of the individual traits which can be assumed for the earliest form of this portion of tradition, is repressed in the version of the story that has been determined by the Son of God conception. The chief stress shifts onesidedly to the bestowal of the Spirit, which is here understood in the sense of equipment and permanent endowment. For that reason not only is the apprehension of Jesus by the Spirit, the rushing power of God, spoken of, but the Spirit comes down in bodily form from heaven and enters

into the human person of Jesus in order to unite with him. The
εἰς αὐτόν, which is characteristic of Mark, may not be toned
down or given a new interpretation; it is meant here also
in the same way as in the *Gospel of the Ebionites*: ἐν εἴδει περι-
στερᾶς κατελθούσης καὶ εἰσελθούσης εἰς αὐτόν.[38.39] The motif of
the Spirit's form, the derivation of which is a difficulty, may
have its real significance in the fact that in person the very
Spirit of God bestowed as a gift takes possession of this chosen
man and unites with him. Hence very much goes to prove that
mention was made of the Spirit's form of a dove first of all in
connection with the Son of God conception, therefore on Hellenistic soil.[40] But therewith the relation of the three basic
motifs got out of place. Originally all disposed in the same way,
they are now very definitely co-ordinated and graded.

The opening of the heavens has now to be regarded primarily
as the necessary presupposition for the bodily epiphany of the
divine Spirit, whilst its eschatological significance still re-echoes
sounding only the retreat. For the heavens must be open that
the dove coming from there may be able to descend; but the
heavens must also be open that the voice of God may be heard.
As the stress has fallen on the bodily descent of the Spirit and
the appointment as Son of God that comes about thereby,
so also the voice from heaven has become first and foremost a
vox interpres. What matters chiefly is the content, not the
coming forth of this voice.[41] The utterance itself no longer
contains Isa. 42:1a exclusively but in its first part leans heavily
on the adoptionist word in Ps. 2:7.[42] That seems particularly
surprising where, with a description of the Spirit, a transition
is effected from a pronouncedly dynamic conception to the idea
of a permanent possession of the Spirit. But on the other hand it
may not exactly be mistaken that the presuppositions of Old
Testament Jewish thought are not abandoned and that the
functional significance of the divinely bestowed office remains
preserved, that therefore the divine sonship understood very
much in a Hellenistic way—for only thus was a transference to
the earthly life of Jesus possible—remains united to an act of
appointment and a bestowal of the Spirit.

The rendering of the voice from heaven that has been handed
down enables us, in the same way as the motif of the form like a
dove, to recognize that we are moving in the realm of a Hellenistic Jewish Christianity. In the long run the apocalyptic motif

of the dawning of the end of time and also the motif of the transference of an actual royal office were no longer decisive. Rather what shows itself here is an understanding of the task and activity of Jesus similar to the one that Hellenistic Judaism had of the behaviour of the Old Testament men of God.[43] Jesus obtains wonderful ability and special status through the Spirit with whom he is equipped. Ps. 2:7 plays a role because of the Son of God title that occurs there and chiefly because of the idea of appointment to office, but not because of the royal functions associated with that.

Here accordingly there appears that understanding of the Messiahship of Jesus which can include His earthly life as well and assumes an equalization with an already Hellenized Son of God concept.[44] The conception of Messiahship in the Jewish sense has to be kept out of this text altogether; it is suited neither to the basic Palestinian nor to the Hellenistic Jewish Christian rendering of the story.[45] Add to this that the happenings at the baptism refer to Jesus alone, but are not understood in the sense of the word of the Psalm as a public enthronement.[46]

The Son of God title has indeed retained a functional significance, but has no longer anything at all to do with the early messianism. Also the adoptionist character of the divine sonship that distinguished Ps. 2:7 has no longer held out clearly, for it is now no longer a question of a man to whom royal authority is transferred, but of a man who is permeated by divine πνεῦμα, which distinguishes him qualitatively. How this could be developed further in the Hellenistic sphere, is shown us impressively in the story of the transfiguration in the rendering of it preserved in Mark.

Let us turn back once again to the earlier form and meaning of the narrative tentatively ascertained above. There, in the context indicated, the Spirit must be understood in a genuinely Old Testament way as an irresistible power of God that descends upon men. Of that we have now a confirmation in the fact that the early v. 12, which forms the transition to the story of the temptation, unquestionably contains precisely this Spirit-concept, which does not at all fit any longer without more ado into the later version of the story of the baptism.[47] But even the piece of tradition in Mk. 1:13 about the temptation of Jesus, which is so difficult in detail, provides a prop for the view of

340

Jesus as an eschatological prophet within the early conception of the baptism narrative, namely in so far as the forty-day stay in the wilderness and also the ministry of angels indicate a Moses-Elias-typology.[48] Certainly Jesus' activity on earth is meant to have a clearly eschatological outlook[49] And similarly as in the case of the early version of the story of the transfiguration it is a matter of His appearance taking place immediately before the beginning of the end of time. It is Jesus' office as the servant who is well pleasing to God to proclaim the coming dominion of God and to confront men with the salvation of God.[50] The later version of the story of the baptism has maintained the eschatological aspect, but repressed it. Here the earthly activity of Jesus itself possesses salvation significance, and in a basic happening, which is referred only to Jesus and which precedes His actual ministry, the presupposition and purport of His earthly history are gathered up.[51]

NOTES

1. Ernst Lohmeyer, *Die Verklärung Jesu nach dem Markus-Evangelium*, *ZNW* 21 (1922), pp. 185–215. This thesis was later abandoned by him, cf. *id.*, *Mk.*, pp. 174f., especially n. 7.

2. Bultmann, *Syn. Trad.*, p. 280; withdrawn in the Supplementary Volume, p. 37.

3. Heinrich Baltensweiler, *Die Verklärung Jesu* (*AThANT* 33), 1959, pp. 31, 35.

4. Further partitive suggestions, particularly from earlier times, are discussed in Joseph Blinzler, *Die neutestamentlichen Berichte über die Verklärung Jesu* (*Nt.Abh.* XVII/4), 1937, pp. 52ff.

5. The appearance of the prophets in v. 4 does not permit of its being detached from the statement in v. 3, but the voice in the cloud in v. 7 is an answer to the word of the disciple in v. 5. That vv. 3f. and vv. 5, 7 belong together should not be disputed.

6. That there exists no actual connection with Mk. 8:27ff., but rather that this was provided only redactionally, is emphasized by K. L. Schmidt, *Rahmen* p. 222. It is indeed not certain whence the time statement originates; on the different views cf. Baltensweiler, *op. cit.*, pp. 46ff.

7. It does not need to be said that the text of Mark is not interested in the "metaphysical qualities of the figure of Jesus", but emphasizes "the functional character of the Messiah as king", so Baltensweiler, p. 117.

8. Lohmeyer, *ZNW* 21 (1922), p. 206, also insists on a contrast

between the Christophany in v. 3 and the theophany in v. 7. This is not obvious, for there it is not at all a matter of an actual theophany. But while originally v. 7 gave the decisive interpretation, this verse is now virtually a mere supplement to, and confirmation of, the revelation event that took place in the metamorphosis.

9. This is added first in the Matthaean and Lukan parallels. That the motif is lacking in the Markan rendering is generally not taken sufficiently into account or is deliberately bypassed, since here we have to reckon with a corrupt text; cf. the celebrated conjecture of B. H. Streeter, *The Four Gospels*, 1924, pp. 315f.

10. Cf. also Billerbeck I, pp. 752f.

11. Cf. especially Joachim Jeremias, art ʽΗλ(ε)ίας, *ThWb* II, pp. 930–943, there p. 932; *id.*, art. Μωυσῆς, *ThWb* IV, pp. 852–878, there pp. 859f.

12. Cf. the συνομιλεῖν in Acts 10:27f. It may on no account be interpreted according to Lk. 9:31, and therefore an announcement of the passion by the heavenly figures is not to be assumed, as it is again and again.

13. We merely observe how naturally ὁ ʼΙησοῦς is used in v. 4 and v. 8.

14. Cf. Jeremias, *ThWb* II, pp. 940f.; *ThWb* IV, pp. 860f.

15. The assumption that eschatological conceptions which were associated with the feast of Tabernacles are active here has much in its favour. Particular reference to it was made for the first time by Lohmeyer, *ZNW* 21 (1922), pp. 191ff. The narrative of the transfiguration was interpreted down to details on the basis of such associations by Harald Riesenfeld, *Jésus transfiguré* (*Acta Seminarii Neotest. Upsaliensis* XVII), 1947. For criticism cf. Noth. *Gott, König Volk im AT*, in *Ges. Studien*, pp. 227ff. Baltensweiler, *op. cit.*, pp. 37ff. also reckons with eschatological expectations which were connected with the feast of Tabernacles.

16. The fact that Elias is given precedence is explained in the best way by far if it is a matter of the office of the eschatological prophet. For the Old Testament is already familiar with the idea of a return of Elias (Mal. 3:23f.), while the conception of an eschatological prophet like Moses is already developed, but a carrying away and personal return of Moses was reckoned with only gradually and in assimilation to the expectation of Elias. The view of a return together of Elias and Moses has precipitated itself most clearly in the Jewish *Vorlage* of Rev. 11:3ff.; cf. Jeremias, *ThWb* II, pp. 941ff. (IV, pp. 867f.).

17. Cf. also regarding this the *Apocalypse of Elias* adduced by Jeremias, *op. cit.*; it is preserved in Coptic, dates in its present form from the third century A.D., and in part has been revised under Christian auspices (ed. G. Steindorff, *TU* NF 2,1899; translation in Riessler, *Altjüdisches Schriftum*, pp. 114ff.).

18. We are referred to this not lastly by the Aramaic ῥαββί in v. 5.

19. Cf. Dalman, *Worte Jesu*, pp. 226ff.; Bousset, *Kyrios Christos*, p. 57, n. 2; Jeremias, *ThWb* V, p. 699; Hooker, *Jesus and the Servant*, pp. 68ff.

20. Cf. Appendix, p. 382. (pp. 372ff.).

21. On no account may it be said precisely in regard to this rendering of the story that Jesus' communion with the Father and His obedience are decisive as marks of the Son designation.

22. In this respect Lohmeyer, *ZNW* 21 (1922), pp. 203ff. has seen something correct. There he intended merely to eliminate v. 3 along with v. 2fin and thus quarried out a portion the ancient traits of which immediately struck him. In his commentary, *Mk*, pp. 174f., he appeals to apocalyptic conceptions for v. 2fin and v. 3; so also Baltensweiler, *op. cit.*, pp. 63f.

23. In late Jewish writings עבד is rendered by παῖς, but to some extent also by υἱός; cf. Jeremias, *ThWb* v, p. 677.

24. G. H. Boobyer, *St. Mark and the Transfiguration Story*, 1942, briefly summarized in the article, "St. Mark and the Transfiguration", *JThSt* 41 (1940), pp. 119–140, wishes to interpret the individual motifs of the Markan rendering of the transfiguration narrative as a representation in advance of the parousia; but that interpretation of it is not convincing. The position of the story after Mk. 8:38; 9:1 doubtless requires an explanation, but that can be obtained only from the redactional framework and is of no consequence for the story itself.

25. Because of this merely quite secondary reference to the resurrection the view that the transfiguration narrative was at one time a resurrection story certainly drops out; so especially Wellhausen, *Mk*, p. 71; Bultmann, *Syn. Trad.*, p. 278. But against that there also tells a series of other reasons, which have been well assembled by Baltensweiler, *op. cit.*, pp. 91ff.

26. In addition reference may be made to the analysis of Hans-Peter Müller, *Die Verklärung Jesu. Eine motivgeschichtliche Studie*, *ZNW* 51. (1960), pp. 56–64. The tensions between the different motifs are clearly perceived, various singularities are pertinently observed, but no convincing solution is obtained: two originally independent stories are said to present themselves in vv. 2a, b, 7, 9 and vv. (2c) 3–6, 8, in the one case the appearance in the cloud and the proclamation are constitutive, in the other the appearance of the luminous form is so.

27. Cf also Baltensweiler, *op. cit.*, pp. 112ff.

28. κατ' ἰδίαν Mk. 6:31, 32; 9:28; 13:3; κατὰ μόνας Mk. 4:10.

29. Lohmeyer, *ZNW* 21 (1922), p. 202.

30. Cf. Johannes Weiss, *EYΘΥΣ bei Markus*, *ZNW* II (1910), pp. 124–133.

31. The motif of the opened heavens crops up in the Old Testament first of all in Ezek. 1:1 in the framework of a prophetic vision: in Isa. 63:19b the eschatological reference is unambiguous.

32. Lohmeyer, *Mk*, p. 22, has brought out well this connection between the opening of the heavens and the voice from heaven.

33. The unconstrued Semitic introduction of φωνή is to be observed; cf. Wellhausen, *Mk*, p. 6; Klostermann, *Mk*, p. 9.

34. On the *Bath qol* cf. Billerbeck I, pp. 125ff. The interpretation of the voice from heaven at the time of Jesus' baptism as the *Bath qol* is frequent, cf. only Klostermann, *Mk*, p. 9; Schniewind, *Mk*, p. 46;

343

Schlatter, *Mt*, pp. 93f.; Traub, *ThWb* V, pp. 530f.; Taylor, *Mk*, p. 161; Cranfield, *Mk*, p. 54. Against that rightly: Lohmeyer, *Mk*, p. 22; Robinson, *Geschichtsverständnis*, p. 22.

35. Cf. Volz, *Eschatologie*, pp. 392f.; Billerbeck II, pp, 128f.

36. Isa. 42:1b may also have been an important connecting link; there, immediately following the word received from the voice from heaven, it is said: "I have put my spirit upon him"; cf. Branscomb, *Mk*, p. 19; Jeremias, *ThWb* V, p. 699, ὁ ἀγαπητός also comes from Isa. 42:1 and is not to be referred to Gen. 22:1. It will be shown in the Appendix, p. 382 (pp. 372ff.) that here there is no reference to the conception of the "suffering" servant of God.

37. Here in any case we must proceed from the dynamical understanding of the Spirit such as was lively through Old Testament tradition.

38. Text of the *Gospel of the Ebionites*, Epiphanius, *Haer*. XXX 13, 7, in Erich Klostermann, *Apocrypha* II (*Kl. Texte* 8), 1929³, p. 14; cf. Hennecke-Schneemelcher, *Neutestamentliche Apokryphen* I, 1959³, p. 103 (published in English by Lutterworth Press, London, 1963.)

39. The εἰς αὐτόν of the Markan text is therefore in my opinion meant quite concretely; with ἐπ' αὐτόν Matt. and Luke have leaned upon the LXX text of Isa. 42:1b. The bodily epiphany of the Spirit has here not a merely symbolical significance, but the Spirit goes down into the person baptized to effect a completely real union with him; κατα-βαίνειν has its fixed place in statements regarding the epiphany of the divine being, as Robinson, *Geschichtsverständnis*, p. 22, brings out pertinently.

40. As regards the dove form of the Spirit reference ought not to be made merely to the many associations in which in the land of the Old Testament and the Near East the dove was connected with the godly man; so Heinrich Greeven, art., περιστερά, *ThWb* VI, p. 68. It remains true especially in the opinion of Billerbeck I, p. 123 "that only to a very limited extent can it be shown that it (the dove) counted as a symbol of the Spirit of God" in the sight of Palestinian Judaism; cf. also Barrett, *Holy Spirit*, pp. 35ff. Accordingly it may perhaps be concluded that in the Judaism of the Diaspora the Spirit of God working on the earth was commonly equated with the dove, and anyhow the representation of the רוח in Ezek. 37 in the synagogue at Dura-Europos could point to that; cf. on this Werner Georg Kümmel, *Die älteste religiöse Kunst der Juden*, *Judaica* 2 (1946), pp. 1–56, there p. 51f.; otherwise Harald Riesenfeld, *The Resurrection in Ezechiel XXXVII and in the Dura-Europos-Paintings* (*Upsala Universitets Årsskrift* 1948/11), pp. 31f., who thinks of Hellenistic "Psyche-like winged beings"; likewise Rudolf Meyer, *Betrachtungen zu drei Fresken der Synagoge von Dura-Europos*, *ThLZ* 74 (1949), especially cols. 35–38. Cf. also the reflections of Goodenough, *Jewish Symbols* VIII, pp. 41ff. on the use of the dove on tombstones, in synagogues and in the thought of Philo (especially pp. 44ff.) At all events in the narrative of the baptism we are concerned with a concrete appearance of the Spirit; Luke's words σωματικῷ εἴδει show

that he understood that quite properly, and by them he has made it clear.

41. Herbert Braun, *Entscheidende Motive in den Berichten über die Taufe Jesu von Markus bis Justin, ZThK* 50 (1953), pp. 39–43, especially pp. 40f. (*Studien*, pp. 168–172, especially pp. 169f.) points out that both the opening of the heavens and the mention of the voice from heaven drop out of later texts; he asks whether a gnostic tendency is involved here, but himself observes that Justin does not harmonize with that. In my opinion the transition indicated above to the Hellenistic under-standing of the story of the baptism provides a very much better explanation. It is shown, e.g. by Johannes Schneider, *Die Taufe im Neuen Testament*, 1952, pp. 25f., how naturally the latter is often made the starting point and that thereby the original characteristics of the statements are unappreciated. He speaks on the whole only of two constitutive elements: the bestowal of the Spirit (in the sense of equip-ment) and the voice from heaven which serves "to explain" that happen-ing. Similarly even Schlatter, *Mt*, p. 91.

42. The wording is transposed as compared with the Massoretic text and the LXX; in conformity with the current style of preaching the σὺ εἶ now stands in front.

43. Cf. Chapter 5, pp. 288ff.

44. Cf. Chapter 3, pp. 189ff.

45. Mention is frequently made of a "Messiah consecration", but at best that is possible only in a very metaphorical sense; cf., e.g., Bult-mann, *Syn. Trad.*, pp. 264, 267;

46. Outwardly in composition with its vision and audition affecting Jesus alone the story of the baptism bears a certain resemblance to the call of a prophet; cf. Schniewind, *Mk*, p. 46; the differences are empha-sized from a one-sided point of view by Bultmann, *Syn. Trad.*, pp. 263f. If we assume the complete text of Isa. 41:1a as the wording of the voice from heaven and judge the coming of the Spirit according to Isa. 42:1b (cf. Isa. 61:1), there is not the least suggestion of the royal messianism. Matthew has altered the form of the story drastically in so far as he has turned the call into a public epiphany. Luke has virtually taken over the text of his *Vorlage* in substance, only he has erased the mention of the baptist; cf. on this Conzelmann, *Mitte der Zeit*, pp. 15, 16ff. The much discussed Western text of Lk. 3:22 has taken over Ps. 2:7 word for word and erased the rest of Isa. 42:1a. This stands at the end of the development and has no claim to originality: on the one hand, in Mark all the weight has already fallen on the Son of God predication, and on the other hand the citation of Ps. 2:7 in the context of the baptism of Jesus already assumes quite a considerable process of re-casting of the messianic motifs.

47. Lohmeyer, *Mk*, p. 27, refers to a difference in nature between the concepts of the Spirit in v. 11 and v. 12; but his distinction, according to which the Spirit is in v. 12 an "angel-like being" who carries out God's command, is a mistake. The Old Testament character of the Spirit concept in v. 12 in the sense of divine power is properly brought out by Eduard Schweizer, *ThWb* VI, pp. 395f.

48. The difficult Markan rendering of the story of the temptation has to be understood from apocalyptic tradition; cf. above all Arnold Meyer, *Die Versuchung Christi* in *Festgabe Hugo Blümner*, 1914, pp. 434–468, especially pp. 444ff. Precisely here we do not succeed with purely Old Testament presuppositions; against Jacques Dupont, *"L'arrière-fond biblique du Récit des Tentations de Jésus"*, NTSt 3 (1956/57), pp. 287–304. This is seen not lastly in the idea of temptation itself, which is determined by the eschatological conflict between God and Satan; cf. Karl Georg Kuhn, Πειρασμός—ἁμαρτία—σάρξ *im Neuen Testament und die damit zusammenhängenden Vorstellungen*, ZThK 49 (1952), pp. 200–222. Even to the motif of association with the wild beasts we have only one late Jewish parallel, *Test. of Napht.* 8, 4 (similarly *Test. of Iss.* 7, 7) and indeed in the sense of a "paradisiacal" procession, therefore signifying the subordination of the beasts; there also the motif of the overcoming of the devil and of the service of angels, referred, however, simply to the pious; cf. A. Meyer, *op. cit.*, pp. 445f. The starting point is the forty days lonely sojourn of Moses, Exod. 34:28, and especially of Elias, 1 Kings 19:1ff., since in the latter case the service of an angel is added: Ps. 91:11–13 also has an effect.

49. Brief reference may be made to *Test. of Lev.* 18 and *Test of Jud.* 24. As is well known, there are in both passages motifs very similar to those in the story of the baptism of Jesus, at one time bound up with the idea of the messianic high priest, at another time with that of the messianic king. Now it must be recognized from this simultaneous use of the motifs in different connections that they were by no means united firmly to a definite salvation figure, but are to be regarded in general merely as significant of eschatological happenings.

50. I am opposed not only to Schniewind, *Mk*, pp. 47ff., who wishes to regard the exaltation as the actual appointment as Messiah, but says that onwards from the baptism the reference is to the concealed Messiah, but also to Cullmann, *Tauflehre*, pp. 15f.; *id.*, *Christologie*, pp. 65ff., who wants to see the consciousness of sonship and of the role of the "suffering" servant of God associated with Jesus' baptism.

51. The latter is well brought out in Robinson, *Geschichtsverständnis*, pp. 20ff.

RETROSPECT

So far as direct overlappings and contacts did not emerge, the several Christological titles have been extensively examined in independence of one another. There has emerged, however, a whole series of common traits, and in conclusion these may now be set together. Certain basic tendencies obviously hold their own in the various conceptions.

The earliest Christology has in all its distinctive features a consistently eschatological orientation. The coming Son of man, the again expected Lord and the Messiah appointed in the last days, stand at the outset of the formation of the tradition. To that there corresponds the fact that the motif of exaltation is altogether lacking not merely in the Son of man conception but also in the earliest Christology. The delay of the parousia, which was already being felt in the early Palestinian primitive church, was not overcome by the idea of the presence of the Lord but by a still more intensive waiting and the summons to trial. On the other hand, it may not be overlooked that the conception of exaltation was early prepared for because the church, filled with the Spirit and knowing that it was at the beginning of the final events, in a certain way anticipated the eschatological accomplishment. The experience of the time was, however, not so considerable as to lead to a new conception.

A looking-back to Jesus' earthly work likewise played a decisive role from the beginning. It is true that in the earliest period the church set its mind against all messianic interpretations of the life of Jesus; the status and the authority of the earthly Jesus were determined for it by the predicates "Master" and "Lord". But presently his earthly work as well was taken into the framework of the Son of man conception, and with the designation "the Son" the early church secured a further declaration regarding Jesus' special power and dignity. Whilst the ideas of Jesus as "Master", "Lord" and "Son" were developed chiefly in view of the doctrine, so also Jesus' work, His impressive bearing and His working of miracles, occupied an important place in the proclamation. Jesus was seen in the

347

light of the Old Testament charismatic persons and above all was understood as the new Moses appearing with full power. This idea did not continue to be preserved as an independent tradition, but in association with other conceptions it had after-effects for long.

At an early time, not only Jesus' teaching and work but also His passion had a place in Christological statements. In the earliest story of the passion an attempt was made to understand Jesus' way to the cross by the thought of Scriptural necessity with a view to surmounting its offence. From this there then emerged in the primitive church a recasting of the Messiah concept. For if Jesus was crucified as "king of the Jews" according to God's will, then must the passion of the "Messiah" be according to God's will. In this way the tradition of the passion united on Palestinian soil with the Messiah title, which henceforward retained this very place as far as it was not generalized and used merely as a proper name. Side by side with the idea of Scriptural proof the idea of vicarious atonement already played a role in the earliest period. It is true that only a part of the tradition is stamped particularly with Isa. 53 and its ideas of universal atonement. The motif of vicarious atonement is present in the tradition of the Lord's Supper, as also in the passion statements which are associated with the Christos title.

The strong influence of the tradition of the passion is shown by the words about the suffering Son of man. First of all, under retention of the leading motif of the Son of man idea, only a "being delivered into the hands of men" was spoken about, but then the thought of Scriptural necessity was taken over, and so finally the motif of atonement supervened. Also the statements about resurrection, which at first were referred exclusively to the parousia and signalled the beginning of the final happenings, at the same time obtained their fixed place in connection with Jesus' passion, as follows from 1 Cor. 15:3b–5 and the long renderings of the words about the suffering Son of man.

A very different stage of tradition is represented by Hellenistic Jewish Christianity; for, on the one hand, the conception of exaltation was developed there and, on the other hand, the Messiah conception was carried over step by step to the earthly Jesus. The conception of exaltation was the first consistent attempt to make allowance for the fact of the delay of the parousia or, to put it more accurately, to correct a view of immediate expectation that in the long run was insufficient and an enthusiastic anticipation of the accomplishment.[1] The Messiahship was now no longer spoken of in regard to Jesus' eschatological work, but already in association with the resurrection so that it was possible to develop the idea of His present activity in this still existing world.

As a second component, the idea of Jesus' heavenly κυριότης came to birth. This was first of all understood in connection with Ps. 110:1 in a strictly functional sense; thus under the influence of the Hellenistic kyrios cult the conception of the divinity of Jesus became increasingly effective, the more so since the Kyrios title of the Septuagint was already in many cases applied to Jesus.

Therewith a decision having important consequences was reached. It did not remain without effect upon the idea of Jesus' work on earth. At the beginning in the domain of Hellenistic Jewish Christianity there stood a singular conception corresponding directly to the exaltation conception, the view of Jesus as "Son of David", which was understood in the sense of a preliminary stage of dignity. But Christology soon drove it out. Already in Palestinian tradition Jesus was understood as a charismatic person and a bearer of the Spirit, and this was now taken up by the θεῖος ἀνήρ-motif and carried further.

The Judaism of the Diaspora had already in pre-Christian times seized upon this Hellenistic idea in connection with the specially distinguished men of God and deprived it of its specifically pagan edge, thus making it possible for Hellenistic Jewish Christianity to connect with it, which was then also made easy by the transference to the earthly Jesus of the Messiah and Son of God conceptions. There supervened the theologumenon of the virgin birth, first in association with the idea of Jesus' Davidic sonship, but later as proof of the conception of His earthly divine sonship.

In spite of these various restatements, genuinely Jewish thought was certainly preserved in that the messiahship and divine sonship of the earthly Jesus continued to be associated with an act of appointment and His special abilities were carried back to the gift of the Spirit bestowed by God.

In Hellenistic Gentile Christianity, so fluid the boundaries could be, the influence of the Old Testament Jewish tradition and of the mode of thought bearing its stamp receded perceptibly. Some traditions, as that of the Son of man, also the later one of Jesus' Davidic sonship, completely disappeared. The Christos title, so far as it did not stand in association with the passion tradition, was understood merely as a proper name; on the other hand, Kyrios and Son of God were considerably transformed under Hellenistic presuppositions and definitely stepped into the foreground. Kyrios came to be the dominating concept in worship and served as the acclamation of Him who possesses divine sovereign power over all the world. Son of God served henceforth first and foremost to designate Jesus the divine being who has come down from His heavenly pre-existence, has suffered death on the earth, but then rose again and has been exalted to the right hand of God that some day He may appear before all the world in His unconcealed divinity.

On Hellenistic soil Christendom seriously endeavoured, in all its remodelling and elaboration of the message of Jesus, to resist every foreign infiltration that assailed the centre of its proclamation. In coming to grips with the mystery religions and also with emperor worship it understood the κυριότης of Jesus as the one position as Lord over all the world conveyed by God to Jesus and adjusted the divine sonship strictly to the thought of the incarnation with a view to setting itself on the defence against all docetism. In this way there was secured in the Christology of Hellenistic Gentile Christianity the conception which lay as a determining factor at the basis of all the further development of the early church.

NOTE

1. A brief reference may be made to Martin Werner, *Die Entstehung des christlichen Dogmas*, 1954, who, following Albert Schweitzer, has energetically undertaken the attempt to solve the problem of the further development of Christian doctrine by setting out from the early thoroughgoing eschatological idea and the delay of the parousia that gradually made itself felt (cf. especially pp. 105ff.). Apart from the questionable opinion expressed regarding the history and proclamation of Jesus, as also apart from the significance which the so-called angel

Christology is assumed to have had in the earliest Christendom (pp. 61ff. 302ff.), the fundamental claim of this statement cannot be disputed without more ado, even if on the other hand it needs to be seen that the delay of the parousia was by no means the only thing at the bottom of the transformation of early Christian theology. The manifold elements in the earliest tradition will need to be worked out much more clearly, and above all it will have to be observed that already there were at hand ideas in regard to Jesus' earthly work and its salvation significance which permitted a reconstruction of the thoroughgoing eschatological conception without that almost chaotic crisis coming about which Werner assumes (pp. 115ff.).

THE ESCHATOLOGICAL PROPHET

In the Judaism of the time of Jesus the conception of the eschatological prophet played a role that was not a small one, and it was operative, so far as we can see, in very different formulations. The early Christian tradition did not remain uninfluenced by it, although the result is still in part only indirectly discernible. Traces of this view are stamped most clearly on the opinion that was formed of the Baptist. But it may not be overlooked that at an early stage of the tradition the person and work of Jesus were also described with the help of this conception. This was certainly blurred and covered over by later Christological statements, yet peculiarities of this antiquated Christology still permit of their being discerned. Since the idea of Jesus as the eschatological prophet has been mentioned repeatedly, the previous history of this conception in late Judaism and the primitive Christian tradition relating to it will now be dealt with somewhat more in detail.

1. *The Expectation of the Eschatological Prophet in late Judaism.*

For an understanding of this expectation it needs to be observed that onwards from a certain point of time in the post-exilic history there was no longer any prophetic mission of the old style. The words of the popular lamentation in Ps. 74:9: "We see not our signs: there is no more any prophet", contain a first clear allusion to the changing situation.[1]1 Maccabees contains quite unmistakable statements: there in 9:27 the time is looked back to "in which for the last time a prophet appeared unto them", and furthermore in 4:46; 14:41 decisions are recorded which were taken with the reservation "until a (faithful) prophet should come". Here it is not yet the eschatological prophet that is thought of,[2] but the presuppositions out of which such a conception could arise are easily discernible. In association with the consciousness of a non-appearance of prophets there stands also the well-known rabbinical theory according to which the prophetic spirit had given way since the time of Malachi and a certain compensation had been given only through the so-called *Bath qol*.[3] This thesis is falsely judged when it is regarded simply as having been invented to support the rabbinical concept of the Canon; it is not to be disputed that behind it there stands an actual extinction of prophetic activity.

On the other hand it must be stated that there can of course be no talk of a complete disappearance of prophecy, and actually there were prophetic utterances of most various kinds in this epoch. Doubtless we are concerned here, as Plöger has well said, "with a survival in completely altered circumstances and in a completely altered form, during which something new actually came into being".[4] In particular there is noticeable here the phenomenon of a spiritually powerful exegesis of Scripture, which played a dominating role in apocalyptic as also in the Qumran community; with all freedom in interpretation there is a characteristic fundamental adherence to Scripture.[5] Beside that there emerged in almost all circles of the Judaism of this period a type of seer who foretold future happenings and interpreted appearances in dreams. Among the Essenes there appears to have been a school of such seers who had developed a distinctive methodology involving contemplative and ascetic practices; the Pharisees also came forward with oracles which they understood according to rabbinical doctrine as effected by the *Bath qol*. On the fringe of the official religious life there survived even still a pronouncedly ecstatic prophetic mission of a very old style, obviously in very barbarous forms, as is shown by the threatening word Zech. 13:4-6 or the behaviour before and during the Jewish War of the curious Jesus son of Ananias, who moved continually through the streets of Jerusalem with his woeful cry. Finally reference must be made to the many prophets of deliverance and prophets of ruin who appeared in the course of the revolt.[6]

The judgment regarding the Hasmonaean John Hyrcanus has a special position within the late Jewish traditions. According to a tradition preserved in Josephus he is said to have held the office of king and high priest and moreover to have also possessed the gift of prophecy.[7] However it may stand as regards the question of the actuality of messianic expectations in the period of the Maccabees, it cannot be disputed that there was a late Maccabean court-ideology which brought the old expectations into association with the new ruling family. The union of the three functions of king, high priest and prophet is in that form doubtless a construction intended to serve as legitimation of the Hasmonaeans.[8]

It is not surprising that in the structure of religious thought in late Judaism hope was transposed to a return of genuine prophecy at the end of time. This expectation is in part difficult to grasp, and was never developed quite clearly and uniformly. At all events it is well not to speak of a "prophetic Messiah" or of a "messianic prophet".[9] For the whole conception of the eschatological prophet has roots which are completely other than those of royal messianism; later contacts of the two conceptions are not to be overlooked, but they are positively of a secondary kind. Another question is whether purely terminologically the designation of the eschatological prophet as an "anointed one" was usual;[10] we are then concerned with the special act in which an office is made over in an anointing and not at the same time with a specific definition of functions in accordance with royal messianism. Precisely in the event of a terminological identity the actual differences have to be attended to all the more accurately.

The expectation of the eschatological prophet evidently moulded itself into two very different forms, connected on the one hand, on the basis of Deut. 18:15-18, with the person of Moses, on the other hand, on the basis of Mal. 3:1, 23f., with the person of Elias. Only if this difference is attended to, can results that are to some extent clear be secured. It is of course not to be expected that the two forms appeared and have been preserved in pure and clear renderings and that no sort of intermingling has taken place. But even a complex state of affairs can be rightly defined only when the single elements intertwined in it are clearly recognized.

(a) The hope of Elias has always been an extremely lively one in Judaism.[11] This also holds good for the New Testament period as follows from various pieces of evidence. The New Testament contains not a small number of allusions which assume a widespread conception, and the late Jewish literature, which, it is true, contains unambiguous material only in later strata, nevertheless permits a series of pretty reliable inferences.[12] The starting point for an eschatological expectation connected with the person of Elias was on the one hand his miraculous removal to heaven (2 Kings 2:1ff.), on the other hand the prophecy in Mal. 3:1, which was interpreted of Elias already at an early time in a secondary addition 3:23f. (4:5f. AV).[13]

The idea of Elias as an eschatological prophet thus found expression in the Old Testament.[14] It is his task at the end of time to lead men to repentance that the purity of families and thereby the spiritual condition of the people may be restored.[15] According to Ecclus. 48:10 he is, following Isa. 49:6, to restore the tribes of Israel, therefore to bring about the right outward conditions. Here as compared with the older view, which attributed to the returning Elias a purely religious office, a certain change is discernible in so far as he is charged with a more political function. Nevertheless mention may not be made right away of an assignment to him of the work of the royal Messiah, there being no talk of an exercise of sovereign power.[16] It is also material that Elias occasionally counts as the immediate forerunner of Jahwe and that there is no place for a royal Messiah in this conception. There are also of course various interminglings and combinations. The equating of Elias with the messianic high priest[17] apparently had not yet come into question in the time of the primitive church, but came about only later; in any case it did not play any role within the primitive Christian tradition. If on the other hand a prophetic gift is awarded to the messianic high priest in the *Testament of Levi* 2:10 (8:2?), that does not need necessarily to be coupled with the task of Elias, but coheres with the fact that in any case the ideas of priest and prophet easily combine.[18] It may first be asked whether an association with the conception of the eschatological Elias presents itself in connection with Taxo, a mysterious figure coming from a priestly family, in the *Assumption of Moses* 9:1ff. Anyhow the name points to the function of Elias as an organizer, and moreover the appearance of Taxo immediately precedes the appearing of the kingdom of God.[19] Elias was indeed never equated with the royal Messiah. On the other hand a position as his forerunner was assigned to him. The age of the evidence for that does not indeed permit of its being referred with certainty to pre-Christian times.[20] But it is nevertheless probable that in the New Testament there has in fact been a going back to such a combination and that it was not first brought about there. For the Qumran texts are also acquainted with the role of the eschatological prophet before and side by side with the two Messiahs, even if at the same time the eschatological prophet does not bear the traits of Elias.[21] Moreover the idea of the appearance of Elias immediately before the coming of Jahwe naturally remained lively and may indeed even have stood in the foreground. At all events for the eschatological prophet expected as Elias it is essential that he appear as a preacher of repentance and confront the people with salvation or judgment.

(b) Besides the prophecy of Elias the promise of a prophet like Moses has played an important role in connection with the conception of the eschatological prophet.[22] Deut. 18:15-18 was of course not worded originally with an eschatological orientation. In Deuteronomy it is rather a matter of Israel standing under permanent charismatic leadership; and the "supreme office in which the actual living intercourse of Jahwe with Israel is to take place is that of the prophet, who will never fail Israel".[23] Whether at the same time a firmly organized institution ought to be thought of, which would be filled up in continuous succession,[24] may be questioned. Certainly the historical work of the Deuteronomist does not allow us to recognize aught of such an idea. The decisive thought was that on and on for ever Israel might reckon on a sending of prophets.[25]

No definite evidence of the hope of an eschatological prophet like Moses can be found in the Old Testament. It can nevertheless be considered whether it has not precipitated itself in the much disputed Ebed-Jahwe-figure in Deutero-Isaiah. Apart from questions as to the state of the text and as to the compass and the origin of the Songs, there still remain for the understanding of them, as is well known, two main problems, that of the individual or collective interpretation and that of estimating the royal and the prophetic elements.[26] After Duhm's delimitation of the Songs[27] the individual interpretation first stood in the foreground; it was then disputed by Eissfeldt[28] and others so that since then more attention has been paid to the collective interpretation, according to which the Servant of God represents the people of Israel.[29] On the basis of the idea of corporate personality[30] a pronouncedly bilateral exposition has been suggested: according to it Israel is the Servant of God in the midst of the people, but on its part is again represented by the king,[31] or, to put the matter somewhat otherwise, behind the Servant of God Israel there simultaneously flashes up the idea of a coming Messiah.[32] The individual exposition merits the preference.[33] But is it then a matter of a royal or a prophetic figure? That certain royal traits are to be met with, is not to be disputed.[34] But on the other hand an attempt to interpret the Servant of God Songs throughout by the king conception, shows that for this there are no unambiguous criteria.[35] Consequently in the case of the Ebed Jahwe we must be concerned with a prophetic figure, as especially Mowinckel and Zimmerli have shown.[36] But if now the person of a prophet has so exclusive a function in connection with eschatological happenings, then the question forces itself upon us whether here a use of Deut. 18:15–18 does not present itself and whether the Servant of God is here represented as a new eschatological Moses. This thesis advocated by Bentzen[37] and others[38] has much in it and merits attention.[39]

On a first glance it seems to stand badly in post-Biblical Judaism[40] so far as concerns evidence for the expectation of an eschatological prophet like Moses. Rabbinical literature presents only very few passages with the basic text Deut. 18:15–18 and everywhere steers clear of eschatological interpretation.[41] But in this connection it is not to be forgotten that for the rabbinate prophecy had altogether only a subordinate significance and was in rank separated from the law and above all from Moses as the lawgiver.[42] The apocalyptic literature also presents no relevant material, but, as in other passages of the New Testament, we have here perhaps to infer a tradition which has precipitated itself in later scriptural documents which are preserved in fragments.[43] That in New Testament times the figure "of the prophet" played a role in the expectation of the end and was distinguished from Elias, is easily recognized from John 1:21, 25.[44] It is easy to suppose that the hope of the eschatological prophet like Moses underlies this.[45] We have then to reckon with a popular expectation which was lively in the time of Jesus.[46] It will certainly not have been uniform and had probably in part detached itself from the scripture passage Deut. 18:15–18.[47] But on the basis of the Qumran discoveries it can be shown clearly that actually this text from Deuteronomy stands in the background and was also used in association with the conception of the eschatological prophet; for in the *Testimonia* from Cave 4 Deut. 18:18f.; Num. 24:15–17; Deut 33:8–11 are made use of one after the other as predictions

357

of the eschatological prophet and the two Messiahs Israel and Aaron.[48] In dealing with the question as to the eschatological prophet like Moses we may not now limit ourselves to the places where that Bible passage occurs; rather we must determine the characteristic traits of this conception and thus bring into prominence the singular type of this expectation.

In late rabbinical literature we come across the sentence: "As the first redeemer, so the last redeemer".[49] The first redeemer is Moses, who led the people out of Egypt; the royal Messiah is regarded as the last redeemer. But it is very much a question whether the conception of the eschatological "redeemer" in analogy with Moses and the conception of the Messiah-king originally belonged to one another. Manifestly the tradition of the eschatological prophet has been associated here with messianism at second hand. Since in the rabbinate Moses was set above all prophets, his eschatological antitype could be not any prophetic figure but at best the Messiah. But whilst traditionally the latter has his real task in the function of ruling and in the exercise of right judgment, in the case of the former redeemer conception miracle stands in the foreground.[50] The time of salvation is not looked at as a restoration of David's kingdom, but in analogy with the miraculous act of deliverance wrought by God at the beginning of the people's history under Moses. The exodus to the wilderness plays an essential role. Besides mention is also made of the happenings which took place at the time of the entrance into Canaan under Joshua. It may not be said without more ado that in this case the Moses typology disappears; rather, precisely as the successor of Moses, Joshua is together with him representative of that first redemption, and for that Ecclus. 46:1 LXX presents an instructive text: διάδοχος Μωυσῆ ἐν προφητείαις, ὃς ἐγένετο κατὰ τὸ ὄνομα αὐτοῦ μέγας ἐπὶ σωτηρίᾳ ἐκλεκτῶν αὐτοῦ.[51]

From this a very significant phenomenon in the history of the Judaism of the time of Jesus—one which in its characteristic features has often not been appreciated sufficiently—permits of its being understood. We may not without distinction class as Messiah-pretenders the various agitators of whom accounts have reached us. Josephus, who has treated them very unfairly and called them impostors and cheats, nevertheless allows it to be recognized that while some appeared with pronouncedly fanatical intentions,[52] others renounced all resort to force, led the people into the wilderness and promised them a great miracle to be wrought by God.[53] To the latter there belongs above all the Theudas mentioned in Acts 5:36, who led a great multitude of men with him and promised a repetition of the miraculous crossing of the Jordan;[54] also the unnamed Egyptian Jew who led the people from the wilderness on to the Mount of Olives and there expected that the walls of Jerusalem, as once those of Jericho, would collapse.[55] Likewise there belong to this group the leaders mentioned only summarily who induced men to make an expedition into the wilderness that there they might have part in miraculous happenings.[56] Both in the case of Theudas and in that of the above mentioned Egyptian Josephus remarks that they appeared with the claim of "prophet".[57] A very much later similar phenomenon in Crete in the fifth century A.D. is reported by the Byzantine church historian Socrates, in which a Jew wished to repeat the passage through the sea and to lead his followers directly into the Holy Land; at the same time it is even said that "he alleged that he was Moses".[58] The typological reference to the time of the first redemption is evident, also the analogy with Moses or Joshua stands out positively,[59] and the title prophet seems here to have had a relatively fixed place.

To the same context there also belongs the Samaritan expectation of the *Ta'eb* (*Taheb*), the "returning one".[60] This eschatological figure has also some messianic features, but is primarily the prophet promised in Deut. 18:15, 18 and indeed the returning Moses himself.[61] He was expected as a prophet and a teacher, but likewise also as a worker of miracles. Apart from Samaritan sources,[62] the one can be seen from John 4:25,[63] the other from a report in Josephus, according to which a Samaritan induced the people to get together on Gerizim that there he might show them the temple utensils which Moses had hidden.[64] To the Samaritan Ta'eb conception there belongs authoritative doctrine. But how about that in the expectation of the eschatological prophet?[65] On the basis of the Moses typology this feature is not at all surprising. The Qumran writings also now present evidence for it: the designation "investigator of the torah" (דורש התורה) occurs in several passages.[66] In the several sections of text it refers to different eschatological figures,[67] but certainly nowhere to the royal "Messiah of Israel".[68]

359

In the remaining late Jewish literature attention has to be paid to an idea that is available admittedly only in late texts, the idea of the rabbis about the Messiah as the bringer of a "new torah".[69] As in the case of the conception of the second redeemer, it may be considered whether an old theologumenon has not been transferred by the rabbinate only at second hand to the royal Messiah, a thesis which is again supported by the Qumran texts. Here and there indeed a very different valuation of the prophets and their relation to Moses comes to expression.[70] Where Moses and the prophets are bluntly separated according to rank even the Messiah can possibly come into question as the eschatological figure in analogy with Moses. In view, however, of the unique status of the torah of Moses there can fall to the Messiah himself only the work of correct exposition as previously done by those skilled in the law, although his knowledge of the law will exceed all present possible understanding of it.[71] The revelation of secrets hitherto hid and the laying down of new ordinances is no business of his. Nevertheless one passage in the rabbinical literature shows that the "new torah" of the Messiah also includes alterations of the old torah.[72] This feature may have been repressed deliberately among the rabbis.[73] Notwithstanding it may be assumed for the whole of late Judaism that the "new torah" of the end of time was understood not in antithesis to, but in analogy with the torah of Moses.[74]

Some further observations must be mentioned briefly. They may admittedly not seem intelligible to us in the picture of the eschatological prophet like Moses which the literature, in this respect a very fragmentary literature, presents to us, yet they may possibly be connected with it. Above all regard ought to be had to them because they may play a certain part in the critical examination of New Testament problems. First of all it has to be pointed out that in late Judaism the designation "Servant of God", besides having many other applications, was used in a special way as a name of honour for Moses, and moreover was also a popular designation of the prophets.[75] On that account it may not be excluded that the predicate was also applied to the eschatological prophet. Then it must be mentioned that the motif of an anointing of prophets, with which the Old Testament is already acquainted,[76] appears in the Qumran writings. In two passages the designation משיחים

is unambiguously applied to the Old Testament prophets;[77] a third passage is disputed: in the *Damascus Document* II, 12 the phrase "he allowed them to recognize his Holy Spirit ביד משיחו" could be read in the plural, and then likewise be referred to the prophets of the Old Testament.[78] On the other hand, however, the whole context CD II, 11ff. alludes so unambiguously to the remnant community of this sect that it is not excluded that here the text should be retained in its singular form; then it would doubtless indicate the teacher of righteousness,[79] who consequently would be equated here, as he is also in some other passages, to the eschatological prophet. This exposition nevertheless remains uncertain, and a reference to the Old Testament prophets is also possible in view of the eschatological position of the sect and inasmuch as it regarded the prophetic writings as a storehouse of still hidden secrets. In any case it may be stated, on the basis of these testimonies, that the idea of an anointing of prophets must have been quite common in New Testament times. Thirdly, the question has still to be put how far the idea of the violent death of the prophets had reacted on the figure of the eschatological prophet. The fact that in late Jewish tradition the assassinations of the prophets was given a perfectly typical interpretation, has already been alluded to in another place.[80] The two eschatological witnesses of Rev. 11:3ff. must also suffer death, and it can hardly be disputed that here Moses and Elijah are thought of.[81] Behind this text there doubtless also stands a Jewish tradition, which is preserved for us in a somewhat different form in the late *Apocalypse of Elijah*.[82] Here an expiatory death is certainly not thought of; this motif is foreign to the whole tradition about the assassinations of the prophets. That has its explanation in the fact that according to the view of Palestinian Judaism in the time of Jesus the death of the fathers of Israel, of the righteous and of innocent children possesses vicarious expiatory power,[83] but not the death of the martyrs. Martyrdom was understood as a sign of judgment and of punishment and made atonement merely for the individual's own sins; accordingly the early tradition is not acquainted with a joyous acceptance of the martyr's death; such a death is to be avoided as far as possible. The few witnesses who go beyond that come either from Hellenistic Judaism (2 Macc., 4 Macc.) or from the time of the 'Amoraim.[84] To that there corresponds the fact that in the New Testament the tradition of the martyrdom of the prophets has been brought to bear not merely on the death of Jesus, but especially on the sufferings of the disciples.[85] As far then as suffering and death supervene upon the conception of the eschatological prophet, we must not reckon with the motif of vicarious atonement and much less still with the thought of the suffering Servant of God of Isa. 53.[86]

The conception of the eschatological prophet in the Qumran writings requires separate discussion because there it stands in the framework of an eschatological conception which was systematically pursued and which moreover was used in various ways in the course of the history of the sect. We must start from the much quoted passage of the *Community Rule*: the members of the community "shall follow the primitive laws (*scil.* those enacted by their founders), by which the men of the community have been kept under discipline from the beginning, until the coming of a (the) prophet and of the Messiahs Aaron and Israel".[87] Quite appropriately then the Old Testament prophecies regarding these three eschatological figures are assembled in the *Testimonia* from Cave 4, and at the same time, as has been mentioned, Deut. 18:18 is applied to the eschatological prophet.[88] The conception of a two-Messiah doctrine already appearing in the post-exilic tradition of the Old Testament, which is also adumbrated in the juxtaposition of a royal and high priestly office in the history of late Judaism,[89] is here combined with the conception of the appearance of the eschatological prophet, which by no means necessarily belongs there; for the idea of the eschatological prophet is altogether self-supporting and independent of any messianism. It is very characteristic of the Qumran community that it did not take over the conception of the eschatological prophetic task of Elias, whose function it is to preach repentance among the people and to prepare Israel for judgment—the people were indeed abandoned as a *massa perditionis*, but took over the Moses typology. It is true that all traits are lacking which would call our attention to the eschatological Moses as a worker of miracles, but the more clearly is this eschatological prophet distinguished as a teacher of the torah. This can be recognized particularly well where the expectation of three eschatological figures is given a modification that is extremely characteristic of the sect's understanding of itself. In a surprising way, namely, the prophet is lacking alongside the two Messiahs in some clearly late texts. The eschatological outlook now turns, as it is said once, "from the day of the taking away of the only teacher to the appearance of the Messiahs Aaron and Israel".[90] The conjecture forces itself upon us that the so-called teacher of righteousness (מורה הצדק) has been identified with the eschatological prophet, whose coming was to precede that of the two Messiahs. To that there corresponds the fact that to this teacher of righteousness, who is of decisive consequence to the existence of the sect, pronouncedly prophetic functions have been assigned and it is precisely to him that the manifestation of the secrets of the Old Testament prophetic writings belongs:[91] thus the title "investigator of the torah" was also conferred on him,[92] and he had issued its rule to the community.[93] It has certainly to be observed that an outlook on a prophetic function in the time of salvation itself nevertheless remains preserved, this being manifestly associated with the figure of the messianic high priest.[94] In one passage a future "teacher of righteousness" is set side by side with the now living "investigator of the torah",[95] and in connection with this it must be observed that both "investigator of the torah" and "teacher of righteousness" are titles which could possibly be conferred on quite different persons.[96] The expectation of a return of the historical "teacher of righteousness" may not be concluded from such a passage.[97] In all the uncertainty which for the present is still attendant on the interpretation of the Qumran texts—and that is associated not lastly with the fact that there various tendencies and documents of different ages are met with[98]—this understanding of the conception of the eschatological prophet and of its application to the historical teacher of righteousness has still something in it.[99] The adhesion to Deut. 18:16, 18 thus gives proof of a Moses typology, in which to the eschatological prophet as the forerunner of both Messiahs there belongs above all the authentic interpretation of the law, the laying down of new ordinances and the revelation of secrets that have hitherto been hidden.[100] The Qumran texts thus in fact exhibit "a rather buried tradition which reaches far back and existed side by side with other streams of messianic expectation up to the time of Jesus and beyond it".[101]

In conclusion the question must be answered how the idea of the eschatological prophet and messianism stand to one another. As has been said, it is wrong straight away and on principle to designate the eschatological prophet as the "messianic prophet".[102] Precisely the Qumran finds show that it is a matter of a figure who is clearly distinguished from the royal Messiah as also from the priestly. And the already discussed tradition about the first and second redeemer, the Moses typology proper, also permits us to recognize that it is a matter of a quite singular type of eschatological expectation. That is also not contradicted by the fact that in the Old Testament and in late Judaism mention can be made of an anointing of prophets and consequently of prophets as "anointed ones", for on the one hand it is a matter here precisely of the assignation of an altogether specific office, and on the other hand the designation is not technical in the same sense as in the case of the royal and high priestly Messiah, as emerges from 1 QS IX, 10f.[103] Because in our customary speech the term "Messiah" belongs to royal messianism and has merely been transferred to the office of the eschatological high priest regarded as an accurate parallel, the designation messianic prophet must be avoided. The situation is of course somewhat different when it is verified that expectations of the eschatological prophet and the messianic king can have largely combined with one another. This presents itself as extremely probable in the Samaritan eschatology and therefore holds good also for the Samaritan prophet who appeared under Pontius Pilate. John 6:14f. also indicates that the two conceptions were beside and in one another: on the basis of the σημεῖον of the multiplication of bread the people recognize the "prophet" in Jesus and desire to make him their "king". A reference to Deut. 18:15ff. may not be disputed,[104] for precisely this miracle is understood as a repetition of the feeding with manna and assumes the Moses typology.[105] We must reckon then with a transition to the idea of the royal Messiah, but this may not simply be brought in everywhere. In the same way there can of course also come about an intermingling or at least an assimilation of elements of the expectation of Elias and of the expectation of Moses. That already emerges from the setting beside one another of these two figures in Mk. 9:4 and Rev. 11:3ff. But elsewhere also single traits may occasionally have been carried over, as e.g. the function of a teacher of the torah to Elias as the eschatological high priest. But on the whole the expectation of an eschato-

logical prophet, independent of royal and high priestly messianism, can nevertheless be assumed for late Judaism, and this
has expressed itself in the two basic forms already discussed,
associated on the one hand with Elias following Mal. 3:1, 23f.,
and associated with Moses on the other hand following Deut.
18:15, 18. Whilst in the first case the preaching of repentance
and the proclamation of the judgment of God must be regarded
as the typical elements, so in the second case must miracle and
authoritative teaching.

2. John the Baptist as the Eschatological Elias

The penitential homily of John the Baptist has a pronouncedly eschatological character and points to the coming
of Jahwe which is close at hand.[107] That John claimed to be
the eschatological prophet, is nowhere discernible. Even the
Baptist's clothing does not permit such a conclusion, for if the
present presentation in Mk. 1:6 par. recalls Elias, yet in this
regard an early prophetic tradition lived on and had not
necessarily a direct reference to the Tishbite.[108] Still less can
the baptism of John be fitted into any such association of ideas,
rather it was precisely this that was regarded as his characteristic
proper and that conferred on him his special status.[109]

Nevertheless it was easy to apply to this preacher of the
coming judgment of God the motif of the eschatological prophet
when there was a desire to designate his function in the salvation history. At the same time, of course, only the conception
of the returning Elias came into question, and actually in
Baptist circles as in primitive Christianity this attained great
significance. The Infancy Story, Lk. 1:5–25, 57–66, in part also
vv. 67–80, may today be claimed with tolerable certainty as a
portion of the tradition of the Baptist community.[110] In Lk.
1:14–17 in the announcement of the angel to Zacharias it is
expressly said that the promised child is to accomplish his task
"in the spirit and in the power of Elias"; he will fulfil the
functions of Elias, will be "great" and walk before God the
Lord.[111] Lk. 1:76–79 also assumes this tradition, although
Elias is not expressly mentioned; instead of that we find there
the predicate $\pi\rho o\phi\eta\tau\eta s$ $\dot{v}\psi\dot{\iota}\sigma\tau o v$. Vv. 76f., 79b keep wholly
within the framework of the promise of Mal. 3:1, 23f. A far-
reaching statement is certainly made in Lk. 1:78, 79a, for by
$\dot{\alpha}\nu\alpha\tau o\lambda\dot{\eta}$ $\dot{\epsilon}\xi$ $\dot{v}\psi o v s$ and the quotation from Isa. 9:1 a messianic

identification mark is certainly intended.[112] Here in fact it can
be asked whether the Baptist community had not taken their
master himself for the Messiah.[113] But it is advisable to bring
in another consideration. As is well known, the period vv. 76–79
is syntactically very far from lucid.[114] When the verses 76f.,
79b, which really belong closely to one another, are taken
together, there results a smooth construction with two parallel
infinitival clauses. Accordingly in vv. 78, 79a we may certainly
be concerned with a subsequent extension.[115] The question then
is whether this insertion comes from the Baptist community
and is to be understood as an attempt to present John as the
Messiah or whether it goes back to primitive Christendom, which
wished to have this understood as a reference to Jesus.[116]
From the composition of the *Benedictus* an unambiguous
answer can be obtained: already for long the seam between
vv. 68–75 and vv. 76–79 has been noticed;[117] the eschatological
hymn vv. 68–75, as can be easily recognized, assumes the
national messianic hope, it is therefore, quite apart from its
assuredly Judaic origin, not possible in the framework of the
Baptist ideas that come to expression in Lk. 1:14–17 and 1:76f.
79b; the genethliacon[118] vv. 76–79 contains in its present
form[119] and in association with vv. 68–75 the idea that the
"prophet of the Highest" is not the forerunner of God, but the
forerunner of the Messiah Jesus, and that suggested itself since
the Kyrios title (v. 76b) had a dual meaning in the primitive
church. Vv. 78, 79a, together with vv. 68–75, are thus a
Christian addition; through the reference to the "dayspring
from on high" the *Benedictus* received its unity in Christ and
became an appropriate conclusion to the story of the infancy of
John, in so far as this child pointed beyond himself to the one
who was coming after him.[120] That in Baptist circles John was
also regarded in some way or other as the Messiah is not
excluded, but is not evident on the basis of Luke I.[121] According to it his status is that of the eschatological prophet in conformity with the person and task of Elias.

Jesus was baptized by John and, as the Synoptic Gospels
still let us see, also repeatedly expressed Himself regarding him.
The so-called discourse about the Baptist Matt. 11:7–19 par.
(Q) represents in its present form a subsequent composition.
Four early and in their basic form certainly genuine single
traditions are here turned to account: the sayings group vv.

7b–9, the word v. 11, the so-called assailant saying vv. 12f., and the parable of the children dancing vv. 16–19; the parable is useful in this connection only, it is true, because of its old but nevertheless secondary exposition in vv. 18f.; originally, however, it had no reference at all to John and Jesus[122] and can therefore be eliminated. V. 10 with the citation Mal. 3:1 and Matt. 11:14f., the statement about John as Elias together with the following "rousing formula", are additions made in composition. Between this and vv. 7b–9, 11, 12f. there is a tension that cannot be mistaken. These single traditions may be briefly dealt with. No additions can be seen in vv. 7b–9 par. It is disputed whether in v. 9b the opinion of the people is rejected and accordingly Jesus intends an accusation of the people, whose enthusiasm for the Baptist had already long ago died away,[123] or whether in v. 9b a response presents itself (similarly as in v.8b) in which Jesus confirms the opinion of the people expressed in v. 9a and at the same time formulates his own judgment regarding the Baptist.[124] The latter may merit the preference, and περισσότερος προφήτου then means that Jesus does not at all wish to have the Baptist fitted into any one of the usual categories, but in this way describes his function simply *per negationem*. Here the question must be asked whether the statement did not receive its original point subsequently from v. 11b.[125] In any case v. 11b presents considerable difficulties which cannot without more ado be cleared away by referring ὁ μικρότερος to Jesus[126] or associating ἐν τῇ βασιλείᾳ τῶν οὐρανῶν in a causal sense with the predicate.[127] But however that may be, v. 11a presents a judgment regarding the Baptist the genuineness of which is not to be disputed; and again a status is ascribed to John which is not characterized by any current predicate of dignity. Vv. 12f., the enigmatical assailant saying,[128] also permits us to recognize this much, that in view of the dawning kingdom of God Jesus assigns to the Baptist a singular task, which is to be understood not from ancient prophecy, but rather from the new man who is pressing his way forward. Therefore as in v. 9b, but implicitly also in v. 11a, John is not regarded as the fulfiller and eschatological representative of prophecy, but is taken completely out of the series of prophets.[129] For this reason the equating of the Baptist to Elias cannot be carried back to Jesus.[130]

As the New Testament lets us see, the primitive church

carefully endeavoured to fit John correctly into its preaching. In doing so it was on the one hand directed by Jesus' own high estimate of John, but on the other hand had to fix accurately the relation of the Baptist to Jesus. It was also easy for it to jump at the idea of the eschatological Elias, except that now John had to be understood not as the forerunner of God but as the forerunner of the Messiah. The earliest evidence for the equating of the Baptist to Elias within the Christian tradition is the already touched upon discourse about the Baptist, Matt. 11:7ff. par. in its made-up condition. As early as v. 11b the judgment on the Baptist is restricted: he may be the greatest among all that are born of women, he still stands nevertheless before the beginning of the time of salvation. Accordingly he is not the watchman at the turning-point of the aeons, who keeps his post onwards from the dawning of the future, but only the last and most significant link in the chain of messengers from God who lead on to the time of salvation. In this sense the word from Mal. 3:1 in Matt. 11:10 about the eschatological messenger holds good of him. This citation has certainly been given— probably under the influence of Exod. 23:20—a Christian adaptation[131] that the messianic reference may be more clearly discernible. Matt. 11:14f. takes up this motif. Moreover the question must be put whether this explicit equating of the Baptist to Elias goes back to the logia source or belongs to the redaction of Matt. The first of these possibilities may be favoured by the fact that Luke does not have the text of Matt. 11.12f. in this context, but in another very loose sequence of sayings (Lk. 16:15–18). On the other hand the "rousing formula" in Matt. 11:15 and actually in the framework of the Q-tradition is surprising, whilst it seems to have its roots rather in the Markan parable tradition or the apocalyptic epistle; moreover the introduction, "if ye will receive it" v. 14a, is noteworthy in this section of text which is otherwise very thetically formulated. Thus the conclusion must be drawn that vv. 14f. goes back to the evangelist,[132] who has thereby continued and made clear the intention to which a start has been given in v. 10.[133] Vv. 16–19 fit into the train of thought of the discourse about the Baptist which is orientated by v. 10: while the Baptist marks the period of asceticism and repentance,[134] the work of the Son of man belongs to the days of the time of salvation, and its time is therefore one of joy; the ministry of the Baptist is thus again demarcated from that of Jesus and is not seen along with it.[135] If Matt. 11:14f. is to be ascribed to the evangelist, then he has been able thereby not only to carry v. 10 further but also to make full use of the portion of tradition Mk. 9:9ff.

Mk. 9: (9f.) 11–13 has undergone much editorial revision: as the conclusion of the story of the transfiguration Mark has formulated in vv. 9f. the thoughts that are important for his Christology and at the same time in v. 9b has utilized a passion and resurrection prediction, the first part of which he has added in v. 12b, whereby he certainly destroys the clear train of thought in vv. 11–13, but in place of that has secured an analogy between the suffering of the Baptist and the suffering of Jesus. Therewith he has emphatically rounded off a thought which already suggests itself in 1:14 and then was decisive for the start of the story of the Baptist's end in 6:17–29.[136] What about v. 13b? Has Mark also added this statement regarding the Scriptural necessity of the suffering of the Baptist because he was interested in the comparison with Jesus? That is hardly likely. The rejection of the two messengers of God also comes to expression in Matt. 11:16–19; besides the death of the Baptist there was the conception of the suffering and death of the returning Elias, wherefore the καθὼς γέγραπται ἐπ' αὐτόν may refer not to the Old Testament but to apocryphal tradition.[137] On the whole it is seen clearly in this section vv. 11, 12a, 13 that the primitive church worked out the whole work and life of the Baptist after the model of the Elias who returns before the time of salvation as the preacher of repentance. Whilst in Mark in this place an explicit identification with the Baptist is wanting, although there is no real doubt about it, Matt. in 17:13 has set it emphatically at the end, a further indication that Matt. 11:14f. is also to be ascribed to the evangelist.[138]

As the last section of text Mk. 1:2–8 has to be discussed. It is frequently assumed that this passage was provided only by the evangelist and that he also set in front the two quotations.[139] On the other hand Lohmeyer maintains the unity of the section; trait by trait, line by line of the Old Testament citation has been taken up ingeniously in the story that follows.[140] These solutions are both unsatisfactory. Wellhausen has already pointed out that such a combination of words of Scripture as presents itself in vv. 2f. is not in the manner of Mark,[141] and the permeation of the narrative section with elements of the citation would have been altogether strange on the part of the evangelist. Wherefore we shall have to reckon with a piece of tradition which had come down and which, unaltered in essentials, was taken up by Mark. That various traditions have flowed together, is not to be disputed. It is shown by the presentation of the Baptist at the Jordan in vv. 4f.; the description of his dress in v. 6 and the double logion in vv. 7f. On the other hand, the quotation from Isaiah that has been set in front has had an effect in the motif of the wilderness preacher in v. 4,[142] and the κηρύσσειν which occurs twice, in v. 4 and v. 7, is also associated with the conception of the crier in the wilderness, although here, as in the description of the baptism in v. 4b, a Christian terminology has had an effect; the unusual phrase κηρύσσειν βάπτισμα[143] is intended to underline John's function as a herald. We must then assume that the history of the evolution of the passage was a somewhat long one. The characteristic which embraces the statements regarding the baptism in Jordan, the clothing and the messianic proclamation, is now the role of the wilderness preacher. Whatever traits recall Elias can be best seen in v. 6, but, as has been mentioned, they are not clear. But that then means that of the citations in vv. 2f. the word from Mal. 3:1, recast as in Matt, 11:10 par., has no actual importance, on the other hand Isa. 40:3 is dominant.[144] While the messianic reference in the first citation comes to expression only in the twice occurring σου, in the second Jesus is spoken of as κύριος.[145] This use of the Kyrios title shows, just as does the dependence on the Septuagint, that here tradition of the Hellenistic church has to be assumed, whilst the citation from Malachi has indeed obtained its New Testament form independently of the Septuagint and very probably in the sphere of Semitic speech. It is an old offence that the citations in vv. 2f. are, when introduced, described as words of Isaiah. Accordingly the suggestion has frequently been made that actually the citation from Malachi is to be regarded as a subsequent interpolation. In favour of that it can be said that this citation is lacking in Matt. and Luke and therefore probably did not stand in their *Vorlage*.[146] On the other hand, however, it is not to be denied that both citations speak of going before and of preparing the way, and therefore may manifestly have been bound together as parallel statements, in which case Isa. 40:3 may later have been put by the side of the early Scriptural proof Mal. 3:1.[147] And Mk. 1:2–8 shows how the Elias motif may then have receded and been almost superseded by the idea of John as the crier in the wilderness.[148] Mark may also have taken over the word from Malachi, whilst Matt. and Luke cut it out because it did not come into question as a citation from Isaiah, did not really define this section of text and besides appeared once again within the Q-tradition.

In conclusion, a glance has to be cast at the conceptions of the evangelists.

Mark has taken up both traditions about John as Elias and as the preacher in the wilderness, and he has given the Baptist an important place by setting his work under the leading idea of ἀρχὴ τοῦ εὐαγγελίου. In this way the intention which was to be recognized in the judgment of Jesus has been retained, and at the same time subordination to Jesus is clearly brought to expression through the idea of John as the preparer of the way, as indeed also in 1:14 where the times of the Baptist and of John are clearly distinguished from one another.

Matthew has taken over the Markan text, has used material from the logia source and, as has already been shown, has especially emphasized the equating of John to Elias.[149] He is also interested in the close association of, as also in the distinction between, John the Baptist and Jesus. Since because of the different beginning of his Gospel the significant heading of the Markan Gospel had to drop out, Matthew brings the Baptist into his Gospel in such a way that in Matt. 3:2 with μετανοεῖτε ἤγγικεν γὰρ ἡ βασιλεία τῶν οὐρανῶν he puts into his mouth the same message as that with which according to 4:17 Jesus also begins his work; the two are distinguished only by their different functions in the history of salvation, and that is made clear by the Old Testament citations in 3:3 and 4:14–16.[150]

Luke has proceeded otherwise. Lk. 3:15 reflects discussions with the Baptist community. This as also his own conception of the history of salvation led him to co-ordinate the figure and work of the Baptist with the time of the old covenant and of the prophets; we need but to compare the ἀπὸ τότε . . . εὐαγγελίζεται in the new rendering of the assailant saying in Lk. 16:16 with Mk. 1:1. Luke has taken over the Q-version of Jesus' discourse about the Baptist; Mk. 1:2–8 and also the story of the baptism in vv. 9–11 have been considerably recast; the characterizing of John as Elias certainly remains standing in the nativity narrative, but Mk. 9:11–13 has been completely cut out.[151] John has proceeded in a yet more radical way. The forerunner has become the witness to Jesus.[152] The predicate Christ as also the designation as Elias or as the prophet are refused by the Baptist himself.[153] Isa. 40:3 is referred to John not now in association with the conception of the eschatological prophet, but in antithesis to it (John 1:20f.).

3. *Jesus as the New Moses*

The question whether and in what way the idea of the eschatological prophet was applied to Jesus, has not been put for a long time and only recently has it received attention.[154]

After his appearance Jesus was first regarded mainly as a rabbi. Certain of his traits, however, did not harmonize with the figure of a scribe and recalled rather the appearance of a prophet. A stock-taking of such peculiarities led to a remarkable comparison with the "ordinary" prophet.[155] There is, however, a series of indications that the idea of the eschatological prophet was carried over to Jesus and that this was apparently done very early; a wider activity of a somewhat modified form within the Hellenistic tradition of primitive Christianity can be comprehended more definitely. Here we are concerned throughout with the type of expectation that bears upon it the stamp of Deut. 18:15ff.[156] On the one hand, that is easy to understand for the reason that Jesus did not appear, as did the Baptist, as a preacher of repentance, and moreover the Baptist community had already taken over the Elias conception. On the other hand, the use of that late Jewish conception is not surprising when we realize that of all previously imprinted ideas of a salvation figure it most easily harmonized with Jesus' earthly work and could be taken over without overmuch remodelling. The Son of man conception was associated with the apocalyptic final happenings, the Messiah conception assumed the taking over of an actual royal dominion and the high priestly messianism was altogether remote, priestly features being foreign to the earthly Jesus. The addressing of Jesus as "Rabbi" and "Lord" was not originally connected either with any designation of dignity or with any conception of salvation. Thus there remained only the expectation of a new Moses. Since Jesus appeared as an authoritative teacher and interpreter of the law and furthermore as a worker of miracles, this conception may even have suggested itself. Since Jesus' death was moreover brought into association with the murder of the Jewish prophets,[157] it itself can have been understood in analogy with the apocryphal tradition of the suffering of the eschatological prophet.[158]

We must proceed from texts in which the designation prophet is expressly included or Deut. 18:15ff. is quoted; and although that means dealing with late evidence, still some characteristic features can be recognized in this way. A very interesting tradition is the discourse of Stephen in Acts 7:2-53. It begins with a long historical summary vv. 2-34, which, as the content and the general use of the Septuagint show, doubtless goes back directly to the Hellenistic synagogue, with the spirit of which it is stamped.[159] The interpolated v. 25—perhaps v. 22b has also been supplied—and the section vv. 35-39a present a Moses typology, at the centre of which stands Deut. 18:15. Jesus is indeed not expressly named as the fulfiller of this promise, but without doubt this whole passage has been drafted in view of His activity. The next double section vv. 39b-43 and vv. 44-50 presents, in immediate connection, a polemic against the Jews who persist in unbelief and their false worship; finally vv. 51-53 brings a concluding accusation bound up with the charge of murdering the prophets and of putting Jesus to death.[160] Even if in vv. 35ff. particular portions of a summary of Jewish history may have been taken over—especially is this to be contemplated in vv. 39b-41 and vv. 44-47—yet vv. 35-53 are Christian in construction and execution, a thing that emerges from the theme as also from the elaborate formal wording, in vv. 39-50 from the association of an informing section with an interpreting prophetic word.[161] The word of threatening from Amos 5:25-27 shows that vv. 39ff. also must be understood typologically and consequently the end of v. 43 must be referred to the catastrophe of A.D. 70.[162] Then at the same time the continuation in vv. 44ff. also explains itself. What presents itself here is by no means, as is usually asserted, just a very loose catchword addition *ad vocem* σκηνή, which on the whole may perhaps be merely accidental; rather the temple worship practised by the Jews is, as the word of the prophet in vv. 48ff.

shows, a service of idols which denies the true godhead of God. That the conclusion vv. 51–53 is Christian is quite obvious; here on the other hand the question now presents itself how far a redactional encroachment by Luke is discernible. The large second portion of the discourse vv. (22b. 25) 35–50 does not show any Lukan characteristic.[163] While so far as the history of salvation is concerned Luke thinks in the schema of prediction and fulfilment and accordingly makes use of Scriptural proof,[164] here such a purely typological way of thinking presents itself as is not usually found in Luke, to whom what matters is the temporal course of events. In Acts 7:22b, 25, 35ff., it is a matter of analogy. According to v. 25 the Jews do not understand that God wills to give them σωτηρία by the hand of Moses, according to vv. 35ff it is a question of the sending of the ἄρχων καὶ λυτρωτής, in v. 36 of his τέρατα καὶ σημεῖα and in v. 38 of the λόγια ζῶντα, which he has received to pass on; in between there stands the citation about the sending of the prophet like Moses. In the same way the statements regarding the idols and the temple worship together with the prophetic judgments are referred to the time of the Jews then living. With this there also harmonizes the inclusive word in v. 51 regarding obstinacy and impenitence with the concluding "as your fathers did, so do ye". The situation is somewhat different in vv. 52f. In both the traditional motifs of the persecuting and killing of the prophets as also the mediation of the law through angels, Luke has certainly also gone back to a document that lay before him, but he binds this up with what is his own: for one thing with the function of the prophets as προκαταγγεί-λοντες, whereby the specific place of the prophets in the history of salvation is stressed; for another with the designation of Jesus as δίκαιος, which is, as Lk. 23:47; Acts 22:14 (also 3:14) show, a characteristic motif of the Lukan Christology; finally the accusation of the Jews as the betrayers and murderers of Jesus is also a genuinely Lukan trait.[165] The redactional encroachment may then be restricted to v. 52b, while Acts 7: (22b) 25, 37–52a, 53 represents a pre-Lukan Moses-Jesus typology that had its origin in Hellenistic Jewish Christianity.[166]

As the second text there has to be discussed the discourse in Acts 3:12–26, which was composed by Luke but works up older material. The reference to the matter of the healing of the cripple in vv. 12 and 16 can be left out of account. Vv. 17f.

with the motif of ignorance and with the prophesying of the
prophets are pronouncedly Lukan, only the formal παθεῖν
τὸν χριστὸν (αὐτοῦ) having been taken over.[167] The admonition to repent in v. 19 belongs to the schema of the discourse,[168]
but possibly v. 19b and certainly vv. 20, 21a is tradition of an
early coinage.[169] V. 21b returns to the idea of prophetic prediction. Then there follows as Christological Scriptural proof,
which in v. 23 also motivates the admonition to repent, the
reference to Deut. 18:15(f.), 19 with inclusion of the αὐτοῦ
ἀκούεσθε, which is lacking in Acts 7:37 but well known from
the story of the transfiguration. Yet a third time Luke in v. 24
brings in the idea of the prophetic proclamation of salvation,
after which there follows in v. 25 an application such as is
made in Gal. 3:8 of Gen. 12:3; 22:18. The concluding v. 26 is
certainly Lukan in its formulation,[170] but the predicate ὁ
παῖς αὐτοῦ expressly referred back through ἀναστήσας ὁ θεός
to Deut. 18:15 must come from a definite tradition. The same
may be asserted of ἐδόξασεν τὸν παῖδα αὐτοῦ in Acts 3:13,
a formulation taken over from Isa. 52:13, which is bound up
with the title, derived from a narrative about Moses, of God as
the God of the fathers (Exod. 3:6, 15). Moreover the section
vv. 13b–15 with its triple climax of accusation is again characteristic of the author of Acts.[171] The discourse is on the
whole his work; Luke has taken over in a stereotyped form the
wording of v. 13a, the phrase about the suffering of Christ in
v. 18 and the portion of tradition in vv. (19b) 20, 21, but this
does not exclude the possibility that he has worked up yet other
early traditions, and that holds good above all for the prophecy
in Deut. 18:15ff. referred to Jesus and also for the different
predicates: δίκαιος is indeed a favourite word with Luke, but it
may have had an early history; also ἀρχηγὸς τῆς ζωῆς, which
has a parallel in 5:31, was not first minted by Luke. For our
context the question has to be asked above all as to the derivation and meaning of ἅγιος. Besides in Lk. 4:34//Mk. 1:24 it recurs
only in Acts 4:27, 30 and there in association with the Servant
of God designation; it is thus not a specifically Lukan word. The
conjecture is easy that in Acts 3:14 also it stands in association
with the Servant of God tradition. Only the central section of
this discourse vv. 17–21 is controlled by the Christos title, the
kerygma vv. 13–15 and the Scriptural proof vv. 22–26 however by the Servant of God title, which stands in connection

with the prediction of the prophet like Moses. Acts 4:30 contains as the conclusion of the church's prayer the phrase διὰ τοῦ ὀνόματος τοῦ ἁγίου παιδός σου ᾿Ιησοῦ and makes it possible for us to recognize the early rooting in liturgy of the designation of Jesus as the Servant of God.[172] It will later emerge that for ὁ ἅγιος παῖς in 4:27 we may have to reckon with early tradition. Accordingly Luke was acquainted with a view which regarded Jesus as the new Moses predicted in Deut. 18:15ff. and designated him as the "holy Servant of God".[173]

In Acts 7:35ff. it is a matter exclusively of the Moses typology and of Jesus' eschatological office as prophet without any association of this with the confession of Jesus' messiahship. In Acts 3:13-26. Jesus as the promised prophet and the Servant of God is also the suffering and returning Christ. Once again the tradition of Jesus as the eschatological prophet has been worked up in another way in Lk. 24:13-35, the story of the Emmaus disciples. This story, which certainly has an early core, has in its present rendering been extended in a twofold way.[174] As additions there are to be regarded: the appendix vv. 33-35 and all the elements which are associated with the conversation, therefore vv. 14, 15a, 17-27, 32. The original story only recorded that the risen Jesus as an unknown traveller met the two disciples and made Himself known to them at a meal, and then disappeared.[175] To that there was added as a completely new focal-point the instructive conversation, furthermore in vv. 33-35 and vv. 21b-24 the linkage with other Easter narratives.[176] Vv. 19-27 are of interest in reference to the matter now being dealt with. Three different elements have been interfused; a statement about Jesus as ἀνὴρ προφήτης in vv. 19b, 21a, then in vv. 20, 21b-24 a summary of the passion and Easter happenings,[177] finally in vv. 25-27 a tradition about the passion of Christ as necessary for Scriptural reasons. Altogether it can be said that the intention is to correct the interpretation of Jesus as a prophet by that of the suffering Christ; but for the question as to the primitive Christian idea of the eschatological prophet this does not at present need to be considered. Vv. 19b brings the motif of potency in deeds and words which also appears in Acts 7:22b, 36, 38. Moreover there belong here as parallels—even if the title prophet is lacking or Deut. 18:15ff. is not mentioned—the passages Acts 2:22 and 10:38, where certainly only deeds are mentioned.[178] That in the tradition about the eschatological prophet like Moses the working of miracles played a decisive role, is already recognizable in late Jewish tradition, and precisely in view of Jesus' earthly life it manifestly attained great significance. Could it be shown that here in fact a very early conception presents itself, then it would follow that Jesus' earthly work was of importance from the beginning at least in a certain stratum of tradition. If it is frequently said with reference precisely to Acts 2:22, 36 that to begin with Jesus' life was regarded as "not messianic", that accords well in the sense that no use was made of royal messianism which however does not mean that no sort of statement was made about Jesus' function as the bringer of salvation; in these passages there is quite certainly no talk of Jesus as a ψιλὸς ἄνθρωπος, such as in later heretical tradition he was understood to have been. In another regard also we must be cautious and may not consider that Jesus is designated an "ordinary" prophet, one, i.e. who stands in a series with the Old Testament messengers of God, even if there is no wording with the definite article. For, if after the long period when there was no prophet at all, a prophet again appeared, then he was certainly the promised eschatological prophet, and his miracles, as also his words, identified him as such. Lk. 24:21a is difficult.[179] In Acts 7:35 λυτρωτής side by side with ἄρχων and δικαστής is the decisive predicate of dignity for Moses, by whose hand God is to give σωτηρία. To λύτρωσις there certainly belongs a mighty working through miracle and the proclamation of God's will, even if in the case of Moses or in the case of Jesus both are refused by the people. It must now be considered whether a future act of redemption is not also in view. It would then be explicable how the idea of the prophet can have been united with the expectation of the return as the royal Messiah of the Jesus who had been removed to heaven (Acts 3:20f.)[180]. In Lk. 24:21, however, there is quite another turn. There the statement about Jesus as a prophet is brought into association with the hope of the realization of an earthly messianic kingdom, a hope which according to these disciples had been disappointed. Such fanatical expectations were of course rejected and replaced by the true, scriptural interpretation of Jesus as the suffering Christ. Nevertheless it remains to ask whether the very carefully worded v. 19b does not take up an early tradition of the post-Easter church, to which the αὐτός ἐστιν ὁ μέλλων λυτροῦσθαι τὸν Ἰσραήλ in v. 21a belongs and which can have had a thoroughly positive, i.e. eschatological meaning. An expectation of the kind restricted to Israel was later regarded as insufficient and was replaced by other conceptions. Yet this remains a conjecture. What the text certainly permits us to recognize is again an application of the prophet conception to the earthly work of Jesus and a close association with the Messiah conception.

The decisive question now is whether the idea, clearly palpable in these texts, of Jesus as the eschatological prophet like Moses reaches back to the early Palestinian stratum of the New Testament tradition and whether it had precipitated itself in independence of the prophet designation and the word in Deuteronomy.[181] Otherwise the objection may be made that it is palpable exclusively in the Lukan writings and in consequence of that ought to be regarded as a Lukan theologumenon. But against that there tells the fact that precisely in the special material of his Gospel Luke has preserved material that in part is astonishingly early; in addition there is the fact that the three texts that have been dealt with, Acts 7:2–53; 3:12–26; and Lk. 24:13–35, contain the tradition that is under discussion in very varied forms; in the discourses of the Acts which he himself constructed Luke has also made use of very early material, even if it remains preserved only in part in its original form.[182]

Inquiry must now be made as to how far the reports of Jesus' work have been determined by the idea of the eschatological prophet. First of all we shall refer to the demand for a sign in Mk. 8:11f. par.; Lk. 11:(16) 29 par. (Q). It is well known that attestation by miracles was not required of the rabbi. The task of the scribe was instruction, even if ability to work miracles occasionally supervened. On the other hand, it is inapposite in the matter of the demand for a sign to think right away of the attestation of messiahship.[183] The attestation miracle has at all times its place in connection with the claim of the prophets, and the Old Testament already contains vehement discussions regarding its meaning and trustworthiness.[184] The sign "from heaven" is not a mighty act wrought by one's own power, but a legitimating miracle granted by God.[185] Jesus refused the demand of His opponents.[186] On the other hand, the church, as will be shown directly, understood a whole series of His miracles in this way. That shows that we must think not just of the attestation of any prophet but in fact of that of the eschatological prophet. Of that there are still other indications; for one thing, attestation by miracle played a decisive role precisely in the case of the agitators of that time who appeared as eschatological prophets;[187] for another, the Johannine version of the demand for a sign in John 6:30f. contains a direct reference to the feeding with manna by Moses.[188]

John 6:30f. is a bridge to the narrative of the miraculous feeding: Mk. 6:35–44 parr.; Mk. 8:1–10 par.; John 6.1–15. We can here dispense with the relation of the different renderings of the story and with their details. The reminiscences of the eucharistic mode of speech in the accounts of the breaking and distributing of the bread are certainly secondary. Originally it was a matter of a miracle of the eschatological prophet who repeats in the wilderness the feeding of the time of Moses.[189] This remains preserved most clearly in the Gospel of John, where, in the acclamation of the people, an acclamation that is elsewhere lacking, it is said: οὗτός ἐστιν ἀληθῶς ὁ προφήτης ὁ ἐρχόμενος εἰς τὸν κόσμον, and where at the same time all misunderstanding in a messianic sense is prevented by the flight of Jesus.[190]

The question must be considered whether the raisings of the dead do not belong to this circle of ideas. In Lk. 7:16 the story of the young man at Nain concludes with the designation of Jesus as προφήτης μέγας. That the article is lacking does not tell against that, [191] there being a parallel in Lk. 24:19b (21a); moreover μέγας is understood in the sense of peculiar distinction; finally the eschatological aspect is made clear by the statement about the visitation of God.[192] Through rabbinical tradition we are acquainted with the idea that at the time of the giving of the law on Sinai there was no sick person and no power over the people was given to the angel of death,[193] and in this passage that may have been utilized typologically. Certainly it must be observed that influences of the Elias tradition can also be present and are clearly in evidence in Lk. 7:11–17.[194] But the basis of the idea of Jesus as the eschatological prophet is still the Moses typology, in which the title προφήτης has also its fixed place.

The take-over of certain features of the Elias tradition may be connected not only with the fact that raising of the dead, temptation and removal have direct parallels there, but also with the fact that Jesus' working of miracles altogether bears upon it the stamp of the Old Testament idea of the charismatic person whom God has endowed. This has already emerged earlier in our discussion of Mk. 1:23f.[195] and is also assumed in Acts 10:38b and in 2:22. It can then hardly be surprising that the conceptions of Jesus as ἅγιος τοῦ θεοῦ and παῖς θεοῦ have united and that occasionally the designation ὁ ἅγιος παῖς θεοῦ also appears (Acts 4:27, 30). The stories of the miracles only rarely allow this conception to be recognized in detail, but the text Matt. 11:2–6‖Lk. 7:18f., 22f. presents important evidence. τὰ ἔργα τοῦ χριστοῦ in Matt. 11:2 and ὁ κύριος in Lk. 7:19 are to be regarded as secondary. The phrase σὺ εἶ ὁ ἐρχόμενος is especially worthy of note, as is also the combination of the citations Isa. 35:5f.; 61:1 together with blessing on those who are not offended in Jesus (vv. 5f.).[196] ὁ ἐρχόμενος can hardly be associated in a fixed terminological sense with a definitive stratum of tradition. "Coming" means all that stands in association with the time of salvation, the new aeon, the dominion of God, the world judge, Elias, the Messiah, etc.[197] If ὁ ἐρχόμενος is used here without being characterized more closely, then thought is centred on the Baptist's statement about the "one coming after me", which was widely disseminated in the earliest Christian preaching.[198] Jesus' answer is anything but "messianic". Working miracles and proclaiming glad tidings is not the task of the royal Messiah.[199] On the other hand, these functions harmonize excellently with the idea of the eschatological prophet.[200] Again the Sinai period is typologically in view, supplemented with Deutero-Isaianic predictions. At the same time the proclamation of Jesus is distinguished not as torah doctrine but as eschatological glad tidings, as intelligence of the dawning of the kingdom of God.[201] The word בשׂר is used religio-technically first in Deutero-Isaiah, as is also the participle מְבַשֵּׂר belonging to it, and in Isa. 61:1 it was already associated with the tradition of the eschatological prophet.[202] It remained lively in late Judaism, even if associated with very different figures.[203] It being obvious that precisely Isa. 61:1 played an essential role in the primitive Christian conception of Jesus as the eschatological prophet, it is not out of the question that the word εὐαγγελίζεσθαι was originally rooted in this stratum of tradition.

The importance of Isa. 61:1 becomes particularly clear in Lk. 4:16–30. This story of Jesus' first appearance in Nazareth cannot be regarded as a Lukan revision of Mk. 6:1–5;[204] the evangelist has also taken over Lk. 5:1–11 from a special tradition and exchanged it for a Markan story. The incorporating of it at the beginning of the ministry of Jesus goes back of course to Luke; but it has already for a long time been observed that this is hardly the intention of the story itself, but rather that traces of its later dating in v. 23b have not even been obliterated.[205] The text is not a unity. There is a seam between v. 22a and v. 22b.[206] Vv. 16–22a is to be regarded as an independent portion of tradition, also the comparison with Elias and Eliseus in vv. 25–27.[207] Vv. 22b–24 assumes a tradition similar to Mk. 6:1–5,[208] but has beyond that the proverb about the physician and the comparison of Jesus' working of miracles in Capernaum and in Nazareth; in vv. 28–30 the refashioned story is brought to a very wonderful close. We must start from vv. 16–22a, where at the focal-point there stands Isa. 61:1f. (58:8), the fulfilment of which in the person of Jesus is stated in v.21 *expressis verbis*. As the task of Jesus there stands at the beginning the εὐαγγελίσασθαι πτωχοῖς and at the end the κηρῦξαι ἐνιαυτὸν κυρίου δεκτόν, and in between these the mighty works are also mentioned. Thus far the text of Matt. 11:5f. par. is very close to this. The specific thing now is that on the basis of Isa. 61:1 a gift of the Spirit and an "anointing" understood in this sense is asserted of Jesus. Acts 10:38a contains the same assertion. It must be considered whether this does not also hold good of Acts 4:27, in spite of the close association intended by Luke with the citation meant messianically of Ps. 2:1f. in vv. 25f.; the phrase ὁ ἅγιος παῖς σου 'Ιησοῦς in v. 27 also proves itself to be an ingredient of the idea of the eschatological prophet like Moses. The different Christological traditions are of course interwoven by the evangelist into a coherent picture such as he has also completed in the discourses of Acts. But precisely the verbal use of χρίειν in contrast with the established *terminus technicus* χριστός shows that here an anointing in the strict sense is thought of, and indeed an appointment to the prophetic office in the sense of Isa. 61:1.[209] Turning back once again to Lk. 4:16ff. we must say that the original conception has been largely obliterated by the addition of vv. 22b–30, for in v. 24,

in the sentence about the despised prophets, the reference is to
the fate of prophets in general and not specially to the fate of the
Israelitish messengers of God who are exposed to persecution
by the obstinate people, and in vv. 25ff. the comparison with
Elias and Eliseus is intended only in a general prophetic
sense.

The observations already made in another place on the
original rendering of the story of the baptism may be included
in this place. The opening of the heavens and the descent of the
Spirit are apocalyptic signs of the dawning of the time of
salvation. The person to be baptized is equipped with the Spirit
and is addressed as the Servant of God by the voice from heaven,
the word of Isa. 42:1a being uttered. Isa. 42:1b like Isa. 61:1
predicates the bestowal of the Spirit; it is not cited in the story
of the baptism, but it is incorporated in the preceding description of the events; the fulfilment of this promise is thus exhibited
concretely. The story of the baptism has therefore its traditio-
historical place first of all within the circuit of the eschatological
prophet conception. In favour of that there also speaks the
Markan version of the story of the temptation, in which
the Moses typology is recognizable although in addition traits of
the Elias tradition are also incorporated.[210]—The story of the
transfiguration in its earliest rendering has also to be fitted into
this context. Here the motif of the bestowal of the Spirit is
lacking, but in its place reference is expressly made through
the ἀκούετε αὐτοῦ to Deut. 18:15 (Mk. 9:7fin). The title Servant
of God and the use of Isa. 42:1 have again to be assumed.
Elias and Moses legitimate the office which Jesus has adjudi-
cated to him in the presence of his intimate disciples. Probably
an eschatological glance is also involved in that, and Jesus is
regarded, as was Elias and at a later time Moses also, as a man
of God carried off to heaven who will appear again with these
two at the end of time.[211]

The conception of the eschatological prophet like Moses was
applied especially to Jesus' earthly work.[212] Mk. 9:2–8 and
Lk. 24:21a, however, permit the conjecture that this had an
eschatological aspect. This appears quite clearly in Rev. 15:2–4,
the picture of the sea of glass and the song of Moses and of the
Lamb, where the deliverance from the Red Sea is equated
typologically with the eschatological consummation.[213] In this
way it was perhaps even possible to understand the time of

salvation in a pronouncedly theocratic way, and that answered not merely to an important tendency within late Jewish expectation but also in like manner to the proclamation of Jesus; even the Son of man conception restricts itself practically to participation in judgement and has no cognizance of any actual special status or particular function of the Son of man at the consummation. On the other hand, the close connection of the ideas of the eschatological prophet and the royal Messiah did not of course remain inoperative, and so the earthly work of Jesus as the promised new Moses was as a rule co-ordinated with his future messianic office, as is the case in Acts 3:12–26 (vv. 20, 21a), where at any rate the idea of being carried away may have been gathered from the figure of the prophet. The carrying away like the violent death can indeed be fitted into this conception without more ado, as Rev. 11:7ff. shows.[214]

The material of tradition in the Gospel of John permits the idea of the eschatological prophet like Moses to be clearly recognized. John 6:1ff., 14f. has already been spoken about. Correspondingly in the dispute of the Jews about the dignity of Jesus in John 7:40ff. the designations the prophet and the Messiah stand side by side with one another. An allusion to the eschatological prophet possibly occurs, John 4:19, 25 within the story of the Samaritan woman being left out of account, in John 3:2, where Nicodemus speaks of the miracle-working teacher sent from God. The situation is similar in John 9:17, granted that the blind man who has been healed designates Jesus as a prophet on the strength of the miracle. We bungle our understanding if in such cases we assume that it is a matter "merely" of popular opinion. We have to reckon with a very early Christological tradition of the primitive church. In such pieces of tradition as Mk. 6:1–5; 6:14–16; 8:28 this has already completely faded, it being there in part only a matter of a prophetic office in the general sense.[215]

From a subject, the primitive Christian paschal expectation, which has recently been studied more accurately, it has become clear that the conception of Jesus as the eschatological Moses played an important role in Palestinian tradition. This expectation precipitated itself especially in the arrangement of the Lord's Supper,[216] but it has also left traces behind elsewhere in the New Testament.[217] Judaism had already connected eschatological expectations with the celebration of the passover, and the primitive church took them over in a very significant remodelling in that it related the conceptions of the exodus and the deliverance under Moses typologically to Jesus (the passover lamb) and connected with that a view of His parousia.[218] The significance of this paschal tradition, which will not be described here in detail, is in my opinion only completely recognized when it is observed that it belongs to the total complex of the idea of Jesus as the eschatological prophet and the new Moses.

The result of our investigation can also be supported by the fact that the characterizing of Jesus as the eschatological prophet has been preserved in late Jewish Christianity.[219] It may not indeed be overlooked that the documents of Jewish Christianity preserved to us, especially the pseudo-Clementines, have preserved the early conception in a form that is much superimposed and transformed with essentially later elements, for on the one hand the Moses typology is here screened by an Adam-Christ-typology, which is moreover connected with the doctrine about the prophet who incarnates himself continuously in history and now finds his fulfilment, "comes to rest" as it is said in the *Gospel of the Hebrews*, in Christ as the true prophet;[220] that in this gnostic ideas come to expression cannot be disputed.[221] On the other hand, the early Jewish Christian tradition is modified by the fact that Jesus as the true prophet reforms Mosaism and for that reason is set antitypically over against Moses.[222] Nevertheless the idea of Jesus as the eschatological prophet and Deut. 18:15ff. as the starting point of a Moses typology can still be clearly recognized.[223] Even as regards the view, the carrying-through of which was certainly late, of a modification by Jesus of the law of Moses, it has to be considered whether it had not a genuine start in the earliest tradition of the primitive church, for in His preaching Jesus Himself sometimes attacked instructions given by Moses and abolished them.[224] His relation to the Old Testament torah does not allow without more ado of its being brought into a schema in such a way that no jot of the Mosaic law is cancelled, as a later theological view wished to have it. The preaching of Jesus does not at all fit smoothly into a Moses typology, and later Jewish Christianity was able to preserve the awareness of this contrast without detriment to the idea of the fulfilment of the promise of Deut. 18:15ff.

It remains to inquire how far the conception of Jesus as the new Moses has precipitated itself in the conceptions of the individual evangelists. This motif plays no role in the framework of the Gospel of Mark, but the more clearly does the Moses typology appear in the Gospel of Matthew. It appears at once in its structure. The great central portion of the Gospel, cc. 3–25, owes its arrangement to five discourses which are concluded respectively with a parallel phrase,[225] and the thesis that the five main sections thus obtained answer to the five Books of Moses is not to be rejected on the ground that in cc. 8ff. there is also a cohering group of miracle stories and that therefore doctrine and mighty works are deliberately set side by side. Not only the distribution of most of the material of the logia source into the five great discourse compositions but also the regrouping of the Markan material in cc. 8f. goes back to the evangelist and is intended to give expression to his intention.[226] Here is the new Moses, who proclaims his torah and accomplishes his miraculous, God-granted mighty deeds. Obviously the idea of the eschatological prophet is accepted and united with the standard Christology of the later church, according to which Jesus is the Son of God and Christos. But for Matthew's understanding it is also for this reason quite correct to speak of Jesus as the bringer of the "messianic torah".[227] That has indeed been disputed recently, as according to Jewish understanding the torah of Moses has everlasting validity, and there can be given only a new interpretation of the same, for which reason a considerable gradual difference in the knowledge of the law is to be expected in the modern world, but not in any case an abrogation or alteration of the Mosaic law.[228] This rabbinical opinion can hardly have been the only and generally authoritative one in New Testament times,[229] and it has moreover to be considered that the primitive church doubtless knew that Jesus had not come merely as an interpreter of the Mosaic torah, but rather that in definite instances he had confronted it in a thoroughly critical way. The idea of the eschatological prophet like Moses was carried over to him without what was contrary to it being simply set aside.[230] Nevertheless Matthew has to a great extent restricted Jesus' contradiction to opposition to the rabbinate; for the rest he has represented the Mosaic law as plainly obligatory and has supported the view that it must be only better expounded and above all better obeyed. For that very reason he was able to take over the motif of the new torah in the sense of a new, obligatory exposition, even if he avoids the concept as such that he may not on any account suggest opposition to the Mosaic law. All the same, however, he has not simply set aside the idea alleged in the matter (antithesis). The new exposition is not different merely in degree. Jesus' doctrine is indeed an exposition of the Mosaic law, but it is one that is new in principle and therefore radically separate from the exposition of the scribes. That in this way Matthew actually thought of a new messianic torah, he makes clear by his distribution of the material of the logia over the five discourses and also by his mention of the mountain in Matt. 5:1.—Further elements of a Moses typology can be recognized in his Gospel. In Matt. 2:13–23, the concluding part of the Nativity Narrative, the childhood of Jesus is related in analogy with the story of the youth of Moses, a complex of tradition already met with in this form.[231] The story of the temptation, which stands, it is true, in connection with the tradition of the eschatological prophet in the Markan but not in the Q-form, is brought by Matthew into an unambiguous relation with Moses in 4:2.[232] In 21:11, 46 he sets even the title of prophet beside the Son of David designation (21:9). Also according to Matt. 23:2, 8–10 it is Jesus, and not the class of the scribes, who is the rightful occupant of the κάθεδρα Μωυσῆς[233] Some observations may be added, admittedly with reserve:[234] the seven Beatitudes in 5:3ff. and the seven woes in 23:13ff. may answer to the seven blessings and curses of Deut. 28,[235] and the close of the last discourse of Jesus in Matt. 26:1f. to the phrase in Deut. 32:45 regarding the completion of all the discourses of Moses to Israel. Whether we can go beyond these analogies that have been mentioned here, is in my opinion very questionable.[236] We must understand clearly that while the Moses typology is indeed significant for Matthew, it is only a single element of his Christology; it is interwoven with many other motifs and is not the sole key to the explanation of his Gospel.

In the Gospel of Luke also is an after-effect of the conception of Jesus as the eschatological prophet discernible? Dabeck has asserted that in the same relation in which the Christ of Matthew stands to Moses the Christ of Luke stands to Elias.[237] This may possibly even explain why some essential passages which characterize the Baptist as Elias are lacking in it. But the material that is adduced as proof is not convincing.[238] A representation of Jesus as Elias is not provable as a leading motif of the Lukan redaction. It has very much rather to be asked whether the Moses typology does not here also play a role. Anyhow in Acts 7:2–53 Luke has incorporated, and in the mission discourse Acts 3:12–26 has Christologically developed, the promise in Deut. 18:15. Certainly all hints and allusions are lacking that Luke carried through the idea of a new exodus, in which case the passion of Jesus would have been understood as the passage through the sea, His resurrection as the miracle of God that works salvation, the forty day period of His appearances as the march to the promised land, and the ascension into heaven as the entrance into the heavenly Jerusalem.[239] Rather we have to think that in the middle portion which is independent of Mark, the Lukan "travel narrative" with its emphatic introduction in 9:51f. and with traits in its construction that have parallels in Deuteronomy, the Moses typology is at least meant to be indicated.[240] This doubtless can be no match for the significance which the motif has in Matthew.

In conclusion reference has to be made briefly to the Gospel of John. Apart from the allusions already touched upon in the material of tradition, it has to be pointed out that the expectation of the eschatological prophet was applied in a very much modified form to Jesus' relation to the Paraclete.[241] Without exhibiting in detail the specific Johannine pursuit of this motif, we may in this place emphasize how strongly the early idea of the earthly work of Jesus as the eschatological prophet, which idea was orientated towards the eschatological consummation at His parousia, was felt afterwards. Only the function of Jesus as the mighty Messiah king who is to appear, is now to a certain extent freed from eschatology and transferred to the Spirit as the Paraclete,[242] and besides the forerunner-finisher schema is modified in the sense that the Paraclete leads back to Jesus and confirms the things that have gone before.[243]

As is evident from the texts that have been dealt with, the conception of Jesus as the new Moses has left behind it manifold traces in the New Testament.[244] Assuredly in most contexts it has only a subordinate place, but the conclusion is easy that it must have been an early and formerly a prevailing idea. If this turns out to be true, then it has to be recognized from it that already in the earliest primitive Christian tradition the earthly life of Jesus had a decisive significance and was orientated directly to His second advent.

NOTES

1. Ps. 74 has probably to be set in a time before 520 B.C., therefore before Haggai and Zechariah; that is the dating favoured recently. On the withdrawal of prophetism in the post-Exilic period and on the later advance of rabbinism cf. J. Giblet, *Prophétisme et attente d'un Messie prophète dans l'ancient Judaisme* in *L'attente du Messie* (*Recherches Bibliques*), 1954, pp. 85ff.; Rudolf Meyer, art. "προφήτης (*Judentum*)," *ThWb* VI, pp. 813ff., 817ff.

2. But just as little may these passages be referred to John Hyrcanus; against R. Meyer, *ThWb* VI, pp. 816f. For a quite different tradition according to which this ruler is said to have been equipped with the prophetic gift, is not in the least indicated in 1 Macc. and may not be introduced.

3. So especially *T. Sota* 13, 2; cf. also Billerbeck I, pp. 125ff.

4. Otto Plöger, *Prophetisches Erbe in den Sekten des frühen Judentums*, *ThLZ* 79, 1954, cols. 291–296; cf. also Werner Foerster, *Der heilige Geist im Spätjudentum*, *NTSt* 8, 1961/62, pp. 117–134.

5. As instances only Dan. 9:1f., 20–27; 1 Q pHab may be mentioned.

6. Cf. Rudolf Meyer, *Der Prophet aus Galiläa, Studie zum Jesusbild der drei ersten Evangelien*, 1940, pp. 42ff.; id., *ThWb* VI, pp. 823ff. A brief survey of the material also in Otto Michel, *Spätjüdisches Prophetentum* in *Neutestamentliche Studien für Rudolf Bultmann* (*BZNW* 21), 1957[2], pp. 60–66. On the late word Zech. 13:4–6 cf. Elliger, *Kl. Propheten* ii, pp. 163f.

7. On John Hyrcanus cf. Josephus, *Bell. Jud.* I 68; *Ant.* XIII 300 cf. 282f.

8. It is not impossible that such a tradition may be preserved in the *Test. of Levi* 8, although precisely the reference to the prophetic gift in 8, 15 is textually uncertain. A reference to the Hasmonaeans was advocated especially by R. H. Charles, *The Apocrypha and Pseudepigrapha of the OT* II, 1913, p. 314. Against this is T. W. Manson, *Miscellanea Apokalyptica III: Test. XII Patr.: Levi VIII, JThSt* 48, 1947, pp. 59–61, who applies the passage to the founding of the Zadokite priesthood by Solomon. Cf. also K. G. Kuhn, *NTSt* I, 1954/55, pp. 168ff, especially p. 172; Ernst Bammel, *ΑΡΧΙΕΡΕΥΣ ΠΡΟΦΗΤΕΥΩΝ. ThLZ* 79, 1954, cols. 351–356; v.d. Woude, *Mess. Vorstellungen*, p. 213,

9. Cf. Gressmann, *Messias*, pp. 285ff.; J. Giblet, *op. cit.*, pp. 85ff. For the distinction also Cullmann, *Christologie*, p. 21.

10. 1 Kings 19:16 and Isa. 61:1 show that the motif of the anointing of an Old Testament prophet is not out of the question.

11. Cf. Georg Molin, *Elijahu. Der Prophet und sein Weiterleben in den Hoffnungen des Judentums und der Christenheit, Judaica* 8, 1952, pp. 65–94; P. Marie-Joseph Stiassny, *Le prophète Élie dans le Judaisme* in *Élie le Prophète (Études Carmélitaines* 35), 1956, ii, pp. 199–255, especially pp. 241ff.

12. The material that comes into question for the New Testament period in Billerbeck IV/2, pp. 764–798; Voltz, *Eschatologie*, pp. 195–197, 200f.; Joachim Jeremias, art. 'Ηλ(ε)ίας, *ThWb* II, pp. 930–942.

13. I refer merely to Elliger, *Kl. Propheten* II, pp. 205f.

14. Besides eschatological tasks there is ascribed to the Elias who has been carried away to heaven the position of a heavenly scribe and an intercessor, also of a helper in the troubles of this world, as is assumed in Mk. 15:35f.; cf. Billerbeck IV/2, pp. 766ff., 769ff.

15. Cf. the slight but yet important alteration in the LXX: the making of peace between fathers and sons is now extended to men and their neighbours; here also for הֵשִׁיב there is the word ἀποκαταστήσει which was later so significant.

16. Isa. 49:6 also is not to be understood as a "Messianic" statement, rather the reference is to a specifically prophetic function; cf. pp. 356ff. above. This likewise impedes an exposition of Ecclus. 48:10 in a messianic sense.

17. Cf. Billerbeck IV/2, pp. 789ff.; Jeremias, *ThWb* II, pp. 934f.

18. That also holds good where an eschatological figure is not specially thought of, e.g. in John 11:51. Cf. on this E. Bammel, *ThLZ* 79, 1954, cols. 351ff.

19. There is, it is true, no talk in the *Assumption of Moses* 9 of the office of the messianic high priest. Moreover this figure called Taxo is vested with traits of the martyrs of 2 Macc. 6f., and that renders it more difficult to fit him in; it may perhaps be asked whether from there by way of the *Apocalypse of Elias* 35 lines of connection can be drawn to Rev. 11:3ff.

20. Cf. Billerbeck IV/2, pp. 784ff.; Jeremias, *ThWb* II, pp. 933f. Besides the rabbinical instances Justin, *Dial.* 8, 4; 49, 1 especially comes into question.

21. Cf. pp. 362ff. above.

22. Here it has to be observed that in contrast with the expectation of Elias there is no thought first and foremost of a returning Moses (Moses redivivus)—that view took shape only later and remained a side-line—but of a prophet "like Moses". A special investigation has been submitted by Howard M. Teeple, *The Mosaic Eschatological Prophet (JBL, Monog. Ser.* x), 1957.

23. Von Rad, *Theologie* I, pp. 106, 292f.

24. So Rolf Rendtorff, art. "προφήτης (AT)", *ThWb* VI, pp. 803f.

25. According to Georg Fohrer, *Elia (AThANT* 31), 1957, pp. 48ff. Elias is represented in the stories in 1 Kings 17–19 as a second, new Moses, of course without his having there an eschatological role.

26. Cf. the surveys of the history of research in C. R. North, *The Suffering Servant in Deutero-Isaiah* (1948), 1956², pp. 6–116; Herbert

Haag, "Ebed-Jahwe-Forschung 1948–1958", *BZ* NF 3, 1959, pp. 174–204.

27. Bernhard Duhm, *Das Buch Jesaja* (1892), 1922⁴, to Isa. 42:1–4; 49:1–6; 50:4–9 (10f.); 52:13–53:12 (today as a rule 42:5–9 is also included).

28. Otto Eissfeldt, *Der Gottesknecht bei Deuterojesaja* (*Beitr. z. Religions-geschichte des Altertums* 2), 1933.

29. Cf. Otto Kaiser, *Der königliche Knecht. Eine traditionsgeschichtlich-exegetische Studie über die Ebed-Jahwe-Lieder bei Deuterojesaja* (*FRLANT* NF 52), 1959, p. 10 and often.

30. Cf. also the short survey in E. Schweizer, *Erniedrigung und Erhöhung*, pp. 153f.

31. So, e.g. Georges Pidoux, *Le serviteur souffrant d'Esaie 53*, *RevThPh* n.s. 6, 1956, pp. 36–46.

32. So Helmer Ringgren, *The Messiah in the Old Testament* (*Stud. Bibl. Theol.* 18), 1956, pp. 39ff., especially pp. 66f.

33. Today this is advocated especially by: Walther Zimmerli, art. "παῖς θεοῦ (AT)", *ThWb* V, p. 665; Mowinckel, *He That Cometh*, pp. 213f.; also Ivan Engnell, "The Ebed Yahweh Songs and the suffering Messiah in 'Deutero-Isaiah'", *Bull. of the John Rylands Library* 31, 1948, pp. 54–93.

34. Zimmerli, *ThWb* V, pp. 662f., 665f.

35. In my opinion that is seen very clearly in the above mentioned investigation of O. Kaiser, who wishes to establish a transference of the king conception to the people (pp. 132ff.).

36. Zimmerli, *ThWb* V, pp. 666ff. identifies the Servant of God with Deutero-Isaiah, following Sigmund Mowinckel, *Der Knecht Jahwäs*, 1921, p. 9; *id.*, *He that Cometh*, pp. 249f., 253f., now prefers to point to another person from the Isaianic-Deutero-Isaianic circle of prophets. Cf. also the discussion with Engnell in Aage Bentzen, *Messias—Moses redivivus—Menchensohn* (*AThANT* 17), 1948, pp. 42ff. The individual and prophetic interpretation is now also favoured by v. Rad, *Theol.* II, 1960, pp. 271f., who at the same time advocates the Deutero-Isaianic authorship (p. 264).

37. Bentzen, *op. cit.*, pp. 51, 64ff.; following and correcting an earlier thesis already advocated by Sellin; otherwise Teeple, *op. cit.*, pp. 56ff.

38. Robert Koch, *Geist und Messias*, pp. 107ff.; Rendtorff, *ThWb* VI, p. 812; v. Rad. *Theol.* II, pp. 273f.

39. Haag, *op. cit.*, pp. 199f. also makes an interesting suggestion: no prophet would venture to speak of "his law" (Isa. 42:4), only Moses and the teacher of wisdom, who comes from quite another tradition, occupy an exceptional position, everywhere else in the Old Testament it is a matter of Jahweh's own torah. Haag infers from this an influence of the wisdom tradition on the figure of the Servant of God. Ought we not to think here rather of Moses?

40. As regards literature see especially: Joachim Jeremias, art. Μωυσῆς, *ThWb* IV, pp. 852–878; Rudolf Schnackenburg, *Die Erwartung des "Propheten" nach dem Neuen Testament und den Qumran Texten* in *Studia Evangelica* (*TU* V/18), 1959, pp. 622–639.

41. Cf. Billerbeck II, pp. 626f.

42. Cf. Giblet, *op. cit.*, pp. 90ff.

43. I may refer merely to the problems of Mk. 9:4 and Rev. 11:3ff. (Elias and Moses).

44. That here there is an underlying Hellenistic view of the prophets —so Wetter, *Sohn Gottes*, pp. 21ff.; cf. also Walter Bauer, *Joh.*, pp. 32ff. —is altogether unlikely.

45. Cf. only Bultmann, *Joh.*, pp. 61f.

46. Jeremias, *ThWb* IV, p. 867.

47. So Schnackenburg, *op. cit.*, pp. 628f.

48. Text in Allegro, *JBL* 75, 1956, pp. 182ff.

49. Passages in Jeremias, *ThWb* IV, pp. 864f. Cf. too CD V, 19, where mention is made of the time "in which Israel was redeemed the first time".

50. The significance which belongs to the miraculous in the conception of the eschatological prophet like Moses is completely misunderstood by Teeple if he regards miraculous doings as a general characteristic of all ancient prophets (p. 88). According to Isa. 11:2 the motif of extraordinary intellectual power in judging certainly belongs to the conception of the Messiah, but not the motif that the Messiah performs miracles. Cf. Billerbeck I, pp. 593f.; Bultmann, *Syn. Trad.*, p. 275; above all Klausner, *Messianic Idea*, pp. 502ff.: "The Messiah—and this should be carefully noted—is never mentioned anywhere in the Tannaitic literature as a wonderworker per se" (p. 506).

51. Strange to say, so far as I can see, no reference has been made anywhere to this passage from Ecclesiasticus, a passage that is important for the entire picture. A similar use of σωτηρία or cognate notion does not occur elsewhere in Ecclus.

52. There came forward with a Messianic claim the Galilean Hezekiah and his descendants Judas and Menahem, also later Simon Bar-Cochba.

53. Thorough discussion of the texts and careful discrimination of the two groups in R. Meyer, *ThWb* VI, pp. 827f., and Jeremias, *ThWb* IV, p. 866.

54. Jos., *Ant.* XX 97f. Theudas appeared in the time of the procurator Fadus, A.D. 44–46.

55. Jos., *Ant.*, XX 169ff.; *Bell. Jud.* II 261ff. This Egyptian appeared in the time of the procurator Felix, A.D. 52–60. Cf. Acts 21:38.

56. Jos., *Ant.* XX 167f.; *Bell. Jud.* II 258ff. Similarly also the weaver Jonathan who appeared in Cyrene after the Jewish War, Jos., *Ant.* XX 188.

57. Jos., *Ant.* XX 97: προφήτης γὰρ ἔλεγεν εἶναι (Theudas); *Ant.* XX 169: προφήτης εἶναι λέγων and *Bell Jud.* II 261: προφήτου πίστιν ἐπιθ εἰς ἑαυτῷ (the Egyptian). On the other hand, in *Bell. Jud.* II 434 it is said of the zealot Menahem that he went to Jerusalem "in the state of a king" and there became "the leader of the sedition".

58. Socrates, *Hist. Eccl.* VII 38; in R. Meyer, *ThWb* VI, p. 827.

59. August Friedrich Gfrörer, *Das Jahrhundert des Heils* II, 1838, pp. 332f., even conjectured that the coming out of Egypt in the case of the unnamed Jew could be connected with the Moses typology.

60. The meaning of the word Ta'eb (Taheb) is certainly disputed.

Instead of intransitively "the returning one" the word can also be interpreted causatively "the restorer". We may then think of Mal. 3:24, but that is very unlikely in view of the exclusive validity of the Pentateuch among the Samaritans. The intransitive understanding of the word is favoured by Adalbert Merx, *Der Messias oder Ta'eb der Samaritaner* (*BZAW* 17), 1909, p. 42; Albrecht Oepke, art, ἀποκαθίστημι, *ThWb* I, pp. 387f.

61. In an interesting way Merx, *op. cit.*, pp. 43f. considers whether or not certain features in the Samaritan texts point to a Joshua redivivus.

62. A thorough investigation of the material and an account of the Samaritan Ta'eb expectation is still lacking; Merx's important work purposed above all to open up new sources, M. Gaster's book, *The Samaritan Eschatology*, 1932, is very much disputed because of its treatment of the sources. Cf. John Bowman, "Early Samaritan Eschatology", *Journal of Jewish Studies* 6, 1955, pp. 63–72.

63. Cf. also W. Bauer, *Joh.*, p. 71; Bultmann, *Joh.*, p. 141, especially n.5; Barrett, *Joh.*, p. 200.

64. Jos., *Ant.* XVIII 85f. This incident took place in Samaria in A.D. 35, when Pontius Pilate was procurator. The adherents are said to have taken arms with them in order, after the accrediting miracle, to begin the holy war; prophetic and messianic elements thus intermingled.

65. A task as a teacher devolves even upon the Deutero-Isaianic Servant of God, cf. merely Isa. 42:4.

66. Cf. CD VI, 8 (exposition of מחקק in Num. 21:18); CD VII, 18 (exposition of כוכב in Num. 24:17); 4 Q Flor 2.

67. In the first case we have to think of the founder of the community, with whom the eschatological happenings have their beginning, in the other two cases of a figure who appears along with the royal Messiah, therefore obviously of the high priestly "Messiah of Aaron".

68. The investigation of the torah has of course great significance even for the individual member of the community; cf. Braun, *Radikalismus* I, pp. 16ff. But here then it is not the דורש התורה but a דורש בתורה who is spoken about; also Kurt Schubert, *Die Messiaslehre in den Texten von Chirbet Qumran*, *BZ* NF I, 1957, p. 193, n. 49. For the rest it may be pointed out that the function of the דורש התורה is of course not limited to the mere exposition of Scripture but extends to the revelation of the secrets hidden in it and in addition to the setting up of new decrees and regulations; 1 Q pHab on the one hand and 1 Q S on the other hand have to be understood in this sense. Cf. Otto Betz, *Offenbarung und Schriftforschung in der Qumransekte* (*WUNT* 6), 1960, pp. 15ff.

69. The material in Billerbeck IV/I, pp. 1ff.; thorough discussion in Gerhard Barth, *Das Gesetzesverständnis des Evangelisten Matthäus* in G. Bornkamm-G. Barth-H. J. Held, *op. cit.*, pp. 144f.

70. Still, in the Qumran texts the prophets are seen quite otherwise in line with Moses; cf., e.g. CD V, 21f.; 1 QS 1, 3. So also the "teacher of righteousness", the founder of the community, is put on a par with the prophets. cf. 1 Q pHab 11, 8f.; VII, 4f.

71. Cf. G. Barth, *op. cit.*, pp. 145ff.; "new torah" can be referred on principle to every novel exposition by a scribe (following W. Bacher).

72. Cf. the passage Lev R 13 discussed by Billerbeck IV/2, p. 1162 and G. Barth, *op. cit.*, pp. 145f.

73. Cf. also W. D. Davies, *Torah in the Messianic Age and/or the Age to Come* (*JBL Monogr. Ser.* VII), 1952, especially pp. 86ff, who would like to establish a very great age for the conception of the new torah; similarly Teeple, *op. cit.*, pp. 23ff.

74. One may think most easily of a radicalization of the torah such as is met with in the Qumran writings; cf. Braun, *Radikalismus* I, pp. 33ff., 113ff.

75. Cf. Jeremias, *ThWb* V, p. 679, n.183 and p. 678, n. 167.

76. It occurs only in two passages: 1 Kings 19:16 (the anointing of Elisha by Elijah) and Isa. 61:1. Mowinckel, *He That Cometh*, p. 254f., has pointed out that the Trito-Isaianic passage 61:1–3 stands in close connection with the Servant of God Songs.

77. Cd VI, 1: The laws of God are given בְּיַד מֹשֶׁה וְגַם בְּמְשִׁיחֵי הַקּוֹדֶשׁ (בִּמְשִׁיחוֹ has to be corrected); 1 QM XI: בְּיַד מְשִׁיחֶיכָה "the times of the wars of thy hand" are made known; cf. also v.d. Woude, *op. cit.*, pp. 20ff., 117ff.

78. This conjecture has to be considered seriously for the reason that in the mediaeval manuscripts of the *Damascus Document* all plural forms of מָשִׁיחַ have been struck out; cf. Karl Georg Kuhn, "The Two Messiahs of Aaron and Israel" in *The Scrolls and the New Testament*, ed. Krister Stendahl, 1957, pp. 59f.

79. The different theses on the passage in v.d. Woude, *op. cit.*, p. 17. Bardtke, *Handschriftenfunde* II, p. 260, also supports the singular construction.

80. There come into question the Jewish *Grundschrift* of the *Ascensio Jesaiae* and the *Vitae prophetarum*; cf. Hans Joachim Schoeps, *Die jüdischen Prophetenmorde* in *Aus frühchristlicher Zeit*, 1950, pp. 126–143. The New Testament passages in Friedrich, *ThWb* VI, pp. 835f.

81. On the thesis of Munck, *Petrus und Paulus i.d. Offb. Joh.*, according to which the reference here is to the martyrdom of the two apostles in Rome, cf. the review by Günther Bornkamm, *ThLZ* 85, 1960, cols. 195f.

82. Cf. the *Apocalypse of Elias* 35, 7ff., where indeed Enoch and Elias appear; also Jeremias, *ThWb* II, pp. 942f. Several motifs are united together in Rev. 11:3ff., thus penitential homily and miraculous doings (repetition of the Egyptian plagues), contest with the antichrist, martyrdom and removal to heaven, further the passage Zech. 4:3, 11–14, usually referred to the two Messiahs, about the two olive trees (here applied in the sense of the anointing of the prophets?); there is also as a specifically Christian feature the function as "witnesses".

83. Cf. Eduard Lohse, *Märtyrer und Gottesknecht*, pp. 78ff.; Moses also plays a part among the fathers whose death has vicarious atoning power (pp. 87ff.).

393

84. E. Lohse, *op. cit.*, pp. 66ff., 72ff., who, it is true, also wishes to draw from 2 Macc. certain conclusions for the Tannaite period (pp. 77ff.).

85. Cf. only 1 Thess. 2:15; Hebr. 11:32ff.; Matt. 5:12.

86. One has to be sceptical of the thesis that the conception of the righteous man who suffers willingly and makes vicarious atonement was everywhere widely disseminated—so E. Schweizer, *Erniedrigung und Erhöhung*, pp. 37f.

87. 1 Q S IX, 10f.: בוא נביא ומשיחי אהרן וישראל.

88. 4 Q Test 5ff.

89. Cf. the already frequently consulted article by K. G. Kuhn, *NTSt* I, 1954/55, pp. 168ff., especially pp. 174ff.

90. CD XIX, 35f.: מיום האסף מורה היחיד עד עמוד משיח(ים) מאהרן ומישראל v.d. Woude, *op. cit.*, p. 37, considers whether יחד or יחוד ought not to be read and then translated "teacher of the community". Instead of this Schubert, *BZ* NF I, 1957, p. 181, n. 9, refers to the *Test. of Benjamin* 9, 2 μονογενὴς προφήτης, but there the text tradition is uncertain, cf. R. H. Charles, *The Greek Versions of the Testaments of the Twelve Patriarchs*, 1908 (reprint 1960), p. 227, and is also closely connected with a Christian interpolation. Quite otherwise Leonhard Rost, *Der "Lehrer der Einung" und der "Lehrer der Gerechtigkeit"*, *ThLZ* 78, 1953, cols. 143–148, who thinks of two quite different historical persons.

91. Cf. 1 Q pHab II, 5–10 and above all VII, 3–5: the text of the Old Testament refers "to the teacher of righteousness to whom God has made known all the secrets of the words of his servants the prophets".

92. CD VI, 2ff.; cf. p. 359 above.

93. Cf. only CD XII, 22f.: "This is the order (סרך) . . . wherein they are to walk in the final time of wickedness until the appearance of the anointed out of Aaron and Israel".

94. CD VII, 18; 4 Q Flor 2. Traditio-historically the explanation of this may perhaps be that here the idea of Elias, not indeed as the eschatological prophet (forerunner), but as the messianic high priest plays a part, for to the latter also the correct exposition of the torah was ascribed; cf. on this Billerbeck IV/2, pp. 789ff., 794ff.; v.d. Woude, *op. cit.*, pp. 54f., 186.

95. CD VI, 10.

96. Cf. v.d. Woude, *op. cit.*, pp. 54f., 67ff.

97. So John M. Allegro, *Die Botschaft vom Toten Meer. Das Geheimnis der Schriftrollen (Fischer-Bücherei* 183), 1957, pp. 129f. J. Carmignac, *Le retour du Docteur de Justice à la fin des jours?, RQ* I, 1958, pp. 235–248, has shown that among the texts known thus far there is no evidence for this.

98. Cf. Claus-Hunno Hunzinger *Aus der Arbeit an den unveröffentlichten Texten von Qumran, ThLZ* 85, 1960, cols. 151f.

99. So Giblet, *op. cit.*, pp. 125, 127ff.; K. Schubert, *BZ* NF I, 1957, pp. 179ff.; *id. Die Gemeinde vom Toten Meer. Ihre Entstehung und ihre*

Lehren, 1958, pp. 100f.; v.d. Woude, *op. cit.*, pp. 67ff., especially pp. 186f.; Schnackenburg, *op. cit.*, pp. 631ff; Gert Jeremias' recent work, *Der Lehrer der Gerechtigkeit (Studien z. Umwelt d. NT* 2), 1962.

100. The question how far the wilderness plays a part in this is difficult to answer, and besides there is connected with it the question as to the meaning of the designation "Damascus".

101. Schnackenburg, *op. cit.*, p. 636.

102. Giblet, *op. cit.*, pp. 85ff., e.g. proceeds from this wrong account to a complete misunderstanding of Theudas and the unnamed Egyptian, in whom he wishes to see merely ordinary prophets because no positive messianic traits of any sort are recognizable. Cf. also Jeremias, *ThWb* IV, pp. 862f. and n. 125.

103. Cf. n. 87, above. Here משיח is not applied to the prophets.

104. Against Bultmann, *Joh.*, p. 158.

105. So rightly Barrett, *Joh.*, pp. 231f.

106. Cf. Teeple, *op. cit.*, pp. 102ff.

107. Against Martin Dibelius, *Die urchristliche Überlieferung von Johannes dem Täufer (FRLANT* 15), 1911, pp. 33ff., 139ff., who assumes an expectation of the Messiah on the part of the Baptist.

108. It is matter of the nomadic ideal advocated for example by the Rechabites, which was retained in certain late Jewish prophetic circles (Zech. 13:4); cf. Ludwig Köhler, *Kleine Lichter*, 1945, pp. 85f.; also Hans Windisch, *Die Notiz über Tracht und Speise des Täufers Johannes*, *ZNW* 32, 1933, pp. 65–87.

109. Whence also the designation ὁ βαπτίζων or ὁ βαπτιστής ascribed to him.

110. Cf. especially Martin Dibelius, *Jungfrauensohn und Krippenkind* in *Botschaft und Geschichte* I, pp. 1ff., especially pp. 8f.; Philipp Vielhauer, *Das Benedictus des Zacharias (Lk. 1; 68–79)*, *ZThK* 49, 1952, pp. 255–272 especially pp. 256. 267.

111. In detail Lk. 1:14–17 contains a whole series of motifs of different kinds: the eschatological joy in v. 14 already points to John's unique position. In v. 15 the μέγας moves him into the vicinity of the elected men of God (cf. Dibelius, *Jungfrauensohn*, p. 4); moreover the ascetic motif, which has certainly been taken from the history of the Baptist, is construed as abstinence from wine and strong drink just as a Nazarite and indeed is understood as an allusion to the men of God who are especially distinguished as charismatic persons; to be filled with the Spirit and to hold prophetic office have at all times belonged together; that the prophets are separated already in their mother's womb is a further Old Testament thought. Then in vv. 16f. there is a description, following Mal. 3:1, 23f., of the task which falls to John as the eschatological Elias. There is no mention here of a Messiah; the reference is to the immediate forerunner of God. That κύριος in v. 17 fin. is referred to God is shown by κύριος ὁ θεὸς αὐτῶν in v. 16b.

112. In detail cf. Vielhauer, *op. cit.*, pp. 263ff.; now also Joachim Gnilka, *Der Hymnus des Zacharias*, *BZ* NF 6, 1962, pp. 215–238, especially pp. 227ff.

113. So Vielhauer, *op. cit.*, pp. 267f.

114. Cf. on this Vielhauer, *op. cit.*, pp. 261f.

115. It may merely be considered whether v. 78a belongs perhaps to vv.76f. and therefore whether the interpolation should be limited to vv. 78b, 79a; but in form and substance v. 78a suits better as transition to the messianic statement in vv. 78b, 79a, at the same time the διὰ σπλάγχνα κτλ must be referred to the whole of vv. 76f.; so also Vielhauer, *op. cit.*, p. 263.

116. Vielhauer, *op. cit.*, p. 264 also says that either is possible.

117. Cf. especially Hermann Gunkel, *Die Lieder in der Kindheitsge-schichte Jesu bei Lukas* in *Festgabe für Harnack*, 1921, pp. 43–60. He has shown with detailed reasons that the first part Lk. 1:68–75 is an eschatological hymn of Jewish provenance, whilst the whole of the second part vv. 76–69 is regarded by him as a Christian addition. Correspondingly he considers Lk. 1:46f., 49–55 as a Jewish hymn and v. 48 as a Christian addition, which is certainly right.

118. Erdmann, *Vorgeschichten*, p. 10, rightly points out that it is a composition of this kind. It is, however, hardly correct to say that the whole Benedictus is a Christian paraphrase of the Magnificat (pp. 31ff.).

119. Like Joh. Weiss, *Lk* in *SNT* I, p. 421 and Dibelius, *Joh. d. T*, p. 74, Pierre Benoit, *L'enfance de Jean Baptiste selon Luc 1, NTSt* 3, 1956/57, pp. 169–194, recognizes only vv. 76f. as interpolation. Vv. 68–75, 78f. go back, he says, to a Jewish messianic hymn, but he considers vv. 76f. as Christian interpretation, just as he also derives the story of the childhood of the Baptist from oral tradition of the primitive church which was first fixed in writing by Luke.

120. The Benedictus in its present rendering has thus the same function as the story of the meeting of Elisabeth and Mary (together with the Magnificat). On the other hand it can be asked what place befitted the early genethliacon vv. 76f., 79b in the story about the Baptist; as a rule it is assumed that in Lk. 1:67–80 we are concerned with a Christian appendix; but suppose there is tradition about the Baptist in vv. 76f., 79b. There would then be a good explanation why in the story of the birth vv. 57–66, which reports the fulfilment of the promise to Zacharias vv. 5–25 and the singular name-giving in accordance with v. 13, no statements of any kind are made regarding the significance of the child and the text falls off somewhat as compared with vv. 5ff., If, however, vv. 76f., 79b belongs to that, then a complete balance is brought about. The transition verse 67 will of course be Christian just as is 1:42c. Either an early tradition has dropped out or, and in my opinion this is more likely, the genethliacon originally followed v. 64 immediately (in which case the present concluding phrase of v. 64 was possibly incorporated only subsequently and leads over to the introductory formula v. 68). Further it may not be overlooked that Lk. 1:80 fits better into the tradition about the Baptist than into the redactional framework, for here statements are made about John (for his waxing strong in spirit cf. 1:15) such as are expressly avoided about Jesus in Lk. 2.40, 52 before His baptism; on the other hand 1:80 stands in close connection with the statement about Elias in 1:14–17, for which perhaps Judg. 13:24f. may be drawn upon. That would mean that besides Lk.

1:5–25, 57–66 the story of the Baptist also contained vv. 76f., 79b and v. 80, in which case this concluding verse led over immediately to a presentation of the public work of the Baptist.

121. Within the New Testament only Lk. 3:15 (red.); Acts 13:25a and John 1:20 can be regarded as allusions to a messianic veneration of the Baptist, but the circumstances assumed in these verses are very much later than those assumed in Lk. 1. A clear tendency to regard the Baptist as the Messiah can be concluded from the pseudo-Clementines and Ephraem; but this may have come about in general only through a coming to grips with Christianity; so Joseph Thomas, *Le mouvement baptiste en Palestine et Syrie (Universitas Catholica Lovaniensis, Dissertationes II/28)*, 1935, pp. 113f.

122. Cf. Dibelius, *Joh. d. T.*, pp. 15ff. Against Jeremias, *Gleichnisse*, pp. 139ff., who wishes to carry back vv. 18f. also to Jesus.

123. Schniewind, *Mt.*, p. 143; Schlatter, *Mt.*, pp. 362f.

124. Dibelius, *Joh. d. T.*, pp. 10f.; Klostermann, *Mt.*, p. 97.

125. Dibelius, *Joh. d. T.*, pp. 12ff. (also p. 8 on the original form of the saying); Klostermann, *Mt.*, pp. 97f.

126. So Franz Dibelius, *Zwei Worte Jesu, II. Der Kleinere ist im Himmelreich grösser als Johannes (Mt. 11:11)*, ZNW XI, 1910, pp. 190–192; again taken up recently by Cullmann, *Christologie*, p. 31.

127. So Schlatter, *Mt.*, pp. 365ff.; the disciple of Jesus who is now smaller than John is greater than he when the kingdom of God is revealed.

128. I refer only to Gottlob Schrenk, art. βιάζομαι, ThWb I, pp. 608ff.; Bultmann, *Syn. Trad.* supplementary vol., p. 25.

129. This is again cancelled in Lk. 16:16 at second hand.

130. Mention may also be made briefly of Mk. 11:27–33, the question of authority, where Jesus confronts his adversaries with the heavenly legitimation of John's baptism.

131. Cf. Krister Stendahl, *The School of St. Matthew*, 1954, pp. 49ff., who also shows that here there is no LXX influence, but a singular text tradition is to be assumed.

132. The logia source may already have had a concluding wording in Lk. 7:29f., to which vv. 31f. was added by way of appendix; it is not likely that it was first provided by Luke. In Matt. on the other hand 11:12f. is a logical continuation and vv. 16ff. follows immediately after the redactional interpolation vv. 14f. Accordingly Matthew must have moved the saying about assailants into this place from another context for material reasons.

133. Cf. Klostermann, *Mt.*, p. 99; T. W. Manson, *The Sayings of Jesus*, 1949², pp. 184f.

134. Otherwise Lk. 1:14. The abstinence which is mentioned in v. 15 has another meaning, cf. p. 395 n. 111 above.

135. Cf. Mk. 2:18,19a: John and his disciples fast, in the presence of the bridegroom the fasting ceases. Originally, however, no marking off of the Baptist from Jesus in the salvation history is implied by that; it is also not intended in Matt. 11:16–19, but emerges from the context of Matt. 11:7ff.

136. Cf. Robinson, *Geschichtsverständnis des Mk*, p. 20.

137. Cf. Klostermann, *Mk.*, p. 89; Lohmeyer, *Mk.*, pp. 183f.; Taylor, *Mk.*, p. 395.

138. Otherwise C. H. Kraeling, *John the Baptist*, 1951, pp. 141ff., who wishes to carry back to Jesus the characterization of John as Elias.

139. Cf. say K. L. Schmidt, *Der Rahmen der Geschichte Jesu*, pp. 18ff.; Bultmann, *Syn. Trad.*, pp. 261f.; Marxsen, *Evangelist Markus*, pp. 17ff.

140. Ernst Lohmeyer, *Die urchristliche Überlieferung von Johannes dem Täufer*, *JBL* 51, 1932, pp. 300–319.

141. Wellhausen, *Mk.*, pp. 3f.

142. Pointed out rightly by Helmut Köster in his review of Marxsen's book in *Verk. u. Forsch.*, 1956/57 (1959), p. 179. It must certainly be observed that the wilderness is also mentioned in Matt. 11:7f. par. The motif has, therefore, not simply been spun out of Isa. 40:3, but in Mk. 1:4 it has to be understood from that Old Testament statement.

143. It cannot be translated by "to call to". Usually what is said is βαπτίζειν (τὸ) βάπτισμα; cf. concordance.

144. Isa. 40:3 was evidently not used in Judaism in an exposition of the kind referred to a definite person, as is shown by the material in Billerbeck I, pp. 96f. and the passage 1 Q S VIII, 14f. ("That signifies investigation of the torah . . .").

145. On the Christological correction at the end and the use of the Kyrios title cf. chapter 2, p. 108.

146. Cf. only Ludwig Köhler, *Kleine Lichter*, 1945, pp. 79f.

147. Cf. Stendahl, *School*, pp. 51f, 215, who indeed quite groundlessly assigns this combination to a Semitic basis, although on pp. 47f. he has clearly pointed out a dependence on the LXX in v. 3 in contrast with v. 2. His supposition that this combination of citations is to be ascribed to the Baptist's community is also irrelevant. But on pp. 216f. he rightly points out that to combine words of Scripture in this way was a Jewish practice.

148. That can also be recognized in the assigning of the combination of quotations Mk. 1:2f. to the prophet Isaiah.

149. Cf. Wolfgang Trilling, *Die Täufertradition bei Matthäus*, *BZ* NF 3, 1959, pp. 271–289.

150. Cf. on this Bornkamm, *Enderwartung* in Bornkamm-Barth-Held, pp. 13f.

151. On the place of the Baptist in the Lukan salvation history cf. Conzelmann, *Mitte der Zeit*, pp. 16ff.

152. John 1:7, 8, 15, 19, 32, 34; 3:26, 28; 5:33. For the rest cf. Dibelius, *Joh. d. T.*, pp. 98ff., 119ff.; Bultmann, *Joh.*, pp. 30f., 57ff.; Cullmann, *Christologie*, pp. 26ff.

153. Cf. recent article by Georg Richter, '"Bist du Elias?" (Joh. 1:21),' *BZ* NF 6, 1962, pp. 79–92, 238–256; 7, 1963, pp. 63–80.

154. Statements in Karl Bornhäuser, *Das Wirken des Christus durch Taten und Worte (BFchrTh* II/2), 1924²; reference has to be made especially to Harald Riesenfeld, *Jesus als Prophet* in *Spiritus et Veritas (Festschrift für Karl Kundsins)*, 1953, pp. 135–148; Cullmann, *Christo-*

logie, pp. 11ff.; G. Friedrich, *ThWb* VI, pp. 847ff., 860f.; Teeple, *op. cit.,* pp. 74ff.; Franklin W. Young, "Jesus the Prophet: a Re-Examination", *JBL* 68, 1949, pp. 285–299, is unsatisfactory because no clear demarcation from the Messiah conception is effected; also Erich Fascher, *ΠΡΟΦΗΤΗΣ,* 1927, provides hardly anything for this formulation of the question.

155. A comparison of Jesus with the Old Testament prophets has of course always played a role; we have merely to think of the conception of the *munus propheticum Christi.* An excellent compilation of all prophetic features in this sense is provided by Charles Harold Dodd, *Jesus als Lehrer und Prophet* in *Mysterium Christi,* 1931, pp. 67–86. Similarly Paul E. Davies, "Jesus and the Role of Prophet", *JBL* 64, 1945, pp. 241–254; C. K. Barrett, *Holy Spirit,* pp. 90ff. Even the comprehensive work of Félix Gils, *Jésus Prophète d'après les Évangiles synoptiques (Orientalia et Biblica Lovaniensia* II), 1957, confines itself in the main to this formulation of the question.

156. On the basis of Mk. 6:15; 8:28 the question could be asked whether Jesus was not actually also regarded as the eschatological Elias; anyhow in these places this has precipitated itself more clearly than an equating of Jesus to the eschatological prophet like Moses. It may not on any account be disputed that a whole series of traits remind us of Elias, but this was not the prevailing conception; rather we are clearly concerned here with separate elements which were taken up into that other view of Jesus as the eschatological prophet.

157. Lk. 13:32f. shows that a reference to the death of the prophets belongs in all likelihood to Jesus' own proclamation; cf. Excursus I, p. 66 n. 56. Moreover there belong here the New Testament passages: 1 Thess. 2:15; Matt. 23:31, 37a; Matt. 23:29, 34–36 par. (also the redactional passages Matt. 21:35; 22:6).

158. Explicit reference may once again be made to the fact that no conception of atonement is associated with that; against Jeremias, *ThWb* V, pp. 710f. Cf. pp. 361f. above.

159. Cf. Martin Dibelius, *Aufsätze zur Apg.,* pp. 143ff.; Hartwig Thyen, *Der Stil der jüdisch-hellenistischen Homilie (FRLANT* NF 47), 1955, pp. 19f.

160. We may not analyse thus: vv. 2–16 the period of the patriarchs, vv. 17–43 the history of Moses, vv. 44–50 the building of the temple, vv. 51–53 conclusion with reference to the Messianic prophecies—so Preuschen, *Apg.,* p. 38; Bauernfeind, *Apg.,* pp. 113ff. and others—because in doing so we completely overlook the actual concern.

161. Against Haenchen, *Apg.,* pp. 239f., who regards vv. 35, 37, 39–43, 48–53 as Lukan interpolations in the early historical summary, to which he also reckons v. 36 and v. 38 (besides vv. 44–47). The twice repeated τοῦτον and the thrice repeated οὗτος in vv. 35–38 gives to this section so uniform a stamp clearly as regards its composition that we do not manage with the assumption of a compilation; and moreover the essential function of these verses also answers to their formal peculiarities. In vv. 39–50 we have to reckon rather with elements of the Jewish account of history, a character of a different kind as compared with that of vv.

2–34 being secured chiefly through the attendant words from the prophets.

162. So rightly Haenchen, *Apg.*, p. 241.

163. Bauernfeind, *Apg.*, pp. 110ff., also assumes that the discourse had a start upon that of Luke although he does not attempt to give the limits of the *Vorlage* in detail. He regards early Hellenistic Christianity as its sphere of origin and holds that even an indirect connection with Stephen's circle is not impossible; similarly also A. F. J. Klijn, "Stephen's Speech—Acts vii. 2–53", *NTSt* 4, 1957/58, pp. 25–31.

164. Cf. the treatment of Scriptural proof in the mission discourses, especially Acts 3:22ff., 13:32ff.

165. Against Haenchen, *Apg.*, pp. 240f. it has to be emphasized that the whole discourse in its present condition, therefore both vv. 35ff. and vv. 52f., has a pronouncedly Christological intention; it is not in any way martyrologically orientated and does not in the least depict the situation of Christians who are always assailed by the persecutions unleashed by the Jews. It is a matter of a Moses typology orientated toward Jesus. In addition there is a typological statement in regard to the Jewish people so far as they have refused the divine saving act, rejected Moses and persecuted the prophets who spoke beforehand of Jesus.

166. In Marcel Simon, *St. Stephen and the Hellenists in the Primitive Church*, 1958, pp. 37f., 39ff., 59ff., the typological character of the discourse is noticed, but this is referred primarily not to Jesus' earthly life, since only the rejection by the Jews is crucial, but to the expected parousia (pp. 74ff.).

167. Cf. chapter 3, pp. 187f.

168. Also Dibelius, *Aufsätze z. Apg.*, p. 142; Ulrich Wilckens, *Missionsreden der Apg.*, pp. 72ff., recently in discussion with Dibelius.

169. Cf. chapter 3, pp. 164ff.

170. Cf. Acts 10:36 with 3:26b.

171. On this Wilckens, *op. cit.*, pp. 37ff.

172. It is widely recognized that an early liturgical phrase stands in the background. Neither here nor in the analogous places *1 Clem.* 59, 2–4; *Did.* 9, 2f.; 10, 2f.; *Mart. Pol.* 14, 2; 20, 2; *Barn.* 6, 1; 9, 2 does a connection with the conception of atonement come to light. In the atomistic exegesis of the then period even the fact that in Acts 3:12 there is a direct citation from Isa. 52:13 says nothing in favour of the conception of an atoning death of the Servant of God. If the title does not crop up alone in the passages that have been mentioned from the apostolic fathers, still the idea that appears most generally is that through the Servant of God ἐπίγνωσις θεοῦ is communicated (*1 Clem.* 59, 2; *Mart. Pol.* 14, 2; *Did.* 10, 2: cf. the thrice repeated γνωρίζειν in *Did.* 9, 2, 3; 10, 2). We have to think here of the Old Testament דַּעַת יהוה; cf. on this Hans Walter Wolff, *"Wissen um Gott" bei Hosea als Urform von Theologie*, *EvTh* 12, 1952/53, pp. 533–554, who points out in an interesting way on pp. 549f. that this דַּעַת יהוה was given in substance "in what actually happened between the departure from Egypt and the entrance into the civilized land of Palestine"; this also would tell in our case in favour of a Moses typology and the use of

παῖς θεοῦ as a prophetic predicate, even if this knowledge about God in the nomistic sense had got out of place in Pharisaic Judaism (cf. Bultmann, art., γινώσκειν, *ThWb* I, pp. 700f).

173. J. A. T. Robinson, "Elijah, John and Jesus: An Essay in Detection", *NTSt* 4, 1957/58, pp. 263–281, calls in question the view that already in Judaism Elias was the forerunner of the Messiah (pp. 269f.) and advocates the thesis that John did not himself wish to be Elias, but expected him (pp. 264ff.). Jesus on the other hand began to put the Baptist's programme into operation, but then after an inner change undertook the task of the suffering Servant of God (pp. 271ff.). Jesus was regarded by the people as a prophet and as Elias. The earliest Christology retained this in this way that, as Acts 3:12ff. permits us to recognize, it understood Him above everything else as a prophet and the suffering Servant of God and waited for His second coming as the Messiah (pp. 276ff.).

174. The story in the form handed down in Luke may not be regarded as the earliest Easter story, as it frequently is; cf. only Bultmann, *Syn. Trad.*, p. 314. Also it is not enough with Dibelius, *Formgeschichte*, p. 191, n.2 to exclude merely vv. 21b–24 or vv. 22–24.

175. I follow the excellent analysis of Paul Schubert, "The Structure and Significance of Luke 24" in *Nt. Studien für R. Bultmann* (*BZNW* 21), 1957², pp. 165–186, especially pp. 174f., who certainly regards as Lukan the speech by the way vv. 17–27 and the elements of the story connected therewith.

176. The appendix vv. 33–35 does not necessarily assume vv. 21b–24. Rather this appendix will have been the first enlargement, to which afterwards only the τὰ ἐν τῇ ὁδῷ καὶ in v. 35 was added.

177. Here above all the Synoptic account is assumed; but in v. 24 a tradition is preserved similar to that in John 20:3ff.; that it is a matter of a pre-Lukan report of the Easter story is confirmed by v. 12, which has been interpolated only subsequently on the strength of v. 24; cf. Klostermann, *Lk.*, p. 233. The same holds good for v. 24 as for v. 34; allusion is made to traditions which have not been preserved in the Synoptic tradition.

178. In Acts 2:22 reference is made to all the miracles which God did by him, in Acts 10:38 there are mentioned especially the "doing good" and the healing of the possessed. Significant for the conception of the eschatological prophet is in the first verse the idea of accrediting (ἀνὴρ ἀποδεδειγμένος ἀπὸ τοῦ θεοῦ), in the other verse the motif of the anointing by the Holy Spirit (see below).

179. Accordingly in Acts 2:22 we have not to think of the Hellenistic θεῖος ἀνήρ; against Bultmann, *Theol.*, p. 133.

180. That the ideas of the eschatological prophet and royal Messiah could possibly touch and overlap has already been stated on pp. 363ff. above. Besides Acts 3:20, 21a we have also to remember 1 Thess. 1:10, where ὁ ῥυόμενος is used side by side with the messianically understood "Son of God", certainly referred here in an apocalyptic way of thinking to the judgment of the world; Rigaux, *Thess.*, pp. 395f. refers to Moses, especially to Deut. 13:5; *Ps. Sol.* 9, 1.

181. "Prophet" occurs as a designation of Jesus in Mk. 6:4 parr. and Lk. 7:16; both passages are dealt with later.

182. Wilckens, in his already mentioned work *Missionsreden der Apg.*, strives in especial to prove that these discourses are specifically Lukan in structure and content and that only in a few exceptional cases can we reckon with earlier tradition. It has in fact to be allowed that as a rule early tradition material has been reckoned with in the discourses of Acts much too readily and as a matter of course. In any case. we must consider how very much the author himself has engaged in fashioning and formulating. The question as to the kerygmatic material is still not settled and must now be answered in a new and better way.

183. So, e.g. Klostermann, *Mk.*, p. 76.

184. I refer merely to Deut. 13:1ff., Jer. 23.

185. This interpretation of ἀπὸ τοῦ οὐρανοῦ is to be preferred to the assumption that a cosmic-apocalyptic sign is thought of.

186. Here it is not necessary to enter into the difficult statement about the sign of Jonah Lk. 11:29; cf. Anton Vögtle, *Der Spruch vom Jonaszeichen* in *Synoptische Studien (Festschrift für A. Wikenhauser)*, 1953, pp. 230–277.

187. Schlatter, *Mt.*, pp. 414f., also refers to Theudas, the Egyptian and the Samaritan.

188. In John 6:32 34 this is then continued antitypically (cf. John 1:17; 9:28); not Moses but Jesus, who Himself has come down from heaven, gives the true bread from heaven.

189. Georg Ziener, *Das Brotwunder im Markusevengelium*, BZ NF 4, 1960, pp. 282–285, points out that the first story of the feeding in Mark contains allusions to Exod. 18:13–27. For the rest cf. in Johannes Behm, art. ἄρτος, *ThWb* I, p. 476 the late Jewish pieces of evidence for the expectation of an eschatological manna miracle, especially *Syr. Bar.* 29, 8, "At that time the supplies of manna will again fall from heaven"; *Qoh. R.* 1 on 1:9. "As the first deliverer caused manna to come down, so will also the last deliverer cause manna to come down."

190. It is by no means conclusive that, as Bultmann, *Joh.*, pp. 157f. maintains, John 6:14f. must go back to the evangelist, even if John was able to make a good use of this feature in connection with the misunderstanding of the miracle by the people.

191. Otherwise Cullmann, *Christologie*, p. 29.

192. So Friedrich, *ThWb* VI, pp. 847f.

193. Cf. the passages in Billerbeck I, pp. 594ff.

194. Cf. Gils, *op. cit.*, pp. 26f., who sets Lk. 7:16 directly under the theme *Jésus, le nouvel Élie*.

195. Cf. Excursus IV, pp. 231ff.

196. It is true that of the six members of the statement in Matt. 11:5 only four can be verified by Old Testament citations. The cleansing of the lepers and the raising from the dead have no direct parallels there; only the *Apoc. of Elijah* 33, 1–3 can be mentioned, yet it must be considered whether such a picture of the work of Jesus as was living in the early church has not operated here, in which case the stories about Elijah and Elisha were probably co-determining.

197. Cf. Johannes Schneider, art. ἔρχομαι *ThWb* II, pp. 666f.; Bultmann, *Syn. Trad.*, p. 168.

198 Literally Matt. 3:11; but cf. Mk. 1:7; Acts 13:25. Moreover in the really formal sense ὁ ἐρχόμενος is used only in Rev. 1:4 by the side of ὁ ὢν καὶ ὁ ἦν.

199. Here we refer briefly to Albert Schweitzer, *Das Messianitäts-und Leidensgeheimnis*, 1901 (1956³), pp. 38ff., 43ff.: *id. Geschichte der Leben-Jesu-Forschung*, pp. 218ff.: *id. Mystik des Apostels Pls.*, pp. 160ff. With the futurity of the kingdom of God there harmonizes only a future Messiah, who moreover must appear as a mighty king. Jesus must have known Himself as the Messiah, but during His public ministry did not reveal that in order that He might be able to fulfil His mission. Accordingly the people understood Him as the forerunner. Even the Baptist had expected as "him who is to come" only the forerunner, who had first to clear the way for the Messiah. But Jesus had regarded the Baptist as Elias. In order not to have to expose His Messianic secret at the time of the Baptist's inquiry, Jesus gave an evasive answer, in which, however, He set His person clearly in the foreground.—But this whole conception is tenable on the strength neither of late Jewish nor of primitive Christian tradition. Nevertheless, difficulties in facing the conventional expository tradition are clearly felt and the problem of the tradition about the forerunner side by side with the Messiah conception is also seen.

200. Friedrich, *ThWb* VI, p. 848.

201. Strobel, *Verzögerungsproblem*, pp. 265ff., connects the Baptist's inquiry with Hab. 2:3 and the late Jewish tradition attached to it, regards ὁ ἐρχόμενος as a characteristic of the "apocalyptic messianism of Qumran and related Essenizing circles" (p. 273), rightly emphasizes in connection with Jesus' answer the significance of Isa. 61:1, misunderstands, however, the singular conception of the eschatological prophet, but treats v. 5 as evidence of an expectation of the Messiah.

202. Cf. Julius Schniewind, *Euangelion. Ursprung und erste Gestalt des Begriffs Evangelium* I, 1927, pp. 34ff., 45f. He is followed by Gerhard Friedrich, art. εὐαγγελίζομαι, *ThWb* II, p. 707.

203. Friedrich, *ThWb* II, pp. 712f.; passages also in Billerbeck III, pp. 8f.

204. So Bultmann, *Syn. Trad.*, p. 31, according to whom Luke knew the tradition vv. 25–27 and the παραβολή in v. 23 besides the Markan story. Cf. also Conzelmann, *Mitte der Zeit*, pp. 25ff., who works out the Lukan meaning of the story, but finally leaves the question of origin undecided (cf. *ibid.*, pp. 29f., n. 2).

205. Wellhausen, *Lk.*, p. 9.

206. Rightly Jeremias, *Jesu Verheissung für die Völker*, pp. 37ff. But his understanding of v. 22a—"they all bore witness against him and wondered that he spoke of the grace of God" and not of the judgment of God (the statement about the day of vengeance is absent from the citation of Isa. 61:2)—by which he wishes to establish the unity of the present story, is not convincing.

207. Wellhausen, *Lk.*, p. 10; Bultmann, *Syn. Trad.*, p. 31.

208. Mk. 6:1–5 is not itself a unity, but in it several elements coalesce.

209. Cf. on this the investigation of J. de la Potterie, *L'onction du Christ, Nouvelle Revue Théologique* 80, 1958, pp. 225–252, who shows very excellently that a high priestly anointing is not referred to in a single New Testament passage, that a royal anointing is referred to only metaphorically in Heb. 1:9, and that on the other hand anointing with the Spirit bears a prophetic character; connections with the Christus title are not recognizable in the New Testament, its etymology playing no role. In one passage, however, de la Potterie goes too far; when namely he at once draws lines of connection from the anointing with the Spirit and the baptism to the idea of the suffering Servant of God and to Jesus' passion.

210. Cf. Excursus V, pp. 337ff.

211. Cf. Excursus V, pp. 334ff.

212. Cf. Riesenfeld, *op. cit.*, p. 147, and Cullmann, *Christologie*, pp. 42ff.

213. Cf. especially Hadorn, *Apk.*, p. 159; Jeremias, *ThWb* IV, p. 856.

214. Certainly we may not generalize this connection of the office as eschatological prophet of the earthly Jesus with his function as the messianic consummator and may not by any means carry it back to Jesus himself as Bornhäuser does. Claude Chavasse, "Christ and Moses", *Theology* 54, 1951, pp. 244–250, 289–296, also wishes to prove that Jesus understood Himself as the new Moses.—Indeed Riesenfeld, *op. cit.*, p. 146, also carries back the motif of the eschatological prophet to Jesus so far as its roots are concerned; but Jesus did not give Himself out intentionally either as the Messiah or as a prophet; only the continuous reference to Old Testament categories and the prototype-accomplishment schema suggested the interpretation of His person given by the church (pp. 144ff.).

215. Cf. chapter 3, p. 192 above. To understand εἷς τῶν προφητῶν in the sense of "the" prophet—so Bornhäuser, *op. cit.*, pp. 129f.—is out of the question for the present text.

216. Cf. Bernhard Lohse, *Das Passafest der Quartadezimaner (BFchr-Th* II/54), 1953, pp. 62ff., 89ff., 138ff. especially.

217. Reference may be made merely to the investigations of August Strobel, *Die Passa-Erwartung als urchristliches Problem in Lc 17, 20f., ZNW* 49, 1958, pp. 157—196; id. *Passa-Symbolik und Passa-wunder in Act xii. 3ff., NTSt* 4, 1957/58, pp. 210–215; id. *Verzögerungsproblem,* pp. 203ff.; Georg Ziener, *Johannesevangelium und urchristliche Passafeier, BZ* NF 2, 1958, pp. 263–274.

218. On this in detail B. Lohse, *op. cit.*, pp. 75ff., 78ff.

219. Similarly as in the case of the theologumenon of the virgin birth, which was unflinchingly attacked by the Jewish Christians, a deduction can here be drawn about the earliest Palestinian tradition.— Cf. Epiphanius, *Haer.* xxix 7, 3: ἕνα θεὸν καταγγέλουσι καὶ τὸν τούτου παῖδα Ἰησοῦν Χριστόν.

220. *Gospel of the Hebrews*, Fragment 4; cf. Erich Klostermann, *Apocrypha* II (*Kleine Texte* 8), p. 6.

221. Cf. on this especially the new investigation by Georg Strecker, *Das Judenchristentum in den Pseudoklementinen (TU* 70 = v/15), 1959, pp. 145ff.; but also Oscar Cullmann, *Le problème littéraire et historique*

du roman Pseudo-Clémentin. Étude sur le rapport entre le Gnosticisme et le Judéo-Christianisme, 1930, especially pp. 170ff.; *id., Christologie,* pp. 37ff. Connections with Gnosticism are energetically but not convincingly contested by Hans Joachim Schoeps, *Theologie und Geschichte des Judenchristentums,* 1949, pp. 98ff.; *id., Urgemeinde—Judenchristentum—Gnosis,* 1956, pp. 23ff., 44ff.

222. On this Schoeps, *Theol. u. Gesch.,* pp. 111ff.

223. Cf. Schoeps, *Theol. u. Gesch.,* pp. 87ff.; *id., Urgem.,* pp. 22f.; Cullmann, *Christologie,* pp. 39f.; Friedrich, *ThWb* VI, pp. 86of.

224. Cf. on this Werner Georg Kümmel, *Jesus und der jüdische Traditionsgedanke, ZNW* 33, 1934, pp. 105–130, especially pp. 122ff.; Günther Bornkamm. art. πρεσβύτερος, *ThWb* VI, pp. 661f.

225. Matt. 7:28f.; 11:1; 13:53; 19:1; 26:1f.

226. The division of the Gospel of Matthew into five parts corresponding to the five Books of Moses, together with introduction and conclusion, was first advocated by B. W. Bacon, *Studies in Matthew,* 1930, pp. 8off. (carried through in detail on pp. 165ff., 339ff.); he includes in the discourses the narrative material that sometimes precedes (3:1–7:29; 8:1–11:1; 11:2–13:53; 13:54–19:1; 19:2–26:2). Stendahl, *School,* p. 27, has objected that in the narrative material there is a much too considerable dependence on Mark and that Matthew has made his arrangement especially for the five discourses. Yet in the Pentateuch also narrative and discourse materials are combined. To that there corresponds the other observation that in cc. 8f. the narrative material has been recast in its composition and set under that leading theme. It is to be observed that in the "discourses" regarding the Baptist and against the scribes (11:7–19; c. 23) the typical concluding phrase is lacking; the sharply delimited discourses are exclusively concerned with the promise of salvation made to the church and with admonition addressed to it.

227. E.g. Schniewind, *Mt.,* p. 53; cf. also his pertinent contrast: cc. 5–7 "The Messiah in word" (p. 37) and cc. 8f. 'The Messiah in deed" (p. 106).

228. So Gerhard Barth, *Das Gesetzesverständnis des Evangelisten Matthäus* in Bornkamm-Barth-Held, pp. 143ff.; similarly also Teeple, *op. cit.,* pp. 77ff.

229. Cf. p. 360 above.

230. Cf. what is said on Jewish Christianity.

231. The Matthaean traits in Matt. 2:13–23 are underlined by Krister Stendahl, "Quis et Unde? An Analysis of Mt. 1–2" in *Judentum—Urchristentum—Kirche (Festschrift für J. Jeremias, BZNW* 26), 1960, pp. 94–105.

232. That is seen with special clearness in Luke, who follows the text of Mark in 4:1, 2a and then from v. 2b adheres to the Q-version, whilst Matt. 4:2 carries over from Q into the beginning of the story of the temptation the 40 days of the Markan narrative (cf. Lk. 4:2b), but, following Exod. 34:28, speaks still more clearly of 40 days and nights.

233. This may be said in spite of the not altogether clear wording in Matt. 23:2. For in any case the singularity of Jesus' office as a teacher is clearly pointed out in vv. 8–10, and from that there emerges the claim to the κάθεδρα Μωυσῆς. But it has not at all been made out with

certainty whether the ἐκάθισαν in v. 2 is actually a Semitism and must be understood as a present (so Wellhausen, *Einleitung*, p. 18; Klostermann, *Mt.*, p. 181); it could also very well look back to a period now ended.

234. Cf. the interesting study of P. Dabeck, *Siehe, es erschienen Moses und Elia"* (*Mt. 17:3*), *Biblica* 23, 1942, pp. 175–189, who in the first part examines the Moses typology of Matthew's Gospel.

235. On the original number seven of the beatitudes in Matt. 5:3ff. cf. Klostermann, *Mt.*, pp. 33f., 37. Otherwise, however, Schniewind, *Mt.*, pp. 40ff., who with reasons that are worthy of notice advocates two times four beatitudes.

236. Again see Dabeck, *op. cit.*

237. So Dabeck, *op. cit.*, pp. 180ff., in the second part of his treatise. Riesenfeld, *op. cit.*, pp. 145ff. follows him without giving further reasons.

238. If single features of the story of the young man at Nain recall 1 Kings 17:9, 23 and if Lk. 9:62 can be compared with 1 Kings 18:37f. and 2 Kings 1:10, 12 (Ecclus. 48:3), that merely helps us to form an opinion regarding the material of the tradition. Other elements such as the ministry of the Spirit, the motif of the journey, the representation of Jesus as a man of love and much prayer can in their generality be claimed much less still. Moreover it may not be overlooked that with Moses in view a pronounced typology can be carried through, but not in the case of Elias, it being a matter of the return of a prophet whose eschatological task is not determined by the picture of the historical Elias (it is significant that all such typological traits are foreign to the tradition about the Baptist). In the details of the Synoptic tradition which recall the story of Elias we are concerned with a representation of Jesus as a "man of God" especially equipped and commissioned; cf. chapter 5, pp. 288ff.

239. So Jindrich Mǎnek, "The New Exodus in the Books of Luke", *Nov. Test.* 2, 1958, pp. 8–23.

240. Cf. on this C. F. Evans, "The Central Section of St. Luke's Gospel" in *Studies in the Gospels* (*Essays in Memory of R. H. Lightfoot*), 1955, pp. 37–53.

241. Cf. on this Günther Bornkamm, *Der Paraklet im Johannesevangelium* in *Festschrift Rudolf Bultmann*, 1949, pp. 12–35.

242. Very various motives have co-operated here. It may not be overlooked that in any case the coupling of Jesus' two functions comes from the stratum of tradition in which His activity as the new Moses and as the returning Messiah were united. Accordingly we may not first of all recur to the Son of man conception, which also is by no means absolutely necessary in the motif of the equipment by the Spirit, of the office as judge and of the (temporary) stay in heaven (somewhat otherwise Bornkamm, *op. cit.*, pp. 20ff.), even if it may not in any way be disputed that apocalyptic motives have had a considerable effect and that diverse elements have coalesced in the figure of the Paraclete.

243. This has rightly been pointed out with emphasis by Bornkamm, *op. cit.*, pp. 27f.

244. On the Moses typology in 1 Cor. 10:1f. and in Hebrews cf. Jeremias, *ThWb* IV, pp. 874, 875f.

INDEX OF SUBJECTS

Old Testament

New Testament

411

413